MORE PRAISE FOR
ANTHONY SUMMERS'
OFFICIAL AND CONFIDENTIAL

"Fascinating and appalling . . . gritty, fast-paced, and disturbing . . . Summers' case against Hoover is overwhelming. . . . It will leave readers alarmed by the vulnerability of democracy . . . [and] convinced that J. Edgar Hoover himself was Public Enemy No. 1."
—*Christian Science Monitor*

"The coup de grâce to the once-feared and admired FBI chief."
—*San Francisco Chronicle*

"Anthony Summers has written an important book that should give all of us pause, especially policy makers. . . . No person should be allowed such untrammeled power, and no person should be in office so long."
—*Philadelphia Inquirer*

"Summers offers fresh details. . . . *OFFICIAL AND CONFIDENTIAL* is sure to disturb the old crime fighter's final rest."
—*Time*

"Brilliant. . . . Anthony Summers has carefully broadened his view to incorporate a thrilling and detailed account of the gangland of the Mafia as he found it in the era of Hoover."
—*Harrison Salisbury*

A Book-of-the-Month Club Featured Alternate Selection

MORE PRAISE FOR
ANTHONY SUMMERS'
OFFICIAL AND CONFIDENTIAL

"A scandalous, best-selling book . . . Twenty years after his death, Hoover's villainy swells. . . . Nazi hunter/Nazi, gangbuster/gangster, gay basher/closet queen, action detective/file clerk: Hoover is the picture of Dorian Gray, melting into depravity. . . ."

— *Washington Post*

"The true scandal is that Hoover was allowed to make the FBI into his own secret police. . . . Americans can only shudder as they contemplate the historical truth about Hoover."

— *Boston Globe*

"*OFFICIAL AND CONFIDENTIAL* does its job of yanking Hoover out of the clouds and dragging him through a very terrestrial pile of mud. . . . Well documented and detailed . . . the facts in this book bury him just fine."

— *Milwaukee Journal*

"Anthony Summers' book is a serious work of scholarship that advances our understanding of J. Edgar Hoover and the FBI."

— Representative Don Edwards,
    Chairman of the House of Representatives
    Civil and Constitutional Rights Subcommittee

MORE PRAISE
FOR ANTHONY SUMMERS'
OFFICIAL AND CONFIDENTIAL

"Well researched . . . a powerful indictment of both the presidents and the Congress that allowed one man to have such enormous power over the nation's law-enforcement machinery—with no real accountability. FBI agents in the field could have been vastly more effective in their war on crime if the issues raised in *OFFICIAL AND CONFIDENTIAL* had been responsibly addressed in the public dialogue while Hoover lived."
— Neil Welch, veteran FBI Agent-in-Charge
and specialist on organized crime

"Explosive . . . From Eleanor Roosevelt to Marilyn Monroe to Richard Nixon and Hoover's own suspicious death, this gripping narrative unfolds in riveting detail."
—*Grand Rapids Press*

"I read *OFFICIAL AND CONFIDENTIAL* with mounting horror, fascination, revulsion. . . . This enthralling book . . . explores the dark side of America, and that includes the presidency, the FBI, the Mafia, and forty-eight years of blackmail, intimidation and fear."
—Paul Theroux

"A pile of garbage, third-hand gossip, innuendo, lies."
—Cartha DeLoach, former close aide to
J. Edgar Hoover, on *Larry King Live*

"Anthony Summers has rendered a great public service. . . ."
—John Dowd, former head of the U.S. Justice
Department's F.B.I. corruption inquiry

Books by Anthony Summers

The File on the Tsar (with Tom Mangold)
Conspiracy
Honeytrap (with Stephen Dorril)
Goddess: The Secret Lives of Marilyn Monroe
Official and Confidential

OFFICIAL · AND · CONFIDENTIAL

The Secret Life of J. EDGAR HOOVER

Anthony Summers

POCKET **STAR** BOOKS

New York   London   Toronto   Sydney   Tokyo   Singapore

A Pocket Star Book published by
POCKET BOOKS, a division of Simon & Schuster Inc.
1230 Avenue of the Americas, New York, NY 10020

Copyright © 1993, 1994 by Anthony Summers

Published by arrangement with G. P. Putnam's Sons,
a division of The Putnam Berkley Group, Inc.

All rights reserved, including the right to reproduce
this book or portions thereof in any form whatsoever.
For information address G. P. Putnam's Sons,
a division of The Putnam Berkley Group, Inc.,
200 Madison Avenue, New York, NY 10016

ISBN: 0-671-88087-X

First Pocket Books printing May 1994

10 9 8 7 6 5 4 3 2 1

POCKET STAR BOOKS and colophon are registered
trademarks of Simon & Schuster Inc.

Cover design by Mike Stromberg
Cover photo courtesy of Bettmann Archives

Printed in the U.S.A.

for Robbyn

I thank the close colleagues and friends who have made this book possible. A long Acknowledgments section will be found in its closing pages. The project lasted for five years and demanded work on a scale I could not have hoped to achieve alone. Some 850 people were interviewed, and storage of the hundreds of thousands of documents required the addition of an entire new floor to my house.

On the investigative team, I am especially grateful to Dr. Kathryn Castle, lecturer in American History at the University of North London, and her husband, Paul Sutton, who spent a year in the United States carrying out extensive research. In San Francisco and Washington, Ingrid Young and Glyn Wright were real Sherlocks when it came to tracking down interviewees and obscure documents. In Ireland, with the assistance of Pauline Lombard, Jeanette Woods typed and retyped the manuscript and organized the ever-expanding archive.

The book was conceived by Putnam's president, Phyllis Grann, who lived up to her reputation as a legendary publisher. Andrea Chambers has been a redoubtable editor. Allison Hargraves, the copy editor, dealt meticulously with a mountain of detail. At Pocket Books, I thank Julie Rubenstein and Liate Stehlik for their patience and efficiency. That doyen of Manhattan agents, Sterling Lord, nursed me and the book through tough times. My London agent, Mark Lucas, provided consistently wise advice.

I shall never be able to repay the debt of gratitude I owe to Robbyn Swan, the fine Washington journalist who joined the project expecting to conduct a handful of interviews, stayed four years—and captured my heart.

To Robbyn, who is now my wife, much more than thanks.

A.S.
Ireland, 1992

OFFICIAL · AND · CONFIDENTIAL

PROLOGUE

October 1971, the Oval Office of the White House
The President of the United States, his Attorney General
and key advisers are wrestling with an intractable problem.
The problem is an old man, a man of whom the Chief of
State is afraid.

Richard Nixon: For a lot of reasons he oughta resign.
. . . He should get the hell out of there. . . . Now it
may be, which I kind of doubt . . . maybe I could just
call him and talk him into resigning. . . . There are
some problems. . . . If he does go he's got to go of his
own volition . . . that's why we're in a hell of a
problem. . . . I think he'll stay until he's a hundred
years old.

John Mitchell: He'll stay until he's buried there.
Immortality . . .

Richard Nixon: I think we've got to avoid the situation
where he can leave with a blast. . . . We may have on
our hands here a man who will pull down the temple
with him, including me. . . . It's going to be a problem.[1]

Seven months later, on May 2, 1972, the President's
"problem" proved to be mortal after all. J. Edgar Hoover,
Director of the Federal Bureau of Investigation, died in
office at the age of seventy-seven. The body was reportedly
found by his housekeeper, lying beside the four-poster in the
bedroom of his Washington home. It looked like just
another nighttime heart attack, and there would be no
autopsy.

Yet someone in Washington—someone powerful—felt
threatened by Hoover even in death. The undertakers,

1

arriving at the house to remove the corpse, were met with an extraordinary sight. At the foot of the stairs, in a straight-backed chair, an elderly man sat staring blankly into space. Coming and going around him, moving in and out of the rooms, were a number of younger men—intent on a mysterious task.

Just four hours after the discovery of the body, the men were searching the house from top to bottom. They were rifling through drawers, taking books off the shelves one by one, leafing through the pages, then moving on. The old man in the chair, the dead man's closest male friend—his lover, according to some—seemed oblivious to what they were doing.

The next day, J. Edgar Hoover's body was carried with great ceremony to the U.S. Capitol, where it lay in state on the black bier that once had borne Abraham Lincoln and eight other presidents. Inside, citizens filed past to pay their last respects, at a rate of a thousand an hour. Outside, a few hundred protesters were listening to a "war liturgy"—a reading of the names of the 48,000 Americans who had been killed in Vietnam.

Mingling with the protesters were ten men from the Nixon White House, on a mission to provoke fights and disrupt the rally. They included several Cuban exiles who had been involved in previous illegal break-ins, and who were soon to be caught red-handed at the Watergate. As they stood waiting that night, just yards from the Capitol where the dead man lay, two of the men talked about Hoover.

What one of them said astonished his comrade. Hoover's home, he confided, had been the target of a recent burglary inspired by the White House. Then he clammed up. To reveal more, he said, would be "dangerous."

The previous day, in the Oval Office, President Nixon is said to have greeted the news of Hoover's death with prolonged silence, then: "Jesus Christ! That old cock-sucker!" Other than that, an aide recalled, he showed no emotion at all.

For public consumption, Nixon treated the death of J. Edgar Hoover as the passing of an American hero. It was

2

he who ordered that Hoover should lie in state at the Capitol —the first civil servant ever to be so honored. He eulogized Hoover as "one of the giants . . . a national symbol of courage, patriotism, and granite-like honesty and integrity."

To millions of Americans, Hoover was a hero. Long ago, in the twenties, he had virtually created the FBI. He had rebuilt and expanded it, in a brilliant reorganization that left him poised for fame as the "Number One G-Man," nemesis of the bandits of the Midwest—Dillinger, Machine Gun Kelly, Alvin "Creepy" Karpis and Baby Face Nelson.

Later, Hoover became much more than the nation's top lawman. Charged by President Roosevelt with protecting the internal security of the United States, he emerged as the nation's champion against its most insidious foes: first the Nazis, then his enemies of choice, the Communists, and all who dared voice political dissent.

Endless publicity had made Hoover a living icon, showered with honors in his own time. President Truman awarded him the Medal for Merit for "outstanding service to the United States." President Eisenhower chose him as the first-ever recipient of the Award for Distinguished Federal Civilian Service, the highest honor a civil servant could receive.

The very name Hoover became synonymous with the safety of the nation, with the core values of American society, and—though few dared say so publicly—with fear. Like many of the eight presidents Hoover served, Richard Nixon had known that fear. His relationship with the Director had been long and filled with irony. As a gangly young man, he himself had applied to be a Special Agent in Hoover's FBI. As a fledgling congressman, he had ridden to success on the crusade against the Left that Hoover had largely inspired. He had found favor, been given a helping hand, had supped with Hoover at his favorite watering holes. He and the old man shared enemies, secrets and hunger for power. When, finally, the younger man came to the presidency, the pinnacle Hoover himself had once yearned to reach, the two had seemed natural allies.

Yet President Nixon, in his turn, had collided with

Hoover. Early on, the elderly Director had become impossible to live with. He cut off liaison with all other intelligence agencies. For reasons of self-preservation rather than principle, he sabotaged the President's battle plan for an intelligence offensive against radical activists. Then he enraged Nixon by soft-pedaling the investigation of Daniel Ellsberg, the government analyst who leaked Vietnam War documents to the press. His erratic public performance made him an embarrassment to the administration. Despite all this, Richard Nixon did not dare fire him.

The President tried to do so, on several occasions. In the fall of 1971, aware that Nixon had summoned Hoover for a showdown meeting, officials sat watching the clock, waiting for news that the Director had finally been forced out of office. The news never came. Though Nixon has never admitted it, the old man fought off disaster with his most trusty weapon: knowledge.

Recently released White House transcripts reveal that the President and his aides were squirming with worry over the damage Hoover could do. On Nixon's orders, aides scurried to retrieve incriminating documents—proving the President had ordered the bugging of newsmen—"before Hoover blows the safe." There were a string of other reasons to be afraid. Hoover, it seems, was aware of some of the White House crimes that preceded Watergate. He even had personal information on Nixon—potential scandal involving a woman.

The Director knew Richard Nixon's sins and secrets, as he knew those of so many others. When he died, there was panic over what information might lie in his office. Nixon's Chief of Staff scrawled a terse note: ". . . find out what's there, who controls it—where skeletons are."

In Congress, many senators and congressmen lived in fear of the files Hoover held on them—or that they feared he held. Now, thanks to the Freedom of Information Act, it is clear their fears were justified. The record proves conclusively that FBI agents routinely reported in detail on the sexual activity of politicians—both hetero- and homosexual. Eyewitness testimony reveals how one prominent Senator was terrorized into inaction by a reading from his own FBI file.

One of Hoover's closest colleagues, William Sullivan, was to describe him—after he was dead—as "a master blackmailer." Yet that is only part of the story. New evidence indicates that this immensely powerful man had a fatal flaw of his own. He was the product of a painful childhood, the son of a mentally ill father and a domineering mother, and his adult life was marred by emotional turmoil and sexual confusion. The Hoover who preached stern moral sermons to America secretly practiced homosexuality—even transvestism.

As Hoover himself repeatedly warned, homosexuals have always been prime targets for compromise by hostile intelligence agencies—not least that of Edgar's bête noire, the Soviet Union. So tormented was Hoover by his secret vulnerability that he once sought help from a Washington psychiatrist.

The suggestion that the blackmailer was blackmailed, though, comes from a different and startling direction. Why, many have asked, did Hoover long neglect pursuit of the most insidious criminal force of all—the Mafia? Several mob figures now assert that, as they understood it, Hoover posed no threat. He and top organized crime figures had "an understanding."

Early in Hoover's career, according to mob interviews, he was trapped by his own homosexuality. Mafia boss Meyer Lansky, who specialized in the use of damaging information to manipulate men in public life, had reportedly obtained compromising evidence—probably photographs. Thereafter, until the Kennedy brothers attacked organized crime, Lansky bragged privately that Hoover had been "fixed."

Behind his mask of public rectitude, it is now evident that this American hero was corrupt. He lived "like an oriental potentate," as a former Deputy Attorney General put it, milking FBI funds and facilities for his private profit and pleasure. Wealthy friends favored him with lavish hospitality and investment tips, and he apparently protected them from criminal investigation.

In the FBI's oppression of civil rights activists and liberals, Hoover's personal venom comes into focus. His rage over the award of the Nobel Peace Prize to Martin Luther King, Jr., was the greater because—for years previously—he had indulged the conceit that he himself deserved the Prize. His fury over criticism by comedian Dick Gregory led him to issue orders designed to trigger a mob attack on the entertainer.

Perhaps an alert public should have realized at the time that Hoover's image was too good to be true. Yet in large measure because the nation's press was so timid, it did not.

"If we didn't have Mr. Hoover and the FBI," a television viewer wrote NBC shortly before the Director's death, "I would like to know how you and I would exist." Many ordinary citizens expressed such sentiments.

Others differed. The poet Theodore Roethke called Hoover "the head of our thought police—a martinet, a preposterous figure, but not funny." Hoover's FBI, wrote novelist Norman Mailer, was "a high church for the mediocre." "It was a relief," said pediatrician Benjamin Spock on hearing of Hoover's death, "to have this man silenced who had no understanding of the underlying philosophy of our government or of our Bill of Rights, a man who had such enormous power, and used it to harass individuals with whom he disagreed politically and who had done as much as anyone to intimidate millions of Americans out of their right to hear and judge for themselves all political opinions."

A former Assistant Attorney General under President Johnson, Mitchell Rogovin, thought Hoover's life had been "a passion play of good and evil. And when there was good, it was hollow."

What manner of man stirred such different responses? He came to be regarded, the *New York Post* once said, "with the same awe and reverence accorded the other monuments of Washington. Only he's closed to the public." That a man with a crippled psyche, capable of great evil, became the trusted symbol of all that was safe and good is a paradox of our time. So too is the fact that, in a tribute after Hoover's death, Chief Justice Warren E. Burger said he had "epitomized the American dream," while renowned psychiatrists consider he would have been well suited for high office in Nazi Germany.

In spite of all the damaging information that has emerged about Hoover in recent years, and in spite of congressional motions to remove the words "J. Edgar Hoover" from the wall of the FBI headquarters, the building still bears that name, in huge gold lettering, as though nothing had changed.

To explore such contradictions is to make a vital journey through our century, a time of deception and self-deception about our values, our freedoms and our heroes. Perhaps, because this man's life spanned a period in which the American dream went so badly wrong, understanding him may help us to understand ourselves.

To bring him into mortal perspective, J. Edgar Hoover—the child and the man—will remain "Edgar" throughout this book. His story began on a freezing New Year's morning, nearly a hundred years ago.

CHAPTER 1

"The Child is father of the Man."

William Wordsworth

"ON SUNDAY JANUARY 1, 1895, AT 7:30 A.M. J. EDGAR HOOVER was born to my father and mother, the day was cold and snowy but clear. The Doctor was Mallan. I was born at 413 Seward Square, S.E. Wash. D.C. . . ."[1]

The boy who was to become the world's most famous police official kept a dossier on himself as a child. Edgar's formal report on his own birth fills a page in a small leather-bound notebook, inscribed on the front, in schoolboy handwriting: "Mr. Edgar Hoover, private." It lies now in a muddle of memorabilia, yellowed papers and faded photographs, stored at the House of the Temple, headquarters of the Masons' Supreme Council, Thirty-third Degree, in Washington, D.C. They transport us into a nineteenth-century world that only a handful of Americans survive to remember.

Edgar was born when the Civil War was still a vivid memory, when the assassination of Abraham Lincoln was no more distant in the past than is that of President Kennedy today. The Union Lincoln had forged still had only forty-five member states. The year 1895 saw talk of war with England over territories in Latin America, and soon there would be conflict with Spain, resulting in U.S. conquest of the Philippines. Just four years before Edgar was born, the white man's war against the Indians ended at Wounded Knee.

Edgar, who would die in the era of the jumbo jet, was born

9

when Edison's two inventions, his Light System and his Moving Picture Machine, were still marvels. The telephone was reserved for government officials and the wealthy. There were less than 150 miles of paved road in the nation, and only a few thousand cars. The bicycle, in exotic variety, was the fashionable thing on city streets.

American cities were already overcrowded, although the great wave of immigration was yet to come. Those earliest immigrants, the blacks, faced renewed persecution as southern states applied racist segregation laws. The morning Edgar was born, a black man was lynched by a southern mob—a common enough occurrence then.

The whitewashed frame house that was Edgar's birthplace—a mile or so from the White House—was insulated from all these miseries. His father, Dickerson Hoover, was thirty-eight when Edgar was born, the descendant of settlers who had moved to Washington in the early nineteenth century.

Later, Edgar's propaganda department would describe Dickerson as "a career man in the government service." This was technically true, but the post he held was not grand at all. Like his father before him, he worked as a printmaker for the government mapmaking department.

Edgar's thirty-four-year-old mother, Anna, "Annie" to intimates, had a classier background. Her forebears had served as senior local officials in the Swiss village of Klosters, now the celebrated ski resort. They had their own coat of arms and a fine ancestral home next to the church. One scion of the family had become a bishop.

Annie's immigrant grandfather had been the first Swiss Consul General to the United States. Her grandmother, besides bearing thirteen children, had found prominence in her own right. A trained nurse known as "Mother Hitz," she had been a Florence Nightingale to wounded Union soldiers camped on Capitol Hill during the Civil War.

Edgar's mother had a privileged upbringing—St. Cecilia's school for girls in Washington, then a convent in Switzerland. The granddaughter who probably knew her best, Dorothy Davy, remembers her as "very much a lady, a very interesting person. She was loving, but she was also very proud. Granddaddy was kindly and gentle, but she was the strong one in that combination."

A family photograph shows Edgar's father as a troubled-looking figure of the Victorian clerical class, cramped in high collar and formal dress, his bowler on his knee. His wife stands behind him, severe in high-necked blouse and dark jacket, her hair piled on top of her head, her lips tightly compressed, trying and failing to smile.

The couple's marriage, fifteen years before Edgar's birth, was remembered in the family as "the largest wedding Capitol Hill ever had." For Annie, such a grand affair may have been in the normal course of things. For Dickerson, of humbler stock, it was probably overwhelming.

Edgar was the last of four children. A male heir, Dickerson, Jr., had been born in 1880, followed by two daughters, Lillian and Sadie. When Edgar was conceived, his parents were still grieving over Sadie's death at the age of three, a diphtheria victim before the age of vaccination.

The earliest photograph of Edgar shows a glum-faced little boy, hunched at his parents' side wearing a brass-buttoned jacket, a watch chain and knickerbockers. By one account, he was a "high-strung" child, "sickly and excessively fearful, clinging to his mother whenever he could." He started at Brent Elementary School in 1901, when he was six and as Theodore Roosevelt was about to become President, and he was a star student from the start.

"I passed 5th highest in the first year with an average of 93.8," Edgar was to write in his leather-bound notebook. The school reports confirm it. From Third to Eighth Grade, Edgar received "Excellent Plus" or at least "Good" in Arithmetic and Algebra, Grammar and Language, Penmanship and Reading, History and Civics.

Not only did the teachers report on Edgar, he made notes about *them*: "Miss Hinkle, 4th Grade, who raised me in discipline . . . Miss Snowden who raised me intellectly [sic] . . . Miss Dalton, 8th Grade, a fine lady who raised me morally . . ." Edgar was never ever, he boasted to his notebook, kept back by the teacher after class.

When he was old enough, Edgar would walk the streets of Washington—safe in those days—to meet his father at his office. Dickerson, Sr., seems to have doted on his youngest child, and both the affection and the father's modest origins shine through the language of a letter Edgar kept. "Dear old man," Dickerson wrote from St. Louis in 1904. "I wish you was [sic] here so that I could fight you in the morning. Mamma might think you ain't strong, but just let her try to fight you and she will find out. . . . Be a good boy. With a big kiss. From Papa."

"Don't study too hard," the father wrote cheerfully. Annie was different. "Study hard both your lessons and your music," she wrote, "and try to be a good boy. . . . Was so glad to hear you were perfect in your spelling and arithmetic. Take care of everything nicely and don't run the streets." Annie was strict, but according to Dorothy Davy, "Edgar, of all her children, was the one she spoiled."

In 1906, the year he turned eleven, Edgar started his own "newspaper." He collected two pages of material each week, and persuaded his elder brother—then twenty-six—to type it up. Edgar called his paper *The Weekly Review,* and sold it to family and friends for one cent a copy.

The *Review* offered snippets of family news along with items about Abraham Lincoln and Benjamin Franklin. One early headline reported the marriage of the President's daughter Alice to the Speaker of the House. Alice Roosevelt, beautiful, brave and outrageous, was the woman of the decade.

By 1908, when he was thirteen, Edgar was keeping a diary. He noted daily temperatures and cloud cover, births and deaths in the family, his income from doing odd jobs, even lists of his own hat, sock and collar sizes.

"All the family," said Edgar's niece Dorothy, "had that horrible thing about organization. Everything had to be organized and catalogued, and the pictures had to be straight on the wall—always. It sounds crazy, but we were all like that."

On Sunday evenings, an old man with a flowing white beard would come to dinner. This was Great-Uncle John

Hitz, from Annie's side of the family, and his visits to the Hoovers' meant a solemn Bible-reading session. The entire family would kneel while Uncle John, a staunch Calvinist, prayed.

Contrary to common assumption, though, neither of Edgar's parents was especially devout. Dickerson considered himself a Lutheran. Annie fitted in but, according to Dorothy Davy, "she was a Catholic, more or less. Edgar's mother attended Catholic schools, and she would die with a crucifix in her hands." Edgar's nephew, Fred Robinette, confirms that Annie was "no Bible-thumper." Neither she nor her husband attended church regularly.

Out of the religious mix came anxiety and confusion. In later life, in an overwrought moment, Edgar's sister Lillian threw the family Bible into the fire. Edgar, who publicly spoke of himself as a Presbyterian, would consult with Catholic priests. One day, he too would abuse the Bible. In childhood, however, he followed in the pious footsteps of his elder brother, Dickerson.

Though Dickerson was serious about his devotions, the church offered more than spiritual solace. It was the keystone of the white Protestant infrastructure, a place where social and career connections were made. At the Lutheran Church of the Reformation, Dickerson found himself a wife.

Young Edgar tagged along enthusiastically. He sang soprano in the choir, served as altar boy and, at thirteen, was baptized into the Lutheran Church by the minister who had conducted his brother's wedding. Edgar went to a Passion play, he noted in his Excelsior diary, attended Sunday school and went to a meeting of a group called Christian Endeavour. "Read a little of the *Gospel of Judas Iscariot,*" he noted one day. "(Great Book)."

The Judas *Gospel,* as one might expect, is a fictional account written from the viewpoint of Christ's betrayer. The Judas concept lodged forever in Edgar's mind; years later he would even have FBI researchers check the biblical details for him. The possibility that he himself might be betrayed— by real or imaginary traitors—would become an obsession.

Edgar's childhood dossier on Edgar suggests that he did

occasionally have fun like other little boys. He celebrated Groundhog Day, dyed eggs at Easter time and—aged fourteen—"gave out Valentines." "Fooled lots of people," he noted with glee on April Fools' Day. He would also claim, years later and less reliably, that when he played cops and robbers he "always wanted to be a robber."

Edgar was fascinated by the new phenomenon of manned flight, and built model airplanes with a friend. In 1909, when he was fourteen, he saw Orville Wright make a flight from downtown Washington to Alexandria and back, demonstrating that sustained air travel was possible. In his journal that day, Edgar proudly noted that he had been "the first outsider to shake Orville's hand."

In the fall of 1909, Edgar started at a new school— walking three miles there in the morning, three miles home at night. These were his first real steps toward fame and power. For Edgar did not go to Eastern High, the school his brother and sister had attended. "His mother," said his niece Dorothy, "didn't consider Eastern good enough for him. So he went to Central."

Central High School was the breeding ground for a Washington elite, a springboard to success. Its advantages have been compared to those of a top British public school, minus the hideous requirements of class and wealth that form the basis of the English system. Like smart British schools, Central placed great emphasis on sport. While Edgar was a pupil, the school team—which included a future general, a future veterans' leader and a future president of the Washington Board of Trade—amazed everyone by thrashing the University of Maryland at football, 14–0. Edgar, however, was no sportsman.

"I always wanted to be an athlete," he would recall ruefully, "but I only weighed 125 lbs. in my first year at High School." As if to prove that he was plucky for all that, Edgar claimed that a sports injury was responsible for his famous "bulldog" profile. A fly ball, he said, had smashed his nose during a school baseball game. According to Edgar's niece Margaret Fennell, however, his squashed-looking nose was the legacy of a boil that healed badly.

Edgar held men with fine physiques in awe. At school it was Lawrence "Biff" Jones, who went on to become a famous football coach at West Point. Biff, the grown Edgar would admit, was the boy on whom he lavished his "hero-worship." "We buddied around together all the time, and it always drew a laugh from our friends to see the big powerful Biff, accompanied by a youngster half his size."

Edgar threw himself full tilt into the other Central High activity that mirrored the English public school: the Cadet Corps. Central regularly sent graduates to West Point, including—in Edgar's generation—Jones and several future generals.

Edgar's school nickname, one which stuck for years, was "Speed." A Hoover-approved biography suggested, improbably, that this referred to his dexterity with a football. Elsewhere Edgar would claim it went back to his childhood, when he earned pocket money carrying packages for customers at the local store. He was dubbed Speed, he said, because he ran so fast with the packages.

Neither explanation was true, according to Francis Gray, a surviving classmate tracked down in 1988. "We called him Speed Hoover because he talked fast. He was so fast, talked fast, thought fast . . ."

The extraordinary rapidity of the adult Edgar's voice would be one of his hallmarks. "Machine gun," "staccato," "like a teamster's whip when aroused" are typical descriptions of the way he talked. "I can take two hundred words a minute," one court reporter was to protest, "but that man must be talking four hundred a minute."

William Sullivan, an FBI Assistant Director who served Edgar for thirty years and then broke with him, had an unkind explanation. "He didn't want a man to ask him any questions," said Sullivan, "so he'd keep talking right up until the last and then all of a sudden break off the interview and shake hands with the fellow and send him on his way."[2] Sullivan's complaint was to be echoed by dozens of newspaper reporters. Edgar the FBI Director did not talk with people. He talked at them.

Even as a teenager, Edgar's mind was closing on the issues

that would dominate his times. Seen with hindsight, his performance in the school debating society is revealing. Cuba, then as now a political irritant, was regularly in the news. In the debating society Edgar argued and won the motion that "Cuba should be annexed to the United States." "Neg.," for negative, he wrote in his Debate Memorandum Book next to the proposition that capital punishment should be abolished. He reasoned:

1. The Bible stands for Capital Punishment.
2. All Christian Nations uphold it.
3. The abolition of it would be deplorable in effect on a country. (Brief made).

Edgar would remain in favor of capital punishment for the rest of his life.

One issue Edgar fought and won in the debating society involved women's rights—specifically, whether women should be given the vote. Edgar was against it—vociferously so.

Not everyone took him as seriously as he took himself. "My speech is too long. I must condense it," Edgar was heard to say after working late into the night preparing for a debate. "You can condense steam, Hoover," retorted Jeff Fowler, editor of the school magazine, "but not hot air."

At seventeen, Edgar's glittering scholastic progress continued. His report cards show that he scored "Excellent" in almost every subject. As he carefully figured out for himself, his average grade was 90 percent or higher. He missed school only four times in four years.

Edgar simply could not bear to come in second. Another contemporary, David Stephens, remembered his reaction when, as a Captain in the Cadet Corps, Edgar's company failed to win the drill competition. "As we marched off the field," Stephens recalled in a letter to Edgar forty years later, "I wondered if you were crying because you were mad or were mad because you were crying."

In March 1913, Captain J. E. Hoover led his company down Pennsylvania Avenue in President Wilson's inaugural parade. Sixteen years of Republican government were coming to an end, and America was entering a period of upheaval. While revolution and war overwhelmed Russia and Europe, labor unrest had become a major issue in the United States. Nearly half the working population were toiling excessive hours in appalling conditions, going home to filthy slums at night. The United States was about to experience a wave of strikes, and a million American socialists would demand the overthrow of capitalism.

Soon company guards would be gunning down workers in Ohio. Members of one union, the Industrial Workers of the World, would be lynched. Others would be jailed. Their right to protest at all was questioned by those who asserted that they, and they alone, were "100 percent American."

At Central High, meanwhile, things went on as usual. Eighteen-year-old Edgar and his peers immersed themselves in the rites and celebrations of graduation year. Edgar Hoover, Francis Gray and their fellow cadets, splendid in blue-and-white uniforms, made their way to the Cairo Hotel for the regimental ball.

"We weren't expert dancers," Gray recalled. "We all wore our sabers, and they got in the way." A dance in those days was a rigidly formal affair, and each young man came armed with a dance engagement book. There were spaces to fill out the names of female partners "engaged" to dance the alternating waltzes and fox-trots, and spaces for the names of chaperones.

Edgar's dance book, which he kept all his life, shows that his parents came along as chaperones. The spaces for female partners, however, remain blank. If Edgar's record is to be believed—and he usually recorded everything meticulously —he did not dance with a single girl.

Francis Gray said Edgar "wasn't a dater, didn't go with girls." His relatives noticed it, too. "Edgar never had any girlfriends," said his niece Dorothy. "Never." Edgar's male friends teased him, claiming he was in love only with the Cadet Corps. "He was," said Francis Gray, "just a fraternity man."

In his yearbook picture, Edgar looks more fragile than his

broad-shouldered friends, his mouth pinched and humorless. The caption beneath his name praises him as "a gentleman of dauntless courage and stainless honor." Edgar was class valedictorian.

"There is nothing more pleasing," Edgar wrote in a final Cadet Corps report, "than to be associated with a company composed of officers and men who you feel are behind you heart and soul. The saddest moment of the year was when I realized that I must part with a group of fellows who had become part of my life."

Edgar the debater signed off with thoughts on the virtues of competition. Debate, he reckoned, was like life— "nothing more or less than the matching of one man's wits against another." And so, armed with a curiously fixed set of certainties for a youth of eighteen, Edgar set forth into the adult world.

As he did so, a family crisis was developing—a tragedy that must have been devastating to a young man coming of age. Edgar's father began losing his mind.

Edgar never discussed his father at all, not even with his closest friends. Surviving relatives, the generation that grew up during World War I, have only a blurred memory of Dickerson Hoover. To them he was "Daddy," a kindly man with a small moustache who liked to take children to the basement to sample his homemade ginger ale. Often, though, Daddy was not home at all.

Dickerson, Sr., was away a lot because, sometime during the war, doctors sent him to an asylum at Laurel, some eighteen miles from Washington. Quite what was wrong with him was not discussed in front of the grandchildren. One of them, Margaret Fennell, remembers only that he "had a nervous breakdown."

Dickerson was fifty-six when Edgar left school. He still worked, as he always had, as a printmaker at the government mapmakers. He earned a living wage, but never enough to dispel the notion that his wife, Annie, had married below her station. He had always played second fiddle to Annie at home. Now, in middle age, Dickerson began to be troubled by depression and irrational fears. Repeated trips to the asylum failed to help, and he went steadily downhill.

In the eight years that remained to him, Edgar's father would become a pitiful figure. His death certificate, in 1921, would say he died of "melancholia," with "inanition" as a contributory cause. Melancholia was the contemporary word for what doctors today call clinical depression. Inanition can be the outcome of extreme depression treated inadequately. The patient loses the will to live, stops eating and dies.

This drawn-out tragedy had a traumatic effect on life at Seward Square. Edgar's elder brother and sister were long gone, in their thirties and married with children. Only Annie and young Edgar remained at home, and they reportedly had little patience with Dickerson, Sr.

"My mother," said Edgar's niece Dorothy, "used to say Uncle Edgar wasn't very nice to his father when he was ill. He was ashamed of him. He couldn't tolerate the fact that Granddaddy had mental illness. He never could tolerate anything that was imperfect."

Dorothy, a retired teacher with wide experience of life's trials, said she thought perhaps "the whole Hoover clan were a little off in the head." Her memories suggest the Hoover family's emotional life was seriously fractured. Dickerson, Jr., was distant, and his sister Lillian was "cold, very cold." The young Edgar, who used to come to Dorothy's home to play croquet, at first seemed "quite fun to be around." Then he changed, becoming a remote figure "inclined to push us all away."

"I sometimes have thought," said Edgar's niece Margaret, "that he really—I don't know how to put it—had a fear of becoming too personally involved with people."

Half a century later, FBI Assistant Director William Sullivan would voice the same opinion. Edgar, he thought, "didn't have affection for one single solitary human being around him. . . ."

"I didn't have any honor or love for him as an uncle," said

Dorothy Davy. "Whatever he did for the country, he was no use as a relative." Other family members confirm—often nervously, as though Edgar were still alive to rebuke them—that he bothered little with family ties. When his widowed sister was struck down by Parkinson's disease, Edgar did little to help. When she died, his appearance at the funeral was so brief as to be insulting.

The only constant family connection for Edgar, far into the prime of his life, would be his mother, Annie. Once they were free of Edgar's father, the burden they had both resented, they became inseparable. Edgar lived at home with his mother until he was a middle-aged man. Only when she died, in 1938, would he leave the house on Seward Square. And when he did find a home of his own, he would live there alone.

CHAPTER 2

"If you work for a man, in heaven's name work for him!
If he pays you wages that supply you your bread and
butter, work for him—speak well of him, think well of
him, stand by him and stand by the institution he
represents."

*Elbert Hubbard quotation, displayed on
Edgar's orders in FBI field offices*

As EDGAR GREW TO MANHOOD, HE CLOSED THE DOSSIER ON
himself that he had kept since childhood. There are no more
diaries, and few intimate letters, to help chart his six
decades of adult life. In accordance with his wishes, his
secretary destroyed his private correspondence—and almost certainly much else besides—after his death.

Enough evidence survives, however, to expose the hidden
Edgar. The man who projected himself to the public as a
stern moral figure, full of integrity, was a walking myth. It
was so carefully crafted that he perhaps came to believe
much of it himself, but it was a myth nonetheless.

What Edgar said of his past, especially of events long ago,
must always be treated with caution. "He was a master con
man," his aide William Sullivan was to say, "one of the
greatest con men the country has ever produced, and that
takes intelligence of a certain kind, an astuteness, a
shrewdness."

In 1913, the year he turned eighteen, Edgar graduated
from high school, and decided to study law.

"I don't really know why I chose law," Edgar would say for public consumption. "You come to a crossroads, and you've got to go one way or the other." The other road beckoning, he claimed, was the Church. In the months before he left school, he said, he was preoccupied with the idea of becoming a minister.

FBI propaganda solemnly repeated this story, portraying a youth who had struggled to choose between one path of good, the Church, and another, the Law. According to this version, Edgar the FBI Director remained a regular church-goer, a boss who kept a well-thumbed Bible on his desk, who took his religion very seriously indeed.

Some of this was simply untrue, some of it the truth stretched beyond recognition. Relatives recall no family talk at all about Edgar being "torn" between religion and law. It was the elder brother, Dickerson, not Edgar, who faced such a dilemma.

Edgar did not fully exploit the "call of the Church" gambit until after the death, in 1944, of the brother who might have contradicted him. In 1990, however, a member of Dickerson, Jr.'s, family emerged to set the record straight. "That thing that keeps coming up about Edgar wanting to be a minister," said Dickerson's daughter-in-law Virginia Hoover, "it just isn't true. In our family, we've always known that."

Was Edgar at all religious? As a child, certainly, he was a zealous leader of Sunday school class. He went on teaching, quirkily dressed up in his high school cadet uniform, well into his teens.

According to the propaganda, this was the start of a lifetime of regular worship. A Bureau-approved article in 1960 would report that he "walks down the aisle of Washington's National Presbyterian Church each Sunday morning at precisely 9 o'clock." It was not true. "Mr. Hoover," the church's former pastor Dr. Edward Elson admitted in 1988, "was not regular in his attendance . . . was present at mainly seasonal affairs."

Leo McClairen, a former FBI agent who acted as Edgar's

chauffeur whenever he traveled south, does not remember his boss going to church once—in twenty years of Christmas visits to Florida.

Edgar's public piety was a sham—as was his version of his decision to go to law school. "We have no lawyers in our family," Edgar said, "and I don't recall that I knew any. But suddenly I took the turn, and knew that's what I wanted to be—an attorney."

In fact, Edgar had a cousin, another John E. Hoover, who was a lawyer, a clerk to five Supreme Court justices and a longtime Justice Department attorney. The family also boasted another very successful lawyer; Annie Hoover's cousin William Hitz was a senior Justice Department attorney. He was quite close to Edgar, according to yet another lawyer relative, Harold Burton, who was to become a U.S. Supreme Court Justice.

George Washington University Law School, where Edgar enrolled in 1913, did not have the prestige of other local universities. It offered, however, a respectable conservative law program, a solid grounding in the nuts and bolts of the legal system. For Edgar, a key advantage was that the course consisted of evening classes, leaving time for wage-earning during the day.

The purse strings at home were tight now, with the two elder children burdened with family commitments. Soon, as their father's health declined, they would be even tighter. Edgar was the man of the house at the age of eighteen, and he needed a job. Annie's cousin William Hitz found him one—as a thirty-dollar-a-week junior messenger in the order department of the Library of Congress.

Every day for the next four years, Edgar would walk the few blocks from Seward Square to his day job at the Library. He studied at the law school from five until seven, then went home to study some more. He kept his twenty-six law notebooks, filled with neat script, all his life.

He became a member of Kappa Alpha, a southern fraternity with origins at William and Mary College in Virginia—a link he would maintain long after his student days were over. GWU graduates, and especially Kappa Alpha men, were to be among his closest associates at the FBI.

A photograph from those days shows Edgar at the center of a group of students, hands thrust deep in pockets, a flower in his buttonhole, a grave expression on his face. "He was slim, dark and intense," a classmate recalled. "He sat off by himself against the wall, and always had the answers. None of us got to know him very well."

As manager of his fraternity house, Edgar proved to be a budding despot. He reportedly "took a dim and moral view of such chapter-house capers as crap games, poker and drinking bouts." He "located our contraband," recalled Dave Stephens, who had also been at Central with Edgar, "and destroyed it by sending it crashing to the concrete areaway." "Speed chastised us with his morality," recalled actor William Gaxton.

While the nickname Speed stuck, some students hit on a crueler one. "We men who received C's," said GWU alumnus C. W. Collier, "called Hoover, who received A's, 'Fatty-pants.'"

Edgar had no time for the slew of writers and thinkers then changing social and political attitudes around the world. Not for him the ideas of Freud and George Bernard Shaw, Karl Marx and John Reed, Pankhurst or Bertrand Russell. His favorite poets, he let it be known, were Edgar Guest and Vash Young and Robert Service, the he-man poet who told America that:

> . . . only the Strong shall thrive;
> That surely the weak shall perish, and only
> the fit survive.

Edgar received his Bachelor of Law degree, without honors, in the summer of 1916. America, meanwhile, was moving closer to entering the war in Europe. There were problems at home—anarchist bombs, strikes, workers' demands for shorter working hours. Henry Ford was forced to agree to equal pay for women—$5 a day—and a woman was elected to Congress for the first time. President Wilson promised that all women would soon get the vote. Then, on April 6, 1917, after he had told Congress "the world must be made safe for democracy," the United States declared war on Germany.

That same day, his mental health now seriously impaired, Edgar's father gave up work for good. Though Edgar was now the highest-paid youth in his grade at the Library of Congress, the family faced penury. On July 25, when he learned he had passed his bar exams, Edgar quit the job at the Library. The next day, for a few dollars more, he began work at the Department of Justice.

Edgar would in future imply that he got the government job on his own initiative. In fact he almost certainly got it thanks, once again, to Bill Hitz. Hitz, by then a judge, had clout. He counted the President and Supreme Court Justice Brandeis among his friends, and himself held a senior post at the Justice Department. With connections like that, it was easy to find a place at Justice for a needy young relative.

Edgar would say his first post had been a "clerkship." His personnel file describes him as having been a "Special Employee." In fact he worked in the mail room. Bruce Bielaski, a senior official, recalled how—on the trolley to work one day in 1917—he found himself talking shop with his neighbor, mail room chief George Michaelson.

Michaelson dropped the name of a young lawyer he had sorting mail, "one of the brightest boys around." "You don't need anybody with brains doing that," said Bielaski. "If you want him," Michaelson replied, "you can have him."

That conversation on the trolley was a fateful one for America. Bruce Bielaski was Director of the Bureau of Investigation, direct forerunner of what we know as the Federal Bureau of Investigation, the FBI.

The Bureau had been created in 1908, in the face of congressional fears that its powers might be used for oppressive political ends, and that it might end up under the control of one man. It was used to probe crimes that involved the crossing of state boundaries, antitrust and banking violations, and—notoriously—offenses against the

Mann Act, which made it a crime to carry a woman across state lines for "immoral purposes."

Bureau Chief Bruce Bielaski did not forget the young man his neighbor had recommended—though he did not bring Edgar into the Bureau. Instead he told John Lord O'Brian, head of the War Emergency Division, about Edgar. On December 14, 1917, the name of "Mr. Hoover, special agent" appeared for the first time in an O'Brian memorandum.

So, a month short of his twenty-third birthday, Edgar shot from sorting mail to deciding what to do with suspect foreigners. Three years of propaganda had brought the nation to a fever-pitch of hysteria about German spying and sabotage—although Bureau operations never caught a single spy or saboteur. It fell to the Justice Department to decide the fate of many German aliens.

The first faded memos of Edgar's prodigious career tell their own story. A German alien aged eighteen arrested on the Texas border for mouthing support for the Kaiser—Edgar recommended detention until the end of the war. Another German called President Wilson "a cocksucker and a thief." Edgar recommended internment again. He was overruled, on the ground that angry talk hardly justified such drastic punishment.

In 1918 Edgar worked on a drive to register all German women in the United States. That June, when *The Washington Post* reported that the work was going slowly, he rushed off a memo denying it. He would detest the *Post* and *The New York Times* all his life, would specifically exclude them from his daily reading, claiming that they "distort and slant the news." "When they throw brickbats at the FBI," he was to say, "I'm happy—brickbats from some people are like bouquets."

Edgar worked seven days a week in 1918, often into the night, and his boss took note. "Hoover," O'Brian observed then, "is a conscientious and honest fellow." Edgar received three pay increases in his first year at Justice, doubling his starting salary. Yet there was something odd about all this. Why had this twenty-three-year-old not gone to war?

All American males between the ages of twenty-one and thirty were required to register for military service within weeks of the declaration of war. As the government raised an army for the war in Europe, the first officers' training camp opened in Washington. Three million men would be drafted before it was over. One hundred and fifty thousand of them would die. There was a surge of righteous anger against young men who avoided the draft. In one roundup alone, 60,000 men were picked up in New York City, 27,000 in Chicago.

Edgar was a perfect draftee: a fit man in his early twenties, with years of officer training behind him at a school with strong links to West Point. Many of his former classmates did march off to the training camps, and some were sent to the trenches in France, but not Edgar.

He would later make much of his readiness to serve his country—once the hell of World War I was over. In 1922 he would obtain a commission as Major in the U.S. Army Officers' Reserve. In World War II, by which time he would be in his late forties, he would hold the rank of Lieutenant Colonel in the Military Intelligence Reserve—and resign only at the insistence of the Secretary of War, who said he could best serve his country as Director of the FBI.

Two decades later, Edgar would tell a newspaper that he stayed out of uniform in World War I for the same reason— because his "superiors persuaded him that he could perform a more valuable service in espionage work." Yet his voluminous staff file, filled with the details of the World War II period, is silent on World War I.

"Espionage work" is an inflated way to characterize Edgar's pen-pushing pursuit of aliens. His name, moreover, does not appear on the register of 102 Department of Justice employees who were given occupational exemption from military service. Sons who could prove they were the family breadwinner were eligible for exemption, but it is not known whether Edgar made such a claim.

Had he wanted to serve, as did so many of his classmates, he would have done so. The youth who enthused about the Cadet Corps more than anyone required, who as a grown man would cultivate military men as friends and contacts, who would one day persecute Vietnam War draft resisters, who would delight in combat metaphors in future speeches, could have been expected to rush to the recruiting office. Yet he flinched from doing so.

Edgar, the man whose bachelor status was to spark endless gossip, considered marriage in the closing months of the war. The episode proved a devastating emotional setback, one that may have played a key role in triggering his sexual ambivalence.

The account comes from Helen Gandy, the woman who served as Edgar's confidential secretary for fifty-three years. In conversations before her death in 1988, the usually tight-lipped Gandy revealed a sad story of frustrated courtship. When he was twenty-four, said the former secretary, Edgar saw a good deal of a young woman named Alice. She, too, worked in the War Emergency Division, and she was apparently the attractive daughter of a prominent Washington attorney—a factor that increased Edgar's interest. Should the end of the war bring the end of his job at the Justice Department, Edgar hoped for a job in his law firm.

On Armistice Day, November 11, 1918, Edgar was visited at his office by a friend named Sidney Kaufman. Kaufman was bursting to tell his news—he and his girlfriend planned to announce their engagement that very evening at Harvey's Restaurant, the Washington watering hole Edgar would patronize all his life. Edgar and Alice were invited to celebrate with them.

According to Gandy, Edgar decided he and Alice would also get engaged that evening. He sent her a note, asking her to meet him en route to the restaurant, at the Lafayette Hotel. Alice, however, did not turn up. She soon became engaged to another man, a young officer who—unlike Edgar—had gone to war.

Helen Gandy did not divulge the full name of Edgar's lost love. There is no reason, though, to doubt the story. Gandy talked about aspects of that evening in 1918 with two FBI officials, and she was a firsthand witness to Edgar's humiliation. She herself had been present at Harvey's that night, as the partner of one of the men at the party, and it was then that Edgar, in his loneliness, first took notice of her.

"Miss Gandy told me they had several dates," Edgar's future aide Cartha DeLoach recalled. "They had a good time, but they weren't attracted to each other in that way. It cooled off, but later—when he needed a secretary—he called her." Gandy, who was already working at the Bureau as a messenger, became a confidential clerk in Edgar's office just months later—and remained at his side from then on.

"The shock never really wore off," Gandy said of the Alice episode. The hurt was the greater because, Edgar discovered, the girl he hoped to marry had been romancing her army officer through the mail—while he was away at the front—all the time she was seeing Edgar. "This," Gandy said, "may have been part of why Mr. Hoover never really trusted women in that way, why he never married."

Edgar must have been thinking of Alice when, in 1955, he made a rare comment on his relations with women: "I was in love once when I was young," he told reporter Fletcher Knebel. "I guess you'd call it puppy love. . . ." He told another interviewer that, in his experience, women he wanted to marry were always involved with someone else.

"Here is something I will confess," Edgar said in an unusually frank interview in 1939. "If I ever marry and the girl fails me, ceases to love me, and our marriage is dissolved, it would ruin me. My mental status couldn't take it, and I would not be responsible for my actions." The phrase about "mental status" was deleted in reprints of the interview.

In the same conversation, Edgar gave away more about his attitude. "I have always held girls and women on a pedestal," he said. "They are something men should look up to, to honor and worship. If men would remember this and keep them there, married life would be better. I have had that idea about women all my life."

Edgar's niece Margaret, who saw a lot of her uncle in the decade that followed the Alice fiasco, never saw him with a woman his own age. She laid the blame on his mother. "Edgar would never have been able to get married," she said. "Nanny was truly the matriarch . . . she would have stopped anything rumored."

Edgar's mother had once tried to do just that. She had tried to prevent her elder son marrying, on the grounds that his intended was not good enough for him. On that occasion she failed, but she would never lose her grip on Edgar.

After the "puppy love" experience, Edgar would say years later, his work took the place of women. "I became attached to the Bureau, and I don't think any wife would have put up with me."

For a decade after the setback with Alice—throughout his twenties—Edgar had no emotional connection with anyone except Annie. He would come home each night to Seward Square, first to the tense house dominated by his father's mental illness, then—after Dickerson, Sr.'s, death—to life alone with Annie. As time passed, even that relationship soured. The strain showed in petty things. Edgar's niece Margaret, who lived with the Hoovers in the twenties, recalled the grown Edgar behaving like a spoiled child. "He was quite a tyrant about food. . . . His breakfast—and this goes back to Nanny running the house for him, although they had a cook—was a full-scale operation. . . . His favorite breakfast was a poached egg on toast, and if that egg was broken, he wouldn't eat it. It went back to the kitchen and another egg was prepared. . . ." Edgar would eat one bite of the second egg, Margaret said, then give it to the dog.

"Nanny," recalled Margaret's sister Anna, "always liked to leave the shades down all through the back and front parlors, so it was a very cool dark atmosphere when J.E. came home in the evening. Then up went the shades. There was no argument about it. He simply would go around and raise the shades and go up to his room. It was a kind of battle of wits on the part of two very intelligent people. . . . You had two very strong personalities here. . . . It was a case of dominating the situation. She ran a beautiful home for him, but he provided the wherewithal to run it beautifully.

And he was very good to her. He'd give her gifts, jewelry, some very nice jewelry. . . ."

For Edgar's brother, Dickerson, who was also helping out with the bills, it was galling to see Edgar bringing extravagant presents home to Annie. Dickerson, now a senior official at the Commerce Department, was jokingly called "the General" in the family. Edgar, the younger man, remained "the Major." "And how is the *attorney* tonight?" Dickerson would inquire mockingly when Edgar appeared. Edgar, increasingly conscious of his status, was not amused.

At work at the Justice Department, Edgar was living up to his mother's expectations and more. In November 1918, two months short of his twenty-fourth birthday, he had been elevated to the grade of Special Attorney, with a salary of $2,000 a year—as much as his father had earned at sixty.

Though still a lowly unknown, Edgar was already working on his image—by altering the way he styled himself. Until now he had initialed documents "JEH" or signed himself "J. E. Hoover," with a flourish to the loop of the "J." That, apparently, would no longer do. "J. Edgar Hoover," the name that was to become part of the American lexicon, was about to be born.

Edgar would claim he first changed his signature in 1933, after being refused credit at a clothing store because another John E. Hoover had failed to pay his bills. Like so much of the past according to Edgar, this was not true. It was on December 30, 1918, two days before his birthday, that the young man's pen hovered over an otherwise dull memorandum for John Lord O'Brian. He signed it, with a truly enormous flourish, "J. Edgar Hoover."

Perhaps, just weeks after his humiliation at the hands of Alice, Edgar simply needed to give his ego a boost. The man who headed the Bureau of Investigation at the time, and who had advanced Edgar's career, styled himself A. Bruce Bielaski. Looking back, waspish Justice Department veterans concluded that Edgar—already imagining himself at the top of the bureaucratic pecking order—was aping Bielaski.

O'Brian, who also propelled Edgar on his path to power,

spoke cautiously about him while he was alive. He survived, however, to the great age of ninety-eight, outliving Edgar by a few months. Before his own death, O'Brian was asked about his role in furthering the career of the youth who became J. Edgar Hoover.

"This," the old man admitted, "is something I prefer to whisper in dark corners. It is one of the sins for which I have to atone."

CHAPTER 3

"I always worry when I see a nation feel that it is coming to greatness through the activities of its policemen."

Cyrus Eaton, industrialist and critic of
J. Edgar Hoover

THE ELEVATION OF EDGAR CAME THANKS TO AN OPPORTUNISTIC Attorney General and his anti-Communist witch-hunt. Were it not for chance, and an odd combination of circumstances, it might never have happened at all.

As America celebrated the end of the war, Edgar's future was uncertain. With the War Emergency Division about to be disbanded, he started looking for a new job. He applied to join the Bureau of Immigration, was turned down, then went to his boss, John Lord O'Brian, and asked for a transfer to the Bureau of Investigation. He did not get that either, but O'Brian mentioned his name to the Attorney General–designate Mitchell Palmer, the "Fighting Quaker."

A clutch of senior officials, including O'Brian, quit the Bureau as soon as possible once Palmer was named for the post. During the war, when he had been Alien Property Custodian, millions of dollars in seized German assets had ended up in the hands of Palmer's Democratic cronies. He had ambitions to be President and saw the Justice Department merely as a stepping-stone. Just when he needed one, a political bandwagon appeared—in the shape of a wave of hysteria about Bolshevism.

Palmer took office in spring 1919, as Lenin was calling for world revolution. After months of horror stories about socialist upheaval in Europe, the American middle classes were shocked by waves of strikes at home—3,000 that year alone. Then a bombing campaign began, including a midnight attack on the home of the new Attorney General. The Senate called for a probe into an alleged plan to overthrow the government, and Congress funded an all-out investigation of radical groups.

The great Red scare had begun. Palmer hired William Flynn, former Chief of the Secret Service, to head the Bureau of Investigation, with Frank Burke, the Secret Service's former Russian expert, as second-in-command. As he cast around for assistants in his own department, Palmer remembered Edgar Hoover—one of only two wartime legal staffers who had asked to stay on.

A Secret Service check on Edgar turned up nothing remarkable—except that his father was now "very ill" in an asylum, and that Edgar was paying the bills. At twenty-four, Edgar became a Special Assistant to Palmer and head of a new section formed to gather evidence on "revolutionary and ultra-radical groups."

His day-to-day chores were directed by Assistant Attorney General Francis Garvan, a counter-subversion zealot with a visceral hatred of foreigners—and Edgar soon became known as "Garvan's pet." The job was tailor-made for the young man who had once delighted in sorting his books and keeping a record of his clothes sizes, then gone on to toil among the stacks at the Library of Congress. He now used his experience at the Library to build a massive card index on left-wingers.

The index proved to be astoundingly efficient by the standards of the time, the nearest thing to today's instantaneous retrieval by computer. Names and cross-references could be located within minutes. Half a million names were indexed during this, Edgar's first big operation, along with biographical notes on 60,000 people.

Edgar immersed himself in Communist literature. "I studied," he was to recall, "the writings of Marx, Engels, and Lenin, as well as the activities of the Third International." Those doctrines, he reported to his superiors, "threaten the happiness of the community, the safety of every individual. . . . They would destroy the peace of the country. . . ."

As a reading of Soviet Communism, this was accurate enough. Yet few historians believe there was any real risk of violent revolution in the United States in the twenties. In the wake of the bombings, however—not least thanks to Palmer and his bright young men—the country lost its balance.

Edgar's chosen assistant was George Ruch, a friend from high school days who held extreme right-wing views. Ruch's concept of democracy is summed up in one of his reports, which expressed astonishment that left-wingers—like other citizens—"should be allowed to speak and write all they wish against this government. . . ."

Later, when Ruch left the Bureau to head the Industrial Police for a Pittsburgh coal company, Edgar would assign agents to train the thugs he used against labor activists. Ruch named his son J. Edgar, and Edgar described Ruch as "one of my most personal friends." He addressed him affectionately as "Blimp."

One way to deal with dangerous radicals, the pair advised their superiors, was to throw them out of the country—by applying a law that made mere membership in radical organizations a deportable offense.

There followed a season of oppression remembered by Judge Lawrence Brooks of Massachusetts, who personally witnessed some of its outrages, as "the sorriest episode in the history of our country, not excepting the era of Senator Joseph McCarthy."

It began on November 7, 1919—carefully selected because it was the second anniversary of the Russian revolution—with raids on the offices of the Union of Russian Workers in a dozen cities. Hundreds of suspected revolutionaries were arrested, many severely beaten. Almost all were subsequently released, either because they were not foreigners at all, or could not conceivably be called revolutionaries. The raids were carried out by police and Bureau of Investigation agents, but "handled" at the Justice Department by Edgar.

The next stage of the operation gave Edgar his first taste of publicity, and one of the few opportunities he ever had to present a case in court. It was he who ensured the deportation of Emma Goldman, known to modern moviegoers as the anarchist, critic of organized religion and campaigner for birth control featured in the film *Reds*. She was also an active proponent of free love, whose intercepted letters were, Edgar said, "spicy reading." As an extreme radical *and* scarlet woman, she was anathema to him.

Getting Goldman deported was a tall order. She had been living in the United States for thirty-four years, since long before Edgar was born, and her father and former husband had become U.S. citizens. Edgar achieved it, however, following a massive probe, claiming that the husband's citizenship had been obtained by fraud and that Goldman's speeches inspired the assassin who killed President McKinley eighteen years earlier.

Four days before Christmas 1919, at two o'clock in the morning, Edgar and Bureau Chief William Flynn boarded a cutter to Ellis Island, in New York Harbor. There they confronted Goldman, her lover, Alexander Berkman, and 247 other deportees, as they boarded the troopship that was to carry them to Russia. Edgar described the experience to the press the next day with relish, promising that "other Soviet Arks will sail for Europe, just as soon as it is necessary, to rid the country of dangerous radicals."

On New Year's Day, Edgar had little time to celebrate his birthday. The countdown had started for the biggest Red Raid of all. On January 2, police and Bureau agents arrested some 10,000 people in twenty-three cities—again with brutality and violations of civil rights. Most of those seized turned out to be innocent and were eventually released.

Attorney General Palmer and his department came under intense criticism. Louis Post, the Assistant Secretary of Labor who ruled on the deportations, described the operation as a "gigantic and cruel hoax." Though Edgar was to claim he had "nothing to do with the raids," had "no responsibility," it is clear he and Ruch were the key men at headquarters on the night of the raids.

Bureau orders, sent to field offices by Assistant Bureau Chief Frank Burke, told agents to "communicate by long distance to Mr. Hoover any matters of vital importance which may arise during the course of the arrests." Burke, according to Agent James Savage, had long since "taken a shine to Hoover, taught him everything he knew, trained him and developed what talents he had."

Edgar used the Bureau to spy on lawyers who represented those arrested or worked to expose the abuse of civil rights. The investigation of the latter, he ordered, was to be "discreet and thorough." One of the targets was future Supreme Court Justice Felix Frankfurter, then a distinguished Harvard Law School professor. Edgar was to keep tabs on Frankfurter for half a century, referring to him privately as "the most dangerous man in the United States." As late as 1961, when Frankfurter was on the Court, an old report surfaced to haunt Edgar. Dated 1921 and signed "J. E. Hoover," it identified Frankfurter as a "disseminator of Bolshevik propaganda." In the flap that followed, Edgar tried to say the report had been issued by someone else.

"Hoover lies when he denies responsibility for the Red Raids," Frankfurter told his law clerk Joseph Rauh. "He was in it—up to his ass."[1]

Edgar claimed he had only been carrying out policy as instructed by others. This was a man, John Lord O'Brian would recall, "willing to carry out orders at any time." Judge Anderson, who presided at the deportation hearings, had no time for such officials. "Talk about Americanization!" he snorted. "It is the business of every American citizen who knows anything about Americanism to resign if given such instructions."

Neither Edgar nor Attorney General Palmer and the rest of his staff suffered the disgrace that should have resulted from the Red Raids. Congressional inquiries dragged on for so long—until a new Attorney General had been appointed under a new President—that everyone responsible escaped retribution.

Edgar had learned lessons he would not forget. For one thing, he now knew that state oppression could work in the United States. In spite of the furor, American Communists had suffered a crippling reversal. Party membership, estimated at about 80,000 before the raids, dwindled to 6,000 by late 1920.

Edgar also discovered it was possible to spy on people and hunt them down—not because of crimes but because of their political beliefs. To avoid being caught in the act, Edgar now knew, it was vital to ensure that—technically, at least—"due process" was always observed. He also learned that a way had to be found to keep the investigator's greatest treasure, his secret files, out of the public eye. Too many embarrassing documents came to light during the Red Raid hearings. Later, as FBI Director, Edgar would perfect a file system that, except on rare occasions, proved inaccessible to outsiders. Documents would be released on occasion, but only when it served Edgar's purpose.

He was also learning about politics and the perils of allegiance to any one man. In June 1920, when Attorney General Palmer went to fight for the presidential nomination at the Democratic Convention in San Francisco, Edgar went along. "At the time," political veterans recalled, "he saw his future tied to Palmer's political fortunes. He served above and beyond the call of duty, and mobilized all his official contacts to serve Palmer's cause."

Later, after Palmer had failed to get the nomination and the Democrats had been defeated, a Senate probe discovered that Edgar and three other officials had traveled to San Francisco at taxpayers' expense. Edgar claimed he had been on a routine investigation of radicals.

The probe could have cost Edgar his job, and he henceforth posed as a man above politics. He never joined a political party and—as a resident of Washington, D.C.— never voted.[2] "I don't like labels and I am not political," he liked to say in public.

This was not true. Edgar was a staunch right-wing supporter of the Republican Party from 1921 until the end of his life. "My associations have been with the Republican interests," he told a former colleague, Denis Dickason, in a private letter after Herbert Hoover's victory in 1929. "The results of the last election are particularly gratifying to me. . . ."

Few of those Edgar called friends were Democrats, and close associates never doubted his allegiance. "Hoover was a Republican from beginning to end," said veteran Justice Department official Patricia Collins.

When it suited him, however, Edgar would conceal this. "He could be all things to all people," said William Sullivan. "If a liberal came in, the liberal would leave thinking, 'My God, Hoover's a liberal.' If a John Bircher came in an hour later, he'd go out saying, 'I'm convinced Hoover's a member of the John Birch Society at heart.' He was a brilliant chameleon."

He was also a turncoat. Assistant Bureau Director Frank Burke, who had gone out of his way to help further Edgar's career, now heard his protégé was calling him "a political hack" behind his back. In his rage, he threatened to "kick hell out of" Edgar. The next time the two men met, recalled Agent James Savage, "the young skinny Hoover had surrounded himself with three husky bodyguards—all on the Department payroll."

Things were going from bad to worse at Justice. Harry Daugherty, Attorney General under the feeble new President Harding, was a political wheeler-dealer even less suited to the job than Palmer had been. Political abuse continued, with a heavy dose of corruption thrown in. It was now, in the Daugherty reshuffle of 1921, that Edgar finally joined the agency that would be his professional home for the rest of his life. On August 22 he was appointed Assistant Director of the Bureau of Investigation. The new Director, William Burns, a cigar-chomping former New York City detective, and something of a playboy, was a man who handed out jobs as political favors.

Daughtery was as gung ho to crush Communists and

radicals as his predecessor. His tactics included spying on congressmen and senators, and some of the results went to Edgar. In the future, Edgar would always say carefully that there had been no snooping on Congress "since I became Director." That would not be true but, when he did become Director, he would cover his tracks.

Edgar's brother Dickerson, less than impressed with Edgar's title—Assistant Director, Bureau of Investigation—continued to tease him. One night, as Edgar walked home alone along Seward Square, he realized he was being followed. A shadowy figure vanished into the bushes behind him, then reappeared, rushing out of the darkness with a bloodcurdling yell—Dickerson! Edgar rushed home to Mother, tormented by his brother's mocking laughter. Annie then took reprisals by stepping up her unkindnesses to Dickerson's wife, whom she had always despised.

Jokes about detectives went down badly with Edgar. He claimed detective work held no allure, that he "detested" crime fiction. Yet he owned a complete set of Sherlock Holmes stories, and was once spotted buying cheap detective magazines at a newsstand.

As Assistant Director, image and status were everything. Sometime earlier Edgar had become a Mason, going through the bizarre initiation ceremony that involved being blindfolded, having a noose placed around his neck and swearing at dagger point never to reveal Masonic secrets. Edgar would go on to become a Knight Templar, a Noble of the Mystic Shrine, on and up into the Masonic atmosphere until—at sixty—he attained the Ancient and Accepted Rite of the Thirty-third Degree.

In the twenties, in an America hooked on jazz and dance marathons, he lived a prim life. He still had no girlfriends, but did see a lot of Frank Baughman, a former classmate he had brought into the Justice Department. Smartly turned out in white linen suits, the two of them would venture out to the new Fox movie theater on Sunday nights. They would remain lifelong friends, though Baughman reportedly "lost his inside track" when he got married.

By his own account, Edgar's one true love at the time was Spee De Bozo, the dog that became his pet in 1922. The dog, an Airedale, accompanied its master each morning to fetch the newspaper, and sat by the table to eat the food Edgar rejected. It was Spee De Bozo's photograph, not that of a friend or relative, that Edgar kept on his desk at work. This was the first in a succession of seven dogs Edgar would own.

Years later, when Spee De Bozo died, Edgar made a production of the funeral. He and three male companions drove to Aspin Hill animal cemetery to watch, their hats on their shoulders, as the white-shrouded corpse was lowered into the earth. "This," Edgar told one of the cemetery staff, "is one of the saddest days of my life."

FBI propagandists often used the dog angle. "I remember one individual," an aide would intone in all seriousness to an audience at Yale University, "on the eve of going to the electric chair, writing Mr. Hoover and asking him to take care of his dog, and also expressing his appreciation of what was done for him." Edgar liked to trot out the story of the arrival of Spee De Bozo's successor, a terrier called Scottie. "I can still see my mother," he would say. "Tears welled into her eyes, her surprise matched only by her joy."

In fact, home life was strained. Most nights, Edgar would retreat upstairs as soon as he got home. Behind his bedroom door, he worked into the night on official papers. Now that he was Assistant Director he sometimes had to make speeches, and the prospect terrified him. From her room next door, his niece Margaret often heard him rehearsing. For some time, she said, he "had a problem with stuttering."

A congressman, watching Edgar at work in pursuit of Communists, had thought him a "slender bundle of high-charged electric wire." He was smoking cigarettes now, a Turkish brand called Fatima, and too many of them. By

1924, still pasty and underweight, he was complaining of stomach problems.

At twenty-nine, Edgar was lonely and under stress. But he was about to make a major step forward in his career, an achievement that would make his mother very happy indeed.

CHAPTER 4

"I certainly do not want to indicate that Hoover did not have some unusual ability in structuring an organization designed to perpetuate a sort of dictatorial control of both the FBI and, so far as he could manage it, the minds and aspirations of American citizens: but so did Adolf Hitler."

Arthur Murtagh, former FBI Agent, 1990

ON MOTHER'S DAY 1924, ANNIE HOOVER PRESENTED HER SON with a star sapphire ring studded with diamonds, one that he was to wear every day for the rest of his life. The previous day, May 10, a date that future agents would be required to memorize, Edgar had been promoted to head the Bureau of Investigation.

The way Edgar told it—and he told it often—he was called in that Saturday by Harlan Stone, the new Attorney General picked to clean up the Justice Department. Stone had started by firing William Burns, and Edgar half-expected to be fired, too. Instead Stone growled, "Young man, I want you to be Acting Director."

Edgar offered this account only when Stone had been dead for years. He left out a less glamorous part of the story. Stone had taken over the Department knowing nobody, with no idea whom to trust. He therefore began consulting cabinet colleagues, including Herbert Hoover, then Secretary of Commerce.[1]

Edgar had long been in touch with his namesake's personal staff. He was especially close to Hoover's closest aide, Lawrence Richey, a former Bureau agent who knew Edgar affectionately as "J.E." Told the Attorney General was casting around for a new Bureau chief, Richey had an easy answer. "Why the hell should they look around," he said, "when they have got one of the brightest young attorneys on the job at the present time?" It was Edgar's name that went to Stone.

Edgar's appointment was not reported in the press, and Stone made it clear the job was not yet permanent. "I want just the right man," he said. "Until I find that man, I intend personally to supervise the Bureau." The Attorney General's priority, after the abuses of the Daugherty period, was to restore confidence. Edgar's was to hang on to his job at a dangerous time, and convince Stone he had made the right choice.

In the old Bureau there was an office known as the "Buzzard's Roost," a room—according to an article generated by Edgar—"where the loafers congregated to swap dirty stories and help polish off the bottle which every returning agent was expected to furnish." Edgar closed it down and fired numerous agents. "Hoover," it was reported, "was as repulsed by the immorality of the roost as by the time it wasted."

Of all his achievements, Edgar's cleanup of the agent corps was the one of enduring worth. Since the start of his tenure, and to the present day, corruption among FBI agents has been virtually unheard of—a rare achievement in any police force. Their integrity has earned the admiration and confidence of the public, and made them the jewel in Edgar's crown.

The new Director did something else that pleased Stone, who had been an outspoken critic of Bureau outrages during the Red scare. He found that Edgar the Red-hunter had suddenly become Edgar the moderate. Within ten days of his appointment, he was assuring a Senate committee that the Bureau would no longer investigate citizens because of their political opinions.

At Stone's request, Edgar met with the Director of the American Civil Liberties Union, Roger Baldwin. Baldwin had accused the Bureau of operating "a secret police system," had himself seen the telephone tapping equipment that Edgar denied existed, had seen Bureau plans to set up a phony union local and pack it with government informants. Now, though, after Edgar's assurances about a "new era," Baldwin wrote to Stone saying he had been "wrong about Mr. Hoover's attitude."

After Edgar's death, however, when Baldwin was ninety-three, he was able to see old Bureau files on the ACLU. These showed that, even during the Stone regime, Edgar continued to receive reports on ACLU meetings—complete with purloined minutes and names of contributors—from an informer in place. The Bureau used police intelligence to spy on the group, and—as late as 1977—was still refusing to say whether such operations had ceased.

Edgar tried to appoint his best friend, the right-wing extremist George Ruch, as his most senior aide. The Attorney General vetoed that plan following a public outcry, but confirmed Edgar's permanent appointment as Director of the Bureau of Investigation. The news was announced on December 22, 1924, ten days before Edgar's thirtieth birthday. (Federal was not added to the name "Bureau of Investigation" until 1935. Only then did it become the FBI.) He would hold the post for forty-eight years, a quarter of the time the United States had existed as a nation.

For the rest of both their lives, Edgar fawned upon Stone and Herbert Hoover, the men most responsible for his promotion. Both received regular letters of adulation, and found FBI agents waiting to welcome them on their travels. Edgar jumped to do confidential research for Hoover, or fix a summer job for Stone's chauffeur—a stream of little favors in return for the break they had given him.

Edgar had escaped from the rubble of the old Bureau. Now, from a small power base, he began to build an empire.

Edgar was to create one of the most powerful organizations in the United States, in some troubling ways the most powerful of all. He would achieve it thanks to a combination of rapid social change, political shifts and a good deal of luck. He brought to the task his own brilliance as an organizer, a shrewd ability to read the national mood and a capacity for self-advertisement unparalleled in public life.

Edgar came to office at precisely the right moment. After the chaos of the Harding presidency, America was putting its faith in efficient administrators, education and the wonders of technology. The new Director responded to all three requirements.

Edgar fired the deadwood along with the crooked agents, and closed more than twenty field offices. Within five years, far from expanding, he would cut the number of agents to 339, a quarter less than when he had taken over. New recruits had to be between twenty-five and thirty-five, and have a background in law or accountancy.[2]

A rookie agent arrived on the job with a letter of appointment from Edgar, a salary of $2,700 a year plus travel allowance, and an obligation to go anywhere in the United States at any time. He presented himself for duty dressed in a suit, white shirt and conservative tie, topped off with a plain straw hat. He signed an oath of office, in the early days a terse statement promising to defend the Constitution "against all enemies, foreign and domestic." Later, newcomers would take an extraordinary pledge, issued over Edgar's own signature. It read like a catechism, with Masonic overtones:

> Humbly recognizing the responsibilities entrusted to me, I do vow that I shall always consider the high calling of law enforcement to be an honorable profession, the duties of which are recognized as both an art and a science . . . in the performance of my duties I shall as a minister, seek to supply comfort, advice and aid . . . as a soldier, I shall wage vigorous warfare against the enemies of my country . . . as a physician, I shall seek to eliminate the criminal parasite which preys on our body politic . . . as an artist, I shall seek to use my skill for the purpose of making each assignment a masterpiece. . . .

One of the new recruits, Edward J. Armbruster, served from 1926 to 1977 as an expert on bank fraud. He was typical of the new breed of agent, a teetotaler and nonsmoker, a Mason and Sunday school teacher, who brought seven of his pupils into the FBI, and lived all his life in the Sears and Roebuck prefabricated house bought the year Edgar became Director. Edgar thought him a paragon, and allowed him to work long past retirement age.

An agent of a later generation, Norman Ollestad, drew this portrait of a veteran colleague. "He surrounded himself with an armor of shibboleths—rings, badges and jeweled pins. He was all battened down. A lion's head clasp kept his tie from going awry, cuff links tightened down his white sleeves. He wore a college ring on his right hand to set him apart from the uneducated, and a Masonic ring on the same hand that protected him spiritually. On the third finger of his left hand he wore a wedding band as a shield against any designing women he might interview."

Leon Turrou, a celebrated first-generation recruit, offered a telling definition of the sort of man Edgar wanted. "He is part and parcel of the great middle class. He will always eat well and dress well, but he will never get that sleek Packard or that sumptuous house. . . . He is a man who for better or worse is married to his job twenty-four hours a day. He belongs to the Bureau body and soul, and is simply on loan to his family and friends. He learns to revaluate his life in terms of his work, divorcing himself from the ordinary pleasures of ordinary mortals and often forgetting how to relax. The motto of his life is 'For God, for country, and for J. Edgar Hoover.'"

Under their breath, agents would come to call Edgar "Kid Napoleon." He was dictatorial and diminutive in stature—estimates of his height vary between 5'7" and 5'10", the higher figure being the one he had entered in his personnel record. Edgar compensated for his lack of height, generations of colleagues noted, with artful devices. The Director sat on a swivel chair, screwed up to the maximum height so that he looked down at visitors, who were ushered to a low couch. His chair and desk, in turn, sat on a slight platform.

"He used to accuse me of wearing built-up shoes so I would be as tall as he was," said Miami agent Leo McClairen. "That was funny, because I stand six foot two." Edgar, however, did have his shoes custom-built, by a personal shoemaker.

Edgar was a hard taskmaster. During Prohibition, which coincided with his first decade in office, he fired agents caught drinking—even off duty. In 1940, long after Prohibition, an agent had his pay cut just for being in the company of a colleague who got drunk in a nightclub. As late as 1960, rookie agents, caught with a half-bottle of Cutty Sark, were threatened with dismissal.

Unmarried agents were expected to live like monks. Once, when Edgar learned that an agent had been caught having sex with a woman in the Knoxville, Tennessee, office, he did not just fire the offending couple. He dispersed almost all the Knoxville staff around the country.

Though Edgar insisted that he had no wish to keep his men unmarried, he tried in the early days to obstruct marriages that failed to please him. At best, prospective wives were given the Bureau once-over. At worst, Edgar used covert means to break up marriages of which he did not approve. One agent's wife received anonymous letters claiming, falsely, that her husband was unfaithful.

In 1959 Erwin Piper, Agent in Charge in San Diego, was forbidden to act as best man to one of his staff because— over the objections of the Catholics in the office—the Catholic agent was marrying a Protestant divorcée. Edgar demoted Piper, even though he knuckled under, for arguing with the objectors in the first place.

Once agents were married, Edgar kept a strict eye on them. Heads of FBI field offices, known as Agents in Charge, were under orders to inform him if colleagues were having affairs outside their marriages. Edgar called such men "double-yolkers."

Generations of agents lived in terror of the inspection teams, known as Goon Squads. Their task was to descend without warning to sniff out the most trivial transgressions

—an airline schedule left in a desk drawer that should contain only official papers, laundry left in the wrong place, dirty clothes left behind a radiator. Edgar would claim his own office got the same treatment, which was not true.

Minor transgressions usually resulted in a letter of censure, and every agent earned a stack of them. Graver sins meant a transfer within hours. To face a series of transfers was to go on "the Bureau Bicycle," the device used to ease out an agent who had committed no fireable offense. A man forced to move every couple of months might resign.

The ultimate sanction, dismissal "with prejudice," spelled long-term disaster. The victim would never again obtain federal employment, and had no reference to help him get another job. For most of Edgar's tenure, there was no one to appeal to once he had decided to fire someone.

An agent's life was dangerous, and became more so in the gangster era of the thirties. Until 1934 agents carried guns only in an emergency, and twenty-two of them died on duty while Edgar was Director. In spite of the risks, and in spite of the draconian discipline, men readily served under Edgar. They received better pay and fringe benefits than similar government employees, and developed an esprit de corps that was the envy of other agencies. As for the dangers, Edgar earned the respect of his agents by personally supervising the manhunt that captured the killer of Edwin Shanahan, the first agent to be killed on duty. He saw to it that widows of murdered agents were looked after with a pension, and guaranteed a clerical job if they wanted one.

Edgar could play the compassionate boss or, without warning or justification, the ogre. One man recalls the readiness with which Edgar gave him a transfer to be near his pregnant wife, another the savage reception he got when—offered a promotion—he asked for a month's delay to look after a newborn child. The promotion was canceled, the agent demoted to the ranks.

Edgar was loved and loathed by his men in equal measure.

In the hungry years of the twenties and thirties, though, he made the Bureau a man's institutional home, very like a branch of the armed services, a shelter from the outside world. Soon instructors were telling recruits, with a straight face, "This is the greatest organization ever devised by a human mind." They were officially instructed to quote Emerson: "An institution is the lengthened shadow of one man"—meaning, of course, the Director. The Bureau became an extended family, with Edgar as a sort of nineteenth-century patriarch, praising or punishing as he saw fit.

Meanwhile, Edgar had made the Bureau unique and indispensable. In an era when much of America had progressed little since the days of frontier justice, Edgar brought modernity to law enforcement. He moved into the Director's office in 1924 hefting several boxes of dog-eared fingerprint cards. These, coupled with 800,000 prints sent to the old Bureau from Leavenworth Penitentiary, were the germ of a technological revolution.

Edgar's dream was "Universal Fingerprinting," the notion that the prints of every citizen—the innocent as well as the guilty—should be recorded. That never happened, but he soon became the custodian of those held by police forces across the country, then those of thousands of federal employees and later—in World War II—those of every soldier, sailor and airman, every worker in war industries.

Edgar's fingerprint bureau grew from one small file room to a huge L-shaped clearinghouse high in the Department of Justice, and eventually to a six-story building occupying an entire city block. By the sixties it was said that the fingerprint cards, stacked one on top of another, would reach 113 times higher than the Empire State Building. By the time Edgar died, a vast computerized Identification Division offered instant access to the whorls, loops and arches of the fingers of 159 million people.

Edgar developed a massive Crime Laboratory, room after room in which rows of experts pored over ballistics evidence and analyzed poisons, hairs and fibers. Other staff members spent their entire working lives immersed in the Rubber Stamp and Printing Standards File, the Checkwriter Standards File, the Safety Paper Standards File, the Typewriter Standards File, the Confidence Man File or the Anonymous Letter File.

The FBI Crime Laboratory quickly became the most advanced in the world—and the key to the expansion of Edgar's empire. The first step was to persuade America's police chiefs, always jealous of their power, that in an increasingly mobile nation a centralized fingerprint system was essential. Once local forces started shipping copies of their prints to Washington, thousands of them every day, the payoff in arrests and convictions proved Edgar right.

The fingerprint and laboratory operations alone changed the Bureau from a small agency with limited jurisdiction to a vital facility upon which all other law enforcement depended. Soon it would offer the Uniform Crime Reports system, a bureaucratic miracle that coordinated millions of crime statistics pumped in from across the nation. Next came the Law Enforcement Bulletin, which started as the first centralized Wanted list and became a slick magazine bringing the Bureau's views—or rather Edgar's—to every policeman in the land. Soon the Bureau had a virtual monopoly on the supply of crime information, not only to the police but to the country at large. Accurate or not, its version became gospel.

The final link with the police would be forged in 1935, when Edgar created the police training school that became the FBI National Academy. In an era when there was no such thing as a professional qualification for policemen, the officers who took the Academy course went home to become the elite. Eventually, of the Academy graduates who remained in law enforcement, one in five would end up running a police department. Graduation exercises became grand occasions attended by presidents and attorneys general, and the Academy was recognized as the West Point and Harvard of law enforcement.

Edgar had been shrewd. He knew there was a deep-seated

fear of a national police force, so he repeatedly went out of his way to say such a force could never work. The police fraternity he created, though, came close to being the very thing he publicly deplored. It depended entirely on the Bureau—and the Bureau, everyone knew, was Edgar.

Edgar always limited the Bureau to what he knew it could do successfully. He avoided accepting a mandate to police drug trafficking, for example, because he feared exposing his agents to corruption, and because there was little chance of easy success. So it was that other agencies dealt with narcotics, violations of Prohibition, smuggling, forgery and immigration offenses. Indeed, while Edgar was Director, the Bureau had jurisdiction over only a minute percentage of the serious crimes committed in the United States.

Edgar readily took on more straightforward targets, those that offered easy prestige. He responded willingly in the thirties, when a series of spectacular crimes convinced the nation it was being overwhelmed by a crime wave. For Edgar, launched on a rocket of publicity designed originally to benefit the government, it would prove the breakthrough that assured his fame.

Edgar succeeded at self-advertisement like no comparable public figure, in the long term because, at the taxpayers' expense, he created Division 8, euphemistically known as Crime Records and Communications. His workaholic confidant Louis Nichols, another graduate of George Washington University Law School, built the division into a bureaucratic Madison Avenue devoted to the greater glory of Edgar and the FBI.

Crime Records had multiple functions. One was to send the public messages that had nothing to do with law enforcement—and everything to do with what Edgar wished to preach. This language appealed to the emotions, especially that of fear, and denounced "moral deterioration," "apathy that is really a sickness," "disrespectful young people," "the depraved deeds of teenage thugs," "moral decay," "anarchist elements," "jackals of the news media," "the menace to the security of our country," "a new specter haunting the Western World"—all those horrors in a single speech. The implication was that only Edgar and his FBI stood between America and disaster.

Edgar developed an insidious language, known to some as "Bureauspeak," for use in sensitive communications. This was used to smear people Edgar perceived as political enemies. The paragraph that follows concludes an inter-agency memo about the "alleged interracial sexual indiscretions" of a lawyer in the Civil Rights Division at the Justice Department:

These allegations were not made directly to representatives of the FBI but were received through a third person. Thus the FBI is not in any position to comment upon the reliability of the source; however, the source has furnished some other information, some of which is of a questionable nature, which leaves considerable doubt as to the credibility of the source.

In this one paragraph of Bureauspeak, Edgar managed to throw doubt on his source, thus protecting the Bureau, while still besmirching the character of his target. The memo, like thousands of others, had absolutely nothing to do with law enforcement.

Such quibbles later became academic. Edgar had been vastly strengthened politically when, on the eve of World War II, President Roosevelt handed him the new mission of protecting national security. Thanks to a mandate intended mainly to ensure effective investigation of Fascists, Edgar was again poised to tackle his enemy of preference, the "radicals."

With Crime Records providing a torrent of propaganda, with a vastly expanded FBI employing more than 3,000 agents by 1946 and with presidential sanction to use police state tools such as wiretapping, the way was clear for a new open season on Reds. Thousands of American citizens were persecuted by the FBI, directly or indirectly, while Edgar fostered the notion that the Communists were somehow responsible for all manner of American social problems—from changing sexual standards to juvenile delinquency.

Edgar's protégé Joseph McCarthy would make similar noises and succumb to his own demagoguery. Edgar survived because he was careful never to take center stage, and because he sustained the illusion of being "above politics," an unimpeachable source for the facts the nation needed to know.

He had long since secured the unquestioning loyalty of a powerful constituency that included the police, federal and state prosecutors, the myriad agencies that now relied on the FBI to perform security clearances, and patriotic organizations like the American Legion. The Legion, which Edgar had systematically wooed and penetrated, virtually deified him.

A series of polls showed that, by the late forties, a majority of the population had come to believe Edgar and the Bureau could do no wrong. Criticism was virtually nonexistent until the mid-sixties, and, when there was any, Edgar found ways to stamp it out. Impertinent journalists were frightened into silence or smeared.

By the end of the war, largely thanks to Crime Records, Edgar also had the Congress in his thrall. The Bureau made contact with and kept files on every single politician who made it to Capitol Hill. Men in key positions were courted assiduously, and most were happy for a chance to share Edgar's limelight. Far from being a supplicant seeking funds, as were most agency heads, he pulled the strings.

Edgar's annual appearance before the House Appropriations Committee was a cakewalk. He would produce an array of wondrous statistics on crime, alleged FBI successes to make the Bureau look good, coupled with dire warnings to justify his latest request for cash. He was never denied a legislative mandate, and his demands were never refused.

From 1924 to 1971 there was not a single public hearing on the FBI budget.

Edgar presented himself as the obedient, even obsequious, servant of authority. In theory his boss was the Attorney General. In practice, once Edgar became a public hero in the thirties, that seniority became nominal. No attorney general dared risk a head-on confrontation with the man who had become a national symbol of integrity and continuity.

The eight presidents he served, of course, had the power to fire Edgar. One or two came close and several yearned to do so, but none succeeded. Edgar had a way of making his services seem essential, and presidents who doubted it dared not offend the powerful forces who believed Edgar's cause was their own.

Edgar's vast filing system was part of his stock in trade. He was proud of it, just as he was proud of his scientific advances. Presidents and politicians, however, had to live with the threat—real or imagined—that those files could bring disaster down on their heads. From routine reports to scandal-filled dossiers, from detailed analyses to random fragments of information, Edgar's paper mountain was both bureaucratic dream and democratic nightmare. Even today, few outside the FBI understand Edgar's record system. While he was alive, no one in the outside world knew anything about it. Edgar's insistence on secrecy, which he defended in the name of protecting privacy, made sure of that.

Edgar's record system included files with names like the OBSCENE file, the SEX DEVIATE program, COINTELPRO, OFFICIAL AND CONFIDENTIAL, PERSONAL AND CONFIDENTIAL, JUNE MAIL, even a DO NOT FILE system, so named to keep reports on illegal Bureau break-ins out of the central record system.[3]

The files remained, always, under the ultimate control of just one man. Edgar's senior men might be brilliant in their specialties or mere time-serving hatchet men. Some were fine men of integrity, others devious creatures capable of great evil. All, though, depended on Edgar in a closed, compartmentalized world that permitted no alliance capable of threatening Edgar's position.

He created this private fiefdom in such a way that—as long as he lived—he had absolute power over those who served him, and the weapons to fend off those who did not. He had, moreover, created an instrument that could be used to undermine civil liberties.

CHAPTER 5

"I want at this time to say that so long as I am Director of the FBI, appointments will continue to be made on merit, without regard to creed, color, or nationality."

J. Edgar Hoover, 1943

THOSE WHO KNEW HIM AT CLOSE QUARTERS DISCOVERED THERE was something obsessive about Edgar. The little boy from Seward Square, the offspring of a disturbed father and an ambitious mother, was insistent that everything should run precisely as he directed, that everything should fit his concept of perfection.

This showed itself in the little things, like Edgar's fixation on tidiness. At home, servants would report, there was hell to pay if a bedspread was even slightly askew, a cushion out of place, an undisciplined leaf neglected on the front path. Edgar's first act on reaching the office each morning, his secretary recalled, was to give his shoes a flick with a duster—in case they had lost their sheen during the ride in the car to work.

At headquarters, which Edgar had everyone call the Seat of Government, an official once found himself in hot water because his office window shade was—in Edgar's opinion— pulled down too far. He said it gave the building "a messy look from the outside."

Like Howard Hughes, the eccentric billionaire, Edgar worried constantly about germs. He waged war against them by insisting his office be kept cold, and later by installing an ultraviolet light reputed to eliminate viruses. A servant, armed with a swatter, was assigned to deal with flies. The

Director shrank from physical contact with strangers, especially those with moist palms.

Edgar defended his fragile self like a nuclear bunker. This was a man, his associates learned the hard way, who never—ever—admitted he was wrong; he could not even admit the possibility. Once, when a Special Agent in Charge felt obliged to point out Edgar was quoting incorrect figures, he sat in silence, red as a beet, until the agent slipped quietly out of the room. Later, Edgar crucified the man who had supplied the statistics.

Edgar's officials became expert at dealing with this problem—on issues that mattered and many that did not. When Edgar refused to accept solid research showing the civil rights movement was not, as he insisted, Communist-inspired, an Assistant Director simply admitted humbly that his report had been "wrong." When Edgar dismissed as "baloney" research confirming the existence of the Mafia, its authors did not argue. When Edgar announced his grief at the killing of an agent who had only been wounded, the man's colleagues jokingly drew straws for who would finish him off. The Director was never wrong.

Edgar could be manic about control. One veteran agent inadvertently ruined a cordial meeting by reminding his boss of the good old days when the Bureau had been smaller, when "you could personally keep track of everything that was going on." Edgar exploded. "I still know personally *everything* that goes on!" he roared. "I still personally *run* this Bureau!" As he ranted on, he reached for the agent's file to score out favorable comments he had made moments before.

The corridor to Edgar's inner sanctum was known as the Bridge of Sighs, and few knew how to handle him better than Sam Noisette, the black receptionist who ushered visitors along it. "If it's snowing and blowing outside," he said, "and the Director comes in and says 'It's a beautiful sunny day,' it's a beautiful sunny day. That's all there is to it."

* * *

At first glance Edgar's corps of agents, the linchpin of his reputation, seemed a representative group. It came to include former farmers, airmen, journalists, a baker, professional football players, cowboys, railway workers and miners. Some had military experience, and Edgar was especially keen on former Marines. He had no interest, however, in hiring blacks, Hispanics or women—and he discriminated against Jews.

Three women were serving as agents when Edgar became Director in 1924. Two he fired within a month. He confirmed the appointment of a third, Leonore Houston, following pressure from her Congressman, but she did not last long. FBI records say she ended up in a mental hospital, "threatening to shoot Mr. Hoover as soon as she was released."

From then on Edgar brushed aside all talk of recruiting women, claiming that they "could never gunfight, and all our agents must know how to do that." He remained unmoved, nearly fifty years later, when two feminists sued the FBI, claiming that rejection of their applications violated their constitutional rights. As soon as he died, though, the policy was changed. Today there are nearly 900 female FBI agents, all fully trained in the use of firearms.

To the women he did employ as clerical staff, Edgar behaved like a martinet. He had grown up in a time when women were arrested for smoking in public, so he forbade them to smoke in the office. He refused to let women wear pants to work until 1971. Only then, persuaded by his own secretary that women needed pants to keep warm in the winter, did he capitulate.

Even at that stage, Edgar was still punishing employees for the way they behaved in private. "When a girl in the Fingerprint Section got pregnant without being married," recalled Miami Agent in Charge Kenneth Whittaker, "Hoover was furious. He wanted to know who investigated her before we hired her. Was she promiscuous? When he discovered she was living with a guy, he fired her at once. He didn't want word to get out that we'd hire girls who'd do that."

Edgar's attitude filtered down to the ranks and generated crude contempt. Female employees were tolerated, said former Agent Cril Payne, "only to perform the boring clerical functions required to keep the Bureau paper flowing. The prevailing attitude seemed to be that it was perfectly all right to bullshit 'em and ball 'em; just don't tell 'em any secrets. . . ."

Edgar was apparently prejudiced against Jews. In Miami Beach, where he stayed every Christmas, he invariably chose hotels that—until World War II—carried the sign NO JEWS, NO DOGS. He referred to the Irish leader Eamon de Valera, in an early report, as "a Portuguese Jew," and fifty years later dismissed Robert Mardian, an Assistant Attorney General during the Nixon administration, as "that Lebanese Jew." In fact, de Valera was part Spanish, but had no Jewish blood, and Mardian was a Christian, of Armenian descent.

Over the years, two Jews became Assistant Directors. Jewish employees were given days off to observe religious holidays, and Jews once made up most of the FBI basketball team. Yet Jack Levine, a Jew who joined in 1960, calculated that only one half of one percent of Bureau agents were Jewish. He found pervasive discrimination, including a supervisor who said there was nothing subversive about the American Nazi Party, because "all they are against is Jews," and an instructor who described an expert witness as "a greasy-looking sheenie."

Edgar hired hardly any Hispanics. "The average Mexican," he said, "is a psychological [*sic*] liar. . . . They have visions probably of making money." "You never have to bother about a President being shot by Puerto Ricans or Mexicans," he told an interviewer. "They don't shoot very straight. But if they come at you with a knife, beware."

Edgar had no foreign friends, and had a knee-jerk distrust of anyone from a foreign country. Except for a couple of one-day excursions across the Canadian and Mexican borders, he never traveled outside the United States. He once ruled that *Newsweek* correspondent Dwight Martin was "not acceptable as an interviewer," because his Chinese wife, from Hong Kong, had met American naval officers while working as a tailor's assistant.

"I guess he was afraid she was a spy," said Martin's colleague Ben Bradlee. "It was so stupid. But the really ridiculous thing was the fact that he had that sort of investigation done on a decent, respected reporter just because he'd requested an interview."

As for black agents, Edgar's attitude was that of most white southerners of his generation. "Coloreds" were fine as the help, but they were to be excluded from the professions. The notion that law enforcement officers should address black people courteously seemed outlandish to him as late as 1966. "Instead of saying, 'Boy, come here!'" he noted scornfully, "they want to be addressed as Mr. . . . ."

Edgar kept the Bureau in a state of apartheid as long as he possibly could. There was one black agent when he took office, an "Uncle Tom" figure called James Amos, who had started out looking after President Theodore Roosevelt's children. He had become an agent thanks to Edgar's predecessor, William Burns, and was used as a penetration agent against black activists. Amos was the first black agent, and would have been the last had Edgar had his way.

Of nine black men who rose from the lower grades in Edgar's first forty years, five served as his personal lackeys.[1] Edgar's first flunky was Sam Noisette, who moved up from messenger to become the keeper of his office door. Each morning, when a buzzer alerted him to his master's arrival in the basement garage, Noisette would wait poised to greet him at the elevator. He stayed on hand until Edgar left at night, obsequious to a fault, addressing visitors in a suitably "darky" accent.

Noisette was a competent artist, and Edgar encouraged him. His painting of the Director's dog, Spee De Bozo, hung in Edgar's home, and others were displayed in the anteroom at the office. Edgar reproached aides who failed to attend Noisette's annual exhibition, and some officials bought pictures just to keep the boss happy.

A second black man, former truck driver James Crawford, joined the retinue in 1934 as head chauffeur and handyman.

He would arrive at Edgar's house at 7 A.M., having first driven the Director's personal car to headquarters to pick up the official limousine, so that no one could claim an official car was being used on private time. Crawford's working day involved driving Edgar to the office, waiting on standby all day, then working until midnight if his boss had a function in the evening. He was to serve Edgar for thirty-eight years, continuing to work as domestic and gardener after ill health forced him to retire from the Bureau.

Two other blacks, Jesse Strider in Los Angeles and Leo McClairen in Miami, were to chauffeur Edgar during his vacations. Once he became established he used Pierce-Arrow and Cadillac armored limousines, custom-built by Hess and Eisenhardt. Except for the President, he was the only federal official to have the use of such vehicles, apparently because of regular threats against his life. The President, however, had only one such car, which was moved around the country as required. Edgar had three (they would cost $30,000 each by the end of his career) at his disposal in Washington, California and Florida—and at one point a fourth in New York City. On occasion, the cars were moved around by military transport aircraft.

Washington folklore had it that Edgar's drivers had to keep the car engine running when they waited for him, even if it meant waiting for hours, so that he was never delayed for an instant. Harold Tyler, an Assistant Attorney General during the Eisenhower administration, discovered this story was true. "Hoover came to our house one night," he recalled. "I thought he'd only stay a short while, but he stayed on and on. I went out for a moment to check on booze or something and I found his driver standing there. He looked very embarrassed and said 'I've run out of gas.' He'd just been afraid to switch off the engine. Hoover just felt he could get away with these things. . . ."

One morning in 1946, on the way to work, Edgar was to hand Crawford an official letter—notification that suddenly, after thirteen years, he was being promoted to the rank of special agent. Noisette was promoted, too, but both went back to their servants' duties once they had attended the agents' training program. They were not real agents, just players in one of Edgar's propaganda games. Leo McClairen, who did become a star agent on the Miami Fugitive Squad, was an exception. He resumed his chauffeur role, however, whenever Edgar visited Miami.

The elevation of a few blacks was merely a plot to placate the National Association for the Advancement of Colored People, which had publicly accused the FBI of having a "lily-white" hiring policy. The Bureau remained a white preserve until the sixties. Jack Levine, the Jewish agent who went through his training in 1961, was appalled to hear instructors refer openly to blacks as "niggers." One told recruits that the NAACP was a Communist front. A first-aid lecturer said that, while the most effective resuscitation method was mouth-to-mouth resuscitation, an alternative system could be used if the victim was black.

Attorney General Robert Kennedy made a sport of nagging Edgar about the need to hire more blacks. He raised the subject again and again, often summoning Edgar back as he was leaving the room to ask, as if it were an afterthought, "Oh, by the way, Edgar, how many blacks have you hired *this* month?" The Bureau's whites-only policy was under serious pressure for the first time.

A handful of blacks suddenly found themselves being asked to join the FBI. Aubrey Lewis, a former Notre Dame football star turned coach, found himself seated next to a high-ranking Bureau official at a Hall of Fame dinner attended by President Kennedy. He was recruited soon after, and in June 1962—along with former Bureau clerk James Barrow—became one of the first two blacks to be admitted to the FBI Academy in Virginia. Both men were soon featured in a carefully orchestrated article in *Ebony* magazine. The Bureau boasted thirteen blacks by the end of that year, out of a total agent force of 6,000 men.

Edgar remained obdurate to the end. "I have not, and will not, relax the high standards which the FBI has traditionally demanded," he blustered once the Kennedys were gone. "Robert Kennedy became very angry with me over this. I would not yield." Edgar and some of his aides claimed there were not enough black applicants good enough to make the grade. Black graduates who were, they said, preferred to take better-paid jobs elsewhere.

Edgar died leaving the Bureau with just seventy black agents, not one of them in a senior post. By 1991 the number had risen to 500, though this was still only 4.8 percent of the total agent force of 10,360. Ugly stories of discrimination against serving black agents continue to surface today.

The sort of agent Edgar did want, veteran agent Arthur Murtagh told a congressional committee in 1978, was "a good white Anglo-Saxon, preferably an Irishman with conservative views . . . another good WASP, and have him apply to the Bureau and see he gets the job—to hell with the qualification. . . ."

Some applicants were rejected just because their faces looked wrong. "Didn't you notice that he has eyes like Robert Mitchum?" an Agent in Charge once asked Murtagh during the screening of a former Air Force Captain. "His eyelids fall down over his eyes. I'd be afraid to recommend him. I got transferred one time for recommending somebody that had acne on his face."

The way a man *thought* was most important of all. "We're not interested," Edgar claimed, "in a man's politics." Not true. The Bureau simply passed over applicants whose earliest interviews indicated liberal ideas, or any deviation from Edgar's concept of the norm. According to former Agent Jack Levine, recruits were "heavily indoctrinated in radical right-wing propaganda." Liberals who slipped through the net were moved sideways, if not out, once their deviations were spotted.

Political control extended even to the FBI dress code, which forbade the wearing of red neckties. Agents ended up politically neutered at best, at worst as right-wing zealots. "Mr. Hoover," said Agent Murtagh, "was able over a period of nearly fifty years to bring in thousands of carefully selected agent personnel who were as politically disposed to the right as he was. . . . The result, because of the way he used those agents, was an unbalanced, damaging influence on American culture."

A few brave agents started speaking out against Edgar's policies soon after he became Director. In 1927 Senator Thomas Walsh, a known critic of the Bureau, received an acid memorandum from a former Agent in Charge, Franklin Dodge. He told of unfair treatment of staff, the twisting of facts to give the Bureau credit that really belonged to the police, illegal pursuit of radicals and improper collaboration with right-wing journalists. Edgar himself, Dodge claimed, had been "junketing around the country" with his "wet nurse" friend Frank Baughman, spending taxpayers' money on personal pleasure trips.

Two years later another former Agent in Charge, Joseph Bayliss, sent a detailed complaint to the Attorney General. He spoke of an agency in which bureaucratic perfection was more important than investigation of crime, of a punishment system that terrorized men and destroyed individual initiative. He accused Edgar, accurately, of giving jobs to his former law school classmates, and of making appointments "to please certain politically influential persons . . . U.S. senators." Bayliss thought his complaint would be ignored —and it was.

Michael Fooner, a member of the Bureau's Technical Section in the thirties, made the mistake of supporting the formation of an FBI branch of the Federation of Government Employees. Forty years later, when he obtained his file under the Freedom of Information Act, he was astonished to discover it was six inches thick. The Bureau had watched him throughout his subsequent career, occasionally letting other government agencies know that he was a subversive character.

"Fear," one agent would complain, "actuates every move made by the employees. . . ."

* * *

In 1929, however, as Edgar marked his thirty-fourth birthday, real success still eluded him. His revamped Bureau might be clean as a whistle, but it was rather obscure. So was Edgar. In an article about a half-dozen Washington officials who all happened to be called Hoover, he was listed last—two below his elder brother Dickerson, by this time an important official at the Department of Commerce.

These were doldrum days in Washington. After the years of drift under Calvin Coolidge, Herbert Hoover was beginning the third consecutive Republican reign at the White House. Within months, this businessman president would fail to realize the gravity of the Wall Street Crash, and would announce the Depression "over" when the real misery was yet to come.

By 1932 more than 13 million Americans, a quarter of the work force, were unemployed. Thousands of men and women stood in soup lines. A million and more were homeless. President Hoover's very name had become synonymous with economic blight. There were Hoover blankets, the newspapers used by the destitute to ward off the cold; Hoover flags, pockets empty of money; and Hoovervilles, the shantytowns of the homeless.

Edgar allowed the Bureau to be used—entirely improperly—to silence one of the President's persistent critics. He sent no fewer than five agents to interrogate the publisher of the *Wall Street Forecast,* George Menhinick, who had been printing articles on the dire state of the nation's banks. "Menhinick," Edgar reported with satisfaction, "was considerably upset over the visit of the agents. . . . He is thoroughly scared, and I do not believe that he will resume the dissemination of any information concerning the banks."

Then, on a March night in 1932, the disappearance of a baby from a nursery in New Jersey brought a much needed diversion for the President and a first taste of fame for Edgar. The kidnapping of Charles Lindbergh's son, and the subsequent discovery of his body, caused an explosion of publicity. In a time of gloom, the aviation pioneer was a symbol of all that was positive about America. The President sent Edgar to the scene of the crime as his personal representative.

The case did not go well. In spite of publicity touting Edgar as a "world authority on crime," his involvement brought no magical breakthrough. Scornful of the Sherlock from Washington, local police told how, spotting a pigeon perched on the eaves of the Lindbergh residence, Edgar wondered aloud whether it was a homing pigeon bearing a message from the kidnappers.

One agent on the case, John Trimble, recalled being "stationed at a hotel in Trenton . . . solely for the purpose of relaying any news break to Mr. Hoover so he could get it to the press. . . ." Edgar, Trimble thought, was just "using the case for publicity purposes."

One of the shrewdest minds on the investigation was that of Elmer Irey, head of the Internal Revenue Service's intelligence unit. It was he who saw to it that part of the ransom money was paid in identifiable notes and certificates, the measure that eventually led to the capture of alleged murderer Richard Hauptmann. Yet Edgar tried to have Irey removed from the case, upsetting Charles Lindbergh in the process.

According to Trimble, Edgar placed Irey and one of his aides under Bureau surveillance. It was the start of a long enmity. Five years later, long after the case was resolved, Irey would still be having his phone checked for signs of Bureau wiretapping.

In early summer 1932, with the economy in a shambles, the Democrats scented victory in the coming presidential election. As they gathered for the Convention in Chicago, one man of influence was nursing a bitter grudge against Edgar. Mitchell Palmer, the former Attorney General who a decade earlier had given Edgar a vital break in the days of the Red Raids, believed his young protégé had betrayed him. Edgar, Palmer believed, was one of those who spread word that he was personally corrupt. Now chairman of the Democratic Platform Committee, he urged that, should the party return to power, Edgar be fired.

On the promise of a "new deal" for the American people, Franklin Roosevelt won the presidency by a landslide. In early 1933, as the inauguration approached, word spread that his Attorney General would be Thomas Walsh, a Senator who identified Edgar with both the Red Raids and later abuses. He said he intended a massive reorganization at the Justice Department, with "almost completely new personnel."

Edgar rushed to ward off the danger. Newly elected politicians, arriving at Washington's Union Station, were surprised to find themselves greeted by smiling agents from the Bureau of Investigation. Mr. Hoover, the agents let it be known, was ready to help in any way possible, even by locating suitable accommodation, as a gesture of his personal goodwill.

In the event, Edgar received an unexpected reprieve. Walsh died of an apparent heart attack aboard the train bearing him to Washington. Talk of firing Edgar continued, however, and his Republican friends rallied around. Herbert Hoover, the outgoing president, interceded at the last possible moment, and in extraordinary circumstances.

On the day of Roosevelt's inauguration every bank in the nation closed its doors—the final economic humiliation for the defeated administration. It was a day of national crisis. Yet, as Hoover cruised down Pennsylvania Avenue in his limousine next to the new president, he found time to put in a word for Edgar. According to a Secret Serviceman who overheard the exchange—and as confirmed years later by Herbert Hoover himself—he said he hoped there would be no change at the top in the Bureau. Edgar, he said, had an "excellent record." Roosevelt said he would look into the matter.

In fact the new president had serious doubts about Edgar, and delayed his decision for months. Edgar was made to feel distinctly uneasy. Suddenly, even his expense account was being questioned. Why had he traveled first-class on a train to New York? Had Edgar used a hotel bedroom in Manhattan for official or personal purposes? The White House received an allegation that Edgar was a member of the Ku Klux Klan, and a congressional ally, John McCormack, hurried to rebut it.

Senator Kenneth McKellar, the ranking Democrat on the Appropriations Committee, begged the new Attorney General, Homer Cummings, to dump Edgar. So did several other members of Congress. McKellar's office had been ransacked during the last months of the Hoover presidency, and he held the Bureau responsible.

Then fate intervened again—this time with the death of Wallace Foster, a former Justice Department official Cummings was considering for Edgar's job. Edgar, meanwhile, was supplying the Attorney General with derogatory material on a key rival for the directorship, New York private investigator Val O'Farrell.

The man who championed O'Farrell for the job, Postmaster General James Farley, was allegedly surveilled by Edgar for months to come. "I think he got an obsession that Farley was a sort of walking symbol of his chances to keep or lose his post," a former agent recalled. "Hoover threw the works at him. A tap was put on Farley's office phones. Others were put on his homes in Washington and New York. . . ."[2]

After months of intrigue, it was Roosevelt himself who decided whether Edgar was to keep his job. One of the men he listened to, significantly enough, was Francis Garvan, Edgar's superior in the days of the Red Raids. "Do not let them lose you that boy Hoover," Garvan wrote the President. "Each day that you have relations with him or his Bureau you will find him more necessary to your comfort and assurance." That was to prove only too true, if not in the complimentary sense Garvan intended.

The deciding vote probably came from Attorney General Cummings, who wanted Edgar to stay on. Roosevelt agreed and, on July 29, 1933, the appointment was announced. A great liberal President had taken the first in a series of steps that would ensure Edgar not only survived in office, but survived to become the nation's most powerful force for right-wing oppression, detested by liberals everywhere.

Cummings, for one, was to regret the advice he had given the President. It was, he recalled ruefully, "one of the biggest mistakes I ever made." He would discover that Edgar was "difficult to handle, could not be controlled, and had the faculty of attracting too much attention to himself."

At the outset, getting attention was exactly what was required. The Roosevelt administration was under pressure to do something about crime, and to be seen to be doing it. In the hard-hit Midwest, where farms lay untended and businesses closed, banks were being robbed at gunpoint and wealthy men kidnapped for huge ransoms. Now was the time of Bonnie and Clyde, Machine Gun Kelly, John Dillinger and Pretty Boy Floyd.

This was a regional problem. The statistics do not support the notion that there was a national crime wave, but the government saw the chance of good headlines in hard times. "We are now engaged," the Attorney General declared, "in a war that threatens our country." He called for a national crusade against crime.

As one kidnapping followed another, Cummings summoned several leading journalists to dinner. He told them, recalled the columnist Drew Pearson, that "he believed the best cure for kidnapping was to build up the FBI, not only in actual strength but in the strength of public opinion behind it. . . . He asked our opinion about the appointment of a top-notch public relations man and those of us present, including Cummings, all agreed on Henry Suydam."

Suydam was a former war correspondent, then working as Washington correspondent for the *Brooklyn Eagle*. He was also a former head of the State Department Information Service, a personal friend of the President's, and would go on to become aide to Eisenhower's Secretary of State John Foster Dulles, and adviser to the Shah of Iran.

Edgar, meanwhile, acquired his own personal scribe, an exotic figure named Courtney Ryley Cooper. Cooper had begun his career as a circus clown, and moved on to become press agent for Colonel William Cody, better remembered today as Buffalo Bill. He was also a writer of pulp westerns, a scribbler who turned out some 750 short stories. Cooper's nonfiction, one reviewer noted, was "not always written with entire regard for actualities."

Cooper, nevertheless, now became the Bureau's Boswell. With Suydam, he pumped out the propaganda that made Edgar a household name. In 1940 he would be found hanged in a hotel room, driven to suicide, according to his widow, by some wrong Edgar had done him.

Many gangsters, and a number of brave lawmen, were to die bloodily in the mid-thirties. Cummings would eventually become just another forgotten Attorney General. Edgar, as ever, would survive, the one public official to emerge from the Depression as a national hero.

CHAPTER 6

> "If this tremendous body of evil-doers could be welded
> into a unit of conquest, America would fall before it, not
> in a month, not in a day, but in a few hours."
>
> *J. Edgar Hoover, on the crime wave, 1936*

IN THE CAMPAIGN AGAINST THE BANDITS, EDGAR'S CHIEF LIEU-
tenant was twenty-nine-year-old Melvin Purvis, his Agent
in Charge in Chicago. Theirs is a tale of friendship and
betrayal, the only episode in Edgar's personal life that is
heavily documented. While virtually no other personal
correspondence has survived, the Purvis family preserved
some 500 letters the pair exchanged between 1927 and
1936. Many are intimate, and they make it clear that Edgar
treated the younger man like no other field agent in Bureau
history.

Purvis' youth had mirrored Edgar's own. The son of a
South Carolina planter, he had captained his school cadet
company and obtained a law degree, and he was a member
of the Kappa Alpha fraternity and the Masons. He was
incredibly hardworking, and so fastidious that he changed
his shirts three times a day. Edgar took a shine to him the
moment he hired him, two years below the regulation
recruiting age.

Edgar dropped his usual rigid formality when he corresponded with Purvis, calling him "Dear Melvin" or "Dear
Mel," and signing himself "J.E.H." and even "Jayee."
Understandably nervous, Purvis stuck to "Mr. Hoover"
until Edgar told him to "stop using MISTER," then moved
on to "Dear Chairman" or "Dear Jayee."

When Edgar's letters to Purvis concerned official business, he laced them with a puerile brand of humor. As a cure for a U.S. attorney suffering from "mental halitosis," his standard epithet for those who disagreed with him, he proposed "the Mussolini treatment—a quart of castor oil administered in equal doses three in succession."

In unofficial notes, Edgar kept harping on the way women fell for Purvis, not least his own secretary, Helen Gandy. At one point he taunted the younger man with claims that Gandy, a good-looking woman in her mid-thirties, had been seen locked in the embrace of another Bureau official. In the fall of 1932 he assured Purvis that, should he come to Washington for the Halloween Ball, Gandy would come dressed in a "cellophane gown."

The following year, when Edgar was fighting for his job, he found time to send Purvis a Bel Air Smoke Consumer, an air circulation device to help ease the younger man's sore throat. He fired off a torrent of notes of concern, three in four days at one point.

All that followed, the ballyhooed chase after the thirties' bandits, took place against the background of this curious relationship. By delivering the bandits, dead or alive, Purvis was to ensure Edgar's fame.

In June 1933, the month before Edgar's reappointment, brewing company president William Hamm, Jr., was kidnapped in St. Paul, Minnesota, then released after payment of a $100,000 ransom. The next day, in Kansas City, Missouri, a Bureau agent and three policemen were mowed down by bandits with machine guns. Another wealthy man, John Factor, disappeared in Chicago two weeks later. Thanks to a new law enacted after the Lindbergh tragedy, agents now had the power to investigate kidnappings, and were permitted to carry guns. The Bureau went to work.

On the face of it, Purvis performed brilliantly. He seemingly solved both the Hamm and Factor kidnappings within weeks, by arresting Roger "The Terrible" Tuohy, a big-time Illinois bootlegger from Prohibition days. Edgar called Tuohy one of the "most vicious and dangerous criminals in the history of American crime." Capturing him, he said, was "a credit to the entire Bureau."

In fact, Tuohy had been spotted not by Edgar's men but by an unarmed policeman out on a fishing trip. Later, when public attention had moved on, he turned out to be innocent of the Hamm kidnapping. Although he was convicted in the Factor case and rotted in jail for a quarter of a century, it was finally established that he had been set up by other criminals. The federal judge who released Tuohy, in 1959, was especially scathing about the FBI's refusal to let the court see relevant files.

Edgar gained further glory in the summer of 1933, when oil millionaire Charles Urschel was abducted from his home in Oklahoma City. After Urschel's release, on payment of a ransom, the gang responsible was pursued across six states, an area the size of central Europe. One of its leaders, George "Machine Gun" Kelly, responded with a stream of letters, some taunting Edgar and his "sissy college boys" as incapable of finding him. He even managed to make threatening telephone calls to Edgar's mother—but never actually fired a gun at anyone.

Edgar's men did find Kelly. It was he, according to Bureau propaganda, who originated the nickname "G-Men"—with the "G" standing for "Government"—as the underworld nickname for Bureau agents. He supposedly shrieked, "Don't shoot, G-Men! Don't shoot!" as agents and police burst into his hideout. This is a nice story, but it is not supported by the accounts of policemen present that day. In any case, criminals went on calling Edgar's agents "the Feds," as they had done previously. Only the press latched on to G-Men, which was probably what Edgar's publicity department intended.[1]

Edgar decided the brains behind the Urschel kidnapping was Kelly's wife Kathryn, who allegedly wrote the ransom letters. Only in 1970 did it emerge that the Bureau had suppressed its own handwriting expert's report, which flatly exonerated Mrs. Kelly. Denied that evidence, she served twenty-six years in prison.

"When a woman does turn professional criminal," Edgar

claimed, "she is a hundred times more vicious and dangerous than a man . . . acts with a cold brutality seldom found in a man." Edgar also told the New York Round Table, in all seriousness, that a female criminal "always has red hair. . . . She either adopts a red wig or has her hair dyed red." Kathryn Kelly had worn such a wig, and Edgar stuck to the bizarre theory for years.[2]

Edgar began his fortieth year, 1934, still keeping up a constant correspondence with his protégé Melvin Purvis. The letters were increasingly intimate, with Edgar worrying whenever the younger man caught a cold. In one note, written around the time Clark Gable was shooting to stardom in *It Happened One Night*, Edgar teased Purvis about the way a newspaper had described him. "I don't see how the movies could miss a 'slender, blond-haired, brown-eyed' gentleman," he wrote. "All power to the Clark Gable of the service."

It is hard to interpret the correspondence as anything other than a homosexual courtship, even though Purvis is not known to have had any such tendencies. Edgar's oddest letter to him, a handwritten one dated April 3, 1934, was a bizarre mix of schoolboy humor and sexual innuendo:

Dear Melvin,

I received the True-Vue and films, bombs, magic trick and your sassy note. What did the True-Vue and films cost? I asked you to get them for me and I intend to pay for them. The films were both educational and uplifting but I thought they would include a series on "A Night in a Moorish Harem" or was it a "Turkish Harem"? Nevertheless it was some night and I am still looking forward to you producing a set. Of course my interest is solely as a censor or as Chairman of the Moral Uplift Squad. The bombs are the best yet. I have already caused Miss Gandy to jump two feet and that is something considering the fact that she is now in the heavyweight class. The damned Magic Trick has me almost "nuts" trying to figure out how it is done.

... Well, son, keep a stiff upper lip and get Dillinger for me, and the world is yours.

> Sincerely and affectionately,
>
> Jayee

Exactly a month before Edgar wrote that letter, John Dillinger had become a Bureau target. He had recently emerged from jail, aged thirty, after serving a long sentence for an attempted holdup. Then, in the space of four months, he had organized a mass escape by former cellmates and, armed with machine guns and bulletproof vests stolen from a police station, begun ranging across the Midwest holding up bank after bank. Three policemen were killed in the process—though apparently not by Dillinger himself.

The bandit was in jail again in Indiana when he pulled his most brazen trick—one that made headlines around the world and put Dillinger on Edgar's hit list. He talked his way out of jail waving a fake wooden gun, stole the sheriff's car and hightailed it into neighboring Illinois. For the first time, by driving a stolen car across a state line, Dillinger had committed a federal offense—and became a prime target for Melvin Purvis.

Things went badly wrong in late April, when Purvis received a tip-off that the bandit was holed up at Little Bohemia, a lakeside resort in Wisconsin. Purvis called Edgar, agreed on a plan and rushed to Little Bohemia with a large posse of agents.

"Nervous Purvis," as other agents called him behind his back, made a thorough mess of the operation. "The fever for action," he admitted later, "dissipated all other emotions. . . ." Purvis and his team blundered into the resort grounds and blazed away excitedly—at innocent customers leaving the restaurant. One man was killed and two wounded. Nearby, a member of Dillinger's gang, Baby Face Nelson, killed one agent and wounded another. All the bandits escaped.

It was the second time in three weeks that Dillinger had made the Bureau look like the Keystone Kops. At Bohemia, according to one source, some of Edgar's fabled agents had "mutinied and taken their superiors into custody." The press began calling for Purvis' resignation—even for Edgar's.

Edgar, rarely silent, said little in public about the incident. Behind the scenes he sent a trusted Washington inspector, Sam Cowley, with thirty handpicked men to form a special Dillinger squad in Chicago. Yet, although Purvis had committed a glaring breach of the rule all veteran agents still recall: "Don't Embarrass the Bureau," he remained Agent in Charge. Jayee was looking after Melvin.

Dillinger, whom Edgar called "a beer-drinking plug-ugly," was rated Public Enemy Number One and featured on Wanted posters all over the United States. Attorney General Cummings said that agents should "shoot to kill—then count ten." Although Dillinger himself was not known to have killed anyone, eliminating him had become a public relations imperative.

For Edgar it was a matter of saving face and, as with Machine Gun Kelly, settling a personal challenge. Dillinger was taunting the Director with a series of defiant postcards. With no word from Chicago of a breakthrough, his correspondence with Purvis took on a tone of stern formality. Suddenly it was no longer "Dear Mel" but "Dear Mr. Purvis":

> June 4: I was very disturbed today when I learned from you that the order which I had issued this morning had not been complied with. . . . You have absolutely no right to ignore instructions. . . .

> June 16: I had occasion this afternoon to try to reach you by telephone. . . . I then learned you had gone to one of the Country Clubs for golf. . . . There is no reason why the Agent in Charge should not leave word where he can be reached at any time. . . .

Very truly yours,

J. Edgar Hoover

On July 21, just when his future prospects seemed to be evaporating, Purvis received the phone call that broke the Dillinger case. An Indiana policeman tipped him off that Anna Sage, a Chicago madam, knew where Dillinger was and was prepared to betray him. Sage, a Romanian émigré in trouble with the law, hoped to be rewarded with a permit to stay in the United States.

Edgar was advised the following day that Dillinger's capture was imminent. In Chicago, Purvis and Inspector Cowley briefed a team of handpicked agents. In early evening, after a call from Sage, they moved into position around the Biograph Theater. In Washington, Edgar was at home with his mother, waiting for news.

Dillinger emerged from the theater at 10:30 P.M., and Purvis gave a prearranged signal. "I was very nervous," he recalled. "It must have been a squeaky voice that called out, 'Stick 'em up, Johnny! We have you surrounded.' . . . Dillinger drew his .380 automatic pistol, but he never fired it. He dropped to the ground; he had been shot."[3]

In the capital, Edgar hurried to his office to hold a midnight press conference. He praised Purvis for "almost unimaginable daring," while Attorney General Cummings sent fulsome praise. Edgar poured scorn on the dead bandit, insisting that his agents had opened fire only when Dillinger went for his gun. In fact, there is evidence to the contrary.

Whatever the truth, Edgar had no regrets. "Personally," he said, "I am glad Dillinger was taken dead. . . . The only good criminal is a dead criminal."

In his 1970 book, *The Dillinger Dossier,* author Jay Robert Nash offered the thesis that Dillinger did not die in Chicago at all, that an underworld fall guy was sent to the Biograph in his place. He cited striking flaws in the autopsy evidence, and detailed supporting testimony. An angry Edgar insisted that Dillinger's identity had been proven through fingerprints, but no hard evidence was ever produced.

Days after the Dillinger shooting he was showing the press

the dead man's straw hat, his smashed spectacles, his fifty-cent cigar and a .38 automatic with a damaged barrel that had supposedly belonged to the bandit. These items remained on show in Edgar's reception room, like hunting trophies, for decades to come. The pistol the public saw, however, was a phony. Its serial number—119702—proves that it did not leave the Colt factory until December 1934, five months after the Dillinger shooting.

Also on public display was a plaster cast of the dead man's face, produced at a Chicago embalming college. It became, a *New Yorker* correspondent noted, "a sort of Kaiser's moustache with the FBI." Years later, when a doctor wrote suggesting it was time the Dillinger exhibit was removed, Edgar was furious. The death mask, with just a hint of a smile about the lips, remains on show at FBI headquarters to this day.

After Dillinger, it seemed at first that Melvin Purvis could do no wrong. Edgar greeted him at Union Station on his triumphal arrival from Chicago, and the headline read: DILLINGER HEROES MEET. "He conducted himself," Edgar wrote privately to Purvis' father, "with that simple modesty that is so characteristic of his makeup. . . . He has been one of my closest and dearest friends."

Purvis was in charge, that fall, when an alleged participant in the Kansas City Massacre, Pretty Boy Floyd, was killed in an Ohio cornfield. Edgar and Purvis were again photographed sharing victory together, with Edgar calling Floyd "a yellow rat who needed extermination." Extermination was what he had received. According to a police officer present at the scene, Purvis ordered another agent to fire into the bandit as he lay wounded on the ground. In a formal complaint, the local police chief said that, instead of going to call an ambulance as requested, Purvis called Edgar to report his latest coup. When he returned, Floyd was dead.

Hardly a week went by without the death or capture of another wanted man. Baby Face Nelson died of his wounds, after killing two agents himself, following a car chase in a

Chicago suburb. In Florida, agents killed Kate "Ma" Barker and her son Fred, a key figure in the Hamm kidnapping and other crimes. Singling out the woman in the case again, Edgar called Mrs. Barker "the she-wolf . . . the brain of the whole organization." In fact, she had been no such thing.

At the height of his season of success, Edgar dumped Melvin Purvis. "He was jealous of him," Purvis' secretary, Doris Lockerman, said in 1988. "Unless you continued to please the king, you didn't continue as a favorite very long. . . . They saw to it that Purvis got no more assignments that put him in the public eye. He found himself spending months interviewing applicants for jobs as agents. Every effort was made to denigrate him, to embarrass him. He was terribly hurt."

In March 1935 Edgar sent Purvis a curt note that began "Dear Sir," and asked him to account for a report that he had gotten drunk at a Chicago party. Purvis called it an "unmitigated and unadulterated lie." Then a newspaper said Purvis had waved a gun about in a Cincinnati store, tried to telephone Edgar, then staggered away. Doris Lockerman recalls no such incidents, and wonders whether the story was planted. "Everyone," she said, "was afraid of Hoover."

Purvis resigned on July 10, by telegram. The man whom Edgar had called his "closest friend" now became the target of his lasting spite. When studio boss Darryl Zanuck offered Purvis a crime consultancy in Hollywood, Edgar intervened to block it. He spied on Purvis when he was preparing his autobiography. Yet Purvis never betrayed Edgar, never published the private correspondence that would have made the FBI Director the laughingstock of the country. He married, served with distinction as a colonel in World War II, ran a local radio station and worked for various congressional committees.

To mention Purvis' name to Edgar, according to a veteran official, was "like dropping a bomb into Mount Vesuvius." His name does not appear at all in *The FBI Story*, the authorized Bureau history published in 1956. There is no character called Purvis in the Hollywood movie of the same name, produced under Edgar's control. When Purvis was in line for a Senate job, Edgar ordered officials to disseminate "derogatory information" about him.

In 1952, when Edgar successfully destroyed Purvis' chances of getting a federal judgeship, his wife suggested a reconciliation attempt. FBI records show the men did meet—for six minutes. "I remember being taken to Hoover's office," recalled Purvis' son Alston. "Hoover started talking on the phone, and ignored my father for about a minute. I saw my father's hands start trembling. Then he said to Hoover, 'You goddamn son of a bitch, when I bring my wife in, you stand up.' Hoover did stand up . . . but that ended the reconciliation."

One morning in 1960, two months after Purvis' appointment as Chief Counsel to a Senate committee, his wife heard the crack of a pistol shot. She found her husband dead, at fifty-six, with a .45 automatic in his hand. Purvis had committed suicide, the press reported, following months of pain from chronic back trouble.

The Purvis family was not so sure. The death came just weeks after the fatal shooting of the old bootlegger Roger Tuohy—right after his release from jail for a kidnapping he had not committed—in a case Purvis had directed. Thirty-six hours before Purvis died, he had been visited by someone driving a large black car with out-of-state plates. The next morning he called a lawyer to discuss his will. Of all the weapons in his large collection, it was the pistol of a thirties gangster that was found in his dead hand the next morning.

Edgar expressed no sadness, made no comments to the press and sent no message of condolence to Purvis' widow. Mrs. Purvis, for her part, sent Edgar a bitter telegram:

WE ARE HONORED THAT YOU IGNORED MELVIN'S DEATH. YOUR JEALOUSY HURT HIM VERY MUCH BUT UNTIL THE END I THINK HE LOVED YOU.

Along with Edgar, another FBI official scribbled negative comments in the file when Purvis died—Associate Director

Clyde Tolson. Long since, in a conversation with socialite Anita Colby, Edgar had added a new wrinkle to the mythology about John Dillinger. "Edgar told me," Colby recalled, "that it wasn't Purvis who got Dillinger, it was Clyde Tolson. He said they just let Purvis take the credit, but Clyde really did it."

This was yet another example of Edgar's capacity for untruth. Bureau records show Tolson was at headquarters the day Dillinger died. He may, however, have been a key factor in what really went wrong between Edgar and Purvis: Clyde Tolson had for some time been Edgar's constant male companion, and would remain so for nearly half a century.

CHAPTER 7

"Words are mere man-given symbols for thoughts and feelings, and they are grossly insufficient to express the thoughts in my mind and the feelings in my heart that I have for you."

J. Edgar Hoover, in letter to Clyde Tolson, 1943

CLYDE ANDERSON TOLSON WAS BORN IN 1900 NEAR LAREDO, Missouri, in the heart of the Corn Belt. His parents were poor, and a move to Cedar Rapids, Iowa, did not bring prosperity. Clyde's father, a Baptist who eked out a living first as a small-time farmer, later as a freight guard on the railroad, told his two sons to go out into the world and better themselves.

Clyde took the train to Washington when he was eighteen, after a year at business college. He was a good-looking young man, with piercing black eyes and an athletic build, a careful dresser who favored cream linen jackets and spectator shoes, but nothing too fancy. He could have passed, the press would note later, "for a slightly studious customers' man or a very junior partner in a brokerage firm."

Clyde got a job as a clerk at the War Department, and flourished. By the time he was twenty, thanks to an appetite for work and an astonishing ability to absorb vast quantities of information, he had become Confidential Clerk to the Secretary of War. Eight years later, feeling it was time to move on, he began attending night classes in law at George Washington University.

As a boy, Clyde and his friends had played a game they

called Jesse James, after the outlaw. Clyde's grandfather's cattle had been stolen by James, so he always wanted to play the role no one else wanted—the Sheriff. He wore a silver star, which he carried in his pocket long after he grew out of schoolboy games. So it was that in 1927, after receiving his law degree, he applied to become a Special Agent at the Bureau of Investigation.

At first it seemed Clyde would be disappointed—the Bureau had no vacancies. Then, early the next year, the Secretary of War sent a personal recommendation. Edgar reviewed the application form, which bore Clyde's photograph. It was his first glimpse of an exceptionally handsome young man, an open face above a fashionable wing collar.

Edgar read glowing references from a succession of distinguished men, government Secretaries, the Judge Advocate General, a Missouri newspaper owner and a Republican National Committeeman. Here was a fellow who, very like Edgar, had been President of his sophomore class, a member of the University Senate and a keen participant in fraternity life. Clyde was so personable that he had been taken along on an official War Department trip to the Panama Canal. He was reportedly "not at all dissipated," and had "shown no particular interest in women."

Edgar hired Clyde, then favored him as no other Bureau recruit would ever be favored—promoting him from rookie agent to Assistant Director in less than three years. Clyde would never have any day-to-day experience in the field. Instead, after just four months in Boston, Edgar brought him back to Washington, "because of an emergency." At headquarters, Clyde filed stern reports on overtime rules, revealing himself to be a martinet after Edgar's own heart. Then, after a token fortnight as Agent in Charge in Buffalo, New York, he was promoted to Inspector and brought back to the capital for good.

A year later, Clyde had become one of only two Assistant Directors in charge of administration. And within weeks of that appointment, Edgar was insisting that Clyde be included on White House invitation lists.

This was blatant favoritism. The rapidity of the young

man's rise may have no parallel in any government agency. Clyde was where he was because Edgar saw in him exactly what he needed—a man who could be both an absolutely trustworthy lieutenant and a compatible companion.

Edgar was highly visible, famous for chattering on like a machine gun. Clyde, colleagues noted, was a "Sphinx," "a shadow," a man so gray he was "invisible if he stood against a gray wall." He "looked worried even when he felt good" and made colleagues uneasy with his long silences.

Many agents have expressed a grudging affection for Edgar, the "Old Man." No one seemed to have a soft spot for Clyde. "Tolson," said Jim Doyle, a former organized crime specialist, "was a No. 1 class asshole. A conniver."

Clyde was "the beady eye," a man of ice who took delight in punishing or firing subordinates. A Bureau black joke had him telling Edgar, "Gee, I'm depressed. I think I'll go home for the day and go to bed." "Clyde, don't do that," came the apocryphal reply. "Just look down the list, pick out somebody and fire him. You'll feel a lot better." Tolson, the story goes, beamed and asked hopefully, "With prejudice?"

Even those closest to the Director, like Edgar's secretary, were wary of Clyde. "Helen Gandy and Tolson," recalled Assistant Director Cartha "Deke" DeLoach, "circled around each other like cats. They both had enormous influence on Mr. Hoover, and both were scared to death of him. Tolson was smarter than Mr. Hoover—he had a razor-sharp mind. His great failing was that he slavishly followed Mr. Hoover's every dictate."

"My alter ego is Clyde Tolson," Edgar liked to say. "He can read my mind." Perhaps, but there was one thing Edgar could not relinquish, even to Clyde—total control. Clyde received cantankerous memos from the Director just like everyone else. If there was a case of athlete's foot in the Bureau gym, it was Clyde who took the flak. If the clock in Edgar's car was slow, it was Clyde who had to explain why. Ten years into his service, Clyde was still getting a slap on the wrist for leaving documents in his clothes closet at the Bureau.

In Clyde's eyes, though, Edgar could do no wrong. "This

is what the Boss wants," he would tell senior colleagues supposedly convened to make a decision, and there the debate would end. "The Director," Clyde said to anyone who would listen, "is the Man of the Century."

To many he seemed a pathetic figure, especially as he aged. Washington gossips would note that he walked humbly a pace or two behind Edgar, changing pace in order to stay in step.

Edgar called him "Junior" in the early days, later just "Clyde." In public, even in the virtual privacy of the directorial limousine, one chauffeur noted, Clyde called Edgar "Mr. Hoover." Former officials, even very senior ones, still cannot bring themselves to say plain "Hoover," two decades after his death. Occasionally, though, Clyde was heard to call the boss something no one else ever called him—"Eddie."

It soon became clear, from their daily rituals, that Edgar and Clyde were more than colleagues. Every day, on the dot of noon, the limousine would bear them to lunch at the Mayflower Hotel. There they would consume hamburgers and vanilla ice cream or, when Edgar was watching his weight, chicken soup and salad. According to the hotel's publicity, Edgar once noticed the FBI's third Most Wanted man sitting two tables away, had him arrested, then resumed eating. Another, less kind account said he looked straight through the criminal and failed to recognize him.

Five nights a week, for more than forty years, except for a break when Edgar quarreled with a new owner, the pair would appear at Harvey's Restaurant, then on the 1100 block of Connecticut Avenue.

"They would come in together and sit up on a little dais," recalled barman George Dunson, "a step up from other people. Mr. Tolson would always face the door, and Mr. Hoover sat with his back to the wall. Mr. Tolson did it so he could watch who was coming in. If anyone tried to get Mr. Hoover, they couldn't come at him from behind." Once Edgar became really famous, the management put a barrier between him and unwelcome strangers, by blocking the aisle with a trolley.

Under an arrangement negotiated by Clyde, the pair consumed all they could eat—in one of the best restaurants in town—for $2.50 and the price of their drinks. For years, they did not even have to pay that. "The check was picked up by Hoover's friend Harry Viner, who ran a big laundry business," said former Washington police inspector Joe Shimon. "His reward was that Hoover made one of his relatives an agent when World War II started. Later, when Harvey's closed down for a while, Hoover sent agents to the restaurant opposite, to try and arrange a special rate. He was a chiseler."

Edgar liked steak, medium rare, and, more exotically, green-turtle soup. He took part in the restaurant's oyster-eating competitions, and usually won. At the end of the evening he would leave carrying a bag of ham and turkey, provided by the management, to take home to his dogs.

Once, when Edgar and Clyde arrived late, to find their regular table was taken, they made a scene and stormed out. Harvey's owner, Julius Lulley, was often the butt of Edgar's peculiar brand of practical jokes. When Lulley's wife complained that her husband would not give her a new fur coat, Edgar had agents photograph him with another woman, then used the pictures to change his mind.

Edgar, who was so stern with his agents about drink, enjoyed whiskey, and officials in distant field offices had to keep up with his changing taste in brands. Edgar never drank much in front of colleagues, and none of them ever saw him drunk. Away from the office, said Miami restaurateur Jesse Weiss, who met Edgar in the thirties, things were different. The mood at private parties could be "real friendly, loose, a lot of guys drinking booze, 'Hooray for Hell, who's afraid of fire?'—that kind of thing. . . ."

The waiters at Harvey's also remember heavy drinking. "Mr. Hoover drank Grand-Dad," said Pooch Miller, who was maître d' for thirty-six years. "I used to give him six miniatures when he arrived, with club sodas to go with them. And after he'd finished drinking we'd bring him his dinner, five days a week." "Today," said Aaron Shainus, whose father owned Harvey's at one point, "Hoover would be considered an alcoholic."

The pair became a Washington legend, one heavy with the innuendo that they were homosexual lovers. Robert Ludlum, in his 1978 novel *The Chancellor Manuscript,* was to write what no one dared say straight out in their lifetime. For Ludlum, Clyde's "soft pampered face—struggling for masculinity—had for decades been the flower to the bristled cactus."

Journalists dropped hints about the couple, though, as early as the thirties. "Mr. Hoover," *Collier's* magazine told readers early in the Roosevelt presidency, "is short, fat, businesslike, and walks with a mincing step. . . . He dresses fastidiously, with Eleanor blue as the favorite color for the matched shades of tie, handkerchief and socks. A little pompous, he rides in a limousine even if only to a nearby self-service cafeteria. . . ."

Edgar kept a thick file on the writer of that article, journalist Ray Tucker, and denounced him as a "degenerate alcoholic." Tucker became convinced that Edgar even placed him under surveillance for a while. "Has anyone noted," asked another columnist, "that the Hoover stride has grown noticeably longer and more vigorous since Tucker charged him with walking with mincing steps?"

Yet another reporter observed that Edgar kept dainty china in his office beside the crime trophies. "He is different," commented a foreign diplomat, "from any police officer I ever knew, in that he uses a distinctive and conspicuous perfume." Edgar ordered a senior aide to say "very, very diplomatically" that he never used perfume. In fact, he did.

The hints about Edgar and Clyde persisted. *Time* ran a piece about Edgar, "seldom seen without a male companion, most frequently solemn-faced Clyde Tolson." When the two friends sought to hide from the press, as when they stayed at the Muehlebach Hotel in Kansas City, they merely attracted attention to themselves. "They were shown," the local paper reported, "to the Muehlebach's pride, the penthouse, No. 1125. . . . When reporters lifted the huge knocker of the door bearing the legend The Penthouse, the door was opened slightly, as in movie mysteries. A man in a café au lait lounging robe appeared. 'I'm sorry,' he said, 'you cannot see Mr. Hoover.'" The reporter thought Edgar "as mysterious as a Garbo smile"—and noted that Clyde was installed next door.

The message to readers was clear. FBI insiders, most of them not sure what to think, just joked about it. In 1939, when top aide Louis Nichols—like George Ruch before him—named his son J. Edgar, agents joked, "If it had been a girl, she'd have been called Clyde."

In the sixties, agents would chuckle about "J. Edna" and "Mother Tolson." The writer Truman Capote, himself homosexual, told a magazine editor he knew Edgar and Clyde were, too. He considered writing a magazine piece about them—one that got no further than its title, "Johnny and Clyde."

Scholars have pointed to the many photographs, most of them pictures of Clyde taken by Edgar, that survived from Edgar's private collection: Clyde asleep, Clyde in a bathrobe, Clyde by the pool. Yet the two friends never openly set up house together. Clyde continued to maintain his own apartment when Edgar bought a home for himself after his mother's death. At the office, say former colleagues, the two men showed no unusual affection for each other. For the forty-four years they were intimates, the deception must have been a constant strain. But a deception it was.

The man who knew them best in the thirties was Guy Hottel, a young executive for AETNA Insurance who shared an apartment with Clyde for years. The three men regularly went fishing, along with Edgar's publicist Courtney Ryley Cooper. Edgar gave Hottel a job as an agent in 1938, as a favor to help him avert an unwelcome transfer by AETNA, and made him head of the Washington field office after perfunctory training. Later, he acted as best man at Hottel's wedding.

Hottel remained confidant and constant companion to

Edgar and Clyde throughout the ten years that followed. Shortly before his death in 1990, he spoke of going on "inspection tours" with Edgar and Clyde that were no more than glorified junkets. He told of vacations in Florida and California, of hobnobbing with the wealthy—the Firestones of tire fame and senior Ford executives.

"We did a little gambling, jai alai, horseracing, shuffleboard," Hottel recalled. "At the Flamingo Hotel, in Miami, they had a court with sides on it, and you could go up there and sunbathe all you wanted in the nude. Hoover liked the sun, but Tolson didn't like it too much." On the record, Hottel limited himself to saying that Edgar and Clyde kept their distance from women. "They didn't date them. They might take them out to dinner, but they didn't date them—you know. . . ."

Hottel had more to say on the subject in the forties when, as Agent in Charge of the Washington field office, he became a problem drinker. Former Police Inspector Joseph Shimon, whose career in law enforcement in Washington spanned three decades, recalls that time.

"When Hottel went on the drunk," said Shimon, "he'd go into different bars and start telling stories about the sex parties at Hoover's house, you know, with the boys. To give you an idea of the influence Hoover had, when Hottel's wife would call in and say, 'He's on a drunk,' we would get an order over the Teletype to the police department, to cover the bars and pick him up right away and send him over to the FBI. That was to keep him from talking. You know, that's tremendous power. That happened so many times. . . ."

Edgar did not fire Hottel. Perhaps, after so many years of intimacy, he simply knew too much. "He wasn't fabricating," said Shimon. "He had attended some of the parties, let's put it that way. According to him, some of the top boys who were holding the top jobs at the FBI were participating. They were kind of promoted over other people. I guess sometimes, in order to be promoted, you had to be one of the boys. . . ."

A further serious allegation came from Jimmy G. C. Corcoran, who had become Edgar's trusted associate while working as an FBI Inspector in the twenties.

"After he left the Bureau," said Shimon, "Jimmy became very powerful politically. During World War II he was a lobbyist, and he was retained by a business group to get congressional help for them to open up a factory—for a $75,000 fee. That was illegal during the war, and we got a tip-off from the Attorney General's office that the FBI were going to set Jimmy up when he went to pick up his $75,000 at the Mayflower Hotel.

"Jimmy was really mad. He went to Harvey's Restaurant and sent word to Hoover that Jimmy Corcoran wanted him to come out right now or he was going to create a scene.

"Hoover came out in the end, and said, 'What's the matter, Jimmy?' and Jimmy called him a lot of dirty words and said, 'What d'you mean trying to set me up?' Hoover said, 'Gee, Jimmy, I didn't know it was you.' And Jimmy said, 'For Chrissake, how many J. G. C. Corcorans do you know? . . . This is what I get for doing you a favor, you dirty S.O.B. . . .' And the outcome was that Jimmy went and collected his $75,000. And he wasn't arrested."

After the incident Corcoran confided to Shimon, and to Washington lobbyist Henry Grunewald, what the "favor" had been. While he was at the Bureau, Corcoran said, Edgar used him to deal with a "problem." He said Edgar had been arrested in the late twenties in New Orleans, on sex charges involving a young man. Corcoran, who had by then left the FBI and had powerful contacts in Louisiana, said he had intervened to prevent a prosecution.

Corcoran was to die in a mysterious plane crash in 1956 near Spanish Cay, a Caribbean island owned by a close associate of Edgar's, oil millionaire Clint Murchison. Most of the documents in his FBI file have since been destroyed. While Corcoran's account may never be proven, it does not stand alone. Joe Pasternak, the veteran film producer remembered for his relaunch of Marlene Dietrich in the late thirties, told of another close call. He knew Edgar, and claimed personal knowledge of a sordid episode that occurred in California. "He was a homosexual," Pasternak said. "Every year he used to come down to the Del Mar racetrack with a different boy. He was caught in a bathroom by a newspaperman. They made sure he didn't speak. . . . Nobody dared say anything because he was so powerful."

There are numerous anecdotes about Edgar and Clyde. Joseph Shimon recalled a story told by an astonished cabdriver who had picked the couple up at National Airport. "He said Hoover was waiting, and rented the cab. It was Tolson who came off the plane. And he said he never saw so much kissing and ass-grabbing in his life. It was the kind of thing that made you feel the rumors were true."

Harry Hay, founder of the Mattachine Society, America's first homosexual rights organization, had homosexual friends who went regularly to Edgar's summer racing haunt, the Del Mar track in California. "In the forties," said Hay, "people I knew would come back and say, 'Guess who was in so-and-so's box today?' And they'd say, you know, 'Hoover and Tolson were there again.' I was gay, the people I was hearing it from were gay and the boxes Hoover and Tolson were in were boxes owned by gay men, in a circle in which they didn't have people who weren't gay. They wouldn't be in that crowd otherwise. They were nodded together as lovers."

The Broadway singer Ethel Merman, star of *Annie Get Your Gun,* met Edgar and Clyde in New York in 1936. They remained in touch for the rest of their lives, and regularly sent affectionate telegrams to her on opening nights. In 1978, when a reporter asked her to comment on Anita Bryant, the antihomosexual campaigner, Merman had an interesting reply. "Some of my best friends," she said, "are homosexual. Everybody knew about J. Edgar Hoover, but he was the best chief the FBI ever had. A lot of people have always been homosexual. To each his own. They don't bother me."

In the thirties Edgar began a long association with the columnist who reigned as the nation's premier purveyor of gossip for thirty years, Walter Winchell. Edgar came to know Winchell, he was to say, "as well as any other living person," and it is the Winchell connection that provides eyewitness corroboration of the affair with Clyde.

Edgar began cultivating the columnist during the gangster wars, when Winchell wrote nice things about him. He assigned Bureau agents to guard him during a visit to Chicago, and entertained him at the Shoreham Hotel in Washington. According to Winchell's friend Curly Harris, the columnist and the FBI Director quickly became close. Winchell was one of the few people ever to address Edgar by the first of his Christian names, "John."

For years thereafter, Winchell regaled readers with a diet of trivia about Edgar, along with some genuine newsbreaks. The source, though he always denied it, was Edgar himself. "The information would come on plain paper, in plain envelopes, without official identification," said the columnist's assistant, Herman Klurfeld. "He'd hold up a letter and say, 'Here it is. Something from John.' Hoover was almost like another press agent submitting material."

It was through Winchell that Edgar first found his way to New York City's Stork Club, billed as "the place to be seen if you wish to feel important." Between 1934 and 1965 patrons included several Kennedys and Rockefellers, Al Jolson and Joe DiMaggio, Grace Kelly and Madame Chiang Kai-shek, the Duke and Duchess of Windsor and H. L. Mencken.

Winchell was close to the Stork's proprietor, Sherman Billingsley. He regularly held court there and was often joined at Table 50, his place of honor, by Edgar and Clyde. Billingsley, a former bootlegger, saw to it that Edgar's food and drink came free. The Stork was soon boasting a highball called FBI Fizz.

On New Year's Eve 1936, around midnight, free-lance photographer Gustave Gale took several pictures of Winchell and his party, all wearing funny hats and festive smiles. One photograph shows Edgar, with Clyde chortling at his side, his hands raised in mock surrender to a comely young woman with a toy gun. The woman, tracked down only recently, was a celebrated fashion model of the day, Luisa Stuart.[1]

That New Year's Eve at the Stork, Stuart and her boyfriend, Winchell's colleague Art Arthur, found themselves seated at Edgar's table for dinner. "The world heavyweight champion, Jim Braddock, was there, too," recalled Stuart, now in her seventies. "I remember there were jokes about race, and Hoover didn't want to go on to the Cotton Club because Gene Krupa, the white jazz drummer, played with blacks there.

"All the same, we did end up going to the Cotton Club, in an FBI limousine. I sat with Art in the backseat. Hoover and Tolson sat opposite us in those two little seats on hinges they have in limousines. And that was when I noticed they were holding hands—all the way to the club, I think. Just sitting there talking and holding hands with each other.

"Hoover got furious after we did get to the Cotton Club. Because not only were there black and white musicians, there was a black and white couple dancing—a black man with a white woman. And Tolson, who had been getting drunk, said something like, 'Well, I'd like to dance with you. . . .' It was an awkward moment.

"I didn't really understand anything about homosexuality in those days," said Stuart. "I was so young, and those were different times. But I'd never seen two men holding hands. And I remember asking Art about it in the car on the way home that night. And he just said, 'Oh, come on. *You* know,' or something like that. And then he told me they were queers or fairies—the sort of terms they used in those days."

Like other lovers, Edgar and Clyde had their ups and downs. Edgar drove Clyde to the hospital, a month before the episode at the Stork, when he was taken ill with appendicitis. At the office, though, he fussed and fumed at Clyde like a nagging spouse. Why, Edgar asked in one memo, did he have to hold doors open for visitors, while Clyde and others "swept through as if members of the British Monarch's Jubilee entourage?"

After the Stork Club episode, Luisa Stuart saw Edgar and Clyde several times at the Sunday brunches Winchell and his wife gave at their Manhattan apartment. "One Sunday," Stuart recalled, "Hoover—'Jedgar,' as we called him—showed up without Clyde, and said Clyde was sick. After he left, people said Clyde wasn't really sick. They'd had a big fight. The word was that Hoover had found Clyde in bed with another man."

One Christmas, Edgar, Clyde and Guy Hottel were staying at Miami's Gulfstream Hotel. At the height of a tiff with Clyde, Edgar stormed into the bathroom and locked the door. Hottel had to force his way in, grab the Director by the shoulders and shake some sense into him.

The bathroom siege was also apparently triggered by jealousy—though not, on this occasion, over another male. Hottel, who was something of a ladies' man, had asked Clyde to make up a foursome for the evening with him and two women. Clyde had accepted and Edgar, piqued at the prospect of being left alone, threw a tantrum.

"One of Guy's jobs," said his brother-in-law Chandler Brossard, "was to sort of calm Hoover down. He was an hysteric. And Guy would often have to stay with him half the night to calm him. One of the most powerful men in America would in effect be under house arrest. He and Clyde had to watch Hoover very carefully."

CHAPTER 8

> "But there's a man in Washington
> Whom not many women see,
> Who's as dark and as handsome
> As a sheik of Arabie."

> *Poem for J. Edgar Hoover, submitted*
> *by woman describing herself*
> *only as "Wisconsin Girl," 1940*

EDGAR HAD DEEPLY AMBIVALENT FEELINGS ABOUT WOMEN, but he did not avoid their company. At times, perhaps, he made a point of being seen with women to dispel rumors that he was homosexual. Perhaps, too, Edgar wanted to prove to himself that he could sustain a heterosexual relationship—something he never really achieved. In the end, he was too crippled emotionally to forge a truly fulfilling link with anyone, even Clyde.

When they met, Edgar and Clyde had much in common. As Edgar was devoted to his mother, Annie, so Clyde doted on his mother. As time passed, and their mothers aged, each man gave time and affection not only to his own mother but to his lover's, too. Clyde even sent Annie Hoover Valentine cards.

As Edgar had been humiliated by a young woman in 1918, so Clyde had been rejected—twice. First there had been his childhood sweetheart, who married another man when Clyde went off to Washington. Then, while he was at law school, a second girlfriend became pregnant by another man and married him. According to a classmate, Raymond Suran, Clyde was devastated. Yet he remained attracted to women, and Edgar found that hard to handle.

Anita Colby, the celebrated thirties model, recalled Clyde having "a crush" on her but never following through. In 1939 he briefly courted Edna Daulyton, a waitress in a restaurant near the Justice Department. "He kind of flirted with me," she remembered, "and he took me out to dinner. He talked to me a bit about cases. We saw each other maybe half a dozen times, but I was leery of him.

"One evening when we were having dinner at the May-flower, Hoover came and joined us. I was shocked. He behaved in such an ugly way to me. He was like a little Napoleon. And there was a closeness between him and Clyde that I didn't understand—something that didn't seem quite natural. It was only afterwards I heard the stories."

Clyde would hold Daulyton's hand and give her a good night kiss on the cheek, but that was all. "One night," she said, "I asked him, 'Is there something funny between you and Hoover?' He went very serious and said something like, 'What d'you mean? Are you saying I'm some sort of abnormal faggot?' I guess I said, 'Well, there's *something* between you and that friend of yours. . . .' Hoover joined us again when we went to eat at a place down near the water. And soon after that I stopped seeing Clyde."

In 1939, when Clyde fell in love with a woman in New York and began talking of marriage, Edgar moved ruthlessly to prevent it. "Hoover suggested," said Guy Hottel, "that I have a little talk with Clyde, tell him to forget it. I did. If Clyde had married, he wouldn't have been there to have dinner with Hoover every night. Hoover was selfish. He liked the setup the way it was, and he had ways of getting his own way."

Ironically, at the very time Edgar snuffed out this relationship of Clyde's he was starting to see women himself. He began to do so immediately after his mother's death, following a long battle with cancer, in 1938.

Annie had always been there, holding court when FBI colleagues came visiting, worrying when Edgar took airplane flights. "I am proud and happy that you are my son," she cabled from her sickbed when the National Institute of Social Scientists honored Edgar for "distinguished services to humanity." Soon after, with Edgar at her side in the bedroom where she had given birth to him, she died.

Thoughts about Annie preoccupied Edgar for the rest of his life. He would astonish virtual strangers with guilt-ridden outbursts about not having spent enough time with her when she was alive. He traveled to Florida each Christmas rather than try to celebrate in Washington, where his first forty-two Christmases had been spent with his mother.

Edgar was seen dining out with an older woman within weeks of Annie's death. His new "favorite person," as Walter Winchell put it, was Lela Rogers, mother of Ginger and a formidable figure in her own right. She was forty-seven, four years Edgar's senior, with two marriages behind her. She was tough, as befitted one of the first female recruits to the U.S. Marine Corps, where she had edited *Leatherneck,* the Corps' magazine. She was politically of the far Right, and would one day tell a congressional committee that the line "Share and share alike—that's democracy" in a movie script was dangerous Communist propaganda. She was to be a founding member of the Motion Picture Alliance for the Preservation of American Ideals.

There were soon rumors that Rogers and Edgar were planning marriage. In New York to promote a play she had written, she received the press standing in front of his silver-framed photograph. Edgar had called at 3 A.M. that morning, Rogers let slip, to fill her in on progress in a murder hunt. "Are you going to get married, or are you just interested in detective work?" asked a reporter. "That," she beamed, "is up to him." Edgar, for his part, fended off the questions with coy answers.

Rogers showered him with gifts—a monogrammed ring, a gold cigarette box. "I think," said her friend Anita Colby, "that Leli was more interested in Edgar than he was in her." Ginger Rogers believed the relationship was a "close friendship, not an affair. I do remember this: Mother always said Edgar Hoover was a loner, and lonely."

Edgar told close friends, though, that the affair was serious. "He was really smitten with her," recalled Effie Cain, a wealthy Texan who met Edgar in the forties. Edgar said as much to Leo McClairen, the trusted black Agent who chauffeured him in Florida. "Mr. Hoover told me one time," McClairen remembered, "he was in love with Ginger Rogers' mother. He told me she was thinking of getting married to him, but something came up. . . ."

Richard Auerbach, a top Bureau official, was also privy to the relationship. "No question," he said. "It was a courtship. I used to make arrangements for her to meet with him in Florida. They were very careful, and marriage remained a possibility for many years to come. It lasted until 1955, when I brought the news to her one day that the President wanted him back in Washington the next morning. And his lady love said, 'This just isn't going to work. I'm going back to L.A. . . .' She turned around and left the room with tears streaming down her face, and I put her on a flight. I don't believe he ever saw her again."

From then on, Edgar kept his distance. "Rogers' letters would come in," said Cartha DeLoach, "and he'd send them over to me unanswered. I'd have an agent in the Correspondence Section do it, and he'd sign them."

There were two other women in Edgar's life in the thirties and early forties. The first was Oscar-winner Frances Marion, screenwriter of *Rebecca of Sunnybrook Farm* and *The Scarlet Letter*. She was seven years older than Edgar, a veteran of several marriages. "Frances told me Hoover was in hot pursuit," her daughter-in-law recalled, "but she wouldn't marry him because of the boys, her sons."

The third, and perhaps most important, liaison was with the actress Dorothy Lamour—heroine of films like *Road to Singapore* and *Road to Hong Kong* with Bob Hope and Bing Crosby. She had first met Edgar as early as 1931, when she was a twenty-year-old former beauty queen working as a singer at the Stork Club. They became close, however, only after Lamour's divorce from her first husband and the death of Edgar's mother.

In her autobiography, Lamour wrote only that Edgar was

g friend." In private, in the seventies, she spoke of
elings. "She just started to glow when his name was
m__ _ed," said acquaintances of hers in California. "But
she told us she knew marriage would not have worked. They
were both too involved in their careers. They were heartbro-
ken, though. It was a really sad story."

After 1942, when Lamour married her second husband,
businessman Bill Howard, Edgar became a regular visitor at
their home. "Nobody else was invited," said Howard. "He
so enjoyed privacy where he could relax. . . . He would do
the barbecuing and we'd sit in the backyard. I didn't fool
with Edgar. I was afraid of him. . . ."

Lamour and Howard lived for years near Baltimore, a
short drive from Washington, and the star was occasionally
seen dining with Edgar at Harvey's. He was sometimes at
her side on film sets, or when she gave interviews, and FBI
agents smoothed the way when she traveled abroad.

"When our boys were born," said Lamour's husband,
"Edgar sent an FBI agent out and had their toe prints put on
little gold coins inscribed on the back with his name." "He
wrote a stack of letters to me signed, 'Uncle,'" recalled
John, the elder of the Howards' two sons. "My brother used
to kid me I was born in an FBI test tube."

When Lamour needed financing for a play, Edgar helped
contact an elusive Texas millionaire. "Clyde Tolson called
the Dallas Agent in Charge," recalled Fort Worth FBI Agent
Joseph Schott. "He got the unlisted phone number, and
Lamour contacted the millionaire and got the money. But
the play was a turkey, and he got mad and called Hoover
and asked how she'd gotten to him in the first place. They
ended up blaming the Agent in Charge, and he got transferred. . . ."

After Edgar's death, during an inquiry into FBI corruption, probers discovered how he spent taxpayers' money to
entertain Lamour. "Witnesses told us about the time he had
a party for Dorothy Lamour," recalled investigator Joseph
Griffin. "She'd sung all those songs about moons, and
Hoover wanted her to have a moon that night. So the FBI

Exhibits Section installed an electric globe way up in a tree in his garden, and rigged it up to look like a moon."

Edgar himself hinted at his feelings about Lamour as late as 1969, during a visit to his home by Arthur and Mara Forbes, managers of the resort he stayed at each summer in California. "In his den," Mara recalled, "her signed pictures were all over the wall. He grinned all over and made no bones about it—it was as if it was the big love of his life, something serious."

Lamour, now seventy-eight, has declined to say more about Edgar on the record than she did in her autobiography. The real nature of their relationship remains one of the mysteries of Edgar's life.

Edgar's sexual torment had effects far beyond his personal life. In his day, as is still often the case today, anything other than evident heterosexuality could destroy a public official. Acutely aware of the danger, Edgar overcompensated. Like several other public figures with a secret homosexual life, Edgar often behaved viciously toward fellow homosexuals.[1] Once, reportedly, this resulted in the destruction of a leading statesman's career.

In the fall of 1943 Roosevelt announced the resignation of Undersecretary of State Sumner Welles. Welles was forty-seven, a brilliant diplomat and one of Roosevelt's personal friends. The President said the resignation was because Welles' wife was sick, but it was really the outcome of a drawn-out homosexual scandal in which Edgar played a key role.

Three years earlier, during a night train journey with fellow Cabinet members, Welles had allegedly tried to bribe several black male Pullman staff members to have sex with him in his compartment. A prolonged whispering campaign followed, and, after trying to protect Welles for many months, Roosevelt decided he would have to go.

Edgar's file on the case suggests he behaved impartially throughout, that he merely looked into the matter at the

President's request, then briefed senior officials—telling them no more than was absolutely necessary. Edgar's memoranda, however, sometimes hide more than they reveal. In the Welles case, others paint a very different picture.

The unpublished diaries of Roosevelt's Secretary of the Interior, Harold Ickes, show Edgar went out of his way to volunteer dirt on Welles—two years before the diplomat resigned and at a time when the President was trying to take the heat out of the scandal. In June 1941, Ickes noted, Edgar said he had "absolute proof that Welles is a homosexual . . . and he did not ask that I hold this information in confidence. . . . To my surprise, I found that Hoover was very talkative."

Author and former *New York Times* correspondent Charles Higham recently stumbled on fresh information about Edgar's role. A former FBI official, now retired, said Edgar connived with one of Welles' sworn enemies, William Bullitt, to destroy him. The incident on the train, the official claimed, was an FBI setup—some of the Pullman staff who went to Welles' compartment were paid to do so.

Historian Dr. Beatrice Berle, widow of Adolf Berle, then Assistant Secretary of State, and a cousin of Welles', recently recalled that her husband, too, was sure the scandal was "a put-up job." Edgar's malice, reportedly, was sparked by his distrust of Welles' liberal tendencies—and by gossip that Welles was especially interested in homosexual sex with young blacks.

On several documented occasions in the future, Edgar would attempt to smear other public men—including Adlai Stevenson, Martin Luther King, and three aides to President Nixon—as homosexuals. There is no evidence that any of the allegations were true.

The Welles case occurred at a time when rumors of Edgar's own homosexuality were circulating among high government officials. Secretary Ickes noted it in his diaries, and Attorney General Francis Biddle delighted in making mocking jokes about it. "Do you think Hoover is a homosexual?" he would say in a loud stage whisper as he and Assistant Attorney General James Rowe walked past

Edgar's office. "Shh . . ." Rowe would respond, cringing with embarrassment. "Oh," Biddle would say, still talking loudly, "I only mean a *latent* homosexual."

The whispers spreading about Edgar made him angry and afraid—and he retaliated whenever possible. Agents around the country received standing orders on the subject. "We had a communication," recalled FBI veteran Joe Wickman, "saying he wanted us to deny any of those allegations that might come in, and how. A report had to be made in every case. He wanted to know who said what."

Ordinary citizens who made passing comments on Edgar's sexuality found that, if their remarks filtered back to the FBI, agents arrived to conduct solemn interrogations. Reports to Edgar usually assured him the offender had recanted, sometimes apparently in a state of abject fear. "Agents were rather vigorous in their treatment of ———— [name censored in released document]," one aide noted, "much more so than their memorandum would indicate."

To disassociate himself further from homosexuality, Edgar would make sweeping public statements about his hunt for "sex deviates in government service." He ordered agents to penetrate homosexual rights groups across the country, collect names of members, record speeches and photograph demonstrations. Such surveillance continued for twenty-three years, long after the FBI had concluded that the activists were in no way "subversive."

Edgar was enraged when the leading group, the Mattachine Society, put him, like other heads of federal agencies, on its mailing list. A few years later, Edgar contrived an assurance to the House Appropriations Committee that "no member of the Mattachine Society or anyone who is a sex deviate will ever be appointed to the FBI."

Both Edgar and Clyde kept up a macho front all their lives. They let it be known that they liked smutty jokes, and would call senior colleagues to offer off-color gags—always about women—for inclusion in speeches. Edgar once gave a transparent "striptease" pen, inscribed "J.E.H.," to President Truman's Attorney General, Howard McGrath. One

New Year's Eve, at Gatti's restaurant in Miami Beach, Clyde was seen presenting the sexagenarian Edgar with his birthday present—a Jayne Mansfield doll.

Edgar railed publicly against pornography, and endlessly demanded stern action against the "peddlers of filth," those "parasites of the most deadly variety." As late as 1960, one agent was criticized in front of dozens of colleagues for possessing a copy of *Playboy* magazine. "The Director," said Bureau officials, "looks upon those who read such magazines as moral degenerates."

Edgar himself not only enjoyed *Playboy* but viewed pornographic movies in the Blue Room, a screening facility in Crime Records. A former Agent in Charge, Neil Welch, remembers how a Washington supervisor had to rush a fresh collection of obscene material—seized during Bureau operations—to Edgar's office. Edgar was furious when agents failed to bring him surveillance pictures that showed black activist Angela Davis having sex with her lover.

Once, said Assistant Director William Sullivan, a senior aide with a passkey indulged the temptation to rummage through Edgar's desk after hours. He found "lurid literature of the most filthy kind . . . naked women and lurid magazines that dealt with all sorts of abnormal sexual activities."

Where sexuality is concerned, one must be careful in attaching labels to people. Commenting on Edgar's behavioral patterns, however, two leading medical specialists have reached similar conclusions. Dr. John Money, Professor of Medical Psychology at Johns Hopkins University School of Medicine, felt Edgar was of a "bisexual, but strongly predominant homosexual orientation."

Dr. Harold Lief, Professor Emeritus of Psychiatry at the University of Pennsylvania and past president of the American Academy of Psychoanalysts, concluded that Edgar was probably "a bisexual, with a failed heterosexuality, because of what I see as the sharp division between lust and love in his history."

* * *

The conflicting pressures of dealing with his sexual confusion in private, while posturing as J. Edgar Hoover, masculine, all-American hero in public, eventually drove Edgar to seek medical help. Probably in late 1946, in the wake of continuing rumors that he was a homosexual, Edgar took his worries to a psychiatrist.

Almost all his adult life, Edgar was a patient of Clark, King and Carter, a diagnostic clinic in Washington that handled many distinguished patients. Dr. William Clark, who founded the practice, usually looked after Edgar himself. Soon after the war, however, puzzled by a strange malaise in his patient, he referred Edgar to a colleague who specialized in psychiatry, Dr. Marshall de G. Ruffin.

A product of Harvard and Cornell, Dr. Ruffin had taught psychology at the School of Aviation Medicine during the war. He would go on to become Mental Health Commissioner for the Superior Court of the District of Columbia, and president of the Washington Psychiatric Society. He accepted Edgar as a patient, says his widow, Monteen, because Dr. Clark "couldn't quite understand what was wrong with him. . . . He was suspicious, so he had my husband see him because of his specialty in psychiatry. It was the group opinion—Hoover needed to see a psychiatrist."

"He was definitely troubled by homosexuality," said Mrs. Ruffin in 1990, "and my husband's notes would've proved that. . . . I might stir a keg of worms by making that statement, but everybody then understood he was homosexual, not just the doctors."

After a series of visits, said Mrs. Ruffin, "my understanding was that Hoover got very paranoid about anyone finding out he was a homosexual, and got scared of the psychiatry angle." Edgar ceased seeing the psychiatrist after a while, but reportedly consulted him again as late as 1971, not long before his death.

Dr. Ruffin's case notes on Edgar are not available. He burned them in the fireplace of his home, along with other patient histories, shortly before his own death in 1984. The surviving member of the practice Edgar attended, Dr. Hill Carter, has refused to discuss Edgar's sexuality.

By 1946, when he first consulted Dr. Ruffin, Edgar's social life had long since lost the high profile of the thirties. Edgar had taken his private life out of the public eye and virtually underground. William Stutz, then a young trainee at Schaffer's flower shop in Washington, offers a glimpse of how he went about it.

"First thing each morning," he said, "a Lincoln limo would pull up outside. The chauffeur, usually a black man, would come in and pick up a carnation, a special variety called Dubonnet that we shipped in by air. Normally he would just carry it out to the limousine and drive away. But one day he gave me the motion to go out to the limo, and the glass was rolled down, and the mature man in the back asked if I had a private telephone line. If I had, he said, he would use it to place some orders. Well, it was Mr. Hoover, and my boss had a line assigned to me to take his orders.

"If that phone rang I dealt with the call. It was usually a man's voice. Apparently Mr. Hoover wore his carnation every morning, but only till twelve o'clock—he complained if it did not stay fresh till noon. More often the call was to make a separate order, a flower for a friend. His favorite was a Cypripedium orchid with green and brownish speckles on the throat, the sort of thing a man could send and still remain macho. It came in a glass vial with a special wrought-iron stand, and it cost him twenty-five dollars a crack."

Edgar's florist bill, Stutz recalled, was about $250 a month. "I never knew who the flowers were for," said Stutz, "whether they were favors for someone, I couldn't tell." Sometimes Edgar sent Stutz on mysterious missions. "I was handed a key in an envelope, and I had to take the usual orchid and deliver it, and return the key when the limo came the next morning. The word was discretion, you know, 'Mum's the word' without exactly saying so. I was to go to a place, get in, put the orchid somewhere and take off. One time I was given a key to an apartment in the Wardman Park Hotel. It had dramatic decor, white furniture with a contrasting carpet. There was a sealed envelope with the flowers. I didn't know if it was for a lady or a gentleman. I didn't ask any questions. . . ."

CHAPTER 9

> "The FBI is a really great organization. Under J. Edgar Hoover its list of achievements is most impressive. The rub comes in the never-ending effort to fit the halo. Any angel can tell you this is a damnably hard job."
>
> *James Lawrence Fly, former Chairman,*
> *Federal Communications Commission, 1956*

IN THE SUMMER OF 1937, EDGAR CELEBRATED HIS TWENTIETH anniversary at the Department of Justice. He was presented with FBI Badge No. 1, in gold, an engraved watch and a cowboy hat courtesy of Tom Mix. He and Clyde were photographed, dapper in cream summer suits, up to their waists in a sea of flowers.

The real cause for satisfaction, Edgar knew, was that he had not only survived to serve under Roosevelt, but was now flourishing. Better than that, he was tasting real political power for the first time. Once Roosevelt had grasped the public relations potential of Edgar as champion of an anticrime campaign, he exploited it to the full. He signed special new crime bills, with Edgar standing behind him. He came in person to open the great new colonnaded Justice Department building on Pennsylvania Avenue. "This modern mass of stone and aluminum," said the press, "this $11,000,000 dream of a crime-free America, dwarfs Scotland Yard, the Sûreté, all of them. It is America's general headquarters in the crime war."

Even if the crime wave was overblown, Edgar's FBI was indeed a vast step forward. The fingerprint operation, the technology of crime detection and the disciplined corps of respected agents were genuine assets. In the midst of all the hyperbole, however, the man responsible was glorified beyond all reason. Where mere praise was due, Edgar was idolized.

A few voices were raised in protest. Tennessee Senator Kenneth McKellar accused Edgar before a Senate committee of using public relations to inflate his image. Edgar dodged the questions, concealing the fact that he had propagandists working full-time for him. Then the questions turned personal. "Did you ever," asked McKellar, "make an arrest?" Edgar was forced to admit that he had virtually no field experience. It had been a somewhat meaningless line of questioning—like asking a headquarters officer whether he had ever killed an enemy soldier—but Edgar was shattered. He had done so much to ensure that the world heard about his macho attitude toward criminals, his "Babe Ruth" build, his alleged fitness and his endless hard work. Now doubt was being cast on his masculinity.

A second attack followed within days, when Congressman Marion Zioncheck mocked him as a "master of fiction . . . a dictator." In an astonishing riposte, Edgar called the congressman "a public enemy" who should be driven from public life.

Two days later, Edgar found an opportunity to prove his mettle. When agents in New Orleans located Alvin Karpis, a kingpin of the kidnap gangs, Edgar chartered a fourteen-seater aircraft—a remarkable initiative in those days—and flew south. He was on hand when an eighteen-strong Bureau posse captured Karpis, caught off his guard, on May 1, 1936.

Edgar's version of the arrest was that he personally disarmed Karpis. The gangster himself, on his release twenty-eight years later, claimed Edgar hid behind a building until agents gave him the all clear. Clyde Tolson even bragged later of having "ripped the joint apart with machine-gun fire," when in fact there was no shooting at all. It was, moreover, a Treasury agent who had tracked Karpis and told the FBI where to find him.

Staged though it was, the arrest worked wonders for Edgar's image. He was front-page news, in personal command as Karpis was flown in shackles to face trial in Minnesota. A week later Edgar was off in another chartered aircraft, flying with Clyde to arrest one of the kidnapper's accomplices. He had silenced congressional critics and shown the nation he was a tough guy after all.

Edgar had been working for some time to bring all law enforcement propaganda under his personal control, to institutionalize public relations in a way that would have been unthinkable in any other government agency. First he engineered the removal of Henry Suydam, the publicist hired by Attorney General Cummings. Then, while Courtney Ryley Cooper poured out flattering books and articles, Edgar picked the man who was to shape the Bureau's public image for more than two decades.

This was Louis "Nick the Greek" Nichols, a college football star from the Midwest who had made the Bureau grade the classic way, with a law degree from George Washington University and membership in the Masons. Nichols' personal files, preserved in filing cabinets with combination locks, reveal that he was both workaholic and sycophant, a man single-mindedly devoted to pleasing his master—both at work and with a stream of expensive presents.

It was Nichols who masterminded the formation of the FBI's Division 8, euphemistically known as Crime Records and described by Edgar as "the blood plasma of the Bureau." So it was—though not as a mere record system. The documents in Nichols' file cabinets and in FBI files, from potted biographies of crooks and lawmen to movie scripts and lecture drafts, reflect a herculean effort to manipulate the American mind to the greater glory of J. Edgar Hoover.

There was no attempt to be evenhanded. Feature articles in major league newspapers were "facilitated" only if Edgar approved of the publication concerned. His favorites were those of the Hearst, Copley and Gannett chains, the *San Francisco Examiner,* the *Washington Star* and, at one stage, the *Chicago Tribune.*

By contrast, as explained earlier, Edgar had a lifelong loathing for *The Washington Post*. "If I ever find myself in agreement with that paper," he once told a colleague, "I'll reexamine my position." In the sixties, at Clyde's suggestion, he formally ruled that no background information on himself should henceforth be provided to *The New York Times, Time* or *Newsweek,* thus discriminating against three major press institutions at a stroke.

The handling of individual reporters—the wooing of some and the persecution of others—became a constant preoccupation. Favored contacts were carefully cultivated, even showered with gifts, such as luggage and golf clubs. Some accepted gratefully, and obliged with the sort of coverage Edgar wanted.

"Dear Chief," wrote NBC newsman Raymond Henle, thanking Edgar for sending along *Masters of Deceit,* one of several books on Communism churned out by Crime Records in the Director's name. "Many thanks for the handsomely autographed copy. . . . Once again you have gone into the forefront in defense of our nation against the Commie rats. *Three-Star Extra* will be right there plugging for this fine volume on March 10. . . ."

FBI files would refer to an approved reporter as "a very reliable contact" or "a close friend of the Bureau." One such friend, in later years, would be Jeremiah O'Leary, who then worked for the *Washington Star*. When O'Leary wrote a "hard-hitting review" of a book by an author Edgar regarded as an enemy, the FBI distributed thousands of copies around the country. For his part, according to the file, O'Leary once even helped the FBI when it was trying to identify another reporter's sources. He also submitted an article for review and, according to the file, "any changes we desired."

Contrary to FBI denials, approved reporters were allowed access to files. Karl Hess, sometime Goldwater speechwriter and founder of the *National Review,* since turned left-winger, remembered: "The difference between being just a reporter and being an anti-Communist crusading reporter —with regular assists from the 'secret' files of the FBI—was considerable in terms of vanity alone. . . ." Such favorites were provided with information on unwatermarked paper, to conceal the source.

"The way they handled public affairs," recalled the journalist Fletcher Knebel, "can only be described as blackmail. Nichols told me, 'Look, we can do a lot for your career—if you'll play ball with us. . . .' I later found out what that meant. When I wanted to interview the mighty Director for *Look* magazine, they'd agree only if I wrote the piece before I did the interview, which is of course all wrong. I'm sorry to say my bosses eventually agreed, and Nichols went through it all like a schoolmarm. The story that came out was really watered down, but not enough for them. The next time I bumped into Hoover, he wouldn't speak to me."

Reporters who did not appreciate the Bureau, Edgar told the Society of Former Agents, were "journalistic prostitutes." He carried on a courteous correspondence with Drew Pearson—who for thirty-seven years wrote the *Washington Post* column presided over today by Jack Anderson—while railing against him in private. He built up a 4,000-page file on Pearson and, according to Roosevelt's Vice President, Henry Wallace, kept him under surveillance during World War II.

The columnist remained uncowed, and persistently criticized Edgar—notably over his laissez-faire attitude toward organized crime. By 1969, when Pearson died, Edgar had been reduced to impotent scribblings in the file. "This whelp," he raged, "still continues his regurgitation." The columnist was "a jackal," his writings "psychopathic lyings."

To Edgar, *New York Post* editor James Wechsler was "a rat." The illustrious Walter Lippmann became just another "coyote of the press" when he displeased Edgar. Tom Wicker, at *The New York Times,* would be described as a "jerk" with "mental halitosis," Art Buchwald as a "sick alleged humorist."

When it could be done secretly, reporters were actively harassed. The huge file on Carey McWilliams, who became editor of *The Nation,* covers thirty-two years of investigation, surveillance and probing into his private life to establish whether he was a Communist. He was not.

Once journalists were identified as enemies, Edgar stopped at nothing to discredit them. He would tell the White House that columnist Joseph Alsop was a homosexual, and *Los Angeles Times* executives that reporter Jack Nelson was a drunk. There is no evidence that either allegation was true.[1]

Such tactics proved highly effective. In the first thirty-five years of Edgar's directorship only one publication—*The New Yorker*—would attempt any reporting at all not harnessed to FBI handouts and grace-and-favor interviews.

Edgar rarely had any trouble with broadcasters, who gobbled up FBI exploits for their entertainment value. This began in 1935, when, through tame reporter Rex Collier, Edgar negotiated a contract giving himself total control over "G-Men," a radio series about famous Bureau cases. Later, the propaganda became more ambitious. Louis Nichols organized the writing of the book *The FBI Story,* which became a Warner Brothers movie of the same name.

Edgar had cultivated Jack Warner for years. As a matter of course, agents greeted him at airports and smoothed his path as he traveled around the world. The actor Jimmy Stewart, who starred in the film, got similar treatment. The television series "The FBI," which would begin in 1965, was totally controlled. Edgar and Clyde read the scripts, while an FBI agent watched over the shooting.

Edgar learned that massive self-promotion paid off as early as 1935, when *Time* put him on the cover—the first of four appearances—and declared that his name was now a household word. Universities and organizations began showering him with awards. Edgar's alma mater, George Washington University, gave him an honorary doctorate in law, and New York University followed suit.

By 1936 millions of Americans were devouring G-Man movies and G-Man literature. Their children sported G-Man badges, toted G-Man tommy guns, slept in G-Man pajamas. One wrote to Edgar addressing him as an "American Jesus."

That same year, a survey of 11,000 schoolboys concluded that Edgar was the second most popular man in the nation, topped only by Robert "Believe It Or Not" Ripley. President Roosevelt came in a poor seventh. Youngsters, according to the poll, would vastly rather be Edgar than President of the United States.

A few brave voices in the press suggested Edgar was "stage-struck." "Some scenario writer," wrote Lee Casey of *The Pittsburgh Press,* "should do a burlesque on the G-Men. These federal agents have had things their own way so long there is a danger they will begin to believe they are half as good as people think they are."

Edgar, it seems, did believe his own propaganda. In the spring of 1936, as the Republican presidential candidates jockeyed for position, he sent agents out to take soundings on his own political chances. One of them, Charles Winstead, talked with William Sullivan about his assignment before his death in 1973.

As Sullivan told it, "Hoover got the idea that he should run for president against FDR. . . . He believed he had become a national figure. He thought that if he had the support of the entire law enforcement community—federal, state, city and county—he could run as a Republican and turn Roosevelt and his crew of liberals out of office. . . . Hoover sent some of his most trusted veteran agents, including Charlie, most of them southerners, on a top-secret mission to test the political waters in the South and Southwest, where the Director thought his support was strongest. Charlie was told to approach local chiefs of police or sheriffs on some minor matter, then redirect the conversation to the subject of J. Edgar Hoover. 'He's a great man,' Charlie would say just as he'd been told to, 'and he's done an awful lot for law enforcement on every level in this country. Many people think we'd be better off if Hoover were president.' Then he would wait for the reaction."

The reaction, Winstead said, was "overwhelmingly negative." A surprised Edgar put his presidential ambitions aside. The election was a second massive vote of confidence in Franklin Roosevelt.

A few months later Edgar received the writer Jack Alexander—a future editor of *The Saturday Evening Post*—in the grand octagonal chamber that was now his inner office. Alexander observed Edgar seated behind his huge mahogany desk, framed by flowers, exotic cacti and flags, and found the scene disquieting.

"A few paces to the rear of the Director," wrote Alexander, "are two tall brass standards, topped by brass eagles and clingingly embraced by furled American flags. Much of the Director's time is spent alone in the impressive quiet of this room, and in other quarters than the underworld there is uneasiness over what he may be thinking. Some persons of liberal and leftish beliefs are uncomfortably reminded by the symbolic eagles, and the magnificent distance between door and desk, of the official lair of Mussolini."

CHAPTER 10

> **"There is only one man in political life that FDR feared. He admitted that man was Hoover."**
>
> *Former aide to Colonel William Donovan,*
> *Chief of the Office of Strategic Services in*
> *World War II*

FRANKLIN ROOSEVELT DID NOT LIVE TO RECORD WHAT HE REALLY thought of Edgar. Edgar, for his part, would claim years later that he and the President had been "very close—personally and officially." This was a compound of fact and untruth.

In public Edgar played the loyal courtier. As always with presidents, he behaved immaculately in formal situations, plied the White House with respectful memos. He escorted Mrs. Roosevelt on a tour of Bureau headquarters. After dinner with Roosevelt, in the wake of the Dillinger shooting, he wrote asking the President for an autographed picture.

Yet, said William Sullivan, "Hoover didn't like Roosevelt. He never passed up on a chance to make a snide remark when FDR's name was mentioned, and he never failed to express his feelings about the president in internal memos. . . . When I was assigned to the Research Division, I'd see those blue ink remarks about Roosevelt. One said, 'He has an Emperor's complex.' "

Edgar thought Roosevelt suspiciously left-wing. "Hoover didn't trust liberals," said Sullivan, "and FDR had surrounded himself with other liberals. Hoover hated Henry Wallace, Roosevelt's Secretary of Agriculture. He hated Harry Hopkins, administrator of some of the most important programs of the New Deal; and most of the rest of the President's staff was also unacceptable to the Director." Roosevelt's New Deal, Edgar told his friend, future U.S. Senator George Murphy, was engineered by the Communists.

Edgar's attitude to the President was mild compared with his dislike of Eleanor Roosevelt. He had grave misgivings about the President's wife, about her enthusiasm for left-wing causes and left-wing friends, and he let the President know it. Once, when American Federation of Labor leader Robert Watt complained that the FBI was investigating him, Roosevelt responded with a smile of resignation. "That's nothing," he said, "to what J. Edgar Hoover says about my wife." Yet the President tolerated Edgar, even relied on him.

Roosevelt, one historian remarked, had "a more spacious view" of executive authority than his Republican predecessors. He saw the FBI as a tool that could be used for much more than law enforcement, that could be pressed into service for reasons of state and for his own political benefit. The President handed Edgar massive new powers, powers he would abuse for nearly forty years.

A month before Roosevelt's inauguration, Adolf Hitler had become German Chancellor. The first concentration camp opened soon afterward. As Edgar was celebrating the capture of Machine Gun Kelly, Hitler withdrew from the League of Nations and announced plans to rearm Germany. As Edgar celebrated the shooting of John Dillinger, the Nazis assassinated the Chancellor of Austria.

By spring 1934, there were fears that rightist groups, including the American Nazi movement, were plotting to undermine the government. On May 8 Edgar went to the White House to discuss the problem with the President and senior members of the Cabinet. The outcome was that for the first time, Edgar gained official sanction to conduct political intelligence.

He began by investigating American Nazis, but soon had targets of a different political stripe. That fall Roosevelt ordered Edgar to investigate striking mill workers in Rhode Island. At Christmas, when the American Civil Liberties

Union asked for a meeting with the President, the White House asked the FBI for a briefing. The ACLU was one of Edgar's pet hates, and on his advice the President turned down the ACLU request. Roosevelt and his advisers soon fell into the habit of calling for Bureau reports on matters that had little or nothing to do with law enforcement. Edgar eagerly obliged. He was becoming, as one historian put it, "the President's intelligence valet."

Stalin had murdered his way to absolute power in Moscow. The Nazis marched into the Rhineland, and civil war broke out in Spain. Roosevelt received troubling warnings, word of a home-based right-wing plot to topple him, and allegations of foreign espionage. On the morning of August 24, 1936, he summoned Edgar to a private meeting that would have far-reaching consequences. We have only Edgar's version of what was said.

"I called you over," Edgar was to quote the President as saying, "because I want you to do a job for me, and it must be confidential." According to Edgar, Roosevelt wanted to know how he could obtain reliable intelligence on Communist and Fascist activity in the United States. Edgar said the FBI could legally do the job, although it was outside the realm of law enforcement, if the request came—technically —from the State Department. The next day, in Edgar's presence, Roosevelt told Secretary of State Cordell Hull that the United States was threatened by Soviet and Fascist espionage directed from outside the country. "Go ahead," Hull is said to have responded, "investigate the cocksuckers!"

To avoid leaks, according to Edgar's memorandum of the meeting, the President wanted no written request from the State Department to the FBI. Instead, Roosevelt said, he would "put a handwritten memorandum of his own in his safe in the White House, stating he had instructed the Secretary of State to request this information to be obtained. . . ."

The Roosevelt presidential library can trace no such memorandum, so there is no way of knowing what scope the President intended the order to have. What is clear is that he issued the directive secretly, without sanction of Congress, and that the Attorney General—Edgar's boss—was informed only after the fact.

As a result of those White House meetings, Edgar's freedom of action was greatly increased. Propaganda had already made him a mythological national guardian, the man who made the American housewife feel safe. Now, by presidential fiat, he wielded raw political power as well.

Immediately after his 1936 meeting with Roosevelt, and before even discussing the matter with Attorney General Cummings, Edgar triggered a massive surveillance operation against trade unionists and radicals. An FBI target list, still preserved in Bureau files, included the steel, coal and garment industries, educational institutions and organized labor. Though Edgar denied it at the time, the Bureau also began recruiting informants and preparing dossiers on political "subversives."

In the spring of 1938, as eighteen alleged Nazi spies went on trial, the President responded to public pressure by making more funds available to the intelligence services. Edgar urged that the cash be used for domestic intelligence, and said it could be arranged without special legislation. Such spying on Americans at home, Edgar wrote to the President, should be pursued "with the utmost degree of secrecy in order to avoid criticism or objections which might be raised by either ill-informed persons or individuals having some ulterior motive." In the fall of the year, at a meeting aboard the presidential train at New York's Pennsylvania Station, Roosevelt gave Edgar the go-ahead.

The Bureau now began hiring new agents in huge numbers—their ranks would swell from less than 1,000 in 1937 to nearly 4,000 by the end of the war. Many of the new recruits would be used to defend national security in wartime. Simultaneously, however, the Bureau gathered vast amounts of information on ordinary people of liberal persuasion, and on innocuous groups like the League for Fair Play (which supplied speakers for Rotary and Kiwanis clubs), the Independent Voters of Illinois, even a Bronx child-care center. There was a massive investigation of the

NAACP, involving extensive use of informants. Edgar saw to it that all information gathered, including that collected on thousands of innocent citizens, was duly filed away for future reference.

The FBI file on the Ford Motor Company reveals that in January 1939, Edgar met with Henry Ford's right-hand man, Harry Bennett. Bennett was a ruthless union-buster, whose special achievement had been to develop a day-to-day working alliance between Ford and the leaders of organized crime. He had personal contact with Detroit's crime boss Chester LaMare, men like Joe Tocco and Leo Cellura, and he arranged Ford franchises for gangsters like Joe Adonis and Tony D'Anna.

Bennett used his underworld contacts to take care of Ford's union problems. He used thugs to organize the beating of United Automobile Workers leader Walter Reuther, one of Edgar's perennial targets, when he and others tried to distribute leaflets near the plant. In time he assembled a private army, armed with pistols, blackjacks and lengths of rubber hose, to break up union meetings and attack labor activists. Edgar got on very well with Bennett, sent him autographed photographs of their first meeting and worked with him as an ally. Edgar's Agent in Charge in Detroit, John Bugas, soon had regular access to Bennett's "vast files on Communist activities." Bennett, Bugas reported, was "a very valuable friend . . . without question one of the best sources of information."

The FBI later discovered that Bennett had purchased many of the Communist names in his files from Gerald Smith, the local Fascist leader. This did nothing to dampen Edgar's enthusiasm for him.

In late 1939, without seeking higher authority, Edgar boldly ordered his staff to prepare dossiers for a Custodial Detention List, an index of people who could be detained in time of war. The list named not only those who sympathized with Germany and its allies, but also those with "Communist sympathies." It included, too, people who had done nothing to deserve suspicion, like Harrison Salisbury of *The New York Times*.

In 1942, on his way to a foreign assignment, Salisbury had problems obtaining a passport. It was not until forty years later, when he obtained his FBI file under the Freedom of Information Act, that he found out why. An eccentric female neighbor had told the authorities that Salisbury was an "employee of the German government." He was a code expert, she believed, because he had recording devices at his home. Salisbury's house was secretly searched and a file opened on him at the FBI. It was this that caused the passport problem. Salisbury's name went onto the Custodial Detention List, marked: "Pro-German—stated he is in employ of German government." Salisbury remained technically liable to arrest and internment, in the event of a national emergency, until 1971.

Edgar would resist bitterly when, in 1940, Attorney General Jackson insisted that the Justice Department—rather than the FBI—assume overall control of the Detention List. The Director found a way not to comply in 1943, when Attorney General Biddle ruled that the Department existed to pursue law-breakers, that it had no business cataloguing citizens according to their alleged "dangerousness," and directed that the Detention List be abolished. Edgar simply ordered his officials to maintain the list, but to call it the Security Index instead. He did this secretly, the Senate Intelligence Committee discovered in 1975, without informing Biddle, who was his boss.

In public, most attorneys general talked as though their relations with Edgar were good. In private, there was often terrific friction. Frank Murphy, a future Supreme Court Justice, who held the office in 1939, would conclude that Edgar had ambitions to become Attorney General himself. He found the Director's behavior alarming. "He is almost pathological," Murphy told Assistant Attorney General Norman Littell. "He can get something on anybody if he starts investigating him; that is his tendency."

Indeed, Edgar kept a file on Murphy himself, one that contained information on his private life, and which stayed open until he died. Parts of the file are withheld to this day.

In June 1939, with war looming in Europe, President

Roosevelt agreed that the FBI—with the War and Navy departments—should take over all intelligence operations. In September, as Hitler signed a nonaggression treaty with Stalin and prepared to invade Poland, the President announced publicly that Edgar was to head the fight against foreign espionage and sabotage. At the same time, he authorized him to gather information on "subversive activities." The orders were vague and designed to respond to a temporary need. Their effect, however, was to give Edgar the nearest thing he would ever have to a charter to conduct domestic intelligence—one he would fall back on for the rest of his career.

Edgar's first use of the new authority caused a storm of protest. In January the arrests of a number of anti-Semitic agitators, on charges of plotting to overthrow the government, ended in fiasco. It emerged that the men had received their inspiration and their weapons from a paid FBI informant, and all charges were dropped.

Then FBI agents in Detroit and Milwaukee seized twelve radical activists on the grounds that, three years earlier, they had recruited volunteers to fight on the loyalist side in the Spanish Civil War. Under an old statute, it was an offense for private citizens to raise an army on U.S. soil for a foreign conflict. The arrests were curious because the alleged offenses had occurred so long ago, and the war in question was over. The new Attorney General, Robert Jackson, swiftly dropped the charges—too late, however, to stifle public outrage.

Edgar's men had swooped down before dawn, broken down doors, ransacked homes, held their prisoners incommunicado for nine hours, strip-searched them twice and allowed them access to lawyers for just one minute before they appeared in court. It was all reminiscent of the Red Raids of 1920—and this time Edgar could not deny responsibility.

Suddenly the press was comparing the FBI to the secret police forces of Nazi Germany and Soviet Russia. In Congress Senator George Norris spoke of "an American Gestapo," calling Edgar "the greatest publicity hound on the American continent." The way things were going, he added, there would soon be "a spy behind every stump and a detective in every closet in our land." As FBI files now reveal, Edgar had a stool pigeon on Senator Norris' own staff in 1940.

Three days after the Detroit raids, Edgar was called in to see the President. Then, with Clyde in tow, he departed on a surprise "vacation" to Miami Beach. There he ensconced himself in a villa attached to the Nautilus Hotel, an island retreat for the very rich, to shelter himself from the barrage of criticism.

In Washington, Edgar's aides lobbied furiously to drum up a counterattack. Behind the scenes, agents investigated everyone who had criticized the arrests of the Spanish Civil War activists. Edgar, meanwhile, tried to get Attorney General Jackson to make a statement in his defense. Jackson hesitated. His predecessor Frank Murphy had made him "very dubious" about Edgar, warning that the FBI spied on government officials and tapped their telephones. Edgar denied such charges and offered to resign, and Jackson ended up issuing a compromise statement, expressing confidence in Edgar and committing the government to the protection of civil liberties.

Edgar survived the crisis because he had the most powerful protector of all, the President. Characteristically, Roosevelt made light of the row. "Edgar," he called across the room at a Washington Press Club reception. "What are they trying to do to you?" "I don't know, Mr. President," Edgar replied. Roosevelt then made an exaggerated thumbs-down gesture with both hands, proclaiming loudly, "That's for them." Everyone present knew Edgar's job was safe for the foreseeable future.

"Hoover continued in his job and added to his power," observed Roosevelt's Interior Secretary Harold Ickes, "because he managed to worm himself into the complete confidence of the President." Edgar achieved that, as he would with future presidents, by sending a stream of political intelligence to the White House.

"He started playing up to him," said William Sullivan,

"telling him little tidbits of gossip about high-ranking public officials whenever he could. . . ." Francis Biddle, who followed Jackson as Attorney General, had the same experience. "Lunching alone with me in a room adjoining my office," Biddle recalled, Hoover began "sharing some of his extraordinarily broad knowledge of the intimate details of what my associates in the Cabinet did and said, of their likes and dislikes, their weaknesses and their associations."

In June 1940, when Roosevelt wrote to thank him for the "wonderful job" he was doing, Edgar responded with flattery. He told the President his note was "one of the most inspiring messages which I have ever been privileged to receive . . . a symbol of the principles for which our nation stands."

The job Edgar was doing, as both men knew, was far beyond the proper responsibilities of an FBI Director. Roosevelt had asked the FBI to "look over" the mountain of critical telegrams he had received after making a broadcast on national defense. Edgar obliged by running name checks and opening files on hundreds of citizens.

FBI political espionage for the White House became routine. In late 1940, when the President asked Edgar to assign an agent to Palm Beach to watch the administration's "friends and enemies," Edgar obliged with "complete coverage."

Roosevelt turned to Edgar for help when, at a time the *Chicago Tribune* was opposing his defense plans, he wanted to boost a rival paper in the city. "FDR used the FBI for all kinds of dirty tricks," said the *Tribune*'s Walter Trohan, who became a trusted Bureau contact. "When the new newspaper, the *Sun,* was trying to put the *Tribune* out of business, the government used the FBI to intimidate newspaper publishers. I took it up with Hoover later, and he said, 'Yeah, but I got a letter directing me to do it.' And he showed me the order. He wanted proof before he did that kind of thing. . . ."

As time went on, Roosevelt often bypassed his Attorney General and communicated directly with Edgar. A long line of future attorneys general, who theoretically had full authority over the Director of the FBI, would have to learn to live with the same humiliation. As Secretary Ickes noted in his diary in June 1941, Edgar had become "so strong that apparently he can dictate who is to be the Attorney General, his titular chief."

Edward Ennis, a senior aide to Francis Biddle, felt that attorneys general were cowed by Edgar's relationship with the President, and by an "even deeper fear that he had files on everybody." The best that could be said, wrote Assistant Secretary of State Adolf Berle, was that Edgar "has run a secret police with the minimum of collision with civil liberties, and that is about all you can expect of any chief of secret police."

The fact was, though, that for the first time in the nation's history, a federal official did wield such power, and his assault on civil liberties would be persistent and serious.

In May 1940, Roosevelt gave the go-ahead for use of that vital tool of any secret police, the telephone tap. On its face, Edgar's track record on wiretapping was entirely respectable. The Bureau's first manual, issued in 1928, said flatly that tapping was "improper, illegal . . . unethical" and would not be tolerated. Edgar had assured Congress that any agent caught wiretapping would be fired.

Though some sought to find loopholes in it, the Federal Communications Act of 1934 had seemed to outlaw wiretapping altogether. And, in spite of an Attorney General's ruling that allowed some tapping with prior approval, Edgar continued to say that he was against it except in life-or-death circumstances, such as kidnappings. The testimony of his own men, however, makes it clear that was not true.

For two months in 1936, five FBI agents were forced to reveal in court, the Bureau mounted round-the-clock wiretaps to investigate a case of interstate theft in New York. The evidence made it clear that this was nothing unusual, that there had been dozens of similar assignments, using the most sophisticated equipment available.

According to other agents, Edgar had on occasion used

bugging to further his own private interests. There had been the time, years earlier, when he ordered taps on the telephones of Roosevelt's Postmaster General James Farley, who wanted him replaced as FBI Director. In 1937, during a clampdown on brothels in Baltimore, reporters had asked Edgar about rumors that telephones were bugged during the operation. "We have to do that sometimes," he said carefully. It later emerged that there had been bugging—enough to fill two volumes of notes on conversations in one brothel alone. Part of their mission, former agents were quoted as saying, had been to get smear material on police officials who had fallen out with Edgar.

"Perhaps only Mr. Hoover himself," Federal Communications Chairman James Fly was to write, "can tell exactly how many times he has instructed his men to break the law that his Bureau was supposed to enforce; but he has chosen not to discuss such details." In 1940, when Edgar was quietly lobbying for looser wiretapping laws, it was Fly's congressional testimony that ensured the legislation was rejected. Edgar detested the FCC Chairman from then on, so much so that—even two decades later in retirement— Fly insisted on meeting a reporter out of doors, for fear his home was bugged by the FBI.

In the spring of 1940, convinced that wiretapping was vital to national security, President Roosevelt overrode the law. He authorized the Attorney General to permit eavesdropping on "persons suspected of subversive activities against the United States, including suspected spies. . . ." This order, Francis Biddle pointed out long afterward, "opened the door pretty wide to wiretapping of anyone *suspected of subversive activities* [Biddle's emphasis]." It was to remain Edgar's basic authority for telephone tapping for a quarter of a century.

Attorney General Robert Jackson was so unhappy about this development that he distanced himself from the issue and let Edgar decide who should be wiretapped. Evidence of the sort of bugging Edgar would approve came less than a year later.

* * *

Harry Bridges, the thirty-five-year-old leader of the Inter national Longshoremen's and Warehousemen's Union, had long been a thorn in the side of management. He was also an irritant to Edgar personally. Five years earlier, when Edgar had briefed Roosevelt on the internal threat from Communists, he had named Bridges as the man who could paralyze the nation's shipping. Even after the union leader came out in favor of a peace agreement with management, Edgar pursued him relentlessly.

Bridges was vulnerable because he had been born in Australia. Edgar claimed he was a Communist, and foreign-born Communists could be deported for membership in "an organization advocating the violent overthrow of the government." Bridges said he had never joined the Party, though he admitted being an admirer of "the Soviet workers' state." The result of his latest deportation hearing was still pending in the summer of 1941.

That August, Leon Goodelman, a reporter for the New York newspaper *PM,* received a call from the secretary of the Citizens' Committee for Harry Bridges. Bridges, he was told, was currently staying at the Edison Hotel on West Forty-seventh Street. He had discovered his telephone was being tapped, and invited the reporter to come and see for himself.

Goodelman found he had a scoop on his hands. Bridges explained he had been staying at the Edison intermittently since early July. He was accustomed to being surveilled by the FBI and became suspicious when, even though he asked for different accommodation, the hotel persisted in giving him one particular room, number 1027. Then, down in the hotel lobby, Bridges spotted an FBI agent who had attended one of his deportation hearings. After identifying two more agents, Bridges decided to experiment. Using the telephone in his room, he called a union colleague to make an appointment at a nearby drugstore. Sure enough, one of the FBI agents turned up at the rendezvous. If they knew about his appointment, Bridges reasoned, then they were listening to his calls.

"I went back to the hotel," he recalled, "went in my door

very fast and dove over to the connecting door, lay down and looked under it into the next room. Two pairs of feet went by my eye and I could see some bunched-up telephone wire on the floor. . . . After tipping off my friends that I was being tapped, I sort of settled down to have some fun with the FBI. I left the room very quietly, and ducked out of the hotel."

Soon, armed with a pair of binoculars, Bridges was watching his room, and the room next door to it, from the roof garden of the hotel across the street. "There were the two guys," he said, "stretched out on the twin beds with their earphones on, thinking I was still in the room." First with colleagues, then with reporter Goodelman and a photographer, the union leader watched his watchers for days. Whenever Bridges left his room, the journalists noticed, one of the agents next door would sit down to work at a typewriter. He was also seen pasting little pieces of paper together—scraps from Bridges' wastebasket.

Then Goodelman used a nail file to pry open the telephone connector box in Bridges' room, revealing a hidden radio induction microphone, a dual-function bug capable of transmitting both speech on the telephone and conversation in the room. The police were called, and the agent on duty next door had to flee via the fire escape. He left behind wires leading through the wall to Bridges' phone, abandoned wiring and a piece of carbon paper. The carbon bore the telltale words "Evelle J. Younger, Special Agent."

The FBI had been caught red-handed. Francis Biddle, who took over as Attorney General that month, faced awkward questions from the Senate Judiciary Committee. "When all this came out in the newspapers," he said, "I could not resist suggesting to Hoover that he tell the story of the unfortunate tap directly to the President. We went over to the White House together. FDR was delighted; and, with one of his great grins, intent on every word, slapped Hoover on the back when he had finished. 'By God, Edgar, that's the first time you've been caught with your pants down.'"

Roosevelt might not have laughed so hard had he known what Edgar was saying behind his back. "Hoover stated quite frankly," Assistant Attorney General Norman Littell wrote in his journal, "that, if he were put on the stand as a result of the reopening of the Bridges case, he would frankly state that he was authorized to tap the wires by the President himself." Hoover, Littell observed, "knows no loyalty to the commander-in-chief. He would just let the chief take the rap for authorizing an illegal act. . . ."

Roosevelt himself had few qualms about the use of wiretaps by the executive. He reportedly used Edgar to tap one of his own former advisers, Tommy "the Cork" Corcoran,[1] and even requested coverage of a serving Cabinet member, Postmaster General Jim Farley. Edgar is said to have balked at that, but passed on Farley's conversations when they were picked up on an FBI bug of someone else. During the run-up to the 1944 election, he would reportedly supply the White House with the results of wiretaps on Republican politicians—an alleged Watergate three decades before the scandal that would topple Richard Nixon.

According to Nixon, Edgar told him "every president since Roosevelt" had given him bugging assignments. As the Senate Intelligence Committee would discover in 1975, Presidents Truman, Eisenhower, Kennedy, Johnson—and Nixon—all used the Bureau to conduct wiretaps and surveillance for purposes that had nothing to do with national security or crime, and which can only be described as political. By ignoring ethics, and on occasion the law, and by using the FBI to do it, they all made themselves beholden to Edgar.

Against that background, it is hardly surprising that Edgar would feel free to deceive Congress on the subject. "In Chicago," veteran FBI surveillance specialist Wesley Swearingen was to recall, "we'd get a call from headquarters a couple of days before Hoover was due to appear before the House Appropriations Committee. They'd tell us he was going to tell the Congressmen we had such and such a number of wiretaps going right now—always a real low figure. We'd have dozens on in our city alone, but this call from the Bureau would instruct us that for now we were to reduce them to only one—say, on Communist Party headquarters. So we'd get in touch with the phone company and say, 'As of midnight Tuesday until midnight Wednesday, that's the only wiretap we want working in Chicago.' Hoover would march in, make his speech, give some low figure that was accurate that day, and the Congressmen would be impressed. Then, Wednesday night, they turned them all back on again."

We shall probably never know how much wiretapping was done solely on the authority of senior FBI officials, without the approval of attorneys general. Records of such taps were maintained by designated assistant directors, but in 1953 Edgar ordered that assistant directors' office files be destroyed every six months. The only such file that survives, that of Lou Nichols, contains substantial information on wiretaps—including a series of reports on John Monroe, a Washington influence peddler who held Edgar's attention not least because he reportedly claimed the Director was "a fairy."

The FBI's surveillance index, started in 1941, contains 13,500 entries. While the identity of the individuals tapped is withheld on privacy grounds, the index establishes that Edgar's FBI tapped or bugged thirteen labor unions, eighty-five radical political groups and twenty-two civil rights organizations.

In 1940, secure in his relationship with President Roosevelt, emboldened by his new and formidable powers, Edgar prepared for World War II.

CHAPTER 11

"Hoover was a megalomaniac, an egomaniac, and a prude of the first order. He was a thorn in our side."

A. M. Ross-Smith, wartime British Intelligence official in the U.S., 1990

FOR EDGAR, THE WAR REALLY BEGAN NEARLY TWO YEARS BEFORE Pearl Harbor, with a letter from a retired boxer. Gene Tunney, the undefeated world heavyweight champion of the twenties, had often met Edgar and Clyde on their frequent visits to Yankee Stadium. Now, in early 1940, he found himself passing on a discreet message from a man he had first met at military boxing events in his youth, a man who had since become a top-level British secret agent.

This was William Stephenson, known to millions today as the protagonist of *A Man Called Intrepid,* the best-selling book about his achievements in World War II. Stephenson, a Canadian the same age as Edgar, was an extraordinary figure—World War I flying ace and prison camp escapee, radio and television pioneer, and hugely successful businessman. His mission, when he asked Tunney to make contact with Edgar, was under the personal command of Winston Churchill.

Churchill, the First Lord of the Admiralty, had been engaged in secret correspondence with President Roosevelt for months. The President fervently wanted to save Europe from the Nazis, but was not yet free to help openly. Powerful forces in the United States were opposed to involvement in the war, and a presidential election was looming. At this critical time, Churchill picked Stephenson as his personal representative in the United States.

In April 1940, in Room 39 at the Admiralty, the two men discussed a momentous secret. With invasion threatening, Britain's military was in utter disarray. The country was virtually broke. But Britain had obtained the captured Enigma machine, the key to decoding German military communications—and potentially the key to victory. Churchill decided that, for now, President Roosevelt should be the one foreigner to know Britain had Enigma. "To him, and to him alone," he told Stephenson, "the truth should be confided. . . . Our daily intelligence summaries should be delivered to him through the FBI."

Edgar himself was not to be privy to the intelligence from Enigma,[1] but his cooperation was vital; and, if the relationship was not to be hamstrung by American neutrality, it had to be a closely held secret. That was why their mutual friend, Gene Tunney, was used to deliver Stephenson's first, informal letter. Its contents remain unknown, but Edgar was persuaded. He telephoned Tunney to say, yes, he would see Churchill's man.

The two men met that April at Edgar's new home on Thirtieth Place, N.W., a house he had bought half-built for $25,000, before his mother died. Annie had not liked the place, but now, two years after her death, he had moved in alone. Before getting down to business, Stephenson reflected on what the house might tell him about the Director of the FBI. He noticed the meticulously ordered clutter of ornaments, the myriad photographs of Edgar himself. He noted, especially, the profusion of male nudes.

"There were," Stephenson would recall, "nude figurines, nudes on the stairway, pictures of rather suggestive male nudes, all over the place." He would soon meet Edgar in the company of Clyde, and recognize them as a homosexual couple. Many years later, Stephenson would refer darkly to having gained some sort of grip on Edgar, something that on occasion made it possible to pressure the Director into cooperating. Roosevelt's adviser Ernest Cuneo, who was also privy to the secret Anglo-American diplomacy, put it more bluntly. He spoke of Stephenson "ruthlessly black-mailing" Edgar.

At that first meeting, Edgar listened to Stephenson's plea for cooperation on intelligence matters. Then said he could do nothing without a specific order from the President. Stephenson returned briefly to London, only to hurry back to Washington in May, when Churchill had become Prime Minister.

In England that month, as Churchill stood in his bedroom shaving, his son Randolph told his father he did not see how Britain could possibly beat the Germans. Churchill's response was to swing around and retort that he would "drag the United States in."

Soon afterward in Washington, following a meeting between Stephenson and Roosevelt at the White House, the President ordered "the closest possible marriage between the FBI and British Intelligence."[2]

Roosevelt was running a great risk, perhaps even of impeachment, by ordering such cooperation with a foreign nation while America remained at peace. Edgar may have shared the risk to some degree. While he was to insist, years later, that he received an instruction from the President in writing, no such document can be traced. Edgar insisted the liaison be kept secret from the State Department. Had it been discovered in 1940—and had the President failed to come to his rescue—Edgar would have faced ferocious attacks by those determined to keep the United States neutral.

The official British history of Stephenson's operation acknowledged that Edgar's initial involvement required "courage and foresight," but included acerbic comments on his character. This was a "prima donna" who tolerated no rivals and was "not overscrupulous either in his methods of removing them. . . ." The price of Edgar's cooperation, the British realized, "was always conditioned by his over-whelming ambition for the FBI."[3]

It is hard to tell quite where Edgar's private sympathies lay, in an administration still not immune to pro-German sentiment, during the long buildup to war. He had received one of Himmler's senior aides in 1938, long after the nature of the Hitler regime had become clear, and he corresponded amiably with Nazi police officials until well into 1939. He made tentative plans, later canceled, to attend an international police convention in Berlin that year.

Critics point out that the FBI finally severed law enforcement contact with Germany only three days before Pearl Harbor. All this, however, may signify little. There was no point, during peacetime, in cutting off contacts that might provide useful information. Certainly, once America was committed to the confrontation with Germany. Edgar responded with enthusiasm.

When war became a real possibility, Edgar made sure that Clyde Tolson, still in his thirties, would not see combat. Should hostilities begin, he told the Navy, Clyde could not be spared for service. In late 1940, when the FBI was preparing to send two high officials to England, Clyde volunteered. Edgar said he appreciated his "fine spirit," then sent someone else to face the rigors of London at war. All the same, Edgar liked to refer to Clyde as "Commander," his rank in the Naval Reserve. Edgar himself, now forty-five, had for years now been a Lieutenant Colonel in the Military Intelligence Reserve. Some military men addressed him by that rank, and he did not object.

As an armchair warrior, Edgar at first impressed the British. He provided the transmitter that gave Stephenson direct communication with his people in London, and the FBI helped prevent sabotage of British ships in American ports. Failing any official power of censorship in peacetime, Edgar came to the rescue when Stephenson needed to intercept letters in the U.S. Mail—FBI agents simply purloined the correspondence from post offices. The Bureau also passed on documents captured from German spies, without informing U.S. military intelligence, which at this stage still opposed liaison with the British.

The liaison, however, was a two-way street. The FBI soon found that its British friends were experts in the ungentlemanly art of opening other people's mail without leaving a trace—and Bureau agents flew to the British colony of Bermuda to learn how.

Stephenson shared with Edgar much of the information flooding in from his agents, not least those in Latin America. A year after cooperation began, no fewer than 100,000 reports had been sent to the FBI from the British base in Rockefeller Center.

Working with the British let Edgar feel he was himself part of the derring-do, an agent in the field. In August 1940, when the Nazis tried to intercept a consignment of scientific data held by a British official at Washington's Shoreham Hotel, it was Edgar who drove across town to secure the material.

Mindful of Edgar's vanity, Stephenson saw to it that the Director got the credit when British work achieved a breakthrough against Nazi spies. "He lived by publicity," recalled Herbert Rowland, one of the British team. "Stephenson avoided publicity at all costs. Inevitably the FBI got the credit. We never minded this."

While Europe burned, American intelligence chiefs indulged in empire-building and chicanery—Edgar as much as his military colleagues. As early as 1939, when the President got tired of interagency bickering, Assistant Secretary of State George Messersmith had been asked to get the heads of the squabbling agencies together. When he invited them to dinner at his Georgetown house, all appeared except Edgar. He did show up at the next meeting, but only after a call from the President threatening him with the sack.

General Ralph Van Deman, who knew Edgar well, warned army intelligence that Edgar was a man "catapulted into a job about which he knows practically nothing. . . ." Secretary of War Henry Stimson thought he "poisons the mind of the President . . . more like a spoiled child than a responsible officer."

There was no pleasing the feuding officials, least of all when Roosevelt began considering Colonel William Donovan for the job of overall intelligence chief. Donovan, fifty-eight in 1941, was a decorated World War I hero, a prominent lawyer and a political force in his own right. Although a Republican, he was vastly respected by Roosevelt, who thought he had the makings of a President himself.

As an Assistant Attorney General, in 1924, Donovan had recommended that Edgar be confirmed as Director of the Bureau. Long since, however, he had regretted doing so. Should the Republicans return to office, he said, he would do all he could to get Edgar fired. Edgar's agents had told him all this. It was thus all the more galling to learn that Donovan was at the center of plans to establish a new intelligence agency.

Donovan and William Stephenson, by contrast, had been forging a partnership of trust. Churchill's agent was swiftly becoming disillusioned with Edgar. From the British viewpoint, he was making poor use of the information supplied to him, and, as one official put it, he "only knew how to think like a cop."

Stephenson needed someone with an instinct for intelligence work, and Donovan had it. Soon "Wild Bill," as the press dubbed him, was flying off to Europe with "Little Bill" Stephenson for a crash course in the ways of British intelligence. The British had vastly more experience in the field than their U.S. counterparts—a fact of life that Donovan appreciated. Edgar, however, burned with resentment.

Britain's Director of Naval Intelligence, Rear Admiral Godfrey, and Commander Ian Fleming—later to become famous as the creator of James Bond—arrived in America in May 1941 to recommend intelligence integration under Donovan and Edgar. Edgar, Fleming recalled, "expressed himself firmly but politely uninterested in our mission. . . . Hoover's negative response was soft as a cat's paw. With the air of doing us a favor he had us piloted through the FBI laboratory and record department and down to the basement shooting range. . . . Then, with a firm, dry handclasp, we were shown the door."

In June 1941, Donovan was indeed named to the new post of Coordinator of Information—to the delight of William Stephenson and the rage of the military intelligence chiefs and Edgar, who called the appointment "Roosevelt's folly." The British records show that, well knowing the extent of Donovan's involvement with Stephenson's team, Edgar began to treat the foreigners with "ill-concealed hostility." This developed into real enmity in late 1941, shortly before Pearl Harbor, with results that may have contributed to that national tragedy.

On August 14, 1941, nearly four months before Pearl Harbor, a senior FBI official sent Edgar a report on Dusan "Dusko" Popov, a Yugoslav who had just arrived in New York. He was a double agent, dealing with the Allies and the Germans at the same time. And thirty years later, when he published his war memoirs, he would startle the world with the claim that he had warned the FBI in advance that the Japanese planned to attack Pearl Harbor. He had tried, he said, to give this information to Edgar personally, but had encountered only a stream of abuse.

Popov, the son of a wealthy industrialist, was twenty-nine in 1941. The ground had been laid for his wartime adventures when, while studying law in pre-war Nazi Germany, he forged a strong friendship with another well-to-do student, a German named Johann Jebsen. In 1940, when Jebsen came to Belgrade and told Popov he was working for the Abwehr, German military intelligence, he asked his friend to do the same. For both men it was the start of a tortuous and dangerous trail—one that would end in death for Jebsen.

Popov was openly opposed to the Nazis, and Jebsen's role with the Abwehr was only a front. He was in fact anti-Hitler and had close links to the Abwehr chief Admiral Canaris, who, scholars now believe, was working against Hitler throughout the war. Asked by Jebsen to go to England as a German spy, Popov promptly made contact with British Intelligence. He was told to play along with the Germans and keep reporting back to the British.

Popov traveled to London by way of neutral Portugal, meeting his German control, Major Kremer von Auenrode,[4] on the way. In London, Lieutenant Colonel T. A. "Tar"

Robertson, a senior officer in Britain's domestic security service, MI-5, decided the Yugoslav was a potentially valuable asset. After an intense induction period, Popov returned to Lisbon to feed the Germans a mass of misleading information prepared by the British.

The Germans took the bait. Popov, code-named "Tricycle" by MI-5, spent the first half of 1941 shuttling back and forth between Portugal and England, always returning to Lisbon with phony information for the Abwehr. In May that year, bemoaning Germany's poor espionage presence in the United States, von Auenrode asked him to go to New York and set up a spy ring. Popov had little choice. He could hardly do otherwise if he was to retain the Germans' confidence. The British, for their part, saw a way to take advantage of the situation.

Stewart Menzies, head of the Secret Intelligence Service, or MI-6, which handled foreign intelligence operations, now approved a plan. Popov would go to the States—as a "loan" to Edgar and the FBI. If he did set up a spy ring, as the Germans hoped, the Allies would use it for deception from the very start. The collaboration, moreover, would strengthen relations with the FBI and give the Americans their own ready-made double-cross operation. Edgar, consulted at the highest level, agreed.

In Lisbon, as Popov prepared to leave for America, he picked up an intriguing piece of intelligence from Jebsen. At a meeting on the cliffs overlooking the Atlantic, Jebsen spoke of a recent journey he had made to Taranto, the Italian naval base that had been devastated in a sneak attack by British planes flying off aircraft carriers. The Japanese, Jebsen told Popov, had pressed the Germans for details of just how the British had carried out the operation. Germany's Air Attaché in Tokyo, Baron Gronau, expected Japan to try a similar surprise attack within six months— around the end of 1941. An attack where? Popov asked. "If my calculated opinion interests you," Jebsen replied, "the Japanese will attack the United States."

Furthermore, when von Auenrode briefed Popov on his American mission, he gave him a list of intelligence requirements. It included a detailed set of requests for intelligence about Hawaii, and several specific inquiries about Pearl Harbor. Of a ninety-seven-line questionnaire for the whole U.S. mission, thirty-five lines were devoted to Hawaii. There were questions about the precise positions of ammunition and mine depots, oil dumps, hangar locations, the submarine base, the anchorages. "You are to go to Hawaii," said von Auenrode, "and as soon as possible."

According to Popov, everything then made sense—the Japanese interest in Taranto, the Air Attaché's talk about a surprise attack, Jebsen's heavy inference that it would be against the United States and, finally, the target: Pearl Harbor.

Popov promptly reported all this to British intelligence and, as his former case officer has confirmed, it was taken very seriously indeed. "I saw the questionnaire immediately," recalled Colonel Robertson. "I was terribly impressed with it, and I thought the first thing we should do was to send the Japanese information over to America. . . ."

Control of Popov now shifted to MI-6, which instructed Popov to pass the intelligence to the Americans as soon as he arrived in New York. "They thought it preferable," he was to recall, "that I be the bearer of the tidings, since the Americans might want to question me at length to extract the last bit of juice."

Popov arrived in New York aboard a Pan Am flying boat on August 12, 1941, and soon met with senior FBI officials, including one of Edgar's Assistant Directors, Earl Connelley, and New York Agent in Charge Percy "Sam" Foxworth. The file shows that he gave them their first sight of the microdot system, the new German intelligence technique by which long messages, photographically reduced to tiny dots, could be concealed in seemingly innocuous correspondence. Popov also delivered the Pearl Harbor questionnaire—in plain text as well as in microdot form.

Foxworth responded cautiously to the information about Pearl Harbor. "It all looks too precise," Popov quoted him as saying. "The questionnaire plus the other information spell out in detail exactly where, when, how and by whom we are to be attacked. If anything, it sounds like a trap." The decisions on Popov and his mission, Foxworth added, would be made in Washington, by Mr. Hoover.

In the partially censored FBI file, virtually all of Foxworth's initial one-page report to Edgar about Popov is blanked out. So is the entire opening section of the twelve-page report made by Assistant Director Connelley. There is no way of knowing what was verbally reported to Edgar, since all concerned are dead. The record does show, however, that Edgar was kept personally advised about Popov. Three weeks after Popov's arrival he scrawled a terse note to Foxworth: "Sam: see Connelley in N.Y. and get this Popov thing settled."

In New York, Popov was by now distinctly unsettled. His regular FBI contact, Charles Lanman, had told him he was not to go to Hawaii, which the Germans expected him to do as soon as possible. Nor was he at this stage given any information to feed back to the Germans, to maintain credibility. "There must be a hitch," Lanman said, "somewhere between your people, the British Security Coordination, I mean, and our office in Washington. . . . Mr. Hoover will be here in New York in two weeks, and will see you then."

The real reason for the delay, the files show, was that Edgar was heading off on his usual vacation with Clyde. Popov, meanwhile, decided to fill in the time with a trip to Florida, where the Germans had also asked him to snoop on U.S. military installations. He decided to take a woman friend along, a prospect that caused consternation at the FBI. Very probably acting on Edgar's personal instructions, agents told Popov this would contravene the Mann Act, the law that prohibited transporting women across state lines for the purposes of prostitution. Popov went ahead anyway.

He spent a week in Florida, traveling in a flashy Buick coupe he had bought in New York. The file shows that to appease the FBI, he rented a separate room for his girlfriend. Later, back in New York with time on his hands, he renewed his courtship of the actress Simone Simon, whom he had known in Paris before the war. According to Simon, their relationship was "very proper," with her mother acting as chaperone.

Finally, Popov wrote in his memoirs, he "encountered" Edgar at the FBI office in New York. "I use the word advisedly," Popov recalled. "There was no introduction, no preliminaries, no *politesse*. I walked into Foxworth's office, and there was Hoover sitting behind the desk looking like a sledgehammer in search of an anvil. Foxworth, dispossessed, was sitting silently in an armchair."

Popov recalled how Edgar looked at him with "disgust," how he at once started ranting and "yelping." He "turned purple" with rage and called Popov a "bogus spy," who had done nothing useful since he arrived. The thrust of the tirade was that the Yugoslav had taken a woman to Florida, "chased film stars" and generally lived high on the hog. Edgar ran a clean organization, he said, and Popov had sullied it.

Popov retorted that he always lived luxuriously, that the Germans—who financed him generously—would think it odd if he did otherwise. He had been ineffective since his arrival only because the FBI had given him so little cooperation. But Edgar only got angrier. The meeting ended within minutes, with Edgar shrieking, "Good riddance!" as Popov departed.[5]

Edgar's defenders hold that he had no reason to take special note of Popov's information, that—four months before Pearl Harbor—it deserved no more attention than myriad other snippets of intelligence. In August 1941, however, Edgar had two good reasons to listen to Popov with care.

The Popov information had not come out of the blue, nor did it come merely with a general recommendation from British Intelligence. It came, according to MI-5's Colonel Robertson, only after careful advance contacts by Guy Liddell, then the organization's Director of Counterespionage. Liddell had met Hoover and believed he had established a better rapport than some of his colleagues.

"One reason we put Popov in touch with Hoover," recalled Robertson, "was that Guy Liddell was very friendly with the Director. He thought the best thing to do was to send Popov and his stuff over to Hoover. He thought— misguidedly, as it turned out—that Hoover would pay attention, since it came from him. The mistake we made was not to take the Pearl Harbor information out and send it separately to Roosevelt."

At the time it was offered, Popov's information may not have rated the attention of the President himself. Robertson insists that the FBI was the "natural" place to send it, and that the British cannot be blamed for Edgar's failure to handle it properly.

Ignoring Popov was even less defensible because his warning did not stand alone. Thanks to the British, Edgar already had firm evidence that the Germans, with the Japanese in mind, were snooping on Pearl Harbor. Earlier that year, as a result of vigilance by British censors in Bermuda, the FBI had intercepted a letter from Captain Ulrich Von der Osten, an Abwehr agent operating in the United States. The letter, mailed after a trip to Hawaii, contained a report on the island's defenses, a map and photographs—notably of Pearl Harbor. "This," Von der Osten's report concluded, "will be of interest mostly to our yellow allies."

There was good reason for Edgar to remember that intercept in August. Another German agent, who was one of Von der Osten's close collaborators, was arrested by the FBI just days after Popov handed over his questionnaire. Yet even though the case was still active and under Edgar's personal supervision, he and his officials failed to spot the linkage between the Von der Osten letter and the Popov information, and to give Popov the hearing he deserved.

After the run-in with Edgar, Popov turned for help to a senior member of the British intelligence team in New York, Charles Ellis. The Director of the FBI, Ellis observed, pulled tantrums every day. He would ask Stephenson to intervene. Stephenson tried and got nowhere.[6] So did an emissary sent from London by MI-6 chief Colonel Menzies. Menzies' concern was that Edgar's obduracy would destroy all the painstaking work that had gone into making Popov a star double agent.

Soon, Popov discovered the FBI had placed microphones all over his Manhattan apartment. Life with his Bureau contacts became a series of verbal skirmishes. He was, however, at last given a trickle of low-grade information to send to the Germans, and clearance to travel to Brazil to meet an Abwehr contact. Popov left New York, not to return until after Pearl Harbor.

So far as one can tell, Edgar did not tell Donovan's department, which existed to coordinate intelligence, about Popov either. Edgar's attitude to British Intelligence in the weeks before Pearl Harbor, the British history notes say dryly, "was quite evidently to suppress its activities if he could."

When Popov's memoirs were published in 1974, two years after Edgar's death, the FBI flatly rejected his allegations. Edgar's successor as Director, Clarence Kelley, said the Bureau "certainly did not receive information which indicated the Japanese would attack Pearl Harbor." According to Kelley, the files showed that Popov "never personally met Mr. Hoover," that his story was more fiction than fact. Thomas Troy, former CIA officer turned intelligence historian, has claimed that Popov "never personally warned Hoover about such an attack. . . . He warned nobody." Popov, both men suggested, was little more than a troublesome playboy.

British Intelligence veterans have said the opposite. John Masterman, the wartime head of Britain's interservice XX, or Doublecross, Committee, which used double agents with legendary success, had assessed Popov for himself from the start, and addressed him affectionately in future correspondence.[7] He considered Popov "a leading and highly placed agent . . . one of the leading figures in the double-cross world."

Montgomery Hyde, who worked with British Intelligence

in New York, thought him "one of the most important British double agents"—a rating endorsed by the author Graham Greene, an MI-6 veteran. Ian Fleming, who also met Popov during the war, may have used him as one of the models for James Bond. Former Commander Ewen Montagu, of Naval Intelligence, thought Popov a man of steel and basic common sense, who "made a great contribution to the Allied victory."

So well regarded was Popov that the British eventually gave him the honorary rank of colonel, British citizenship, the Order of the British Empire, the Distinguished Service Medal and a Modigliani painting—a gift from the royal family. He was godfather to the nieces of MI-6 Chief Stewart Menzies.

FBI files contain no written record of a meeting between Edgar and Popov, but that proves nothing. Edgar made an art form of concealing information in alternate file systems, or simply not recording it at all. Edgar's office records, released only in 1991, show that he was indeed in New York in late September 1941, the approximate time of the meeting alleged by Popov—a fact Popov could not have known when he wrote his memoirs.[8]

Popov did not concoct his story in the seventies to create a publishing sensation, as detractors suggest. He reported the episode to his superiors at the time. William Stephenson, who disliked saying anything that would damage Anglo-American relations, avoided public comment on the Popov controversy. He discussed it in private, however, with his biographer, coincidentally also named William Stevenson.

"Our conversation was not for publication at the time," said writer Stevenson. "But he was very clear. He said Popov had indeed met Hoover—he knew all about it. He thought it was a terrible failing in Hoover, who had this straitlaced attitude that shut him off from realities. Stephenson had no doubts about Popov's credibility, and he thought the FBI had totally failed to pick up on what Popov was trying to tell them about Pearl Harbor."

Popov also reported to his case officer, Colonel Robertson. "He was debriefed when he got back to London," Robertson recalled, "and he certainly reported that he'd seen Hoover. He was not going to make up a story of the nature he reported to us, that he and Hoover had had an awful row. I can't see any reason for him to make up such a story."

Chloe MacMillan, who worked with British Intelligence in Portugal, met with Popov when he eventually returned there. "He did see Hoover, I'm sure," said MacMillan, "and he did give them his warning about Pearl Harbor before it happened. When I saw him months later, he was still so depressed about what had happened." Other contemporaries had similar memories.[9]

British officials, moreover, had no doubts about the value of Popov's information on Pearl Harbor. In a 1945 report, written at the time for official consumption only, Masterman said it had "indicated very clearly that . . . Pearl Harbor would be the first point to be attacked, and plans for this attack had reached an advanced state by August 1941."

William Stephenson, who saw the Popov questionnaire, found it "striking." He was especially impressed by the fact that it requested data about the harbor depths at Pearl Harbor—so soon after the British had pioneered the use of air-launched torpedoes against the Italian base at Taranto. When he saw that, he recalled years later, he "had no doubt that Pearl Harbor was *a* target, and perhaps *the* target."[10]

The FBI file shows that by October 20, 1941, seven weeks before Pearl Harbor, the Bureau had shared a paraphrased version of the Popov questionnaire with U.S. naval and military intelligence. It seems almost certain, however, that they did not receive the crucial backup information that went with it—Popov's report on the statements of Jebsen, Baron Gronau and Major von Auenrode. Without those factors to put the questionnaire in perspective, its impact must have been greatly diminished.

The White House fared even worse than the Army and the Navy. Three months before Pearl Harbor, Edgar did send a description of the microdot system, along with two of

Popov's microdots, to President Roosevelt's aide General Edwin Watson. The President himself saw the material within twenty-four hours. He did not, however, see the microdots with the questions about Pearl Harbor. Edgar did not send those to Roosevelt, although he himself knew their contents—the laboratory report on all the microdots had come in the very day of the letter to the White House.

Edgar's ego had got the better of his intelligence. As he rushed to show off his knowledge of a new German espionage device, it does not seem to have occurred to him that the contents of the microdots might be more important than the dots themselves. There is no sign in the record that Edgar ever did tell the White House about either the Pearl Harbor questions or the other Popov information.

Rear Admiral Edwin Layton, who was Fleet Intelligence Officer at Honolulu in 1941, later prepared a massive study on the Japanese attack. He concluded, even without the new evidence assembled in this chapter, that Edgar "dropped the ball completely" in his handling of the Popov information. "His failure," declared the Layton account, "represented another American fumble on the road to Pearl Harbor."

CHAPTER 12

> "Hoover had shown his total incompetence for sophis-
> ticated wartime intelligence early on. His handling of
> the 'Popov Affair' might well have been a tip-off for his
> future legendary secretiveness and over-simplified way
> of thinking."
>
> *William Casey, CIA Director*

EDGAR WAS IN NEW YORK FOR THE WEEKEND WHEN THE JAPANESE airplanes came screaming out of the skies over Hawaii. It was 1:25 P.M., East Coast time, 7:55 A.M. at Pearl Harbor. Intelligence chief William Donovan was also in the city, watching the Brooklyn Dodgers play the New York Giants.[1]

Four and a half thousand miles away, at the FBI office in Honolulu, a young radio technician named Duane Eskridge was testing equipment. Eskridge, the Bureau's first such expert, had been hired four months earlier to set up a new Bureau communications system. His first weeks on the job, in Washington, had been spent attending to the headquarters radio—call sign WFBI—which then consisted of only FBI1, Edgar's limousine, and one other car. Eskridge had to be on duty early in the morning to respond when Edgar announced "FBI1 in service" on his way to work. There were no other messages, so Eskridge simply sat around all day waiting for Edgar to call in again on his way home at night. On December 7, in Hawaii, such foolishness was abruptly forgotten.

"I was making test transmissions when the Jap planes came in," Eskridge recalled. "I went up on the roof to see what was going on, and I could see them flying overhead.

147

They were real low, you could see the pilots with their helmets on. In fact I went and got a .45 automatic from the vault and started shooting at them. It didn't do any good, of course, but that was my reaction."

Eskridge remembered he was a radio operator, not a sharpshooter, and hurried back to his transmitter to begin sending what he believes may have been the first news of the attack. "I sent the news in Morse code, in clear text, to San Diego," said Eskridge. "The operator there thought I was kidding, and I had to repeat it. Then he immediately called his Agent in Charge, who called the weekend duty supervisor in Washington. I have always assumed he called Hoover, and that Hoover called the White House. No one could have got through much faster."

In fact the first news of the catastrophe reached the President within half an hour, through the Navy communications network. For all Eskridge's efforts, it was nearly an hour before headquarters staff patched a call through to Edgar, from the Agent in Charge in Honolulu, Robert Shivers. Then Edgar moved quickly. Long before the final toll was in—2,400 dead, 1,300 wounded, eleven ships sunk and 118 planes destroyed—he was on his way by air to Washington.

Back at headquarters, Edgar issued a torrent of orders. Guards were placed on Japanese diplomatic missions, ports and airports closed to Japanese travelers, mail and telephone links severed. Warrants were issued for the arrest of hundreds of suspect Japanese.[2] Edgar reported to the White House that night that all these measures, planned in advance on a contingency basis, had been efficiently carried out.

For a week or so after America's declaration of war, Edgar acted as government censor. The White House asked him to intervene on December 12, when it learned that columnist Drew Pearson was about to publish details of the scale of the naval disaster. "I got a phone call from J. Edgar Hoover during dinner," Pearson recalled, "in effect threatening to put me in jail unless we killed the story giving the real story on Pearl Harbor. I told Edgar that he was nuts, that there was no law by which he could put me in jail, and that he was not the man to interpret the law. He admitted all this, said that Steve Early at the White House had called him up and asked him to throw the fear of God into me."

That story was killed, and Pearson soon had cause to ponder the extent of Edgar's penetration of the media. On the orders of the Chief of Staff, two generals visited NBC to ask that both Pearson and Walter Winchell be taken off the air. The odd thing, Pearson recalled, was that Edgar later revealed in a phone conversation that he had a "transcript of what happened at the meeting." This could mean only that the NBC office had been bugged.

What the "real" Pearl Harbor story was, of course, remains the subject of fierce debate. Only two things are certain. American intelligence failed because of an inability to extract what really mattered from a mountain of incoming data and draw the correct conclusion. Then, after the disaster, there was a rush to cover up and to pass the buck. Yet, while much has emerged to discredit the military, few have questioned the performance of the FBI.

Immediately after the attack, Edgar began trying to lay the blame on others—anyone other than the FBI. In a report to the President, five days later, he claimed that the Army in Hawaii had previously been sent warning of the "entire plan" and timing of the Japanese attack by intelligence colleagues in Washington. There is no evidence that the military received any such warning, and the rest of Edgar's outburst was packed with inaccuracies. Fortunately for him, the memorandum remained hidden in the Roosevelt papers until after his death.

In the same report, Edgar told how—some thirty-six hours before the attack—the FBI had intercepted a telephone call between Mrs. Mori, a dentist's wife on Hawaii, and a caller in Japan. Their conversation, which lasted forty minutes at a cost of $200, had included discussion about weather, searchlights, and what type of flowers were presently in bloom. Agent in Charge Shivers, said Edgar, had decided the conversation was suspect the moment he saw the transcript on Saturday afternoon. He at once informed the Navy and the Army, but the military response had been woefully inadequate.

It is true that General Short, the Commanding General in Hawaii, failed to give the Mori call the attention it deserved. But new research raises a question as to how well the FBI itself performed after intercepting the mysterious conversation. A check of the record and with surviving witnesses reveals a discrepancy in dating. Edgar told the White House the intercept was made on the afternoon of December 5, translated and transcribed, and passed to the Navy and the military on the evening of Saturday, December 6, the eve of the attack. Agent in Charge Robert Shivers also said the call came in on the fifth.

The official transcript, however, dates the call as having taken place on Wednesday, December 3. Two of four surviving FBI staffers interviewed in 1990 were sure the intercept was made as early as Wednesday. A third thought Thursday, and only one agreed with Edgar and Shivers, that the call came in as late as Friday. One of the witnesses, former agent George Allen, was the "sound man" who installed the tap that picked up the Mori call. He said in 1990 he was certain the call came in on Wednesday evening, and that the transcript went to Washington the next morning. "I'm as clear as a bell on that," he recalled. "We worked on it Wednesday night, and finished it up Thursday morning."

Did the Mori call, then, come in earlier than the official inquiries were told? Though its meaning remains obscure to this day, scholars agree the call was a coded conversation with a Japanese spy. If the call was known to FBI headquarters four days before the attack, was it passed as promptly as it could have been to the military authorities? Given more time, intelligence officers might have found a way to follow through—perhaps with a fruitful interrogation of Mrs. Mori.

Another clue suggests that, before the Mori call, the FBI possessed some specific intelligence—something indicating where and when the Japanese onslaught would occur—that was not acted upon. The head of the Honolulu Police

Espionage Bureau, John Burns, never forgot a visit he received from Shivers a week before the raid. Evidently upset, the FBI man told Burns to close his office door, then confided, "I'm not telling my men this but I'm telling you. . . . We're going to be attacked before the week is out." He was so upset, Burns recalled, that there were tears in his eyes. Burns got the impression Shivers' information had come from headquarters in Washington. Shivers had served with the FBI since 1920, was close to Edgar and in direct touch with him at the time.

A month after Pearl Harbor, when the Roberts Commission of inquiry was holding hearings in Hawaii, Shivers made more strange comments: "You will be one of the ones to be called before the investigation," he told Burns. "What are you going to tell them?" Burns said he would tell the truth. "You really gonna tell the truth?" Shivers responded. "Exactly the truth?" "Yes sir," Burns replied, "including what you told me."

As it turned out, the Commission did not question Burns. It did call Shivers, but nothing in his testimony reflected his prophetic talk with Burns. Incredibly, although he was responsible for domestic security, Edgar himself was never questioned about Pearl Harbor by any official inquiry. The Army Board asked him to appear in August 1944, but he declined, on the grounds that "absence from the city . . . will make it impossible."

The record shows that Edgar was indeed away, taking a four-week vacation with Clyde. He got away with sending in an affidavit instead, and never did submit to questioning about Pearl Harbor by any of the official inquiries.

The findings of the most thorough probe, conducted for the Secretary of War by Henry Clausen, remained unpublished until 1992, when Clausen published his book *Final Judgment.* Its litany of interservice follies includes an explanation of how and why, just five days before Pearl Harbor, Naval Intelligence abruptly stopped monitoring the phones of the Japanese Consul in Honolulu. The decision, Clausen disclosed, was the result of a "childish dispute" between FBI Agent Robert Shivers and Captain Irving

Mayfield of Naval Intelligence. Shivers had exacerbated a liaison problem, testimony revealed, by playing the bureaucrat and sending a formal complaint to telephone company officials. "I could not help asking myself," Clausen recalls, "what might have happened if Mayfield and Shivers had simply hung in there, discussed the matter calmly and kept the Navy's phone taps in place." If the bugging had been continued, Clausen believes, it might have yielded vital last-minute clues to Japanese intentions.

For his part, Edgar kept up his recriminations against others, not least by suggesting that he had proposed the bugging of Tokyo's diplomats in Hawaii and had been ignored. The Japanese consul had sent most of his reports over commercial circuits operated by RCA and Mackay Radio. Unlike the overseas telephone link, which was bugged with the authority of the Attorney General, neither the FBI nor the military had had authority to tap those circuits. By demanding the right to do so, Edgar had collided with an old adversary, Federal Communications Chairman James Fly.

The record shows that Edgar had wanted the FCC to monitor all telephone and cable traffic between the United States and Japan—along with Germany, Italy, France and the Soviet Union—and to supply the FBI with the results. Fly and his officials repeatedly refused, explaining that such eavesdropping was against the law. The only way he could cooperate, said Fly, would be if the law was changed, or in response to a direct order from the President.

According to *The FBI Story,* the history of the Bureau as authorized by Edgar, Fly was still resisting when Pearl Harbor was attacked. The implication was that, had it not been for Fly's obstinacy, the disaster could have been averted. Fly offered a very different account.

"The Radio Intelligence Division of FCC," he said, "did monitor foreign and potential enemy traffic, particularly the enciphered messages on the Tokyo/Berlin circuit. . . . We did not have cryptologists. The RID picked up the pre-Pearl Harbor traffic and funneled it to the FBI, Army and Navy Intelligence and the State Department. Finally Hoover requested that we discontinue this service for the stated reason of the FBI's inability to break the code. But the FCC at my instructions continued to send the traffic to the FBI. In this line of monitoring, the RID picked up the crucial coded 'winds' messages. These messages were on the desks of the Federal Bureau of Investigation on Sunday, December 7, when Hoover was in New York for the weekend. And the fleet went down."

The "winds" messages were the basis of a Japanese contingency plan, sent to diplomatic missions on November 19, advising them that in the event of normal communications being severed, the order to burn their codes would be transmitted in the guise of a broadcast weather report. *"Higashi no kaze ame,"* "East Wind Rain," would indicate an impending break with the United States. Such a message was picked up by U.S. monitors on December 4, but the commanders in Hawaii were not informed. Documents on the subject were subsequently concealed from the official boards of inquiry.

The record shows that the FCC did monitor Japan's traffic, did intercept a key "wind" message on December 4 and did pass it on to Naval Intelligence within twenty-four hours. There is no reason to doubt Fly's claim that the information also went to the FBI well before the raid.

Dusko Popov heard the first confused news of the attack aboard ship in the Caribbean, on his way back to New York. "The seriousness of the moment," he recalled, "could be read on everyone's face. Except mine. It was the news I had been awaiting. . . . I was sure the American fleet had scored a great victory. . . . I was very, very proud that I had been able to give the warning to the Americans four months in advance. . . . Then the news started trickling in. . . . The Japanese had scored a surprise attack. . . . I couldn't believe what I was hearing. . . . We knew they were coming. . . . Somewhere, somehow, there had to be an explanation."

Back in New York, Popov asked his FBI contacts what had gone wrong. Had his warning been ignored? Agent in

Charge Foxworth told him not to ask questions, to "walk in step." "Searching for the truth beyond your reach," Popov recalled Foxworth saying, "may be dangerous. It may stir up an idea in Mr. Hoover's head. . . . Mr. Hoover is a very virtuous man."

Two of the British officers involved, Ewen Montagu and Montgomery Hyde, saw Popov at this time. "I could see," Hyde recalled, "how angry he was with the FBI, who he was convinced had never taken any action on his earlier warning about the Japanese and Pearl Harbor."

Popov's relations with the Bureau eventually collapsed altogether. The FBI refused to let him know what information it was transmitting to Germany—over a "clandestine" radio—purporting to come from Popov. "From the German point of view," recalled Montagu, "he had suddenly changed. He had provided them with no information of any value. He had not built a spy network. Most dangerous of all, he could not hope to provide answers to the really intensive questioning about the radio traffic that had been transmitted in his name. . . ."

In the summer of 1942, in spite of the mortal risk that he would be unmasked as an Allied agent, Popov returned to his work in Portugal. He managed to regain the Germans' confidence, then played a key role in feeding them phony plans for the Allied invasion of occupied Europe.

Popov's friend Johann Jebsen, who had warned of a surprise attack on the United States and who continued to filter vital information to the Allies, did not survive. He was taken by the Gestapo, questioned under torture and shot.[3]

In the safety of Washington, meanwhile, Edgar is said to have extended his insinuations about Pearl Harbor to include President Roosevelt himself. In February or March 1942, according to former U.S. Air Force Colonel Carlton Ketchum, Edgar joined a group of politically like-minded associates, including Republican Congressman George Bender, former Assistant Attorney General Joseph Keenan and Senate Majority Secretary Leslie Biffle, at a private dinner at the Army-Navy Club. What Edgar was to tell the gathering, guests were admonished, was strictly off the record.

"Mr. Hoover said," Ketchum recalled, "that he had had warnings from repeated sources from early fall 1941 to just a few days before the Pearl Harbor attack . . . and that these warnings became more specific from one time to another. . . . He said that, much more important, the President had had warnings during all of that time. . . . Hoover was told by the President not to mention to anyone any of this information, but to be handled [*sic*] in the judgment of the President, and not to pass them on within the FBI. . . . There was discussion in the group at this point, that the Army and Navy commanders could have been warned well in advance . . . so that the casualties would have been minimized. There were some rather bitter things said about the President's conduct."[4]

Recent research indicates the possibility that, in line with his expressed desire to "drag" the United States into the war, Winston Churchill may have withheld last-minute intelligence warning of the Pearl Harbor attack. Most scholars, however, find it unthinkable that Roosevelt shared such foreknowledge and permitted the destruction of Pearl Harbor. Had he had advance warning, he would surely have seen to it that the Navy was ready for battle, perhaps at sea. Any aggression against American territory by Japan, even successfully defended, would have triggered a declaration of war.

Yet Ketchum's story cannot be dismissed. Research confirms that Edgar was on intimate terms with the politicians named as the audience for his charge that the President suppressed vital Pearl Harbor intelligence. If the account is accurate, Edgar was among the first to make the allegation.

In the summer of 1942, six months after Pearl Harbor, a team of American secret agents took on a highly sensitive mission. Contrary to all international rules, they were to steal the secret codes used by the embassies of neutral countries that favored Germany. This involved breaking in at dead of night, cracking safes, photographing codebooks and escaping without getting caught.

Working under Edgar's rival William Donovan, the team pulled off this feat several times. Late one night, however, when the agents were inside the Spanish embassy in Washington, two FBI cars screeched to a halt outside and very deliberately turned on their sirens and flashing lights. Donovan's men had to abort the operation, and several of them were arrested. Donovan had no doubt that Edgar was personally responsible.

It had not been enough for Edgar to have control of intelligence operations throughout Latin and Central America. He had been enraged because Donovan, now a general, had been appointed head of the wartime intelligence body, the Office of Strategic Services, and he was obstructing him at every opportunity. "The Abwehr," Donovan commented, "gets better treatment from the FBI than we do." Donovan's Spanish embassy operation cut across existing FBI surveillance, so Edgar simply sabotaged it. On the eve of the landings in North Africa, his action came close to exposing vital Allied operations.

The agent who led the break-in, Donald Downes, later recalled how Donovan protested to the White House—to little avail. "No President," one of his aides commented, "dare touch John Edgar Hoover. They are all scared pink of him." "We had taken all imaginable precautions," Downes lamented, "all except one—the possibility of betrayal by someone high enough in the American government to know what we were doing."

Edgar's relations with William Stephenson, a staunch Donovan supporter, had sunk to an all-time low. Edgar sent an aide to whisper in the ear of Assistant Secretary of State Adolf Berle, a man with little affection for the British, that one of Stephenson's men was using smear tactics to try to force his removal from office.

Former MI-6 official A. M. Ross-Smith, the controller of the accused agent, said in 1990 that Edgar's allegation had been "completely untrue—absolute balls. It originated with a paid informant, a German-American who made up the story just to please his FBI paymasters. Hoover was just using it to further his own ambitions."

False or not, the episode mushroomed into a high-level international row. The British ambassador, Lord Halifax, was summoned to a meeting with Berle and Attorney General Biddle. Edgar was not satisfied even when the "offending" English official hastily left the country. It was impossible, he insisted, to continue working with the British. "Does J. Edgar," sighed William Stephenson around this time, "think he's fighting on Bunker Hill against us Redcoats? Or has he heard of Pearl Harbor?"

For all their differences, circumstances forced the intelligence warlords to coexist. Donovan turned the OSS into a brilliant success, especially in Europe, and Stephenson labored on in New York.[5] With internal security and Latin American intelligence to handle, Edgar had more than enough on his plate. According to one qualified source, however, he found time to dream of a different kind of glory.

J. Edgar Nichols, son of Edgar's close aide Lou Nichols, remembers his father reminiscing about a fantastic scheme. "Mr. Hoover, my father and a third man whose name I don't know developed a plan to go behind German lines and assassinate Hitler. They actually presented this plan to the White House, and it got bucked to the State Department, and they got taken to task by Secretary of State Hull. What they had in mind was a three-man assassination team, and my father talked as though he and Mr. Hoover somehow hoped to take part themselves. My understanding is that this was no joke—they really did hope something would come of it."

If Edgar was yearning for a new chance to play center stage, he got it. Suddenly, at the height of his squabbles with Donovan and the British, fate delivered a spectacular burst of favorable publicity. At midnight on June 13, 1942, a German submarine surfaced off Amagansett, at the eastern end of Long Island. It disgorged four men laden with arms, explosives and cash—German saboteurs with orders to cause havoc in factories vital to the war effort, and panic in the population. The team might have succeeded had its leader not betrayed the operation almost at once. That inconvenient truth, which would have made nonsense of Edgar's propaganda, was suppressed.

The leader of the commandos, thirty-nine-year-old George Dasch, had lived in the United States for many years before the war. On his return to Germany, it seems, he quickly lost faith in the Nazi regime. During training for the American mission, he seemed less than zealous and oddly disinterested in sabotage techniques. He saw his role, he was to say in a memoir after the war, as ensuring that the mission misfired.

That nearly happened without his help. The Germans ran into a lone Coast Guardsman on the beach, then let him go after thrusting money into his hand to keep quiet. By the time he raised the alarm, however, the Germans had vanished, leaving equipment and explosives behind in a poorly concealed cache.

The FBI joined the search for the saboteurs within hours, and Edgar rushed to see Attorney General Francis Biddle. "His eyes were bright," Biddle recalled, "his jaw set, excitement flickering around the edge of his nostrils." The rest was a great FBI success story—or so it appeared to the public.

Two weeks later, Edgar called a victorious press conference to announce that eight would-be saboteurs, including a second group seized in Florida, had been caught. He appeared regularly at the military tribunal that followed. Lloyd Cutler, a member of the prosecution team and more recently counsel to President Jimmy Carter, thought Edgar carried himself "like a general, very much in control of his troops, the agents. We were handed the case prepared by the FBI, and Hoover kept us at arm's length from his men."

All the commandos were sentenced to death, and six of them went to the electric chair. Edgar recommended the sentences be carried out, and personally organized the executions. Only two of the Germans, George Dasch and a comrade named Ernst Burger, had their sentences commuted to long jail terms.

Thirty years later, Edgar would still be talking of the case as one of his "most important accomplishments." As late as 1979, a bronze marker commemorating the capture was placed in a Justice Department hallway. In fact, as Edgar well knew, the FBI's role had been negligible.

Far from being tracked down by intrepid Bureau agents, Dasch had deliberately betrayed his fellow saboteurs. He began by phoning the FBI in New York and identifying himself as "Franz Daniel Pastorius," the German code name for the operation. He said he had just arrived from Germany, would shortly have valuable information to deliver to J. Edgar Hoover and asked that Washington be informed.

Even then, the Bureau nearly blew it. The agent who took Dasch's call responded by exclaiming, "Yesterday, Napoleon called!" and slamming down the telephone. No one passed the word to Washington as Dasch had requested.

He did, however, give himself up to the FBI in Washington, and provided the Bureau with all the information necessary to locate his fellow saboteurs. He was acting, he explained, with the full knowledge of his comrade Ernst Burger. Later, he recalled, FBI agents asked him to plead guilty, to keep quiet about his dealings with the Bureau, on the assurance of a presidential pardon within months. Instead, he languished in jail for five years, and was deported after the war.

U.S. Army Intelligence, meanwhile, believed Edgar's arrest of the saboteurs had been premature and had wrecked plans to intercept other raiders expected to land a few weeks later. "Secretary of War Stimson was absolutely furious," recalled Lloyd Cutler. "Hoover grabbed all the glory. He just wanted headlines."

He got them, and the Senate Judiciary Committee recommended that he be awarded a Congressional Medal of Honor, normally awarded only to those who had performed valiantly in battle. Although Edgar sent a stream of fawning notes of thanks to his supporters on Capitol Hill, the idea was dropped. On July 25, however, the twenty-fifth anniversary of his arrival at the Justice Department, he was celebrating anyway. Edgar posed beside a giant postcard of congratulations and sat for color photographs—still a novelty in those days—with Clyde at his elbow.

Then Edgar went off on yet another vacation with Clyde, cheered by anniversary congratulations from the President himself. Edgar responded with a gushing letter, telling Roosevelt the years under his leadership had been "some of the happiest years of my life." "You may rest assured," he wrote, "that you may continue to count upon all of us at the FBI. . . ."

The truth behind the formal flattery was very different. For a long time now, Edgar had been snooping on the President's wife.

CHAPTER 13

"If there had been a Mr. Hoover in the first half of the first century, A.D., can you imagine what he would have put into his files about a certain trouble-maker from Nazareth, his moral attitudes and the people he consorted with?"

New York Times *reader's letter, 1970*

EDGAR AND CLYDE LOATHED ELEANOR ROOSEVELT. ONE OF THE reasons he never married, Edgar liked to say, was that "God made a woman like Eleanor Roosevelt." He called her the "old hoot owl" and mimicked her high voice in front of senior colleagues. Mrs. Roosevelt was in her late fifties in World War II, and she was not physically attractive. While her husband sought solace with other women, contemporaries wondered about Eleanor's passionate friendships outside the White House—some with women known to be lesbians. Edgar sniggered about these things behind the First Lady's back.

"The President," he told an aide on his return from a White House meeting, "says the old bitch is going through the change of life . . . we'll just have to put up with her." He once descended unexpectedly on W. C. Fields, the comedian, asking to see certain "interesting pictures." Fields did, indeed, have three trompe l'oeil miniatures of the President's wife. The right way up, they were ordinary pictures. Upside down, they were grotesque anatomical views of a woman's vagina. Edgar thought them hilariously funny, and took them away with him.

It was Mrs. Roosevelt's politics, though, that Edgar could

not abide. She was deeply committed to a host of liberal causes, more deeply—many thought—than a woman of her era should have been. Above all, she campaigned persistently for decent housing and fair treatment of America's black citizens—and that really rankled Edgar. He once watched, glowering, at the Mayflower Hotel when she attempted to bring two black men into the restaurant. Told of rumors that black women in the South were joining "Eleanor Roosevelt Clubs," he ordered agents to investigate.

"Whenever a black would speak out," said William Sullivan, "he attributed it to Mrs. Roosevelt." "Hoover called her a nigger lover, and worse," recalled Clyde's friend Edna Daulyton. "Clyde felt the same. He said she should mind her own business and not stick her nose into her husband's affairs. He said the White House was wide open to the wrong kind of people."

Mrs. Roosevelt sometimes invited potential embarrassment because, as her husband's biographer Ted Morgan put it, she was "a soft touch." In her pursuit of liberal causes she bumped up against Communists and radicals, and plain oddballs, and seemed to think the President's wife could do so with impunity.

Edgar, who had long since infiltrated the Communist Party, was told what Mrs. Roosevelt had supposedly said about him to a Communist friend. "Now you see what a bastard Hoover is," she was quoted as saying. "That's how he covers up his Fascist attitude. You should have seen Franklin. . . . He said this was just another proof of the duplicity of that smug would-be Himmler."

Such reports made Edgar even angrier. As late as 1960, he would still be speaking of the widowed Eleanor as "really dangerous." According to former agent G. Gordon Liddy, "He attributed a lot of the leftish positions that President Roosevelt took to her malevolent influence. He said he was often able to solve problems he had with Communists only after he learned they originated with Eleanor Roosevelt. Then he would go to her husband—and Roosevelt would overrule Eleanor in Hoover's favor."

What survives of Edgar's file on the First Lady is 449

pages long. While Edgar was alive it sat in one of two large file cabinets behind Miss Gandy's desk, one of the supersensitive files that were kept separate from the main system. Some former aides say they were so placed to restrict access to a handful of senior staff—thus protecting the subjects of the files, many of them prominent public figures. Many, however, believe the files were a storehouse of human foibles, ammunition for actual or potential blackmail.

Mrs. Roosevelt got wind of Edgar's temerity in January 1941, when she learned FBI agents had investigated both her social secretary, Edith Helm, and a second aide, Malvina Thompson. The agents had probed deep into the private lives of the women, asking questions of Thompson's neighbors, interrogating desk clerks about comings and goings at her hotel room. They even grilled people in Helm's hometown in Illinois.

When Mrs. Roosevelt protested, Edgar tried to brush her off with a smooth reply. The check on Mrs. Helm was a routine one, he insisted, undertaken because the woman worked for a committee linked to the Council for National Defense. There would have been no investigation, he said, had the FBI known the women worked for the President's wife. Unimpressed, for both women were well known in Washington, the First Lady fired off another letter.

"I do not wonder," she wrote this time, "that we are beginning to get an extremely jittery population. . . . This type of investigation seems to me to smack too much of the Gestapo methods." Edgar had to apologize, but the long-term effect was probably to inflame him even more against Mrs. Roosevelt. Word of the episode had flashed around Washington—and to humiliate Edgar was to make him more dangerous.

Recent scholarship has given some credence to the notion that the President's wife had a secret sex life. Her 1992 biographer, Blanche Cook, suggests she may have had physical relationships with Earl Miller, the state trooper who served as her bodyguard, and with Lorena Hickok, the lesbian reporter who covered the White House for the Associated Press. No one has gone as far as Edgar, who suspected Mrs. Roosevelt of having affairs with several men, including her black driver, an Army colonel, her doctor and two leaders of the National Maritime Union.

The two labor leaders, both former sailors, used to joke about cultivating the First Lady to gain access to the President. "Goddamn it, Blackie," one was overheard saying to the other on an FBI bug, "I've made enough sacrifices. Next time *you* service the old bitch!"

This was almost certainly no more than a coarse joke, but Edgar took it seriously. Here was promising material—information suggesting that the President's wife was sleeping with two labor leaders, one of them a leading member of the Communist Party. Edgar sent the President a cascade of reports on the two men, but kept the sex angle to himself. Then, at the height of the war, he began to concentrate on one of Eleanor's left-wing male friends—Joseph Lash.

Lash was thirty when he met Eleanor, then fifty-five, at a 1939 session of the House Un-American Activities Committee. Lash was not a Communist, but a fervent anti-Fascist who had visited the Soviet Union and Spain during the Civil War, then returned to become a radical student leader. To Edgar he was a subversive who deserved investigation. Eleanor, however, took Lash under her wing, invited him to meet the President at the White House, lent him money and tried to further his career.

On Edgar's orders, FBI officials prepared an eleven-page memorandum on Lash in 1941. The following January, agents broke into the New York headquarters of the American Youth Congress, of which Lash was a leader, and photographed the First Lady's correspondence with the group's officials. The same month, when Lash's application to join the Navy was turned down, Mrs. Roosevelt wrote to Attorney General Biddle.

"I wonder," she asked, "if it would be possible for you to run down for me through the Federal Bureau of Investigation . . . what they really have on Joe Lash." Biddle referred the inquiry to Edgar, who replied smoothly that "the FBI is conducting no investigation." This was a common Bureau circumlocution. In Bureauspeak, the collection of information was different from a full inquiry. In fact, Edgar's closest aides had been discussing Lash with the naval authorities.

Drafted instead into the Army, Lash spent the weeks that followed with Mrs. Roosevelt clucking solicitously around him. She paid for champagne and the band at Lash's farewell party in New York. Edgar took note of all this, and of the fact that Lash stayed in White House accommodations when on leave from his base near Washington.

By November 1942, Edgar was sending "extremely confidential" information—its nature still censored in a document released by the FBI in 1990—to a general in Army Intelligence. The next month, following an FBI burglary at the offices of the International Student Service, an FBI report referred to Lash and Eleanor Roosevelt and their "unusual friendship." "This," one of Edgar's aides wrote, "is nauseating."

In April 1943, when Lash had been posted to Illinois, Edgar sent more information to the military authorities, specifically to the Army Counter-Intelligence Corps. Then, three months later, on instructions from the White House, the corps was drastically reduced in numbers and merged with another unit. By 1944, it had been virtually dismantled. Why?

The answer lies in a two-page report sent to Edgar's office on December 31, 1943, and stored ever since in his files. It was from Agent George Burton, reporting on contacts with two counterintelligence colonels. The unit's surveillance of Lash, Burton reported, had covered his meeting with Mrs. Roosevelt at a hotel in Chicago. The President himself had found out and summoned General Strong of Army Intelligence to the White House with the relevant records. "The material," Agent Burton reported,

> contained a recording of the entire proceedings between Lash and Mrs. Roosevelt which had been obtained through a microphone which had been planted in the hotel room. This recording indicated quite clearly that Mrs. Roosevelt and Lash engaged in sexual

intercourse during their stay in the hotel room. . . .
After this record was played Mrs. Roosevelt was called
into the conference and was confronted with the information and this resulted in a terrific fight between the
President and Mrs. Roosevelt. At approximately 5:00
A.M. the next morning the President called for General
Arnold, Chief of the Army Air Corps, and . . . ordered
him to have Lash outside the United States and on his
way to a combat post within ten hours. . . . It was
learned that the President had ordered that anybody
who knew anything about this case should be immediately relieved of his duties and sent to the South Pacific
for action against the Japs until they were killed. . . .

Today it is difficult, if not impossible, to ferret out the
truth behind this astonishing document. It is peppered with
inaccuracies, and other surviving documents fall short of
establishing for sure whether or not Eleanor Roosevelt had
an affair with Joe Lash. The file shows that the Army's
sleuths, who regularly opened Lash's mail, discovered he
was receiving a stream of letters from both Mrs. Roosevelt
and a fellow radical, Trude Pratt. Pratt, then still married to
another man, was going through a complicated courtship
with Lash, with intimate encouragement from the President's wife.

Mrs. Roosevelt's many letters to Lash were filled with
political chitchat and torrents of affection. "Joe dearest,"
began one letter written in February. ". . . I feel so excited
about the thought of hearing your voice. What will I do
when I actually see you? . . . I am glad you drink your milk
and hope some day you get enough sleep. . . . I am enclosing
a letter that came with a valentine from Trud. . . . I pray St.
Valentine too that he may bring us all together but that is
because *I* need you very much. . . . I must close so bless you
dear and a world of love. E.R."

Army Intelligence was watching on March 5, when Mrs.
Roosevelt had the first of two rendezvous with Lash in
Illinois hotels. She checked into Room 332 of the Urbana-

Lincoln Hotel in Urbana, accompanied by her aide, Malvina Thompson, told the desk she wanted no publicity and reserved an adjacent room, Number 330, for "a young friend." Joe Lash checked into his room that evening, and he and the First Lady stayed upstairs, except for one visit to the dining room, until they left the hotel thirty-six hours later.

Mrs. Roosevelt wrote another "Joe dearest" letter on the train that bore her away. "Separation between people who love each other," she wrote, "makes the reunion always like a new discovery. . . . Bless you dear. Thanks for such a happy time. All my love E.R." Mrs. Roosevelt wished Lash well for his meeting with Trude Pratt the next weekend.

The Army's secret agents were there in strength a week later, when Lash and his wife-to-be had a tryst at the same hotel. This time the bedroom was bugged, and the microphones picked up the sounds of frequent lovemaking. They also picked up a call from the couple to Mrs. Roosevelt at the White House.

Within days, a senior officer in Army Intelligence, Lieutenant Colonel Boyer, was writing an astonishing letter to a superior in Washington. The letters between Lash, Trude Pratt and Mrs. Roosevelt, Boyer said, were evidence of a "gigantic conspiracy." In fact there is nothing conspiratorial in the letters. The Colonel, however, intended to wait for another opportunity, then burst in on Lash having intercourse with Mrs. Pratt and arrest him on a morals charge.

Before the couple could meet again, Lash had another rendezvous with the President's wife. It was in a bedroom at the Blackstone Hotel in Chicago, according to the report in Edgar's file, that hidden microphones overheard Lash and Mrs. Roosevelt having sex.

After that rendezvous, the pair again exchanged breathless letters. "I can't tell you," wrote the First Lady, "how I hated to say goodbye. I loved just sitting near you while you slept. . . ." "I'm sorry," Lash wrote when he got back to base, "I was such a drowsy soul after dinner, but it was nicer drowsing in the darkness with you stroking my head than playing gin rummy. . . ." Lash also wrote to Trude Pratt, telling her that Mrs. Roosevelt had taken him shopping and insisted he buy some "garish underwear."

According to Lash, Eleanor was tipped off about the bugging by the management of the Blackstone Hotel. Furious, she raised the matter at the White House when she got back to Washington—with dire consequences for the Army Counter-Intelligence Corps. When Lash was posted to the Pacific, the President's wife went to San Francisco to say goodbye. "The hard part of loving," she wrote afterward, "is that one has to learn so often to let go of those we love."

What to make of it all? Did the President's wife sleep with Lash at the Blackstone, or anywhere else? Lash, who obtained the FBI and Army files in 1978, denied it; he expressed his outrage in *Love, Eleanor,* a memoir about what he maintained was an intimate but innocent friendship with Mrs. Roosevelt. His widow, Trude, agreed. "I am not aware that Mrs. Roosevelt ever had an affair, at any period during our friendship," she said in 1992. "So far as the alleged tapes are concerned, what may have happened was that Joe came to the hotel from his Army base terribly tired, and Mrs. Roosevelt may have said, 'Lie down on my bed and rest.' And she probably sat next to him and stroked his forehead. She was a very affectionate person, but the sex allegation is ludicrous. The President did become furious, but because he learned about the snooping, not because of any affair. Mrs. Roosevelt said a lot of people were punished because of it."

One of the Roosevelts' six children, Franklin, Jr., joined his name to Joe Lash's denials. His elder sister, Anna, however, added an interesting item of information. She recalled that as late as 1944, a year after the Blackstone episode, an officer brought her a bundle of what he described as "love letters" from Lash to Eleanor, which the censor had intercepted. She took them to her father, as the officer had requested, and he took them from her without a word. Whatever the President's feelings were, he concealed them.

The 1943 letters certainly show that the First Lady was

extraordinarily indiscreet. If she thought she could meet repeatedly with a young man in hotel bedrooms with impunity, she was also naive in the extreme. Yet she was fifty-eight years old at the time, a quarter of a century older than Lash, and the letters show she was acting all along as matchmaker between her young protégé and his married girlfriend. It seems unlikely, if not entirely impossible, that she was nevertheless sleeping with the young man.

Yet clearly a recording of sex activity did exist. Did the Army somehow confuse its evidence of Lash's intercourse with his future wife, Trude Pratt, with its reports of his meetings with Mrs. Roosevelt? Perhaps, but the one item that might resolve the truth is missing. According to a former Army Intelligence Colonel, it did still exist, "well out of circulation," as late as 1967.

Edgar, for his part, made sure that Agent Burton's report, eventually joined by the Army surveillance reports and copies of Mrs. Roosevelt's letters to Lash, went into the bulging file cabinet in Miss Gandy's office. There they remained until 1953, when an opportunity arose to make use of them.

In 1953, when Republican president-elect Eisenhower was keen to remove Eleanor Roosevelt from the U.S. delegation at the United Nations, Assistant Director Louis Nichols briefed Eisenhower's aides on the alleged affair with Lash. The aides took it seriously. In 1954, when the *New York Post* was critical of Eisenhower, Nichols found a way to disinter the allegation again. Pointing out that Lash was now a *Post* correspondent and that Mrs. Roosevelt was close to the paper's editor, he suggested Edgar carry the smear to the President himself.

Much later, when Assistant Director William Sullivan fell out with Edgar, he sent him a passionate indictment of the Bureau's failings. "Mr. Hoover," he wrote,

> you have regularly told the public FBI files are secure, inviolate, almost sacred. Years ago, when I first discovered this was not true at all, I was stunned. But we had created in time a certain atmosphere in the FBI diffi-

cult to describe. .... We have leaked information improperly as you know, on both persons and organizations. My first recollection was leaking information about Mrs. Roosevelt, whom you detested. . . .

Whatever President Roosevelt knew of Edgar's role in the Lash affair, he apparently lost patience with him long before the end of the war. "Mrs. Roosevelt said her husband was very upset with Hoover," Trude Lash recalled. "I had the impression the President had asked her not to discuss the details, but it was clear he was turning away from Hoover. Hoover knew it, and tried to make himself seem indispensable by finding out things Mr. Roosevelt needed to know. As I understood it, however, the President said privately that he would dismiss Hoover as soon as possible."

For Roosevelt, the Lash episode was not the only factor. He was angry, in the fall of 1943, when he was forced to dump Sumner Welles, his valued Undersecretary of State and personal friend, in order to prevent a scandal about his alleged homosexual activity. According to Dr. Beatrice Berle, widow of Assistant Secretary of State Adolf Berle, Edgar's role in the whispering campaign against Welles led to a terminal rift between the Director and the President.[1]

"After it was all over," she said in 1990, "Roosevelt told Hoover to get out, and he never received him again." The President did distance himself from Welles' principal persecutors. And the files at the Roosevelt Library contain no more long private discussions with Edgar, and no genial correspondence, from this point on.

It had been said that, having raised Edgar up for his own political purposes, the President planned to curb his powers when the war ended, perhaps even to remove him from office. If so, he did not live to do it.

CHAPTER 14

"We are a fact gathering organization only. We don't clear anybody. We don't condemn anybody. Just the minute the F.B.I. begins making recommendations on what should be done with its information, it becomes a Gestapo."

J. Edgar Hoover, July 14, 1955

AT 5:00 P.M. ON APRIL 12, 1945, HARRY TRUMAN HURRIED, alone and unprotected, along a deserted passage beneath the Capitol. Then, half-guessing the meaning of the summons to the White House, the sixty-year-old Vice President broke into a run. Two hours later, in the Cabinet Room, he found himself taking the oath of office as the thirty-third president of the United States. Franklin Roosevelt, worn out after twelve years in office, had died of a massive cerebral hemorrhage.

Abroad, the end of the war was approaching. American troops were advancing on Buchenwald concentration camp, where 50,000 Jews had been murdered. The Soviet army was fighting on the approaches to Berlin. Hitler would soon commit suicide in his bunker; Mussolini would be shot by Italian partisans. Germany would surrender and, three months later, after President Truman had unleashed the atomic bomb, so would Japan.

In the midst of all this, and not for the first time, Truman was worrying about Edgar and the FBI. As a senator, he had objected publicly when the Bureau was absolved of all blame for Pearl Harbor. Now, in his first weeks as President, he was alarmed by what he learned about the FBI

—bloated in size and power—that Roosevelt had left behind.

A month after taking office, Truman expressed these feelings in one of his celebrated memos to himself:

> May 12 1945
>
> We want no Gestapo or Secret Police. FBI is tending in that direction. They are dabbling in sex life scandals and plain blackmail when they should be catching criminals. They also have a habit of sneering at local law enforcement officers. *This must stop.* Cooperation is what we must have.

Edgar scurried to shore up his position, scouring the Bureau for someone known to Truman who could serve as the new FBI liaison agent to the White House. "Mr. Hoover wants you to know," the chosen man told the President, "that he and the FBI are at your personal disposal and will help in any way you ask." "Any time I want the services of the FBI," Truman retorted, "I'll ask for it through my Attorney General."

When the emissary took this message back to Edgar, recalled Assistant Director William Sullivan, "Hoover's hatred knew no bounds." Truman had put him in his place as would no other leader except Kennedy, and he had lost his special access to the seat of power.

Even so, Edgar found a way to draw the Truman White House into his web. The President agreed that his military aide, General Harry Vaughan, should liaise directly with Edgar—and Edgar promptly made the relationship conspiratorial. "There's going to be a lot of talk," he warned Vaughan. "When you come over, I advise you to come in on Pennsylvania, get on the elevator, go to the seventh floor, walk around to the other bank of elevators, go down to the third floor, walk around to this bank of elevators, come up to the fifth floor, and come into my office. You and I have legitimate things to talk about. It's the President's business, it's my business, it's your business, it's nobody else's business."

Another Truman aide, John Steelman, knowingly encouraged a new form of covert communication between the FBI and the White House. Previously, under Roosevelt, Edgar's men had passed on political information, the sort of material the FBI had no business handling in the first place, by reading briefing papers aloud to presidential aides. Afterward, to avoid leaving a paper trail, the documents would be carried back to FBI headquarters. Now Curtis Lynum, one of Edgar's new emissaries, dreamed up a refinement of the system.

"One day," he recalled, "I cut off the top and bottom of the memo I was reading from and handed the memo to Mr. Steelman, who said, 'Why can't we do this on all messages you bring?' I replied that I would take the matter up with Mr. Hoover." Edgar jumped at the idea. Sensitive intelligence was henceforth sent to the Truman White House on unwatermarked paper with no FBI letterhead and no signature, information that could never be tracked back to its source.

In the first weeks of his presidency, according to Harry Vaughan, Truman learned how Roosevelt had used Edgar to tap telephones for political information. "What is that crap?" the President is said to have cried when shown transcripts of a bug on Tommy Corcoran, the political fixer who had defected from the Roosevelt camp. "Cut them all off. Tell the FBI we haven't got any time for that kind of shit."

If Truman did say this, he soon changed his mind. FBI files contain some 5,000 pages reflecting eavesdropping on Corcoran during the Truman years. Edgar personally supervised the taps, which were operated from an apartment on Thirteenth Street, N.W., "one of the central plants," the files describe it, under the direction of Edgar's friend Guy Hottel.

Wiretaps aside, Edgar sent the Truman White House tidbits of political intelligence of all kinds—a warning that a scandal was brewing or advance information about a newspaper series critical of the President. And Truman accepted it. Perhaps he felt there was little harm in taking advantage of Edgar's political espionage service, if he could stall more serious FBI abuse of civil liberties. By permitting political wiretapping, however, he made Edgar custodian of a secret that, if leaked, could have imperiled the administration.

Truman made himself beholden to Edgar, and that was the way Edgar liked things to be. There was, too, a significant skeleton in the President's political cupboard, his long-standing link with the crooked Democratic Party machine in Kansas City, Missouri, his home state.

Truman had risen in the world as a protégé of Tom Pendergast, the political boss who, when necessary, enforced his rule with the help of the Mafia. It was Pendergast who had sent Truman to the U.S. Senate, a connection that, Truman confided to his wife, would be "a lead weight on me from now on."

Edgar was aware of all this. He had himself been in Kansas City when Pendergast had been indicted for tax evasion several years earlier, and knew he had a potential weapon. During the presidential contest of 1948, he would leak information on Kansas City corruption to help Truman's opponent, Governor Dewey.

Yet, knowing of Truman's personal dislike for him, Edgar still felt vulnerable. He had his agents report to him on every shift in the political wind, every rumor that his own job was at risk. He became insecure to the extent of paranoia.

"Hoover was frightened of his life with Truman," William Sullivan recalled. "I know that personally. During his entire career in the White House, Truman had *nothing* to do with Hoover and wouldn't let Hoover get anywhere close to him."

Two years into his presidency, Truman ended Edgar's hopes of achieving his most ambitious dream, control over foreign intelligence. This was something he had been angling for as early as 1940, when he proposed an FBI Special Intelligence Service, with agents stationed all over the world. This was the dream he was nurturing when he fought his hated rival, William Donovan, for control of overseas intelligence. Though forced to settle for jurisdiction over just a slice of the global territory, Latin America, his real ambition remained worldwide.

Before the war was over, Edgar had again been talking privately of a worldwide network of FBI agents. In London, U.S. diplomats suspected he already had undercover men in place in the embassy code room, snooping on State Department communications. Donovan's men watched the FBI nervously.

In November 1944, at Roosevelt's request, General Donovan had produced a blueprint for peacetime intelligence. It foresaw a "central intelligence authority" under the personal supervision of the president and, Donovan hoped, with himself at its head. Edgar said there was no need for such an agency, and pressed for a return to pre-war arrangements, with the FBI holding the reins. Suddenly there was a string of press attacks on Donovan's plans, warning of the dangers of a "Super Spy System." Donovan was convinced that one of the stories, based on a top-secret memorandum, had been deliberately planted by Edgar.[1]

Edgar's machinations came to nothing, however, with Truman in the White House. The President told Budget Director Harold Smith he was "very much against building up a Gestapo" at the FBI. Far from allowing it to expand, he thought the Bureau should be "cut back as soon as possible to at least the pre-war level."

Edgar went on lobbying to secure what he claimed was his turf. Generals and admirals, congressmen and senators were persuaded to plead his cause at the White House. They obliged because they, too, had territory to protect, and because some believed Edgar's claim, dating back to the war, that Donovan's OSS was "hiring a bunch of Bolsheviks." A check conducted after the war, by Edgar's own agents, identified no Communists in what remained of the organization.

Truman turned a deaf ear to Edgar's claim to both domestic and foreign intelligence. "One man shouldn't operate both," he told his aide Harry Vaughan. "He gets too big for his britches." The President rarely agreed to see Edgar, and slapped him down hard when they met to discuss this issue. "Hoover tried to argue with the President," said Vaughan. "Truman said no, and when Hoover persisted, he said, 'You're getting out of bounds.'"

The President eventually approved the creation of the Central Intelligence Agency, as a response to the real threat of Soviet subversion, but with no role for Edgar. The CIA was to be responsible to the President, through a National Security Council, and its focus was to be on intelligence evaluation rather than field operations. (The "covert action" capacity, for which the Agency is now best known, was a later development.)

Though Donovan never headed the Agency, Edgar also had to swallow the fact that it was essentially the general's brainchild. The creation of the CIA, moreover, stripped Edgar even of his wartime windfall, the territories south of the Mexican border. The FBI's various overseas posts, in London, Paris and Rome, Ottawa and Mexico City, survived only for liaison purposes. Nevertheless, Edgar defiantly continued intelligence-gathering in Mexico, which duplicated CIA operations far into the future.

"So furious" was Edgar about the creation of the CIA, said William Sullivan, "that he gave specific instructions that under no circumstances were we to give any documents or information to the newly established CIA. . . ." "Hoover pursued a scorched-earth policy," said future CIA Director Richard Helms. "He cleaned out all the files, wouldn't allow his agents to talk to the new CIA people about sources. We got nothing worth having. He just cleaned the place out and went home in a sulk."

Edgar's standoff with the Agency would last until he died. "When requests came in from the CIA," said Sullivan, "legitimate, authorized requests, Hoover would drag his heels, meet half the request and ignore the other half." This pettiness led to a head-on clash with Truman's second CIA Director, the illustrious General Walter Bedell Smith.

"It is mandatory for you to give the CIA full cooperation," Smith told Edgar. "If you want to fight this, I'll fight you all over Washington." Edgar backed off, but his file on Smith shows contempt. "Smith is a stinker," Edgar scrawled on one report, "and not a little one either." Relations with other Agency heads were even worse. According to CIA Counter-Intelligence Chief James Angleton, Edgar did not sit down with a CIA Director more than five times in his entire career.

For a while after the war, Edgar seemed less surefooted, less certain of his direction. He clung to hopes of becoming Attorney General, under some future Republican administration, but had put presidential dreams behind him. Some thought he might quit the FBI. There was speculation that he would become Baseball Commissioner.

On the personal front, this was a time of increased rumor-mongering about Edgar's homosexuality. Once, at a dinner attended by the highest law officials in the land, Edgar was overwhelmed with embarrassment when a female entertainer—one of the Duncan Sisters—tried to sit on his lap. According to those present, he actually fled the room, and the story was around Washington within days. When, in a genuine mistake, the American Mothers' Committee named Edgar one of the nation's "Best Fathers of the Year," the newspapers simpered: "Oh dear . . . Mr. Hoover is a bachelor." Few could have missed the innuendo.

It was at this time that Edgar's worry about his homosexuality drove him to consult Dr. Ruffin, the Washington psychiatrist. The visits soon ended, however, because Edgar was afraid to trust even the doctor.[2] From now on, he merely tried to suppress homosexual rumors whenever possible, using FBI agents to intimidate the press.

In public as in private, Edgar was forever on the defensive against enemies real or imagined. To remain America's "J. Edgar Hoover," he needed to be seen to be fighting a clearly identified foe, and with massive public support.

The enemy of choice—whether it was substance or shadow—had always been Communism. Or, as Edgar pronounced it, "Commonism." And now, just as his image seemed to be losing its focus, history made him fashionable again. The Cold War against the Soviet Union and its satellite states gave Edgar a new lease of life as an American hero. Behind the scenes, his spying on American citizens mirrored some of the excesses of the Communism he decried.

CHAPTER 15

> "The FBI's war against Americans who were not
> criminals but who did not measure up to Director
> Hoover's idea of an acceptable citizen, is a blot on our
> claim to be a free society."
>
> *Congressman Don Edwards,*
> *former FBI Agent and Chairman of*
> *the House Subcommittee on Civil and*
> *Constitutional Rights*

ON HIS FIFTY-FIRST BIRTHDAY, NEW YEAR'S DAY 1946, EDGAR
opened the door of his home in Rock Creek Park to a
Presbyterian pastor, Dr. Elson. The two men then prayed
together in what Elson called "a spiritual act of mutual
dedication," one they would repeat each New Year's Day for
the rest of Edgar's life. A week later, at a Club of Champions
ceremony in New York, Edgar knelt to kiss the sapphire ring
of the Roman Catholic Archbishop of New York, Francis
Spellman.

With Spellman at his side, Edgar told the assembled
throng that "Come what may, when thirty million Catholics assert themselves, the nation must pause and listen.
There are only 100,000 Communists who are organized and articulate, but they are motivated by fanatical
frenzy."

The frenzy came, rather, from Edgar and right-wing
zealots like Spellman. American Communists, Edgar told an
audience of senior policemen, were "panderers of diabolic
distrust who are concentrating their efforts to confuse and
divide. . . . It behooves us to be on guard for an enemy that

brazenly and openly has advocated the corruption of America. . . ."

Former Assistant Director Charles Brennan, an FBI specialist in hunting subversives, would recall wryly that even Bureau insiders never really knew quite what enemy they were fighting. "There was never any substantive understanding of what Communism meant," he recalled. "The word was just used as a general category for that which was foreign, unfamiliar and undesirable. . . ."

Edgar, more than any other individual, would be responsible for the long episode of anti-Communist hysteria from which American society has never fully recovered. Edgar's own figures credited the Party with a mere 80,000 members at the peak of its popularity, in the glow of the wartime alliance with the Soviet Union. In a population of 150 million, that was a percentage of .0533—and less than a third of American Communists were industrial workers likely to threaten economic stability.

President Truman probably had it about right. "People," he said, "are very much wrought up about the Communist 'bugaboo' but I am of the opinion that the country is perfectly safe so far as Communism is concerned—we have far too many sane people." What the President thought in private, however, was submerged by Republican electoral gains and a chorus of right-wing demands for action.

In 1947, to appease the right, Truman ordered that all new civilian employees of the federal government be investigated for "loyalty." Serving employees suspected of "disloyalty" could henceforth be brought before loyalty boards —with no right to know or challenge their accusers. Truman had deliberately entrusted much of the work not to the FBI but to the Civil Service Commission—a snub that led Edgar to take a momentous decision.

He obliged Congressman Parnell Thomas, soon to be jailed for operating a kickback racket, by agreeing to address the House Un-American Activities Committee. Edgar had never made such an appearance before and, by doing so in March 1947, was publicly confronting the administration he served. That he could do so, and get away with it, was a measure of his power in the country.

"This is a big day for me," Edgar told a friend as he set off to make his speech. Communism, he told the congressmen, was being spread by "the diabolic machinations of sinister figures engaged in un-American activities." American liberals, he added pointedly, had been "hoodwinked and duped into joining hands with the Communists."

Edgar stopped short of attacking the liberal President by name, but the effect was the same. Truman was furious. "Pres. feels very strongly anti FBI," noted an aide. "Wants to be sure and hold FBI down, afraid of 'Gestapo.'" Yet Truman was also a realist. "J. Edgar," he told Clark Clifford, "will in all probability get this backward-looking Congress to give him all he wants. It's dangerous."

Edgar did get what he wanted—full control of the loyalty investigations. He had made his declaration of independence, established himself as the standard-bearer of the anti-Red crusade.

One man needed no conversion. During the HUAC hearing Edgar had taken several questions from a freshman Congressman named Richard Nixon. Leaning across to Edgar, attorney Bradshaw Mintener muttered that Nixon had faked smear evidence to beat his Democratic opponent in the recent campaign. "I know all about that," Edgar replied, "but, so far as law enforcement is concerned, he looks to me as if he's going to be a good man for us."

A decade earlier, as a young law student, inspired by a recruiting speech given by one of Edgar's aides, Nixon had applied to become an agent. His appointment had been approved, then canceled, apparently because the FBI deemed him to be "lacking in aggressiveness." Now that he was a Congressman, Edgar had no doubts about Nixon. The two men met that year, and both would soon be engaged in the protracted effort to ruin State Department official Alger Hiss, the controversy that became Nixon's first step on the road to the White House.

Edgar was suddenly the hero of 1947. His face, framed by

the Stars and Stripes, stared from the cover of *Newsweek*, telling the nation "How to Fight Communism." He was being taken seriously, and taking himself much too seriously.

In the midst of the wrangle with President Truman, Edgar learned that *Love for Three Oranges,* the theme tune for two films and a radio show about the FBI, had been written by the Soviet composer Sergei Prokofiev. "We ought to be able to utilize music by someone other than a well-known Communist," Edgar scrawled on a memorandum. "Please get together on this, and *quickly."* Aides scrambled to oblige, solemnly probing Prokofiev's background and holding high-level conferences. There is not a glimmer of a sign that anyone realized how silly it all was.

Nationally, the purge began in Hollywood, when the House Un-American Activities Committee staged its assault on the film industry. Edgar, who thought Hollywood smelled of the "dank air of Communism," played a leading role from the start—in secret. "I want to extend *every* assistance to the Committee," he told aides months before the hearings began. His Los Angeles Agent in Charge, Richard Hood, passed on FBI file information on suspect members of the film community. The committee's team of investigators was led by Allen Smith, a Bureau veteran with close links to Edgar, and heavily weighted with other former agents.

The hearings were a circus, with throngs of giggling women mobbing "friendly" witnesses, such as Gary Cooper, Robert Taylor and Walt Disney, who testified that Communists at his studio were trying to use Mickey Mouse to spread Communist propaganda. A 1993 biography revealed that—in secret—Disney had previously provided the FBI with information on political activity in Hollywood.

Edgar's former girlfriend, Lela Rogers, made a memorable appearance. In her opinion, *None but the Lonely Heart,* directed by Clifford Odets, was highly suspect—the more so because of a scene in which a son tells his mother: "You are not going to work here and squeeze pennies from people poorer than we are." The committee concluded Rogers was "one of the outstanding experts on Communism in the United States."

"Unfriendly" witnesses and those who opposed the hearings, such as John Huston, Katharine Hepburn, Lauren Bacall and Humphrey Bogart, were vilified. The Hollywood Ten, a group of artists who refused on principle to say whether they had ever been members of the Communist Party, were jailed for contempt of Congress. They would emerge to find their careers ruined, because, to butter up the committee, Hollywood's film bosses had declared them "blacklisted."

The Un-American Activities Committee's assault on Hollywood lasted until 1953, with Edgar playing a punitive role in the wings—as the actor Sterling Hayden discovered. Hayden had briefly been a member of the Communist Party, and, worried about his past, he wrote through his attorney asking Edgar for advice. "Get it on the record," Edgar advised, promising to help Hayden "if anything comes up." The actor promptly confessed his past folly in a formal statement to FBI agents.

For Edgar, this was an opportunity for fresh persecution. Far from protecting Hayden, he forwarded his confession to the Un-American Activities Committee. The actor was summoned to testify, panicked and named many friends and colleagues who had also joined the Party. He regretted having been "a stoolie for J. Edgar Hoover" for the rest of his life.

FBI file 100-382196 contains the lowdown on a minor Hollywood actor—"6'1" tall, weight 175 lbs, blue eyes and brown hair"—named Ronald Reagan. The future president, who was spending as much time on union activity as on acting, was on the board of HICCASP, the Citizens' Committee of Arts, Sciences and Professions, which the FBI considered a Communist front. His brother Neil, however, was spying on HICCASP meetings for the Bureau, and warned Ronald it would be wise to resign. Instead, Ronald acted as an FBI stool pigeon, too.

Soon he was phoning his brother at midnight from a pay phone at the Nutburger stand on Sunset Boulevard, to pass on information about the latest HICCASP meeting. As the Bureau's Confidential Informant, code number T-10, Reagan took to calling FBI agents to his house under cover of darkness, to tell of "cliques" in the Screen Actors Guild that "follow the Communist Party line." He reeled off the names of the actors and actresses in question and, in an appearance arranged at Edgar's personal suggestion, did so again during a secret appearance before the Un-American Activities Committee.

Edgar investigated citizens who were not Communists and who had broken no law. Concerned about articles that, in his view, were "severely and unfairly discrediting our American way of life," he was to order an FBI study to look for "subversive factors" in the backgrounds of prominent writers and editors. Out of a hundred people picked at random, agents identified "pertinent factors" that might account for the way forty of them were writing. Reports on them were turned into unlabeled blind memoranda, untraceable to the FBI, for Edgar to circulate "on an informal and confidential basis."

Over the years, Edgar's literary targets would include America's most honored writers. Some, like Dorothy Parker, Dashiell Hammett and playwright Lillian Hellman, were indeed involved with Marxist causes. They were trailed, surveilled and had their mail opened. When Hammett died—a veteran of both wars—the FBI schemed to prevent his burial at Arlington Cemetery.

Numerous other famous writers had no links to Marxism but were investigated all the same. There is a 400-page file on Nobel Prize–winning novelist Pearl Buck. Agents opened her mail, too, even though she did nothing more subversive than write about racism and join the ACLU.

We now know Edgar kept files on Nobel Prize winner Thomas Mann, Erskine Caldwell, Sinclair Lewis, William

Saroyan and Carl Sandburg. The FBI tagged Ernest Hemingway "leftist" and "phony," and kept a file on his wife Mary as well. It reported on John Steinbeck, who alarmed the FBI because he "portrayed an extremely sordid and poverty-stricken side of American life," as well as Irwin Shaw, Aldous Huxley, John O'Hara, Arthur Miller, Tennessee Williams and Truman Capote. Rex Stout, creator of investigator Nero Wolfe, was deemed to be "under Communist influence," and there was even a file on E. B. White, author of the children's classic *Charlotte's Web*.

Files were also kept on painters and sculptors, including Georgia O'Keeffe and Henry Moore—even on Picasso, who never set foot in the United States. Great scientists were also targeted. Edgar thought Dr. Jonas Salk, discoverer of the polio vaccine, suspect enough to merit a four-page warning letter to the White House, because he was a member of the American-Soviet Medical Society. Salk was said to be "far left of center," and had a brother in the Communist Party.

Edgar had started collecting information on Albert Einstein in 1940, because he attended pacifist meetings alongside Communists, and because he had supported the Republican cause in Spain. After the war, when the physicist realized he was being watched, he grew deeply disillusioned. "I came to America," he said in 1947, "because of the great, great freedom which I heard existed in this country. I made a mistake in selecting America as a land of freedom, a mistake I cannot repair in the balance of my lifetime." At the time of his death, the FBI dossier on him had grown to thousands of pages. They contain no evidence that he was ever disloyal.

The actor Charlie Chaplin, one of Einstein's friends, embodied all that triggered fear and anger in Edgar. Foreign-born, in England, he lived a rich heterosexual life, and he was a utopian "internationalist" who cheerfully hobnobbed with Communists. He was also one of the most famous men on earth, more famous than the Director of the FBI, and universally adored.

The Bureau had considered Chaplin dangerous even

before Edgar became Director, when officials worried that his "Communistic" movies would infect "the minds of the people." They were still worrying in 1942, when he made speeches calling on the United States to help the Soviet Union against the Nazis. Edgar's chance to persecute Chaplin, however, came when a deranged young actress, Joan Barry, claimed he was the father of her unborn child.

Edgar thought Chaplin could be prosecuted under the Mann Act (the law with which he threatened wartime agent Dusko Popov), because the actor had paid for Barry's train trips across the country. Under his personal supervision, FBI agents were soon sifting through Chaplin's financial records, interrogating friends and business colleagues and asking his servants whether the actor had "wild parties and naked women."

Chaplin was cleared in the Barry case when blood tests showed he could not be the father of the child. Edgar's harassment, however, continued. He sent information about the actor to Hollywood gossip columnists, even dispatched men to the Library of Congress to hunt down a report that, a quarter of a century earlier, *Pravda* had called Chaplin "a Communist and a friend of humanity."

Thousands of man-hours of research turned up nothing, but Edgar did eventually succeed in hounding Chaplin from the United States. It was his advice to the Attorney General that was to lead to the actor being banished from the country in 1952, on the grounds that he was an "unsavory character." Edgar also told immigration officials of Chaplin's alleged "moral turpitude" and his security background—on notepaper that could not be tracked back to the FBI. References to the Bureau's use of bugging and anonymous sources were carefully deleted from the relevant reports.

Years later, long after Chaplin had settled in Switzerland, Edgar kept him on the Security Index, the list of those to be arrested in case of a national emergency. As late as 1972, when the actor was invited to Los Angeles to receive a special Oscar, Edgar was to lobby against granting him an entry visa. Chaplin was admitted, and received a rapturous welcome. His FBI file is 1,900 pages long.

In 1975, three years after Edgar's death, a congressional committee ordered a detailed check on the domestic security files of the ten largest FBI offices. This indicated that no less than 19 percent of the Bureau's total effort was still devoted to hunting "subversives." Yet criminal conduct was discovered in only four out of 19,700 investigations—and none of those involved national security, espionage or terrorism.

In the fall of 1947, President Truman watched what Edgar was doing, and worried. "Dear Bess," he wrote to his wife after a crisis in the Secret Service:

> . . . I am sure glad the Secret Service is doing a better job. I was worried about that situation. Edgar Hoover would give his right eye to take over, and all Congressmen and Senators are afraid of him. I'm not and he knows it. If I can prevent it, there'll be no NKVD or Gestapo in this country. Edgar Hoover's organization would make a good start towards a citizen spy system. Not for me . . .
>
> Lots of love,
>
> Harry

In 1948, an election year, the Republican Party leadership hoped to return to the White House after fifteen years in the wilderness. Edgar, who so often declared himself above politics, found a way to help them undermine the President —by stirring up new panic about the Red enemy within.

The game this time, which could not have been played without Edgar's collaboration, was to expose alleged Communists high in the Truman administration.

It started in July 1948, when a woman the press called the "blond spy queen" appeared before the Un-American Activities Committee. This was Elizabeth Bentley, a plump, middle-aged former Communist whose lover, now dead, had been a known tool of the Soviets.

Bentley said she had acted as a courier from 1938 to 1944, passing sensitive information from high-level sources in Washington to superiors in the Communist underground. The high-level sources, Bentley alleged, had included a senior aide to President Roosevelt and two officials in the Truman administration, William Remington at Commerce, and Harry Dexter White, a former Assistant Secretary of the Treasury.

Four days later, before that sensation had died down, came the testimony of *Time* editor Whittaker Chambers. He, too, was a former Communist, and his startling claim remains a cause célèbre to this day.

Chambers claimed that Alger Hiss, a distinguished former State Department official, was also a secret Communist, one of several in a cell formed specifically to infiltrate the government. Hiss denied the charge, but Chambers produced a mass of classified documents that, he claimed, Hiss had passed to him.

Whatever the truth of the Bentley-Chambers allegations, the brutal outcome was that many lives were ruined, and four men died. White was felled by a heart attack after defending himself passionately before the committee. William Remington was bludgeoned to death in prison after being convicted of perjury. Laurence Duggan, a former State Department official smeared by Chambers, died in an unexplained fall from the sixteenth floor of a New York office building. Marvin Smith, a Justice Department attorney involved in the Hiss case, committed suicide, and Chambers himself tried to.

Alger Hiss was eventually convicted of perjury—the jury believed he lied when he said he had not passed documents to Chambers. He served three and a half years in prison and, now in his late eighties, has continued to protest his innocence.[1]

Edgar's attitude to White and Hiss had been distinctly downbeat—until it became timely to embarrass President

Truman. The Director had known about the Hiss allegation as early as 1942, and had dismissed it then as "either history, hypothesis, or deduction." Elizabeth Bentley's trips to Washington, supposedly to pick up secrets from traitors, had gone unchallenged for years, in spite of the fact that Jacob Golos, her lover—a long-exposed Communist operative—was a prime target for FBI surveillance.

In 1948, when White's possible guilt became a public issue, former Treasury Secretary Henry Morgenthau asked Edgar privately whether he thought White was guilty. Morgenthau's son, today New York District Attorney, still has his father's contemporaneous note of Edgar's response, scribbled on an old envelope. Edgar's opinion, according to the note, was that there was "nothing to it."

Edgar knew, but did not mention publicly, that the key source in the entire espionage investigation, Soviet defector Igor Gouzenko, had specifically said White was not one of the American traitors. Yet it was reportedly Edgar who leaked the White allegations in the first place, by feeding information to the Senate's Internal Security Subcommittee. He did so through his aide Lou Nichols, a man so adept at passing information for Edgar that he became known as "the cleanest leak in Washington."

Alger Hiss was sent to jail on the basis of only one piece of hard evidence: a Woodstock typewriter said to produce type that matched both the copies of official documents produced by Chambers and letters known to have been typed on the Hiss family typewriter. Hiss, backed by some of the expert witnesses, has claimed the machine was doctored specifically in order to frame him.

We may never know whether Edgar did stoop to such tactics to set up an innocent man. But documents now available show that, in 1960, he was open to the notion of using forgery to neutralize a Communist Party member by "exposing" him to colleagues, fraudulently, as an FBI informer. His only admonition to his agents was to make certain the deception "insures success and avoids embarrassment to the Bureau."

Told that the scheme involved typewriter forgery, Edgar

raised only a mild objection, but not to the idea itself. "To alter a typewriter to match a known model," he advised, "would take a large amount of typewriter specimens and weeks of laboratory work."

Whether the FBI framed Hiss or not, it is clear that milking the affair for political purposes meant more to Edgar than seeing justice done. He had been working covertly to leak the accusations as early as 1945, long before Chambers went public. The word was spread first by William Sullivan, then one of Edgar's favored officials, in briefings to a right-wing Catholic priest, Father John Cronin.

Sullivan, significantly, was the man to whom Edgar would one day entrust COINTELPRO, a program specifically designed to discredit and harass targeted groups by all means available, including forgery of documents.[2]

Father Cronin, for his part, reportedly passed on the Hiss allegations, first in a report to America's Catholic bishops, and, in 1947, to Congressman Richard Nixon. Nixon said in a recent interview that "the FBI and Hoover played no role whatsoever in the Hiss case thing. Hoover was loyal to Truman. . . . There was no way that he was going to have his boys running about helping the Committee."

According to Father Cronin, however, Nixon got constant feedback, thanks to FBI agent Ed Hummer. Hummer "would call me every day," Cronin recalled. "I told Dick [Nixon], who then knew where to look for things. . . ." The FBI file, meanwhile, confirms out of Nixon's own mouth what he denied forty years later. In December 1948, at a secret meeting in his hotel room, he told agents he had "worked very closely with the Bureau and with Mr. Nichols during the last year" on the Hiss case.

Long before the Hiss case, Nichols had become a familiar face in the office of another Republican member of the Un-American Activities Committee, Congressman Karl Mundt of South Dakota.[3] Mundt was also close to Edgar. "They had private dinners together," his former assistant Robert McGaughey recalled, "and they belonged to the same poker club. The Senator always said to me, 'If there's anything you want brought up, we'll discuss it over the game tonight.' "[4]

Edgar fed Mundt information on Hiss from 1945 onward, McGaughey revealed. During the intense 1948 phase, he said, "Nichols was up in the office, say, twice a day. . . . There was a lot of exchange of suggestions, coming from Mr. Hoover more than from Mr. Mundt, letting us know where to look for information."

Was Mundt given access to FBI files? "Files? Yeah," said McGaughey. "Let's put it this way. He had access to see information that was in the files Mr. Hoover had. This was a personal relationship."

Edgar found a way to cover himself. If a politician asked to see an FBI file, he would promptly write denying access. McGaughey reveals, however, that the agent who hand-carried the negative reply to Capitol Hill would simultaneously pass on the information requested, sometimes verbally, sometimes typed on plain, untraceable paper. The file copy of the denial, meanwhile, would be preserved at headquarters, "proof" that the request had been turned down. Other evidence of connivance with conservative politicians was simply destroyed.

In 1992, from post-Communist Moscow, came official backing for Alger Hiss' denials of wrongdoing. Dmitri Volkogonov, a respected military historian and close adviser to President Yeltsin, announced his findings following a review of Soviet files. He called the accusations that Hiss had been a spy "completely groundless."

"Not a single document substantiates the allegation that Mr. A. Hiss collaborated with the intelligence services of the Soviet Union," said Mr. Volkogonov. "The fact that he was convicted in the fifties was a result of either false information or judicial error."

President Truman, who never believed Hiss was guilty, had no doubt as to what the case had really been about. "What they were trying to do, all those birds," Truman was to say years later, "they were trying to get the Democrats.

They were trying to get me out of the White House, and they were willing to go to any lengths to do it. [The Republicans] had been out of office a long time, and they'd done everything to get back in. They did do just about anything they could think of, all that witch-hunting. . . . The Constitution has never been in such danger. . . .''

For all the scare-mongering, only four American Communists would be convicted of espionage offenses while Edgar was Director of the FBI.[5]

Edgar's priority in 1948 was to secure his power base, by helping to get Harry Truman out of the White House. That spring, over hot dogs at Yankee Stadium, Edgar talked privately about the coming election with the journalist Walter Winchell. "He said he was upset with Truman," recalled Winchell's assistant Herman Klurfeld. "The President had restricted his power, and he resented it. He thought Truman should be replaced by someone else."

Edgar climbed onto the bandwagon of the candidate most likely to dislodge Truman, that of Republican Thomas Dewey. It was six years now since the FBI had started collecting information on Dewey, and the signals had been mixed. During the last campaign, agents had learned, Dewey had said privately that the right place for Edgar was a jail cell.

Later reports were more positive, and in 1948, according to William Sullivan, Edgar was dreaming of political advancement under a President Dewey. As the primary campaign began, he secretly placed Bureau resources at Dewey's disposal.

"With the help of the FBI," Sullivan recalled, "Hoover believed Dewey couldn't lose. . . . In exchange for his help, the Director believed that when Dewey became President he would name Hoover as his Attorney General and make Nichols Director of the FBI. To complete the master plan, Tolson would become Hoover's assistant. It would have been a nice setup, because with Nichols at the heim, Hoover would have had the FBI as tightly under his control as if he had never left. . . . Hoover's ambitions didn't stop at the Justice Department. If he couldn't be President, Hoover thought it would be fitting if he were named to the Supreme Court, and he planned to make his term as Attorney General a stepping-stone to that end."

Dewey accepted Edgar's help, Sullivan claimed, and agents assembled briefing papers to help Dewey prepare for his broadcast debate with his primary opponent, Harold Stassen. "There was such a rush to get the material to him," said Sullivan, "that it was sent in a private plane to Albany, New York. . . . The FBI helped Dewey during the campaign itself by giving him everything we had that could hurt Truman. . . . We resurrected the President's former association with Tom Pendergast, political czar of Kansas City, and tried to create the impression that Truman was too ignorant to deal with the emerging Communist threat. We even prepared studies for Dewey which were released under his name, as if he and his staff had done the work. I worked on some of these projects myself."

Edgar became seriously ill with pneumonia that fall and was in Miami Beach recuperating on Election Day, November 2, 1948. Clyde and Lou Nichols had been telling him what most people believed, that Dewey was sure to win. The next day the *Chicago Tribune* ran its famous headline, DEWEY DEFEATS TRUMAN, only to be confounded by news that the opposite had happened. Truman was back in the White House.[6]

"A heavy gloom settled over the Bureau," Sullivan recalled. From Florida, Edgar sent a furious memorandum blaming Nichols for having "pushed me out on a limb." Edgar, said Sullivan, "never could admit that he had made a mistake."

Yet on Inauguration Day, January 20, 1949, Edgar was still Director of the FBI. He invited the twenty-one-year-old actress Shirley Temple, whom he had known since her days as a child star, to join him on his office balcony to watch the parade pass along Pennsylvania Avenue. Wearing what

Temple recalls as "his best Santa Claus smile," Edgar gave her a present—a tear-gas gun disguised as a fountain pen.

Edgar had survived, but he could never feel safe. Always, whatever his other worries might be, there loomed the threat of his own sexuality.

194

"It is almost impossible to overestimate Mr. Hoover's sensitivity to criticism of himself or the FBI. It went far beyond the bounds of natural resentment to criticism one feels unfair. The most casual statement, the most strained implication, was sufficient cause for Mr. Hoover to write a memorandum to the Attorney General complaining, and impugning the integrity of its author."

*Nicholas Katzenbach,
former Attorney General*

RECORDS NOW AVAILABLE SHOW THAT, IN MARCH 1949, DETAILS of Edgar's private life reached President Truman. A high Democratic official—his name is censored out of the document—noted in his journal that a colleague (name also deleted):

gave me some very bad news about J. Edgar Hoover. I hope it is only gossip. Geo. [*perhaps Truman's confidant George Allen*] suggests I see the President alone.

The "bad news" was very probably about Edgar's homosexuality. "One time," Truman confided to the author Merle Miller, "they brought me a lot of stuff about his personal life, and I told them I didn't give a damn about that. . . . That wasn't my business. . . . I said to him, 'Edgar, I don't care what a man does in his free time: all that interests me is what he does while he's on his job.'"

The President was justifiably angry, three months later,

when he received an FBI report on the heterosexual adventures of two of his own aides. Charlie Ross, his Press Secretary and friend, had supposedly "chased a couple of gals around the deck" during a boat trip. The same report raked up a youthful love affair of Dave Niles, his trusted Administrative Assistant. "Being a victim of Cupid," Truman snorted at a Cabinet meeting, "is not being a victim of Moscow propaganda."

Here was the President of the United States being bothered with FBI gossip about his aides' dalliances with women, when he had just been briefed on Edgar's own behavior. In Edgar's case, by comparison, there was at least cause for concern. A homosexual FBI Director, in charge of the nation's internal security, was a classic target for any hostile intelligence service—especially that of the Soviet Union.

That same month, June 1949, saw Edgar publicly humiliated over the case of Judith Coplon, a young Justice Department employee accused of giving information to the Soviets. Coplon had been caught meeting a Soviet diplomat while carrying a purse stuffed full of summaries of FBI reports. Then, to Edgar's horror, the judge at her trial ruled that, to establish the authenticity of the material found in her purse, the FBI would have to release the originals of the documents.

This would be the first time that raw FBI files had ever been made public, and Edgar was worried not because they contained supersecret data, but because they were a mishmash of unchecked tittle-tattle. Edgar protested, right up to the President, but in vain. The documents were produced in court, and proved as embarrassing as Edgar had feared.

It emerged that, even during the trial, the FBI had been bugging privileged conversations between Coplon and her attorney. Agents had then hastily destroyed the resulting records and disks, in a cover-up that could only have happened with Edgar's approval. During those weeks, which Edgar would recall as "pretty rough going," Truman came as close as he ever would to firing his FBI Director.

Edgar was not used to taking knocks, and certainly not in

the glare of national publicity. The Coplon debacle came just weeks after he and Clyde, resplendent in white suits and waist-deep in gladioli, had held court at celebrations marking his silver anniversary as Director. Now, brought down a peg or two by a blast of criticism, Edgar felt deeply insecure. At fifty-four, the paranoia in him had long since excluded the possibility that he himself could be wrong about anything.

Edgar's list of perceived enemies was expanding. Now he would take on liberals, the church, even the publishing industry, with a venom. He was enraged by an article in *Harper's Magazine* that fall, in which the historian Bernard De Voto said the FBI reports uncovered by the Coplon case were "as irresponsible as the chatter of somewhat retarded children." A furious Edgar called for information on De Voto, and his aides knew how to please him. They solemnly reported a flaw in the Pulitzer winner's personality. De Voto, they declared, exhibited the "Harvard intellectual liberal attitude, devoid of practicality . . ."

"I like a country," De Voto had written, "where it's nobody's damned business what magazines anyone reads, what he thinks, whom he has cocktails with. I like a country where what we say does not go into the FBI files along with a note from S-17 that I may have another wife in California. . . . We had that kind of country only a little while ago, and I'm for getting it back. It was a lot less scared than the one we've got now."

There was now concern about the FBI on college campuses. At Yale, a student magazine reported, FBI agents were influencing academic appointments by feeding the Provost with derogatory information on teachers. A distinguished physicist, Professor Henry Margenau, had been berated by agents for addressing a youth group of which the Bureau disapproved. He had knuckled under, and now consulted the local FBI office before accepting speech invitations.

William F. Buckley, Jr., future right-wing pundit, then editor of *The Yale Daily News,* played a leading role in the furor that followed these revelations. In secret, he sent the

FBI blind copies of his letters on the subject to fellow student journalists, and suppressed a letter to the *News* from a student editor at Harvard. Edgar's master of propaganda, Lou Nichols, promptly identified Buckley as a future ally.

While Edgar denied that his agents had infiltrated Yale, the record shows that there was an FBI "liaison officer" in the university. Today it is known that the Bureau opened files on thousands of teachers, throughout the education system. "The entire teaching profession," University of Chicago president Robert Hutchins would soon declare, "is now intimidated."

The fear was usually generated, as at Yale, by quiet interrogations of radicals, FBI whisperings to college officials, followed by discreet firings. There was nothing quiet about the fuss a few years later, when Professor Howard Higman, a sociology teacher at the University of Colorado, made the mistake of mocking Edgar personally.

The episode began when one of the professor's students, a former Miss America named Marilyn Van Derbur, used Edgar's book *Masters of Deceit* to contradict the professor's thesis that the Soviets would have been able to build the Bomb anyway, without help from American Communists. Higman responded by scoffing at Hoover's book and saying he "disapproved of the rise in the United States of a political police. . . ." Told of this by an informant, Edgar retaliated by triggering a nationwide flood of stories and letters denouncing the professor.

In 1991, when he obtained his partially censored FBI file under the Freedom of Information Act, the professor was astounded to find that it totaled some 6,000 pages, covered many years and included investigations not only of him but of his children. "Can't we set a fire under the University of Colorado," Edgar had written, "for having such a character on its faculty?" "We need to meet some of these academic punks in their own back yard," wrote an aide, and an FBI official flew to Colorado to give a "forceful" lecture to Higman's students and colleagues.

"I was wrong to have said the FBI was a political police," the professor commented. "I've discovered since it is a *church.* That you don't contradict J. Edgar Hoover, because he's infallible."

It is now known that, in the fifties and sixties, the FBI penetrated more than fifty colleges and universities. It obtained the collaboration of many senior academics, including at various times the presidents of Yale and Princeton and the dean of students at Harvard, to identify and oust faculty members thought to be Communist or of the extreme Left.

Not even men of religion were safe from Edgar's punitive hand. In Brooklyn, at the Church of the Holy Trinity, the Reverend William Melish and his father drew heavy right-wing criticism for promoting American-Soviet friendship. The FBI, Melish recalled, soon found an insidious way to chastise him. "The headmaster of the Polytechnic Preparatory School, where I had gone as a boy, was the secretary of the parish. A number of 'Poly Boys' were in the FBI, and they were deliberately sent to call on the headmaster about me. They tried to persuade him that he should do something about getting rid of me. Almost every member of the vestry at one point or another was pressured by the FBI. . . . One of my sermons at Holy Trinity, in which I accused the FBI of invading religious freedom, was sent to J. Edgar Hoover. Hoover had it sent to all his bureaus. He personally thanked the informant. . . ."

Melish and his father were eventually driven out of their church, in spite of the overwhelming support of their parishioners. It would be twenty years before the younger Melish had a kind of consolation, when he was asked to return as assisting priest.

Some people, it is said, pull the blinds down over their minds when they reach their fifties. Edgar fitted the stereotype, with the difference that he institutionalized the failing. Those who criticized the Bureau were subject to investigation. Those who found fault with Edgar himself suffered his fury, the fury of a man with 3,000 agents and huge financial resources at his disposal.

In the summer and fall of 1950, Edgar abused his power in an outrageous attempt to stifle free speech. It began when he learned that William Sloane Associates, the New York publishing house, was shortly to publish a book on the FBI by Max Lowenthal, a personal friend of President Truman's. Lowenthal had been squirreling away documentation on the FBI and its Director since the late twenties, when he had been Secretary of the National Commission on Law Enforcement. What he had learned worried him, and now he was bringing forth a 500-page critique.

Edgar's machinations to crush the book began the moment he learned of its existence. He asked his friend Morris Ernst, a prominent New York attorney, to sabotage the book by approaching the publisher behind the scenes. Correspondence shows the FBI was assailing the book's "distortions, half-truths and incomplete details" long before publication.

Lowenthal's son, John, believes he knows how Edgar knew of his father's book before it came out. The family home, he says, was raided by burglars who "seemed more interested in going through my father's papers than in his possessions."

In September, as if spontaneously, Republican Congressman George Dondero delivered a ten-minute diatribe against Lowenthal in the House. Dondero was one of Edgar's stable of tame congressmen, a man who could be relied upon to do the Director's bidding—in this case to smear Lowenthal for alleged Communist connections. Next came a sudden summons for the author to appear before the Un-American Activities Committee. The record of the hearing was leaked to the FBI's friends in the press in November, the day before the Lowenthal book was published. When the book received a favorable review, another of Edgar's political friends, Bourke Hickenlooper of Iowa, rose in the Senate to lambaste the reviewer.

The personal files of Edgar's propaganda chief Louis Nichols, long locked away in steel file cabinets in the Nichols family garage, demolish Edgar's denials that he spoon-fed confidential information to members of Congress. On occasion, Edgar even wrote their speeches for them.

The Nichols files contain an original draft of Congressman Dondero's denunciation of Lowenthal. Line by line, paragraph by paragraph, the speech made by the Congressman merely parroted a diatribe prepared at the FBI on plain paper, without signature. It is the cover note, apparently from Nichols to Edgar, that gives the game away:

> I am attaching a documentation to the details on Max Lowenthal. . . . I checked every reference to Lowenthal in the Bureau. You will observe that several items were obtained from technicals. I feel safe in using these because of the phraseology used in each instance. In many instances, it is the only way we can tie Lowenthal in with some of these buzzards. . . . If you approve the matter as it now stands, you could just tell Miss Gandy to pass the word to me that the project is O.K. . . . You may destroy the old copy I sent you. . . .

"Technicals" was current Bureau jargon to describe wiretaps. Lowenthal's FBI file shows that agents had been collecting information on him for nearly thirty years, and had tapped his phone for extended periods. Other material now being used to smear Lowenthal, Nichols told Edgar, had been obtained thanks to a "black bag job"—an illegal burglary. Handwritten notes indicate that Edgar himself edited and approved the final FBI draft that was given to Dondero to read.

Lowenthal's book sold badly, though not necessarily because of the attacks in Congress. Such criticism can boost sales rather than limit them. "One of our objectives was to kill the sale," William Sullivan revealed years later. "We even went to some stores and asked them not to stock it. . . . We spent an enormous amount of time and taxpayers' money."

At the White House, President Truman had ignored a long and plaintive letter from Edgar about Lowenthal—a letter in which he craftily avoided mentioning that the offending book was all about the FBI. Truman, who had already seen the book in manuscript, merely sent Edgar's letter on to Lowenthal for his entertainment. The President said he "got a great kick" out of reading the book, and praised the author for his "wonderful service to the country."

That was in private. Asked at a press conference whether he had read the book, Truman said he had not. He dared not show his true feelings about Edgar in public, let alone fire him. In the country at large, Edgar's popularity was now at a new high. For a generation frightened by Soviet possession of the atom bomb, the start of the Korean War, the Rosenberg espionage affair and the recent indictments of American Communist leaders, it was easy to believe Edgar's claims that the nation was riddled with subversives.

In the words of the then Attorney General, Howard McGrath, Edgar had "gotten too big to handle." And in the world of power politics, he had become one of the handlers.

CHAPTER 17

"We don't have free speech in this country. . . . This is grown-up politics, and it's stupid and dangerous."

Hubble Gardner, character in the movie
The Way We Were, *set in the McCarthy era*

"LISTEN, YOU BASTARDS," THE DRUNKARD SHOUTED AT A GROUP of reporters. "I just want you to know I've got a pailful of shit, and I'm going to use it where it does me the most good."

It was February 1950, and Joseph McCarthy had just made his sensational claim that the Truman State Department was knowingly harboring more than 200 members of the Communist Party. The claim was bogus but, in an America awash with fear of Communism, the Senator from Wisconsin was about to become a hero.

Over the four years that followed, and as Chairman of the Senate Subcommittee on Investigations, McCarthy was to play grand inquisitor, hurling wild charges at two presidents, dozens of decent officials and a parade of mostly innocent citizens. Today "McCarthyism" is a word in the dictionary: "the use of indiscriminate, often unfounded accusations, sensationalism, inquisitorial investigative methods." Yet Edgar cultivated the Senator, fed him information and persisted in helping him when he ran amok.

Ten months before the fantastic accusation about the Truman State Department, Edgar had gone to the Senate Radio Room to join the forty-one-year-old McCarthy in a fifteen-minute broadcast to the people of his home state. This was a rare gesture of support for a junior politician, irreconcilable with Edgar's supposedly nonpartisan status, and it was not publicized in Washington. Later, in the Wisconsin newspapers, Edgar endorsed McCarthy for re-election.

Edgar had been briefed on McCarthy, as he was briefed on every member of Congress. Yet when he recorded the broadcast, he praised the Senator's previous service as a judge—praise that had to be edited out of the tape. McCarthy had recently been censured by the Wisconsin Supreme Court, and came close to being disbarred as an attorney.

Edgar knew McCarthy was disreputable, yet he took him under his wing long before he became a national figure. The Senator dined with Edgar and Clyde at Harvey's and visited the track with them on weekends. He was reportedly the only elected official allowed to use Edgar's private box at Charles Town in West Virginia, in his absence. Edgar was "crazy about McCarthy," according to a race-going companion, former Secretary of the Democratic National Committee, George Allen.

When McCarthy was challenged to produce proof of his charges about the State Department, he phoned Edgar to ask for help. Edgar at first chided him, not because of what he had said but for the tiresomely specific way he said it. False allegations were best left rather general. Then the Director ordered a search of the files for anything that might support the Senator.

"We were the ones," William Sullivan recalled, "who made the McCarthy hearings possible. We fed McCarthy all the material he was using. I knew what we were doing. I worked on it myself. At the same time, we were telling the public we had nothing to do with it."

Other sources, with no ax to grind, confirm it. "He did feed stuff to McCarthy, a great deal of it," said Edgar's journalist friend Walter Trohan. "Joe would tell me himself that he'd got this or that from the FBI." Ruth Watt, chief clerk to McCarthy's committee, later admitted having received "a lot of FBI reports."

McCarthy's first chief investigator, Donald Surine, was a former FBI agent, and so were other key staff members. The

Senator's future wife, Jean Kerr, turned to Edgar for help when McCarthy was pursuing a secretary married to an FBI agent. The agent found himself transferred, along with his wife, to Alaska.

"Any success the FBI has had," Edgar was to tell the Senator in a letter, "is due in no small measure to the wholehearted support and cooperation we have always received from such fine friends as you."

In 1951, as the country prepared for an election, a Republican Congressman floated the idea of Edgar as a "favorite son" candidate for president. "What an inspiration to the youth of America!" a Chicago citizen responded. "The truly great statesmen are those men with ability and leadership, combined with honesty and ideals, and to me J. Edgar Hoover is synonymous with all these attributes." "If he will run," wrote a Missouri businessman, "he will be elected by the greatest majority any President ever received."

Instead of running for the White House, the man who claimed he was above politics became one of the kingmakers. Edgar joined himself to the clique of fabulously wealthy Americans now pushing Dwight Eisenhower and Richard Nixon toward the White House.

On an August night, around the pool of an exclusive California hotel, Edgar discreetly circulated among the guests at a Nixon fund-raiser. Though he was the host, Edgar's role went unmentioned in the press. There were few guests, and few were necessary. "I think there were about twenty of us," recalled Barbara Coffman, one of the "poorer" guests, "and some gal came up to us and said, 'I only got a million dollars. How about you?' It was a fun party, very casual."

Among the millionaires present were two of the wealthiest men in the world: Texan oil moguls Clint Murchison and Sid Richardson. Richardson, then aged sixty-one, was the wildcatter stereotype, a rough-tongued bachelor with a limp and a penchant for bourbon and late-night poker games.

Murchison, at fifty-seven, a powerhouse of energy, was married to Virginia, his second wife, after whom he named his flagship airplane. Between them the two men had assets in excess of $700 million, not counting as much again in untapped oil reserves.

Recognizing Edgar's influence as a national figure, the oilmen had started cultivating him in the late forties—inviting him to Texas as a houseguest, taking him on hunting expeditions. Edgar's relations with them were to go far beyond what was proper for a Director of the FBI. And although the Murchison milieu was infested with organized crime figures, Edgar considered him "one of my closest friends."

"Money," the millionaire used to say, "is like manure. If you spread it around, it does a lot of good." Murchison and his Texas friends spread a great deal of dollar manure on the political terrain. They had traditionally been conservative supporters of the Democratic Party—until the presidency of Harry Truman. He enraged oilmen by publicly denouncing their tax privileges, and by vetoing bills that would have brought them even greater wealth. Murchison habitually spelled Truman's name with a small *t*, to show how little he thought of him.

Murchison's political instincts were of the far, far Right. He was a fervent supporter of states' rights, reportedly funded the anti-Semitic press and was a primary source of money for the American Nazi Party and its leader, Lincoln Rockwell, who considered Edgar "our kind of people."[1]

During the Truman years, musing in private about the perfect political lineup, Edgar had named Murchison and Richardson as ideal candidates for high office—or at least as financial backers for politicians to his liking. Murchison had been obliging ever since. He threw money at Edgar's friend Joe McCarthy, placed airplanes at the Senator's disposal and promised him support "to the bitter end."

In the 1952 presidential race, the Texans put their money —literally—on Dwight Eisenhower. Sid Richardson had flown to the general's Paris headquarters the previous year, armed with a five-page document setting out why he should run for president. From then on the pressure never ceased. Murchison lobbied ceaselessly, little caring whether Eisenhower ran as a Democrat or a Republican, so long as he ran.

In August, at an unpublicized meeting in California, Eisenhower discussed the Democratic front-runner, Illinois Governor Adlai Stevenson, with Edgar and Murchison. They concluded, Murchison wrote to a friend, that Stevenson would be "used by radicals to destroy America's proud traditions." That month, in Washington, someone began spreading a rumor that the Governor was a "queer." The FBI was almost certainly behind it.

Edgar had been hostile to Stevenson since, three years earlier, he had made a mildly critical remark about Bureau efficiency. Agents had gone to work gathering derogatory material, and Edgar supplied Eisenhower with information on Stevenson's 1949 divorce. In the spring of 1952, shortly before Stevenson's selection by the Democrats, Edgar received a report claiming Stevenson and Bradley University president David Owen were "the two best known homosexuals in the state." Stevenson, supposedly, was known to fellow homosexuals as Adeline.

The report, which originated with disgruntled Illinois policemen and a student basketball player, was secondhand. Stevenson's biographers make no mention of any homosexual tendency. At the FBI, however, the Governor's name went into a special file marked "Stevenson, Adlai Ewing— Governor of Illinois—Sex Deviate."

In July, on the same day Stevenson announced his candidacy, a senior FBI official prepared a nineteen-page memorandum—including the homosexual smear and suggestions that Stevenson had once harbored Communist sympathies. Edgar had also ordered the writing of a "blind memorandum," on paper without a letterhead, summarizing the homosexual allegation. The rumor was spread that summer, Democratic officials believed, by Edgar's close associate Guy Hottel.

In October, a crucial point in the campaign, Senator

McCarthy used a nationwide television address to produce the "coldly documented background" on Stevenson. Waving papers in his hand, he branded the Democratic candidate as a wartime Communist collaborator and a covert member of a left-wing organization. The "documentation," none of which held water when analyzed, was supplied by former FBI agent Donald Surine, the principal liaison between McCarthy and the Bureau.[2]

These were the dirtiest blows in one of the nation's dirtiest campaigns. They left Stevenson deeply dispirited, wondering whether he could continue at all. In November 1952, three months after his California strategy meeting with Murchison and Edgar, a landslide vote sent Dwight Eisenhower to Washington.

"Politics," Eisenhower's friend George Allen wrote in his memoirs, "runs on juice—on the kind of influence by which the proper man can get a ticket fixed." Allen, mutual friend to the new President, Murchison, Richardson and Edgar, plumbed the Eisenhower administration for political juice with the dedication his friends applied to oil.

By a secret agreement, even before the inaugural, Allen and Billy Byars—another oilman friend of Edgar's—arranged to finance Eisenhower's Gettysburg farm. They also funneled money to him "for his share of the farming operation." Byars subsidized Mamie Eisenhower's brother-in-law Gordon Moore, by establishing a racing stable on his land.

Sid Richardson, for his part, made secret payments to Robert Anderson, shortly to become Secretary of the Treasury, and poised to influence presidential policy in favor of domestic oil producers. The Eisenhower administration issued sixty oil leases on government reserves during its first term, compared to only sixteen in the previous fifty-five years.

Speaker of the House Sam Rayburn, a Texan who knew the ways of oilmen, watched in despair as Eisenhower doled out key federal posts to the barons of commerce. "This fellow Hoover," the Speaker growled, "helped him do it. This fellow Hoover is the worst curse that has come to government in years."

"I was close with General Eisenhower," Edgar would recall. "He was a great man and a great President." According to former Attorney General William Rogers, Edgar thought the eight Eisenhower years "the best and happiest" of his career. So they were, in the sense that he had absolute security of tenure. Sugary notes sped regularly from FBI headquarters to the White House. Edgar used Seattle Agent in Charge Richard Auerbach, who had once been secretary to a Republican senator, to cultivate the President's elder brother.

Eisenhower gave Edgar the National Security Medal, and Edgar gave the President the first ever "gold badge of honorary membership of the FBI." "I wish," Eisenhower would tell Edgar after he left the White House, "there were about a thousand J. Edgar Hoovers in key spots in the government."

Behind the courtesies, however, there was disagreement. Eisenhower's papers reveal his concern that loyal Americans should not be persecuted for alleged Communism. He loathed McCarthyism, which Edgar supported to the very end. Later, Edgar would deplore Eisenhower's decision to welcome the Soviet leader Khrushchev to the United States. He thought it created an "atmosphere favorable to Communism among Americans."

Eisenhower compromised himself less than his Democratic predecessors in the use of the FBI for personal political intelligence. He may not have done so at all. "With Eisenhower," recalled Ralph de Toledano, a correspondent in whom Edgar confided, "Hoover never knew whether he would receive praise or blame. . . . He didn't really like Eisenhower very much." In fact, predatory as ever, Edgar pried into the President's private life as he had into that of President Roosevelt.

Eisenhower's wartime romance with his female chauffeur,

the young Irishwoman Kay Summersby, had been a time bomb ticking beneath the 1952 election campaign. Republican leaders considered Summersby's 1948 memoir, *Eisenhower Was My Boss,* potentially explosive—even though it said nothing of the couple's real intimacy. Copies of the book mysteriously vanished from Washington stores and from the New York Public Library.

Three years later, in September 1955, Joe McCarthy's aide, Donald Surine, would pass along some information to the FBI. For the past six weeks, Surine said, Summersby had been staying at Washington's Shoreham Hotel under an assumed name. Edgar at once ordered intense investigation. Agents made numerous "pretext calls," including one to Summersby herself, in an attempt to find out if she had really been staying in Washington.

The only possible explanation is that Edgar wanted to know whether the President had revived his affair with Summersby. It was his custom to let presidents know he knew of their peccadilloes, in the guise of merely keeping them informed. The file does not reveal what Edgar did with the Summersby information, which reached him the day before President Eisenhower suffered his first heart attack.

Since 1953, Edgar and Clyde had spent extended summer vacations as guests of Clint Murchison at the Del Charro, a hotel he owned in La Jolla, in southern California. Edgar had been a regular visitor to the town since the thirties, and told the press it was a place where he "felt God was near." His annual pilgrimage was dedicated to the horseracing at nearby Del Mar, as was that of Murchison and Sid Richardson, racing refugees from Texas, where betting on horses was illegal.

Murchison had bought the Del Charro in a fit of pique when another establishment failed to place a complete floor at his disposal. "Our father which art in Dallas," went the prayer of the hotel staff, "Murchison be thy name." The Lone Star flag fluttered in the Pacific breeze when the millionaire and his pals were in residence. Celebrities such as John Wayne, Zsa Zsa Gabor, Elizabeth Taylor and a couple of her husbands, along with the less famous but much monied, came and went in private planes. The hotel was small, and its astronomical room charges—the equivalent of $700 a night at today's rates—drastically limited the clientele.

After Murchison took over in 1953, Edgar and Clyde never stayed anywhere else. Their stay in Bungalow A, one of seven reserved for the tycoon's special friends, became an annual ordeal for local FBI agents. A respectful tap at the door would bring first a delay, then Clyde snapping, "What the hell do you want?" He is remembered as petulant, unreasonable, "madder than a scorpion" over trifles. Even Murchison nicknamed him "Killer."

Former agent Harry Whidbee still has the list of Edgar's vacation requirements: direct phone lines to Washington; three oscillating fans—the Director detested air-conditioning; new light bulbs for every lamp; two 5″ × 8″ unlined white paper pads; two rolls Scotch tape, with dispenser; six sharpened No. 2 pencils; two bottles Scripps Permanent Royal Blue ink, No. 52—no one else in the Bureau was allowed to use this brand; a basket of fruit; and whiskey—Jack Daniel's for Edgar, Haig & Haig for Clyde, gift-wrapped and paid for by the local Agent in Charge, whether he liked it or not.

There was panic one year when subordinates forgot a vital item—Edgar's favorite ice cream. When he insisted on having it, late at night, agents persuaded a local manufacturer to open his plant after hours. An FBI stenographer then dressed up as a waitress to serve the boss his precious dessert.

Even on vacation, the pair were rarely seen in anything but suit and tie. Edgar's alternative uniform, a staff member recalls, was a "loudest of loud, shocking blue Hawaiian shirt, worn with suit pants." Edgar never used the hotel's kidney-shaped pool. Proximity to water, he told the Nixons at La Jolla, made him "desperately uneasy." "The two of them always sat with their backs to the wall, even when they had dinner by the pool," recalled longtime hotel official Arthur Forbes. "That was for security. It was sad, watching the way those two men lived."

Clint Murchison made sure Edgar and Clyde wanted for nothing at the Del Charro. When Edgar mentioned that on Florida vacations he "could pick fruit right from the trees at the door," he awoke the next morning to find his patio planted with orange, peach and plum trees, and a grapevine. The grapes, the staff recall, had been laboriously wired to the branches during the night.

The favors Edgar accepted from Murchison made a mockery of his public pose as a man of thrift and incorruptibility. "It came to the end of the summer," recalled Allan Witwer, the Del Charro's first manager, "Hoover had made no attempt to pay his bill. So I went to Murchison and said, 'What do you want me to do?' 'Put it on my bill,' he told me. And that's what I did."

According to Witwer and his successor, Arthur Forbes, Murchison and associates paid Edgar's huge accommodations charges at the Del Charro every year until his death, nearly two decades later. Witwer has preserved a copy of the 1953 bill, covering July 28 to August 28, at his home in Maine. It is marked simply "Murchison," and was sent on to the millionaire's secretary, Ernestine van Buren. In the fifties, Witwer said, most of Edgar's bills were covered by Delhi-Taylor, a Murchison company.

The 1953 bill alone amounted to $3,100, or $15,755 at today's rates. If that was the average charge (and the hotel rate increased over the years), then the eighteen summers that followed brought Edgar hospitality worth nearly $300,000. That figure may be on the low side, for Edgar's vacation sometimes lasted nearly two months. In addition, his journeys to California were usually logged as official "inspection trips," meaning that taxpayers footed the travel expenses. Since 1950, Edgar's FBI salary had been more than that of a Congressman or a member of the Cabinet.

Just months before his death, in an off-the-record talk

with *Los Angeles Times* Bureau Chief David Kraslow, Edgar would admit having accepted this largesse. Plaintively, as though it made everything all right, he said he had paid for his own food and drink.

Nineteen fifty-eight, as few adult Americans could have failed to notice, saw publication of Edgar's book *Masters of Deceit*, touted as a manual on "Communism in America and How to Fight It." Because Edgar was the author, it became a massive best-seller, selling 250,000 copies in hardcover and 2,000,000 in paperback. The book became required reading in many schools. In a formal announcement, the Justice Department said the royalties were to go to the FBI Recreation Fund.

Masters of Deceit was not written by Edgar, nor was it even his idea. The book grew out of a suggestion by Assistant Director William Sullivan, was written by four or five Bureau agents assigned to the job and was "polished up" by Fern Stukenbroeker, an agent with a Ph.D. who worked in Crime Records. Agents all over the country were required to promote the book and to place "reviews"—written in advance at the Bureau—with friendly newspapers. *"Masters of Deceit,"* went the in-house joke, "written by the Master of Deceit who never even read it."

After Edgar's death, an official inquiry would establish that thousands of dollars of FBI Recreation Fund money had been diverted to uses other than the "athletic and social functions" for which the fund had been created. Moreover, only a fifth of the income from the book went to the fund at all. Edgar rebuffed suggestions that the remainder should go to a heart or cancer charity, and divided it among himself, Clyde, Lou Nichols and Bill Nichols (no relation), a journalist brought in to help with the final draft.

"I just don't remember," was Lou Nichols' reply, when asked years later how much he received. Edgar was more forthright—in private. Each of the four men, he admitted, received $72,000—about $340,000 at today's rates.

Edgar's friend Clint Murchison, who owned a controlling interest in Henry Holt, the publisher of *Masters of Deceit*, had virtually instructed the company to buy the book, and, his secretary, Ernestine van Buren, recalled, he "stressed his desire that Hoover be given an especially favorable contract."

Despite dire warnings to FBI recruits never to speculate on the stock market, Edgar and Clyde grew rich thanks to investment tips—and a special "no lose" arrangement provided by their Texas friends. Edgar invested in oil and insurance companies and railroads, areas in which Murchison and Richardson specialized. Some holdings, in Gulf Life, the Chesapeake & Ohio Railway and Texas Oil and Gas, coincided directly with the millionaires' own interests.

Edgar and Clyde always invested the same amounts in the same oil concerns. As late as 1973, after Edgar, Murchison and Richardson had died, Clyde was making $4,000 a month from one oil investment alone. "People who were in the oil business," said former FBI Assistant Director John Mohr, "would call him on the phone and tell him, 'We've got a good one going here; do you want to get in on it, Clyde?'"

When he died in 1975, Clyde would leave $725,000, almost $1,800,000 at today's rates. Edgar's published estate, most of which went to Clyde, included $122,000 in oil, gas and mineral leases. Unless he lost a great deal in the years before his death, the real fortune may have been far greater. The following episode reveals that Edgar and Clyde invested huge sums, twice as much as the whole of Edgar's declared estate, in just one Texas oil project.

In 1961, while sorting out his late father's affairs, the Massachusetts businessman Peter Sprague came across correspondence showing that Edgar and Clyde were major investors in Santiago Oil and Gas, a Texas oil drilling company. The former president of Santiago, Leland Redline, confirms it, and documents show Edgar continued to invest in Texas oil. "I know we made them a profit," said Redline, "but the amounts varied from year to year. Their profits were no business of mine."

As Sprague recalls it, documents showed Edgar and Clyde put huge sums into Santiago Oil—around three quarters of a million dollars in today's figures. "The question struck me," he said, "where did they get all that money? Certainly not from saving their FBI salaries. . . ." Sprague passed the records to New York District Attorney Robert Morgenthau.

"Basically," Morgenthau said in 1988, "these were wires sent to Hoover telling him of his drilling ventures. What caught my eye was these were federal leases—and Hoover was an official of the federal government. Had he helped his principal to get those leases? Was the investment income in effect a finder's fee? This could have been what they call in the trade a 'carried' interest, a reward for bringing the lease or oil prospect to the principal's attention. That would have been improper for someone in a federal agency, like Hoover."

Some information on the links between Edgar's oil ventures and Clint Murchison, evidence that could have destroyed him, reached federal officials over the years. Telltale business records were sent to the desk of William Hundley, head of the Organized Crime Section at the Justice Department during the Kennedy administration. "There wasn't enough to make a criminal case," Hundley recalled. "But it was wrong. He shouldn't have done it."

John Dowd, who headed a Justice Department probe into FBI corruption after Edgar's death, was appalled by what he learned of the oil investments. "Hoover did have oil ventures with Clint Murchison," Dowd confirmed in 1988. "If the drilling company hit a dry hole he'd get his money back. Everything was a sure thing. It had to be a sure thing. If not, he'd get his money back, be it stocks, bonds or oil ventures. It was extraordinary."

According to William Sullivan, Edgar "had a deal with Murchison where he invested in oil wells and if they hit oil, he got his share of the profits, but if they didn't hit oil, he didn't share in the costs. . . . One time, he got into serious trouble on his income tax manipulations, and we had to send an accountant from New York to Houston, Texas, where apparently the operations existed. He told me afterwards, 'Good God Almighty. If the truth were known, Hoover would be in serious trouble. . . .' Apparently he did straighten it out. But he did say that Hoover had done something that was a serious violation of the law."

The Bureau's Chief Clerk, Albert Gunsser, looked after tax matters for Edgar and Clyde in later years—and a grateful Clyde was to leave Gunsser $27,000 in his will.

In the late summer of 1953, as Edgar was enjoying Murchison's hospitality at the Del Charro for the first time, Joe McCarthy turned up unexpectedly at the hotel. Edgar told reporters it was just a coincidence, but the evidence suggests it was a crisis meeting between protégé and patron.

The start of the Eisenhower presidency, the previous year, had given the Senator the chairmanship of the Subcommittee on Investigations, his opportunity to hold the repellent hearings for which he would become infamous. And his chief Counsel during that season of political terror was one of Edgar's most favored acolytes, Roy Cohn.

The gifted son of a New York Supreme Court judge, Cohn had a good deal in common with Edgar. He was already identified with the far Right when he arrived in Washington, at the age of twenty-five, and—although he denied it until his death from AIDS in 1986—he was homosexual. Like Edgar, he made a point of attacking fellow homosexuals and campaigners for homosexual rights.

Cohn obtained a job at the Justice Department thanks to George "Sok" Sokolsky, a columnist close to Edgar who checked in with the FBI each day for advice on what to write. He was also close to Walter Winchell and got his first audience with Edgar within minutes of requesting it. Edgar urged him to defy his superiors, press ahead with a planned prosecution of alleged American Communists at the United

Nations and keep in touch. "It was obvious," Cohn recalled, "that I was trusted."

It was Edgar who recommended Cohn to Joe McCarthy, and Edgar attended the celebrations when the Senator appointed him Chief Counsel. McCarthy and his mentor were becoming closer by the month, as Cohn discovered when he attended a series of private dinners at the apartment of the Senator's fiancée, Jean Kerr.

Edgar would arrive accompanied by Clyde, always on time, always fastidiously dressed. Unlike McCarthy, he could never be persuaded to take off his jacket, until the night the Senator jokingly asked whether he had a tape recorder in his pocket. Edgar relented and ate dinner in his shirtsleeves.

Cohn brought an unpaid "chief consultant" to the subcommittee, and Edgar was linked to him, too. This was David Schine, a handsome, blond twenty-six-year-old Harvard graduate who was Cohn's constant companion—and the target of gossip that they were lovers. His hotelier father, Myer, regularly played host to Edgar and Clyde on their Christmas visits to Miami Beach.

Edgar was not deterred by the darker side of Myer Schine, who admitted to the Kefauver Committee that he had a deal with the mob for gambling operations at his hotels. He and Clyde accepted Schine's hospitality at the Gulfstream, an exclusive set of beach apartments in Miami Beach, and at the Ambassador Hotel in Los Angeles. Schine, like Murchison at La Jolla, paid the bills.

McCarthy turned up in La Jolla in 1953 as his popularity was waning. All manner of powerful people, including the President and many right-wingers, felt that enough was enough. The Senator arrived at the Del Charro in a state of disarray. He got drunk, abused hotel employees and threw his fiancée into the pool with her clothes on.

Edgar picked that moment, when other public figures were distancing themselves from McCarthy, to speak out warmly about him. "I view him as a friend," he told a local reporter. "Certainly he is a controversial man. He is earnest and he is honest. He has enemies. Whenever you attack Communists, Fascists, even the Ku Klux Klan, you are going to be the victim of the most extremely vicious criticism. . . . When certain elements cease their attacks on me, I'll know I'm slipping. McCarthy is an ex-Marine. He was an amateur boxer. He's Irish. Combine those and you're going to have a vigorous individual who is not going to be pushed around."

McCarthy had begun his slide largely thanks to the arrogance of the man Edgar had sent to help him. The following summer, millions watched televised hearings revealing that, during a hunt for Communists in the military, Roy Cohn had abused congressional privilege by trying to prevent his pal Schine from being drafted. When that failed, he tried to pressure the Army to grant Schine special privileges. Cohn was forced to resign in July 1954, and McCarthy's own ruin seemed inevitable.

He responded, once again, by running to join Edgar and Clint Murchison at La Jolla. Cohn, who came with him, was turned away at the door because he was a Jew. Murchison had a "No Jews" policy at the Del Charro. No blacks were admitted, either, except servants. In between drinking bouts, McCarthy played shuffleboard with Edgar or sat talking, one arm draped around the Director's shoulders.

If McCarthy was hoping for public support from Edgar, he was to be disappointed. Edgar had been playing a double game all along, emphasizing his role as nonpartisan FBI Director in public while giving the Senator virtually unlimited support in secret.

Meanwhile, knowing that Eisenhower detested McCarthy, Edgar told the President that the Senator's activity was now impeding the hunt for Communists. In the Senate, he let it be known that, while he valued McCarthy's work, he was critical of his methods. All along, he maintained the fiction that no FBI documents were being supplied to the McCarthy team.[3]

McCarthy kept in touch with the FBI long after the Senate set the seal on his disgrace with a formal notion of censure.

Even in his last days, when he was in the terminal stages of alcoholism, he was proposing Edgar as the right man to succeed Eisenhower as President. In 1957, when McCarthy died of cirrhosis of the liver, Edgar, Roy Cohn and Richard Nixon were among the vast crowd at the funeral.

Some who knew him said McCarthy never really believed in his own anti-Communist rhetoric, that he was just a cynical opportunist. And astonishingly, given that he made it his lifetime crusade, Edgar's zeal may have been just as hollow by the fifties. "Of course he wasn't sincere," said William Sullivan. "He knew the Party didn't amount to a damn. . . ."

By 1956, in part thanks to unrelenting FBI pressure, membership of the American Communist Party had slipped from its 1944 peak of around 80,000 to a mere 20,000. The figure would continue to plummet, to 8,500 in 1962 and 2,800 by 1971. Edgar would obscure this decline by ceasing to publicize membership figures, and responding to inquiries by saying the figures were secret.

To the extent it did survive, the Party was crippled by the penetration activities of innumerable FBI informants. "If it were not for me," Edgar was to tell Abba Schwartz, Assistant Secretary in charge of security at the State Department in 1963, "there would not even be a Communist Party of the United States. Because I've financed the Communist Party, in order to know what they are doing."

"How do you think I'm going to get my Appropriations out of Congress if you keep downplaying the CP?" Edgar would exclaim angrily to William Sullivan toward the end of his life. Sullivan, who specialized in monitoring the Party's activities, later declared publicly that the Communist "threat" had long been "a lie perpetuated on the American public."

All this indicates that, by the end of the McCarthy era at any rate, not even Edgar himself was sincere about the anti-Communist effort known at the FBI as The Cause. Above and beyond everything, however, Edgar believed in

Edgar. Those in Congress who marched to his tune, like McCarthy, he used. Those who did not, he found ways to crush.

From the early fifties on, in the words of Senator Estes Kefauver, Edgar's hold on Congress gave him "more power than the President."

CHAPTER 18

"J. Edgar Hoover was like a sewer that collected dirt. I now believe he was the worst public servant in our history."

Former Acting Attorney General Laurence Silberman, the first person to peruse Hoover's secret files after his death

EDGAR DENIED TIME AND AGAIN THAT HE KEPT FILES ON THE personal lives of politicians and public figures. "The supposed secret dossiers," he said, "do not exist." The politicians, however, did not believe him. In 1958, a group of senior U.S. senators held a special meeting to discuss what to do if Edgar should suddenly die. If that happened, they decided, a delegation would rush to FBI headquarters and demand to see the files.

The bottom line was fear, and in some unlikely quarters. Senator Karl Mundt, a Republican of the far Right and a staunch supporter of the Internal Security Subcommittee, was ostensibly one of Edgar's vocal advocates. One night in 1960, however, Mundt poured out his true feelings to his aide Henry Eakins.

"Hoover," he said, "is the most dangerous man in the United States. He has misused his office. There are things I know that Hoover has done to congressmen and senators, things that should never have happened. He has things on them." Later, worried about having spoken so openly, he implored Eakins not to repeat what he had said while Edgar remained in office.

Thanks to a Senate investigation in 1975, we now know

that the FBI also kept files containing "information of a personal nature" on the following famous members of Congress: Carl Albert, Hale Boggs, Edward Kennedy, George McGovern, Mike Mansfield, Wilbur Mills, Abraham Ribicoff, Adlai Stevenson and Lowell Weicker. While Edgar was alive, senators and congressmen could only guess at the nature of such files. Then, a few months after his death, an FBI agent in Ohio was caught investigating a Democratic election candidate. For more than twenty years, it was revealed, the Crime Records Division had run a "Congressional Relations Service"—supposedly with the purpose of gathering public-record information on politicians for "internal use."

FBI officials well knew that the very existence of such an operation was potentially explosive. "These matters," warned an instruction to field divisions during a primary campaign, "should be handled with *extreme* discretion to avoid the implication that we are checking on candidates."

Yet that was exactly what Edgar was doing. "Hoover," said William Sullivan, "had a complete file developed on each incoming congressman. He knew their family backgrounds, where they had gone to school, whether or not they played football, and any other tidbits. . . . Bureau indices were immediately reviewed to see if what we had was good or bad. Could he be looked upon as a person to cultivate and use, to draw into our stable on Capitol Hill? Or should he be looked upon as one who would be unfriendly to the Bureau?"

As an election approached, congratulatory letters from Edgar were prepared for all candidates. When the results came in, winners' letters were rushed around the country, the notes to the losers trashed. A "friendly" politician found himself courted by the FBI wherever he went. If he traveled to foreign capitals where the Bureau had offices, escorts were there to greet him at the airport. "We went out of our way," Sullivan recalled, "to make it clear, 'We are pleased with you.'"

On Capitol Hill, politicians were watched by men well placed to serve as Edgar's spies. From 1943 on, FBI agents were "loaned" to congressional committees as investigators. Others ostensibly "left" their Bureau jobs altogether to work as congressional staffers.

Edgar's key bridgehead in Congress was the House Appropriations Committee, which holds the purse strings of government agencies. By the seventies, no fewer than twenty-eight FBI agents were attached to that committee alone. John Rooney, the Chairman of the subcommittee that controlled the FBI budget, was the Bureau's cherished friend. The Democratic Congressman from Brooklyn kept just one signed photograph on his office desk—of Edgar. He lavished praise on the Director at every opportunity. "I have never cut his budget," Rooney said, "and I never expect to." Edgar, who turned down requests to testify before the House Committee on Crime, made an annual ritual out of his appearance before the Appropriations Committee, a platform from which to preach his view of the world and to reel off statistics suggesting the Bureau had achieved an extraordinarily high rate of convictions—usually around 96 percent of crimes committed.

These figures were cooked. The superb conviction rate referred only to the number of cases that came to court, not to the number of investigations undertaken. Many of the apparent successes, such as auto theft convictions, were actually achieved by local police. Over the years various public bodies and scholars have cast doubt on Edgar's statistics. Warren Olney, an Assistant Attorney General in the fifties, thought them "hogwash." They were never challenged, however, by Rooney's Appropriations Committee.

Edgar protected Rooney even though the Congressman was, in the words of crime consultant Ralph Salerno, "up to his ears in collusion with organized crime." Washington lobbyist Robert Winter-Berger, who said he personally saw Rooney accept a cash-filled envelope from a mob emissary, called him the "key connection for the underworld" on Capitol Hill.

An FBI report in 1967 noted that, in spite of allegations that Rooney had accepted a $100,000 bribe, the Bureau had "conducted no inquiry." The following year, when another candidate contested Rooney's seat, Edgar obliged when the Congressman asked him to spice his annual testimony with "anything timely that would perk up the ears" of his constituents. Furthermore, he supplied Rooney with the criminal record of an associate of his electoral opponent.

In 1970, when Rooney was challenged again, Edgar sent him details of a police charge against his rival, arising from a long-ago fraternity party, enabling Rooney to claim the candidate was "a fugitive from justice." Rooney held on to his seat by a narrow margin.

Congressman John McCormack of Massachusetts, Speaker of the House in the sixties, also had a special relationship with Edgar. "I met Hoover around 1962," Winter-Berger recalled, "when McCormack would send me over to the FBI to pick up files for him. If McCormack wanted some information to use against someone—a girlfriend the guy shouldn't have or some nefarious dealings—Hoover would help him. It might be someone in the House whose arm McCormack wanted to twist on a vote. Or someone in government he wanted to bring pressure on. McCormack couldn't send an ordinary messenger to pick up that sort of thing, so he used me. I'd go over to Hoover's office, and he personally would give me the file. He knew what I was coming for, and he'd have it waiting."

Winter-Berger also recalled something that put him off. "When I was leaving, Hoover would pat me on the rear end, sort of the way they do athletes when they've had a good game, except that we were alone in his office and I certainly wasn't an athlete. I was thirty-six then, and he was thirty years older than me. I thought it was out of order for the head of the FBI to do that, and I eventually became uncomfortable and started trying to get out of going over there."

Edgar dined regularly with Congressman—subsequently Senator—George Bender of Ohio, later widely condemned for his corrupt links with the Teamsters Union. Edgar energetically promoted the congressional career of Senator Thomas Dodd, who regularly made warm speeches about the Bureau. Dodd, a former FBI agent, had once been described in a memo from Edgar's office as "absolutely no good . . . a scoundrel." In the sixties, however, when Dodd was exposed for corruption, the Bureau helped him cover his tracks. "Nothing," recalled the Senator's former aide James Boyd, "could have been more effective for intimidating potential witnesses into silence. . . . FBI agents had been instructed not to take any information concerning Dodd."

The way Edgar secured a man's allegiance, and by contrast silenced potential enemies, was ruthless. FBI agents were forever on the alert to record human failings. "We had a general instruction," said former senior agent Curtis Lynum, "to record anything we might need in the future, in what we called a 'Zero file.' I was skiing with my wife once when I was serving in Nevada, and we saw a man in a homosexual embrace with a teenage boy outside a chalet. We both recognized the guy, a big name in the business circles of Las Vegas. I wished I hadn't seen it, but I had. I figured it might be important later on, so I reported it to my Special Agent in Charge. I probably put a recommendation 'File for future reference.' But the SAC could look at that thing and say, 'This is a prominent guy. I guess I'd better send that back to Washington for indexing.' It was a well-established procedure. I made those decisions myself when I became an SAC. I'd think, 'Maybe I'd better send that to Mr. Hoover.'"

Long before a new member of Congress boarded his plane for Washington, said William Sullivan, FBI files had been scoured for any references: a criminal record perhaps, an occasion the name had come up in any investigation, however incidentally, any mention of a sexual or ethical lapse. "The leadership of the Bureau knew exactly what he wanted," Sullivan said, "every bit of derogatory information on every congressman, every senator . . . and on anybody else in Washington. He didn't have to make any requests—they'd feed it to him."

After Edgar's death, by one official count, the Bureau was holding 883 files on senators, 722 on congressmen. Some are still withheld, others have been shredded. Many, as former Assistant Director Nicholas Callahan has claimed, no doubt contained nothing sinister, just "informative material." A scattering of surviving documents, however, prove that politicians' fears were well founded. Many come from the files designated "Official and Confidential," which were closely held in locked file cabinets in Edgar's office suite. His secretary, Helen Gandy, reportedly took the keys home with her each evening.

The dirt in Edgar's files was often sexual in nature. In 1948, when Senator Vandenberg of Michigan was a dark-horse Republican presidential candidate, aides kept Edgar up to date on gossip about him. OC file 50 shows that the Senator expressed himself "deeply indebted" to the FBI for passing on information about his relationship with a woman not his wife. This was a direct clash of interests. Edgar was poking around in the private affairs of a potential presidential candidate at the very time he himself was dreaming of advancement under the man he wanted in the White House, Thomas Dewey.

In the late thirties, Clyde's woman friend Edna Daulyton had listened in horror as Edgar and Clyde discussed Congressman Harold Knutson, a Republican from Minnesota, over dinner at the Mayflower. "It was clear to me," Daulyton recalled, "that they'd done something awful, something very detrimental to that congressman. I didn't exactly understand what they'd done, or why. I was very young and I didn't ask questions."

Knutson, who served in Congress from 1917 until 1948, was a bachelor who lived with a male Mexican companion. A rumor, never published, suggested he was involved in a homosexual scandal—successfully hushed up. "I heard," said his fellow congressman George MacKinnon, now a federal judge, "that someone had allegedly caught him buggering a younger man. It was put about by someone who didn't like him." The word in Washington police circles was that Edgar was somehow involved. Some even whispered that he was himself involved in the homosexual scandal. Whatever the truth, Edna Daulyton remembered something

Edgar said that evening at the Mayflower. It stuck in her mind, she said, because it was so cold and vicious. Congressman Knutson, Edgar remarked, would "always be in our pocket now. . . ."

The Official and Confidential files show that between 1958 and 1965 Washington Agents in Charge systematically collected scandal on politicians. Politically damaging tidbits were culled from the reports of agents engaged in other investigations, from human eavesdroppers on the Hill and from electronic devices, and hand-delivered to Edgar.

An FBI roundup of information, dated June 13, 1958, and including a passage headed "Government Circles," tells Edgar what Agent Conrad Trahern overheard "in the cafeteria of the Senate Office Building." Parts of the document, reproduced below, were censored by FBI officials before its release under the Freedom of Information Act in 1989.

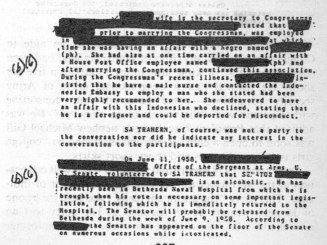

(b)(6)

wife is the secretary to Congressman ▆▆▆▆▆▆▆ tated that ▆▆▆▆▆▆▆ prior to marrying the Congressman, was employed in ▆▆▆▆▆▆▆ at which time she was having an affair with a Negro named ▆▆▆▆▆▆ (ph). She had also at one time carried on an affair with a House Post Office employee named ▆▆▆▆▆▆ (ph) and after marrying the Congressman, continued this association. During the Congressman's recent illness, ▆▆▆▆▆▆ insisted that he have a male nurse and contacted the Indonesian Embassy to employ a man who she stated had been very highly recommended to her. She endeavored to have an affair with this Indonesian who declined, stating that he is a foreigner and could be deported for misconduct.

SA TRAHERN, of course, was not a party to the conversation nor did he indicate any interest in the conversation to the participants.

(b)(6)

On June 11, 1958, ▆▆▆▆▆▆▆ Office of the Sergeant at Arms, U. S. Senate, volunteered to SA TRAHERN that SENATOR ▆▆▆▆▆▆▆ is an alcoholic. He has recently been in Bethesda Naval Hospital from which he is brought when his vote is necessary on some important legislation, following which he is immediately returned to the Hospital. The Senator will probably be released from Bethesda during the week of June 9, 1958. According to ▆▆▆▆▆▆▆ the Senator has appeared on the floor of the Senate on numerous occasions while intoxicated.

Edgar responded that he "deeply appreciated" this information. The report was followed, on July 7, by a summary of an interview with a photographer for the Democratic National Committee, describing how politicians had suppressed a compromising photograph. There was gossip on a Guggenheim family member—he had attended a masked ball with someone other than his wife—and information on a Washington "telephone answering service for homosexuals."

The report of August 8 ends with smear information on a member of the Senate:

advised SA Joseph
1. Woods on August 7, 1958, that Senator ▮▮▮▮▮
prepares a personal check each month
in the amount of $500, payable to ▮▮▮▮▮ is a "party girl"
stated he had heard that ▮▮▮▮▮ is a "party girl"
and that she may now be living with Senator ▮▮▮▮▮
at the Shoreham Hotel, Washington, D. C.

Unless otherwise indicated, the foregoing
material has been obtained from confidential technical
sources.[1]

That same month Edgar was told about an aide to Congressman James Morrison of Louisiana who had been conned out of $254 while attempting to attend a live sex show. He learned that a congressional critic of Army security regulations—name censored—was consorting with a person with "the morals of an alley cat." He was advised that President Eisenhower's nephew Michael Gill was soon to open a club for politicians, staffed by "college girls in low-cut blouses and short, short skirts."

An October 1958 report told Edgar of a farewell celebration at the Mayflower for Senator William Jenner of Indiana. "This party," the document reads, "was paid for by one of Jenner's wealthy Texan friends. . . . The party cost an estimated $2500." Most of the rest of the report, on former congressman Harold Velde and an aide to Congressman Leslie Arends, remains censored. A November document, on the forthcoming election for Governor of New York, quotes someone with "a big file of dirt" on Nelson Rockefeller.

On June 9, 1959, Edgar received this report:

Dear Mr. Hoover:

      You may be interested in the following information furnished by ▓▓▓▓▓▓▓▓▓▓ a local prostitute ▓▓▓▓▓▓▓▓▓▓▓▓▓▓ Special Agent Amos M. Teasley on June 9, 1959, that she had spent the afternoon of June 8, 1959, with Senator ▓▓▓▓▓▓▓▓▓▓ in his private office in the Senate. She also said she had sexual intercourse with the Senator during the afternoon "on the couch in the Senator's office".

      You will recall ▓▓▓▓▓▓▓▓▓▓ previously associated with ▓▓▓▓▓▓▓▓ but this is the first occasion she has been with him in recent months.

      Sincerely yours,

      James H. Gale
      James H. Gale
      Special Agent in Charge

On May 16, 1960, as the Nixon-Kennedy fight for the presidency intensified, agents rushed to send Edgar information supplied that same day by a Washington prostitute. She spoke of sex with various congressmen at the Mayflower, at home and, in one case, "in his office at the Capitol." Edgar's men were especially busy cultivating prostitutes that fall, in the closing stages of the election campaign. Agents were actually present on September 2, when a whore received a call from a Senator to arrange a midmorning appointment. Later, as the report relates:

Agents were advised when the Senator arrived and upon his departure, he was overheard ▓▓▓▓▓▓▓▓▓▓▓▓ "It was wonderful." After he had left the premises ▓▓▓▓▓▓▓ commented that the sexual ability of the Senator was "pretty good".

In gathering such information, agents assumed it would be passed on to Hoover. "There was no thought of my taking any undue liberties with anyone's privacy," said Agent in Charge Joseph Purvis, who signed some of the reports in the series. "These were things that I thought would be of interest to Hoover, primarily. It was a matter of advising him of things that I thought would be useful."

Former Agent Conrad Trahern, however, had no illusions. "Hoover," he declared, "treated people wrong. He was a despot. He did everything to impose on people on Capitol Hill who were screwing broads and that sort of thing. . . . But the policy was to make J. Edgar Hoover happy, and I reported what I knew."

According to Norman Koch, an FBI fingerprint specialist in World War II, scavenging for dirt had long been routine. In the forties, he recalled, colleagues complained of "spending all their time investigating public official number so-and-so rather than Public Enemy Number One. They were digging into the background of anyone who might pose the slightest danger to the Director, and the idea was to find anything that could be used as leverage should any of these men dare to challenge his authority."

Gordon Liddy, best known for his role in the Watergate affair, was an FBI agent in the fifties and early sixties. In Washington, where he worked in the propaganda department known as Crime Records, he learned firsthand exactly how compromising information was handled.

"Say there was a bank robbery someplace. An informant might tell us the man to look for was holed up in the Skyline Motel, about six blocks south of the Capitol in Washington. Agents search the motel, and in the process they come across Senator X in bed with Miss Lucy Schwartzkopf, age fifteen and a half. They make their apologies and withdraw. But everything has to go into the record. The Supervisor who gets the report may think there's no need to keep stuff on the peccadilloes of Senator X, but he has no authority to destroy it. The report has to go up to the Director's office."

In Edgar's office, said Liddy, a summary would be prepared for Miss Gardner of Crime Records. Those involved in congressional liaison, like Liddy himself, would come across it sooner or later. "Say the Director was expecting to meet Senator X or if the Senator's name had come up in some way, I would have to prepare a memorandum. I would check out the card held by Miss Gardner, and if there was something noteworthy I would write a note—perhaps a blind memorandum, 'For the Director Only.' It would say something like, 'The Director may wish to recall that Senator X was involved in such-and-such an incident, and is not very discreet.'"

Sometimes, said Liddy, Edgar might send an official to meet with the compromised politician soon after receiving the initial report. "The messenger would simply say Mr. Hoover apologized for the intrusion into the Senator's privacy, assure him it came up in the course of legitimate inquiries and tell him not to worry, this had been removed from the file. The whole point was to let the [Senator] know that Hoover knew. That's why, when Hoover would go before the Appropriations Committee and say he wanted something, they'd give him anything. Anything, because they were afraid of what he had."

Others corroborate Liddy's statement. "I learned a lot," said former CIA Director Richard Helms, "from fellows who had worked in Hoover's office before joining us. I used to hear how certain senators and congressmen would get caught in cathouses over in Virginia. When the report came in, Hoover would put it in his personal safe. If there was any problem with that senator, he would say, 'Don't worry, I've got those papers right in my safe. You don't have a thing to worry about.' . . . . He played a very skillful game."

Emanuel Celler of Brooklyn, a Democratic Congressman for fifty years, many of them as Chairman of the House Judiciary Committee, told *New York Post* publisher Dorothy Schiff that he was afraid to speak his mind about Edgar's abuses because the FBI had a hold on him. In public, he continued to speak of Edgar as a "most exemplary" public servant.

"It was not uncommon," said veteran Agent Arthur Murtagh, "to learn of some politically damaging information about some leading figure in politics as having been developed by the Bureau; and then, always at a time when it would be most damaging to the individual, the information would in some way show up in the *Chicago Tribune* or some other friend of the Bureau."

Walter Trohan, the *Chicago Tribune* reporter who was close to Edgar, recalled talking with some of the victims of such tactics. "Some of Hoover's overwhelming support on the Hill," he said, "was due to what I can only call blackmail, polite blackmail."

Senator Sam Ervin, remembered for his presiding role during the Watergate hearings, behaved differently in 1971 when, as Chairman of the Subcommittee on Constitutional Rights, he vetoed a probe of FBI abuses. "I think," he said of Edgar, "he has done a very good job in a difficult post." According to William Sullivan, Ervin was "in our pocket. It was financial, something like the Abe Fortas affair. This is why he came out praising the Bureau."[2]

Edgar liked to send dirt on politicians to the White House. "I know he had a dossier on me," recalled former Florida Senator George Smathers, "because Lyndon Johnson read it to me. Johnson called me in the middle of the night—he loved to do that—and said, 'These are rumors the FBI have been picking up about you. . . .'[3] He also read me the file on Senator Thruston Morton, the former Chairman of the Republican National Committee, and the one on Barry Goldwater. There was a lot about Nixon in there, too. A lot of people were very nervous. . . .'"

"Information," President Nixon would reflect after his disgrace, "was one of the primary sources of Edgar Hoover's power. He usually knew something about everything that was going on, and that knowledge made him as valuable to his friends as it made him dangerous to his enemies."

CHAPTER 19

"The allegation that Mr. Hoover used FBI files as a power broker or as blackmail, or something of that nature, is probably one of the greatest distorted allegations in the history of mankind."

Cartha DeLoach, former FBI Assistant Director, 1982

POLITICIANS WERE NOT THE ONLY PUBLIC FIGURES ON WHOM Edgar gathered information. Over a period of thirty years, starting in 1945, FBI wiretappers learned the private thinking of at least twelve Supreme Court justices—Chief Justices Earl Warren and Frederick Vinson, Associate Justices Felix Frankfurter, Hugo Black, William Douglas, Stanley Reed, Robert Jackson, Frank Murphy, John Harlan, Potter Stewart, Harold Burton and Abe Fortas. Some of the justices were overheard holding telephone conversations with other targets of Bureau surveillance. References to justices in yet other surveillances were duly logged and filed. The Constitution protects the Supreme Court from such intrusions, but Edgar did not have the transcripts destroyed. He preserved them, and on occasion used them to advantage.

Justice Douglas' conversations were picked up during the wiretapping of political maverick Thomas Corcoran, on behalf of the Truman White House. Truman, who read the transcripts himself, decided in 1946 not to nominate Douglas as Chief Justice, a choice that determined the shape of the Supreme Court for many years to come. What he learned about Douglas from Edgar's wiretaps may well have influenced his decision.

Douglas' liberal views infuriated Edgar, and he kept a running dossier on him. The Justice had been married four times, and three of his wives were much younger than he; Bureau summaries kept Edgar up to date. "Information has been received," read one entry, "that Douglas frequently becomes intoxicated at parties and has a habit of pawing women. . . ." The Bureau also checked up on Douglas' friends, noting that some were "of doubtful loyalty." The Justice himself suspected that his chambers were bugged.

In 1957, while investigating an allegation about a "ring of left-wing law clerks," the FBI collated information on the political attitudes of the justices themselves. Edgar's files show, too, that he had three sources on the Supreme Court during the Rosenberg spy case in 1953. Not even talk in a car was safe. When Justice Burton discussed a case in an FBI limousine, the accompanying agent reported straight back to Edgar.

While 20,000 pages of records on the Supreme Court and federal judiciary have been released, the FBI insists that others, notably electronic surveillance transcripts, "must be kept secret in the interests of national defense or foreign policy." More court battles lie ahead before the public can see just what intelligence Edgar obtained on the nation's justices.

Judge Laurence Silberman, who examined the Official and Confidential files while serving as Acting Attorney General in 1974, concluded that Edgar "did not have one ounce of scruple" about using wiretaps and hidden microphones. Today it seems certain he used them against members of Congress, as the politicians themselves long suspected.

In 1956, at the height of an election campaign, Senator Wayne Morse found himself on hands and knees in his living room, peering up the chimney and poking about under the furniture, hunting for hidden microphones. A Secret Service agent had warned him that both his office and his home were bugged, and quoted some of Morse's conversations to him to prove it. Though he never found a bug, Morse believed the FBI was responsible.

In 1965, when the Judiciary Committee called in experts to "sweep" Senate corridors, they reported a "strong indication of bugs" in the offices of Senators Maurine Neuberger and Ralph Yarborough, the liberal Democrat from Texas. A bug was later found in Yarborough's desk intercom, and he believed it had been installed by the FBI on behalf of President Johnson. Johnson boasted at the time that he was privy to every call that went in or out of the Senate offices.

Members of Congress wondered and worried and held meetings in the Speaker's office, but felt impotent to do anything. The issue was not aired publicly until the year before Edgar died, when Senator Joseph Montoya and House Majority Leader Hale Boggs claimed the FBI had been bugging congressional phones. Boggs accused Edgar of using "the tactics of the Soviet Union and Hitler's Gestapo." Edgar issued a flat denial and circulated derogatory information on Boggs, typed on the usual untraceable paper, to influential people. The row blew over.[1]

According to Boggs' son Thomas, however, the Congressman had proof of his charge—transcripts of bugged conversations, supplied to him by Bureau officials with uneasy consciences. An investigator for the Chesapeake and Potomac Telephone Company, moreover, told Boggs that his own home telephone had been tapped by the FBI.

In his denial, Edgar insisted that agents had long-standing orders to abort operations rather than follow a suspect into a building on Capitol Hill. Court testimony, however, later established that an agent working a corruption case had taped a conversation in the office of Senator Hiram Fong, using concealed equipment. Others had sent an informant into Congressman John Dowdy's office on a similar mission, and the FBI had tapped several calls between Dowdy and the informant, with Edgar's approval.[2]

According to Bernard Spindel, an electronics specialist, FBI bugging of Capitol Hill was routine in the mid-sixties. In 1965, while checking a congressman's phone, he found a bugging device wired into Congress' telephone frame room.

Then, using a detector, he tracked a multi-line Alpeth cable that was spliced into the one serving both houses of Congress and their hearing rooms. The cable terminated at the old Esso Building at 261 Constitution Avenue, in a room rented by the Justice Department.

"I was able to monitor senators' and congressmen's conversations on that cable," recalled Spindel's partner Earl Jaycox, "and it was one that shouldn't have been carrying their calls. We understood from our conversations with telephone company employees that the cable had been put in at the direction of the FBI."[3]

Spindel was to have testified about all this to the Subcommittee on Invasion of Privacy, chaired by Senator Edward Long, the Democratic senator from Missouri. Then, on the eve of the hearing, he was told Senator Long had reached an "understanding" with the FBI, that he was not to discuss FBI operations on the stand. When Spindel tried to do so anyway, Long silenced him. "We will not," he said, "go into this area." The reason, according to Long's Chief Counsel Bernard Fensterwald, was that the Senator had been blackmailed into submission by the FBI.

For eight years in the sixties, Long did battle with what he called "the snooping monster," the invasion of citizens' privacy by the tappers, microphone planters and mail openers of modern life. He also wanted something that was then just a pious hope, a Freedom of Information Act to give citizens access to government records.

In 1963, as chairman of a Judiciary subcommittee, Long began to probe government efficiency. Fired by the discovery that state agencies spent $20 million on eavesdropping equipment each year, he ordered an inquiry. The resulting hearings ground on for more than three years, and spelled the Senator's ruin.

When Long decided to hold hearings specifically on the FBI, Edgar was furious. "Pressure," an aide had earlier advised, "would have to be applied so that the personal interest of Senator Long became involved, rather than any ideological basis." Years later, in a sworn affidavit, Fensterwald gave this account of what followed in 1966.

236

"The FBI," Fensterwald said, "knew they were going to be the next subject of the committee hearings. Hoover's man [Assistant Director] Cartha DeLoach made an appointment and came to Long's office with another agent. They never come alone. Long had me sit in on it, probably because he expected it to be about our FBI investigation. I doubt that he knew it was going to be 'This Is Your Life, Senator Long.' They had a file folder with them, and DeLoach said something like, 'Senator, I think you ought to read this file that we have on you. You know we would never use it, because you're a friend of ours, but you never know what unscrupulous people will do. And we just thought you ought to know the type of stuff that might get around and might be harmful to you.'

"They handed him the folder, a fairly thin one, as I recall. And Long just sat there and read it for a few minutes. Then he closed the file, he thanked them and they went on their way. The next thing I knew we had orders to skip over the FBI inquiries and go on to whatever other agency was next. I think there were some perfunctory face-saving hearings, but we never got into the heavy stuff—the wiretapping and so on."

DeLoach, who has denied the Fensterwald allegation, was Edgar's principal go-between with Senator Long. He wrote of one visit to Long: "I asked him point-blank whether or not he intended to hold hearings concerning the FBI at any time. He stated he did not. I asked him if he would be willing to give us a commitment that he would in no way embarrass the FBI. He said he would agree to do this. . . . I told Senator Long that, to sum up, it was our understanding that we had a commitment from him that he would not bother the FBI. He stated this was true and that we could have his word in this regard. . . . He stated that at the conclusion of his hearings he intended to use the FBI as a shining example for other agencies to follow.

"It is important," DeLoach wrote, "that we stay in touch with Senator Long in view of his changeable personality. While *we have neutralized the threat* [author's emphasis] of being embarrassed by the Long Committee, we have not yet eliminated certain dangers. . . . We therefore must keep on top of this situation at all times."

A year later Long was the subject of an exposé in *Life* magazine. It reported that Long had received payments from Morris Shenker, chief counsel to Jimmy Hoffa, the crooked leader of the Teamsters Union. His probe of federal snooping, *Life* claimed, was inspired by Teamsters cronies and had blunted government efforts to fight organized crime.

A Senate ethics committee inquiry found no facts to support these allegations. Long had focused on privacy before the suspect payments were made, and he and Shenker also shared clients who had nothing to do with Hoffa. The *Life* article and the ensuing furor, however, wrecked Long's political career. He failed to win reelection in 1968.

Another member of Congress, also a prominent campaigner for the privacy rights of American citizens, fell foul of the FBI and *Life* magazine in circumstances that suggest the Bureau maliciously fed *Life* false information.

In the mid-sixties, Cornelius Gallagher was regarded as one of the best and brightest of the Democratic Party's young men. A Korean War hero from Bayonne, New Jersey, he had been in Congress since 1958. Six feet tall, silver-haired in his early forties, he soon became congressional adviser to the Arms Control Agency and a delegate to the Disarmament Conference. He was friendly with the Kennedy brothers and was mentioned as a possible Vice President to Lyndon Johnson in 1964.

Like Senator Long, Gallagher's major domestic interest was what he perceived as the encroachment of the Big Brother mentality. He worried about the thousands of people whose private lives, thanks to modern gadgetry, were no longer private at all. He wondered about data banks and the growing use of lie detectors, about genetic engineering and the psychological testing of children. Who had access to such information? What safeguards did the citizen have?

The result of the Congressman's worrying was the creation in 1963 of the Subcommittee on Privacy, an outgrowth of the House Committee on Government Operations. Private business, educational bodies, even medical institutions, drew much of its fire. Soon, however, in part because the FBI and the IRS pried personal information out of credit bureaus, the committee's work began to give both those agencies bad press.

It was not what Gallagher was doing so much as what he refused to do that brought the first clash with Edgar. The trouble began when he came under unexpected pressure from the Teamsters Union and from Roy Cohn, Edgar's protégé from the McCarthy days.

Cohn, who said he was speaking on Edgar's behalf, astonished the Congressman by *urging* him to hold hearings on evidence of illegal FBI and IRS surveillance. The purpose, Cohn explained, was to embarrass former Attorney General Robert Kennedy, on whose authority the wiretaps had been installed.

When Gallagher refused to hold hearings, saying it was outside his committee's mandate, Cohn responded with wheedling and threats. "Mr. Hoover wants to give you a big buildup," he said. "If you're their friend, anything you need you get. But if you're not a friend, and you don't cooperate, that means you're an enemy."

Months later, while signing correspondence one evening, Gallagher paused at a letter he knew nothing about. "In the letter, which was all typed and waiting for my signature, I was asking the Attorney General to supply my committee with copies of the authorizations for the bugging of Martin Luther King. I knew about that bugging, because John Rooney had taken great delight in playing the sex stuff to me. But I had no plans to ask for the files, and I had dictated no such letter. I called in my secretary and asked where the letter had come from."

Gallagher's secretary, Elizabeth May, recalled the incident vividly. "Roy Cohn," she said, "had dictated the letter to me on the telephone. He indicated that he was following FBI instructions. I typed up the letter and left it for the Congressman with the rest of his mail. I thought he must know about it. When Mr. Gallagher asked me what it was, and I told him, he was really wild. He called Cohn right away."

At a new meeting with the Congressman, Cohn told Gallagher the letter was "another chance" for him to cooperate, and urged him to send it. When Gallagher refused, Cohn told him: "You're gonna be sorry. . . ." The Congressman ignored the threat and pressed on with his privacy hearings.

At Easter 1967, there was a mysterious burglary at Gallagher's house by raiders apparently interested only in documents. Police contacts told the Congressman it was "an FBI job." "Then," Gallagher recalled, "a top guy I knew at Bell Telephone told me the FBI was bugging our phone."

The real body blow, however, was an article that fall in *Life* magazine. It focused on "the Fix," the blackmail and bribery that guarantees the mob the blind eye, or the active assistance, of police and elected officials. Specifically, *Life* named the mobster "Bayonne Joe" Zicarelli, and claimed he was "on the best of terms with the widely respected Democratic representative from Hudson County, Congressman Cornelius E. Gallagher. . . ." The politician and the mafioso, said the magazine, had regular "get-togethers," sometimes for Sunday brunch, at a suburban inn.

Gallagher strenuously denied the relationship, but complained to *Life* executives in vain. When he considered suing for libel, lawyers warned the case would generate more adverse publicity and that public officials rarely win libel cases. Then, in July 1968, three *Life* reporters interviewed the Congressman at his office. He readily admitted two innocent encounters with Zicarelli, who was a prominent figure in the area, but again denied compromising contacts.

That same month, Gallagher's attorney, Lawrence Weisman, asked him to fly to an urgent meeting at Newark Airport. What they had to discuss, he said, could not be discussed on the telephone. At Newark, Weisman explained that he had spent part of the day at Roy Cohn's office. At Cohn's suggestion, he had listened in on an extension as

Cohn talked on the telephone with Cartha DeLoach of the FBI.

DeLoach allegedly claimed the Bureau had "incontestable" proof that a missing New Jersey gambler, Barney O'Brien, had died of a heart attack in the Congressman's house "while lying next to Gallagher's wife." The body had supposedly been removed by Kayo Konigsberg, a gangster linked to Zicarelli. According to Gallagher and his attorney, DeLoach made it clear he had recently been in touch with *Life.* "If you still know that guy," DeLoach was quoted as saying, "you had better get word to him to resign from Congress. He's not going to last more than a week after the story hits."

The story hit on August 8, 1968, and it was one of the most savage attacks on a public figure in the history of twentieth-century journalism. THE CONGRESSMAN AND THE HOODLUM, shouted the headline. Gallagher was described as "a man who time and again has served as the tool and collaborator of a Cosa Nostra gang lord."

At the core of the story was what appeared to be a journalistic scoop, drawing on transcripts of an eight-year-old wiretap on Mafia boss Zicarelli. According to *Life,* they showed that the mob boss had reached out to the congressman to get the police off his back:

Gallagher: I got hold of these people [Bayonne Police] and there will be no further problem.
Zicarelli: I hope so, because they're ruining me.
Gallagher: They damn well better not.
Zicarelli: They're doing a job on me like was never done before.
Gallagher: I laced into them.

The *Life* exposé sparked prolonged public debate. To the astonishment of many, however, the Congressman was reelected that year with a healthy majority. He continued his campaign for privacy rights and for laws to limit the powers of the IRS and the Bureau of the Budget.

It was an IRS investigation in 1972 that brought the ruin the *Life* article had failed to achieve. Gallagher was charged with evading taxes and helping a local official to do the same. He pleaded guilty, following an impassioned speech to the House about his ordeal, and went to jail for seventeen months.[4] Meanwhile, thanks to a redrawing of constituency boundaries, his congressional seat ceased to exist. Gallagher received messages of support and sympathy from Gerald Ford, then Vice President, former Secretary of State Dean Rusk and many others. Rusk has characterized Edgar as "a veiled blackmailer."

The House Ethics Committee found no evidence that the Congressman had ever been involved with organized crime. *Life* had run its story about the supposed cadaver in Gallagher's house in spite of the fact that its alleged source, Kayo Konigsberg, was in the Mental Center for Federal Prisoners at the time. He later said the *Life* account was "a phony" and that the FBI had tried to persuade him to "frame-up" the Congressman.

There is no evidence that the damning "transcript" of conversations between Gallagher and the Mafia boss Zicarelli ever existed in the files of any law enforcement agency. In 1968 the IRS, the CIA, the Narcotics Bureau, the Secret Service, the New York City Police, the Manhattan District Attorney and the New York Rackets Bureau all pleaded ignorance. As for the FBI, Attorney General Ramsey Clark said he was advised that "the FBI does not have and has not had any transcripts or logs that could be the basis for the quotations in the *Life* magazine story. . . ." Nor have any such transcripts turned up in the thousands of documents that have since been made public.[5] A review of FBI files in Newark, New Jersey, has produced none, and agents who worked the Zicarelli case in the sixties said they knew of no such evidence.

Life reporter Sandy Smith, who obtained the "transcript" in 1968, had made his name as an organized-crime special-ist while working for the *Chicago Tribune,* a paper especially favored by the FBI. In 1965, when *Playboy* consulted Smith about an article by a former agent critical of the FBI, he recommended it be rejected and passed it on to the Bureau. Bureau documents describe Smith's value to the FBI as "inestimable" and say he was "utilized on many occasions."[6]

While Smith has refused to comment, former *Life* reporter Bill Lambert, who also worked on the Gallagher story, recalled that his colleague was so close to the FBI that he was "almost like an agent." It was possible, he agreed, that someone at the FBI might have fed him a phony transcript. Former Assistant Director DeLoach, for his part, has admitted he knew Smith well in 1968, but had no comment on the *Life* story. "I do not," he claimed, "recall the Neil Gallagher matter."

Another key figure in the story, however, did remember. In 1986, when Roy Cohn knew he was dying, he was told that Gallagher's wife was still tormented by the allegation about O'Brien, the gambler who had supposedly died in her arms. Cohn then signed a formal letter stating that the O'Brien allegation had come from DeLoach. He quoted DeLoach as saying that if Congressman Gallagher "did not stop his hearings in evasion [*sic*] of privacy, he would make the information public." Cohn passed on the threat, he now confessed, just as Gallagher had claimed.

In 1992, still a popular figure in New Jersey, Gallagher turned seventy-one. A measure of his confidence in his innocence is that he agreed to give the author free rein with any documents on him the FBI might release under the Freedom of Information Act. More than four years after applying, not one document has been forthcoming.

Mitchell Rogovin, who was an Assistant Attorney General at the time of the exposé, spoke of "all the leaking to *Life* magazine" by the Bureau in those days. It was, he said, "part and parcel of the retributive mode that went on. . . . This was one of a lot of cases. . . ."

Former Attorney General Ramsey Clark has expressed grave concern about the Gallagher case and that of Senator Long. The leaking of unproven information to the press, he said, was "inexcusable." "This," he had sighed at the height of the crisis, "is the work of the old man down the hall."

This was the dark side of Edgar, the most insidious violation of his office. Most Americans saw only the other side, the formidable propaganda machine and the impressive corps of agents.

"J. Edgar Hoover," *Newsweek* declared in 1957, "has become as bipartisan as the Washington Monument, as much an institution as the Smithsonian."

CHAPTER 20

"The FBI is a closely knit, cooperative organization of more than 14,000 men and women. I like to speak of it as a 'we' organization."

J. Edgar Hoover, 1956

ONE DAY IN 1959, AS THE LIGHTS CAME UP IN A SCREENING ROOM at FBI headquarters, Edgar was observed to be weeping. He had just watched a preview of Hollywood's movie *The FBI Story*, and he was crying with happiness. He thought the film, which portrayed a super-efficient agency staffed by a happy band of exemplary agents, "one of the greatest jobs I've ever seen."

In his address to the Appropriations Committee that year, Edgar catalogued a battery of impressive facts. The Identification Division now held more than 150 million fingerprints on file, and most of those submitted by police had been successfully identified. The Laboratory had made 165,000 scientific examinations, an all-time high. FBI investigative staff had performed more than three million hours of overtime. The FBI National Academy had celebrated twenty-three years of training law enforcement officers. Three and a half thousand agents, along with 10,000 other Bureau employees, had as usual achieved a near-perfect conviction rate. Chairman Rooney thanked the "eminent Director," and dismissed him after perfunctory questioning.

Within the FBI, a generation of agents were beginning to ask questions. The structure of the organization had not changed since the reshuffle of 1924, but there were now two

245

FBIs. There was the Field, with its corps of brave, hard-working agents serving in the front line against crime; and there was FBI Headquarters—the Seat of Government, as Edgar liked to call it—with its ever-expanding bureaucracy made up of men who had been office-bound for years. Communication within the Field was becoming a sterile business. Many active agents thought of headquarters as a place for timeservers and promotion-hunters, a source of meaningless paperwork and fatuous orders.

British MI-5 officer Peter Wright, at the FBI on a liaison visit, thought the Seat of Government a "magnificent triumphalist museum" peopled by vacant-looking staff. At a meeting with Edgar and two Assistant Directors, he was shocked to see how the aides "for all outward toughness and the seniority of their positions . . . were cowed."

Fear was woven into the fabric of FBI life. Edgar punished Acting Assistant Director Howard Fletcher, who had tried to change an unfair wages system, by excluding him from promotion. Bernard Brown, Assistant Agent in Charge in New York, was demoted and transferred to the boondocks for commenting to a journalist without permission. One man—his name is deleted from the FBI release—was reported for telling a risqué joke to a class at the FBI Academy. "I regret very much having told such a story," he told Edgar in a groveling letter. "I want to assure you, as I did Mr. Tolson, that I do not consider myself a joke-ster. . . . I have, of course, learned my lesson."

The myth of the infallible Director had been institution-alized. "Boys," an instructor told a group of rookie recruits, "J. Edgar Hoover is an inspiration to us all. Indeed, it has been said, and truly, 'The sunshine of his presence lights our way.'" Lectures to recruits were approved in advance by Edgar and his aides.

The first test for new agents came at the end of the training course, when they filed into the presence to shake Edgar's hand. As they waited in the anteroom, men were seen frantically wiping their hands on their pants. A moist palm was enough to end an agent's career before it began. So were pimples or a bald head.

Once, as a group of recruits left his office, Edgar summoned the instructor back. "One of them," he snapped, "is a pinhead. Get rid of him!" Afraid to ask which man Edgar meant, the instructor surreptitiously checked his pupils' hat sizes. There were three men with small heads, all of them size 6⅞. To placate Edgar, and to protect Training Division officials, all three were fired.

"In our class," said former agent Jack Shaw, "we had a kid from Kansas called Leroy, who'd been a schoolteacher. He had a high-pitched voice, and this didn't fit with the Bureau stereotype: tall, commanding, blond, blue-eyed, the perfect accent. Word came down about this, so they worked on Leroy to lower his voice. He got it to a manly level, and he was smart and sharp in every other way. But when he went for his final test, the Assistant Director looked at him and said, 'Have your ears always protruded like that?' Leroy had large, flapping ears, and they told him his ears were wrong. He left that day."

An agent who lost his gas credit card received a letter of reprimand from Edgar. Agent Francis Flanagan was talking on the phone one day, hat on and cigarette in mouth while trying to keep a key informant on the line, when Edgar walked in. His punishment, for failing to spring to his feet, was an immediate transfer to Sioux Falls, South Dakota.

During the fifties word reached headquarters from San Francisco that a nude belly dancer had performed at an agent's retirement party. Edgar ordered all 200 partygoers to file a report, but not one admitted having seen the dancer. Each claimed he had been in the men's room during the performance. For once, by sheer weight of numbers, Edgar's wrath was thwarted.

In the sixties, a clerk called Thomas Carter would be subjected to an inquisition because of an anonymous letter claiming he had slept with a young woman. Carter admitted spending the night with the woman, who was his fiancée, but insisted he had done so "clothed in Bermudas and a sports shirt." One of his roommates was then asked if he had heard the bed creaking. He had not, but Edgar fired Carter anyway. Carter sued, arguing unfair dismissal, and the courts decided in his favor.

Grown men tolerated such nonsense because an agent's job had great advantages. It was well paid, sometimes exciting, and there was the prospect of retirement after twenty years, a decent pension and a second career based on the FBI background.

There was also safety in numbers. It was an unlucky man who attracted the full blast of Edgar's wrath or who suffered under the worst of his centurions. In offices far away from the throne, agents found ways to function as well as the system would permit—and at its best it was very good indeed. As in the Army, men put up with the sillier rules, kept their noses clean and got on with the job.

Yet the rules seem to have become increasingly absurd. Field agents, for example, had to spend a minimum number of hours out of the office, even when there was nothing to do. This was obligatory at times when the headquarters' inspection team was expected. "Stay out of the office," one official told his men. "If you've seen all the movies, then go to the library or someplace. . . . The main thing is to stay out of here."

"Since we weren't allowed to drink coffee in the office except before 8:15 A.M.," former agent Jack Shaw recalled, "agents used to go down to Casey's Kitchen on Sixty-seventh Street. John Malone, the Assistant Director in Charge, would position himself in the lobby of the office to catch them coming back. He was infamous for shouting, 'Hey, you there!' as an agent came in through the swing door. Sometimes the agent would turn right around and go out again, with Malone chasing him out into the street, yelling."

Word sometimes reached the agents at Casey's that "Cement-head" Malone, one of Edgar's closest associates, was on his way to flush them out. "Seventeen or eighteen guys would abandon their breakfasts and clear out through the fire escape, rushing pell-mell, brushing pedestrians aside."

For the agent and his family packed off to the other end of

the nation for some trivial transgression, there was nothing to laugh about. "The worst thing," said a former Agent in Charge who suffered such punishment, "is what happens to you in the eyes of your family. 'You must have done something wrong or Mr. Hoover wouldn't have demoted you,' they say. You can't ever explain it, even in your own family. You lose faith in yourself. The things that used to be true aren't true anymore. I don't think Mr. Hoover really understood this phase of his disciplinary actions, because he never had a family—wife and kids, I mean."

The massive file on Agent Nelson Gibbons, who served from 1954 to 1962, is a catalogue of calculated cruelty. Gibbons came to the FBI after war service in the Marines and a spell on the police force. He proved an outstanding agent, attracting six commendations and for years no censures at all—a state of grace achieved by few. He was brave in action against armed criminals and won praise from Edgar for unmasking a Soviet spy. Gibbons became a Resident Agent, running a small FBI office on his own, at the age of thirty-three.

His troubles began only in 1958, when—at sixty-three—Edgar began worrying excessively about his health. There was nothing significantly wrong, but, not least judging from the bewildering number of doctors he consulted, he had become something of a hypochondriac. That year Edgar read an insurance company prospectus that listed ideal weights in proportion to height. It told him he was overweight, and, according to the FBI press office, he went on a diet that brought his weight down from 203 pounds to 170.

What the Director did for his health, agents were expected to do, too. Agents in Charge were charged with monitoring the weight of every man in the Bureau. As a health precaution, properly administered, the idea had merit. As an iron rule, rigidly enforced under pain of punishment, it was a disaster.

It was certainly that for Agent Gibbons, a thickset fellow, nearly six feet tall, who usually weighed more than 190 pounds. He weighed in at 195 when Edgar's checks started, and the examiner recommended he lose seven pounds.

Gibbons tried hard to conform, even though his own doctor thought his weight reasonable given his size. The agent duly lost seven pounds, but then his weight began straying up into the low 190s again. That was not good enough for headquarters.

In 1960, after being turned down for promotion because of the weight issue, Gibbons made a declaration of independence. He said he was happy with his weight at 190 and asked to see Edgar—a right theoretically extended to all agents. Edgar refused, ordering Gibbons to be transferred to Detroit and weighed every thirty days.

Gibbons was now on the Bureau "bicycle." Soon he was moved again, to Mobile, Alabama, then—two months later—to Oklahoma City. There he was twice censured and suspended without pay. Yet senior officials reported he had "no surplus fat," and he continued to work out at the YMCA. For all the abuse, he said he wanted to go on working for "the best organization in the world."

Unimpressed, Edgar condemned Gibbons for not being a "team worker" and transferred him again—to Butte, Montana. Then again, to Anchorage, Alaska, where petty punishment continued. At last, after a fatuous interrogation as to whether and how often he might have gotten drunk while in the Marines, long before he joined the FBI, Gibbons cracked. He quit his post and cabled Edgar, saying he felt "mentally unable" to continue.

Though Gibbons never suffered mental illness, before or after this ordeal, the FBI found a psychiatrist who diagnosed him as "paranoid." He was retired on a disability pension, an event Edgar perceived as some kind of victory. "Good riddance," he scrawled on a final memo, "of bad rubbish."

Nelson Gibbons was lucky. In New York, while on a crash diet to meet Edgar's weight standards, Agent George Blue collapsed and died at his desk.

The experience of Jack Shaw and his wife May, ten years later, was another Orwellian nightmare. Agent Shaw, a law graduate and former Marine captain, had served with distinction since 1963. He was thirty-seven years old and the father of four children under the age of ten when he enrolled for master's degree classes at New York's John Jay College of Criminal Justice, a prestigious course for law enforcement personnel. Once qualified, Shaw hoped, he would go on to become an instructor at the FBI Academy.

When his sociology professor made some harsh criticism of the FBI, Shaw jumped to defend it. Later, however, he decided to prepare a detailed critique of the organization's good and bad points. A bad point, he wrote, was that the Bureau had become ossified. "We are not simply rooted in tradition," he wrote, "we're stuck in it up to our eyeballs. And it all revolves around one key figure, the life and exploits of J. Edgar Hoover."

Though this was hardly the stuff of revolution, Shaw was apprehensive. "I feel certain," he wrote his professor, "that all of what I have said will be retained by you in complete confidence. In the Bureau's eyes, of course, however academically intended, my statements would constitute a prima facie case of *heresy*. I would prefer not to be martyred this calendar year."

Martyred he was, because of his own openness. Shaw made the mistake of giving the draft of the letter to a trusted FBI secretary to type. She in turn gave it to a colleague, and the private communication was private no more. The agent was soon being interrogated by Assistant Director Malone.

"It was clear from the start that my head was on the platter," Shaw recalled. "The inquisition went on and on, from 4:00 P.M. till about 9:00. I tried to tell Malone this hadn't been some covert, clandestine operation. No harm had been done. I hadn't even mailed the critique to my professor yet."

Reason, however, played no further part in relations between Shaw and the FBI. He was suspended "for possible insubordination and criticism of the Bureau" and told to hand in his badge and gun and go home. There he heard his sentence: one month's suspension without pay, six months' probation and a transfer to Butte, Montana, for failing to report his professor's original criticism of the FBI.

An FBI official called the president of John Jay College,

Dr. Donald Riddle, saying that no FBI students would attend the school while Shaw's professor remained on the faculty. The professor stayed, so the FBI men departed, as did others—studying at American University, in Washington, D.C.

Jack Shaw, meanwhile, sat at home worrying about his future and about his wife, who was sick. In her condition a move to Montana was out of the question, so Shaw resigned. Edgar accepted the resignation "with prejudice," a blot on Shaw's record that would make it virtually impossible for him to get work with another federal agency or a major company. A star FBI agent had been destroyed over a private letter no one had yet read, which had never even been sent.

Within months of Shaw's resignation, his wife's illness was diagnosed as terminal cancer. At first, as she lay desperately sick in the hospital, her husband's FBI colleagues rallied around. Two agents offered to give blood for her transfusions, then shamefacedly retracted. They had been told not to associate with Shaw, because he was "in touch with enemies of the Bureau."

The Bureau even used false pretenses to spy on Shaw as he sat in the hospital with his dying wife. The wife of another agent, a nurse, showed up in uniform in two different hospitals and chatted with Shaw as if out of genuine sympathy. Later, when Shaw saw his FBI file, he found detailed reports of the conversations. The nurse had been commended by her husband's superiors for "penetrating Shaw's inner circle."

After his wife's death, Shaw took his case to the American Civil Liberties Union. Senior senators raised the issue in Congress, and the former agent became a cause célèbre. The FBI settled the matter with a cash payment and removal of the "with prejudice" slur from his record. Shaw is today an Assistant Commissioner in charge of investigations for the Immigration and Naturalization Service.

Edgar had written his damning "with prejudice" notation, a virtual sentence to unemployment, in the full knowledge that Shaw's wife was seriously ill. Shaw and others who

complained, he said, were "malcontents or crybabies."
Edgar never accepted that he had been wrong.

The cult of the personality reigned at the FBI in a way
unparalleled in American government, outside the presidency. When Edgar and Clyde traveled, men worked feverishly to smooth their way. Gas station toilets were inspected
in advance in case the Director should need to use the
facilities. A faulty generator in one of Edgar's limousines
triggered a nationwide operation. Agents got help from the
management of Cadillac, delayed a commercial flight and
rushed about with sirens wailing, to get the part to Cleve-
land in time. In Edgar's hotel suite, agents quickly removed
bottles of liquor that had been only partially consumed. For
fear of being poisoned, Edgar reportedly insisted on drinking from newly opened bottles.

Across the country, agents were taught the wisdom of
writing regularly to congratulate their boss on his birthday,
the anniversary of his appointment or simply to tell him he
was wonderful. "He loved to get those letters," said William
Sullivan. "You couldn't be too lavish in telling him what a
great job he was doing for the country. Tolson had a
standard phrase that he used all the time: 'The Director will
go down in history as the greatest man of the century.'"

In 1958, Agent Arthur Murtagh sent Edgar a courteous
letter commenting on Bureau personnel policy, and mailed
it, according to routine, through Roy Moore, his Agent in
Charge. Moore, a mild-mannered man of vast experience,
astonished him with his response.

"Art," Moore said, "I can't send that letter. . . . You don't
understand Bureau politics. . . . You must understand that
you're working for a crazy maniac and that our duty is to
find out what he wants and to create the world that he
believes in, and to show him that's the way things are. . . ."

These comments would be quoted twenty years later, in
sworn testimony to a congressional committee. In the late
fifties, although many men thought Edgar had lost his
mental balance, few dared to say so out loud.

Four years after Edgar's death, during a Justice Department inquiry into the misuse of FBI funds, it would emerge that Edgar had been corrupt. It had started with little things. A well-timed gift, his officials learned, could win the master's favor. It might be a birthday cake, sent from Miami to Washington on an agent's lap. Or, at headquarters, a regular supply of flowers. "He really liked pretty flowers," said Cartha DeLoach. "That was a good thing to give him. I personally or my group made sure that we gave him azaleas. That was his favorite."

The higher the official, the more costly the giving. "Hoover was always hitting us for gifts," said William Sullivan, "and we'd have to buy extremely expensive ones. They handled it very cleverly. It would always come out of Tolson's office to us. . . . For example, I was told he wanted a garbage masher. We Bureau officials paid for it out of our own pockets." It was wise to pay up. Edgar reportedly kept a record of those who rendered tribute and those who didn't. His own gifts to colleagues, on the other hand, were usually purchased at government expense.

Edgar lived virtually free, at taxpayers' expense. The FBI Exhibits Section, which made displays for official use, had been Edgar's personal building contractor. His house in Rock Creek Park, the Justice Department report revealed:

> was completely painted and major maintenance performed inside and out every year while he vacationed in California. The Exhibits Section designed, constructed and built a portico on the front of his house, and a lighted fish pond complete with pump. Shelves, telephone stands, and other furniture was built and furnished. A handcrafted oriental fruitbowl was made. . . . Home appliances, air conditioners, stereo equipment, tape recorders, television sets and electric wiring were serviced and repaired by Radio Engineering Section employees. . . . Employees were on call night and day for complete repair and maintenance of the entire home and grounds.

FBI men serviced Edgar's lawn mower and snowblower, maintained his yard, replaced sod twice a year, installed artificial turf, planted shrubbery, constructed a deck at the rear of the house, erected a redwood fence and laid a flagstone court and sidewalks. When Edgar complained of the smell of bacon at breakfast, the FBI installed a powerful fan. When he fussed that his television took too long to warm up, FBI technicians labored to solve the problem. If even a light bulb failed, the FBI replaced it.

Tolson, who fancied himself an inventor, has been credited with dreaming up two items of gadgetry: a bottlecap opener and a system to open and close windows automatically. The bottle opener is remembered as a "Rube Goldberg flop." When it failed to work, an official recalled, "Tolson or Hoover came up with the idea to gold-plate the things and give them away to 'friends of the Bureau.'" Edgar's millionaire friends, such as Clint Murchison, were among the recipients.

The window system was later installed, with accompanying propaganda fanfare, in President Johnson's bedroom at the White House. The Justice Department inquiry, however, established that the gadgets were developed not by Tolson but by the FBI laboratory, at public expense.

Deputy Attorney General Harold Tyler, who supervised the probe, concluded that Edgar "lived like an Oriental potentate." Edgar declared he would eat ice cream only out of a round package—so it was flown in and kept in a freezer in the basement of the Justice Department. He wanted sides of beef from Colorado—they were flown in, too, all for free.

"There were the craziest things," recalled John Dowd, the prosecuting attorney who led the investigation. "Hoover had a heated toilet seat, invented in the FBI laboratory. When he decided it was either a quarter of an inch too high or too low, it had to be redone. Then there was the raccoon turd. One day Hoover opened the door of his patio, and there was a turd. He had the laboratory come and remove it, to get it analyzed. It was priority number one that morning. No matter what official business they had in the goddamn lab, it was 'You identify that turd and report.' Tolson was going apeshit, threatening to fire people and asking again and again, 'What is it? What is it?' Some guy in the lab said, 'Hey, it's gotta be a wild animal. I've got a friend at the Smithsonian.'

"So they took the turd to the Smithsonian, and the Smithsonian identified the turd. There were berry shells in it that raccoons eat. So they told Hoover it was raccoon shit. Hoover ordered a trap built to destroy that raccoon. They built a trap and installed it on the patio. And the following morning the neighbor's cat was spread all over the wall of the house.

"When you saw the whole picture," said Dowd, "it wasn't funny at all. This was the Director of the FBI helping himself, using his power to obtain whatever he wanted. He didn't have any out-of-pocket expenses like the rest of us."

The investigators also stumbled on the "safe" oil investments by Edgar's millionaire friends, the hundreds of thousands of dollars' worth of free accommodation at La Jolla and the vacation transport paid for with Bureau funds. The labor for work done by FBI employees at Edgar's home, thousands of man-hours of it, had been provided free. It was clear, too, that much of the cost had been paid out of shadowy FBI "special funds."

Suspicion focused on the FBI Recreation Fund, ostensibly created to promote athletic activities for ordinary agents, and its subsidiary, the Library Fund. No one could explain why the fund bore this name; it had little to do with books. Edgar's aides had destroyed its records soon after his death. Fund money had paid for Edgar's personal public relations, and Exhibits chief John Dunphy admitted having pilfered petty cash to pay for "nonofficial projects or 'gifts' to the Director."

Few of the miscreants were punished. Former Assistant Directors John Mohr and Nicholas Callahan, both deemed to have violated the law, escaped prosecution thanks to the statute of limitations. Callahan, still in office when the inquiry began, was forced to resign. John Dunphy pleaded guilty to converting FBI property to his own use, and he too resigned.

Had they been alive, Edgar and Clyde would have faced prosecution and dismissal. Statements by prosecutor Dowd and Michael Shaheen, of the Justice Department's Office of Professional Responsibility, indicate the pair were guilty of several federal offenses, including private use of government property and accepting gifts from lesser-paid employees. The scale of Edgar's abuse would have made him liable to up to ten years in prison and automatic dismissal.

Dowd, the former head of the Department Strike Force formed to fight organized crime, remembered above all the atmosphere of fear he encountered at the FBI. "There I was," he said, "interviewing employees who were just as scared as the loan sharks, bookies and all the other people I'd had to deal with in pursuing Mafia chieftains. There were people in my office absolutely trembling, relating twenty or thirty years of this sordid conduct. They were still afraid, even though Hoover himself was dead. I've investigated corruption for many years, but I've seen no greater betrayal of the public trust."

It seems, however, that Edgar was guilty of an even greater dereliction of duty. For his own secret reasons, he refused to confront the Mafia.

CHAPTER 21

"The art of the police consists in not seeing what there is no use seeing."

Napoleon Bonaparte

ONE OF THE LAST MAFIA BOSSES OF THE OLD TRADITION, CARMINE "The Doctor" Lombardozzi, was asked in 1990 about the mob's attitude toward J. Edgar Hoover. Lombardozzi, known as "the Italian Meyer Lansky," continued to direct financial operations for the Gambino family until his recent death. "J. Edgar Hoover," he replied, "was in our pocket. He was no one we needed to fear."[1]

The growth of the American Mafia coincided precisely with Edgar's career. Its seeds had been sown when Edgar was a little boy, when Italian and Sicilian immigrants poured into the United States bearing the bacillus of Cosa Nostra, "Our thing." They formed ghetto gangs that battled the authorities and one another, and began to practice their specialty, extortion enforced by violence.

While Edgar was growing up, the gangs remained disparate and unstable. But by the time he became FBI Director, in the spring of 1924, Prohibition had opened 200,000 speakeasies. The bootlegger was in business by popular demand, and few cared that bootlegger was synonymous with crook. This was when the mob empire was founded, on a basis of booze, prostitution, loan-sharking and labor racketeering.

The names that made the fortunes—Luciano, Costello, Capone, Siegel, Torrio, Dutch Schultz, Longy Zwillman— were in league with the captains of Prohibition commerce, liquor dealers like Lewis Rosenstiel, forging alliances that were to make them multimillionaires when liquor became legal again. In time, at least two of these characters would forge relationships with Edgar. Around 1930, following their first high-level conferences, the nation's top criminals divided the United States into agreed spheres of influence operating under a formal alliance.

Edgar's life and rise to power ran parallel to that of the mob, in significant phases. Professionally, his early performance was fairly good. The Bureau responded well in the early twenties, when it was used to enforce Prohibition in Ohio. It was Edgar's agents who first arrested Al Capone in 1929—for contempt of court—although the Internal Revenue Service eventually sent him to jail.

In the thirties, Edgar concentrated on soft targets, kidnappers and bandits like Dillinger, but he did seem seriously interested in the mob. He set up the Hoodlum Watch, which required all Bureau offices to collate information on local crime bosses, and he announced a national drive against racketeers, or "organized business criminals."

In 1935, not to be upstaged by Thomas Dewey, then Special Prosecutor for New York, Edgar declared Dutch Schultz "Public Enemy Number One." Soon he was sounding like a crusader against organized crime. "Racketeering," he said early the following year, "is a problem which, if not solved, will destroy eventually the security of American industrial life and the faith of our people in American institutions."

In 1937, as Baltimore society danced the night away at the Preakness Ball, Edgar personally led dozens of agents on raids against the city's brothels. Clyde, who was at his side, earned the nickname "Slugger" for knocking out a man who resisted arrest. The premises targeted were operated by Italian gangsters, and—according to notes kept by the agent who organized the operation—Edgar "was interested in the big racketeers and the tide of dirty money that flowed from the houses to the racketeers and through them filtered out to local protectors, police, small-time politicians and even ultimately into the coffers of state political machines."

There could hardly be a more succinct description of the way organized crime works. And Edgar pressed on. In August, after swoops in three states, Edgar made a point of telling newsmen that one of those arrested—for running prostitution rackets—worked for Charles "Lucky" Luciano.

Edgar was getting to the heart of things. Luciano, specialists agree, was the father of organized crime in America, founder with Meyer Lansky of the national syndicate, a key man behind the Atlantic City mob convention of 1929 and the victor in the gang wars that followed. He had been in prison since 1936, following his prosecution by Dewey for vice offenses, but still wielded vast power. On the outside Meyer Lansky, Frank Costello and Joe Adonis continued to run the empire of crime. In targeting the Luciano network, Edgar was threatening the heartland of the Mafia.

Then, abruptly, Edgar's attitude changed. From the late thirties on, the FBI's war with organized crime became a nominal affair, a thing of occasional sound but no fury at all. The American criminal, Edgar was insisting by 1938, was "not of a foreign country, but of American stock with a highly patriotic American name." Comforting words for crime bosses with names like Costello and Luciano, Genovese and Adonis, Lansky and Siegel.

World War II was boomtime for organized crime, a boom boosted by new rackets and black marketeering. The New York mob leadership won official approval by helping to protect the waterfront against Nazi saboteurs, thus easing the way for Luciano's release and deportation. After the war, Costello, Lansky and the crime empire flourished out of control, while Edgar did nothing.

Sometimes it was as if he was deliberately thwarting progress against the mob—as in the case of James Ragen, owner of a racing-wire service covering half the country. Whoever controlled that wire had enormous power over gambling operations, and in 1946 the Mafia tried to muscle in. Ragen resisted and began telling the FBI all he knew about the rackets. Yet Edgar refused to provide protection —and the mob killed Ragen.

"The Ragen affair," said William Roemer, later the FBI's star expert on the Chicago mob, "is a very, very significant moment for any study of J. Edgar Hoover and organized crime. When Ragen started talking, the FBI opened a real operation against organized crime in the city for the first time ever. But as soon as Ragen was killed, Hoover dropped the investigation. For eleven years afterwards, that was the end of it."

According to the then Attorney General, Ragen's revelations led to "very high places," including Henry Crown, the Chicago financier, and the Annenberg family, which had originally owned the racing-wire service. Edgar, however, claimed "the people Ragen pointed to had now reformed."

Pete Pitchess, the longtime Sheriff of Los Angeles County, was an FBI agent in the forties. "Organized crime," he recalled, "was just not a concern of the Bureau. We knew it existed, but there were hardly any prosecutions, and we knew this was FBI policy. I myself had to deal with Bugsy Siegel [a key associate of Meyer Lansky who opened up the West Coast to syndicate operations]. When Siegel took it upon himself that he would like to talk to me, I was afraid even to tell the Bureau.

"I didn't tell the Agent in Charge I was going to see him. We'd stand at a street corner on Sunset Boulevard, in front of the old La Rue restaurant. Siegel gave me information on his enemies, but we just put it in some intelligence file—we didn't dare call it 'Mafia.' That, we'd been told, didn't exist. So we simply dumped it in a file, or quietly passed it on to the police."[2]

Neil Welch, a distinguished former SAC who eventually made organized crime his specialty, became an agent in the early fifties. "When I was in Boston," he recalled, "I used to investigate theft of interstate shipments—whole truckloads of freight—that was totally dominated by Mafia union racketeering and the Teamsters Union. It was frustrating; we were trying to solve the theft of a single shipment of shoes, or chickens, when it was obvious to us all that the answer wasn't in that approach. The whole thing was controlled by organized crime, yet it was never made the subject of investigation. It was just inexcusable blindness. I don't know how you can have the responsibility that Hoover did, and the FBI did, and just ignore it, for all practical purposes."

In 1951, millions of Americans watched on television as a procession of gangsters appeared before the Senate Special Committee to Investigate Crime in Interstate Commerce, remembered today as the Kefauver Committee. After hearing 800 witnesses, it concluded that there was indeed "a nationwide crime syndicate known as the Mafia," and that there were "indications of a centralized direction and control" by Frank Costello and Meyer Lansky and others.

Edgar had appeared before the committee to congratulate its members on having revealed "the unholy alliance between the criminal element and officialdom," and to mouth courtesies to the senators. Behind the scenes, it was a different story.

Senator Kefauver revealed to Jack Anderson, then a young reporter, that Edgar had tried to prevent the committee from being established in the first place. "He told me the FBI tried to block it," Anderson recalled. "They worked with the Senate Majority Leader, Scott Lucas. Hoover knew that if the public got alarmed about organized crime, the job would go to the FBI. And he didn't want the job."

Kefauver's Assistant Counsel, Joseph Nellis, was still angry in 1990, when he recalled the way Edgar treated the committee. "We had a long series of meetings with him off the record, at which he told us, 'We don't know anything about the Mafia or the families in New York. We haven't followed this.' He told us what we were learning about the Mafia wasn't true, but we didn't believe him. It was dreadful. We tried to enlist the FBI's help in every major city, but got none. Hoover was polite to the senators—he had to be, because they controlled his purse strings. But he gave us nothing."

Heavily censored documents in Kefauver's FBI file strongly suggest Edgar gathered smear material on the Senator. He forbade agents to join other law enforcement officials at a meeting with Kefauver and refused requests for FBI protection of committee witnesses—even after two had been murdered.

Edgar told the committee organized crime should be dealt with not by the FBI but by local police forces. Given the chance to call for new laws giving the FBI wider jurisdiction, he said the existing laws were just fine. When the committee recommended the creation of a national crime commission, Edgar made sure it did not happen.

In 1953, more than a year after Kefauver's report had been issued, FBI Assistant Director Alan Belmont wrote a memo to Assistant to the Director D. M. Ladd. "Maffia [*sic*]," he wrote, "is an alleged organization. . . . The organization's existence in the U.S. is doubtful." This was the truth according to Edgar, a truth maintained at the top of the FBI, in defiance of all the facts. The street agents who actually encountered organized crime had to behave as if black was white.

"During the early 1950s," recalled veteran agent Anthony Villano, "two agents caught a made guy [formally enrolled mafioso] in midcrime. . . . He relaxed and started to tell them war stories—Mafia war stories. They were astonished at his recitation of the table of organization in criminal circles. They wrote it all down and filed reports in New York. None of the brass believed a word of it; after all, the Director had announced that organized crime didn't exist. It was filed and forgotten."

"At headquarters," recalled former agent William Turner, "there wasn't even a section working on organized crime. In the field, what we did get on top mobsters was just dropped into the General Investigative Intelligence file—to be forgotten."

During the writing of this book, three former Attorneys General, a District Attorney, the former police chief of a major city, a congressional consultant on organized crime, several former Justice Department officials, a professor of law and nineteen former FBI employees, including several Assistant Directors, were asked why Edgar failed to tackle organized crime. None had a satisfactory explanation. Some thought that, because cases would be difficult to make, Edgar was afraid his annual statistics would suffer—that the FBI would appear to be slipping. Some thought he feared contact with gamblers and hoodlums would corrupt his agents. Others mentioned Edgar's supposed animosity toward Harry Anslinger, the head of the Narcotics Bureau. Because Anslinger saw the hand of the mob everywhere in the narcotics rackets—so went this theory—Edgar automatically rejected the notion.[3]

Some pointed to the excuse Edgar himself offered in the sixties, after change had been forced on him. "The truth of the matter," he claimed, "is that the FBI had very little jurisdiction in the field of organized crime prior to September 1961." This was not true. The FBI had had some local jurisdiction in crimes of violence since 1934, and many federal statutes covered mob activity. In any case, when Edgar did want a change in the law, Congress generally obliged. On the question of organized crime, he never asked.

Edgar's claim about having no jurisdiction, said the historian Arthur Schlesinger, Jr., "was a transparent fraud." "If they want to do it," said Director of Prisons James Bennett, "it's within the jurisdiction of the FBI. If they don't want to do it, they tell you it's outside the jurisdiction of the FBI."

Former FBI official Neil Welch could conclude only that Edgar's attitude was a mystery. "None of the usual excuses," he said, "are convincing. Hoover and his top people knew of the existence of the Mafia. They knew from the agents' reports that routinely referred to it, certainly all through the fifties. . . . Hoover's attitude was so contrary to reality as to be a reason for great speculation. It's a mystery. . . ."

The clues that explain Edgar's behavior lead back to the mid-thirties. It was then, as the American Mafia was establishing itself, that he had begun enjoying national celebrity.

Egged on by the columnist Walter Winchell, he started making regular weekend trips to New York, there to enter a social world that put him perilously close to organized crime.

The danger started with Winchell himself. Any decent crime reporter makes it his business to know criminals on a personal basis, but Winchell did not know where to draw the line. The journalist was on close terms with Owney "The Killer" Madden, a mob associate of Meyer Lansky's. He intervened with the *Herald Tribune* when it made repeated references to Madden's murderous past, then accepted a new car from the mobster as a reward.

Winchell was on first-name terms with Lansky himself, and often dined with him in New York and Florida. As the mobster's widow has revealed, the columnist even asked Lansky's permission before writing sensitive stories about the mob. He knew Frank Costello—Winchell called him "Francisco"—even better. They both had apartments at 115 Central Park West and met there frequently. In the fifties, when Costello was targeted by the Kefauver Committee, Winchell rushed out an article saying what a good, misunderstood fellow he was.

The Stork Club, where Edgar and Clyde joined Winchell as regulars, was infested by the mob. The nominal proprietor, Sherman Billingsley, was a former bootlegger with several convictions. Yet Edgar gave him a character reference for his gun permit and spoke of him as "a very good friend." Costello, who may have been the club's real owner, leaned on the unions for Billingsley when necessary.

It was the same in Florida, where Edgar vacationed regularly. His favorite Miami haunt, from the late thirties, was Joe's Stone Crabs restaurant—also frequented by Capone, Costello and Lansky. Lansky, who stamped on industrial trouble at Joe's as Costello did at the Stork, liked to come in for a pink gin. The restaurant's owner, Jesse Weiss, agreed in 1988 that he was on close personal terms with gangsters while simultaneously "very, very, very close friends" with Edgar.

"Jesse had friends the Bureau was looking for," Mrs. Weiss recalled. "Edgar would be sitting there, and there might be some of these fellows sitting at the other side of the dining room." Sometimes Weiss puzzled over the way Edgar ignored a man's known crimes. "I'd ask him, 'You had so-and-so on him for twenty years, for Christ's sake. Why didn't you do anything?'"

Edgar was protective, at the highest level, of millionaire developer and casino owner Del Webb, best known to the public as the owner of the New York Yankees baseball team. "The Las Vegas casinos," Edgar would one day assure President Johnson, "represent the worst element of the Cosa Nostra—except, of course, for Del Webb's."

"Hoover gave Webb a pass. He was his buddy," said Justice Department attorney William Hundley, who was present at the White House that day. "No bugs went in on Webb's places." FBI sources and mob security personnel confirm that establishments owned by Webb went uninvestigated.

Webb was deeply involved with organized crime for thirty years, an involvement he concealed with a series of fronts and middlemen. Through proxies, he was in business with Lansky, Bugsy Siegel and a string of other criminals. Webb and Edgar, observed the former FBI Agent in Charge in Las Vegas, were "very close friends." When Edgar visited the city, he reportedly stayed at Webb's hotels, free of charge. Like Edgar, Webb was a frequent guest at the Del Charro, Clint Murchison's hotel in California.

The Del Charro was small, and in its comparative privacy Edgar rubbed shoulders with a bevy of white-collar crooks. Those welcomed at the hotel in the fifties included Ed Levinson, John Drew and Ray Ryan, all notorious names to rackets investigators. Drew once departed leaving a valuable antique, a bottle of pre-Prohibition whiskey, as a present for Edgar.

Far from avoiding such men, Edgar socialized with them. The hotel manager, Allan Witwer, saw him huddled with Art Samish, California's political fixer supreme and mob front man, soon after Samish emerged from a long stint in jail. The pair lounged around talking, said Witwer, "without apparent embarrassment to either of them."

By 1959, the year he saw Edgar with Samish, such encounters no longer astonished Witwer. It had been different five years earlier, when Dub McClanahan, oilman and gambler, came to stay—and sat by the pool talking with Edgar each morning. The manager thought of McClanahan as just another friend of Clint Murchison's—until a friendly FBI man enlightened him.

"My office faced the swimming pool," said Witwer, "and one of the agents was in there with me one evening. He looked out the window—we had torches by the pool at night—and he saw McClanahan, and he said, 'Allan, what's he doing here? D'you know who he is?' And I said, 'Sure.' And he said, 'I bet you don't. He's a partner of New Orleans Mafia boss Carlos Marcello.' And I said, 'Well, tell Hoover that! He has breakfast with him every morning.' I got a kind of shock that Hoover would allow McClanahan to be with him at all."

McClanahan remained Edgar's regular poolside companion at the Del Charro until 1959, when he went on trial for tax evasion.[4] Another, reportedly, was Johnny Roselli, the West Coast henchman of Chicago Mafia boss Sam Giancana. "I knew Hoover," Roselli would say breezily years later. "I'd buy him drinks, and we'd talk. It was fun to be with the Director of the FBI like that."

In the mid-fifties, as Murchison's two sons became more involved in the business, the family's money became inextricably involved with Mafia money. The Murchisons' affairs were probed constantly between 1955 and 1965—by two congressional committees and no fewer than nine federal agencies.

In the early fifties, according to a Senate committee, 20 percent of the Murchison Oil Lease Company was owned by the Vito Genovese crime family. Handridge Oil, a Murchison-owned outfit, was the subject of a deal with Las Vegas gamblers involving massive security violations. There were also to be deals with Jimmy Hoffa, the crooked boss of the Teamsters Union, and Clint, Jr., established financial ties with Mafia boss Marcello.

It was Edgar who suggested the Murchisons hire one of his own former administrative assistants, Thomas Webb. A seventeen-year FBI veteran, Webb was to have an interest in the Murchison meat deal that was part of the Bobby Baker scandal during the Johnson presidency. According to Baker, he and Webb once traveled together to make a political contribution—cash in a white envelope, no questions asked. Webb, Baker said, was "the fixer for the Murchisons in Washington, the bagman." Also, according to Baker and others, he "worshiped" Edgar.

It was a Murchison aide who introduced Edgar to Washington lobbyist Irving Davidson. Davidson has been linked to the Teamsters and organized crime. He was involved in the Murchison meat deal and, more recently, was the go-between for Clint Murchison, Jr., and Carlos Marcello during the sting operation that sent the Mafia boss to prison in 1983.

"I'm a great admirer of Mr. Hoover, and I did have access," said Davidson. "We used to have parties before the Redskin games, at Tom Webb's house or my house, and Hoover always came to them. He was a darned good friend. I lived around the corner from him, three quarters of a block. I'd go over and say hello to him and Clyde Tolson. If Mr. Tolson was sick I'd bring him a Cowboy jersey or some Polish kielbasa."[5]

In the late fifties, while monitoring a bug on Murray "The Camel" Humphries in Chicago, surprised agents heard their boss' name mentioned. Humphries was the head of the "Connection Guys," the criminal group with special responsibility for corruption of public officials. He was talking, with evident knowledge and interest, about Edgar's friendship with Clint Murchison.

"Murchison owned a piece of Hoover," Bobby Baker mused in 1990. "Rich people always try to put their money with the sheriff, because they're looking for protection. Hoover was the personification of law and order and

officially against gangsters and everything, so it was a plus
for a rich man to be identified with him. That's why men
like Murchison made it their business to let everyone know
Hoover was their friend. You can do a lot of illegal things if
the head lawman is your buddy."

Everywhere they went, Edgar and Clyde indulged a
passion for horseracing. At Hialeah in Florida and Del Mar
in California, at Bowie and Pimlico in Maryland, Charles
Town in West Virginia and Belmont in New York, Edgar's
face was familiar for forty years. Edgar and Clyde had
special tables, and usually complimentary boxes, at every
track. There was a horse called Director J.E. in Maryland, a
J. Edgar in Texas and a J. Edgar Ruler in California. At
Laurel, in Maryland, they still run a J. Edgar Hoover
Handicap.

Racing, and the gambling that went with it, became an
addiction for Edgar. An in-house joke had it that the FBI
agent whose hair grayed fastest was the man who had to get
the Director to the track through rush-hour traffic. Headquarters staff were dispatched to the Library of Congress to
dig out racing information. Edgar issued standing orders
that he was not to be bothered on Saturdays and, according
to DeLoach, once defied an order by President Johnson to
return for a meeting with Cabinet members. Racing got
Edgar overexcited. After a run of luck one afternoon, former
Speaker Tip O'Neill recalled, he took another man's car by
mistake and drove it all the way back to Washington.

Edgar encouraged his oil millionaire friends in 1954
when, not content with owning a hotel near Del Mar, they
bought the track itself. The group they bought it from was
headed by Al Hart, a liquor distributor with links to the
Chicago mob—another dubious character with whom
Edgar had socialized.

"At first," said Del Charro manager Witwer, "Murchison
and Richardson were not only turned down by Hart and his
directors, they were practically thrown out of the office. And
Murchison said, 'If those fellas won't deal with me, we'll

sick old J. Edgar on them.' And Hoover sent two FBI agents out to call on Hart. I heard this from the agents themselves afterwards. And then Hart sold."

All the profits from the track, Murchison claimed, were to go to Boys Inc., a fund established by the Texans "for the benefit of underprivileged boys." To present a respectable front, he picked a revered war hero, General Holland Smith, to serve as president. "I think $200 a month for General Smith," he wrote, "is good propaganda. . . ."

Murchison guessed wrong. The general resigned after a few months, noting that in spite of clearing $640,000 at one meeting, "not one cent has been turned over to Boys Inc. I do not know where the money went. It is my considered opinion that no money will be transferred to Boys Inc. for at least five years, if then. I hope I have given you a fair idea of what I think of Mr. Murchison and Mr. Richardson. . . ."

Skeptics, including the California tax authorities, said the Del Mar scheme was just another moneymaker for the millionaires. Because the profits were supposed to go to charity, they could not be taxed—and the state wanted the tax. Murchison counterattacked with every asset at his disposal, including the obliging Edgar.

"I know Clint Murchison," Edgar told the racing press, "and I think he would be the last person in the country to use such a plan as a clever tax or business subterfuge. . . . This work helps directly in making the nation sturdy, for Communist penetration is currently directed mainly at labor and youth organizations."

Some Del Mar profit did go to charity over the years, but eminent critics did not share Edgar's confidence. "This dodge," said former President Herbert Hoover, Chairman of Boys' Clubs of America and normally one of Edgar's allies, "is as old as the hills. They do not give *all* profits to charity." George Allen, racing enthusiast and intimate of Murchison and Edgar, admitted years later, "It was a racket, if you want to know . . . a tax racket."

Edgar behaved at the track as though he did not know what everyone in law enforcement knew, that racetrack gambling was the single most important source of revenue for organized crime. Police intelligence in California learned that he regularly used bookmakers linked to the mob.

In Florida, Edgar asked Phil "The Stick" Kovolick, a heavy for Meyer Lansky, for the winning numbers. At one stage, crime reporter Hank Messick learned, "gangsters began taking advantage of Hoover's ignorance by getting themselves invited to his box at the track and posing with him for pictures. It became something of a game. . . ."

Edgar was not so ignorant. He once boasted about shady gambling to Robert Mardian, an Assistant Attorney General in the Nixon administration. "He told me," Mardian recalled, "that he was once in an illegal race parlor down in Florida where you could have dinner and place bets and so on. And the Miami police raided the place. He laughed and said, 'Well, what a shock they got when they found me there! They cleared out faster than you can imagine.'"[6]

FBI propagandists, who apparently understood the risks better than their boss, regularly let it be known that Edgar placed only small bets. "Temperance and moderation in everything," he was quoted as saying, and he was duly photographed standing at the $2 window. The truth was otherwise.

"We all used to laugh about that," said Del Charro manager Allan Witwer. "At Del Mar, when he'd been authoritatively tipped, Hoover would place two-*hundred*-dollar bets" ($1,000 at today's rates). To avoid being observed making large bets, insiders recalled, he would send companions—often FBI agents—to place the bets for him.

Edgar made light of suggestions that racing was penetrated by the mob. "The FBI," he was quoted as saying, "has much more important functions than arresting gamblers all over the place." And, all the while, he carried on an amicable relationship with one of the most notorious gambling bosses in the country, the mob boss known as "Prime Minister of the Underworld."

CHAPTER 22

"Intelligent gangsters from Al Capone to Moe Dalitz and Meyer Lansky have always been fierce, voluble defenders of the capitalist faith, and to that extent they were and are J. Edgar Hoover's ideological kinsmen."

Albert Fried, historian

EDGAR HAD A RELATIONSHIP WITH MOB CHIEFTAIN FRANK Costello that lasted for years, and has never been satisfactorily explained. It started, apparently, with a seemingly innocuous meeting on a New York street.

Edgar recalled the occasion himself, in a private conversation with the veteran journalist Norma Abrams—a confidence she kept until shortly before her death in 1989.

"Hoover was an inveterate window-shopper," said Abrams. "Early one morning in the thirties, he told me, he was out walking on Fifth Avenue and somebody came up behind him and said, 'Good morning, Mr. Hoover.' He turned to see who it was, and it was Frank Costello. Costello said, 'I don't want to embarrass you,' and Hoover said, 'You won't embarrass me. We're not looking for you or anything.' They talked all the way to Fifty-seventh Street together, but God protected them, and there was no photographer around, or anyone. . . ."

The contact was renewed, as Edgar explained to Eduardo Disano, a Florida restaurateur who also knew Costello. "Hoover told me he and Costello both used apartments at the Waldorf," Disano recalled. "He said Costello asked him to come up and meet in his apartment. Hoover said he told him by all means he would meet him, but not in his room, downstairs. . . . I don't know what they talked about. Hoover was a very quiet man about business."

If Costello was trying to cultivate Edgar, it worked. Once they even took the risk of sitting together in the Stork Club. Costello was soon referring to Edgar as "John"—a habit he presumably picked up from Winchell. The mobster was to recall with a chuckle the day Edgar in turn took the lead and invited him for coffee. "I got to be careful about my associates," Costello told Edgar. "They'll accuse me of consorting with questionable characters. . . ."

In 1939, when Edgar was credited with the capture of racketeer Louis "Lepke" Buchalter, it was Costello who pulled strings to make it happen. This was the time the mob would remember as the Big Heat, when Thomas Dewey, then District Attorney, brought unprecedented pressure on organized crime. The heat was on, especially, for the capture of Lepke, the man they called the head of Murder Inc.

Shortly before midnight on August 24, Edgar called in newsmen to hear a sensational announcement. He, personally, had just accepted Lepke's surrender on a New York street. It made a fine tale—Edgar, in dark glasses, waiting in a parked limousine for his encounter with one of the most dangerous criminals in America. Edgar said the FBI had "managed the surrender through its own sources," and it emerged that his friend Winchell had played a role as go-between. Edgar was covered in glory, to the rage of Dewey and the New York authorities, who said he had operated behind their backs.

He had indeed, thanks to a neat piece of manipulation by the mob. Lucky Luciano, issuing orders to Costello and Lansky from prison, had decided that to relieve law enforcement pressure on mob operations Lepke must be made to surrender. Word went to the gangster that he would be treated leniently if he surrendered to Edgar—a false promise, as it turned out, for he was to end up in the electric chair. Costello, meanwhile, met secretly with Edgar to hammer out the arrangements.

The beauty of it all, Luciano would recall, was that they achieved two things at once. They won relief from law enforcement pressure and simultaneously ensured that Edgar and Dewey—even the ego-obsessed Walter Winchell —each got their "piece of the cake." For supreme practitioners of the Fix, the sacrifice of Lepke was a job well done.

William Hundley, the Justice Department attorney, had a glimpse of the way Costello handled Edgar. It happened by chance in 1961, when Hundley was staying at the apartment of his friend—and the mobster's attorney—Edward Bennett Williams. "At eight o'clock in the morning," Hundley recalled, "there was a knock at the door. There was a guy there with a big hat on, and this really hoarse voice. It was Frank Costello, and he came in, and we sat around eating breakfast. . . . Somehow the subject of Hoover came up, and Hoover liking to bet on horseracing. Costello mentioned that he knew Hoover, that they met for lunch. Then he started looking very leery of going on, but Ed told him he could trust me. Costello just said, 'Hoover will never know how many races I had to fix for those lousy ten-dollar bets.' He still looked leery, and I guess he didn't want to say much more."

In Costello, Edgar had one of the most powerful tipsters in gambling history. One of his primary mob functions was to control betting and fix races. Those who failed to cooperate got hurt, or worse. Edgar's relationship with him is corroborated by sources both inside and outside the mob. "Costello did give tips to Hoover," said Walter Winchell's colleague Herman Klurfeld. "He got them from [betting-parlor operator] Frank Erickson and passed them on through Winchell. . . . Sometimes Costello and Hoover met directly. Now and then, when Hoover was in the barbershop at the Waldorf, so was Frank Costello."

Chicago Mafia boss Sam Giancana reportedly had an inside track on the relationship. His half brother Chuck has claimed that Costello "worked the whole thing out. He knew Hoover was just like every other politician and copper, only meaner and smarter than most. Hoover didn't want an envelope each month . . . so we never gave him cash outright; we gave him something better: tips on fixed horse races. He could bet ten thousand dollars on a horse that showed twenty-to-one odds, if he wanted . . . and he has."[1]

In 1990, aged eighty, New York mob boss Carmine Lombardozzi said Costello and Edgar "had contact on many occasions and over a long period. Hoover was very friendly towards the families. They took good care of him, especially at the races. . . . The families made sure he was looked after when he visited the tracks in California and on the East Coast. They had an understanding. He would lay off the families, turn a blind eye. It helped that he denied that we even existed. If there was anything they could do for him, information that did not hurt family business, they would provide it."[2]

George Allen, Edgar's racecourse companion for forty years and a prominent public figure who had no connection to the mob, recalled a conversation between Edgar and Costello. "I heard Hoover in the Stork one night," he said, "tell Costello that as long as he stayed out of Hoover's bailiwick, he'd stay out of his."

Since Costello's principal business was gambling, and since gambling was not a federal offense, it could be said that Edgar's remark merely reflected the legal situation of the day. Other clues, however, suggest that his laissez-faire attitude went deeper. In the early fifties, when there were efforts to have Costello deported to Italy, there was no pressure from the FBI. According to Walter Winchell's friend Curly Harris, who knew both Edgar and the mobster, Edgar once went out of his way to protect Costello from his own agents.

"The doorman at Frank's apartment building," Harris remembered, "told him that there were a couple of FBI guys hanging around. So Frank got hold of Hoover on the phone and told him, 'What's the idea of these fellows being there? If you want to see me you can get to me with one phone call.' And Hoover looked into it, and he found out who the fellows were and why they were doing that. He said they weren't under any orders to do it, they'd taken it on themselves. He was very sore about it. And he had the agents transferred to Alaska or someplace the next day. . . . He and Costello had mutual friends."[3]

To Costello, and to his associate Meyer Lansky, the ability to corrupt politicians, policemen and judges was fundamental to Mafia operations. It was Lansky's expertise in such corruption that made him the nearest there ever was to a true national godfather of organized crime.

Another Mafia boss, Joseph Bonanno, articulated the principles of the game. It was a strict underworld rule, he said, never to use violent means against a law enforcement officer. "Ways could be found," he said in his memoirs, "so that he would not interfere with us and we wouldn't interfere with him." The way the Mafia found to deal with Edgar, according to several mob sources, involved his homosexuality.

The mob bosses had been well placed to find out about Edgar's compromising secret, and at a significant time and place. It was on New Year's Eve 1936, after dinner at the Stork Club, that Edgar was seen by two of Walter Winchell's guests holding hands with his lover, Clyde.[4] At the Stork, where he was a regular, Edgar was immensely vulnerable to observation by mobsters. The heavyweight champion Jim Braddock, who also dined with Edgar and Clyde that evening, was controlled by Costello's associate Owney Madden. Winchell, as compulsive a gossip in private as he was in his column, constantly cultivated Costello. Sherman Billingsley, the former bootlegger who ran the Stork, reportedly installed two-way mirrors in the toilets and hidden microphones at tables used by celebrities. Billingsley was a pawn of Costello's, and Costello was said to be the club's real owner. He would have had no compunction about persecuting Edgar, and he loathed homosexuals.

Seymour Pollack, a close friend of Meyer Lansky, said in 1990 that Edgar's homosexuality was "common knowledge" and that he had seen evidence of it for himself. "I used to meet him at the racetrack every once in a while with lover boy Clyde, in the late forties and fifties. I was in the next box once. And when you see two guys holding hands, well come on! . . . They were surreptitious, but there was no question about it."

Jimmy "The Weasel" Fratianno, the highest-ranking mobster ever to have "turned" and testified against his former associates, was at the track in 1948 when Frank Bompensiero, a notorious West Coast mafioso, taunted Edgar to his face. "I pointed at this fella sitting in the box in front," Fratianno recalled, "and said, 'Hey, Bomp, lookit there, it's J. Edgar Hoover.' And Bomp says right out loud, so everyone can hear, 'Ah, that J. Edgar's a punk, he's a fuckin' degenerate queer.'"

Later, when Bompensiero ran into Edgar in the men's room, the FBI Director was astonishingly meek. "Frank," he told the mobster, "that's not a nice way to talk about me, especially when I have people with me." It was clear to Fratianno that Bompensiero had met Edgar before and that he had absolutely no fear of Edgar.

Fratianno knew numerous other top mobsters, including Jack and Louis Dragna of Los Angeles and Johnny Roselli, the West Coast representative of the Chicago mob. All spoke of "proof" that Edgar was homosexual. Roselli spoke specifically of the occasion in the late twenties when Edgar had been arrested on charges of homosexuality in New Orleans.[5] Edgar could hardly have chosen a worse city in which to be compromised. New Orleans police and city officials were notoriously corrupt, puppets of an organized crime network run by Mafia boss Carlos Marcello and heavily influenced by Meyer Lansky. If the homosexual arrest occurred, it is likely the local mobsters quickly learned of it.

Other information suggests Meyer Lansky obtained hard proof of Edgar's homosexuality and used it to neutralize the FBI as a threat to his own operations. The first hint came from Irving "Ash" Resnick, the Nevada representative of the Patriarca family from New England, and an original owner-builder of Caesars Palace in Las Vegas. As a high-level mob courier, he traveled extensively. In Miami Beach, his Christmas destination in the fifties, he stayed at the

Gulfstream, in a bungalow next to one used by Edgar and Clyde. "I'd sit with him on the beach every day," Resnick remembered. "We were friendly."

In 1971, Resnick and an associate talked with the writer Pete Hamill in the Galeria Bar at Caesars Palace. They spoke of Meyer Lansky as a genius, the man who "put everything together"—and as the man who "nailed J. Edgar Hoover." "When I asked what they meant," Hamill recalled, "they told me Lansky had some pictures—pictures of Hoover in some kind of gay situation with Clyde Tolson. Lansky was the guy who controlled the pictures, and he had made his deal with Hoover—to lay off. That was the reason, they said, that for a long time they had nothing to fear from the FBI."[6]

Seymour Pollack, the criminal who saw Edgar and Clyde holding hands at the races, knew both Resnick and Lansky well. When Lansky's daughter had marital problems, it was Pollack who dealt with her husband. He and Lansky went back to the old days in pre-revolutionary Cuba, when Havana was as important to the syndicate as Las Vegas. "Meyer," said Pollack in 1990, "was closemouthed. I don't think he even discussed the details of the Hoover thing with his brother. But Ash was absolutely right. Lansky had more than information on Hoover. He had page, chapter and verse. One night, when we were sitting around in his apartment at the Rosita de Hornedo, we were talking about Hoover, and Meyer laughed and said, 'I fixed that son of a bitch, didn't I?'" Lansky's fix, according to Pollack, also involved bribery—not of Edgar himself, but men close to him.

Lansky and Edgar frequented the same watering holes in Florida. Staff at Gatti's restaurant in Miami Beach recall that the mobster would sometimes be in the restaurant, at another table, at the same time as Edgar and Clyde. One evening in the late sixties, they were seated at adjoining tables. "But they just looked at one another," recalled Edidio Crolla, the captain at Gatti's. "They never talked, not here."

If Edgar's eyes met Lansky's, though, there was surely an

involuntary flicker of fear. "The homosexual thing," said Pollack, "was Hoover's Achilles' heel. Meyer found it, and it was like he pulled strings with Hoover. He never bothered any of Meyer's people. . . . Let me go way back. The time Nevada opened up, Bugsy Siegel opened the Flamingo. I understand Hoover helped get the okay for him to do it. Meyer Lansky was one of the partners. Hoover knew who the guys were that whacked Bugsy Siegel, but nothing was done." (Siegel was killed, reportedly on Lansky's orders, in 1947.)

According to Pollack, Lansky and Edgar cooperated in the mid-fifties, when Las Vegas casino operator Wilbur Clark moved to Cuba. "Meyer brought Clark down to Havana," Pollack said. "I was against him coming. But I understand Hoover asked Meyer to bring Clark down. He owed Clark something. I don't know what. . . . There was no serious pressure on Meyer until the Kennedys came in. And even then Hoover never hurt Meyer's people, not for a long time."

Like Frank Costello, Lansky did seem to be untouchable—a phenomenon that triggered suspicions even within the Bureau. "In 1966," noted Hank Messick, one of Lansky's biographers, "a young G-Man assigned to go through the motions of watching Meyer Lansky began to take his job seriously and develop good informers. He was abruptly transferred to a rural area in Georgia. His successor on the Lansky assignment was an older man who knew the score. When he retired a few years later, he accepted a job with a Bahamian gambling casino originally developed by Lansky."

Also in the sixties a wiretap picked up a conversation between two mobsters in which, curiously, Lansky was referred to as "a stool pigeon for the FBI." The Royal Canadian Mounted Police, taping a conversation between a criminal in Canada and Lansky in the United States, were amazed to hear the mob chieftain reading from an FBI report that had been written the previous day.[7]

There was no serious federal effort to indict Lansky until 1970, just two years before Edgar died. Then, it was the IRS rather than the FBI that spearheaded the investigation. Even the tax evasion charges collapsed, and Lansky lived on at liberty until his own death in 1983.

New information indicates that Lansky was not the only person in possession of compromising photographs of Edgar. John Weitz, a former officer in the OSS, the predecessor of the Central Intelligence Agency, recalled a curious episode at a dinner party in the fifties. "After a conversation about Hoover," he said, "our host went to another room and came back with a photograph. It was not a good picture and was clearly taken from some distance away, but it showed two men apparently engaged in homosexual activity. The host said the men were Hoover and Tolson. . . ."

Since first publication of this book, Weitz has revealed that his host was James Angleton, a fellow OSS veteran and—in the fifties—a top CIA officer. A source who has been linked to the CIA, electronics expert Gordon Novel, has said Angleton showed him, too, compromising pictures of Edgar.

"What I saw was a picture of him giving Clyde Tolson a blowjob," said Novel. "There was more than one shot, but the startling one was a close shot of Hoover's head. He was totally recognizable. You could not see the face of the man he was with, but Angleton said it was Tolson. I asked him if they were fakes, but he said they were real, that they'd been taken with a special lens. They looked authentic to me. . . ."

Novel said Angleton showed him the pictures in 1967, when he was CIA Counter-Intelligence Chief and when Novel was involved in the furor swirling around the probe into the investigation of the assassination of President Kennedy by New Orleans District Attorney Jim Garrison. "I was pursuing a lawsuit against Garrison, which Hoover wanted me to drop but which my contacts in the Johnson administration and at CIA wanted me to pursue. I'd been told I would incur Hoover's wrath if I went ahead, but Angleton was demonstrating that Hoover was not invulnerable, that the Agency had enough power to make him come to heel. I had the impression that this was not the first time the sex pictures had been used. Angleton told me to go see Hoover and tell him I'd seen the sex photographs. Later, I went to the Mayflower Hotel and spoke to Hoover. He was with Tolson, sitting in the Rib Room. When I mentioned that I had seen the sex photographs, and that Angleton had sent me, Tolson nearly choked on his food. Hoover told me something like, 'Get the hell out of here!' And I did. . . ."

With Angleton dead, there is no way to follow up this bizarre allegation. While Novel is a controversial figure, his account of seeing compromising pictures must be considered in light of other such references—not least that of former OSS officer John Weitz. For Novel added one other significant detail, that "Angleton told me the photographs had been taken around 1946, at the time they were fighting over foreign intelligence, which Hoover wanted but never got."

During his feud with OSS chief William Donovan, dating back to 1941, Edgar had searched for compromising information, sexual lapses included, that could be used against his rival. His effort was in vain, but Donovan—who thought Edgar a "moralistic bastard"—reportedly retaliated in kind by ordering a secret investigation of Edgar's relationship with Clyde. The sex photograph in OSS hands may have been one of the results.

It may be significant, too, that compromising pictures are reported as having been in the hands of both the OSS and Meyer Lansky. The OSS and Naval Intelligence had extensive contacts with the Mafia during World War II, enlisting the help of criminals in projects including the hiring of burglars and assassins, experimentation with drugs, the protection of American ports from Nazi agents and the invasion of Sicily.[8] Lansky helped personally with the latter two operations, meeting with Murray Gurfein, a New York Assistant District Attorney who later became one of Donovan's most trusted OSS officers.[9]

At least once, Lansky worked alongside U.S. intelligence officers on exactly the sort of operation likely to turn up smear material on prominent public men. In 1942, he arranged for the surveillance of a homosexual brothel in Brooklyn suspected of being the target of German agents. "Clients came from all over New York and Washington," Lansky recalled, "and there were some important government people among them. . . . If you got hold of the names of the patrons you could blackmail them to death . . . take some pictures through a hole in the wall or a trick mirror and then squeeze the victim for money or information."[10]

There is no knowing, today, whether the OSS obtained sex photographs of Edgar from Lansky, or vice versa, or whether the mobster obtained them on his own initiative. A scenario in which Lansky obtained pictures thanks to the OSS connection would suggest an irony: that Edgar had tried and failed to find smear material on General Donovan, that Donovan in turn found smear material on him and that the material found its way to a top mobster, to be used against Edgar for the rest of his life.

CHAPTER 23

"For like Caesar's wife, the FBI Director must not only
be above suspicion but be seen to be so."

Smith Hempstone, journalist, 1971

IN NOVEMBER 1957, THE ZEAL OF A RURAL POLICEMAN ESTAB-
lished what competent law enforcers had long accepted, that
there was indeed a Mafia, a vast national organization
directed by known godfathers of crime.

On a routine inquiry about a bad check, Police Sergeant
Edgar Croswell of Apalachin, New York, stumbled on an
extraordinary gathering. Sixty-three top mobsters, from
fifteen states, were assembled at the palatial home of a
Sicilian killer, Joe Barbara, for what could only be described
as a Mafia convention.

For all Edgar's denials, events of recent months had made
anyone who read the newspapers aware of organized crime.
Gang warfare in New York had been making headlines for
months: Frank Costello shot and wounded in the lobby of
his Central Park apartment building; Frank Scalise, a henchman of Albert Anastasia, killed in the Bronx, his brother
Joseph missing, reported shot, the body apparently dismem-
bered and dumped; then one of the great Mafia sensations of
the century, Anastasia, Costello's key protector, the man
reputed to have been chief executioner of Murder Inc.,
riddled with bullets in the barbershop of the Park Sheraton
Hotel.

The Eisenhower government realized something had to be
done. According to former Attorney General William Rogers, however, Edgar had to be dragged "kicking and scream-

ing" into action. He obstructed, especially, the task force known as the Special Group on Organized Crime, set up by Rogers in response to Apalachin.

The Group's Chicago office was headed by Richard Ogilvie, a future Republican Governor of Illinois, a man revered by those in the FBI who did try to work against organized crime. Edgar, Ogilvie recalled, "ordered that the FBI files, containing the very information we needed on organized crime, were to be closed to us. Furthermore, he forbade any agents even to talk to members of the Special Group. . . ."

Edgar refused to see the Group's chief, Milton Wessel, dismissing him as a "Pied Piper" and, in writing, as "a real rat." FBI agents investigated Wessel and may have tapped his home telephone. When the Group concluded that nationwide organized crime existed "without any doubt," Edgar derided its members as people who "look at 'Mr. District Attorney' on TV too frequently."

In order to appear to be taking an interest in organized crime, however, Edgar suddenly discovered an old statute—the Hobbs Act—under which the FBI could investigate racketeers. Two weeks after the Apalachin gathering, startled Agents in Charge received instructions to embark on a new project, the Top Hoodlum Program.

The agents called the project THP, and it called for each field office to produce a list of exactly ten suspect members of the underworld. That was, of course, ridiculous. While one town might have trouble identifying more than a couple of gangsters, another, like Chicago, could point to dozens. For all that, the agents went to work with a will. In Washington, Edgar agreed that William Sullivan—then Chief of Research and Analysis—should report on the nature of organized crime. At last, it seemed, Edgar was interested in reality.

In the two years that followed, the FBI gathered intelligence on organized crime as never before. Then, just as his agents were starting to make real progress, Edgar quietly let things slide. The campaign against the mobsters first slowed, and then ground to a virtual halt for no apparent reason. A possible explanation is that Edgar had become the target of fresh blackmail—through one of Frank Costello's allies, Lewis Solon Rosenstiel.

Rosenstiel, sixty-six in 1957, was a hulking figure who favored amber-tinted glasses, which he rarely removed, and large cigars to go with his status as one of the wealthiest men alive. As a young man, he had entered the liquor trade thanks to an uncle who owned a distillery. Then, during Prohibition, he had built up massive whiskey stocks for the day America could drink legally again. By the end of World War II his company, Schenley, had become the leading U.S. distiller, with profits of $49 million a year. By the late fifties he owned a luxury house on East Eightieth Street in Manhattan, a 2,000-acre estate in Connecticut, a mansion and yacht in Florida and a large private airplane.

The public Rosenstiel wore the mantle of business tycoon and philanthropist. He gave $100 million over the years to Brandeis University, the University of Notre Dame and hospitals in New York and Florida. Secretly, he was in league with the nation's top mobsters and had a corrupt relationship with Edgar. According to new information, he also joined Edgar in bizarre sex orgies, at the very time the FBI was under pressure to pursue organized crime at last.

Rosenstiel's lifelong involvement with the Mafia came to light only in 1970, when the New York State Legislative Committee on Crime established that he and mob characters had formed a consortium to smuggle liquor during Prohibition. When Prohibition ended, committee investigators learned, Rosenstiel had appeared at a business meeting flanked by Frank Costello. "Costello was there," a witness said, "to give them a message that Rosenstiel was one of their people. You know, if there were any problems they would see to it. Here's where you had the Jew with the brains coming in with the Italian with the muscle."

Rosenstiel also had long-standing links to Meyer Lansky. He and the gangster "owned points together" in mob-operated businesses, including a Las Vegas casino. During the committee's investigations, the millionaire was observed playing host to Angelo Bruno, the Philadelphia Mafia boss.

Many of the committee's leads were supplied by Rosenstiel's fourth wife, Susan. At fifty-two, she was emerging from a decade in the divorce courts, during which Rosenstiel had spent half a million dollars attempting to concoct phony evidence. Embittered though she was, Crime Committee Chairman John Hughes had no doubts about her testimony. His Chief Counsel, Edward McLaughlin, now a New York judge, remembers her as an excellent witness. "I thought her absolutely truthful," he said. "The woman's power of recall was phenomenal. Everything she said was checked and double-checked, and everything that was checkable turned out to be true."[1]

Most of Mrs. Rosenstiel's testimony to the committee was behind closed doors, in executive session, and remains sealed. Two decades later, interviewed at her home in France, she still had the keen recall that so impressed the New York investigators. By her account, to live with Rosenstiel was to live with the command structure of organized crime.

Her first date with the millionaire, in 1955, was dinner at the Waldorf accompanied by Lansky associate Joe Linsey. He was there again during the honeymoon cruise, along with Robert Gould, a Schenley distributor who had been jailed for black marketeering in World War II. Mrs. Rosenstiel later met Sam Giancana, the Chicago Mafia boss, and Santos Trafficante, the Florida crime chieftain. She was also introduced to Al Hart and Art Samish, both shady operators in the liquor business who had met Edgar at the Del Charro hotel in California. At Rosenstiel's birthday parties, famous hoodlums drank elbow to elbow with judges and local government officials. Cardinal Spellman, another of Edgar's friends, was a regular guest.

During 1957, a time of crisis for the mob—the year of the Apalachin conference and feuding over who was to dominate New York—Rosenstiel stayed in constant touch with Frank Costello. He visited him during a brief spell in jail, then received him as a guest at his home on East Eightieth Street. Earlier that year, on a trip to Cuba, the millionaire had introduced his wife to Meyer Lansky—an experience she described vividly to the New York Crime Committee.

"We arrived in Havana," Susan testified, "and then we went to the National Hotel. . . . We had a very big suite, and it was filled with flowers. . . . I looked at the card, and it said, 'Welcome, Supreme Commander, to Havana. Meyer and Jake.' So I asked my husband who Meyer and Jake were, and he said, 'That is Meyer and Jake Lansky, very good friends. . . .'"

The Rosenstiels dined with Lansky that evening. He paid all their bills in Havana and provided unlimited credit for gambling. The millionaire, for his part, regularly returned the hospitality when the mobster was in New York or Florida. Lansky found one of the grander dinner parties a positive ordeal.

"I had two butlers," recalled Mrs. Rosenstiel, "double service, with Mouton-Rothschild to drink. The butlers were trained always to have white towels around the bottles so my husband couldn't see it wasn't one of his champagnes. And we had this marvelous dinner. I was using my beautiful gold dinner service that had belonged to Queen Marie of Romania. They ate the dessert and then the butlers brought the little finger bowls, with little flowers in them. And some of them thought at first it was an extra dessert. Meyer Lansky went to taste it and hurt his teeth on the bowl.

"Then we went upstairs to the sitting room, and Lansky said, 'Can't I have a decent cup of coffee?' He had, you know, just a little demitasse. My husband thought himself quite a pianist, and he said to these men, 'Well, boys, what would you like to hear me play?' They said, 'Play anything.' So he did, and when he finished he said to Lansky, 'Meyer, what do you think I was playing, what composition?' I think Lansky had only heard of Beethoven, so he said Beethoven. And Rosenstiel laughed, and he said, 'You goddamn son of a bitch, I composed that myself.' They all had to applaud."

Susan Rosenstiel was aware that her husband had business deals with Lansky. "He was always having under-the-table transactions, and for that he didn't want to use the banks. Just cash. And Lansky used to put up a lot of money. Once, later, they gave my husband some kind of big payment at the Sands Casino in Las Vegas. There were thousands and thousands and thousands of dollars in bundles of cash."

Contrary to denials by Edgar's two propaganda chiefs, Lou Nichols and Cartha DeLoach, Rosenstiel was also close to Edgar. "They knew each other very well," said Sidney Stricker, the son of Rosenstiel's longtime attorney, who himself worked for Schenley. Jesse Weiss, owner of Joe's Stone Crabs restaurant in Miami Beach, confirmed the relationship. "Rosenstiel and Edgar were social friends. They came to my place together when they were in Miami." Edgar sometimes flew with Rosenstiel in his private plane.

Recently released FBI documents show that Hoover was aware of Rosenstiel, and extended Bureau assistance to him, as early as 1933. In 1939, Meyer Lansky used Rosenstiel as a go-between while plotting the surrender to Edgar of the gangster Louis "Lepke" Buchalter. In 1946, Edgar and Clyde were guests of honor at a barbecue thrown by leading liquor companies, including Rosenstiel's. The FBI files show that the millionaire's friendship with the Director began in earnest with a meeting at FBI headquarters in 1956.

By the fifties, Rosenstiel was surrounded by familiar figures from Edgar's world. There was George Sokolsky, the Hearst columnist who churned out right-wing propaganda, much of it gleaned from daily calls to the FBI. Sokolsky had long since acted as a mouthpiece for Edgar. Now, in return for regular handouts, he also parroted Rosenstiel's views.

Closest of all was Roy Cohn, now a high-profile New York attorney. His services were at the disposal of Lewis Rosenstiel—not that he had any genuine affection for the man. He would be disbarred, twenty years later, in part for "helping" Rosenstiel sign a document naming Cohn as his trustee and executor—when the millionaire was senile and in a terminal coma.

Rosenstiel trusted Cohn "as a son," and Cohn indulged

his eccentricities. The pair was once observed on a yacht, cruising past the West Point Military Academy with a recording of General MacArthur's farewell speech blaring forth from a loudspeaker. The Rosenstiel clique liked to address one another as if they were members of some secret army. Cohn, like Lansky, called Rosenstiel "Supreme Commander." The millionaire called Cohn "Field Commander," another crony "Sergeant-at-Arms" and so on.

Rosenstiel cultivated Edgar assiduously. He quietly bought up 25,000 copies of *Masters of Deceit* for distribution to schools around the country. In the sixties, he would contribute more than a million dollars to the J. Edgar Hoover Foundation, a fund established to "safeguard the heritage and freedom of the United States of America . . . to perpetuate the ideas and purposes to which the Honorable J. Edgar Hoover has dedicated his life . . . and to combat Communism." The foundation still exists today, under the aegis of Cartha DeLoach. It makes grants to those planning careers in law enforcement, to the Scripps Clinic in California, where Edgar had his medical checkups, to Boys' Clubs of America, and the Freedoms Foundation, an ultra–right-wing organization that aims "to preserve and improve the Distinctive American System of Freedom."

There was nothing innocent about Edgar's relations with Rosenstiel. "I learned," his wife said, "how much Hoover liked the races, that he was a big gambler. My husband was friendly with several Lansky bookmakers—Red Ritter and Max Courtney and Charlie 'The Brud' Brudner—and he would call them at the Eden Roc and give them Hoover's bets. And Hoover didn't have to pay off. If he won, he won. My husband would send the money through Cohn. If Hoover didn't win, he didn't pay."

Rosenstiel called in such favors, Susan said, by using Edgar to obtain the release of jailed associates, to "help with the judges" when Rosenstiel was involved in litigation—even to "put in a word" with the tax authorities.

Susan Rosenstiel met Edgar in the fall of 1957, when he came to the town house on East Eightieth Street. "It was supposed to be a bit cloak and dagger," she recalled.

"Nobody was to know he was coming. He didn't come with Clyde Tolson; he came alone.

"I remember thinking he didn't look like the head of the FBI. He was rather short, and he seemed distant, arrogant. You could see he had a grand opinion of himself, and they all went along with it. Everything he said they agreed with. They talked about Lou Nichols' coming over from the FBI to work for my husband. After about half an hour, I was given the wink to leave. I went upstairs to my room." Soon, after twenty-three years as Edgar's closest assistant, Nichols quit the FBI to perform the same function for Lewis Rosenstiel.

Within months, according to Susan Rosenstiel, Edgar was involved in an episode remembered as an outrageous example of congressional corruption. This was the passage in 1958 of the Forand Bill—a piece of legislation incomprehensible to the general public but crucial to Rosenstiel's fortunes. Schenley Liquor was facing serious trouble because of a miscalculation made eight years earlier. At the start of the Korean War, the millionaire had guessed that hostilities would continue for a long time—causing shortages of several of the ingredients needed to make whiskey. On that assumption, Schenley had produced and stored millions of gallons of liquor, far more than usual. When shortages came, Rosenstiel gambled, prices would skyrocket —and he would make a fabulous profit.

It never happened. The war ended in 1953, and there was no shortage. Rosenstiel had no market for his whiskey hoard. In 1958, the liquor would become subject to a crippling government tax—$10.50 on each gallon. The only solution was to get the tax law changed, which meant bringing pressure on Congress.

It was at that time that Nichols, Edgar's influence man on Capitol Hill, came to work for Rosenstiel. He at once began bombarding politicians with phone calls and requests for meetings, and his lobbying succeeded. Congress passed the Forand Bill, named after the Congressman of that name, freeing liquor companies from punitive tax on stored whiskey for a dozen extra years—ample time to dispose of their stocks. For Rosenstiel, it meant bonanza as well as salvation. The bill saved the company between $40 and $50 million, and the value of Schenley stock soared by $33 million in a single day.

A few months before the passage of the bill, according to Susan Rosenstiel, she was present at a meeting in New York attended by her husband, Edgar, Nichols, Cohn and Sokolsky. "Hoover," she said, "told them the bill would pass. He said it would cost a great deal of money, but it would be worth it. His involvement was talking to certain congressmen and senators." Nichols, said the millionaire's wife, was "the bagman." "He carried the money to the politicians. The Schenley plane was like a shuttle, taking cash down to Washington."

According to Mrs. Rosenstiel, prominent politicians accepted money from Rosenstiel. Lyndon Johnson, then Senate Majority Leader, allegedly received half a million dollars. She was present, at her husband's Connecticut estate, when Rosenstiel personally handed a large sum of money to Emanuel Celler, the Chairman of the House Judiciary Committee. And, says Mrs. Rosenstiel, the whole corrupt operation was conducted with Edgar's knowledge and approval.

FBI records released in 1991 establish that Rosenstiel twice visited Edgar in his office in 1958, at the time the Forand Bill was going through its most crucial stages.

Susan Rosenstiel's final and most sensational revelations suggest her husband and Roy Cohn involved Edgar in sex orgies—thus laying him more open than ever to pressure from organized crime.

Susan Rosenstiel's previous marriage had collapsed because her first husband was predominantly homosexual. Now, she concluded, she had made a similar mistake. Her husband seemed little interested in having sex with her, but went to great expense to have her dress up in clothes that made her look like a little girl. She discovered, meanwhile, that he enjoyed sex with men.

"One day," Susan recalled, "I came into my husband's bedroom and found him in bed with Roy Cohn. It was about nine o'clock in the morning. I was shocked, just shocked. He made some sort of joke about it being so he could be alone with his attorney. And I said, 'I've never seen Governor Dewey in bed with you,' because Dewey was one of his attorneys, too. And I walked out."

Roy Cohn flaunted his homosexuality around Susan. He openly caressed one young man, a former congressional associate, in front of her. He seemed to take pleasure in telling her about the sexual proclivities of her husband's friends—including, especially, the homosexuality of Cardinal Spellman.

Sometime in 1958, probably in the spring, Rosenstiel asked his wife whether, while living in Paris with her previous husband, she had ever witnessed an orgy. "A few weeks later, when Cohn was there, he commented that I was a 'regular' and knew what life was, that my first husband had been gay and I must have understood because I'd stayed with him for nine years. And they said how would I like to go to a party at the Hotel Plaza? But if it ever got out, it would be the most terrible thing in the world. I told them, 'If you want to go, I'll go.' Cohn said, 'You're in for a big surprise. . . .'"

A few days later Rosenstiel took his wife to the Plaza, the venerable hotel overlooking New York's Central Park. They entered through a side entrance and took an elevator to a suite on the second or third floor. She had the impression her husband had been there before. "He knocked," Susan recalled, "and Roy Cohn opened the door. It was a beautiful suite, one of their biggest, all done in light blue. Hoover was there already, and I couldn't believe what I saw."

According to Mrs. Rosenstiel, Edgar was dressed up as a woman, in full drag. "He was wearing a fluffy black dress, very fluffy, with flounces, and lace stockings and high heels, and a black curly wig. He had makeup on, and false eyelashes. It was a very short skirt, and he was sitting there in the living room of the suite with his legs crossed. Roy introduced him to me as 'Mary' and he replied, 'Good evening,' brusque, like the first time I'd met him. It was obvious he wasn't a woman, you could see where he shaved. It was Hoover. You've never seen anything like it. I couldn't believe it, that I should see the head of the FBI dressed as a woman.

"There was a bar set up with drinks, and we had drinks. Not too much. I think it was about then that Roy muttered to me that Hoover didn't know that I knew who he was, that I'd think he was someone else. I certainly didn't address him the way I had at other times, as Mr. Hoover. I was afraid of my life by then.

"The next thing, a couple of boys come in, young blond boys. I'd say about eighteen or nineteen. And then Roy makes the signal we should go into the bedroom. It was a tremendous bedroom, with a bed like in Caesar's time, with a damask spread, blue, I think, like the suite. And they go into the bedroom, and Hoover takes off his lace dress and pants, and under the dress he was wearing a little, short garter belt. He lies on the double bed, and the two boys work on him with their hands. One of them wore rubber gloves."

After a while, said Susan Rosenstiel, the group returned to the living room. "Cohn had brought up some food. Cold stuff, so as not to have room service. So we had a little something to eat.

"Then Rosenstiel got into the act with the boys. I thought, 'You disgusting old man . . .' Hoover and Cohn were watching, enjoying it. Then Cohn runs to get himself satisfied— full sex—with the two boys. Those poor boys. He couldn't get enough. But Hoover only had them, you know, playing with him. I didn't see him take part in any anal sex. Rosenstiel wanted me to get involved, but I wouldn't do it."

Later the Rosenstiels went home in their limousine, leaving Cohn and Edgar, with the boys, in the suite. Rosenstiel would not discuss Edgar's part in the evening's events, but Cohn later laughed about it. "He said, 'That was really something, wasn't it, with Mary Hoover?' He told me, as if it had happened before, 'I arrive at the Plaza first, with his clothes in a suitcase.' Cohn said Hoover came in through the side entrance on Fifty-eighth Street, so he didn't have to go through the lobby. I guess he made it his business not to be followed. . . ."

A year later, according to Susan, Rosenstiel asked her to accompany him to the Plaza again. She agreed, in return for an expensive pair of earrings from Harry Winston's, and the procedure was the same as on the previous occasion. Cohn ushered them into a suite to find Edgar, again attired in female finery. His clothing this time was even more outlandish. "He had a red dress on," Susan recalled, "and a black feather boa around his neck. He was dressed like an old flapper, like you see on old tintypes.

"After about half an hour some boys came, like before. This time they're dressed in leather. And Hoover had a Bible. He wanted one of the boys to read from the Bible. And he read, I forget which passage, and the other boy played with him, wearing the rubber gloves. And then Hoover grabbed the Bible, threw it down and told the second boy to join in the sex."

When they got home that night, the Rosenstiels quarreled. Lewis rebuffed his wife's questions and never again asked her to go to the suite at the Plaza. She saw Edgar only once more, in 1961, when he and Cardinal Spellman visited the Connecticut estate.

Susan Rosenstiel has insisted she could not possibly have been mistaken, that Edgar was definitely the man in female dress at the Plaza. Her account remained consistent, and she signed a sworn affidavit that it is true.

She was permitted to witness Edgar and the others in such a situation, she surmised, "because they wanted a woman present. I guess it gave them some sort of extra thrill. And if I'd said anything, they'd have said I was crazy, that Hoover hadn't been there. It would have been my word against theirs, and no one would have believed it."

People who knew Rosenstiel say he was bisexual. Roy Cohn was indeed homosexual and regularly hired young male prostitutes. The facts of Edgar's life, meanwhile, fit the Plaza scenario well enough. He regularly traveled to New

York City, and without Clyde. Former Agent John Dixson, who served in New York during that period, often had the task of meeting Edgar when he arrived at Penn Station, after traveling alone from Washington. He would be taken by car to the Waldorf, his usual hotel, and left to his own devices.

Nor is it odd that Clyde Tolson was not present at the Plaza. Thirty years had passed since the first flower of his affair with Edgar, and he was no longer the handsome young man who had attracted Edgar in 1928. He was fifty-eight and, unlike Edgar, his health was failing rapidly. He was hospitalized repeatedly during the fifties for a serious eye ailment and for problems with duodenal ulcers. It was the start of a decline that would lead to open-heart surgery and several strokes.

Edgar and Clyde always remained intimate friends. When Clyde's mother was dying, Edgar traveled to be at his side in Iowa. When Edgar made a token appearance at the funeral of his sister, Lillian, Clyde was there with him. At work, each could depend entirely on the other, and that was perhaps the real bond between them. Physical love, however, had probably run its course.

There is another account of Edgar's interest in dressing up as a woman, one that refers to an episode in Washington in 1948, ten years before the orgies at the Plaza. It comes from two men, successful professionals in their fields, both heterosexuals, who have requested anonymity. For several months that year, they said, they frequented a Washington watering hole called the Maystat that was noticeably, though not exclusively, used by homosexuals. At the Maystat they were befriended by Joe Bobak, a fifty-year-old Army Supply Sergeant serving at Fort Myers. "Bobak," one of the witnesses recalled, "was decidedly gay, a bit swishy. He knew senior officers at the Pentagon, even senators and congressmen who were also gay. It was a strange group to us, and we were fascinated."

One evening in 1948 the two young men sat in a car outside the Maystat with one of Bobak's regular companions, a younger man in his mid-twenties. With a conspiratorial air, the younger man produced five or six photographs for the others to examine. "The picture he showed us first," one of the witnesses recalled, "was of a man dressed up as a woman—the whole thing, wig, evening gown and everything. It was easily recognizable as J. Edgar Hoover.

"He was lying across a bed, in this evening gown. I think the wig was light-colored, or blond. But the face was completely recognizable. Hoover made an ugly-looking woman. Nothing sexual was going on, at least not in the pictures we saw. No one else was in that first picture. It was like he'd just laid down there. I think you could also see a bedside table in the shot. At first we thought it might be Hoover's head stuck onto another body, a sort of trick picture, phonied up. But the other four or five photos made it clear to us they were authentic—they were taken from different angles, with other people visible, and Hoover was in all the shots. It was a party scene.

"The way we were shown the pictures was all rather matter-of-fact. The people in that group knew, or behaved as if they knew, that he was gay. We also met two other guys, through Sergeant Bobak, who said they had been to gay parties Hoover attended. Bobak said he had been to Hoover's house. The boy with him had glommed on to the pictures somehow, swiped them or got hold of prints.

"At that tender age, it didn't occur to us that anyone in the gay crowd intended to use the pictures for blackmail. It was more as if they were a curiosity, to be giggled about in the group. It sounds strange now, but at that age—we were only about twenty then—I don't think it fully occurred to us what it would mean to attach that kind of stigma to a major public figure. It seemed funny to us, kind of laughable. We just looked at the pictures and handed them back and talked about them once or twice afterwards. And that was all. We soon moved away from that circle of people."

There is no question of collusion between these two witnesses and Susan Rosenstiel. The men who saw the photographs, moreover, knew nothing of Edgar's connection with Rosenstiel. It seems likely they did see the pictures, and did recognize the grotesque man in female garb as Edgar.

Sexual adventuring was folly for Edgar, and especially in the company of a man like Rosenstiel. Several sources told the New York Crime Committee that Rosenstiel had his Manhattan home wired from roof to basement with hidden microphones, so that he could spy on visitors and staff. The man who installed the system, security consultant Fred Otash, said it was rigged to tape conversations for hours on end. Conversations in the library, where Edgar met with Rosenstiel and his cronies, were recorded as a matter of routine. The millionaire was quite capable of having the sex sessions at the Plaza bugged or arranging for Edgar to be photographed in his female costumes.

Meyer Lansky, who claimed Edgar was no threat, that he had been "fixed," was Rosenstiel's close associate. Mrs. Rosenstiel quotes her husband as saying that "because of Lansky and those people, we can always get Hoover to help us." The mobster's insurance policy, according to associates, was photographic evidence of Edgar's homosexual activity. The evidence suggests that in the late fifties, at a difficult time for the mob, the episodes at the Plaza may have renewed that insurance.

In July 1958, soon after the first Plaza episode—and in order to be seen to be responding to the uproar about the mobsters' conference at Apalachin—Edgar asked his Domestic Intelligence Division to produce a study on organized crime. Though the full two-volume report remains classified, its summary conclusion stated:

Central Research has prepared a monograph on the Mafia for the Director's approval. This monograph includes the following points on the Mafia: The Mafia does exist in the U.S. It exists as a special criminal clique or caste engaged in organized crime activity. The

Mafia is composed primarily of individuals of Sicilian/ Italian origin and descent. . . .

This, of course, was contrary to Edgar's stated belief, and his response was perverse. In private he seemed grudgingly to accept that the Mafia existed. He exploded, however, when he heard the report had been sent to other top law enforcement officials, including Attorney General Rogers.

Edgar ordered all the circulated copies to be retrieved within hours of delivery. No one outside the Bureau ever read the report, which Edgar referred to thereafter as "baloney."[2]

In 1959, meanwhile, Edgar made public speeches saying he hoped "to keep such pressure on hoodlums and racketeers that they can't light or remain anywhere." In September, in Chicago, an FBI surveillance microphone hit the jackpot. Sam Giancana was overheard referring repeatedly to "the Commission," the cabal that ruled organized crime nationwide. He even ran through the names of its members, ticking them off one by one.

Agents regarded this as a major breakthrough, but it did not move Edgar to change his stance. Three years later he would still be insisting that "no single individual or coalition of racketeers dominates organized crime across the nation."

By late 1959, agents working on the new Top Hoodlum Program realized something was badly wrong. Agent William Turner, on an inspection visit to the Bureau's Los Angeles office, concluded the program was "dead in the water." In Chicago, the specialist staff was cut from ten agents to five. "Mr. Hoover seemed to lose interest," recalled Chicago's Bill Roemer. "Organized crime was no longer his top priority."

In New York, agent Anthony Villano was told by his superior that recent operations against the Mafia were probably "only a temporary operation designed to satisfy criticism and would be disbanded after the heat died down." In New York, where 400 agents were working on

Communism that year, just four were assigned to organized crime.

Edgar's much-trumpeted onslaught on the mob had turned out to be a phony war. It would become real enough, however, just two years later. In Attorney General Robert Kennedy the mob chieftains—and Edgar—would meet real opposition at last.

CHAPTER 24

> "Hoover passed along gossip to the President he served, and that practice could raise questions in a President's mind. What did Hoover know about him? In theoretical terms, that put Hoover in the position of a veiled blackmailer."
>
> *Dean Rusk, former Secretary of State*

In October 1955, Joseph Kennedy had returned from a foreign vacation to an America in turmoil. President Eisenhower had just survived his near fatal heart attack, and many doubted whether he would be fit enough to run in 1956. Would the Democratic candidate be Adlai Stevenson? If so, would Kennedy's thirty-eight-year-old son John be on the ticket for Vice President?

The Kennedy political machine was beginning to roll. The prize that had eluded the father was now on the horizon for the son. That fall day, however, Joseph Kennedy enthused about a very different possibility—that within twelve months America might elect President J. Edgar Hoover. At home in Hyannis Port, the family headquarters in Massachusetts, he dictated this letter:

Dear Edgar,
I think I have become too cynical in my old age, but the only two men I know in public life today for whose opinion I give one continental both happen to be named Hoover—one John Edgar and one Herbert— and I am proud to think that both of them hold me in some esteem. . . . I listened to Walter Winchell men-

1. Edgar's father, Dickerson, suffered from mental illness. His mother, Annie, hoped for great things from her youngest child. 2. Edgar as a toddler, at the turn of the century. 3. Though a zealous company commander in his school Cadet Corps, Edgar did not join up in World War I.

4.5.6. In 1921, Edgar joined the Bureau of Investigation, the precursor of the FBI; by 1936, when he turned forty-one, his name had become a household word.

7. After meeting Edgar at a dinner party in 1918, Helen Gandy became his loyal secretary for fifty-three years. **8. 9.** Despite rumors that Edgar and Lela Rogers *(above)*, mother of Ginger, would wed, friends said the only woman he was ever serious about was Dorothy Lamour.

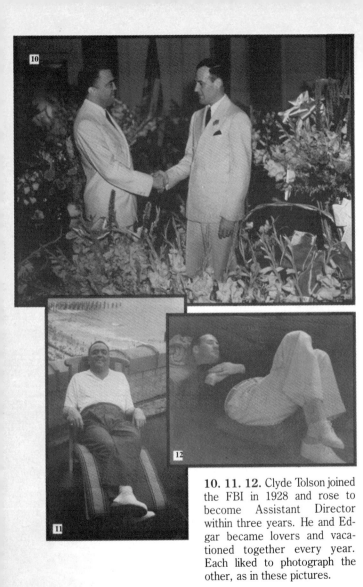

10. 11. 12. Clyde Tolson joined the FBI in 1928 and rose to become Assistant Director within three years. He and Edgar became lovers and vacationed together every year. Each liked to photograph the other, as in these pictures.

13. Luisa Stuart, a young model, met Edgar and Clyde at Manhattan's Stork Club on New Year's Eve, 1936. Afterward, she saw them holding hands in a limousine. 14. Besides Clyde, Edgar's close confidants in the early years were George Ruch *(second from right)* and Guy Hottel *(right)*.

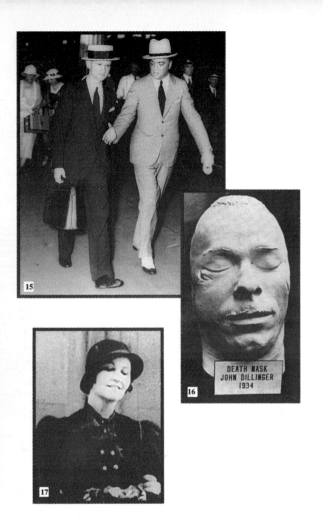

15. Edgar flirted with Agent Melvin Purvis, who led the chase for bandit John Dillinger in the early thirties. **16.** Dillinger's plaster death mask remains on display today at FBI headquarters. **17.** Edgar claimed that Kathryn Kelly, wife of thirties bandit Machine Gun Kelly, was the typical female criminal, "a hundred times more vicious than a man."

18. A master of propaganda, Edgar curried the favor of friendly reporters such as Walter Winchell, here pretending to eavesdrop on the Director and Vice President John Garner in 1939. **19.** Through his Crime Records Department, Edgar ran a powerful public relations operation. This *Time* cover, in 1949, was one of four devoted to him.

TIME
THE WEEKLY NEWSMAGAZINE

J. EDGAR HOOVER

20. Though Franklin Roosevelt vastly increased Edgar's power, the Director thought both the President and the First Lady dangerously left-wing. **21.** Years later, FBI aides leaked documents suggesting Eleanor Roosevelt was romantically involved with leftist writer Joseph Lash; Mrs. Roosevelt poses with Lash and his fiancée, Trude Pratt. **22.** Double Agent Dusko Popov brought the FBI a warning that the Japanese would soon attack Pearl Harbor, but Edgar failed to pass the information on to the White House.

23. Testifying before a Senate subcommittee in 1953, Edgar caused a sensation by claiming former President Truman had ignored FBI warnings about a suspected Communist traitor. He appeared flanked by Clyde Tolson *(left)* and his propaganda specialist, Louis Nichols *(right)*. **24.** Edgar covertly supplied information to Senator Joseph McCarthy and vacationed with him in California. *(Left to right)* Edgar, Royal Miller (Clint Murchison's brother-in-law), Tolson and McCarthy.

25. 26. Texas oil millionaire Clint Murchison *(top)* paid Edgar's vacation hotel bills and shared his and Clyde's passion for horseracing. **27.** Another friend, liquor tycoon Lewis Rosenstiel, made sure Edgar's sexual preferences were accommodated.

28. 29. 30. Edgar claimed the Mafia did not exist. He accepted racing tips from Mafia boss Frank Costello *(top left)*. Meyer Lansky *(top right)* claimed he had "fixed" Edgar, ensuring that he would have no trouble from the FBI. Dub McClanahan, an associate of mobster Carlos Marcello, was a regular vacation companion.

31. 32. Edgar encouraged publication of damaging material about John Kennedy, like the photograph *(above)* snatched as he left a girlfriend's house one night in 1958. Yet when Marilyn Monroe died, both brothers were forced to use the FBI to cover up their affairs with the actress.

28. 29. 30. Edgar claimed the Mafia did not exist. He accepted racing tips from Mafia boss Frank Costello *(top left)*. Meyer Lansky *(top right)* claimed he had "fixed" Edgar, ensuring that he would have no trouble from the FBI. Dub McClanahan, an associate of mobster Carlos Marcello, was a regular vacation companion.

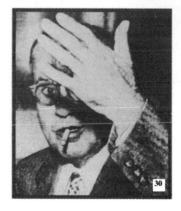

31. 32. Edgar encouraged publication of damaging material about John Kennedy, like the photograph *(above)* snatched as he left a girlfriend's house one night in 1958. Yet when Marilyn Monroe died, both brothers were forced to use the FBI to cover up their affairs with the actress.

33. Martin Luther King was visibly shaken after a 1964 meeting with Edgar, who wiretapped the civil rights leader and tried to smear him. **34.** Aubrey Lewis, recruited in 1962 after pressure from Robert Kennedy, was one of the first authentic black agents. Until then, Edgar used blacks merely as servants.

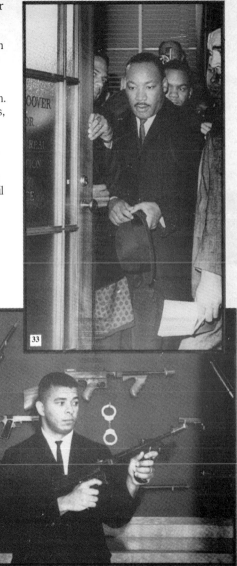

35. 36. 37. Edgar spotted Richard Nixon as a "good man for us" as early as 1947. Later, he apparently used his knowledge of Nixon's secrets, including his relationship with Hong Kong hostess Marianna Liu *(center)* to avoid dismissal. The President responded with flattery, visiting the Director at home *(bottom)*.

38. Until the end, Edgar and Clyde lunched regularly at Washington's Mayflower Hotel. **39.** The Director and his longtime companion watched the 1969 inaugural parade, the last Edgar would see, from their office window.

40. In his final years, retired agents presented Edgar with a bust of himself. **41.** The Director lay in state in the Capitol on Lincoln's bier, and was given a hero's funeral. President Nixon eulogized him as "one of the giants . . . a great force for good in our national life."

tion your name as a candidate for President. If that should come to pass, it would be the most wonderful thing for the United States, and whether you were on a Republican or Democratic ticket, I would guarantee you the largest contribution that you would ever get from anybody and the hardest work by either a Democrat or Republican. I think the United States deserves you. I only hope it gets you.

My best to you always.

Sincerely,

Joe

The notion that Edgar might yet run for the White House was merely a flattering gesture by his old congressional allies. Yet Edgar framed Joe Kennedy's letter and kept it on his office wall for the rest of his life. It was part of a vast correspondence of mutual admiration.

The FBI file on the elder Kennedy suggests a man taking out political insurance. At sixty-seven, he was a figure of immense power but dubious history. Biographers agree that, like Lewis Rosenstiel's fortune, a great part of the Kennedy fortune derived from Prohibition bootlegging in league with organized crime. Frank Costello liked to say he had "helped Joe Kennedy get rich," that they had been partners.

Kennedy's years as Ambassador to London, at the start of World War II, had sealed his personal political fate. He thought the Germans were the right leaders for Europe, opposed America's entering the war and believed Hitler was bluffing. He said he would cheerfully "sell Poland down the river," and that influential American Jews threatened the peace of the world. Learning that Kennedy was also scheming against him politically, President Roosevelt summoned him home, persuaded him not to withdraw his support during the 1940 election, then fired him.

Roosevelt thought Kennedy a "thief," "one of the most evil, disgusting men I have ever known." Harry Truman said he was "as big a crook as we've got anywhere in this country." Kennedy and Edgar, however, had an enduring relationship.

They had met, some say, as long ago as the twenties, when Kennedy was financing movies in Hollywood. He introduced Edgar to a clutch of movie stars—decorative females who looked good at his side and belied the rumors about his homosexuality. A quarter of a century later, Edgar and Clyde had become occasional guests at the Kennedy winter retreat in Florida. When there were first discussions about setting up a J. Edgar Hoover Foundation, Kennedy promised a large contribution. He once offered Edgar a princely salary to join the Kennedy organization as "security chief."

From 1943, for his part, Kennedy was a Special Service contact for the FBI, complete with Bureau symbol and running file, ready to use his influence in industry and the diplomatic world "for any advantage the Bureau might desire." Years later, knowing Edgar's jealousy of the CIA, he leaked to Edgar what he learned as a member of Eisenhower's board on Foreign Intelligence.

From 1951 the FBI maintained a Resident Agency, staffed by four agents, at Hyannis Port. Since it had no other discernible purpose, unkind observers said it existed "solely to appease and serve the Kennedys." Bureau agents buttered up "the Ambassador," extended courtesies to the family—and kept Edgar briefed on what its members were doing.

Edgar's career seemed assured as the fifties drew to a close. He was already laden with honors, and President Eisenhower doled out a new one, the President's Award for Distinguished Civilian Service. Officials in Indiana declared a J. Edgar Hoover Day in 1959, and another was planned for Illinois.

Above all, Edgar remained close to the seat of power and to the man he hoped would be the next president. As politicians geared up for the 1960 election, Edgar was seen a good deal with his protégé of the McCarthy era, Vice President Richard Nixon. It was, rather, a matter of Nixon making sure he was seen with Edgar. They went to the races together and, when Edgar celebrated his thirty-fifth year as Director, Nixon came to his office to pay obeisance.

Nixon was the clear Republican favorite, but the Party's popularity was at its lowest ebb in twenty years. Edgar, like many others, covered his bets. He ordered agents to supply Nixon with research material for his speeches and kept a weather eye on the Democrats.

The Democrats were juggling Joseph Kennedy's son John, now forty-two, the senator from Massachusetts; veteran contender Adlai Stevenson; Senator Hubert Humphrey; and Lyndon Johnson. For all his father's blandishments, John Kennedy was not the candidate Edgar preferred. If there was to be a Democrat in office, he favored Johnson.

Edgar had known Johnson since the thirties, when he had first come to Washington, and they had been close neighbors since the forties. Edgar sometimes visited the Johnsons for dinner or Sunday brunch and—he told colleagues—filled in as baby-sitter for their daughters. They came to think of him as an uncle and helped look for his dogs when they strayed. The Johnson home, Edgar said, "was a place where you could get the best chili con carne and the best mint julep in Washington."

Lyndon Johnson, one of Washington's craftiest manipulators of men, understood early on the importance of making Edgar his friend or—more important—ensuring he never gave him cause to become an enemy. Johnson's political closet was bulging with skeletons. There were corrupt business deals, and women, and above all there were the allegations of ballot-rigging in 1948, when Johnson won election to the Senate by just eighty-seven votes.[1]

During the outcry following that election, Edgar had made a personal visit to Austin, the Texas state capital, and was seen closeted with Clint Murchison and Sid Richardson, who had backed Johnson. The FBI's probe of the vote fraud was conducted, observers recalled, with "a notable lack of investigative and prosecutorial vigor." According to the definitive study of the case, it soon "disappeared without trace."

Johnson referred to Edgar privately as "that queer bastard." He fawned over him, however, in a steady stream of complimentary letters. "I think you and all your men are tops," he scrawled on one. "I see them under all circumstances and when I do I'm proud that I am a public servant." In the last weeks of the Eisenhower administration, Clyde Tolson lobbied frantically for a special law to ensure that, should Edgar retire he would continue to receive his full salary. This was achieved, not least thanks to pressure from Majority Leader Johnson.

Edgar reciprocated. He was observed visiting Room S-208, the hideaway Senate office known as the Johnson Ranch East, to proffer advice. He even flew to Texas in November 1959 to make speeches extolling Johnson's virtues. During a whistle-stop tour, including a visit to the Johnson ranch, the Senator bear-hugged Edgar for the cameras. Edgar then returned to Washington after a meeting with oil millionaire Billy Byars, a regular vacation companion in California and—like Murchison—one of Johnson's financial backers. Disregarding all the proprieties, the Director of the FBI had been making a campaign appearance on behalf of a presidential candidate.

Clint Murchison, the kingmaker who had played a key role in bringing Eisenhower to power, had something on all the political horses. The big money went to Nixon, as it had in the past and would in the future. He even sent an aide to deliver $25,000 in cash to the Kennedys. This, though, as Bobby Baker put it, was "just betcopping." Edgar's friend Murchison was really rooting for Lyndon Johnson, a candidate sure to protect the interests of the big oil companies.

Murchison cared about power, not party labels, and one man—Edgar—remained a fixture on his political agenda. Two years before the election, when right-wing senator William Knowland had presidential hopes, the millionaire offered this advice in a letter to Johnson: "If you can work Knowland, Nixon and Hoover together," he told his fellow Texan, "you can control the United States."

In 1960, with Johnson's name replacing Knowland's, the

same formula applied. And as the campaign got under way, Edgar began considering the strengths—and weaknesses—of the young man who did not fit any agenda but his own, John Kennedy.

"When John Kennedy was making a strong challenge for the presidency," recalled Cartha DeLoach, "Mr. Hoover asked Clyde Tolson, and Tolson told me, to make a thorough review of the files. They knew all about Kennedy's desires for sex, and the fact that he would sleep with almost anything that wore a skirt. 'Joe Kennedy told me,' Mr. Hoover said, 'that he should have gelded Jack when he was a small boy.'"

The FBI file of dirt on John Kennedy had been opened at the start of World War II, based on British MI-5 reports on his social life while visiting his father, then Ambassador to Britain. He was just twenty years old, and the reports were merely random intelligence filed by a foreign ally. Then, in 1940, Edgar began receiving reports about a twenty-eight-year-old beauty named Inga Arvad, currently living in Washington.

Arvad was a journalist and socialite, Danish-born but with associations in Nazi Germany. She had interviewed Hermann Göring and Adolf Hitler, and by one report went to bed with the latter. She described Hitler in print as "very kind, very charming . . . not evil as he is depicted . . . an idealist."

At first Arvad rang no alarm bells at the FBI. Ironically, as a reporter for the *Washington Times Herald*, she charmed her way to meetings with the Bureau's top brass. She wrote flatteringly of Edgar's secretary, Helen Gandy, with her "masculine intelligence and womanly intuition," and of Clyde, with his "intelligent eyes" and a smile "like a good boy expecting the promised candy bar." Clyde even introduced Arvad to Edgar at a party.

In late 1941, however, officials scurried for cover. Arvad's interviews were suddenly declared to have been "unsatisfactory." Edgar himself had ordered a probe that revealed that "a young Ensign of the U.S. Navy known as Jack . . . has apparently been spending the night with Miss Arvad in her apartment."

Kennedy, then serving with Naval Intelligence, had been introduced to Arvad by his sister Kathleen. By January 1942, FBI surveillance records confirm, they were having a passionate affair. Kennedy called her "Inga-Binga." She called him "Honeysuckle" and "Honey Child Wilder." They talked of marriage, a match—friends recalled—that his father violently opposed.

To separate the lovers, the Navy transferred Kennedy out of Washington, a move that only increased their ardor. Edgar's agents listened to hidden microphones as the couple made love, "on numerous occasions," in Room 132 of the Fort Sumter Hotel in Charleston, South Carolina. The surveillance was dropped for a while when Arvad began to suspect she was being bugged, then resumed in the summer of 1942. By that time Kennedy's meddlesome father had arranged for his son's transfer to the Pacific, where his heroism after the sinking of PT-109 would bring lasting fame.

Like a million wartime romances, the affair with Arvad lasted only months. The FBI's surveillance had been a legitimate way of handling a potential security risk, and the lovers had done nothing disloyal. It was, however, the start of lasting bitterness between Kennedy and Edgar.

In March 1942, when Arvad realized she was being surveilled, she was overheard telling Kennedy she intended protesting directly to Edgar. She was going to say, "Now, look here, Edgar J., I don't like everybody listening in on my phone. . . ." In fact, Arvad told Ronald McCoy, her son by a subsequent marriage, Kennedy went with her to confront Edgar. As McCoy recalled it, "Jack was furious. Through his father or through Arthur Krock, he knew everybody, so he and Mother went to see J. Edgar Hoover. Hoover told them his investigation showed she was *not* a Nazi spy or did anything for them. So Jack asked Hoover if he would give them a letter saying she wasn't a Nazi spy. Hoover said he couldn't, because if he gave her a letter and then she went out and started working for them tomorrow, his ass was on the line."

That first encounter sowed the seeds of future discord. Pique aside, Kennedy sensed danger long before Edgar became a threat to the Kennedy presidency. Exposure of the affair with Arvad—a suspected Nazi spy—could have been disastrous. In 1946, the moment he became a career politician, Kennedy began worrying about Edgar's dossier.

"When Jack came down to Congress," recalled his friend Langdon Marvin, "one of the things on his mind was the Inga-Binga tape in FBI files—the tape *he* was on. He wanted to get the tape from the FBI. I told him not to ask for it. . . . Ten years later, after he beat Henry Cabot Lodge in the Massachusetts senatorial race, Jack became alarmed. 'That bastard. I'm going to force Hoover to give me those files,' he said to me. I said, 'Jack, you're not going to do a thing. You can be sure there'll be a dozen copies made before he returns them to you, so you will not have gained a yard. And if he knows you're desperate for them, he'll realize he has you in a stranglehold.'"

Perhaps Kennedy did betray his fear. Just after his election to the Senate, the record shows, he asked for "the opportunity of shaking hands" with Edgar. From then until 1960, Kennedy went out of his way to flatter the man he privately called "bastard." Even at his wedding, he found time to tell the Hyannis FBI agent he was always available to "support Mr. Hoover." Just weeks later he piled on the flattery, saying the FBI was the only agency "worthy of its salt." His brother, Robert, for his part, was said to be "more enthusiastic than ever about J. Edgar Hoover."

Edgar wrote polite replies, filed the letters and continued to collect smear material. He was to learn that, one night in 1958, a couple named Leonard and Florence Kater had been disturbed by the sound of pebbles being thrown at an upstairs window. The window belonged to their twenty-year-old lodger, Pamela Turnure, a secretary in Kennedy's

Senate office. The man Turnure let in that night was Kennedy himself, and he became a regular nocturnal visitor.

The Katers, strict Catholics, became obsessed about the man they called the "philanderer." They rigged up a tape recorder to pick up the sounds of the couple's lovemaking and snapped a picture of Kennedy sneaking out in the middle of the night. They spied on him for months on end, even after Turnure moved out of their house.

Something odd happened in the course of this persecution. Kennedy told an aide he thought his home telephone or his secretary's was being tapped. The aide, acting on his own initiative, asked the FBI to check it out. Then, apparently after speaking further with Kennedy, he called back to ask the FBI to "just forget the whole matter." Kennedy, we can assume, was appalled at the notion of asking Edgar for any such favor—not least if, as he may have feared, the Bureau itself was involved in the bugging.

Edgar learned of Kennedy's affair with Turnure soon enough anyway, thanks to the Katers. In the spring of 1959, with the election campaign approaching, they mailed details of the "adulterer's" conduct to the newspapers. The press shied away, but one company—Stearn Publications—sent the Katers' letter on to Edgar. Soon, according to one source, he quietly obtained a copy of the compromising sex tapes and offered them to Lyndon Johnson as campaign ammunition.

"Hoover and Johnson both had something the other wanted," said Robert Baker, the Texan's longtime confidant. "Johnson needed to know Hoover was not after *his* ass. And Hoover certainly wanted Lyndon Johnson to be president rather than Jack Kennedy. Hoover was a leaker, and he was always telling Johnson about Kennedy's sexual proclivities. Johnson told me Hoover played a tape for him, made by this woman who had rented an apartment to one of John Kennedy's girlfriends. And she turned the tape over to the FBI. . . ."

One senior official, William Sullivan, said flatly that Edgar tried "to sabotage Jack Kennedy's campaign." Surviving records suggest Agents in Charge had standing orders to report everything they picked up on him. In March 1960 the New Orleans office quoted an informant who:

> had occasion to overhear a conversation which indicated that Senator Kennedy had been compromised with a woman in Las Vegas, Nevada. . . . He stated that when Senator Kennedy was in Miami, Fla., an airline hostess named [name deleted] was sent to visit Sen. Kennedy.

Edgar had the woman's name and address within hours. Another report, filed a few days later from Los Angeles, remains totally censored. It is marked merely "Memo, John F. Kennedy, U.S. Senator, Information Concerning, Central Research Matter."

In April, as Kennedy's primary victories began to panic the Johnson camp, DeLoach reported a source who:

> noted on the top of Kennedy's desk a photograph openly displayed. This photo included Senator Kennedy and other men, as well as several girls in the nude. It was taken aboard a yacht or some type of pleasure cruiser. . . . The thing that disturbed him most was that the Senator would show such poor judgment in leaving this photo openly displayed. . . . Members of the guard and cleaning services were aware of the photograph and Kennedy's "extracurricular activities" were a standard joke around the Senate Office Building.

On the very day of the nomination, July 13, DeLoach received a summary of "highlights" of the Bureau's Kennedy file. It included a reference to the Inga Arvad affair in World War II and to "affidavits from two mulatto prostitutes in New York." It also raised a factor far more ominous than the sexual allegations, yet inextricably linked to them —"the hoodlum connections of Senator Kennedy."

John Kennedy, like his father before him, had apparently

slipped into his own shabby relationship with organized crime. He was compromised by it, and not only because of sex—caught, even before the presidency began, in the tangle of intrigue that may eventually have led to his assassination.

Edgar, himself long since neutralized by the mob because of his homosexuality, would gradually discover the extent of the younger man's folly.

The Kennedy connection with the Mafia had not ended with Prohibition. Joseph Kennedy had maintained personal and business ties to the mob. His Chicago agent in the forties was a Miami gangster—eventually shot dead following a deal with the syndicate. He had played golf from time to time since the thirties with Johnny Roselli, the Chicago mob's man on the West Coast.

John Kennedy followed the same perilous road. According to Meyer Lansky's widow, Kennedy met Lansky when he visited Cuba in 1957—even took his advice on where to find women. Not long afterward, in Arizona, he went to mass with "Smiling Gus" Battaglia, a close friend of Mafia chieftain Joe Bonanno. Later, he met Bonanno himself.

In 1960, when the Kennedys were pursuing the presidency, Joe Kennedy had meetings in California with numerous gangsters. He mended fences with Teamsters leader Jimmy Hoffa, whom his son Robert—in sharp contrast to the father and the elder brother—had long been pursuing.

At the height of the campaign, the elder Kennedy reportedly met with an assortment of organized crime bosses at Felix Young's restaurant in New York. "I took the reservations," said Edna Daulyton, then working as a hostess at Young's, "and it was as though every gangster chief in the United States was there. I don't remember all the names now, but there was John Roselli, Carlos Marcello from New Orleans, the two brothers from Dallas, the top men from Buffalo, California and Colorado. They were all top people, not soldiers. I was amazed Joe Kennedy would take the risk."

Thanks to a variety of sources, including FBI wiretaps

and mob associates, it is now clear the Kennedys used the mob connection as a stepping-stone to power. They asked Carlos Marcello to use his influence to win Louisiana's support for Kennedy at the Convention. He refused—he was already committed to Lyndon Johnson—but Chicago Mafia boss Giancana proved helpful.

Giancana and Roselli, Joe Kennedy's golfing friend, would later be overheard on an FBI wiretap discussing the "donations" they had made during the vital primary campaign in West Virginia. According to Judith Campbell, who became the candidate's lover in the spring of 1960, John Kennedy himself took outrageous risks to enlist Giancana's help. He met secretly with the Mafia boss at least twice and even sent Campbell to him as a courier, carrying vast sums of money in cash.

"I felt Jack was entrusting me with something that was very important to him," Campbell recalled. "I didn't know where the money was going to go when it left Sam, but I knew it had to do with the campaign. . . . Someone was being paid off, something was being bought with this money."

A mass of information suggests that is exactly what was going on. The Kennedy millions, along with contributions from the mobsters themselves, were used to buy votes both during the primaries and—in Chicago—in the close-run election that sent Kennedy to the White House.

From the start, Edgar knew something of all this. As early as March 1960—the very month Kennedy began discussing Giancana with Judith Campbell—word reached FBI headquarters that:

> members of the underworld element . . . Joe Fischetti [a Giancana associate] and other unidentified hoodlums are financially supporting and actively endeavoring to secure the nomination for the presidency as Democratic candidate, Senator John F. Kennedy . . . to assist Senator Kennedy's campaign whereby . . . hoodlums will have an entre [sic] to Senator Kennedy. . . .

In July, on the eve of the Convention in Los Angeles, Robert Kennedy was told that Edgar's agents had been trying to dig up information about the conduct of the West Virginia primary. A long FBI report containing "an extensive amount of derogatory information" on his brother was supposedly on its way to the Justice Department.

If John Kennedy was worried by such reports, he did not show it. His antics with women during the Convention caused near panic among Democratic officials. We now know he was juggling Judith Campbell, Marilyn Monroe, whom he had known on and off for years, and sundry call girls. Los Angeles law enforcement noted his use of whores from a mob-controlled vice ring. This, too, would eventually be reported to Edgar.

Kennedy often shrugged off warnings that his womanizing might one day ruin him. "They can't touch me while I'm alive," he said to one intimate, "and after I'm dead, who cares?" "Jack," said Senator George Smathers, "felt he could walk on water so far as women were concerned." Reckless womanizing was a flaw in Kennedy's character that imperiled everything he strove for, and Edgar was one of the first to spot that flaw.

According to one compelling account, Edgar used his knowledge to influence the selection of the vice presidential candidate at the Democratic Convention in Los Angeles in 1960.

The Democrat Edgar favored, Lyndon Johnson, had gone to the Los Angeles Convention not just to win the nomination for himself, but to see Kennedy beaten. "LBJ," said the political wags, stood for "Let's Block Jack." It was a dirty fight. Johnson's men spread the word that Kennedy suffered from Addison's disease—which was true—and that his father had been pro-Nazi, which was not unfair. Both sides accused the other of buying delegates' votes. When Kennedy money and superb organization defeated Johnson on the first ballot, he was furious.

"He barked at aides, cursed, slammed down telephones," recalled Johnson's aide Bobby Baker. "He refused to go and thank his exhausted campaign workers. I did not know it at the time, but LBJ had learned that the Knight newspapers on the West Coast would be out with a midnight edition saying John F. Kennedy was considering three men for the vice-presidential spot—and that LBJ was not among them."

Less than twenty-four hours later, all that had changed. After a day of hectic speculation, Johnson stepped before the cameras to announce he was to run alongside Kennedy as the candidate for the Vice Presidency. "Jack Kennedy has asked me to serve," he said smoothly. "I accept."

Hardly anyone had expected this development. And over the years historians have tried repeatedly to analyze the tense negotiations between the Kennedy and Johnson camps that led to Johnson accepting the vice-presidential slot.[2] Kennedy himself told his aide Pierre Salinger cryptically that "the whole story will never be known. And it's just as well it won't be." "The only people who were involved in the discussions were Jack and myself," said Robert Kennedy. "We both promised each other that we'd never tell what happened."

According to new testimony, what happened was blackmail. For John Kennedy, a key factor in giving Johnson the vice-presidential slot was the threat of ruinous sex revelations, revelations that would have destroyed the "American family man" image so carefully seeded in the national mind, and snatched the presidency from his grasp. The blackmailers, by this account, were Johnson himself—and Edgar.

The new information comes from Evelyn Lincoln, John Kennedy's personal secretary for twelve years, before and throughout his presidency, and herself a part of the Kennedy legend. She lived and breathed the Kennedy saga, took her boss' intimate telephone calls, saw his most secret correspondence, watched him agonize over crucial decisions. She was also at his side in Los Angeles.

Intensely loyal to the President's memory, Mrs. Lincoln will say no more about his sex life than is necessary to make her point about the episode in Los Angeles. She has now, however, admitted that her boss was a "ladies' man." Then, with a chuckle, she blamed it on the ladies. "Kennedy didn't chase women," she laughed. "The women chased Kennedy. I've never seen anything like it. . . ."[3]

During the 1960 campaign, according to Mrs. Lincoln, Kennedy discovered how vulnerable his womanizing had made him. Sexual blackmail, she said, had long been part of Lyndon Johnson's modus operandi—abetted by Edgar. "J. Edgar Hoover," Lincoln said, "gave Johnson the information about various congressmen and senators so that Johnson could go to X senator and say, 'How about this little deal you have with this woman?' and so forth. That's how he kept them in line. He used his IOUs with them as what he hoped was his road to the presidency. He had this trivia to use, because he had Hoover in his corner. And he thought that the members of Congress would go out there and put him over at the Convention. But then Kennedy beat him at the Convention. And well, after that Hoover and Johnson and their group were able to push Johnson on Kennedy.

"LBJ," said Lincoln, "had been using all the information Hoover could find on Kennedy—during the campaign, even before the Convention. And Hoover was in on the pressure on Kennedy at the Convention."

Whatever Edgar had on Kennedy at this stage, it was apparently enough. His agents' reports had filled him in on some of the recent womanizing, and there was also the ugly information about the Mafia connection. There was, too, the dossier Kennedy himself had long been worried about: the voluminous file, complete with tape recordings, on the candidate's wartime affair with Inga Arvad.

In 1960 only fifteen years had passed since the war. Had voters learned that Kennedy had had a serious affair with a woman he knew to be close to Hitler and Göring, many—not least the vital Jewish constituency—might well have turned against him. Some believed that his father's supposed Nazi sympathies would count against him anyway.

During their day of decision over the Vice Presidency, the brothers did their worrying alone in a bedroom, away from their aides. As John paced up and down and Robert slumped on a bed, Lincoln moved in and out of the room with messages. She heard enough, she says, to understand that Edgar's smear information on Kennedy was at the heart of their dilemma. "It was the information J. Edgar Hoover passed to Johnson—about womanizing, and things in Joe Kennedy's background, and anything he could dig up. Johnson was using that as clout. Kennedy was angry, because they had boxed him into a corner. He was absolutely boxed in. He and Bobby tried everything they could think of, anything to get Johnson out of the way. But in that situation, they couldn't do it."

Once he had decided on Johnson, John Kennedy tried to make little of it. "I'm forty-three years old," he told his aide Kenneth O'Donnell. "I'm not going to die in office. So the vice presidency doesn't mean anything. . . ."

Lyndon Johnson saw it differently. "I looked it up," he would tell Clare Boothe Luce later. "One out of every four presidents has died in office. I'm a gamblin' man, darlin', and this is the only chance I got."

Evelyn Lincoln's account, if accurate, is evidence that Edgar's interference in the American political process was even more insidious than previously feared. It suggests, in effect, that he subverted the democratic system as ruthlessly as any secret police chief in a totalitarian state.

Edgar soon had an opportunity to test his power. The very day after the Convention a press report forecast that—if elected—Kennedy would fire Edgar.

"Clyde Tolson called me," recalled Cartha DeLoach, "and said, 'We ought to have some feeling as to his intentions regarding the Director. Why don't you get one of your friends in the press to plant a question at a press conference?' I called a vice president at UPI, a good friend, and asked him to ask Kennedy whether he would keep Hoover on. He did ask that question, and John Kennedy's response was immediately, without hesitation, 'That will be one of the first appointments I will make.'"

Indeed, less than three weeks after his nomination, Kennedy had committed himself to reappointing Edgar. Three months later, the night after his election, Edgar's name came up after dinner with friends at Hyannis Port.

"It was a joyous, silly, fun evening," recalled Ben Bradlee, then Washington Bureau Chief for *Newsweek*. "Jackie Kennedy and my wife, Tony, were both extremely pregnant, and I remember the President said, 'OK, girls, the election's over, you can take the pillows out now!' We talked about what we should call him now that he was elected, and he said, 'Well, Prez sounds pretty good.' Then, as a sort of joke, he said to Bill Walton and me, 'I'll give each of you guys an appointment, one job to fill. What do you want?' And one of us said, 'Well, one guy you can't reappoint is Allen Dulles,' who was CIA Director. And the other said, 'I don't give a shit what you do, so long as you don't reappoint J. Edgar Hoover.' And he just laughed. . . ."

Bradlee was close by the next morning as the new president placed a call to Edgar. "He was telling him how much he wanted him, was counting on him, to stay on. . . . Laid it on a bit thick, I thought."

Kennedy's decision to reappoint Edgar was front-page news within hours. "He never discussed it with any of us," said Kenneth O'Donnell. "I think he made up his mind— 'We're not going to rock the boat at this moment.' He would not discuss it with me."

As President, Kennedy would make light of the Edgar problem. He dismissed Edgar as a "master of public relations." "The three most overrated things in the world," he liked to say, "are the state of Texas, the FBI" and whatever was exasperating him most at the moment. In private, he fumed.

Kennedy told the columnist Igor Cassini, a family friend, that he "knew" Edgar was a homosexual. "I talked to him about it," said the novelist Gore Vidal, "and he gave me one of those looks. He loathed Hoover. I didn't know then that Hoover was blackmailing him. Nor did I realize how helpless the Kennedys were to do anything about him."

The bottom line was fear. "All the Kennedys were afraid of Hoover," said Ben Bradlee. "John F. Kennedy was afraid not to reappoint him," said the columnist Jack Anderson. "I know that because I talked to the President about it. He admitted that he'd appointed Hoover because it would've been politically destructive not to."[4]

On the day Kennedy was elected, Edgar wrote him an unctuous letter. "My dear Senator, Permit me to join the countless wellwishers who are congratulating you on being elected President of the United States. . . . America is most fortunate to have a man of your caliber at its helm in these perilous days. . . . You know, of course, that this Bureau stands ready to be of all possible assistance to you. . . ."

Hours after writing the letter, Edgar asked Philip Hochstein, editorial director of the Newhouse newspaper group, to fly down to Washington from New York. "When I got to his office," Hochstein recalled, "I offered my congratulations on the announcement of his reappointment by the President-elect. He replied in a surly manner and said, 'Kennedy *isn't* the President-elect.' He said the election had been stolen in a number of states, including New Jersey, where my office was, and Missouri, where Newhouse had recently bought a paper. . . .

"It was quite a harangue, and I think Hoover wanted me to be part of a crusade to undo the election. I didn't do it, and I didn't tell anyone at the time. But later I saw what Hoover had told me reported accurately in a book by an author who knew Hoover well. Hoover wanted it published, one way or another. . . . I remember, too, he called in an assistant—DeLoach, I think. He asked me to join DeLoach afterwards, that DeLoach had some interesting things to tell me. And the conversation with DeLoach was about Jack Kennedy's women. . . ."

"I think he's dangerous," Robert Kennedy would say of

Edgar after his brother was dead. "But it was a danger we could control, that we were on top of, that we could deal with. There wasn't anything that he could do."

Robert knew this was far from the truth, that Edgar had been a constant maddening irritant to the Kennedy presidency. And, by the time John Kennedy flew to Dallas, dealing with the Director of the FBI had become a nightmare.

CHAPTER 25

"A man cannot be too careful in the choice of his enemies."

Oscar Wilde

SOON AFTER THE INAUGURATION, WORKERS AT THE JUSTICE DE-partment received strange orders. They were to retrieve a neglected piece of statuary from storage, dust it off and display it prominently in the Department hallway at Tenth Street and Pennsylvania. Then orders came to remove it—only to be followed by a fresh command to put it back again. And so on, several times.

The statue was of Stanley Finch, the forgotten first-ever head of the Bureau, one of three who had preceded Edgar as Director. Most people were by now under the im-pression that Edgar was *the* Director, the only one there ever had been. The resurrection of Finch's bust was a re-minder that there had been life before Edgar and, by im-plication, there would be life afterward. The orders to take it away, went the whisper, came from Edgar. The orders to put it back came from Attorney General Robert Ken-nedy.

The President's brother had not wanted to run the Justice Department—he rightly anticipated protests about nepo-tism, lack of experience and youth. Still only thirty-five, he had never even practiced law. His one sure qualification was his loyalty to John Kennedy, in times that promised to be stormy.

"I need you," the new president had told Robert over bacon and eggs a month after the election. In the end it was as simple as that. Robert Kennedy became the youngest Attorney General in 150 years.

Robert had consulted Edgar, among others, before bowing to his brother's will. And Edgar had told him, in an opaque sort of way, to take the job. When he did, Edgar wrote an obsequious note to say he was "very happy" and praised him in the press. Yet each man, behind the other's back, knew this was hypocrisy. "I didn't like to tell him that," Edgar muttered to William Sullivan, "but what could I say?" "He spoke of it," said Cartha DeLoach, "as the worst damn advice he ever gave in his life."

John Kennedy's right-hand man, Kenneth O'Donnell, recalled talking with Robert when he emerged from seeing Edgar. "I said, 'Bobby, just tell me exactly what he said,' and he told me Hoover advised him to take it. But if I listened to the words carefully, [Edgar] was hoping he wouldn't. . . . I knew Hoover wouldn't want him. He doesn't want the Attorney General to be more important than him. . . . He couldn't want Bobby to have it, he couldn't want that."

The official portrait of Robert Kennedy, hanging today in the Criminal Division of the Justice Department, shows a slim young man with rumpled hair, in leather jacket and T-shirt. The pictures of sixty-three of his predecessors are all, by contrast, sober-faced, predictable fellows in formal dress. Edgar wore the same drab uniform, kowtowed to the same conventions. More important, previous Attorneys General had been his superiors only in theory. For nearly thirty years, since the Roosevelt days, he had answered only to the President. With the arrival of Robert Kennedy, all that changed.

Kennedy burst into the Justice Department determined to effect change. Not satisfied with the office usually used by Attorneys General, he took over the great wood-paneled chamber normally used for conferences. Not content with the government furniture, he replaced it with large sofas, a sailfish over the mantel, and a stuffed tiger by the fireplace. He fixed drawings done by his seven children on the wall with Scotch tape, and sometimes the children themselves appeared in the office. Often his dog, Brumus, a grouchy Labrador, lay growling on the rug.

When Kennedy wore a tie, it was Ivy League, and it often hung cheerfully askew. His blue button-down shirt gaped open at the neck, and the Attorney General's legs spent half the day on the vast desk, not under it.

An Attorney General in shirtsleeves, Edgar told a colleague, looked "ridiculous." He and Clyde looked on in confusion, during a visit to Kennedy's office, as the younger man sat throwing darts at a target on the wall. Their amazement turned to outrage when some of the darts missed altogether, piercing the "government property" paneling.

Soon aides were reporting the discovery of beer cans on the ground outside, supposedly tossed from the Attorney General's window. One wintry day, Edgar told friends, Kennedy had water pumped into the Department courtyard so his children could skate.

Years later, after Robert had been killed, Edgar would refer to him derisively as the "Messiah of the generation gap." Edgar had spent nearly forty years drilling conformity into his men and was rarely seen out of a tie, even on vacation. The Kennedy style, on what he viewed as his personal territory, offended him deeply.

Sometimes the affront was personal. Edgar was not amused, agents recall, when Kennedy took him to lunch at a People's drugstore. Even the Labrador made its contribution to Edgar's discomfiture—on the floor outside his office. Kennedy had a tendency to appear without notice in the Director's office, something no one in government had ever presumed to do. One afternoon he pushed past a horrified Miss Gandy to find the Director taking a nap.

Kennedy insisted on instant communication with Edgar and began by ordering the installation of a buzzer with which to summon the Director at will. Edgar had it removed, only to be confronted by telephone engineers putting in a hot line. The first time Kennedy used it, recalled former Assistant Director Mark Felt, "Hoover's secretary answered. 'When I pick up this phone,' Kennedy snapped impatiently, 'there's only one man I want to talk to. Get this phone on the Director's desk immediately.'"

There was such a phone, and Edgar never came to terms with it. He would sometimes pick it up only to hear one of Kennedy's children giggling on the other end. "Shall I get Hoover over here?" former Justice Department attorney William Hundley recalled Kennedy saying. "And he would hit the goddamn button, and the Old Man would come in all red-faced. They'd start fighting with each other right there in front of me. No other Attorney General had ever done that to Hoover. I couldn't believe it."

In a stroke, Robert Kennedy had broken the mold that Edgar had fashioned over decades. He was asserting the authority of the Attorney General, which Edgar had eroded, and he was severing Edgar's most treasured link of all, his one-to-one contact with the President himself. John Kennedy's secretary, Evelyn Lincoln, cannot recall a single phone call between the President and Edgar during the entire administration.

From the White House, Kenneth O'Donnell made it clear this was deliberate policy. If Edgar tried to call the President, he would be blocked by either Evelyn Lincoln or O'Donnell himself. "It gets back to the crux. . . . Bobby is the boss, and for the first time in Hoover's life he can't go over the boss's head."

Having a boss at all was something that, at sixty-six, Edgar could never have borne easily; having Robert Kennedy as his boss was unthinkable. It was not just that Kennedy's style was the antithesis of everything Edgar stood for. He had a driven quality, an absolute insistence on getting his own way that—when it did not inspire love and loyalty—triggered bitter enmity. It certainly triggered Edgar's.

In the company of "his" people, Edgar pulled no punches. He told Roy Cohn the younger Kennedy was an "arrogant whippersnapper." He spoke of him to Richard Nixon, just months into the presidency, as "that sneaky little son of a bitch." He sounded off about it on vacation, to the Weiss family in Florida and to his friends at the Del Charro. Billy

Byars, Jr., the son of the oilman, recalls him "raving about Robert Kennedy, saying god-awful things. He despised him and didn't hide the fact."

When it suited him, on the other hand, he lied. "Attorney General Kennedy and I," Edgar wrote to Cardinal Cushing, a friend of the Kennedy family, "have worked most cordially together. . . . We have not had a single difference."

Kennedy's people, meanwhile, found Edgar very strange indeed. Joe Dolan, a slim young lawyer, found himself lectured about weight problems for forty-five minutes— then briskly dismissed. John Seigenthaler, Kennedy's administrative assistant, was harangued first about the way key newspapers were supposedly infiltrated by Communists, then about Adlai Stevenson's alleged homosexuality. Edgar subjected first Robert, then the President himself, to a long briefing on the alleged homosexuality of Joseph Alsop, the distinguished journalist.

It was all bizarre to the Kennedys. For the first time, perhaps, men in power dared voice the notion that Edgar was not entirely sane. "He was out of it today, wasn't he?" Robert murmured to Seigenthaler when he emerged from Edgar's lecture about Communists and pederasts. Kennedy staffers began to talk about Edgar's "good" and "bad" days.

"He acts in such a strange, peculiar way," Robert Kennedy was to say in 1964, on an embargoed basis, in an interview intended for use by future historians. "He's rather a psycho. I think it's a very dangerous organization. I think he's become senile and rather . . . frightening."

Sometimes through Robert, and sometimes in memos to the White House, Edgar quickly began playing on the President's weakest characteristic: his womanizing. Ten days after the inauguration, an Italian magazine had published comments by Alicia Purdom, wife of the British actor Edmund Purdom. She claimed that in 1951, before either of them was married, she and Kennedy had had an affair. Had Joseph Kennedy not stepped in to end it, they would have married.

This was not picked up in the American press. Edgar, however, alerted by his man in Rome, promptly informed the President's brother. Available information, and a heavily censored file, suggests the matter had been a worry even before the election, and that the family had paid a vast sum of money to hush the matter up. Allegations would reach Edgar that the reported affair with Purdom had involved a pregnancy. Stage by stage, as more of this came to his attention, he made sure the Kennedys knew he knew.

By now Pamela Turnure, who had been involved with the President in his Senate days, had—ironically—become press secretary to the President's wife. Her former landlady, Florence Kater, still obsessed with the affair, once again tried to stir up trouble. Robert Kennedy's office asked the FBI whether it knew anything about the matter and was told untruthfully that it did not. Edgar was playing games, and the brothers—mindful of how Edgar had used his Kennedy sex file to propel Lyndon Johnson toward the vice presidency—had to live with it.

They also had to live with efforts by Edgar, from the very beginning, to torpedo White House nominees he did not like. Pierre Salinger, who had been named as Press Secretary, was astonished to get a call from *Time* inquiring about an allegation that he had received Communist training as a child. Salinger cleared the matter up—his "Communist training" had consisted of a vacation spent at a summer camp run by the Longshoremen's Union—and *Time* explained that the tip-off had come from Edgar's office. Then Edgar personally warned John Kennedy that Salinger had once been in jail. This was true. As a young reporter for the *San Francisco Chronicle,* he had posed as a prisoner to write a series of articles on jail conditions. Salinger's appointment went ahead.

As John Kennedy examined FBI reports on potential appointees, he was astounded by their keyhole quality, by the obsession with sexual innuendo. One celebrated episode involved the account of how an American ambassador, caught with a married woman, had escaped through a bedroom window without his trousers. Pressed by the FBI for his reaction, Kennedy eventually sent word that he "wished his diplomats could run faster." Told of a White House secretary's promiscuity, he just chuckled. "Great," he said. "I never knew she was that way."

The banter stopped, however, when the extent of Edgar's snooping dawned on John Kennedy. "He was shocked at the welter of scandal," learned Hugh Sidey, then as now a *Time* correspondent in Washington. "He gasped and told his aides that he would never again read another such dossier." "I don't want any part of that stuff," the President told Kenneth O'Donnell. "I don't want to hear about it. I'd like to see the report they've got on *me*. . . ."

As an agent at headquarters, Gordon Liddy saw files on Kennedy. From mid-1961, while on a headquarters assignment that included research on politicians, he perused numerous $5'' \times 7''$ cards packed with file references to the President's past and present. "There was a lot," he recalled. "It grew while I was there, and kept growing."

Edgar's knowledge of the President's bedroom secrets, exposure of which could most certainly destroy him, remained a constant threat. With just a sliver of an electoral majority, and with reelection in 1964 far from certain, the Kennedys could not afford to alienate the multitude of voters for whom Edgar represented order, the public good and the American Way. In the short term, at any rate, they were saddled with him.

When Robert Kennedy sent U.S. marshals to Alabama to protect the Freedom Riders, civil rights activists demanding the right to use public transport, he confronted more problems with the FBI. As white bigots attacked blacks in the state, Kennedy was told, Edgar's agents just took notes and did nothing. FBI headquarters, which received specific warnings of collusion between the Ku Klux Klan and local police, failed to alert the Justice Department. Edgar was reluctant to do anything to alienate a vital constituency, the southern conservatives who supported him in Congress. And that put him on the side of the racists.

Edgar's immediate fight over racism, however, was sparked by Robert Kennedy's pressure on him to hire black agents. At first, rather than admit the only such "agents" were his own black servants, he simply took no notice. Later, at Kennedy's insistence, a few blacks were hired.[1] For Robert Kennedy, though, civil rights took second place to a crusade that rankled even more with Edgar—the pursuit of organized crime.

On February 4, 1961, not two weeks into the presidency, Drew Pearson used his regular radio broadcast to report the first major battle in the younger Kennedy's war with Edgar. "The new Attorney General," Pearson said, "wants to go all out against the underworld. To do so, Bobby Kennedy proposes a crack squad of racket busters, but J. Edgar Hoover objects. Hoover claims that a special crime bureau reflects on the FBI, and he is opposing his new boss."

Both Kennedy brothers had served on the Senate rackets committee, John as Senator and Robert as Chief Counsel. John, though, admitted that he had done so only because his brother asked him to. His priorities were those of a politician, Robert's those of a zealot.

It was Robert, in his first Senate probe, who had exposed the extent to which organized labor was intertwined with organized crime. He had toppled Teamsters leader Dave Beck and sent him to jail. Then, in a second probe, he had struggled to nail Beck's corrupt successor, Jimmy Hoffa, an intensely personal feud that brought bitter confrontations with Hoffa and mafiosi like Giancana—live on national television.

Joseph Kennedy, with his long-standing ties to organized crime, thought all this madness. He tried to smooth things over during the run-up to the 1960 election, but Robert was beyond persuasion. As Attorney General, his fight against organized crime was to be more than a just cause, almost an obsession.

Robert hurtled into the Justice Department determined to bring real power to bear against the mob for the first time. Edgar greeted him, even before he had formally taken office, with an exhortation to fight Communism. "The Communist

Party U.S.A.," said his memorandum, "presents a greater menace to the internal security of our Nation than it ever has." Kennedy disagreed. "It is such nonsense," he said that year, "to have to waste time prosecuting the Communist Party. It couldn't be more feeble and less of a threat, and besides, its membership consists largely of FBI agents."

Robert already knew Edgar was delinquent on organized crime. While in the Senate he had asked to see files on the mobsters arrested at Apalachin and had found the response pathetic. "The FBI," he recalled, "didn't know anything, really, about these people who were the major gangsters in the United States. That was rather a shock to me. . . . I sent the same request to the Bureau of Narcotics and they had something on every one of them."

While Robert was on the road probing organized crime for the Senate, agents in far-flung FBI offices had received specific orders not to help him at all. The orders came directly from Edgar.

Before taking office, Robert had proposed a national crime commission, an intelligence clearinghouse to coordinate the work of the various agencies. Edgar had publicly shot down the notion, claiming such a federal authority would be "dangerous to our democratic ideals." He dismissed as pests those who suggested it. For him they were just that, for they demanded a coordinated fight against the national crime syndicate, something Edgar claimed did not even exist.

A collision was inevitable. Luther Huston, an aide to the outgoing Attorney General, went to see Edgar a few days after the inauguration. "I had to wait," he recalled, "because the new Attorney General was there. He hadn't called or made an appointment. He had just barged in. You don't do that with Mr. Hoover. Then my turn came and I'll tell you—the maddest man I ever talked to was J. Edgar Hoover. He was steaming. If I could have printed what he said, I'd have had a scoop. Apparently Kennedy wanted to set up some kind of supplementary or overlapping group to take over some of the investigative work the FBI had been doing. My surmise is that Mr. Hoover told Bobby, 'If you're going to do that, I can retire tomorrow. My pension is waiting.' "

News of the rift quickly leaked to the press. In Florida, after a round of golf with Tony Curtis, Joseph Kennedy tried to cover up. "I don't know where those ridiculous rumors start," he told a reporter. "Nothing could be further from the truth. Both Jack and Bob admire Hoover. They feel they're lucky to have him as head of the FBI. Hoover is a wonderful, dedicated man—and don't think Jack and Bob don't realize it."

Behind the scenes, the father begged his sons to humor Edgar. A meeting at the White House in February 1961, one of only six occasions on which John Kennedy agreed to see Edgar during the presidency, was probably to arrange a truce. There was no stopping Robert, however, on organized crime. He got around Edgar's rejection of a crime commission by quadrupling the staff and budget of Justice's Organized Crime Section, and rammed expansion through whether Edgar liked it or not.

In the key target areas, New York and Chicago, the FBI resumed the drive Edgar had allowed to slacken once the fuss over Apalachin had died down. The New York office, where less than a dozen agents were working organized crime when Robert took office, would end up with 115 men assigned to the task. In Chicago, the team expanded from six agents to about eighty.

To demolish Edgar's old "no jurisdiction" excuse, Robert rushed through new laws. In 1960 a mere nineteen members of organized crime had been indicted. In the first year of the Kennedy presidency, 121 were indicted and ninety-six convicted.

FBI agents assigned to organized crime now came into their own. They liked Robert Kennedy and respected the way he came in person to consult them in the field. "Bobby got the fight going again," recalled Chicago's Bill Roemer. "He was a great and most capable guy."

"Kennedy and his people came in full of piss and vinegar," said Neil Welch. "They were down at the office on Saturdays, sending messages out all over the place. Kennedy was just so young and enthusiastic. We thought it was delightful. He just ran roughshod all over the mechanisms that had kept all the other Attorneys General at bay. It annoyed the hell out of Hoover. He couldn't control it."

"It's a disgrace," Edgar told Agent in Charge Kenneth Whittaker. "Kennedy's immature, impetuous. He'll destroy in five minutes the respect the FBI has built up over the years." "When Kennedy was after Hoffa," Whittaker recalled, "and going around the field divisions telling agents in charge what to do, the word came down that, hey, he might be the Attorney General, but we weren't to do anything without clearance from Bureau headquarters."

For all Edgar's obstruction, Robert's criminal targets were rapidly becoming enraged. Carlos Marcello and Sam Giancana became prime targets, mercilessly harassed by the agency that had left them at peace for so long.

The Kennedy family's different attitudes to organized crime were at their most extreme, and most potentially dangerous, when it came to Giancana. As the man who had reportedly helped John win the election with illegal vote-buying, Giancana had hoped for an easy ride from the Kennedy Justice Department. What he got was a tough, ceaseless onslaught and, as his half brother Chuck put it in 1992, the mobster felt "double-crossed." "Here I am helping the government," Giancana's henchman Roselli was overheard saying on a wiretap, "and that little son of a bitch is breaking my balls."

On the evening of July 12, 1961, Giancana walked into a waiting room at Chicago's O'Hare Airport, on a routine stopover to New York, accompanied by his mistress Phyllis McGuire. Waiting for him were a phalanx of FBI agents, including Bill Roemer, one of the mobster's most dogged pursuers. Giancana lost his temper, and revealingly so.

He knew, he told the agents, that everything he said would get back to J. Edgar Hoover. Then he burst out, "Fuck J. Edgar Hoover! Fuck your super boss, and your super super boss! You know who I mean; I mean the Kennedys!" Giancana piled abuse on both brothers, then snarled, "Listen, Roemer, I know all about the Kennedys, and Phyllis knows more about the Kennedys, and one of these days we're going to tell all. Fuck you! One of these days it'll come out. . . ."

At the time, Roemer had no idea what Giancana meant. Today the "all" is less mysterious. There was the Kennedy vote-buying, the plotting against Castro—and, of course, the womanizing. The mobster was in regular contact with Judith Campbell, the lover the President used as go-between. He was also close to Kennedy's brother-in-law Peter Lawford and would one day be overheard reminiscing with him about "the girls they used to produce for the Kennedys." The inference was that Robert, too, was not innocent of womanizing.

In early September 1961, according to former FBI Supervisor William Kane, an informant told the Bureau Robert Kennedy had recently been seen "out in the desert near Las Vegas with not one but two girls, on a blanket. Somebody in organized crime had taken telephoto pictures . . . and the word we got from our informants was that they were going to use it to blackmail the Attorney General. This was confirmed several times over from several different sources."

Kane said Edgar digested this, then sent Courtney Evans, his liaison with the Justice Department, to warn Robert Kennedy. Kennedy listened without comment. Then he simply asked what Evans was doing for the holiday—it was Labor Day weekend—and ended the meeting.

Former Assistant Director Evans, though famously discreet, agreed the exchange "probably did happen as described. There were many times I had to go in with that sort of information. Mr. Hoover would give instructions and I would carry them out. There was, I know, an effort to bring pressure on the presidency by organized crime."

It is unlikely that at this stage, even with his resources, Edgar fully comprehended the complexities of the Kennedy relationship with organized crime. He simply did what he knew best—collected dirt, let the brothers know he had it and obstructed Robert Kennedy in ways that amounted to insubordination.

A Justice Department official, dispatched to the FBI's Chicago office to improve liaison, arrived to find the Agent in Charge had left town. Knowing Kennedy's man was on the way, Edgar had deliberately ordered him to Des Moines, Iowa. At headquarters he deliberately snubbed Kennedy himself. "The entire time Bob was Attorney General," said Joe Dolan, "he had a Tuesday and Thursday lunch in his office with the Assistant Attorneys, myself and others invited, including Hoover. Hoover came to a couple of the lunches the first month, and after that he was a no-show."

If Robert visited a field office, Edgar stayed away. When he did travel himself, there was a galling reminder that things had changed. Once there had been a picture of Edgar on the wall of every office, a lone Big Brother presence. Now it was flanked by one of President Kennedy, distributed across the country on the instructions of his brother.

This was a war of attrition. Yet Edgar and the brothers Kennedy continued to act out, as one writer has put it, "an Oriental pageant of formal respect." Perhaps the Kennedys, used to years of inane courtesies between Edgar and their father, half-hoped to coexist with Edgar by stroking his ego, remembering his anniversaries and praising him in public. They would humor the old man, even if they thought him half-crazy. Edgar, an old hand at the game, sent this handwritten note to Robert on June 9, 1961:

Dear Bob,
. . . Your confidence and support mean a great deal to me, and I sincerely trust I shall always merit them.

Sincerely,

Edgar

A note from the President, December 5, 1961, when Edgar received his latest award:

Dear Mr. Hoover,
The Mutual of Omaha Criss Award is further proof of
the high esteem in which all America holds your record of untiring effort in the field of federal law enforcement. . . . I am proud to add my congratulations
to you and to express again my gratitude for your
outstanding contributions to the nation.

Sincerely,

John F. Kennedy

Edgar, who replied that he was "touched," had just
received a tip-off that the President was planning to fire him.
Agents were deployed in an intense investigation, as assidu-
ous and as painstaking as that into any crime. Yet a few days
later "Edgar" was thanking "Bob" for the invitation to his
Christmas party, and making his excuses.

The Kennedys had a less than festive Christmas in 1961.
On December 19, on the golf course at Palm Beach, the
President's father suffered a debilitating stroke. His right
side and face were paralyzed, and though he lived on for
eight years he would never speak intelligibly again. A few
months earlier, when the press had carried stories of quar-
reling between John and Robert and Edgar, Joseph had been
at hand to calm things down. From now on, though Edgar
was to visit him during his recuperation, his role as peace-
maker was over.

Nor would Joseph be there, henceforth, to intervene in his
sons' tangled relations with the Mafia. From now on, the
boys were on their own.

CHAPTER 26

> "Aside from the moral issues, the morass of potential
> blackmail in which the Attorney General found himself
> must have appalled him. . . . How could the CIA and
> John Kennedy have been so stupid? . . . The potential
> for blackmail extended beyond Giancana. J. Edgar
> Hoover would also be able to hold these stories over
> John and Robert Kennedy as long as they lived."
>
> *Harris Wofford, former Kennedy aide, 1980*

ON JANUARY 6, 1962, THE COLUMNIST DREW PEARSON MADE A
daring prediction: "J. Edgar Hoover," he said, "doesn't like
taking a back seat, as he calls it, to a young kid like
Bobby . . . and he'll be eased out if there is not too much of
a furor."

It was only a brief comment in a radio broadcast, but
what Pearson said made ripples in Washington. Three days
later, in a note to his brother, Robert Kennedy begged the
President to keep a favorable reference to the FBI in his
State of the Union address. "It is only one sentence," he told
the President, "and it would make a big difference for us. I
hope you will leave it as it is."

On January 11, before the assembled throng of senators
and congressmen, John Kennedy spoke of Vietnam, of civil
rights and of taxes. Few could have noticed or cared as he
rattled off a line praising the FBI—for its "coordinated and
hard-hitting effort." This was a sweetener for Edgar, but the
time for meaningful sweeteners was past.

A month earlier, Edgar's spies had warned him not only
that the Kennedys were planning to fire him, but that a

specific candidate, State Department Security Director William Boswell, was in line for his job. And soon, having not deigned to see Edgar for the past year, Kennedy sent word that he "desired to speak with Mr. Hoover."

Edgar stepped out of his limousine at the northwest gate of the White House at one o'clock on March 22. He was ushered into the Oval Office, and then he and the President took the elevator to the dining room in the Executive Mansion. The only other person present was Kenneth O'Donnell.

The meeting was a long one. Four hours later, as Edgar was leaving, Kennedy aides Theodore Sorensen and Arthur Schlesinger were on the way in. Their names were anathema to Washington conservatives, and the President refrained from introducing them. As he explained to them a few moments later, he "did not want to upset Mr. Hoover too much."

It may never be known whether or not Kennedy tried to fire Edgar that day. The Kennedy Library says it has no record of what was said at the lunch. Nor does the FBI— even though Edgar normally wrote a memo following a visit to the White House. We do know the meeting went badly. Kenneth O'Donnell, interviewed years later, would say only that the President eventually lost patience. "Get rid of that bastard," he hissed to his aide. "He's the biggest bore."

Since the mid-seventies, when a Senate inquiry probed the nation's darker intelligence secrets, the encounter has had a special significance. Edgar sat down with the President armed with dirt more explosive than even he was used to—much of it, ironically, obtained thanks to Robert Kennedy's pursuit of Mafia boss Sam Giancana.

Edgar had learned, even before Eisenhower left office, that there was a plot to kill Fidel Castro and that Giancana was somehow involved. Early in the Kennedy presidency he discovered Giancana was working with the CIA; and by March 1962 he knew that Judith Campbell, who was in touch with Giancana and Johnny Roselli, was one of the President's lovers. While his attention was drawn to this by his agents, Edgar may even have learned something of it directly from Roselli, who is said to have socialized with him at La Jolla.

Edgar knew, too, of Giancana's threat to "tell all" about the Kennedys and, from a recent wiretap, that Giancana and Roselli had discussed obtaining a "really small" receiver for bugging conversations. In that same conversation they had spoken of "Bobby" and when he would next be in Washington.

The Director of the FBI, then, had evidence that the President of the United States was intimate with a young woman who was close to a Mafia boss who was involved with the CIA in a plot to assassinate a foreign leader—a plot that Edgar had every reason to suspect the President had authorized. And that, all the while, the FBI was ruthlessly pursuing that same Mafia boss on the orders of the President's younger brother.

Any Director of the FBI would have been justified in bringing such a scenario to the President's attention. With his malice toward the brothers and with the threat of dismissal hanging over him, Edgar must have relished doing so.

Judith Campbell, now known by her married name, Exner, has revealed that Edgar indeed brought her name up that day. "Jack called me that afternoon," she said. "He told me to go to my mother's house and call him from there. When I did, he said the phone in my apartment wasn't safe. He was furious. You could feel his anger. He said that, at their meeting, Hoover had more or less tried to intimidate him with the information he had. He'd made it clear that he knew about my relationship with Jack, even that I'd been to the White House, that I was a friend of Sam and Johnny Roselli, and that Jack knew Sam, too. Jack knew exactly what Hoover was doing. Knowing that Jack wanted him out of office, he was in a way ensuring his job—by letting Jack know he had this leverage over him."

According to Campbell, there was something even more damaging to hide. Early in the presidency, Kennedy had repeated his folly of the election period—by meeting again with Giancana. The new contacts, Campbell said the President told her, "had to do with the elimination of Fidel Castro." Kennedy also used Campbell as a courier, on some twenty occasions, to carry sealed envelopes to Giancana.

Campbell's account cannot be dismissed. It is specific in dates and details and is supported by travel documents, her annotated appointment book and official logs recording three of her visits to the White House. Giancana's half brother Chuck has also spoken of contacts between the Mafia boss and Kennedy during the presidency and of Campbell's delivering envelopes.

Most historians now accept that the Kennedy brothers were involved in the Castro plots. After the Bay of Pigs debacle, we know, they no longer trusted the CIA. It is therefore conceivable that, given his existing relationship with Giancana, the President may have chosen to deal directly with the mobster about Castro murder plans. To have done so would have been foolhardy, but it would fit with Kennedy's love of intrigue.

According to Campbell, the President said the envelopes he sent to Giancana contained "intelligence material" to do with the plots. The envelopes were sealed, however, and she never saw the contents for herself.[1] Whatever they contained, John Kennedy was playing a horrendously dangerous game. Giancana had hoped that his help—first in getting the President elected and then with the Castro operation—would be rewarded with federal leniency. Yet Robert Kennedy's onslaught on organized crime not only included Giancana among its targets; he was singled out for especially intensive harassment.

According to his half brother Chuck, the mobster felt that the President had reneged on a bargain. To a mafioso, to break a bargain is a sin commonly punished by death, and Giancana was a murderer by profession. Again according to his half brother, he was to play a key role in planning Kennedy's assassination in Dallas.

It is not clear how fully Edgar understood the Giancana scenario in March 1962, only that he knew plenty and told the President so. "My impression from Jack," Judith Campbell has said, "was that Hoover had intimated to him that he knew I had been passing material from Jack to Sam." According to Cartha DeLoach, Edgar returned from the meeting saying he had told the President he knew "a great deal" of what was going on.

Even so, records suggest, the brothers soon made themselves even more dependent on Edgar. Unless his brother had been keeping the Castro plot a secret from him, which seems highly unlikely, Robert had long known about Giancana's involvement. Yet it was vital for Robert, as it was for his brother as President, to protect himself from being linked to the plots. A paper record was therefore concocted, including a memo by Edgar claiming that he and Robert had learned of the CIA's use of Giancana with "great astonishment." The writing of that memo alone left the Attorney General indebted to Edgar.

Contrary to previous assumptions, the President did not sever his connection with Judith Campbell after the March meeting with Edgar. White House phone logs show that contacts between him and Judith Campbell continued at least through the late summer of 1962. According to Campbell, she and the President simply used other telephones to evade FBI wiretaps. Kennedy, his secretary Mrs. Lincoln recalled, suspected Edgar of bugging even the White House itself. Even so, says Campbell, she and the President went on seeing each other for months to come, and she continued to meet with Giancana.

Increasingly harassed by the FBI, Campbell asked the President for help. "I was sort of begging him," she recalled, "saying, 'Jack, do something. I can't handle this'—because I was being followed. And he would always reply, 'Don't worry about it. You're okay, you haven't done anything wrong. You know Sam works for us.'"

Still, the President was infuriated. "Jack spoke of Hoover with great irritation," Campbell recalled. "It was in the sense of, 'I wish he'd get out of my hair.' It was very obvious he wanted to be rid of Hoover."

* * * *

The President could not risk trying to dump his FBI Director. The Giancana mess aside, Edgar was now armed with knowledge of a battery of other Kennedy follies. Even before the March confrontation, Edgar had let the President know he knew about the use of prostitutes during the 1960 Convention. He knew, too, about an old relationship that could prove as politically damaging as the current ones.

In early March a small New York magazine, *The Realist,* ran a story headlined THE STORY BEHIND THE RUMOR ABOUT PRESIDENT KENNEDY'S FIRST MARRIAGE. The rumor was that Kennedy had been briefly married, in 1947, to a Florida socialite named Durie Malcolm. Malcolm had merited an entry in a privately printed history of her family, and it stated flatly that among her several husbands was "John F. Kennedy, son of Joseph P. Kennedy, one time Ambassador to England."

If true, the "other marriage" story was dynamite. It would mean that the first Catholic president had been divorced, which was against his professed religion, and—since he had concealed the fact—had deceived the nation. Research to date has established only that Kennedy and Malcolm did know each other in the forties, well enough to stir up speculation in a Florida gossip column.[2]

An entry in FBI files shows that in November 1961, when the rumor first reached the Bureau, an agent promptly perused Malcolm's family history in the New York Public Library. His report, and similar ones from New Jersey and Massachusetts, went straight to Edgar. He then brought the matter to Robert Kennedy's attention.

The file, however, does not tell the whole story. In a rare interview after Edgar's death, his secretary, Helen Gandy, indicated that her boss had been onto the "other marriage" as early as 1960, and that he and Richard Nixon discussed using it for election dirty tricks.

Soon after Edgar's lunch with the President in 1962, the story began appearing in the press. First the *Thunderbolt,* the racist organ of the National States Rights Party, came out with a front-page story: KENNEDY'S DIVORCE EXPOSED! IS PRESENT MARRIAGE VALID? Right-wing organizations distributed hundreds of thousands of copies of Malcolm's family history around the country. The syndicates and wire services started digging. A United Feature column, by Henry Taylor, was withdrawn at the last moment. Then Walter Winchell asked, "Why hasn't the White House debunked it?" By the time the debunking came, in *Newsweek,* it had become a serious embarrassment.

Ben Bradlee, the magazine's Washington Bureau Chief, has told how that story came to be written. "I talked to the President about doing a story, based largely on *Thunderbolt* and the hate sheets. The FBI had made an investigation and some FBI documents were made available by Kennedy's press secretary. The condition was that we could have them overnight, and never again. Salinger was the intermediary between us and the FBI. Chuck Roberts and I stayed up all night with the documents, writing the story in some motel. . . . I don't know what the terms were on which Kennedy got that stuff from the FBI. . . ."

Edgar, then, had ridden to the rescue, a rescue that might never have been necessary had it not been for the stories written by Winchell, Henry Taylor and *Thunderbolt.* Winchell had long been manipulated by the FBI. Henry Taylor's massive FBI file shows he and Edgar had been pals for years. Edgar had supplied him with information, and he had dutifully written stories attacking Edgar's critics. Taylor's column on the "second marriage" was killed only at the eleventh hour, when Edgar intervened at the request of the White House.

Thunderbolt would also dredge up the old story about Kennedy's affair with his Senate secretary, Pamela Turnure. The headlines read: JFK ACCUSED OF ADULTERY, and the article appeared after Turnure's former landlady, who had recorded the sounds of the couple's lovemaking, wrote letters to several public officials. Edgar was one of the recipients, and according to Bobby Baker, Lyndon Johnson's former aide, the *Thunderbolt* publication was no coincidence. "Johnson told me," he recalled, "that Hoover had given him the sound tapes on that woman during the 1960 campaign. Then, during the presidency, he made sure the information got to people they thought would use it. Not the regular press, but scurrilous publications. . . ."

Like *Thunderbolt*.

It all suggests that Edgar secretly fanned the flames of both the Turnure gossip and the "other marriage" to his own advantage. Then, when the marriage story had done its damage, he put Kennedy in his debt by supplying background for the *Newsweek* rebuttal.

As if this was not enough, there was the Hollywood connection—the President's alleged involvement with the actress Angie Dickinson, and Marilyn Monroe's affairs with both brothers.

Dickinson is said to have become one of John Kennedy's lovers sometime before the inauguration. "Angie and JFK disappeared for two or three days in Palm Springs during the period before Kennedy assumed office," recalled photographer Slim Aarons, a Kennedy friend. "They stayed in a cottage and never emerged. Everyone knew about it."

"Everyone" was meant to include only Kennedy insiders, but reporters who traveled with the Kennedys got wind of such things. *Newsweek* reporter Dick Schumacher recalled how he opened a door at Palm Springs, spotted Dickinson relaxing on a bed and promptly "forgot" what he had seen. The predominantly male press corps of those days liked Kennedy and somewhat envied his success with women. They believed that a politician's private life was his own business, not to be probed or written about. Secret Service agents took the same view and protected him as best they could. FBI agents did what they were trained to do, and reported to Edgar.

An account of how Edgar found out about Angie Dickinson comes from a former agent whose squad liaised with the Secret Service. "It happened," said the agent, who asked to remain anonymous, "when Kennedy was on the West Coast on political business. He flew from Burbank Airport to Palm Springs by chartered aircraft, with Angie Dickinson on board, and they took a detour—via Arizona. When they did get to Palm Springs, Kennedy got off alone, I guess to stop the press seeing Dickinson.

"The problems came later. The plane on that trip had been an executive aircraft with a bedroom. The copilot, who was employed by Lockheed, had bugged the bedroom and taped the conversation. And afterwards he tried to use the tape, anonymously, to extort the President for a large sum of money. His letter was intercepted by the Secret Service, and they called the FBI. Our goal was to get that tape back. Find it, get it back. No publicity. We checked on the airplane's crew, and the copilot was kind of shady. So, when he was abroad on a trip we bribed the manager of his apartment to let us in.

"We found the tape recording hidden in the wall, near an electric socket. It was a large tape, the old-fashioned sort. We took it and we resealed the goddamn thing, so the guy wouldn't even know at first it was gone. The Bureau gave us very exact orders after we found the tape. They didn't want it mailed. They wanted it sent by personal messenger to the Director. We talked to Lockheed and they fired the guy. There was no prosecution, to keep it quiet. And that was that. But Hoover had the tape."

Cartha DeLoach confirms that information came in on the Dickinson affair. Homer Young, another former agent, recalled how, when the President's ardor cooled, the FBI was brought in to help out.

"The Secret Service," said Young, "would call the FBI in Washington, who would call the Bureau in L.A. to get them to call the FBI Resident Agent in Palm Springs—because the Secret Service had no representative there. And our guy would have the job of telling Angie to knock it off, to stop trying to get through to the President, to stop calling the White House. . . ."

Even as Edgar received his information on Dickinson, he was assiduously monitoring yet another dalliance—with the most famous Hollywood beauty of them all.

* * *

Oddly enough, Marilyn Monroe was a pinup in the lives of both Edgar and President Kennedy. Her nude calendar shot, along with other pictures of naked women, graced the walls of the basement bar at Edgar's home in Washington. They were there, some assumed, to deflect speculation about the Director's homosexuality.

In 1954, when he was undergoing back surgery, Kennedy had stuck a poster of Monroe on the wall of his hospital room. It showed her in shorts, standing with her legs apart, and the patient had it fixed upside down, so her feet stuck up in the air.

The evidence suggests Monroe and Kennedy had an affair of sorts in the early fifties. They were certainly in touch, and sleeping with each other occasionally, during the election campaign of 1960. The President's brother-in-law Peter Lawford, who talked about the relationship shortly before his death, recalled taking photographs of Monroe and Kennedy in the bathtub.

Such encounters continued into the first and second years of the presidency. The most famous blonde in the world was smuggled into Kennedy's suite at New York's Carlyle Hotel, even on board Air Force One, disguised in a black wig and sunglasses. Such escapades would have been dangerous at any time, and Monroe's state of mind made them especially so.

Few except Monroe's psychiatrists and closest friends knew how desperately Monroe was floundering. Her marriage to playwright Arthur Miller was in ruins and—as a longtime abuser of barbiturates—she was in a narcotic nosedive. There was a brief, anguished stay at a psychiatric clinic, then more doctors, more drugs and episodes of heavy drinking. Monroe suffered abrupt mood swings, from elated highs to black despair.

No public man with an image to protect should have gone anywhere near her. Yet John Kennedy continued to see Monroe, and Edgar was watching. Gordon Liddy, then an agent in Crime Records, was aware of the continuing coverage. "The stuff on the brothers and Monroe," he recalled, "was very, very closely held."

It has been clear for some time now that Monroe came under electronic surveillance during the Kennedy presidency. Interviews with private detectives and technicians leave no doubt of it. Confusion remains, however, as to who commissioned the bugging and who received the "take."[3]

Teamsters leader Jimmy Hoffa, a prime target of the Kennedy Justice Department, almost certainly received some compromising material. He said as much to fellow prisoners when he later went to jail, and his attorney, William Buffalino, confirmed it in a 1990 interview. Some bugging, meanwhile, may have been commissioned by mobster Sam Giancana.

By 1962, according to his brother, Giancana had lost patience with the Kennedys. Still under constant pressure from the Justice Department, he hired surveillance experts to collect all possible dirt on the Kennedy brothers. If collaborating with them had failed to help, the mobster intended to try blackmail, a tactic at which the Mafia excelled.

Peter Lawford had long since been under surveillance on the orders of someone else—Edgar. The sound specialist who installed the bugs is still operating today and has revealed his role only on the formal understanding that his name is not used.

"The job at the Lawford house," the source said in 1991, "was done for the Bureau, through a middleman. I installed the devices on FBI orders. They were in the living room, the bedrooms and one of the bathrooms. An intermediary for Hoover came to me to arrange the installation, I guess at the end of the summer, in 1961. The formal reason given was that Hoover wanted information on the organized crime figures coming and going at the Lawford place. Sam Giancana was there sometimes. But of course the Kennedys, both John and Robert, went there, too.

"Hoover's intermediary told me that, as Attorney General, Robert Kennedy had given strict orders that the house was *not* to be bugged. But it was covered, on Hoover's personal instructions. Jimmy Hoffa did get one of the Kennedy-Monroe tapes, but only because it was leaked to him by one of the operatives. He wanted to make a buck and Hoffa's people paid $100,000—a lot of money back then. But that surveillance was commissioned by the FBI, and almost all the tapes went to the FBI. J. Edgar Hoover had access to every goddamned thing that happened at the beach house, including what happened when the Kennedys were there, for nearly a year. Draw your own conclusion."

One of the men who monitored the bugs at the Lawford house was private investigator John Danoff. He told how, during a presidential visit in November 1961, he listened in on a tryst between Kennedy and Monroe. "To my amazement," Danoff recalled, "I started to recognize the voices—because of the President's distinct Bostonian accent and Marilyn Monroe's voice. . . . Then you heard them talking and they were going about disrobing and going into the sex act on the bed. . . ."

For Edgar, tapes of scenes like this were just the beginning of the harvest. On February 1, 1962, Monroe met Robert Kennedy for the first time, at a dinner party in the Lawford house. Later that night, the actress was to tell a friend, the two of them talked alone in the den. In characteristic fashion, she had prepared questions of topical interest and asked whether it was true that J. Edgar Hoover might soon be fired. Robert replied that "he and the President didn't feel strong enough to do so, though they wanted to."

According to the man who installed the bugs, that conversation would have been picked up by the hidden microphones. For Edgar, reading the transcript in Washington, Kennedy's words must have held some comfort. He now knew, for sure, from the mouth of one of the brothers, that the Kennedys were afraid to dismiss him—for the time being. That gave him all the more reason to go on watching, to keep on piling up compromising information.

Edgar would have known about Robert's comments on his future, and about the sex session with Monroe at the Lawford house, well in time for the lunch at the White House in March 1962. Yet whether or not he mentioned Monroe that day—along with Judith Campbell—John Kennedy blithely saw the actress again within forty-eight hours, on a trip to California. "It was obvious," said Philip Watson, a Los Angeles County official who saw them together, "that they were intimate, that they were staying together for the night."

In Washington in the weeks that followed, the tension between Edgar and the Kennedys continued. Robert Kennedy and Edgar now rarely cooperated with each other about anything. Formal courtesies continued, with the President telephoning Edgar to congratulate him on his thirty-eighth anniversary as Director. Edgar sent a pleasant acknowledgment. Then, the same day, he refused to show up at a cake-cutting ceremony organized by Robert.

The Monroe saga, meanwhile, took a strange turn. John Kennedy saw the actress once more, on May 19 in New York, but apparently never again. According to Peter Lawford, Edgar had warned him off, saying the Lawford beach house "had very likely been bugged by the Mafia." He did not, one may be sure, say it had been bugged on his own orders.

Unfortunately for the Kennedys, Monroe would not accept that the affair was over. Back on the Coast, she plunged into black despair, losing herself in drugs and barbiturates. "Marilyn," Lawford recalled, "began writing these rather pathetic letters to Jack and continued calling. She threatened to go to the press. He finally sent Bobby Kennedy out to California to cool her off."

In the course of calming Monroe, however, Robert followed his brother into her embrace. "It wasn't Bobby's intention," said Lawford, "but they became lovers and spent the night in our guest bedroom. Almost immediately the affair got very heavy. . . ." Soon, Lawford said, Monroe was saying "she was in love with Bobby and that *he* had promised to marry her. It was as if she could no longer tell the difference between Bobby and Jack."

A number of witnesses, and the surviving phone records, support Lawford's account. They also support his statement that Robert in turn soon tried to distance himself. He did so too late, however, to avoid being drawn into Monroe's psychiatric collapse. And too late to avoid falling into a double trap—the surveillance ordered by the criminals, Giancana and Hoffa, and the web spun by Edgar.

Edgar knew early on. On June 27, according to Monroe's housekeeper, Robert Kennedy arrived at the actress' home alone, "driving a Cadillac convertible." A memorandum from the Los Angeles Agent in Charge, William Simon, landed on Edgar's desk within days. "I remember it coming in. I was shocked," recalled Cartha DeLoach. "Simon reported that Bobby was borrowing his Cadillac convertible for the purpose of going to see Marilyn Monroe." From now on, agent sources say, the Attorney General's California comings and goings were effectively under Bureau surveillance.

During the June visit, heavily censored FBI documents indicate, Monroe had lunch with the Attorney General at Peter Lawford's house. Their conversation included a discussion about "the morality of atomic testing." At that critical time in the Cold War, anything Robert Kennedy said about such matters would have been of interest to Communist Intelligence. For Edgar, aware that Monroe had numerous left-wing friends, the development meant that his gratuitous snooping could now be justified as an authentic security concern.

On Saturday, August 4, Monroe was found dead. The autopsy report gave the cause of death as "acute barbiturate poisoning due to ingestion of overdose," and the Coroner decided it was "probably" suicide. Others have theorized that the overdose was not taken by mouth but administered by someone else—perhaps by injection, perhaps rectally.

Sam Giancana's half brother Chuck claimed in 1992 that the Chicago mobster had Monroe murdered in precisely that fashion. "By murdering her," he said, "Bobby Kennedy's affair with the starlet would be exposed. . . . It might be possible to depose the rulers of Camelot."

Whether Giancana had a hand in the death or not, the evidence suggests the account given to the public was untrue. There are unresolved questions, above all, about Robert Kennedy's behavior that weekend.

The Attorney General was in California at the time, to

address the American Bar Association and to take a vacation with his family. A mass of testimony, supported in the eighties by that of Peter Lawford, suggests Kennedy flew to Los Angeles on August 4 for a showdown with Monroe. According to Lawford, who admitted accompanying his brother-in-law to Monroe's house, there was an ugly quarrel. "Marilyn," he said, "allowed how first thing Monday morning she was going to call a press conference and tell the world about the treatment she had suffered at the hands of the Kennedy brothers. Bobby became livid. In no uncertain terms he told her she was going to have to leave both Jack and himself alone—no more telephone calls, no letters, nothing."

According to Lawford, the row ended with hysteria from Monroe, a struggle in which she was subdued, then an urgent call for help to her psychiatrist, Dr. Ralph Greenson. Dr. Greenson did come over, believed he had calmed Monroe down and went off to dinner.

It was he, according to the official account, who would be summoned by the housekeeper in the early hours of the following morning to find Monroe dead in bed. Yet statements by police officers, ambulance men, the housekeeper, doctors and others suggest the following scenario: After desperate calls by Monroe to the Lawford beach house, Kennedy and his brother-in-law returned to her home. They found the actress either dead or dying and phoned for an ambulance. One or both of them may have joined the ambulance on a last-hope drive to a hospital—only to turn it around when it became clear Monroe was dead. The body was then replaced in the bed, and the President's brother left town rapidly the way he had arrived, by helicopter and aircraft. Dr. Greenson confirmed privately, years later, that Robert Kennedy was present that night and that an ambulance was called.

For Robert Kennedy, back in northern California resuming his scheduled activities, the crisis was far from over. On the morning of Monroe's death, Los Angeles Chief of Detectives Thad Brown was called to headquarters because of a "problem." A crumpled piece of paper, found in

Monroe's bedclothes, bore a White House telephone number.

A remarkable cover-up followed. The problem of that scrap of paper, and many other embarrassments, simply evaporated. Records of Monroe's telephone calls were made to disappear, in part thanks to Captain James Hamilton of Police Intelligence, a longtime friend of the Attorney General. It was not the police, however, who retrieved the records of Monroe's last phone calls. As a reporter discovered at the time, they were removed from the headquarters of General Telephone by midmorning on the day after Monroe's death. And, according to the company's Division Manager, Robert Tiarks, they had been taken by the FBI.

A former senior FBI official, then serving in a West Coast city, confirms it. "I was on a visit to California when Monroe died, and there were some people there, Bureau personnel, who normally wouldn't have been there—agents from out of town. They were on the scene immediately, as soon as she died, before anyone realized what had happened. I subsequently learned that agents had removed the records. It had to be on the instructions of someone high up, higher even than Hoover."

The former official understood at the time that the orders came from "either the Attorney General or the President." "I remember the communications coming in from the Los Angeles Division," said Cartha DeLoach. "A Kennedy phone number was on the nightstand by Monroe's bed." Monroe's death, it seems, at last brought home to the President the scale of the risks he was running. The White House log shows he took a call from Peter Lawford at 6:04 A.M. on the morning Monroe was found dead, an hour after Lawford had hired security consultants to bury all evidence of the brothers' affairs with Monroe. Another of John Kennedy's lovers, Judith Campbell, called the White House twice the next day—once in the afternoon and again in the evening. A note in the log indicates that Kennedy was in conference, with the scrawled addition "No." At about this time, it seems, the perilous Campbell liaison was ending at last.[4]

If mobsters had hoped to use the Monroe connection to destroy Robert Kennedy, they were thwarted by the successful cover-up. That cover-up, however, worked largely thanks to Edgar. By grabbing the telephone records on their behalf, he made the Kennedys more beholden to him than ever.

On August 7, just forty-eight hours after that favor, Robert Kennedy did something quite remarkable. A few hours earlier W. H. Ferry, Vice President of the Fund for the Republic, set up by the Ford Foundation to promote civil liberties, had lambasted Edgar's scaremongering about Communism as "sententious poppycock." Robert Kennedy, we know, shared that view. Now, however, he leaped to Edgar's defense, effusively praising his stance on Communism. "I hope," he said piously, "Hoover will continue to serve the country for many, many years to come."

Photo agency files contain not a single picture of Monroe with either Kennedy brother, not even of her very public meeting with the President after singing "Happy Birthday" from the stage of Madison Square Garden. Once, though, Globe Photos did have two such photographs. "In one of them," said a former senior executive, "he was looking up at her. You could see the admiration in his eyes. It was a great picture."[5]

A fortnight after Monroe's death, two men visited Globe's offices. "They said they were collecting material for the presidential library," said the former executive. "They asked to see everything we had on Monroe. I had a stock girl look after them, and then—afterward—we found that everything was gone, even the negatives."

The staff at Globe remember only one thing about the men who took the photographs. They introduced themselves as FBI agents and had badges to prove it.

Months after Monroe's death, even though the case was purely a police matter, agents were still interviewing potential informants on the subject. Edgar's old journalistic mouthpiece Walter Winchell would later write an article virtually accusing Robert Kennedy of the star's murder. In

1964, with help from the Motion Picture Alliance for the Preservation of American Ideals, a right-wing activist called Frank Capell published a booklet linking Robert Kennedy to the events surrounding Monroe's death. Perhaps not coincidentally, one of the founders of the Motion Picture Alliance was Edgar's old friend Lela Rogers, who—according to her daughter Ginger—was still in contact with the Director.

Later in the sixties, ranting on about the Kennedys during his California vacations, Edgar would rarely fail to bring up Monroe's name. Years later, at home in Washington, he would respond to a question about the case from a young neighbor, Anthony Calomaris. "He said she was murdered," Calomaris recalled, "that it wasn't a suicide, that the Kennedys were involved."

In the fall of 1962, the chill between Edgar and Robert Kennedy had become a freeze. "It became a total rift," said former FBI Assistant Director Courtney Evans. "The phone contact between them ended. The special phone just sat on the desk unused."

The President, for his part, would see Edgar only twice more in the year that remained to him. The brothers were staying as far away from Edgar as possible, biding their time. For at last, on the horizon, they could see a chance to get rid of him.

CHAPTER 27

> "Mr. Hoover's capitulation to his personal pique was
> irresponsible and clearly contrary to the personal inter-
> ests of Presidents Kennedy and Johnson, constitutional
> government and the nation."
>
> *Nicholas Katzenbach,*
> *former Attorney General, 1976*

INSTEAD OF SUNNING HIMSELF IN MIAMI BEACH, HIS USUAL RE-
treat over the holiday, Edgar spent New Year's 1963 by
himself, holed up in a New York hotel, recovering from
prostate surgery. He was lonely and feeling his age, and
suddenly his age mattered.

In two years' time he would be seventy, the mandatory
retirement age for federal officials. Only an Executive Order,
signed by the President, could prolong his reign at the FBI.
And in two years' time, it seemed likely, John Kennedy
would be secure in his second term. Unless something
unexpected happened, Edgar's insurance policies were
about to run out.

In February, Edgar gave a charade of an interview. "My
relations with Robert Kennedy," he said solemnly, "have
always been pleasant and cordial, as well as my meetings
with the President." Was there any truth to rumors that he
might retire? "No truth whatever," said Edgar. "I expect to
be here a long time. . . . The President has power to extend
my term of office."

President Kennedy intended to do no such thing. The
brothers had had enough, and the retirement-at-seventy rule
promised to be a way to dump their persecutor without
being seen to be firing him. It was now a question of hanging

on, of fending Edgar off until after the 1964 election. Then, with Edgar's seventieth birthday just weeks away, he would be replaced.

The dismissal was to come gift-wrapped. "Robert Kennedy told me," said Deputy Attorney General Nicholas Katzenbach, "they intended to give Hoover a glorious ceremony." "I remember speculating how they were going to go about it," said Courtney Evans, Edgar's liaison with the Kennedys. "Perhaps they could make him Ambassador to Switzerland—the country his family came from."

The names of possible replacements were now going the rounds—Courtney Evans among them. Robert Kennedy had long since sounded out John Connally, then Governor of Texas. Connally recalled: "I said, 'Bobby, you're not going to be able to get rid of J. Edgar Hoover.' But he assured me the time would come, and he would."

Speculation about Edgar's successor became a kind of sport. "Some friends of mine with mischief in them," remembered Joe Dolan, "were sitting around trying to think of the most unlikely successor to J. Edgar Hoover. And one of them said, 'Adam Yarmolinsky!' He was a very bright lawyer, the assistant to McNamara, over at the Department of Defense. But he looked kind of evil, a bit like a gnome, a schemer, and apart from that he was absolutely not the guy you appoint to head the FBI. It was just a joke, but it got back to Hoover within hours. I guess he didn't understand that his leg was being pulled."[1]

Word of the Kennedys' intentions spread through the Bureau, from the highest aide to the lowliest rookie agent. "It was common knowledge, according to Justice Department gossips," recalled Norman Ollestad, "that in 1964 the Director would definitely be out."

"The way it came to me," said Justice Department aide William Hundley, "was that the President had said to Bobby, 'I can't do it now. But when I'm reelected I'm going to get rid of him, make him Boxing Commissioner or something.' And when I'd bitch to Bobby about Hoover, he'd say, 'Wait, just wait.' That kind of comment kept getting back to Hoover, and that was it. . . ."

"From then on," recalled Courtney Evans, "the Director wouldn't have anything to do with the Kennedys—beyond the formalities. He was *so* incensed and mad."

Through the spring and summer of 1963, Edgar went on scratching at the old sore—Kennedy womanizing. On May 29, he wrote to Kenneth O'Donnell raking up the old affair with Jacqueline Kennedy's press secretary, Pamela Turnure. A week later it was another salvo about the President's 1951 involvement with Alicia Purdom, letting the Kennedys know he knew about the alleged half-million-dollar payoff to keep Purdom quiet. Edgar kept up a steady stream of information on this, spicing a later memo with a reference to the alleged pregnancy.

At about this time, in 1963, the Kennedys began trying to play Edgar's game in reverse. When Abba Schwartz of the State Department Bureau of Security reported some new example of Hoover meddling, the President responded with, "Tell it to Kenny [O'Donnell]. He's keeping a record on all this." The Kennedys were doing what Edgar did to others, keeping a dossier on *him.*

Unfortunately for the President, Edgar was way ahead. June 1963 brought brand-new woman trouble, the sort that could not be shrugged off. As the Kennedys wrestled with the mounting civil rights crisis, Edgar quietly opened a new file code-named "Bowtie." It was to grow to more than a thousand pages, and its subject was a scandal that on the surface appeared to be another nation's problem.

Britain's Minister for War, John Profumo, had confessed to having slept with a woman simultaneously involved with the Soviet Naval attaché in London, Yevgeny Ivanov. He resigned, but the crisis continued. The government of Prime Minister Macmillan, who had backed Profumo to the end, was shaken to its foundations. The press, meanwhile, fueled the controversy with daily revelations about the orgies and adulteries of the British establishment.

In Washington, President Kennedy was paying more than ordinary attention. "He had devoured every word written about the Profumo case," noted Ben Bradlee. "He ordered all further cables on that subject sent to him immediately."

Bradlee assumed the President was merely fascinated by the sexually exotic aspects of the story. But it was more than that. According to persistent reports, he himself had dallied with two of the young women linked to the scandal.

As he combed the reports from London, Kennedy must have been especially concerned about references to a twenty-two-year-old prostitute of Anglo-Czech parentage named Mariella Novotny. In early 1961, she had been in New York and, she said later, was procured for the President-elect by Peter Lawford. They had sex several times in Manhattan, once in a group involving other prostitutes. As in the Profumo case, there was a potential security angle. Novotny's name was being linked to an alleged Soviet vice ring at the United Nations.[2]

In the third week of June 1963, John Kennedy brought up the Profumo affair in a conversation with Martin Luther King. After a tumultuous two years, the civil rights leader was facing a fresh crisis—thanks to the FBI. Edgar, who had long since written King off as "no good," had been telling Kennedy the black leader was under Communist influence.

Specifically, he had persuaded Robert Kennedy to authorize a wiretap of one of King's advisers who, Edgar alleged, was an active Soviet agent. This was just another of Edgar's irrational obsessions, but the Kennedys could not be sure of that. They were afraid exposure of such links could bring disaster, not only on King but on the administration for supporting him.

So it was that on June 22, before addressing a group of civil rights leaders at the White House, the President took King by himself into the Rose Garden. He begged him to get rid of two colleagues Edgar claimed were Communists, then asked if he had read about Profumo in the newspapers. "That," he told King, "was an example of friendship and loyalty carried too far. Macmillan is likely to lose his government because he has been loyal to a friend. You must take care not to lose your cause for the same reason."

Kennedy went further. "I suppose you know," he said, "you're under very close surveillance." He warned King to be very careful about what he said on the phone, that if

J. Edgar Hoover could prove he had links with Communists, he would use it to wreck pending civil rights legislation.

As the meeting with the President ended, King found himself wondering why Kennedy had taken the precaution of ushering him out into the garden to talk. "The President," King told an associate later, "is afraid of Hoover himself, because he wouldn't even talk to me in his own office. I guess Hoover must be bugging him, too."

On June 23, the President left Washington for Europe, on the tour remembered today for the *"Ich bin ein Berliner"* speech and the pilgrimage to Ireland. He also visited London to see Prime Minister Macmillan. The evening he arrived, as he dined with the British leader, Kennedy learned the Profumo case was about to touch his presidency. The noon edition of the New York *Journal-American* that day carried the headline: HIGH US AIDE IMPLICATED IN V-GIRL SCANDAL. The opening line read: "One of the biggest names in American politics—a man who holds a 'very high' elective office—has been injected into Britain's vice-security scandal. . . ." The report stopped short of naming the President, but the implication was clear.

The report stayed in the paper for one edition and was then dropped without explanation. Robert Kennedy had moved swiftly. He telephoned his brother in the middle of the dinner with Macmillan, FBI files show, and the President expressed "concern." The FBI representative in London, Charles Bates, was ordered to brief Kennedy the next morning before he left for Italy. "If anything develops," the President told Bates, "anything at all, we'd like to be advised. Get it to us in Rome."

In Washington, forty-eight hours after publication of the *Journal-American* story, the authors of the article faced the Attorney General in his office. The paper's Managing Editor, Pulitzer Prize winner James Horan, and Dom Frasca, remembered by a colleague as "the best investigative reporter" on the paper, had been hauled from their homes in New York and flown to the capital in the Kennedys' private jet.

The two journalists have since died, but their ordeal at the hands of Robert Kennedy was recorded by the FBI. According to the file, the President's brother asked the newsmen to name the "high U.S. aide" who, according to the article, was being linked to the Profumo scandal. Horan replied that the reference was indeed to the President and that, according to the newspaper's sources, it involved a woman he had known shortly before he was elected President.

"It is noted," Edgar's liaison man Courtney Evans reported, "that the Attorney General treated the newspaper representatives at arm's length. . . . There was an air of hostility. . . ." When the reporters refused to reveal their sources, Kennedy followed up ruthlessly. According to Mark Monsky, godson of the *Journal-American*'s owner Randolph Hearst, the President's brother threatened to bring an antitrust suit against the paper. Hearst's editors then dropped the story.

After this confrontation with the reporters, Robert Kennedy betrayed how vulnerable he felt about Edgar. He tried to persuade Courtney Evans "not to write a memorandum" to Edgar about the meeting. According to Charles Bates, Edgar had been delving into the case for some time. "There was a big flap," Bates recalled. "My HQ sent cables saying 'Is this true? What can you find out?'"

On the evening of June 29, as the President dined with Macmillan, Bates had sent Edgar coded telegram 861, marked VERY URGENT. Of twenty lines, seventeen have been excised by the censor. What remains reads: ". . . [Name censored] talked about President Kennedy and repeated a rumor that was going around New York. . . ." A second document provides more background. A report addressed to William Sullivan, by then Assistant Director in charge of Counter-Intelligence, offers—between the censored chunks —information that:

One of [name blanked out] clients was John Kennedy, then presidential candidate. [Name] stated that Marie Novotny, British prostitute, went to New York to take [name's] place, since she was going on pre-election rounds with Kennedy.

Before it was silenced, the New York *Journal-American* had referred to a second mystery woman, "a beautiful Chinese-American girl now in London." The highest authorities, said the paper, "identified her as Suzy Chang. . . ."

Suzy Chang was an aspiring actress and model. There is no evidence she was a prostitute, but she did move in the wealthy London circles associated with the Profumo case. Tracked down in 1987, she admitted having known Kennedy. "We'd meet in the 21 Club," she said nervously. "Everybody saw me eating with him. I think he was a nice guy, very charming." Then she laughed. "What else am I going to say?"

A mass of FBI and Immigration Service documents show Chang did travel to New York in 1960, the year she was alleged to have gone with John Kennedy. She was also there in 1961, and over the Christmas period at the end of 1962. The most revealing document notes that late in 1963 "Chang arrived in US at New York, via Flight 701. . . . She was the [blanked out section in report] . . . She was questioned regarding the 'Profumo Affair.'"

The Profumo case was treated with the utmost gravity in Washington. Defense Secretary McNamara, CIA Director John McCone, Defense Intelligence Agency boss General Joseph Carroll, and usually one of Edgar's senior aides, attended a series of meetings. The case was handled at the FBI by two Assistant Directors. Progress reports, which remain almost entirely censored, went to the office of President Kennedy, to his brother—and to Edgar. "To find that the President was perhaps involved with somebody in the British security scandal!" exclaimed Courtney Evans, recalling the gravity of those days. "Nobody was grinning. . . ."

Except, perhaps, for Edgar. By the time the President returned from Europe he had a pile of information on Suzy Chang, and probably on Mariella Novotny, too. Heavily censored documents show Edgar was in contact with his New York office about Chang just twenty-four hours before the *Journal-American* story broke in that city.

He had long used the *Journal-American,* like other Hearst papers, to fuel fears about the Red Menace. There were even former FBI men on the paper's staff. Edgar's phone logs show that he talked regularly with Richard Berlin, head of the Hearst conglomerate. Berlin oversaw an editorial policy of fierce opposition to the policies of the Kennedy administration.

He and Edgar, moreover, were both close to Roy Cohn, who was acting as attorney for an American involved in the Profumo case and said by a central figure in the scandal to have "arranged sex parties for JFK in London." A telltale handwritten note on one of the FBI's Profumo documents reads: "Roy Cohn has this info."

President Kennedy had been compromised by his relations with Judith Campbell, Marilyn Monroe—and now Novotny and Chang—all in circumstances that touched on national security, all discovered by Edgar. Yet all that summer the brothers and their FBI chief kept up a pretense of cordiality.

Edgar wrote to "Dear Bob" to congratulate him on the birth of his eighth child, a son named Christopher. He commiserated with the President when his newborn son died less than two days after birth. The brothers wrote polite letters back.

All the while Edgar was up to his tricks, using the press to distort the facts on organized crime, bringing pressure to brand Martin Luther King a Communist, trying to get Robert Kennedy to authorize wiretaps—not just against close colleagues but against King himself. In August, even as he was offering sympathy over the loss of the President's baby, Edgar had agents urgently investigating a lead about yet another woman, yet another potential security risk.

Ellen Rometsch, a lovely young refugee from East Germany, had come to the United States in 1961 with her husband, a West German army sergeant on assignment to his country's military mission in Washington. She had looks like Elizabeth Taylor and soon became known as a "party girl." One of the men Rometsch met during the social whirl was Bobby Baker, secretary to the Senate Majority Leader and a close associate of Lyndon Johnson's, and she was soon appearing in low-cut dress and fishnet tights at the exclusive Quorum Club, near the Capitol, which Baker had helped to found.

One of the club's patrons in the late summer of 1961 was Bill Thompson, a railroad lobbyist and an intimate friend of the President's. A wealthy bachelor, he was privy to many of the secrets of Kennedy's love life and had been present at one of the earliest meetings with Judith Campbell.

"We were having cocktails at the Quorum," Baker recalled, "and Bill Thompson came over to me. He pointed to Ellen and he said, 'Boy, that son of a bitch is something. D'you think she'd come down and have dinner with me and the President?' So I had her meet Thompson, and she went down and saw the President. And he sent back word it was the best time he ever had in his life. That was not the only time. She saw him on other occasions. It went on for a while."

Rometsch was loose-lipped, however, and began to talk about her relationships with men in Washington. Someone tipped off the FBI about her, and in July 1963 agents came to ask questions. As a recent refugee from the East, and one who had once been a member of Communist youth organizations, Rometsch might have been a Communist plant. Soon, with the cooperation of the German authorities, she and her husband were quietly shipped back to Germany.

The matter might have ended there were it not for the scandal that exploded, three weeks after Rometsch's departure, around Bobby Baker, the man who had arranged many of her introductions to Washington politicians. The focus of the Baker case was on financial corruption, not sex, but—behind the scenes—the Quorum Club connection triggered an explosive allegation.

"Information has been developed," read a top-level FBI memo written on October 26, that pertains to possible questionable activities on the part of high government officials. It was also alleged that the President and the Attorney General had availed themselves of services of playgirls.

The remainder of the text of the memo is censored as released by the FBI, and its source is not identified.

That same Saturday, in Iowa, *The Des Moines Register* ran a front-page story reporting the Rometsch expulsion for the first time. The FBI investigation, said the paper, "established that the beautiful brunette had been attending parties with congressional leaders and some prominent New Frontiersmen from the executive branch of Government. . . . The possibility that her activity might be connected with espionage was of some concern, because of the high rank of her male companions."

Clark Mollenhoff, who wrote the *Register* story, was one of Edgar's "friendly" reporters.[3] His article added that Senator John Williams, the Republican from Delaware, "had obtained an account" of Rometsch's activity. It would later emerge that the Senator had come into possession of documents from the FBI, a leak that only Edgar could have approved. His information, the *Register* reported, included a list of Rometsch's "government friends," and he intended to present it to the Senate Rules Committee, the body investigating Bobby Baker, the following Tuesday.

Now the Kennedys performed urgent damage control. In a series of panicky calls to Edgar's office, a White House aide begged the FBI to prevent the *Register* story from being published in other newspapers. The President himself, he said, was "personally interested in having this story killed." The Bureau refused to help.

Publication of the story on a weekend, and in an out-of-town newspaper, offered a small breathing space. The Attorney General called La Verne Duffy, a Kennedy friend, and dispatched him on the next plane to West Germany. His mission was to silence Rometsch before the press got to her. It was reported a few days later that "men flashing U.S. security badges saw Mrs. Rometsch Sunday and got her to sign a statement formally denying intimacies with important people." Letters Rometsch later sent to Duffy thanked him for sending money and assured him, "Of course I will keep quiet. . . . "

At home, very early on Monday morning and just twenty-four hours before Senator Williams' planned speech to the Senate Rules Committee, Robert Kennedy called Edgar at home. As the man with access to the facts, Edgar was the one person likely to be able to persuade the Senate leadership that the hearing would be contrary to the national interest and—because members of Congress were likely to be dragged in—contrary to the interests of Congress, too.

Edgar's notes of the call from Kennedy, and of a later meeting at the Justice Department, leave no doubt of the Attorney General's humiliation. The President's brother was a supplicant, begging Edgar to bring the Senators in line.

That afternoon, as the capital buzzed with impending scandal, Edgar briefed Mike Mansfield, the Democratic leader in the Senate, and Everett Dirksen, his Republican counterpart. To ensure total secrecy, they met at Mansfield's home. What Edgar said at the meeting is censored in the FBI record, but it evidently did the trick. Before the afternoon was out, Senate plans to discuss Rometsch had been canceled.

The crisis was over, but it had been desperately serious. The Rometsch affair had threatened to become a Profumo-style sex and security disaster that could have forced the President into resignation. The cover-up had been achieved at great cost and left the Kennedys more indebted to Edgar than ever. The power struggle had lasted nearly three years, and they were losing.

Three months earlier, in the face of pressure from the FBI, Robert Kennedy had refused a Bureau request to wiretap Martin Luther King on the unfounded suspicion that he was under Communist control. Since then, in the week Ellen Rometsch had flown back to Germany, there had been the great civil rights March on Washington. A quarter of a million people had descended on the capital to hear

King speak of his dream of freedom and to sing "We Shall Overcome." For millions it was a moment of inspiration, of hope for progress. For Edgar, a southerner born in the nineteenth century, it merely inflamed his fear of King.

Edgar had again pressed the Attorney General to authorize a wiretap on King. Again Kennedy hesitated, knowing discovery of such surveillance would be politically disastrous. Then, bowing to the pressure, he authorized just one tap. In October, when Edgar demanded taps on four more King telephones at the height of the Rometsch affair, Kennedy caved in. The telephone taps, along with microphone surveillance, would continue until 1966.

On October 26, the morning he and Edgar discussed Ellen Rometsch, the Attorney General had found himself in an impossible situation. On the one hand he was virtually begging for assistance with the Rometsch problem. On the other, he was angry at Edgar for disseminating an outrageously misleading report—that Martin Luther King was "knowingly, willingly, and regularly taking guidance from Communists." When he tried to remonstrate, Edgar just stonewalled. The Kennedys had lost control of J. Edgar Hoover.

There would have been "no living with the Bureau," Kennedy told an aide, if he had not approved the King wiretaps. Once he did, though, the Kennedys were mired even deeper. "It was a trap," wrote King's biographer Taylor Branch. "Hoover would possess a club to offset Kennedy's special relationship with the President. . . . How could Kennedy hope to control Hoover once he had agreed to wiretap King? There was a Faustian undertow to Kennedy's dilemma, and he did not feel strong enough to resist."

Edgar picked October 29, the day after he had rescued the President from the Rometsch scandal, to discuss his future with Robert Kennedy. What of the rumors on Capitol Hill, he asked, that he was about to be fired? Kennedy assured him, Edgar noted with satisfaction, that the rumors were unfounded. Two days later he went to lunch with the President at the White House.

It must have been an extraordinary encounter, and deeply

humiliating for the President. At the height of the Rometsch crisis, he had been forced to break his own rule and telephone Edgar directly. Now they were face-to-face. The Kennedy archives list the meeting as "off the record," but we know a little of what transpired from the President's friend Ben Bradlee.

"He told me Hoover had talked to him about that German woman," Bradlee recalled, "that they'd looked at pictures of her, and Hoover had discussed what she did with various politicians." Kennedy said nothing to Bradlee about the dirt Edgar had on him and his brother.

The President's aide David Powers, meanwhile, has hinted that Edgar's future was discussed at the meeting. And, according to Bradlee, Kennedy decided he would have to have Edgar over more often. "He felt it was wise—with rumors flying and every indication of a dirty campaign coming up."

There had been only six meetings between Edgar and John Kennedy since 1961, and there would never be another. Twenty-two days after that last secret encounter at the White House, the President flew to Dallas.

CHAPTER 28

"Hoover lied his eyes out to the Commission, on Oswald, on Ruby, on their friends, the bullets, the gun, you name it. . . ."

Congressman Hale Boggs,
House Majority Leader and former member of
the Warren Commission

EDGAR LEARNED OF THE ASSASSINATION THE WAY THE WORLD'S newsmen did, from the UPI teleprinter installed in his office. The first flash bulletin came in at 1:34 P.M., Washington time, four minutes after the shooting, as the President's limousine sped toward a Dallas hospital.

Nine minutes later, with UPI saying Kennedy was "perhaps fatally wounded," Edgar picked up the direct line that neither he nor the Attorney General had used for months. Robert Kennedy was at home eating lunch, and the call was transferred to him there. "I thought something must be wrong," the President's brother was to recall, "because Hoover wouldn't be calling me here." Moments later he hung up, gagged and turned away.

Edgar merely noted, in a five-line memo, that he had passed on the news. Edgar's voice, the Attorney General would recall, had been "not quite as excited as if he was reporting the fact that he found a Communist on the faculty of Howard University [Washington's predominantly black college]. His conversations with me on November 22 were so unpleasant."

Edgar would never offer a word of commiseration—he just sent one of those terse formal notes of his. In the nine months Robert Kennedy was to remain in office, the two men would rarely speak. When the direct-line phone next rang, Edgar merely waited until it stopped. Then he ordered, "Put that damn thing back on Miss Gandy's desk, where it belongs."

When Edgar called Kennedy a second time, forty minutes after the shooting, he was still talking only of "critical" wounds. The Attorney General, who had better sources, set him straight. "You may be interested to know," he snapped, "that my brother is dead."

That evening, Edgar went home to watch television. The next day he went to the races.

"The track raced on the Saturday, the day after Kennedy died," said Bill Koras, an official at Pimlico, "and Mr. Hoover was there. He used our little private office and was there most of the day conducting business about the assassination. Mr. Tolson was with him, and he went down to place the bets."

Within hours of the murder, before leaving his office, Edgar had written an ingratiating letter to Lyndon Johnson, the man who had gambled—correctly—that fate might bring him the presidency.

My dear Mr. President,
I was indeed shocked by the brutal assassination today of President Kennedy and I want to offer my deepest sympathy on the Nation's tragic loss of your personal friend.
    My staff and I want to reaffirm our earnest desire to be of assistance to you in every possible way.

This was pure hypocrisy. Edgar well knew that Johnson and the Kennedys had at best tolerated one another. By contrast, he and Johnson had long been exchanging letters of mutual admiration. In one, just months earlier, the Vice President had expressed his "complete and utter devotion" to Edgar.

Johnson's first calls as President were to two former leaders—Truman and Eisenhower—and to Edgar. Within days, at the White House, he would be pouring out his concern that he might be assassinated himself. Edgar offered the use of one of his own bulletproof cars, and Johnson responded emotionally. He thought, Edgar noted, "I was more than head of the FBI—I was his brother and personal friend . . . that he had more confidence in me than anybody in town. . . ."

In one of his notes as Vice President, Johnson had spoken of continuing to rely on Edgar "in the years ahead." Now, his accession to power offered Edgar the likelihood of reprieve from the forced retirement that, under Kennedy, would soon have been his fate. Meanwhile, there was a most sensitive game to be played—tidying up after Dallas.

Thanks to two conflicting official verdicts, millions of Americans remain confused about the assassination. The initial inquiry, the Commission chaired by Chief Justice Earl Warren, concluded that the President had been killed by twenty-four-year-old Lee Harvey Oswald, former Marine and recently returned defector to the Soviet Union, acting on his own. Yet as we now know, four of the Commission's own eminent members had doubts. And in 1978, Congress' Assassinations Committee decided that there had "probably" been a conspiracy.

The committee believed Oswald was only one of two gunmen and that the murder was most likely planned by the Mafia. Others, pointing to evidence that Oswald had links to U.S. intelligence, wondered if it was quite so simple. Even a former chief of the CIA's Western Hemisphere Division, David Phillips, himself a committee witness, in 1988 declared his belief in a plot involving "rogue American intelligence people."

There might never have been such confusion had the Warren Commission not had to rely on the FBI for the vast majority of its information. Edgar's priority from the start was to protect himself and the Bureau and to insist that Oswald was the lone assassin. Less than four hours after the shooting, Assistant Attorney General Norbert Schlei was astonished to hear the Director declare himself "quite convinced they had found the right party." Yet called upon to brief the new head of state the next day, Edgar was less positive. Jotting down what Edgar told him, President Johnson wrote:

> Evidence not strong . . . not strong enough to get conviction. . . .

There was no more talk about weaknesses in the evidence the day after that, when Oswald had in turn been shot by Jack Ruby, and with no further prospect of a trial. "The thing I am concerned about," Edgar told the White House two hours after Oswald's murder, "is having something issued so we can convince the public that Oswald is the real assassin." Soon the President was saying he hoped he could "get by" with a hastily prepared FBI report.[1]

Of the few FBI veterans prepared to discuss the Kennedy assassination, two senior officials[2] and a field agent tell a story of rush to judgment and information distorted. "Hoover's obsession with speed," said Assistant Director Courtney Evans, "made impossible demands on the field. I can't help but feel that had he let the agents out there do their work, let things take their normal investigative course, something other than the simple Oswald theory might have been developed. But Hoover's demand was 'Do it fast!' That was not necessarily a prescription for getting the whole truth."

Agent Harry Whidbee was assigned to talk to people who had known Oswald in California, where he had served during his stint in the Marines. "I remember distinctly," he said in 1988. "It was a hurry-up job. Within three weeks a letter of general instruction came to the field divisions. We were effectively told 'They're only going to prove he was the guy who did it. There were no co-conspirators, and there was no international conspiracy. . . .' I had conducted a couple of interviews, and those records were sent back again and were rewritten according to Washington's requirements."

There are numerous stories of badgered witnesses and edited evidence. Two of President Kennedy's senior aides, Kenneth O'Donnell and David Powers, both believed shots had come from behind the fence in front of the motorcade —rather than from the building behind it, where Oswald supposedly lay in ambush. "I told the FBI what I had heard," O'Donnell recalled, "but they said it couldn't have happened that way. . . . So I testified the way they wanted me to."

As Attorney General, Robert Kennedy would normally have played a key role in the investigation. But he remained traumatized and away from his office for weeks after the assassination. According to a senior FBI official, Edgar ordered aides to get the Bureau's assassination report out of the Justice Department "before Bobby gets back."

Edgar opposed inquiry by any body other than the FBI. Then, once Johnson decided he had to have a presidential commission to ward off calls for independent investigation, Edgar wanted to head it himself. When the job went to Chief Justice Warren, Edgar interfered from the start. He opposed the Chief Justice's choice of Warren Olney, a former head of the Criminal Division at Justice and an expert on organized crime, as the Commission's Chief Counsel. Lee Rankin, who was appointed, would conclude belatedly that "the FBI couldn't be trusted."

Edgar used Cartha DeLoach to liaise secretly with two members of the Commission: Senator Richard Russell and Congressman Gerald Ford, the future President. DeLoach gleaned details of the Commission's secret deliberations from Ford, and supplied him with a secure briefcase to carry documents on a ski trip. Ford, said William Sullivan, was a member of the FBI's "congressional stable . . . 'our man' on the Warren Commission. It was to him that we looked to protect our interest and to keep us fully advised of any development that we would not like . . . and he did."

Bobby Baker, Lyndon Johnson's former aide, has offered

an explanation for Ford's readiness to help the FBI. For a period in the year preceding the assassination, he and Ford both had access to a "hospitality suite" at Washington's Sheraton-Carlton Hotel rented by a mutual friend, the lobbyist Fred Black. "Like me," Baker said, "Jerry Ford had a key to the suite. And sometimes Black would tell me not to use the room, because Ford was meeting someone there."

For two months in 1963, as later emerged during court proceedings against Black for tax evasion, the hotel room in question was bugged by the FBI. Baker speculates that the surveillance targeted against Black picked up compromising information on Ford, that it was passed on to Edgar, who then used it to pressure Ford into cooperating during his spell on the Warren Commission.

Edgar had long buttered up Chief Justice Warren, to the extent of running FBI checks on his daughter's boyfriends. Now, however, he treated him as a nuisance. "If Warren had kept his big mouth shut," Edgar scrawled on one memo, "these conjectures would not have happened." He sent agents hunting for derogatory information on the staff of the Warren Commission.

At least one Commissioner felt pressured to toe the FBI line on the assassination. According to his son Thomas, House Majority Leader Hale Boggs "felt personally intimidated by the FBI's visits to see him. It was, you know, 'We know this and that about you, and a lot of things could come out in public about you . . .' My father tried not to let it affect his judgment."[3]

Former Deputy Attorney General Katzenbach, who stood in for Robert Kennedy in the wake of the assassination, would recall ruefully that Edgar and the FBI had a virtual monopoly on vital information. "I did not know what was going on," he said. "Nobody else in the government knew." Had they known, neither Katzenbach nor the Warren Commission would have placed any trust at all in Edgar. The FBI concealed evidence from the Commission and, in one damning episode, destroyed it.

Early on, Warren staffers became suspicious about a

discrepancy between the original of Oswald's address book and the FBI's typed inventory of its contents. In the FBI version one page had been retyped, omitting some information that had appeared in the original. And part of the excised material was the name, address and car license plate number of an FBI agent, James Hosty.[4]

Hosty was the Dallas agent who, according to the Bureau, had had the routine job of checking up on Oswald because of his background as a former defector. He testified that he never met Oswald, but left a message with Oswald's wife not long before the assassination, asking him to call. If that was all, why then did the Bureau try to conceal the Hosty relationship from the Commission?

The FBI denied that it had, offering a complex bureaucratic explanation for the omitted entry. Commission staff remained skeptical. "We never forgot the incident," said attorney Burt Griffin. "It established in our minds that we had to be worried about them."

This leads on to a horrendous discovery, something the Commission never found out. Oswald had told his wife's close friend Ruth Paine that he had left a note at the Dallas office of the FBI following the Hosty visit. After the assassination, told by an agent that this was not so, Mrs. Paine decided it had been just a tall story. In 1975, however, a congressional committee learned that the alleged assassin had indeed left a note at the FBI office two weeks before the assassination—addressed to Agent Hosty.

According to a receptionist, the note was a warning by Oswald that he would blow up the FBI office if they did not "stop bothering my wife." According to Hosty, there was no threat of violence—merely a warning that Oswald might "take appropriate action and report this to the proper authorities."

That note is not part of the official record because, Hosty testified, Dallas Agent in Charge Gordon Shanklin ordered him to destroy it. The note was in Shanklin's possession after the assassination. Two days later, when Oswald had been shot, Shanklin produced the letter from a desk drawer.

He told Hosty, "Oswald's dead now. There can be no trial. Here—get rid of this." Hosty then tore up the note in Shanklin's presence, took it to the lavatory and "flushed it down the drain."

Who originally issued the order to destroy Oswald's note, and why, may never be known. Shanklin is dead and former Agent Hosty refuses further comment. Agent Cril Payne, who served in Dallas during the inquiry that followed Hosty's revelations, thinks it "inconceivable" that the note could have been destroyed without clearance from Washington. "The prevailing office rumors," he added, "were that J. Edgar Hoover had personally ordered the destruction of the note." According to two Assistant Directors, William Sullivan and Mark Felt, headquarters officials did know about the note at the time. It was Edgar, said Sullivan, who ordered that its very existence be kept secret from the Warren Commission.

"We didn't think," former Commission Chief Counsel Rankin has since said ruefully, "that he would deliberately lie. . . . There is an implication from that note and its destruction that there might have been more to it. . . ." Rankin was thinking of the bombshell that for a while threatened to change the course of the Warren inquiry, when the Attorney General of Texas, Waggoner Carr, reported "an allegation to the effect that Lee Harvey Oswald was an undercover agent of the FBI."

Edgar flatly denied to the Commission that either Oswald or Ruby had ever been FBI informants. Yet it later emerged that the FBI had no fewer than nine contacts with Jack Ruby, long before the assassination. He was even listed in FBI files as a P.C.I.—Potential Criminal Informant. If Edgar misled the Commission about Ruby, what of Oswald?

The alleged assassin's widow, Marina, has said she believes he "worked for the American government." The former security chief at the State Department, Otto Otepka, recalled uncertainty, months before the assassination, as to whether the returned defector to the Soviet Union was "one of ours or one of theirs."

Two witnesses from New Orleans, where Oswald spent time before the assassination, said they saw Oswald in the company of FBI agents there. A Dallas deputy sheriff, Allen Sweatt, was quoted as saying the Bureau was paying Oswald $200 a month at the time of the assassination and had assigned him an informant number.[5]

The Commission, however, never conducted a thorough probe of such claims.[6] It ended up, the Assassinations Committee staff concluded in 1979, "doing what the members had agreed they would not do: Rely mainly on the FBI's denial of the allegations."

Commission Chief Counsel Rankin was puzzled from the start by the FBI's stance on the assassination. Normally Edgar never tired of saying it was the Bureau's job to offer facts, not conclusions. This time everything was different. "They haven't run out all the leads," Rankin told the Commissioners, "but they are concluding that Oswald was the assassin . . . that there can't be a conspiracy. Now that is not normal. . . . Why are they so eager to make both of these conclusions?"

Some believe it was Edgar's obsession with protecting his reputation that led him to shut out everything else. He scurried to send secret letters of censure to seventeen agents and officials—all men who had been involved in handling the Oswald case before the assassination. Had they performed properly, Edgar claimed, Oswald's name would have been on the Security Index. Later, when the Warren Report gently chastised the Bureau for not having been alert enough, he punished some of the same men all over again. "The Bureau," he said, "will never live this down." Yet Oswald was not known to have said or done anything violent, anything at all that justified a warning to the Secret Service, the agency responsible for protecting the President. Edgar's retribution against his own agents was merely a vindictive device to cover his own back.

The Assassinations Committee reported in 1979 that the FBI probe of Kennedy's murder had been "seriously flawed," "insufficient to have uncovered a conspiracy." The committee's own investigation, meanwhile, identified men who had said the President was going to be killed, along with associates who acted highly suspiciously before and after the assassination. It appears, moreover, that the FBI was aware in 1963 of all or most of the clues the committee followed sixteen years later.

Edgar, former aides confirm, gave personal attention to all aspects of the assassination. "He got everything, knew about everything," Cartha DeLoach recalled. "We didn't dare hold anything back." Yet Edgar ignored a mass of information that, when the Assassinations Committee came upon it years later, would suggest conspiracy.

More than three years before the assassination, when Oswald was an obscure defector living in the Soviet Union, a memo about him had gone forth under Edgar's name. "There is a possibility," it warned the State Department on June 3, 1960, "that an imposter is using Oswald's birth certificate."

According to a former Army Intelligence colonel, Philip Corso, high-level U.S. officials said within weeks of the assassination that they knew two Oswald birth certificates, and two Oswald passports, had been in circulation before the assassination—and had been used by two different men. Speaking in 1992, Corso cited two sources—Passport Office head Frances Knight and William Sullivan, then head of the FBI's Domestic Intelligence Division. Corso said it was in large measure his briefing on this matter that led Senator Richard Russell, one of the members of the Warren Commission, to doubt the lone-assassin theory.

There is some evidence that a few months after Edgar wrote his 1960 "imposter" memo, someone was masquerading as Oswald. In January 1961, an American and a Cuban exile negotiated to buy ten Ford pickup trucks from a dealer in New Orleans. The dealer remembered the incident after the assassination, dug out the old sale form and found that his memory was not playing tricks. One of the truck purchasers had identified himself as Oswald, representing an organization called Friends of Democratic Cuba. The dealer's form was withheld by the FBI until 1979, yet the lead had great potential significance.

Friends of Democratic Cuba was an anti-Castro group, and the attempt to buy trucks occurred during the buildup to the Bay of Pigs invasion. FBI agents were out asking about Lee Oswald's business dealings within two weeks, and Passport Office concern about a possible imposter followed soon after. It seems that while the real, pro-Communist Oswald was far away in the Soviet Union, someone of the opposite political persuasion may have been using his name in the United States.

The coincidences proliferate. Gerard Tujague, a senior member of the same anti-Castro group, had once employed the real Oswald as a messenger. And a leading member of the group, in 1961, was Guy Banister, a man of mystery not least because of his close relations with the FBI.

Guy Banister served with the Bureau for twenty years, seventeen of them as a Special Agent in Charge, and he was one of the handful of veterans who had worked alongside the Director in the field, during the recapture of escaped convicts in 1942. His Bureau career had ended in 1955, following major surgery and a warning to his wife that "as a result of brain damage, he would develop increasingly unpredictable, erratic conduct."

The Banister who returned to Louisiana, the state of his birth, was a man disintegrating. His state of mind shifted from feisty to choleric to violent rage. Alcohol made the problem worse, and the pills prescribed by his doctors brought little relief.

None of this deterred Banister from his self-appointed role as superpatriot and crusader against Communism. He was a member of the John Birch Society and the paramilitary Minutemen, an investigator for Louisiana's Committee on Un-American Activities and publisher of a racist tract called the *Louisiana Intelligence Digest*. He believed plans for racial integration were part of a Communist plot against the United States, and he worked feverishly in support of the CIA-backed campaign to topple Fidel Castro. On a journey to Europe he reportedly met with French terrorists plotting the assassination of President de Gaulle.

Like many former Bureau agents, Banister was a private detective, and he kept up his contacts with the Bureau at the highest level. "Guy was in touch with J. Edgar Hoover long after he left," said New Orleans Crime Commission Director Aaron Kohn, and the New Orleans office of the FBI was close by Banister's detective agency. According to his secretary, Delphine Roberts, "Mr. Banister was still working for them. I know he and the FBI traded information." FBI records confirm this, and a CIA document identifies Banister as one of the "regular FBI contacts" of a Cuban exile leader.

In the old days in Chicago, Banister's anti-Communist squad had been one of the most effective teams in the country. And in 1963 in New Orleans he ran penetration operations against the Left, hiring young men to inform on pro-Castro and civil rights organizations—just the sort of operation the FBI was running at the time.

Oswald was in New Orleans that summer, making a show of himself as a pro-Castro activist—the very sort of "Commie" Banister deplored. Yet the evidence suggests they had a secret working relationship with each other. According to his secretary, Banister even provided Oswald with office space. "Don't worry about him," Delphine Roberts quotes her boss as saying. "He's with us, he's associated with the office. . . ."

One of Banister's associates, former Eastern Airlines pilot David Ferrie, has also been linked to Oswald. They apparently met for the first time in the fifties, when Oswald was a teenage cadet and Ferrie an instructor in the Civil Air Patrol. By the early sixties Ferrie's life, like Banister's, had become a constant round of anti-Castro scheming and right-wing politics.

Numerous witnesses would recall having seen Oswald in the company of two men, one of them almost certainly

Ferrie, less than three months before the assassination. They arrived together in a black Cadillac, acting oddly, during a black voters' registration drive in Clinton, a town north of New Orleans. Even then, local civil rights activists suspected, they were undercover FBI agents.

One of Banister's investigators, Jack Martin, blew the whistle on his boss and Ferrie immediately after the assassination. He made, then retracted, an allegation that Ferrie had been involved with Oswald and in planning the murder. Ferrie himself, meanwhile, charged frantically around New Orleans quizzing Oswald's former landlady and neighbors about a library card. Other information suggests Oswald may have been carrying a library card when arrested, one with Ferrie's name on it.

Banister, for his part, spent hours after the assassination drinking heavily with investigator Martin. The session ended with Banister accusing Martin of going through his confidential files, then beating him over the head with a .357 Magnum revolver. The fracas started, according to Martin, when he asked Banister: "What are you going to do, kill me like you all did Kennedy?"

This would seem to be more than enough to have become a serious focus of the investigation, yet the FBI let the matter drop after perfunctory inquiries. Guy Banister was interviewed, but was asked no questions at all about Oswald. Neither his name, nor Ferrie's, appears in the Warren Report. Banister was found dead of an apparent heart attack, with a gun at his side, before the Commission finished its work. Ferrie was to die in 1967, a possible suicide, after New Orleans District Attorney Jim Garrison had reopened the case and was about to call him before a grand jury.

A clue to the Banister connection was handed to the FBI on a platter, but it was not passed on to the Warren Commission. Some of Oswald's pro-Castro leaflets had been stamped with the address 544 Camp Street, the building that housed Banister's detective agency. Yet the FBI memorandum on the leaflets, which might have alerted the Warren

Commission attorneys to this coincidence, concealed it. It listed Banister's address as 531 Lafayette Street, a reference to the alternative entrance to the 544 Camp building, which stood on a corner. The Commission's attorneys, poring over reports in Washington, had no way of knowing that fact. The FBI knew it very well, but kept the Commission in the dark.

Had Edgar provided the full picture on Banister and on David Ferrie, the Commission would have surely paid more attention to something very serious, the possibility that the Mafia had a hand in the assassination. Years later, Congress' Assassinations Committee expressed suspicion that two specific Mafia bosses might have been involved—Santos Trafficante of Florida and Carlos Marcello of New Orleans.

Marcello, like Trafficante and Sam Giancana, had been targeted by the Justice Department on Robert Kennedy's orders. He also held a peculiarly personal grudge. Within weeks of taking office in 1961, the President's brother had arranged for his abrupt deportation to Guatemala as an undesirable alien. When the mobster slipped back into the United States, Kennedy began renewed efforts to kick him out for good. David Ferrie had worked for Marcello's attorney, Wray Gill, since early 1962—in parallel with his work for Guy Banister. Ferrie and Banister had both helped prepare Marcello's defense against charges that he had used a phony birth certificate to avoid being deported.

Had the Marcello angle been pursued, much else would have come out. Oswald's uncle and surrogate father, Dutz Murret, with whom the alleged assassin stayed in 1963, worked in Marcello's gambling network. Jack Ruby, who had many mob associations, was in touch with Nofio Pecora, a Marcello lieutenant, three weeks before the assassination. Pecora, in turn, was close to Oswald's uncle. After the assassination, witnesses claimed that one Marcello associate had been seen handing Oswald cash, and that another had discussed the suitability of a foreign-made rifle to "get the President."

The FBI dropped such leads. Marcello's name appears neither in the Warren Report nor in any of its twenty-six volumes of evidence. Nor do those of Santos Trafficante or Sam Giancana.

The CIA failed to tell the Commission about its use of the Mafia in its plots to kill Castro, which had continued until early 1963. So did Edgar, who had known about them for a long time. Chief Justice Warren's investigators were thus denied a vital opening, a chance to make sense of the triple tracks confronting them—U.S. Intelligence, the mob and the exiles.

"Because we did not have those links," said Commission attorney Burt Griffin, now a judge, "there was nothing to tie the underworld in with Cuba and thus nothing to tie them in with Oswald, nothing to tie them in with the assassination of the President." The CIA, and Edgar with his New Orleans leads, did have the link. They held the key to the labyrinth and withheld it from the Commission.

Information from numerous sources suggests the principal Mafia leaders were linked to the case. The secretary to Guy Banister, the former FBI agent said to have manipulated Oswald, said he was visited before the killing by Giancana's henchman Johnny Roselli. Giancana's half brother has claimed the Chicago Mafia boss plotted the assassination in concert with Marcello, Trafficante and CIA operatives.

Frank Costello, the old Mafia overlord who helped Marcello build his criminal empire, said before he died that Oswald was "just the patsy" in the President's murder. Frank Ragano, the former attorney of Teamsters leader Jimmy Hoffa, said he was sent to discuss the President's murder with Trafficante and Marcello in early 1963. He gained the impression "they already had such a thought in their mind. . . ."

Most compelling, perhaps, is what the new generation of FBI agents learned during surveillance of Trafficante and Marcello as late as 1975. "Now only two people are alive," FBI microphones overheard Trafficante say, "who know who killed Kennedy." Trafficante himself died of natural causes in 1987, but Marcello lives on. Some years ago, according to Joseph Hauser, an FBI plant, he admitted that Oswald had worked as a runner in his betting operation in 1963.

The most serious information pointing to Trafficante and Marcello raises the possibility that the FBI was gravely negligent *before* the assassination. According to Jose Aleman, a wealthy Cuban exile, Trafficante made ominous remarks about the President at a business meeting as early as September 1962. The Kennedys, said the mobster, were "not honest. They took graft and they did not keep a bargain. . . . Mark my word, this man Kennedy is in trouble, and he will get what is coming to him." When Aleman demurred, saying he thought the President would be reelected, Trafficante said quietly, "You don't understand me. Kennedy's not going to make it to the election. He is going to be hit."

In Louisiana that same month, Marcello and two close associates met to discuss an oil project with Ed Becker, an entrepreneur from California. And as the whiskey flowed, the mobster talked angrily about his ordeal at the hands of Robert Kennedy. Finally, uttering a Sicilian oath, he exclaimed that the Attorney General was "going to be taken care of. . . ."

According to Becker, Marcello referred to President Kennedy as a dog, with his brother Robert being the tail. "The dog," he said, "will keep biting you if you only cut off its tail." If the dog's head were cut off, the biting would end.

The more Marcello ranted on, the more serious he seemed. According to Becker, he "clearly stated that he was going to arrange to have President Kennedy murdered. . . ." As "insurance" for the assassination, he spoke of "setting up a nut to take the blame."

The Marcello threat was first reported in a 1969 book by Pulitzer Prize winner Ed Reid, the Trafficante comments in *The Washington Post* in 1976. Congress' Assassinations Committee, however, inadequately probed the claim common to both of them—that the FBI was fully informed at the time.

Aleman, a valued FBI contact, would later insist that he told Bureau agents about Trafficante's remarks soon after they were made in 1962. After the assassination, he said, two agents rushed to see him, made him go over his story again, then asked him to keep the conversation confidential.

Available FBI files contain no reports showing that Trafficante's comments, or the Marcello threat, were reported as claimed. Paul Scranton, one of two former agents whom Aleman said he told of the Trafficante comments before the assassination, has refused to deny or confirm the claim. "I wouldn't want to say anything to embarrass the Bureau," he told *The Washington Post* in 1976.[7]

Ed Becker, for his part, has said from the start that he, too, quickly informed the FBI. "When I got home from Louisiana," he said, "I found that Bureau agents wanted to see me. They obviously knew I'd been seeing Marcello and asked why. I told them about the oil deal I'd been trying to set up and what Marcello had said about killing Kennedy. But they never came back to me. Although I talked to the congressional inquiry in the seventies, the FBI has never questioned me about it to this day."[8]

In 1962, when Ed Becker saw Marcello, he was working part-time for a former FBI agent turned private investigator, Julian Blodgett. Blodgett, who once also served as chief investigator for the Los Angeles County District Attorney, revealed in 1992 that Becker had told him of the mobster's threat less than two days after it was made. As a law enforcement professional, he responded by calling the FBI immediately.

"I took it seriously," said Blodgett. "Becker described the circumstances very carefully, and I considered him reliable, as I still do. I at once notified one of my Bureau contacts, a Supervisor in Los Angeles. He was a very dedicated man, and I am sure he reported it. A subject as vital as that would have been made a matter of record and transmitted to Washington."

Blodgett is an agent of the old school, steeped in respect for J. Edgar Hoover. He is mystified that FBI files supposedly contain no record of his report, nor of Becker's. Memos in the file do, however, show that in 1967, when the author Ed Reid was planning to publish Becker's account, Edgar and senior aides mounted an operation designed to destroy Becker's credibility. Agent George Bland visited Reid and tried to convince him that Becker was "a liar and a cheat." Becker's statement that he reported the Marcello threat to the FBI was removed from the book as a result.

Edgar had assured the Warren Commission that the FBI would keep the Kennedy assassination "in an open classification for all time," that "any report from any source will be thoroughly investigated." Yet far from investigating, he did everything possible to suppress Becker's story when it surfaced in 1967. This was, said the Assassinations Committee, "a violation of the Director's promise." Today with the statement by former Agent Blodgett that the threat was reported more than a year *before* the assassination, the violation looks even worse.

Edgar was required by law to warn the Secret Service of all threats to public officials. As a matter of routine he did indeed pass on the sort of menaces uttered daily by drunks and maniacs across the country. There is no sign, however, that the FBI told the Secret Service of the many violent remarks about the Kennedy brothers picked up on wiretaps of top mobsters.[9] Nor is there any evidence that the FBI passed on Marcello and Trafficante's talk of assassination.

On the eve of the President's murder, Jack Ruby ate dinner at a Dallas restaurant owned by Joseph Campisi, an intimate of Carlos Marcello and his brothers. Campisi talked with Ruby then, and would later visit him in jail. Another regular visitor to the restaurant was Joseph Civello, head of the Marcello-controlled Dallas Mafia. Civello had associated with Sergeant Patrick Dean, the Dallas policeman in charge of security when Ruby shot Oswald.

A witness told the FBI Ruby was close to Civello, and Edgar passed that information on to the Warren Commission, in the most bland language possible, failing to mention that Civello was a top Mafia figure controlled by Carlos Marcello. Nor did he point out something else—that Civello was a close friend of Clint Murchison, Jr., the son of one of Edgar's very best friends.

Irving Davidson, the Washington lobbyist who counted himself a friend of Edgar's and the Murchisons, had known Marcello since the early fifties. He styled himself the mobster's "door opener and arranger" and when the Kennedys succeeded in kicking Marcello out of the country for a while, he was said to be the one man in Washington who had the mobster's phone number abroad. Davidson was to be the liaison between Marcello and Clint Murchison, Jr., at the time of the sting operation that finally sent Marcello to jail in 1983.

Murchison, Sr., like almost all oilmen, had backed Johnson for the White House in 1960, and his fears about Kennedy turned out to be justified. The young President made no secret of his opposition to the oil moguls' extraordinary tax privileges, and moved quickly to change them. Murchison and his associates, it turns out, were linked to the assassination saga by a series of disconcerting coincidences.

George de Mohrenschildt, an oil geologist who knew Murchison and had worked for one of his companies, was on intimate terms with alleged assassin Oswald. He would be found shot dead in 1977, an apparent suicide, on the day an Assassinations Committee investigator called to arrange an interview.[10]

Within four days of the assassination, the FBI received a tip-off that Clint Murchison and Tom Webb—the FBI veteran the millionaire had hired at Edgar's suggestion— were both acquainted with Jack Ruby. While they denied it, Ruby had met one of Murchison's best friends, Humble Oil millionaire Billy Byars.

Byars was close to Edgar. They used adjacent bungalows

at Murchison's California hotel each summer. The phone log for the Director's office shows that, aside from calls to Robert Kennedy and the head of the Secret Service, Edgar called only one man on the afternoon the President was shot—Billy Byars.

Byars, Sr., is dead. His son Billy, who was a student in the early sixties, saw Edgar at the Del Charro the following summer. "I was there for one or two weeks," Byars recalled in 1988. "They would eat together, my father, Murchison and Hoover, and the others. Hoover seemed to be in a very strange frame of mind. He was having a better relationship with Johnson, evidently, than he had with President Kennedy—by a long shot. His relationship with Bobby Kennedy had apparently almost driven him over the edge. He used to talk about that constantly, and once I had the chance to ask him directly about the assassination.

"I asked him, 'Do you think Lee Harvey Oswald did it?' And he stopped and he looked at me for quite a long time. Then he said, 'If I told you what I really know, it would be very dangerous to this country. Our whole political system could be disrupted.' That's all he said, and I could see he wasn't about to say any more."

President Johnson, who should have been privy to the best intelligence on the assassination, believed there was a conspiracy. "Just a few weeks later," recalled Madeleine Brown, the woman who says she was his mistress, "I mentioned to him that people in Dallas were saying he himself had something to do with it. He became really violent, really ugly, and said it was American Intelligence and oil that were behind it. Then he left the room and slammed the door. It scared me."[11]

Johnson seems to have swung back and forth, certain there had been a conspiracy yet unsure where to pin the blame. His suspects varied from some Vietnamese faction to Fidel Castro to U.S. Intelligence. In 1967 he told his aide Marvin Watson that he felt "the CIA had something to do with this plot." At the time of his death in 1973, he was still

383

wondering whether the CIA-Mafia plots to kill Castro, on which he was briefed soon after taking office, had somehow boomeranged.

Months after the assassination, in the privacy of his office, Edgar told a visitor that the case was "a mess, a lot of loose ends." Why, then, did he steer the Warren Commission so insistently toward the lone-assassin theory, when there were clues demanding investigation of elements of U.S. Intelligence, the Mafia—even his own oil millionaire friends? Was he merely doing President Johnson's bidding, covering up information that would exacerbate the crisis? Or was he, too, under a different kind of pressure?

"I got a way," Carlos Marcello once said during a Louisiana election. "No matter who gets in there, you know I'm going to find a fuckin' way to get to 'em. I don't care who it is." Along with the other factors that may have left Edgar compromised by the Mafia, there is the report of an occasion long ago when he had been arrested for a homosexual offense in New Orleans.[12] Just as he may have had no choice in his failure to pursue the Mafia for years before the assassination, Edgar may have had no choice but to drop the leads that pointed to the mob in November 1963.

The most telling postscript to the assassination may be the fate of Robert Kennedy's crusade against organized crime. Before the murder, the President's brother had been succeeding in his struggle to force Edgar to confront the mob. Whether Edgar liked it or not, the FBI had become what it had never been before: a force the Mafia had cause to fear.

Fifteen weeks before Dallas, an FBI wiretap in Florida had picked up a conversation between two men who knew Edgar. One was Alvin Malnik, an attorney who would one day be identified as "one of Meyer Lansky's trusted people" and whom Edgar had befriended on a visit to Miami Beach. The other was local restaurateur Jesse Weiss, host to numerous mobsters and—every Christmas—to Edgar.

The log of the wiretap shows that the two men discussed the continuing crackdown on organized crime, and—with Robert Kennedy now in the ascendant—Edgar's waning influence:

> **Weiss:** They're taking the play away from him.
> **Malnik:** Hoover is a lost . . .
> **Weiss:** Cause.
> **Malnik:** A lost cause, that's all . . .
> **Weiss:** They take everybody's picture—license numbers and everything . . .
> **Malnik:** Well, that's not even bad, but when they go breaking into private property trying to get evidence, that's the limit . . . the lowest.
> **Weiss:** And then it's laughable. Once upon a time, you know, you walked into the FBI . . . intimidate . . .

Poor reception apparently blurred the rest of Weiss' comment, but the transcript resumes:

> **Malnik:** Sure! It doesn't mean anything anymore . . . it doesn't mean anything. . . . Does Hoover realize this great transformation that's happened within his own organization?
> **Weiss:** I spoke to him. Two weeks ago I was in Washington before he went to California—he goes out to California every year. . . . It's like he . . . He told me the same thing: "Shucks, the Bureau is shot!" "What the hell," he says. "But what can I do? . . . The Attorney General is the boss of the Bureau. He runs it . . . dare you to fight him."
> **Malnik:** That's right . . .

Just weeks after that conversation, Robert Kennedy complained to his brother about the FBI's failure to bring pressure on Mafia boss Carlos Marcello. It was an issue that became moot when the President was assassinated.

"The minute that bullet hit Jack Kennedy's head," said Justice Department aide William Hundley, "it was all over. Right then. The organized crime program just stopped, and Hoover took control back." "Those people," Robert Kennedy said bitterly of the FBI a fortnight later, "don't work for us anymore." In the months that followed, stunned by grief, he faltered in his drive against the mob. Edgar took full advantage.

"Pursuit of organized crime did continue," recalled veteran Chicago agent Bill Roemer, "but not with the same intensity." Field agents soon found they had less money to spend and fewer clearances to install bugs against organized crime figures. "The whole Mafia effort," said William Sullivan, "slacked off again."

The figures confirm it. At the end of the Kennedy administration, members of the Justice Department's Organized Crime Section were working 6,699 man-days in the field each year. Three years later the figure had dropped by half. Days spent prosecuting mobsters before grand juries dropped 72 percent, days in court 56 percent, court briefs prepared 82 percent.

The President was dead, his brother a lame duck Attorney General. Edgar, by contrast, was back on top. On May 7, 1964, even while Edgar was secretly frustrating the work of the Warren Commission, Congress honored his fortieth year at the FBI with Resolution Number 706. It praised "one of the most remarkable records of service to God and country in our Nation's history." It referred to Edgar's "strong moral determination" and his "unrelenting battle" against America's criminal underworld.

The next day, in a Rose Garden ceremony at the White House, President Johnson unveiled Executive Order 10682. With Edgar beside him, he announced he was waiving the compulsory retirement rule, due to take effect when Edgar turned seventy, seven months later. He praised Edgar as "quiet, humble . . . an anathema to evil men," and promised he could stay in office "for an indefinite period of time."

"The Roman Senate," commented Loudon Wainwright in *Life*, "conferred god status on a few emperors while they were still in office, and more or less the same thing has just happened to J. Edgar Hoover. Not that he hasn't been at least a demi-god for a long time. . . ."

CHAPTER 29

"You don't fire God."

Charles Brennan,
former Assistant Director of the FBI

ON JUNE 4, 1964, THE HISTORIAN WILLIAM MANCHESTER WAS ushered into Edgar's office on the fifth floor of the Justice Department. In the anteroom, aides had pointed out a new life-size bust of the Director, in bronze. Now, seated like all guests on a chair that forced him to gaze upward, he stared in fascination.

"In the foreground," Manchester recalled, "there was a miniature of the bust I had seen outside. It was looking at Hoover, and Hoover was looking at the bust. And between me and him there was an American flag, made of a sort of filmy gauze material. I was looking through the gauze at Hoover, and his complexion was red, white and blue."

Manchester, who was researching his epic work *Death of a President*, was there to discuss the day of President Kennedy's assassination. A few weeks earlier, at the White House, the professor had gone through another bizarre experience. Fearful of being interviewed, President Johnson had insisted on listening from another room as Manchester staged a "dress rehearsal" question-and-answer session, with an aide standing in for the President. He never did sit for an interview. Now, closeted with Edgar, Manchester realized the Director of the FBI did not want to talk about the assassination. He wanted to talk about himself.

"He would drift off into the early thirties," said Manchester, "and recall chasing Dillinger and Pretty Boy Floyd and all that. I couldn't keep him on the subject, and, in my opinion, he was really senile already."

Johnson's Undersecretary of State, George Ball, once met Edgar to discuss State Department security. "His counsel was totally fatuous," said Ball. "He indulged in such a rambling and seemingly endless monologue . . . I found it intolerable to sit and listen to such nonsense. So I finally excused myself to take a pretended telephone call in my conference room, then ducked out the back way. I questioned his competence."

"I used to go to his office rather than asking him to come to mine," said Nicholas Katzenbach, "partly as a courtesy, but also because I could leave his office. I could never get him out of mine. He would never listen at all, he'd just ramble on. He was closer to senility than anybody thought. . . . Yet next to the President, this was the most powerful person in the country."

Soon after the assassination, a new photograph of Lyndon Johnson appeared on Edgar's office wall. "To J. Edgar Hoover," read the dedication. "Than whom there is no greater—from his friend of thirty years." The president's widow, Lady Bird, who wrote gushingly of Edgar while he was alive, proved more reserved in 1988. "I wouldn't," she said, "consider him a friend of ours." Others are more blunt. "Johnson didn't like him," said *Time*'s White House correspondent Hugh Sidey. "He had a great regard for Hoover's clout, but he was very suspicious of him. When Johnson talked with me about him, he seemed kind of contemptuous."

"Johnson would call me up on the phone," said Katzenbach, "and he'd say, 'Goddamnit, can you do something about Hoover for me? The phone calls he makes! The bastard talks for hours. . . .'" Edgar, for his part, had no real fondness for the new president. "Johnson," he warned senior colleagues early in the new administration, "may become very dictatorial. We must keep our guard up."

The fact of it was that Johnson would use Edgar, when Edgar was prepared to be used, but could not hope to dictate to him. "The President," his former press secretary George

Reedy admitted, "recognized that Hoover was very powerful. He had so much information on everybody. . . ."

Johnson betrayed his fear. "Every once in a while," said William Sullivan, "he'd call Hoover and say, 'Now I'm going to ask you again. Tell me now, did you have a tap on me when I was a Senator?' Johnson had a hell of a guilty conscience. I guess he assumed that if we had a tap on him when he was a Senator, he'd be in real trouble."

Edgar had known too much about Johnson, for too long, not to pose a threat. He knew about the ballot-rigging of 1948 that had brought him to the Senate, and he had an inside track on the corruption that made the President rich. Two years earlier—responding to an appeal for help from Johnson—Edgar had used FBI clout to squash press interest in the Billie Sol Estes fraud scandal.

The FBI records on Johnson's relationship with Estes are withheld to this day, as are many of the papers on his corrupt aide Bobby Baker and on the Ellen Rometsch sex and security scare.

Though not in the same league as his predecessor, Johnson too had his share of extramarital adventures. As in the case of Kennedy, a mistress has survived to claim Edgar had knowledge of one of them and used it to ensure his survival.

Madeleine Brown, a Texan in her mid-sixties, has said she and Johnson enjoyed an on-off liaison for two decades. She said they met at a Dallas reception in 1948, when he was a congressman and she a twenty-four-year-old assistant in an advertising firm, and that Johnson fathered her son Steven, born three years later. The son bore a resemblance to the former president.

It was during the Kennedy era, when he was Vice President and her son Steven was ten, that Johnson first told his mistress Edgar had become a threat. At one of their trysts at Austin's Driskill Hotel, said Brown, he confided that he had "a big problem." "Hoover," he told her, "wants me to try to influence Kennedy to keep him on as FBI Director. He knows about you and Steven, and he's calling in his marker."

Johnson's solution, Brown said, was to push her into a

"paper marriage" hastily organized by Jesse Kellam, the confidant who had introduced them years earlier. "It was done to stop any gossip, and it worked, especially later, when he moved into the White House."

"What Lyndon told me," Brown said, "was that he was afraid of Hoover, that Hoover wanted him to intervene with the Kennedys not to fire him. 'I want you to go through with the marriage,' he told me, 'to help me get my balls out of Hoover's vise grip.'"

Bearing in mind the various ways in which he was compromised, one is left to ponder the fact that, as President, Johnson moved quickly to prolong Edgar's tenure. "The nation cannot afford to lose you," he told Edgar when he made the announcement. Perhaps, rather, it was Johnson who could not afford to risk Edgar's wrath.

Perhaps, too, Johnson and Edgar reached some sort of accommodation. Edgar's Official and Confidential files, and the main Bureau folders on the President, contain little compromising material: nothing on Madeleine Brown and only limited coverage of the corruption scandals in Johnson's life.

According to *The Washington Post,* "tapes and memos once existed concerning Johnson's backdoor activities. Some of this embarrassing material was removed from the files and sent to him at the White House." Clyde Tolson reportedly removed other sensitive documents immediately after Edgar's death.

Washington insiders have a fund of coarse Johnsonian sayings, and one of the most famous refers to Edgar. Pressed by a young aide to replace him, the President is said to have replied, "No, son, if you've got a skunk around, it's better to have him inside the tent pissing out, than outside the tent pissing in."

Edgar now had better access to the White House than at any time in his four decades as Director. There followed a four-year period of manipulation that Richard Goodwin, an aide under both Kennedy and Johnson, has likened to the access Soviet Secret Police Chief Beria had to Stalin.

Word went out from Edgar to build special facilities for

Johnson at Austin, Texas, the nearest FBI office to the LBJ ranch. A brand-new office was opened at Fredericksburg, even closer to Johnson's home. Soon an FBI agent was traveling regularly aboard Air Force One, although presidential security was a Secret Service responsibility. Happily for interagency relations, the head of the Secret Service was himself a former FBI agent.

Cartha DeLoach now became Edgar's link to the President. He had been a favorite for more than a decade, an enforcer of Bureau discipline (including Edgar's hypocritical code of sexual behavior), a manipulator of the press, and congressional ringmaster. It had been DeLoach, on the eve of the Kennedy presidency, who prevailed on Johnson and Congressman John Rooney to ram through a law ensuring Edgar a bountiful retirement deal should the Kennedys force him out.

DeLoach was appointed liaison to the White House within hours of Kennedy's assassination—replacing Courtney Evans, who had seemed to get on with the Kennedys rather too well. It was DeLoach who drafted the formula that kept Edgar on as Director after his seventieth birthday. He, rather than a White House aide, even wrote the proclamation.

DeLoach shuttled between the FBI and the White House for five years and became intimate with the First Family in a way unprecedented for a mere agency official. There were lunches at the White House, domino sessions with the President, an Easter weekend with the Johnsons at Camp David. "Quite soon," he recalled, "the President was consulting me frequently, particularly about government appointments."

When Johnson had trouble getting through to DeLoach's home number—a teenage daughter was hogging the phone —he sent technicians to install a hot line. "They had instructions to put it in the bedroom," Edgar's aide recalled. "The President would call at all times, day and night."

"Dear Mr. President," DeLoach wrote in a gushing letter early in the administration:

Thank you for allowing Barbara and me to have a "moment of greatness" with the world's number one family yesterday afternoon. The informality, yet quiet dignity you possess, never ceases to inspire me. . . . The telecast was excellent. . . . I received a call at 9:00 P.M. last night from my elderly Mother [sic] . . . to report that "Mr. Johnson is the best thing that has ever happened to this Nation. . . ."

Sincerely,

Deke

The President liked to say he wanted men around him who were "loyal enough to kiss my ass in Macy's window and say it smelled like a rose." DeLoach was the perfect candidate, an ambitious assistant dedicated to ensuring not only that Johnson's will was done, but that it coincided with Edgar's.

Edgar too played the sycophant. One of the President's public appearances, Edgar told Johnson, "brought out your humbleness. . . ." "I only wish," he gushed after a press conference, "our Washington Senators baseball team had an outfielder as capable of fielding some of the hot ones you handled. They were certainly loaded but you handled them like a Mickey Mantle."

The two men were linked by fear. Edgar's was the chronic fear of a forced end to his rule. Johnson's hidden terrors are only now being unveiled. Two senior aides, Richard Goodwin and Bill Moyers, became so alarmed by the President's state of mind that, secretly and unbeknownst to each other, they turned to psychiatrists for advice. "The diagnosis was the same," Goodwin revealed in 1988. "We were describing a textbook case of paranoid disintegration, the eruption of long-suppressed irrationalities. . . . The disintegration could continue, remain constant or recede, depending on the strength of Johnson's resistance."

Others, like former press secretary George Reedy, believe the President was "a manic depressive." Johnson worried constantly about the danger of assassination and was obsessed with the notion that survivors of the Kennedy administration were plotting his downfall. He came to believe the press wanted to destroy him, that the press corps and government were riddled with Communists.

Edgar had fulminated against enemies real or imagined all his life, and his policeman's function had long since taken a backseat to politics. In the Johnson presidency, the combination of psychoses made a dangerous mix. Vital checks and balances, designed to ensure the separation of the executive from law enforcement, simply lapsed.

For both men, the first obvious enemy was Robert Kennedy, who remained Attorney General until September 1964. Johnson thought him "that little runt," and Kennedy considered Johnson "mean, vicious, an animal in many ways." For all that, Kennedy felt Johnson needed him to win the coming election, and he saw himself as Johnson's vice presidential running mate. It was a delusion. Johnson spurned Kennedy and his people from the start.

Edgar and Kennedy acted out a similar charade. In January 1964, at a party in the Justice Department, Kennedy gave Edgar a delayed Christmas gift, a set of gold cuff links embossed with the Department seal, the Attorney General's initials and his own.

While others received the same gift, Kennedy had made a point of including the Director, perhaps as a last-ditch attempt to ease the tension. Edgar responded with a "Dear Bob" note, saying the cuff links would be "a constant reminder of a friendship I shall always treasure."

Even as he wrote it, a stream of FBI information was going to President Johnson on Kennedy people still working at the White House. Though much of it was requested by Johnson, the tone of the FBI correspondence leaves no doubt of Edgar's complicity.

Edgar stirred up trouble at every opportunity. In February, from Minneapolis, his Agent in Charge reported gossip about a dinner at which members of the "Kennedy crowd" had supposedly plotted to "create a situation whereby the

President would be forced to pick the Attorney General, Robert Kennedy, as his running mate." Edgar sent DeLoach to pass on the story, unchecked and uncorroborated, to President Johnson.

Johnson loved sleaze, and Edgar indulged the appetite, especially when it concerned the Kennedys. One of Edgar's Assistant Directors, who asked not to be identified, tells the following story: "We supplied Johnson with a full field investigation report on a young woman who had worked as a hostess on the Kennedy plane and supplied sex services to John Kennedy. Kennedy had brought her into the White House as an assistant press secretary—for obvious reasons. When Johnson came into office we turned up some nude pictures taken when she was still a senior in high school. They went to Johnson, and he took them out of the report folder and put them in his desk. This little girl would come in to clear the Teletypes, and the President would take out these pictures and then give her a good looking over. It became quite a joke around the White House. . . ."

In the first year of the Johnson presidency there was a possibility that Edgar himself might be exposed. *Life* magazine reporter William Lambert, probing the origins of Johnson's wealth, conducted interviews with Allan Witwer, the former manager of the hotel owned by the millionaire Clint Murchison, friend to both Johnson and Edgar. Witwer told how Edgar had freeloaded at the hotel; he produced the bills to prove it and revealed that Edgar rubbed shoulders with organized crime figures there.

While Lambert found Witwer credible, *Life*'s top executives and its attorneys shied away. Already under pressure from the White House for doing the Johnson series, they thought it folly to take on J. Edgar Hoover as well. Lambert passed his information on to Robert Kennedy, who urged old friends at the Justice Department to investigate. It was hard, however, to prove Edgar had broken the law, and his corrupt involvement with Murchison remained a secret.

When Kennedy left the Justice Department and ran for the Senate, Edgar leaked smear material on him to the press. When wiretapping became a controversial issue, he blamed

Kennedy for wiretaps conducted during his time as Attorney General. The viciousness and guile of it all is evident from a report filed by Cartha DeLoach. President Johnson, DeLoach reported, wanted:

> to get word to the Director that the Director might desire to bring "the facts" concerning Kennedy's authorization of wiretapping before a Congressional Committee. . . . [Johnson aide] Watson stated the President was most anxious to see that the Director would not get hurt in connection with this matter. He wants to put Kennedy in his place. The President obviously wants to get these facts out, inasmuch as Kennedy will be seriously injured, as far as the left wing is concerned, if such facts become known. At the same time, as the Director knows much better than I do, there are far better ways of getting these facts out than through the medium of a Congressional Committee.
>
> Respectfully,
>
> C. DeLoach

Years later, under questioning by the Senate Intelligence Committee in 1975, DeLoach acted naive. "I was an investigator, not a politician. . . . I didn't know whether it was political or not. We didn't know what was in the minds of the White House personnel or the President. . . ."

Recently he was more forthright. "President Johnson," DeLoach said, "knew how to twist arms. He knew how to use people. And he recognized early in the game that to have the FBI on his side and to use the FBI as a tool would be of assistance to him."

None of this had anything remotely to do with the legitimate business of the FBI—law enforcement and the protection of national security. Yet DeLoach acknowledged his role without a glimmer of an awareness of ethical wrongdoing. He was, he said, just taking orders. "I kept the

Director constantly advised at all times. I did nothing, at any time, that Mr. Hoover was not fully advised of."

Those who served in the Johnson White House still shudder at the memory of the effects of Edgar's mischief. In 1965 the FBI man in London, Charles Bates, picked up allegations that the British Prime Minister, Harold Wilson, was sexually involved with his aide Marcia Williams. He reported this to Edgar—along with a story that Wilson was a tool of the Soviets—just before Wilson visited Washington.

"Next time I saw Hoover," said Bates, "he told me the Wilson information was 'terrific.' He had sent it straight over to President Johnson. When he told me that I thought, 'Oh Jesus!' It was just raw intelligence, and I kind of hoped they'd never use it."

When they did, it caused great diplomatic embarrassment. "Johnson didn't like Wilson," said Undersecretary of State George Ball, "because Wilson wasn't supporting him over the Vietnam War. Hoover knew his subject. He knew what pleasure Johnson would get out of any pornographic or scatological information about anyone he didn't like. The President showed me the gossip on Wilson with great glee. Then, when Wilson brought Marcia Williams along to the first meeting, Johnson got hold of me and said, 'Keep that woman out.' I had to make some excuse, telling Wilson the meeting was confined to the government officials directly concerned. It was very awkward."

Today competent sources agree that Edgar's "terrific" information on the British Prime Minister was part of a smear campaign cooked up by Wilson's political enemies. "Hoover was a very malign influence," said Ball. "I hated those preposterous canards. . . . They tended to influence the President's attitudes to the point of distorting policy."

The Secretary of Defense, Robert McNamara, soon collided with Edgar—partly because he insisted on communicating with the FBI through the correct channel, the office of outgoing Attorney General Robert Kennedy. To change his mind, Edgar sent derogatory material on Kennedy to the President, who then read it aloud to McNamara. Edgar told Johnson the Defense Secretary was part of a Kennedy conspiracy to get him out of the FBI. McNamara, who suspected Edgar of bugging public officials, told the President Edgar was "a menace" and should be fired.

Johnson, however, seemed more committed to Edgar than to his own Cabinet members. Should they abandon him by resigning, he warned, two men were going to "follow their ass to the end of the earth": J. Edgar Hoover and the head of the Internal Revenue Service.

Judge Laurence Silberman, the former Deputy Attorney General who examined Edgar's Official and Confidential files in 1974, concluded that Johnson used the FBI as "his private political police force." Edgar supplied him, by one estimate, with 1,200 dossiers on individual U.S. citizens.

Members of the press were especially vulnerable. "I know the FBI picked up cocktail party chatter," said Richard Goodwin. "It all went into the files. I remember Johnson talking about certain columnists' cars being parked in front of the Soviet ambassador's house, and he must have got that from the FBI. As we got deeper into the Vietnam thing, Johnson became obsessed with the idea that the opposition was coming from some Communist subversive source."

"You know, Dick," the President told Goodwin one day in 1965, "the Communists are taking over the country. Look here . . ." Then, showing Goodwin a manila folder, "It's Teddy White's FBI file. He's a Communist sympathizer." This would have come as news to all who knew Theodore White, author of the Making of the President books.

Edgar sent Johnson material on numerous journalists, including NBC's David Brinkley, columnist Joseph Kraft, and *New York Times* veteran Harrison Salisbury. He also sent a dossier on Associated Press reporter Peter Arnett, most recently distinguished for his valorous coverage of the Gulf War for Cable News Network.

In 1965, furious over press leaks, the President demanded

information on Peter Lisagor, Washington bureau chief of the *Chicago Daily News.* Edgar sent DeLoach scurrying to discover the source of a Lisagor story about the presence of Soviet bombers in Hanoi. The resulting report offered an answer to the question, with some malicious gossip thrown in. The source, DeLoach decided, had been:

> Marguerite Higgins, who was formerly employed by the *New York Herald Tribune.* Miss Higgins is widely known around Washington. Her reputation is spotty. The newspapermen refer to her as "mattress-back Maggie." She is currently married to retired Lieutenant-General William E. Hall. Miss Higgins is very close to Peter Lisagor. . . . My source feels that Miss Higgins obtained this information from her husband. . . .

Citizens who sent telegrams to the President criticizing policy would have been appalled to know the FBI ran checks on them. So would members of the U.S. Senate, had they known how Johnson sat in the White House chuckling over FBI reports on their sex lives. He would slap his thigh in delight as he read about a senator's visits to a brothel.

A 1968 memo, reporting presidential curiosity about Senators Stephen Young and William Fulbright, Chairman of the Foreign Relations Committee, sums up the conspiratorial atmosphere:

> Marvin Watson [presidential aide] called last night at 7 P.M. Watson stated that he and the President wanted to make certain that the FBI understood that when requests were made by the President, Watson, or Mrs. Stegall [White House secretary], concerning matters of extreme secrecy, the FBI should not respond in writing by formal memorandum. Watson stated that what the President actually wanted was a blind-type memorandum which bore no government watermarks or letterhead signifying the source of the memorandum. . . .

Edgar simply scrawled "OK." This was a technique he had been using for decades. The President was soon bragging that he knew within minutes what Senator Fulbright had said at lunch at the Soviet embassy.

Never was secrecy more necessary to Johnson, or FBI acquiescence more unethical, than in August 1964, during the Democratic Convention in Atlantic City. When the delegates poured into town, FBI wiretaps and bugs were ready at key locations, with DeLoach heading a force of no fewer than twenty-seven agents, a radio technician and two stenographers. Secure phone lines linked a control center in the Old Post Office Building with the switchboards of the White House and FBI headquarters in Washington. After talks with the White House, Edgar was mounting a massive surveillance operation.

Johnson's nomination was a foregone conclusion, but he was haunted by the memory of his defeat by the Kennedy brothers in 1960. "He was afraid," said Clark Clifford, "that because they had planned a tribute to John F. Kennedy and Bobby was to deliver it, he might very well stampede the Convention and end up being the vice presidential nominee." Waiting and watching in Washington, Johnson juggled the timetable to ensure nominations were completed before Robert Kennedy appeared to eulogize his dead brother. Only then did the President descend on Atlantic City to be acclaimed the victor.

Some wondered how Johnson had managed to manipulate the Convention so brilliantly. "The interesting question," wrote Walter Lippmann, "is why he had such complete control. . . ." The FBI files supply the answer.

"We were able to keep the White House fully apprised," read a DeLoach report, "by means of informant coverage . . . by infiltration of key groups through use of undercover agents, and through utilization of agents using appropriate cover as reporters." "Through cooperation with the management of NBC News," read another memo, "our agents were furnished press credentials."

NBC executives have denied all knowledge of this, suggesting that the phony passes were supplied by officials of the Democratic National Committee. DeLoach, for his part, has said the ruse proved very successful. We can only guess how often the FBI used this trick. Later, during the Nixon administration, an agent would be caught asking questions at a press conference.

While DeLoach has suggested the Bureau's primary task at the Convention was to preempt violence, former Agent in Charge Leo Clark told a different story. He was warned in advance, he told a Senate committee, that the mission was to be concealed from the Secret Service. Prevention of violence was just the cover story.

The FBI's primary job, Clark revealed, was to snoop on senators and congressmen, key convention delegates, civil rights activists—and Robert Kennedy. He was present when DeLoach reported by telephone direct to the President and to Edgar. Therein lay an irony, for in principle only Kennedy—as Attorney General—had the authority to approve electronic surveillance.

The President later told Edgar the "job" in Atlantic City was one of the finest he had ever seen. "DeLoach," Edgar scrawled on a report, "should receive a meritorious reward."

Everything appeared to go swimmingly after the Convention—for Johnson and for Edgar. Robert Kennedy departed for the Senate. The Warren Report came out, seemingly closing the door on the Kennedy era itself. Then, on October 14, 1964, with the election just weeks away, a sex and security scandal burst upon the Johnson presidency.

News broke that Walter Jenkins, Johnson's closest aide, had been arrested in a YMCA toilet, two blocks from the White House, having sex with a retired Army soldier. Jenkins admitted the offense, resigned and took refuge in a hospital room, suffering from "exhaustion." A rapid FBI inquiry concluded that he had never compromised national security.

Nagging questions remained, however, as to how and why the arrest had been kept secret for a week after it occurred.

Nor was it clear why the FBI, supposedly so effective in its security checks, had failed to tell the White House of Jenkins' arrest for a similar lapse, in the very same toilet, nearly six years earlier. Edgar's public statement, moreover, failed to mention that Jenkins, a colonel in the Air Force Reserve, had tried to use his influence to reinstate a fellow officer dismissed for sex offenses.

Edgar's public attitude on homosexuality was normally at least condemnatory, often cruel. On this occasion, however, he visited Jenkins in the hospital and sent him flowers. Jenkins' brother William was a veteran FBI agent, and his secretary, Mildred Stegall, was at one stage being paid out of the FBI budget. Jenkins and his family were socially close to DeLoach and his wife.

It was Edgar, according to William Sullivan, who came up with the idea of trying to get a doctor to say Jenkins "has a brain injury and he's definitely not a homosexual. It's because of his brain injury that he acted in such a peculiar, unusual manner on this particular evening." The President's friend Abe Fortas did try to cajole a psychiatrist, Dr. Leon Yochelson, to spin such a yarn, but he refused.[1]

With Edgar's certain connivance, and probably at his suggestion, Johnson tried to turn the Jenkins case around to damage the Republican candidate for the presidency, Senator Barry Goldwater.

Years later, asked whether there had been FBI surveillance of Goldwater in 1964, DeLoach said he "would doubt seriously whether such a thing ever happened. . . . The request was made of me to make so-called name checks of Senator Goldwater's staff. I came back and told Mr. Hoover about it and Mr. Hoover said, 'What do you recommend?' And I told him I recommended we do nothing, and he said, 'I agree with you.' And that's exactly what we did, nothing."

Other information has since become available. As the Jenkins case developed, Johnson burst into the office of his aide Bill Moyers. "Hoover was just here," he snapped, "and he says some of Goldwater's people may have trapped Walter—set him up. I told Hoover to find the ——— [expletive deleted in Moyers' account]. . . . I told him I want to know every one of Goldwater's people who could have done this thing. . . . You call DeLoach and tell him if he wants to keep that nice house in Virginia, and that soft job he has here, his boys had better find those bastards."

Senator Goldwater, as it happened, was the commander of the 999th Air Force Reserve squadron, the unit in which Jenkins had served. The two men had traveled together on Air Force planes. On the strength of that, three days after Jenkins' resignation, two FBI agents arrived to question the Senator. He was busy campaigning, and the interrogation irritated him. Had Goldwater known what was really going on, he would have been even angrier.

"I knew DeLoach pretty well," said Robert Mardian, later an Assistant Attorney General under President Nixon, "and I had been western regional director for Goldwater. Long afterwards, DeLoach told me how they had been ordered by Hoover to bug the Goldwater plane. . . ."

An FBI report to DeLoach, dated nine days into the Jenkins probe, shows that sixteen members of Goldwater's staff were also investigated. One, it said, "frequently dated prostitutes . . . in his office." This report was generated "according to the instructions of the Director."

President Johnson did receive an FBI dossier on his opponent. He even read extracts aloud over the telephone to Democratic Senator George Smathers. As for Edgar, he probably had his own motive to try to torpedo Goldwater. In private, but unbeknownst to him in the presence of a former FBI agent, the Senator had made the mistake of saying he would dump Edgar if elected President.

In the wake of the Jenkins sensation, Edgar also responded to a Johnson request to "bring him everything we have on Humphrey." The reference was to Senator Hubert Humphrey, the President's own running mate in the election campaign. FBI reports on the Humphrey team, including a (still censored) "allegation" about the Senator himself, went to the White House within days.

Triumph in 1964 did little to calm Lyndon Johnson. One day the next year, sitting beside his swimming pool in Texas, Johnson talked gloomily about the deepening crisis in

Vietnam. "I'm going to be known as the president who lost Southeast Asia. I'm going to be the one who lost this form of government. The Communists already control the three major networks and forty major outlets of communication. Walter Lippmann is a Communist and so is Teddy White. And they're not the only ones. You'd all be shocked at the kind of thing revealed by FBI reports."

"Lyndon," said his wife, Lady Bird, "you shouldn't read them so much. . . . They have a lot of unevaluated information in them, accusations and gossip which haven't been proven." "Never mind that," the President growled, "you'd be surprised at how much they know about people. . . . I don't want to be like a McCarthyite. But this country is in a little more danger than we think. And someone has to uncover this information."

Edgar fed Johnson's neuroses until the end of his presidency. And all the while he had been orchestrating the most vicious character assassination of his career, aimed at a man today revered as a hero, Martin Luther King.

CHAPTER 30

"The way Martin Luther King was hounded and harassed is a disgrace to every American."

Senator Walter Mondale,
later Vice President, 1975

IN LATE 1963, WHEN *TIME* MAGAZINE NAMED MARTIN LUTHER King its Man of the Year, Edgar was furious. "They had to dig deep in the garbage," he scrawled on the wire copy of the announcement, "to come up with this one."

Edgar's attitude on race—his reluctance to hire black agents and his opposition to the civil rights movement—has been explained as a legacy of his origins. He had been born in a time of virtual apartheid in the South, when blacks were expected to be servants and grateful for it. A black maid had waited on Edgar's family when he was a child, and he attended a whites-only high school. Years later, when the school admitted black students, outraged alumni returned to tear down the insignia of an institution they regarded as a bastion of white respectability.

Edgar's prejudice, however, had deep-seated personal origins. Through his youth and into middle age, a rumor circulated in Washington—a rumor of which he was certainly aware—that Edgar himself had black blood in his veins.

In 1958, while researching articles on Edgar for the *New York Post,* reporter William Dufty enlisted the help of a black agent in the Bureau of Narcotics to obtain a clandestine interview with Edgar's black manservant, Sam Noisette. As the three men talked, Dufty realized the two

405

blacks were repeatedly referring to Edgar as "some kind of spook," even "soul brother." Dufty had many black friends —he had co-authored Billie Holiday's biography *Lady Sings the Blues*—and remembered having heard offhand remarks along the same lines. He later realized that, in the black communities of the East, which also claimed Clark Gable and Rudolph Valentino as their own, it was generally believed that Edgar had black roots.

The writer Gore Vidal, who grew up in Washington in the thirties, has a similar memory. "Hoover was becoming famous, and it was always said of him—in my family and around the city—that he was mulatto. People said he came from a family that had 'passed.' It was the word they used for people of black origin who, after generations of interbreeding, have enough white blood to pass themselves off as white. That's what was always said about Hoover." "There was a sort of secret admiration among blacks for those who were able to pass," said Dufty. "Fooling white people was easy, but fooling blacks was next to impossible."

Early photographs of Edgar do have a negroid look. His hair was noticeably wiry, and a 1939 article refers to his "dark skin, almost brown from sunburn. His coloring . . . gives a striking contrast to the crisp, white linen suit." Was there then some truth to the story?

As was often the case in those days, no birth certificate was registered when Edgar was born in 1895. The document that was eventually issued, in 1938, states simply that both his father and mother were "white." The ancestry of his mother is well documented, a line of solid burghers easily traceable to their ancestral home in Switzerland. His father's family history, however, amounts to no more than a series of conflicting reports of descent from German, Swiss or British immigrants, settlers who arrived in America 200 years before Edgar's birth. There had been plenty of time for racial intermingling.

After Edgar's death, even Helen Gandy would speak of "an early story" that Edgar had black blood. She spoke of the rumor during an interview, then dropped the subject.

"Hoover himself had to know what people said about

him," said Gore Vidal. "There were two things that were taken for granted in my youth—that he was a faggot and that he was black. Washington was and is a very racist town, and I can tell you that in those days the black blood part was very much the worst. People were known to commit suicide if it was discovered that they had passed. To be thought a black person was an unbelievable slur if you were in white society. That's what many people flatly believed about Hoover, and he must have been so upset by it. . . ."

Whether or not the rumor was true, it must have caused endless distress to Edgar, whose public posture was that of the white nativist, suspicious of all that seemed alien. Just as he compensated for his secret homosexuality by lashing out at fellow homosexuals, so Edgar's worry about his racial identity may have shaped his behavior toward blacks. To those who knew their place—servants like Noisette, James Crawford and the rest—he played the decent, paternalistic boss. Those who sought to rise above their station, as perhaps he sensed he himself had done, he had at best no time for.

Born in an era when black men were regularly lynched for rape—if the victim was white—Edgar preferred to shrug off the miseries of black Americans. As with organized crime, he was content to ignore the law enforcement problems that arose, or to claim "lack of jurisdiction."

The attorney Joseph Rauh never forgot the angry non sequitur of an answer Edgar gave when asked to probe the attempted murder of a white labor leader in the forties. "Edgar says no," Attorney General Tom Clark told Rauh. "He's not going to send the FBI in every time some nigger woman says she's been raped."[1]

Though Edgar mounted some effective operations against the Ku Klux Klan, his priorities became obvious once blacks began to demand their rights. "When I was working in the South in the fifties," said Arthur Murtagh, "there was simply no comparison. The Bureau only investigated the Klan when a murder had been committed and the press forced them into it. Far more time and effort went into investigating black militants. . . ."

During the Kennedy presidency, Edgar became involved in the struggle over race whether he liked it or not. The civil rights campaign, and the violence with which southern whites responded, was the major domestic policy issue. Edgar was forced to stop stonewalling requests for help by the Civil Rights Division of the Justice Department and to join the federal government in confronting the nation's race problems.

FBI agents suddenly found themselves investigating police brutality and preventing abuse of black voters' rights. The Bureau had been dragooned into taking on such duties, and Edgar resented it.

Martin Luther King, the pacifist preacher's son from Atlanta, was a black man who did not know his place, who had won something Edgar had lost—the attentive ear of the President and the Attorney General of the United States.

Although King had been in the public eye for some five years, Edgar had lumped him together with advocates of violent struggle, such as Malcolm X. "We wouldn't have any problem," he had once grunted over lunch with Johnson in his senatorial days, "if we could get those two guys fighting, if we could get them to kill one another off. ..."

Now King could not be laughed off. In May 1961 a sketchy FBI report had given Edgar the idea that the black leader might have links to the Communist Party—and revealed that the FBI had yet to investigate him properly. Edgar scrawled in the margin "Why not?"—two words that marked the start of a seven-year vendetta.

Forty years earlier there had been a dress rehearsal for this. In 1919, as a young official, Edgar had played a leading role in hounding a black leader of an earlier generation, Marcus Garvey. A Jamaican by birth, Garvey offered American blacks a fantastic dream of a mass exodus to Africa, where he promised to establish a black Empire. Edgar strove to get Garvey jailed or deported, and achieved both.

He was obsessed, too, about the great singer and actor Paul Robeson, a political activist who spoke out for the poor and racially downtrodden. Over three decades FBI agents kept Robeson under surveillance, bugged his phone calls and spread false rumors that he was a member of the Communist Party. The harassment was such that Robeson's son believes the Bureau "neutralized" his father during the fifties by slipping him hallucinogenic drugs—a charge impossible to investigate because FBI records on Robeson are still censored on the grounds of "national security."

Edgar's pursuit of Garvey and Robeson was a blueprint for the future. The attempts to establish they were Communists, the use of black stool pigeons as penetration agents, and electronic bugging to snoop on their private lives were all tactics that Edgar would use against King.

"King is no good anyway," Edgar had written early in the Kennedy presidency. Then, his obsession was to convince Washington the civil rights movement was controlled by Communists—whether the evidence supported the accusation or not. In October 1963, after rejecting his own agents' advice that there was no such control, he had embarked on a massive surveillance operation against King—phone taps for which he had extracted permission from Robert Kennedy under pressure[2] and hidden microphone installations never formally sanctioned by anyone.

By late 1963 the recordings had yielded nothing to brand the black leader a Communist, but a good deal to raise questions about his private morality. The Reverend King enjoyed sex, and he did not let the fact that he was a minister of the church, and married, cramp his style. "I'm away from home twenty-five to twenty-seven days a month," he told one friend. "Fucking's a form of anxiety reduction." As he traveled the country, King sought relaxation in the arms of three regular mistresses, and on occasion with prostitutes. Many of his retinue, including his close friend Reverend Ralph Abernathy, did the same.

Philandering might have remained King's secret safety valve, tolerated by those around him, had it not been for the FBI. Sleeping with women has yet to become a federal offense, but to Edgar and his aides the knowledge of it seemed to offer a powerful weapon. In December 1963, after a marathon nine-hour meeting at Bureau headquarters, the focus changed. The question of possible Communist links would henceforth be only the nominal reason for surveillance, masking an altogether different purpose.

Edgar's aides now plotted to achieve the "desired result" of "neutralizing King as an effective Negro leader." It could be done, they hoped, by exposing him as a "clerical fraud," an "immoral opportunist." There was to be a "counterintelligence move to discredit" King, using ministers, "disgruntled acquaintances," "aggressive" newsmen, "colored" agents, even Dr. King's wife and housekeeper, and by "placing a good-looking female plant in King's office." The Attorney General was told nothing of this plan.

A fortnight later, when it was learned King was about to arrive at Washington's Willard Hotel, agents scrambled to install microphones and tape recorders. The resulting fifteen reels of tape, gathered during a two-day stay, included the sort of thing the FBI wanted—the sounds of a somewhat drunken party involving King and his colleagues and two women from the Philadelphia Naval Yard.

A day later, while FBI stenographers were still transcribing the tapes, Assistant Director Sullivan dictated a new memo. "King," it read:

> must . . . be revealed to the people of this country and
> to his Negro followers as being what he actually is—a
> fraud, demagogue and moral scoundrel. When the true
> facts concerning his activities are presented, such
> should be enough, if handled properly, to take him off
> his pedestal. . . . When this is done . . . the Negroes
> will be left without a national leader of sufficiently
> compelling personality to steer them in the proper
> direction. This is what could happen, but need not
> happen if the right kind of a national Negro leader
> could at this time be gradually developed so as to
> overshadow Dr. King and be in a position to assume
> the role of leadership of the Negro people when King
> has become completely discredited.

Sullivan's suggested replacement for King was Samuel Pierce, a Republican attorney who would one day, after serving as Secretary of Housing under President Reagan, become the target of a corruption probe. Edgar scribbled "OK" beneath the suggestion, adding that he was "glad the 'light' has finally, though dismally delayed, come to the Domestic Intelligence Division."

"Highlights" of the Willard tapes were brought to Edgar like hunting trophies. "They will destroy the burrhead," he responded excitedly. Edgar personally phoned President Johnson's aide Walter Jenkins to describe the material, then sent Cartha DeLoach to the White House with a transcript.

DeLoach, who heard one of the King surveillance tapes, claimed it featured King with "hundred-dollar-a-night prostitutes, committing sexual acts in front of eight, nine, ten, eleven men gathered around the bed, naked, drinking Black Russians. . . ." It is not clear how DeLoach could count how many men there were, or know they were naked, by listening to a sound tape.

Edgar thought King "a tomcat with obsessive degenerate urges," and insisted on coverage of what one FBI report called "the entertainment." When King went to Honolulu a crack Bureau team, complete with lock-picker, was flown in from the mainland. King's party included two female companions, but the snoopers were frustrated on that occasion—the sound of the television and air-conditioning drowned out other sounds.

Edgar's spies had more luck in Washington. King was overheard mockingly allotting his companions bawdy titles and telling off-color stories about sex and religion. They included a crude sex joke about the late President Kennedy and his widow, Jacqueline. Earlier, apparently because of fears the Attorney General would alert King, Edgar had withheld the results of the surveillance from Robert Kennedy. Now he saw to it that the transcript of King's "vilification" of the late President was shown to his brother. Robert was appalled.

President Johnson listened to some of the original recordings and once spent an afternoon discussing them with Edgar. Nothing Edgar said or did about King, however, deterred Johnson from his growing commitment to civil rights. Whatever his failings in other areas, it was he who rammed through a mass of new race legislation, the most radical measures since the Civil War.

A tearful Martin Luther King would telephone Johnson, overwhelmed with emotion, after the President's 1965 address to Congress on black voting rights. Edgar sat stoically in the gallery of the Capitol as Johnson invoked the words of the Baptist hymn that was the anthem of King's movement, "We Shall Overcome." When King opposed the Vietnam War, however, the President's exasperation would betray what he knew. "Goddamnit!" he told an aide. "If only you could hear what that hypocritical preacher does sexually. . . ."

Edgar used King to play on the President's known fears. According to Richard Goodwin, the Director suggested that "Bobby Kennedy was hiring or paying King off to stir up trouble over the Vietnam War. It was total nonsense. If you haven't seen those files of his, you can't believe how flimsy the information was. Bobby did nothing to stir up King. King was against the war long before Bobby was."

Edgar's effort to ruin King was in high gear in the spring of 1964. The news that Marquette University in Milwaukee intended to give King an honorary degree sent an agent rushing to persuade officials to change their minds. This was especially "shocking" news—the university had given Edgar the same honor in 1950. The agent received a cash award for his successful intervention.

The National Council of the Churches of Christ, briefed by William Sullivan about King's "personal conduct," promised it would never again give King "one single dollar." On Edgar's orders the same smear went to the Baptist World Alliance. Agents were told to thwart publication of magazine articles by King, and even a book.

Edgar's vendetta was pursued at a time of constant racial tension and mayhem. The long-running drama of 1964 was the disappearance, presumed murdered by the Ku Klux Klan, of three young civil rights workers in Mississippi. The first FBI response was sluggish—one agent even said "a thrill of joy went up my spine" when he heard the news. This was the FBI King deplored, and it was now forced to change its ways.

President Johnson bulldozed Edgar into action. "There's three sovereignties involved," he told a colleague. "There's the United States and there's the state of Mississippi and there's J. Edgar Hoover." On this occasion, the United States prevailed. Over Edgar's protests, agents were sent to open a large new office in Jackson, Mississippi, and Johnson dispatched Edgar by presidential jet to declare it open.

Using intelligence, lavish bribes and strong-arm tactics as tough as the Klan's, a team of the FBI's best agents did eventually solve the Mississippi murders and enforce federal law in the state. In Washington, Edgar went on smearing King. He supplied James Eastland, the Democratic Senator from Mississippi, with surveillance film of King walking into a hotel with a white girl. One of his officials, meanwhile, informed Berl Bernhard, staff director of the Civil Rights Commission, that King was a sexual "switch-hitter," a bisexual.

In a conversation with Carl Rowan, then Director of the U.S. Information Agency, Congressman Rooney told of listening to an FBI tape in which the black leader invited his colleague Ralph Abernathy to have sex with him. Rowan, himself black, tried to explain to Rooney that the kind of sex talk he quoted was characteristic, harmless joshing between black males. Rooney, however, spread scandal about King at every opportunity.

Using a stool pigeon to obtain access and infrared cameras, the FBI also obtained pictures of King naked in a bathtub and lying on a bed, with his associate Bayard Rustin, a known homosexual, seated beside him. When he saw two of the pictures, apparently slipped out by the FBI to bring pressure on the black leadership, Rustin was horrified. "In both cases," he said, "I was conferring with Martin in the only time available to me. Nothing, absolutely nothing, took place."

This aspect of Edgar's smear operation failed to influence anyone—except, perhaps, his closest congressional supporters. It should be stressed, moreover, that no biographer has reported a homosexual relationship between King and Abernathy, or Rustin, or anyone else.[3]

In September 1964, when King was due to visit the Vatican, Edgar's friend Cardinal Spellman was asked by the FBI to persuade Pope Paul VI not to grant King an audience. To Edgar's astonishment, the Pope ignored the advice. Then came news that the civil rights leader was to receive the Nobel Peace Prize. King, in the hospital suffering from exhaustion, thought it the "foremost of earthly honors, not for himself, but for the movement." Edgar was beside himself with rage.

"The mores of this country has [*sic*] certainly sunken to a new low," he scribbled, overlooking the fact that the Nobel was awarded by foreigners. "He was the last one in the world who should ever have received it," he said. "I held him in utter contempt. . . ." King, Edgar thought, deserved only the " 'top alley cat' prize."

Bitterness was compounded by jealousy, for Edgar had long hankered after a Nobel himself. Herbert Jenkins, the longtime police chief of Atlanta, talked with him at this time. "For years and years," Jenkins later revealed, "Hoover had tried unsuccessfully to win the Prize. Many prominent Americans had been asked by Hoover to write the Nobel Committee . . . but every year Hoover was passed over. . . . Then along comes a Negro southerner who is awarded the Prize. It was more than Hoover could stand. It just ate away at him."

Edgar doled out dirt on King to any officials whose duties might somehow touch on the Nobel—at the State Department, the USIA and the United Nations. In London, FBI representative Charles Bates received orders to fly to Scandinavia "to tell our ambassadors there what kind of guy he was. My orders came direct from Hoover." Bureau technicians prepared to go to Oslo to bug King when he arrived for the Nobel ceremonies, a flagrant contravention of the rules confining the FBI to operations in the United States.

In Washington, Edgar took an extraordinary step. After refusing their interview request for months, he suddenly agreed to see a group of eighteen female journalists. During a monologue lasting three hours, he told them how unfair the Warren Commission had been to the FBI, about "bleeding-heart judges" and how Fidel Castro was "trying to brainwash the Puerto Ricans." Then, quite coolly, he told them Martin Luther King was "the most notorious liar in the country."

Hovering at his master's side, Cartha DeLoach frantically passed Edgar notes warning him to stipulate that his last remark was off the record. "Mr. Hoover threw the notes away," DeLoach recalled. "He told the women he wanted it on the record . . . and they rushed for the phones."

Calling King a liar was front-page news. Edgar went through the motions of saying the "lie" had been King's claim that agents in trouble spots were southerners, likely to be racist themselves. That squabble, though, had occurred two years earlier. Now Edgar was hinting at something else. King, he added, was "one of the lowest characters in the country . . . I haven't even begun to say all I could on this subject."

Some Bureau officials felt, as one put it, that the "boss had flipped." So did King. "Mr. Hoover has apparently faltered," he told a reporter, "under the awesome burden, complexities and responsibilities of his office." As FBI eavesdroppers listened, he told intimates Edgar was "old and broken down . . . senile . . . should be hit from all sides," until President Johnson brought him to heel.

Edgar yearned to say something even stronger, not least when King asked to meet with him to discuss the Bureau's failings. "I can't understand why we are unable to get the true facts before the public," the Director wrote William Sullivan. "We can't even get our own accomplishments published. We are never taking the aggressive [*sic*] . . ."

The men around Edgar answered the call. A week after the press conference, with the Nobel ceremonies nearing,

Newsweek Bureau Chief Ben Bradlee reported a development to Attorney General Katzenbach. DeLoach, he said, had been telling *Newsweek* about "some interesting tapes involving Dr. King."

Katzenbach, greatly alarmed, flew with the head of the Civil Rights Division, Burke Marshall, to brief the President in Texas. Though Johnson acted concerned, he merely warned the Bureau that its operation was backfiring.

DeLoach has repeatedly denied Bradlee's story. In 1975, in Senate testimony, he said he did "not recall" talking to reporters about the King tapes. "No offer," he said recently, "was ever made by me, Hoover, Tolson or anybody in the Bureau to the best of my knowledge—and I would swear this on a stack of Bibles—to play those tapes."

Bradlee, who later became editor of *The Washington Post,* was no less adamant. "DeLoach asked me if I was interested in looking at transcripts. He was making me the offer to look at them. . . . I told him I had no interest."

A long list of distinguished reporters had similar experiences. John Herbers of *The New York Times* recalls "a special agent . . . one of the people that worked for DeLoach . . . told me about these things that they had on King. He was holding the tapes out for me, in case I wanted to hear them. I thought they were off base."

At the *Los Angeles Times,* David Kraslow listened "nauseated" as an FBI man tried to read him a "juicy section" of a King tape over the telephone. Transcripts were "made available" to columnist Jack Anderson, who refused to publish. According to Mike Royko, of the *Chicago Daily News,* a former agent raised the subject after a golf game. "He very casually brought up King and asked if I would be interested in reading some transcripts that concerned illicit sex things. . . . I thought, 'How dumb can they be?' I was totally sympathetic to King and his movement."[4]

On King's home turf, agents tried a different tack with Eugene Patterson, editor of the Atlanta *Constitution.* Patterson was told when King would be arriving at a Florida airport on the way to a secret meeting with a woman. "Why not," said the agent, "have a reporter and photographer there? Expose him to the South and the world."

Patterson, who won a Pulitzer Prize for his editorials urging racial justice, turned the FBI down flat. "The agent who failed to persuade me," said Patterson, "paid the price by being transferred to New Orleans on the pretext that he was forty-one pounds overweight. I had great sympathy for him, for it had been totally out of character for him to make the approach. He did it because he was terrified of Hoover —they all were."

Edgar himself showed photographs—purporting to link King with Communists—to Hearst's Mark Monsky. He mentioned the sex tapes over lunch to *Washington Star* editor Newbold Noyes, a man DeLoach thought could be "led around by the nose," and reportedly played them to Eugene Lyons of *Reader's Digest*.

Not one newspaper obliged Edgar by running the sex smear, but nor did any editor have the guts to expose him for what he was up to. Word of the FBI dirty tricks, meanwhile, soon filtered back to King himself.

Horrified at the potential damage, he now urged government contacts to arrange the meeting with Edgar he had been requesting. On December 1, 1964, just days before the trip to Oslo, Edgar, King and their aides sat down together in the Director's office.

"Mr. Hoover was very, very cold," Ralph Abernathy recalled, "and Dr. King tried to be very, very warm. Mr. Hoover sat there in his blue suit and would not smile at all. He called us 'boys.' . . ." The black men sat perplexed as Edgar launched into a fifty-minute monologue on the FBI's work in the South and on his efforts to hire black agents. "The old man," King was later heard saying on a Bureau wiretap, "talks too damned much."

"Mr. Hoover gave Martin a lecture," Ralph Abernathy recalled, "reminding him he was a man of the cloth. . . . He said, 'You boys, if you're doing nothing wrong, you don't have to worry about anything. But if you're doing something wrong, we know about it. . . .'"

That was apparently the closest Edgar came to revealing he had sex dirt on King. For King, who may already have known about the suggestive pictures the FBI had of him with Rustin, the omission brought no comfort. "Martin responded by becoming nervous and eating his nails," said Abernathy. "He was troubled. . . ."

King looked that way when he emerged to tell the press he and Edgar had "a much clearer understanding." Had he retracted anything he had said about Edgar? "No," he said, and ducked into an elevator. In the corridor, even as he met with Edgar, an FBI official had been trying to interest a newsman in pictures of King with a woman.

Anxiety about the FBI compounded the fatigue that had recently sent King to the hospital. On the long flight to Europe he fretted about it aloud. His wife, Coretta, who accompanied him to Oslo, remembers his deep depression. "It was a time when he ought to have been happy. . . . But he was worried that the rumors might hurt the movement, and he was worried about what black people would think. . . . Somehow he managed all the official functions. . . ."

King returned to the United States to a tumultuous welcome, and a private jet provided by New York's Governor Nelson Rockefeller to carry him on his way. Edgar, meanwhile, rushed a letter about King's "personal conduct" to Vice President–elect Hubert Humphrey, because he had greeted King at a reception in the Waldorf-Astoria.

In early January 1965, at home in Atlanta, Coretta King opened a small box that had been forwarded from King's headquarters. It contained a reel of tape, which aides assumed was a recording of one of her husband's speeches. Her husband's voice was indeed on the tape, but this was no speech. And with it came an unsigned, typed note that read, in part:

KING,
    In view of your low grade [censored at FBI] I will not dignify your name with either a Mr. or a Reverend or a Dr. And, your last name calls to mind only the type of

King such as King Henry the VIII [censored words]. King, look into your heart. You know you are a complete fraud and a great liability to all of us Negroes. . . . You are no clergyman and you know it. You are a colossal fraud and an evil, vicious one at that. . . .

King, like all frauds your end is approaching. You could have been our greatest leader. . . . Your "honorary" degrees, your Nobel Prize (what a grim farce) and other awards will not save you. King I repeat you are done. . . .

King, there is only one thing left for you to do. You know what it is. You have just 34 days in which to do [sic] (this exact number has been selected for a specific reason, it has definite practical significant [sic]. You are done. There is but one way out for you. You better take it before your filthy, abnormal fraudalant [sic] self is bared to the nation.

Soon King was listening to the accompanying tape with his friend Abernathy. "There were muffled voices," Abernathy recalled, "that seemed to come from a faraway room. . . . I recognized Martin and then myself. . . . Then there were other sounds. . . . Clearly what we were hearing were whispers and sighs from a bedroom."

The two men sat in silence when King switched off the tape. Then Abernathy said simply, "J. Edgar Hoover." He was right, as a Senate committee established a decade later. The tape was a composite, made up of several surveillance recordings and prepared in the FBI laboratory. Edgar's aide William Sullivan had told a trusted agent, Lish Whitsun, to fly to Florida with the package and mail it to Mrs. King from a post office near Miami Airport.

Edgar had the satisfaction of knowing the victim's reaction within twenty-four hours. "They are out to break me," King was overheard saying on a wiretap, "out to get me, harass me, break my spirit." According to relatives and close friends, he fell into a deep depression, tormented by insomnia.

A few days later, when Bureau agents tracked King down to a secret hideaway, they called in a false fire alarm. Fire trucks arrived, sirens blaring, and King guessed at once who had sent them. One local agent has since recalled that this was deemed "a good prank, something to be proud of." As if he too were proud, Edgar sent a report on King's emotional crisis to the White House.

The motive for mailing the tape, had the package not been delayed by a mail pileup, had been to "scare King off" from collecting his Nobel Prize—the honor Edgar himself so coveted. Sullivan said years later that the idea originated with Edgar and Clyde, and the record shows that the tape was mailed the day after a demand by Edgar for aggressive action.[5]

The harassment continued, and for a while King became even more depressed. Then he rallied. After an intense discussion with Abernathy, he decided not to give in to the pressure in any way. "We were not going to let Hoover and the FBI turn us around," Abernathy recalled in 1989, "because we were fighting a just cause."

Martin Luther King was killed on April 4, 1968, at the age of thirty-nine, the day after making a speech anticipating his own death. Felled by a single rifle shot as he stood on a motel balcony in Memphis, Tennessee, he died within minutes. Poor black communities across the country exploded in grief and rage. The nation's leaders joined King's widow at a funeral attended by 150,000 people.

Edgar was not among the mourners. Although the public was told he was personally running the murder investigation, he spent the following morning having his photograph taken for public relations purposes. The next day he did what he had done after President Kennedy was killed—went to the races. In the weeks that followed, he failed to show up for meetings with the Attorney General to discuss the progress of the inquiry.

Two months later, following a manhunt, a small-time

criminal named James Earl Ray was arrested in London and extradited to the United States. He pleaded guilty to King's murder and was sent to jail for ninety-nine years.

That, however, was not the end of the story. Ray's guilty plea was the basis of a deal between his attorney and the prosecution. He immediately recanted the plea and requested a mistrial. Then the judge died, and——in spite of repeated legal efforts——the evidence against Ray has never been tested in court. Now aged sixty-five, he is still in jail.

Few believe Ray acted alone. William Sullivan, who took part in the 1968 investigation, had serious doubts. And ten years later, after a massive new inquiry, Congress' Assassinations Committee concluded that there had indeed been a conspiracy. It suspected Ray had been hired to shoot King, and that his two brothers were also involved.

After Ray's arrest, asked whether there was any evidence of conspiracy, Edgar said, "None whatsoever." The day after the guilty plea, he approved this proposal by DeLoach:

> I would like to suggest that consideration be given to advising a friendly newspaper contact on a strictly confidential basis, that Coretta King and Reverend Abernathy are deliberately plotting to keep King's assassination in the news by pulling the ruse of maintaining that King's murder was definitely a conspiracy and not committed by one man. This, of course, is obviously a rank trick in order to keep the money coming in to Mrs. King and Abernathy. We can do this without any attribution to the FBI and without anyone knowing that the information came from a wiretap.

Ralph Abernathy had two main suspicions at the time. His first thought was that the Ku Klux Klan was behind it. His second, he recalled, was that King had been killed "by someone trained or hired by the FBI and acting under orders from J. Edgar Hoover himself."

In 1988, in a television interview from prison, Ray said he made his original confession only under pressure from the

FBI. He claimed agents threatened to jail his father and one of his brothers if he did not do so. He had been framed, Ray alleged, to cover up an FBI plot to kill King.[6]

The Assassinations Committee did not believe the Bureau was involved in the murder. It did, however, conclude that the inquiry into the crime was inadequate. No one has satisfactorily explained why it was two weeks before the FBI issued an alert for Ray, a prisoner on the run from jail, when his fingerprints had been found on personal belongings found near the scene of the crime. The belongings even included a radio bearing Ray's prison identification number —00416.

Former Atlanta agent Donald Wilson is bewildered to this day by his superiors' actions during the hunt for Ray, recalled the strange reaction when he and a colleague spotted a man they believed to be the suspect. "We saw the guy when we were driving near an apartment Ray was known to have used. . . . He was the spitting image of Ray, and we thought, you know, 'This is it, this is our future. We're golden!' We got on the radio to the control post and said we wanted to detain the man and ask for identification. But the radio came back and said we were to take no action, return to the office and sign out. We looked at each other in disbelief, but we did as we were told.

"I'm not saying it *was* Ray," Wilson said. "The point is that it could well have been. He wasn't apprehended till much later, by the police in London. Why were we stopped? The top people were calling the shots, including someone they'd sent down from Washington. I was really suspicious even then. I thought there was something wrong going on. . . ." Arthur Murtagh, who was also serving in Atlanta at the time, had misgivings, too. "I was told we weren't to talk about conspiracy," Murtagh recalled. "I think it was a political decision."

Murtagh recalled the depth of hatred whipped up by Edgar's long vendetta. "When they announced King's death on the radio," he said, "my colleague literally jumped in the air and said, 'We finally got the son of a bitch!' I don't know what he meant by '*We* got him,' but that's what he said. . . ."

Even if Edgar and the FBI had no part in the actual crime, they must surely bear some of the blame. "Among the kind of paralegal groups they did business with," said King's colleague Andrew Young, "it is quite possible that one of those groups took it upon themselves to plan and execute Martin's assassination—knowing that the FBI would be pleased with it and wouldn't give them too much trouble. . . . They created the climate in which Martin's assassination was acceptable."

Character assassination of King continued even while his murder was being investigated. "Hoover sent word through one of his appointed leaks," said Jack Anderson, "that they had a line on the assassination. They said King had been playing around with a dentist's wife in Los Angeles, and they thought the dentist might have killed King in revenge. I couldn't ignore the lead, so I went to see her—she was a very beautiful woman. She more or less admitted she and King had been lovers.

"What the FBI had told me seemed to fit together, until I talked to the husband. It was obvious that he had neither the inclination nor the ability to have killed King, and that the FBI story was false. My conclusion was that Hoover was hoping I'd bite and run a story—because the effect would've been to discredit King. The real story he wanted out was that King had been running around with other men's wives."

Edgar later strove to prevent King's birthday from being declared a national holiday, and approved a scheme to persuade members of Congress that King had been a "scoundrel." Such briefings, he stressed, should be conducted *"very cautiously."* The politicians were briefed, and King's birthday was not declared a holiday until 1983.

In 1975 President Ford would declare that those responsible for the FBI smear operation against King should be brought to trial. The FBI Director who succeeded Edgar, Clarence Kelley, agreed with him. By then Edgar was dead, as was Clyde. Other officials involved were still alive, but none was ever charged.

* * *

423

There was no grief in Edgar's office, two months after King's assassination, when Robert Kennedy was murdered in Los Angeles. "Goddamn the Kennedys!" William Sullivan had heard Clyde Tolson say in 1963, after President Kennedy's death. "First there was Jack, now there's Bobby, and then Teddy. We'll have them on our backs until the year 2000." In the summer of 1968, when it began to look as though Robert might win the presidency, Clyde startled colleagues at an executive meeting. "I hope," he said, "that someone shoots and kills the son of a bitch."

Now someone had, and Edgar was roused from sleep by President Johnson to be told that, as in 1963, he would rely on the FBI for the best information. Yet today, as in the case of the Dallas assassination, the murder of Robert Kennedy remains a historical muddle. The notion that only Sirhan Sirhan was responsible is increasingly in doubt. The initial FBI report on the crime, released only after Edgar's death, indicated that twelve or more bullets were fired. Sirhan's gun was capable of firing only eight. A wealth of other evidence, moreover, indicates that two gunmen were involved.

The first autopsy pictures of Kennedy were rushed to Edgar personally, to be joined in his Official and Confidential files by gruesome color pictures and medical reports. Of all the famous deaths in the Director's long career, they are the only death pictures thus preserved.

Edward Kennedy, too, was a victim of Edgar's spite. In 1962, when he first ran for the Senate, the youngest of the brothers was embarrassed by the revelation that he had been suspended from Harvard for getting a friend to take an exam in his place. It was Edgar, according to FBI sources, who ensured the story got into the newspapers.

By 1967 Edgar had written Kennedy off as "irresponsible," a judgment vindicated two years later when the Senator abandoned a female companion in the wreckage of his sunken car at Chappaquiddick. The accident was a local police matter, but Edgar would readily oblige when the Nixon White House asked him to send agents looking for additional dirt. He loved to gossip about the tragedy, sometimes for hours on end.

In the summer of 1968, with Robert Kennedy gone, Edgar's horizon seemed free of serious opposition. It was an illusion.

CHAPTER 31

"Mr. Hoover served with distinction, but he served too long. . . . Those who had recent contact with him knew that age increasingly impacted his judgment. We all—the Presidents, the Congress, the Attorneys General, the press—knew that, and yet he stayed on struggling against change and the future."

Nicholas Katzenbach,
former Attorney General, 1975

"THE GREATEST ENEMY," EDGAR HAD SAID, "IS TIME," BUT HE acted as though he could hold the clock back. In 1968, when he turned seventy-three, the familiar bulldog profile seemed little changed. Edgar's doctors pronounced him fit, and aides passed on the reassuring news to the press. They said as little as possible about Clyde Tolson.

Though five years Edgar's junior, Clyde had undergone open-heart surgery and suffered the first of several strokes. So feeble was his eyesight that he would soon need help to read his mail, and sometimes he did not make it into the office at all. Edgar could not stand to see his friend show his weaknesses in public. When Clyde stumbled and fell at the track in California, Edgar ordered an accompanying agent not to help him. "Leave him alone," he snapped. "Let the dumb asshole get up by himself."

Clyde "retired" when he reached the automatic retirement age of seventy, but only for a day. By dint of some bureaucratic sleight of hand, Edgar promptly rehired him. Clyde continued to get "outstanding" performance reports and, in spite of his failing eyesight, was issued a new service revolver. FBI propaganda insisted that the Director and his right-hand man were hale and hearty, as indomitable as ever.

Increasingly, however, people who mattered were unconvinced. A group of Los Angeles agents wrote to the Attorney General complaining of the Director's "rapidly advancing senility and increasing megalomania." Two former agents dared to write books criticizing him, and Edgar found that old suppression techniques no longer worked. Even the conservative press, he found, was now prepared to run articles mocking him and asking how much longer he could remain Director of the FBI.

History was leaving Edgar behind. In the past he had always known how to maneuver, how to respond to change in ways that left the FBI looking good. Now he failed to see how Middle America, his traditional constituency, was changing. The tide of opinion was running in favor of civil rights, a factor the FBI could have exploited by being seen to enforce the law. Instead, Edgar ranted on about supposed Communist influence on the black movement and about Martin Luther King's "lies." Millions of Americans were turning against the Vietnam War, but Edgar exacerbated the situation by having his agents infiltrate the protest groups and sending agents provocateurs to disrupt demonstrations. The manipulator of public opinion had lost his touch.

Then, when Edgar's decline and fall seemed inevitable, along came Richard Nixon.

It was as if some historical magnet had pulled the two together. Twenty-one years had passed since Edgar first cast an approving eye on Nixon. He and his wealthy friends, the Texas oilmen, had nursed Nixon on his way to becoming Vice President in 1952. Nixon had been seen repeatedly at Edgar's side, on trips to the races and at baseball games, before the 1960 upset that swept Nixon into the political wilderness.

Even in the wilderness Edgar had been there, a sympathetic houseguest at the Nixon home in California. "Hoover," Nixon would say ruefully when Edgar was gone and when Watergate dragged him down in disgrace, "was my crony."

In 1968, as Nixon reached for the presidency, he committed himself to keeping Edgar on as soon as his campaign went into high gear. Edgar leaked information designed to hurt the Democratic opposition. He laughed off a bid, meanwhile, to get him to run for Vice President alongside the southern conservative George Wallace. Dreams of a place for himself at the White House were long past—what Edgar wanted now was safe passage in a seaworthy Republican ship.

All the gang were there, the millionaires and the middlemen. That summer, funds flowed into the Nixon coffers from Clint Murchison in Texas and Lewis Rosenstiel in New York. Louis Nichols, once Edgar's political fixer and now Rosenstiel's, became one of Nixon's political advisers.

Edgar covered his bets. He knew Vice President Hubert Humphrey, now the leading Democratic contender, still had a good chance of winning. He raised no objection, therefore, when Humphrey's people asked for the "same service" at the Convention that the FBI had given Johnson four years earlier. This time, however, there would be no electronic surveillance; when Edgar asked Attorney General Ramsey Clark for approval, he was turned down flat.[1]

Edgar worried about his fate should Humphrey become President. In the White House, a depressed Lyndon Johnson worried—again—about his personal safety. "Tell Edgar Hoover," he told an aide, "that I have taken care of him since the beginning of my administration, and now that I am leaving, I expect him to take care of me. . . . There will be any number of crackpots trying to get at me after January 20, 1969."

In November, when Nixon scraped home to victory, Edgar wrote Johnson a last obsequious letter:

My dear Mr. President,

You have afforded me many pleasant moments for many years. As a personal friend, neighbor and subordinate, I have enjoyed your company. . . . Clyde Tolson and Deke DeLoach join me in expressing appreciation for your kindness. They, too, are very grateful for the time spent with you.

Sincerely,

Edgar

Within two days of writing this farewell note, Edgar was closeted with Nixon at New York's Pierre Hotel, telling him of Johnson's illicit use of the FBI during the campaign. "Hoover told me the cabin on my plane was bugged for the last two weeks," Nixon would recall. "Hoover told [Attorney General–to-be] Mitchell and me separately . . . Johnson ordered it."

FBI files contain no evidence that Nixon was bugged, only that checks were made on the phone records of his running mate, Spiro Agnew, because Johnson suspected Republican sabotage of the Vietnam peace talks. Yet as Nixon's aide H. R. Haldeman confirmed, Edgar not only claimed the bugging had occurred, he played on Nixon's fears in other ways.

"When you get into the White House," the Director warned, "don't make any calls through the switchboard. . . . Little men you don't know will be listening." Edgar claimed that presidential communications, run by the U.S. Army Signal Corps, were insecure—that "the President should know that if he talked on those lines he would probably be monitored."

"We were to find that Hoover always came in with a little bag of goodies," Haldeman recalled, "tidbits of information that he doled out, alarums and excursions on which your imagination would feed. He would roll his eyes skywards, without offering a firm conclusion—all to create an impression of how useful the Bureau could be to the President."

Edgar must have hoped for a smooth run, a return to the power and privilege he had exercised during the last Republican administration, when Nixon had been Vice President.

Haldeman, watching him with Nixon at the Pierre, thought they greeted each other "like old pals." "Edgar," Nixon said, "you are one of the few people who is to have direct access to me at all times."

Yet Nixon's counsel John Ehrlichman, also present, thought his boss said this "ostentatiously, for effect." Haldeman thought Nixon doubted Edgar's competence and was secretly considering firing him. Even as he was making promises to Edgar, Nixon was approaching others to fill the post.

At a meeting in Palm Springs, Nixon dangled the job in front of Pete Pitchess, Sheriff of Los Angeles County, a Goldwater conservative and a former FBI agent. Pitchess responded with care. "Hoover," he noted, "hasn't yet said he's retiring." "No," said Nixon, "but he's told me he's going to, on his birthday." "Ah," Pitchess responded, "but *which* birthday?" Nixon changed the subject.

Why did Nixon fail to follow through? "He was afraid," said Pitchess. "Every goddamn president was afraid of Hoover—Johnson, even Kennedy. All of them, afraid. I was close to Nixon, but he wouldn't be specific. He just said, 'I have to handle Hoover with kid gloves.'"

John Connally, who served Nixon as Secretary of the Treasury, saw it, too. "Nixon would like to have forced Hoover to retire, but he was not prepared to force it. He didn't trust him. He was fearful. . . ."

Even after Edgar was dead, Nixon would be speaking of his power, in awe, almost as if Edgar were still alive to wield it. "He's got files on everybody, goddamnit!" Nixon was to say in 1973, wishing Edgar were there to rescue him from Watergate.

President Johnson had told a friend there was a fat FBI dossier on Nixon. One might have expected it to be bulging with reports of connections to white-collar crime or of dubious business deals. The one item we know about, however, comes as a surprise. It links Richard Nixon with a woman, and an exotic one at that.

* * * *

The story began in 1958, when Nixon, then forty-five, married and serving as Vice President, met Marianna Liu, a Hong Kong tour guide in her twenties. This was a chance encounter, but the two met again in Nixon's wilderness years, when he traveled to Hong Kong on business. Liu believes they saw each other each year between 1964 and 1966, when she was working as a hostess at the Den, the cocktail lounge of the local Hilton. The two were photographed together.

By her own account, Liu and a waitress friend visited Nixon and his traveling companion, the controversial businessman Bebe Rebozo, in a suite at the Mandarin Hotel. She—and eventually Nixon, after an initial "No comment" —has denied any sexual activity. Liu said that when Nixon next came to Hong Kong, she was in the hospital and he sent her flowers and a bottle of her favorite perfume.

The former FBI representative in Hong Kong, however, remembers that the Nixon relationship with Liu caused a security flap. "One of my contacts in another U.S. agency," said Dan Grove, now a security consultant, "came to see me one morning and said one of his sources, Marianna Liu, was seeing Nixon. He thought I should be aware of this, because there was a suspicion she was a Chinese Agent, that she was seeing U.S. Navy officers. He said he knew Nixon had had a top-secret briefing on the People's Republic of China, and that made his contact with Liu a risk."

Grove went to the Hilton that lunchtime to talk to Liu. "My colleague," he recalled, "just said to her, 'You were with a big man last night, weren't you?' And she said, 'Yes, how did you know?' He said, 'Who was with you?' And she replied, 'His friend, Bebe Rebozo.' Marianna and a girlfriend had spent the day and evening with them.

"It was not FBI jurisdiction, but I decided that I'd report it if I found she had any record of visas for the U.S. It turned out she did have a couple, and her background didn't quite check in the different applications—a classic indicator of a possible intelligence background. I checked with the British Special Branch, and they came back and said, 'She's on record with us.' She'd come to their attention as a possible

Chinese Intelligence Service agent. They'd never followed up because all her activities seemed to involve the Americans, rather than British subjects. . . . I reported this to the Bureau, to Assistant Director Sullivan, and I got a reply saying something like, 'Mr. Nixon's personal life is of no interest to this Bureau. . . . Make your checks and close the file.'"

According to Liu's attorney, FBI records confirm that her contact with Nixon set alarm bells ringing, that Nixon himself came under surveillance in Hong Kong—to the extent of his being photographed through his bedroom window with infrared cameras. The surveillance, Grove suspects, was carried out by the British, at the request of the CIA.

A 1976 FBI memorandum shows that Grove's memory is accurate:

From: DIRECTOR FBI   August 18, 1976
Subject: MARIANNA LIU—ISCH [Internal Security Desk China]
Bureau file concerning caption matter brought to the attention of this Bureau by Legal Attaché Hong Kong letter dated 10.12.67 wherein suspicions of possible Chicom intelligence involvement of subject were inferred but not substantiated by Special Branch, HK Police . . . and a U.S. [name of agency deleted] representative indicated he had heard . . . subject [regularly saw] VP Nixon when he visited HK. . . .

"When Nixon got elected President," Grove recalled, "I was in the office one Sunday morning, and I saw a picture of Liu with Nixon in a newspaper—if my memory serves me right it was at the inaugural ball. I thought, 'How did she get in there?' I'd asked for visa applications to be monitored and was supposed to be notified if she tried to enter the U.S. . . . Since I hadn't been, I sent in an official letter marked 'Personal attention of Mr. Hoover.' Our instructions were that any possible hostile activities against senior

U.S. government officials were to go to the Director personally. . . . But he did not respond to my letter."

None of this proves that Nixon and Liu slept together, and—whatever other agencies may have done—the FBI in Hong Kong never investigated the allegation. Unchecked sexual innuendo, however, had always been grist for Edgar's mill. According to William Sullivan, Edgar read the information on Liu "gleefully" and personally showed the report to Nixon before he became President.

Nixon's companion in Hong Kong, Florida real estate millionaire Bebe Rebozo, was his closest confidant. He has since been linked to a string of suspect business deals, including the suspected funneling of campaign funds to Nixon's personal coffers. Edgar told Kenneth Whittaker, his Agent in Charge in Miami, to be especially "attentive" to Rebozo—and to watch him carefully.

We cannot know what passed between Edgar and Nixon concerning the trips to Hong Kong or about Marianna Liu. For Nixon, however, there was one certainty. Blameless though his relations with Liu may have been, exposure of the security flap—during the election campaign or during his presidency—could have wounded him gravely, even fatally. And Edgar had the file.

Just before Christmas 1968, weeks after their meeting at the Pierre, Nixon announced Edgar's reappointment as Director. He also gave him a raise to $42,500 a year, a fortune at the time.

Nixon's inaugural parade took place under conditions of unprecedented security. Edgar's agents used dirty tricks to thwart anti–Vietnam War protesters—false housing forms to disrupt accommodation arrangements for out-of-town demonstrators and phony CB radio broadcasts to confuse the organizers.

The office windows on Pennsylvania Avenue were all closed by order of the Secret Service, with one exception. As they had so many times before, Edgar and Clyde stood peering down from their balcony at FBI headquarters, watching the birth of another regime.

Nixon told neither of his key aides, Haldeman and Ehrlichman, about the Marianna Liu problem. Nor did he mention any other reason he might have to fear Edgar. He simply ordered Ehrlichman to establish himself with Edgar as "his friend and White House confidant."

Ehrlichman's first mission was to reassure Edgar about a project he held dear, the building of a grand new headquarters for the FBI. It had been eight years since Congress had agreed that the FBI should have a new building. It was to be a concrete edifice, eleven stories high at its tallest point, facing onto Pennsylvania Avenue between Ninth and Tenth streets. And Edgar was already fighting with the planners.

He was worried that open arcades on the new building would give "free access to alcoholics, homos and whores." Columns, he thought, would provide cover for lurking assassins. For public consumption, he let it be known that he did not want the building named after him. In private, he admitted that was exactly what he wanted. "It was," said his friend Walter Trohan, "the dearest thing to his heart."

Ehrlichman assured Edgar that building operations would be expedited, then sat back and listened to one of the Director's monologues. "He was doing a selling job on me," Ehrlichman recalled, "telling me what we should look out for. Communism, the Kennedys, the Black Panthers. . . . He spoke of all the black movements with passion and hatred."

"I hardly had a chance to say anything," the aide complained afterward to Nixon. "I know," the President replied, "but it's necessary, John. It's necessary." Nixon went out of his way to humor Edgar. He went along to the FBI Academy to be made an honorary FBI agent—three decades after trying to become a real one. He brought Edgar to Camp David for the weekend, with the ailing Clyde in tow.

Edgar went on playing the game he knew so well, doing favors, making himself seem indispensable. When Nixon picked John Mitchell, a wealthy lawyer without obvious qualifications, to serve as Attorney General, he reportedly asked that the usual stringent FBI checks be waived. Edgar had no problem with Mitchell, whom he described as "honest, sincere and very human. . . . There never has been an Attorney General for whom I've had a higher regard." Mitchell was to wind up serving nineteen months in jail for conspiracy, obstruction of justice and lying under oath during the Watergate crisis.

In the early days, Nixon had Edgar over to the White House almost every month. "He'd come in at breakfast," the President would recall. "He got us information. There were times when I felt the only person in this goddamned government that was standing with me was Edgar Hoover. . . . He was giving me the stuff that he had . . . little things."

During the Nixon presidency, the FBI institutionalized the supply of dirt to the White House under the code name "Inlet." Edgar ordered field offices to look out for six categories of information, including "items with an unusual twist or concerning prominent personalities which may be of special interest to the President. . . ."

Nixon's officials were unimpressed. Henry Kissinger and Alexander Haig laughed openly over redundant reports on the late Martin Luther King. "The FBI investigative work I saw was of poor quality," said John Ehrlichman, "rumor, gossip and conjecture . . . often hearsay, two or three times removed. When FBI work was particularly bad I sent it back to Hoover, but the rework was seldom an improvement."

At the White House, Haldeman leafed through information on U.S. politicians, picked up while surveilling foreigners. Edgar, he thought, was just "lobbying . . . trying to pique the President's curiosity." Haldeman was uneasy, too, about Edgar's access to the Oval Office through Rose Mary Woods, the presidential secretary later to become celebrated for her "accidental" erasure of one of the Watergate tapes. She had worked for Nixon since the early fifties, and Edgar was on first-name terms with her.[2] Under pressure from Haldeman, the President agreed to try to "minimize the connection." It was a turning point in his relationship with Edgar.

"FBI Director Hoover," *Newsweek* reported in May 1969,

"no longer enjoys direct access to the White House. . . ." Realizing Nixon's advisers were responsible for the change, Edgar struck back in characteristic fashion. That month, using Rose Mary Woods to ensure the message got through, he passed on an astonishing allegation—that Haldeman, Ehrlichman and a third aide, Dwight Chapin, were homosexual lovers.

"We found out," said Haldeman, "one night when Mitchell and Ehrlichman and I had been out with the President for a dinner cruise on the *Sequoia,* the presidential yacht. When we came back, Mitchell's limo dropped Ehrlichman and me off. Mitchell got out of the car, walked us away so the driver wouldn't hear and told us Hoover had come up with this homosexual report. It came from a bartender who was a source for the FBI on stuff like this. We were supposed to have attended homosexual parties at the Watergate complex. There were dates, places, everything. Well, every factual allegation he made was totally false and easily disproven. Mitchell advised us to give depositions to the FBI, that it would be useful for us to have in our records. We did as he suggested.

"Mitchell's conclusion," said Haldeman, "was that this was an attempt by Hoover to lay a threat across our path, to keep us in line, remind us of his potential." "I came to think," said Ehrlichman, "that Hoover did this to show his claws, or ingratiate himself to Nixon—probably both. It was my early introduction to the way the game was played."

This was just the start of the game. In midsummer, after more bizarre statements by Edgar about Robert Kennedy and Dr. King, former Attorney General Ramsey Clark—and *The Washington Post* in an editorial—called for his resignation. The President, it was reported, was looking for a way to dump him.

Nixon denied the rumors. In October, to the astonishment of aides, he left the White House to dine at Edgar's home—a compliment he had not paid even to Cabinet members. He made sure photographers were there to see him bid Edgar an affable good night on the doorstep. Yet,

Ehrlichman said, "the President seemed uncomfortable that evening. He left as early as he decently could."

After the first calls for his resignation, probably in July, Edgar had quietly visited Nixon to discuss a new report from one of his agents. Marianna Liu, the President's Chinese friend, was shortly to be granted permanent residence in the United States. One of her sponsors was listed as William Allman, a businessman with whom Nixon had stayed in Hong Kong. Another was Raymond Warren, a Nixon-era immigration official who lived in Whittier, California, Nixon's hometown.

Nixon has since denied having used his influence to help Liu obtain U.S. residence. According to William Sullivan, however, the FBI's information was that the woman had been given "top priority." Marianna Liu was admitted to the United States, went to live in Whittier and reportedly saw Nixon again after her arrival.

Years later, asked about reports that she visited the White House, Liu became upset. "I'm not saying anything else about me and Mr. Nixon," she cried. "Are you trying to get me killed?"

On New Year's Day 1970, as Edgar turned seventy-five, Nixon telephoned to wish him Happy Birthday. Again he made sure the press knew, and again he said there were no plans for Edgar to retire. A few months later, on reading a fresh news report that he planned to resign, Edgar scrawled a petulant note—"I will not."

A new gag was now making the rounds in Washington. Plans were being made, it was said, to make Edgar's reappointment automatic—in the year 2000.

Terrorized as they were by Edgar's homosexual smear, the President's aides would have been interested in an account of what he himself was up to in 1969. Much later, information reached the police that, on vacation in California with Clyde, he went to great lengths to indulge a sexual interest in teenage males.

The story is told today by Charles Krebs, one of a group of Los Angeles homosexuals who kept close company in the late sixties. One of Krebs' friends was Billy Byars, Jr., wealthy son of the oil magnate who had used the bungalow next to Edgar's at the Del Charro hotel in La Jolla. As a result of his acquaintance with Byars, Jr., said Krebs, Edgar made the contacts necessary to have teenage boys brought to him at La Jolla.

Byars was thirty-two in 1969, a part-time filmmaker, fitness enthusiast and dilettante. He went on to produce *The Genesis Children,* an X-rated movie with scenes featuring naked male adolescents. He was indicted in 1973, along with fourteen other men, shortly after Edgar's death, during a police inquiry into other movies that featured sex acts involving young boys. Byars was by then abroad, reportedly in Morocco, and stayed out of the United States for many years to come.

According to Krebs and others, Byars' house in Los Angeles, at the summit of Laurel Canyon, was for a while a haven for adult homosexuals and male teenagers. Some of Byars' friends were aware, as Del Charro staff and Byars himself confirm, that their host knew Edgar and sometimes saw him at La Jolla. They noticed that a card arrived from Edgar one Christmas and that a fifteen-year-old youth at the house talked openly of having met Edgar at the Del Charro. "Hoover bawled me out," he complained, "for having long hair, but I told the old faggot where to go. No way was I getting a haircut."

"It was accepted in our circle that Hoover and Tolson were homosexual," Krebs recalled. "The impression I had from Byars was that Hoover and Tolson had had a sexual relationship with each other when they were younger, but not anymore. They were just two old aunties together in old age, but they were queens. On three occasions that I knew about, perhaps four, boys were driven down to La Jolla at Hoover's request. I think the arrangements were made by one of Billy's friends, an older man.

"I went down to La Jolla with the group a couple of times, and we spent a good deal of time at a bar called Rudi's

Hearthside, where the Hoover rendezvous were. We'd go to the Hearthside with the boys, the fifteen-year-old and another youngster. Hoover and Tolson would be driven there in a limo, always at night. I saw them and their security a couple of times—guys in suits and pointy shoes who looked like crooks. I'd be left behind and they'd go off in two cars, Hoover's and the one carrying the boys. The way I heard it, they'd drive to a reservoir up in the hills. The two cars parked headlight to headlight, with a cover car down the hill. And the boys would go and get in the Hoover car, and that's where they'd do their business."[3]

Detective Don Smith of the Los Angeles police vice unit interviewed the juvenile witnesses in the 1973 sex-movie case. "This was a group of homosexuals," he recalled, "some of them pedophiles. There were a number of Hollywood people, also doctors, lawyers, schoolteachers, a head of a corporation. These were upstanding community leaders, but that was their quirk. . . . The kids knew them as 'Uncle Mike' and 'Mother John,' not by their real names. They'd describe the vehicles the guys were driving in and the chauffeurs who got out and made the pickups. The kids brought up several famous names, including those of Hoover and his sidekick."

Charles Krebs expresses anger at the memory of the expeditions to La Jolla. "Here was J. Edgar Hoover, himself a homosexual. Any law they ever brought up to help homosexuals, he shot it down. Anyone they thought homosexual who tried to get a job, he shot them down. He built dossiers on them and had people follow them around. Anyone who was a faggot he hated. Yet he was doing the same thing."

CHAPTER 32

"Justice is only incidental to law and order."

J. Edgar Hoover, 1968

IN APRIL 1969, A BROODING PRESIDENT NIXON CALLED EDGAR to discuss the unrest sweeping the nation about Vietnam. Nixon was worried about student unrest, about draft resisters and the possibility of a mutiny by troops in the field. It was the sort of thing, he felt, that "brings down governments." Edgar's response was to compare the situation to the Russian revolution of 1917. Rambling on about "bleeding hearts," he told Nixon that campus rebellion could be solved if "presidents of the universities showed more guts and expelled the individuals. . . ."

Later, when Ohio National Guardsmen fired into a crowd at Kent State University, killing four young people and wounding eight, Edgar had no compassion. "The Guardsmen used as much restraint as they could," Edgar informed presidential aide Egil Krogh. "The students invited and got what they deserved."

In fact, official investigations showed, the students were shot when they were hundreds of feet away from the Guardsmen, too far to be any threat. None of those killed were militants. A tape of the incident shows that the fatal salvo was preceded by a single gunshot. "This could have been fired," wrote the historian William Manchester, "either as a signal or from fear, by Terence F. Norman, a spurious 'free-lance photographer' who was really an informer on the FBI payroll. . . ."

All Vietnam protests, however peaceful, were infiltrated

by FBI agents. On Edgar's orders, informants were paid to report on the plans—and private lives—of peace activists. Some of the victims were famous. Jane Fonda, trailed by the FBI long before her controversial visit to North Vietnam, was reported as arriving at an airport "disheveled and dirty." Her address book, containing "names, addresses and telephone numbers of many revolutionary and leftist groups," was confiscated and Xeroxed for FBI files. The actress' mail was opened, her phones bugged, her bank records examined. She became, for the Bureau's record, "Jane Fonda: Anarchist."

The famous were at least somewhat protected by their celebrity. There was no such protection, however, for the obscure Scott Camil, a two-tour Marine veteran, home from Vietnam with his wounds, nine medals and grave misgivings about the war. After Camil helped found Vietnam Veterans Against the War and threw away his medals in front of the Capitol, Edgar ordered a "full-scale aggressive investigation." The former Marine was put out of circulation, first on kidnapping charges, which were dropped, then for possession of marijuana. Agents have since admitted they had been told to find a way, any way, to "neutralize" Camil as a peace activist.

The instrument for the most serious abuses of the period was the Bureau's COINTELPRO project, originally launched thirteen years earlier to undermine the Communist Party using dirty tricks—fake documents, bogus phone calls and fabricated news stories.[1] In 1968, with Edgar's approval, agents concocted a letter to *Life* magazine signed by Howard Rasmussen of Brooklyn. Rasmussen did not exist, and the purpose of the letter was to smear a leader of the Youth International Party, better known as the Yippies. Morris Starsky, an Assistant Professor at Arizona State University who happened to be an antiwar activist, lost his job after an anonymous letter was sent to college officials. That letter, too, had been dreamed up at the FBI.

The FBI worked to divide and disrupt, to set one radical group against another. Bureau artists churned out bogus fliers attacking the "crap" influence in the New Mobilization Committee Against the War in Vietnam, then submitted a copy to Edgar. It was labeled "Obscene," with the apologetic explanation that it was necessary to use bad language to get through to the New Left.

The FBI, established to prevent crime, now provoked it. Robert Hardy, a former Bureau informant in New Jersey, testified that agents urged him to persuade antiwar activists to break into the offices of the local draft board. "They told me," he said,

> all they wanted was evidence of a conspiracy. . . . In the course of the next month, upon the instruction of my FBI agents, my leadership role increased to the point that it became absurd. I was not only encouraging the group to raid the Camden draft board, I was initiating all the plans to do so. I provided them with the tools they needed—ladders, ropes, drills, bits, hammers. . . . On instructions, I once tried to give them guns, but they refused. . . . All this was paid for by the FBI.

Far from settling for evidence of conspiracy, said Hardy, his control agent told him the break-in was to be allowed to go ahead. It did, and the protesters were caught red-handed. Hardy's Bureau contact told him the orders "had come direct from the little White House in California. . . . The FBI again had gotten its man. The country could now see positive proof that the administration was correct in warning the country about the threat from the Left. . . . I will never forget the role I played in this abuse of American justice."

The fact that the FBI denied Hardy's story is no reason to doubt it. The Bureau was conducting itself just as badly in other areas. The black movement, and especially the militant Black Panthers, came under ruthless attack. Unlike the mainstream civil rights movement, the Panthers preached revolution. Many were armed and dangerous, others not. Edgar lumped them together as "the greatest threat to the internal security of the country."

People the Panthers approached for funds, such as church groups and women's organizations, were shocked to receive copies of the *Panthers' Coloring Book for Children*, depicting black children killing white policemen. The Panther leadership disapproved of the book and had ordered all copies be destroyed. The FBI, however, obtained copies and circulated them—to deter possible donors.

The Newark Agent in Charge proposed the sending of a fake telegram, supposedly from within the Panthers' organization, warning that white "supporters" were sending poisoned food donations to Panther charities. To "prove" it, he suggested, the Bureau laboratory could "treat fruit such as oranges with a mild laxative-type drug by hypodermic needle or other appropriate method and ship fruit as a donation from a fictitious person. . . ." Incredibly, Edgar's office thought the plan "had merit," and rejected it only "because of the lack of control over the treated fruit in transit."

A vicious campaign was mounted to discredit Jean Seberg, the movie actress remembered for her role as Joan of Arc. Because the actress was among the Panthers' several prominent white backers, this suggestion went to Edgar from Agent Richard Held, a COINTELPRO specialist in Los Angeles:

Bureau permission is requested to publicize the pregnancy of JEAN SEBERG, well-known white movie actress, by Raymond Hewitt, Black Panther Party . . . by advising Hollywood Gossip-Columnists in the Los Angeles area of the situation. It is felt the possible publication of Seberg's "plight" could cause her embarrassment and serve to cheapen her image with the general public. It is proposed that the following letter from a fictitious person be sent to local columnists:

I was just thinking about you and remembered I still owe you a favor. So—I was in Paris last week and ran into Jean Seberg, who was heavy with baby. I thought she and Romaine [sic] had gotten together

*again, but she confided the child belonged to
Raymond Hewitt of the Black Panthers. The dear
girl is getting around! Anyway, I thought you might
get a scoop on the others. Be good, and I'll see you
soon.*

Love,

Sol

The FBI had discovered from a wiretap that Seberg was pregnant. To conceal that fact, Edgar recommended that the sending of "Sol's" smear letter should be delayed "until Seberg's pregnancy would be obvious to everyone." Just two weeks later, however, Los Angeles columnist Joyce Haber ran a story referring to an unnamed actress who was evidently Seberg. "Papa," it said, "is said to be a rather prominent Black Panther." The story was repeated by the *Hollywood Reporter* and—three months later—by *Newsweek,* which identified Seberg by name.

As the FBI well knew, Seberg was already emotionally disturbed and under psychiatric care. Soon after the publicity started, she took an overdose of sleeping tablets. The baby she was carrying was born prematurely days after the *Newsweek* story, but survived for only two days. The infant's father was almost certainly neither a Black Panther nor Seberg's estranged husband, the French novelist Romain Gary, but a Mexican she had met while making a movie.

The actress became obsessed about the loss of the baby and—when she learned of it years later—about the sinister role of the FBI. She committed suicide in 1979, almost nine years to the day after the child's death. "Jean Seberg," said the grieving Romain Gary, "was destroyed by the FBI."

None of this emerged until after Edgar was dead, and—in spite of the evidence in its files—the FBI has never admitted leaking the Seberg smear to the press. Bill Thomas, then City Editor of the *Los Angeles Times,* says he recalls only that the story came from "a law enforcement source." Richard Held, the agent who initialed the original proposal to headquarters, now heads the San Francisco office of the FBI. He will say only that his memo was "a bureaucratic requirement in response to pressure from someone in Washington."

Edgar sent a report on Seberg to the White House, describing her as a "sex pervert . . . presently pregnant by Raymond Hewitt of the Black Panthers," the very day the first gossipy item appeared in the *Los Angeles Times*. He sent a copy of the report to the Attorney General.

Former FBI Assistant Director Charles Bates, who has studied the Seberg file, had no doubt of its origin. "This got the okay from Washington. It was probably given to the press orally, to avoid detection. But the Director saw this—his marks are on the papers. He knew about it. There's no excuse, and the FBI should admit it."

Dick Gregory, the black comedian, was targeted with potentially fatal malice—on Edgar's orders. He had three faults: He was black, he was a vociferous supporter of the civil rights movement and he had referred publicly to Edgar as "one of the most dangerous men in this country." Edgar therefore sent orders to the FBI office in Chicago, where Gregory lived, to:

develop counter-intelligence measures to neutralize him. . . . This should not be in the nature of an exposé, since he already gets far too much publicity. Instead, sophisticated completely untraceable means of neutralizing Gregory should be developed.

In some intelligence circles, "neutralize" is said to be synonymous with "kill." It did not mean that at the FBI, but Edgar's next order might well have resulted in Gregory's death. He noted that Gregory had recently made an outspoken attack on organized crime, calling its members "the filthiest snakes that exist on this earth." And he told Marlin Johnson, the Chicago Agent in Charge, to:

Consider the use of this statement in developing a counter-intelligence operation to alert La Cosa Nostra to Gregory's attack. . . .

Edgar's order can be read only as incitement to have Gregory beaten up, perhaps killed, by the mob. Johnson, now retired, has refused to say whether or not he carried out the instruction. Gregory survived.

FBI dirty tricks, the Senate Intelligence Committee later discovered, provoked "shootings, beatings and a high degree of unrest" in the Black Panther movement. For two Panthers in Chicago, the FBI tactics brought sudden death. Fred Hampton and Mark Clark died in a hail of gunfire, and three others were wounded, when police burst into their apartment at 4:00 A.M. on December 3, 1969. It later emerged that the police had fired ninety-eight rounds, the Panthers—maybe—one.

In 1982, after persistent litigation, the survivors were awarded $1.85 million in damages against the police, in a case that revealed the killings had been the direct result of action by the FBI. The Bureau had provided the police with detailed information on Hampton's movements, along with a floor plan of the apartment. Veteran agent Wesley Swearingen quoted a Chicago colleague as telling him: "We told the cops how bad these guys were, that the cops had better look out or their wives were going to be widows. . . . We set up the police to go in there and kill the whole lot."[2]

Elmer "Geronimo" Pratt, a former Panther leader in California, is still in jail today for the alleged murder of a woman during a robbery. As revealed on CBS's "60 Minutes," however, the FBI concealed the fact that key testimony at his trial was provided by a Bureau informant. Pratt is now on Amnesty International's list of people who, for political reasons, did not receive a fair trial.

Edgar, it is now known, had personally ordered that a way be found to put Pratt out of circulation. He was fully briefed on all Bureau operations against the Panthers, and ensured that they were among the most closely held secrets in FBI history.

From the standpoint of the Nixon White House, Edgar did not do enough to counter radical movements. In 1969 and early 1970, bombings or bomb threats were running at eighty every day. There were 400 threats on one day alone in New York City. Blasts ripped through the Manhattan offices of IBM, General Telephone and Mobil Oil. Forty-three people were killed, and property worth $21 million destroyed.

It was, President Nixon recalled, a "season of mindless terror." Few were caught and, of 40,000 incidents, 64 percent were by bombers whose identity and motive were unknown. The men around Nixon had grumbled from the start about the paucity of FBI intelligence on things that really mattered—as distinct from dirt on people's private lives. There were other things, however, that seemed intolerable in the present situation.

Relations between the FBI and the other intelligence agencies were at an all-time low. Edgar had been hostile and uncooperative toward the CIA since the forties, when he had been thwarted in his desire to do its work himself. Yet while he rarely deigned to meet with Directors of the CIA, his agents had long found ways to cooperate with the Agency. In the spring of 1970, however, in a fit of pique over a trifling formality, Edgar ordered all liaison to cease. In a city where there is rarely unanimity on anything, the news shocked everyone in the secret world.

Edgar's veteran liaison with the CIA, Sam Papich, was so appalled that he tendered his resignation. "I hope you will share my alarm," he wrote Edgar. "I am absolutely convinced that the intelligence services of Great Britain, France, West Germany and others are well penetrated by the Soviets. . . . The break in relations between the FBI and CIA will provide a basis for promoting further rifts. . . . I appeal to you to leave the door open."

Edgar was not listening. He was shortly to sever the FBI's

links with the National Security Agency, the Defense Intelligence Agency, the military services and the Secret Service—with everyone, indeed, except the White House.

As old men isolate themselves, so Edgar was trying to isolate the FBI. Nixon's aides thought the situation the height of folly, especially at a time of crisis. They were frustrated, too, to discover that agents were now inhibited in their ability to perform "black bag" jobs—Bureauspeak for illegal break-ins. Edgar had smiled on such operations for decades, only to call a halt in 1966, when Bureau methods came under unprecedented scrutiny. This formal order had been a device to protect Edgar's rear, not some sudden rush of respect for the proprieties. And black-bag work had continued, though more cautiously. The young men around Nixon, however, had no time for an old man's caution.

In April 1970, H. R. Haldeman went to the President with complaints about Edgar and suggestions for change. Nixon listened, and ordered the nation's intelligence chiefs to conduct a rapid review of the security situation—a process that turned out to be a humiliating charade.

Aware of Edgar's scorn for his peers at other agencies, Nixon played to his vanity by making him chairman of the review committee. Less adroitly, he appointed a presidential assistant, Tom Huston, to coordinate it. Though very right-wing, Huston riled Edgar from the start. He was young—twenty-nine—highly intelligent and well read, and he sported sideburns and longish hair. Edgar wrote him off as a "hippie intellectual."

For a long time now, albeit reluctantly, Edgar had been sending an aide to meetings of the nation's most prestigious intelligence group, the U.S. Intelligence Board. His attitude to that body is well summed up by an incident during the Nixon era—when each agency was asked to provide a small plaque, bearing its seal, for display on the conference room wall. Edgar had sent one three feet in diameter, three times larger than anyone else's. Now, as chairman of Nixon's review committee, he behaved accordingly.

At a first meeting Edgar astonished everyone with introductory remarks saying the President merely wanted a history of the current unrest. When colleagues had to put him right, explaining that Nixon wanted to know what was wrong with intelligence on the radical movements, Edgar turned crimson. Then he abruptly ended the meeting.

Two weeks later Edgar angered the rest of the committee by adding his own footnotes to a text all the agencies had already approved. Then, at the signing session, he amazed everyone by reading the entire forty-three-page document out loud. After each page, as Edgar went around the table asking for comments, he would get Huston's name wrong. It was "Mr. Hoffman" or "Mr. Hutchinson," anything that began with H, but never the correct name. This meeting also ended in discord.

Huston's recommendations, approved by the President, called for more surveillance of "domestic security threats," the monitoring of internal communications used by American citizens, fewer restrictions on opening mail, more informants on college campuses, a full-scale resumption of black-bag jobs and the establishment of an umbrella group, linking all the agencies, to manage internal security.

That any president could have approved such a package, the Senate Intelligence Committee would one day declare, was "deeply troubling." Edgar also objected vociferously, but not on reasons of principle. "Hoover was for the Huston plan," Nixon said in 1988, "but only if *he* did it. He did not trust the CIA, he didn't trust anybody else. He was paranoiac, almost, about doing anything that would make him get in bad with the media. . . ."

Tom Huston fought a fierce rear-guard action. He sent a "Top Secret—Eyes Only" message to Haldeman, pointing out that Edgar was the only official raising objections:

> At some point, Hoover has to be told who is President. He has become totally unreasonable. . . . The Director of the FBI is paid to take risks where the security of the country is at stake. . . . If he gets his way it is going to look like he is more powerful than the President. . . .

Nothing happened. Richard Nixon never was one for confrontations. Edgar went off on vacation to La Jolla. Tom Huston was moved sideways, and eventually resigned. Yet, in a way no one could have understood fully at the time, the ground had shifted. Edgar had alienated men whose actions were to determine his own last days, the future of the FBI and the history of the nation.

William Sullivan, long one of Edgar's most trusted aides, emerged embittered from the Huston confrontation. Like several of his colleagues in the Domestic Intelligence Division and like Sam Papich, of CIA Liaison, Sullivan had long been grumbling about restrictions in the fight against domestic terrorism. He had also started playing a double game, simultaneously urging Huston on while letting Edgar think he was defending Bureau policy.

There was more than self-preservation at stake, for the men around Edgar had long been eyeing the succession. If Edgar was to be replaced from within, Sullivan and DeLoach were the two main contenders. According to DeLoach, "Sullivan would go to the extent of writing eight-page letters to Mr. Hoover saying effectively, 'You're getting old for your office. You deserve to be compared with Konrad Adenauer and Charles de Gaulle. Think of them as the greatest leaders in the world, and you are like them.' And Mr. Hoover would call me over and read me those damn letters, and I would almost regurgitate."

In the midst of the Huston furor, DeLoach decided there was no longer any point in waiting for Edgar to retire. He decided to take up a long-standing offer and go to work for one of the President's close friends, Donald Kendall, as a vice president of Pepsico. "I went in to see the old man," DeLoach recalled, "and we talked for two hours and forty-seven minutes, him doing ninety-eight percent of the talking. And when I got up to leave he said, 'If you decide to leave, come back and let me know.' I said, 'That's what I came in to tell you,' and he said, 'Well, I thought you were one who would never leave me.'"

In the two weeks that followed, Edgar refused to speak to DeLoach and cut him off from top-level mail. Then he did something that upset not only DeLoach, but Clyde and Miss Gandy, too. He appointed William Sullivan to step into DeLoach's place, to become Assistant to the Director, number three man in the Bureau, right behind the ailing Clyde. Not that it made any difference to Edgar. "I will never," he told DeLoach, "leave the directorship of the FBI."

"Whatever you say," Edgar insisted that day, "I think Sullivan's loyal to me." Sullivan had been loyal for the past thirty years. But now, with his newfound friends in the Nixon administration, with one eye on the directorship and the other on his deep differences with Edgar, he was not trustworthy at all. Sullivan became a Judas, waiting for the moment to betray.

At the White House, Huston was replaced by a young man named John Dean, and he soon reached the conclusion now shared by many in the Nixon hierarchy. "Hoover," he was to recall, had "lost his guts." Quietly, in the months that followed, Dean worked behind the scenes to further the domestic intelligence plans Edgar had snuffed out. Frustrated by Edgar's intransigence, the brash young men at the White House now began to work around him.

It was a trend that would lead everyone involved down a trail of treachery.

CHAPTER 33

> **"I know Nixon was afraid of him. . . . Knowledge is powerful, and he had knowledge of the most damaging kind."**
>
> *William Sullivan,*
> *former Assistant to the Director, 1975*

ON CERTAIN WINTRY MORNINGS IN 1970, WHILE EDGAR WAS still sleeping at his home on Thirtieth Place, a young man with a Pancho Villa moustache would park outside, walk rapidly down the alley beside the house and pick up the garbage. This was not, however, the garbageman. He was Charles Elliott, a rookie reporter for *Washington Post* columnist Jack Anderson.

An hour or so later, as Edgar climbed into his limousine to go to work, Elliott would be watching. During the day, when he knew his quarry was away, he stood on the doormat emblazoned with the initials J.E.H., beside the mailbox topped with a roosting eagle. He peered through the glass of the front door at the bronze life-size bust of Edgar, dominating a foyer crammed with mementos. Then he interrogated the neighbors.

The *Post* published the results of the snooping on New Year's 1971, as Edgar began the last full year of his life. "We decided," Anderson wrote, "to turn the tables on J. Edgar Hoover and conduct an FBI-style investigation into his private life." In fact, the garbage was less than revelatory. It produced some handwritten dinner menus, on stationery headed "From the Desk of the Director," one of them featuring crab bisque soup, spaghetti and meatballs with asparagus, peppermint ice cream and strawberries. There was evidence that the great man drank Black Label whiskey and Irish Mist, Coca-Cola and club soda, took Gelusil for indigestion and cleaned his teeth with Ultra Brite.

An enraged Edgar called Anderson, accurately enough on this occasion, "the top scavenger of all columnists." Elliott, who had actually removed the garbage, came home one evening to find two "FBI types" on his doorstep. They snapped photographs of him, then ran for their car. Elliott's roommate, who happened to be the son of an FBI agent, later made it clear Elliott was no longer welcome in the apartment.

Subsequent *Post* columns contained serious revelations. Anderson disclosed that Edgar's millionaire friends had long been picking up the tab for his summer vacations in California. He said Edgar had accepted more than a quarter of a million dollars in royalties from *Masters of Deceit* and two other books on Communism he had not even written. "This is an offense," Anderson pointed out, "that, if it had been committed by some other government official, the FBI might have been asked to investigate."

If those articles scared Edgar, a third must have shaken him to the core. "Competent sources," Anderson wrote, "told us that Hoover had consulted Dr. Marshall de G. Ruffin, the society shrink, about his nightmares." Anderson was perilously close to one of Edgar's most sensitive secrets, for it was Ruffin whom Edgar had consulted years earlier about his homosexuality.[1]

Edgar was rattled. He talked about Anderson with Attorney General Mitchell and, after the story about the psychiatrist, with Mitchell's deputy, Richard Kleindienst. "With these jackals," he said, "I wouldn't put anything past them. . . . I have been undecided whether to sue for libel or not." "If they spelled your name right," Kleindienst advised, "leave it alone."

Clyde Tolson, Anderson reported, was now too "feeble" to do his job properly. It was true. Clyde suffered another stroke that year, failed to recognize his own nephew when he visited him in the hospital and found it hard to follow conversation. To hide his faults when he did go to work, Clyde was henceforth smuggled out of his apartment by a back door. A discreet arrival at the office was easy—via the underground parking lot and an elevator that stopped near his office. Yet that year Edgar gave his friend a special bonus for excellent service. "Mr. Tolson," he wrote, "performs his tasks quickly and with outstanding accuracy. . . . His services are without parallel."

Edgar's own schedule, never as grueling as his publicity suggested, was now very light. "By the time I left in 1970," said Cartha DeLoach, "he would come in at nine on the dot, stay until eleven forty-five, go to lunch at the Mayflower and come back around one. Then he would close his doors until three and go right on home. I never could get him during that time. That was his workday, every day."

Out-of-town officials now found Edgar virtually inaccessible. "Months and months went by," said Neil Welch, "when he wasn't seeing anybody. It'd been regular as clockwork that he saw all Agents in Charge once a year. But for the last year and a half he cut them all off. We just couldn't get any information—just total silence. Nobody had seen him, nobody could see him. Asking how he was was like it must've been trying to find out how the Tsar was, in Russia. . . ."

What the public now saw was a cantankerous old man, issuing blasts of bigotry at his enemies—not least those unable to answer back, like Robert Kennedy and Martin Luther King. When former Attorney General Ramsey Clark criticized him in a book for his "self-centered concern for his own reputation," Edgar promptly proved him right. In a three-and-a-half-hour harangue to a reporter, he labeled Clark "a jellyfish and a softy."

At the Nixon White House, the unease grew. One reason for keeping Edgar on had been the fear of jettisoning a national institution, a man assumed to have overwhelming public support. That assumption was no longer valid. Fifty-one percent of those questioned in a Gallup poll thought Edgar should retire. "J. Edgar Hoover," said one

Washington columnist, "has spent too much time being a demigod." Lawrence Brooks, a ninety-year-old former judge who had observed Edgar in action since 1919, was moved to quote Abraham Lincoln. "We must," he said, "disenthrall ourselves."

In February 1971 Nixon's speech writer, future presidential contender Patrick Buchanan, advised him that Edgar was now a political liability and should be replaced as soon as possible.

> He has nowhere to go but down; and he is going down steadily. . . . With each of these new picayune battles in which he involves himself, his place is being sullied. . . . My strong recommendation would be to retire Hoover now in all the glory and esteem he has merited and deserved; and not let him—for his own sake and ours—wind up his career a dead lion being chewed over by the jackals of the Left.

The memo went to a president preoccupied. At home, Nixon was beset by the highest unemployment figures in a decade. Abroad, he was embroiled in the U.S.-supported Vietnamese invasion of Laos, a public relations disaster, soon to be followed by ugly revelations about the My Lai massacre. Vietnam had become an albatross for Nixon, as it had been for Johnson. While he applied himself to such problems, Edgar piled embarrassment on embarrassment.

In a time of fervent feminism, Edgar was still dithering over whether or not secretaries should be allowed to wear pants. "It is absolutely essential," he had written a year earlier, "that we conduct sufficient investigation to clearly establish the subversive ramifications of the Women's Liberation Movement." Now, in a blaze of publicity, he turned down two female applicants for the job of agent. They sued. Then he fired two female clerks for working with the peace movement in their spare time.

In March 1971, burglars broke into the FBI field office in Media, Pennsylvania, escaping with nearly a thousand documents—including some that exposed Bureau surveillance of students, radicals and blacks for the first time. One, at least, bore the telltale letters COINTELPRO, code word for the Bureau's most secret dirty-tricks operations. Styling themselves the Citizens' Commission to Investigate the FBI, the thieves sent copies of the documents to newsmen and politicians. They were never caught—and Edgar had to close down COINTELPRO.

Angry voices were raised in Congress. Senator George McGovern, gearing up to fight Nixon for the presidency in 1972, publicly protested Edgar's savage treatment of Agent Jack Shaw, forced to resign for venturing criticism of the FBI in a private letter.[2] "I cannot believe," McGovern said, "that we want our great nation to become a land where our personal privacy and our personal freedom are jeopardized by the abuse of power by a police official who seems to believe he is a law unto himself."

Behind the scenes, Edgar rehearsed the old routine. Agents trawled fruitlessly through McGovern's record seeking something, anything, to discredit the Senator. Edgar scribbled a furious note about "psychopathic liar McGovern." Clyde got twenty-one Bureau officials to fire off letters supporting Edgar, and sent one himself. The file copy bore a spiteful note: "The address of this letter has deliberately been phrased to avoid referring to McGovern as 'Honorable.'"

Senator Edmund Muskie, meanwhile, discovered the FBI had recently surveilled a series of countrywide rallies by environmentalists—including himself. Congressman Henry Reuss learned—from one of the documents stolen in Pennsylvania—that agents had investigated his daughter, a student at Swarthmore College. "The FBI," said Reuss, "has an important responsibility to investigate crime . . . not to compile dossiers on millions of Americans, congressmen's daughters or not, who are accused of no wrongdoing."

Such protests paled beside the outburst of House Majority Leader Hale Boggs, in April, when he made speeches accusing the FBI of wiretapping members of Congress and infiltrating the universities.[3] "When the FBI adopts the tactics of the Soviet Union and Hitler's Gestapo, then it is time—it is way past time, Mr. Speaker—that the present Director thereof no longer be the Director. . . . The time has come for the Attorney General of the United States to ask for the resignation of Mr. Hoover."

Edgar learned of Boggs' attack within minutes, from the congressional ticker. He had already seen an early copy of the latest *Life* magazine, its cover adorned with his own cartoon image, a disgruntled old man's face done up to look like a statue from the days of imperial Rome. The headline read: THE 47-YEAR REIGN OF J. EDGAR HOOVER, EMPEROR OF THE FBI, and the story suggested that reign should end. Edgar knew that *Newsweek,* too, was preparing a cover story. Its headline would be: HOOVER'S FBI: TIME FOR A CHANGE?

According to his memo of record, Edgar offered to resign that afternoon. He called Attorney General Mitchell, who was sunning himself at Key Biscayne, to break the news of the Boggs speech. "I wanted him to know and the President to know," Edgar wrote afterward, "if at any time my presence embarrasses the Administration—if it is felt I may be a burden or handicap to the re-election—I would be glad to step aside."

If Edgar did offer to resign, neither Mitchell nor anyone else in the Nixon administration remembered the momentous event.[4] For men who hoped to be rid of Edgar, moreover, he and the President responded oddly to the Boggs episode. Nixon said he thought Edgar was "taking a bad rap," and Mitchell demanded that Boggs "recant at once and apologize to a great and dedicated American." A few weeks later he defended Edgar aggressively when a reporter asked the Director if he planned to retire. "You're so far off base," Mitchell snapped, "that I'm going to belt you one. . . . Why, he's the most outstanding individual who has ever had anything to do with law enforcement."

Nixon and his officials had no choice but to grovel to Edgar. For he now possessed information that strengthened his hold over the President—a hold that, even in the clamor for his resignation, made dismissing him unacceptably risky.

Two years earlier, in the spring of 1969, Nixon and Henry Kissinger had been enraged by a series of news stories that in their view compromised national security, especially on Vietnam. They thought the stories had been leaked by trusted officials, and asked Edgar and the Attorney General how best to track down the culprits. As a result, the FBI began a wiretapping operation that targeted six of Kissinger's aides, eight other officials and four prominent journalists. The bugging continued until 1971.

It was Edgar, according to Kissinger, who proposed that course. In his memos for the record, however, he made it appear otherwise. "J. Edgar Hoover," Kissinger wrote in his memoirs, "invariably listed some official outside the FBI hierarchy as requesting each wiretap, even in cases where I had heard Hoover himself specifically recommend them to Nixon."

What Edgar had done was to lure the administration into danger, while—as Kissinger put it—"protecting his flanks." He saw to it that the taps were authorized by Attorney General Mitchell, in writing.

The fact that the targets included eminent correspondents—William Beecher and Hedrick Smith of *The New York Times,* Marvin Kalb of CBS and columnist Joseph Kraft—made the surveillance especially sensitive. The effort produced not an iota of evidence to identify the leaks, but a time bomb of potential trouble for the President.

The fact that Nixon had approved the bugging meant that the buck would stop with him if it were exposed. Such a revelation might wreck his chances of reelection in 1972. Edgar knew the President feared exposure, for Nixon ordered that summaries of the tapped conversations be delivered only to H. R. Haldeman in person, in sealed envelopes.

The man in charge of the wiretap operation was William

Sullivan, the highest-ranking official in the Bureau below Edgar and Clyde. He, too, knew that secrecy was essential. On Edgar's orders, copies were kept to a minimum, one for the White House and one for Edgar. "This is a White House operation," Edgar told Sullivan. "It's not an FBI operation and we're not going to put them in the FBI files. . . ." The transcripts were closely held, first in Edgar's office, then in Sullivan's.

Transcripts under Edgar's control were a potential weapon for use against Nixon. In April 1971, according to three sources, he used it—just days after Congressman Boggs' claim that the FBI had been tapping politicians. He did so, specifically, after Richard Kleindienst, the Deputy Attorney General, declared himself in favor of a congressional inquiry into Boggs' allegations.

If he was to be pilloried for illegal bugging, Edgar had no intention of suffering alone. He angrily called Kleindienst and rambled on at length. The Deputy Attorney General, weary of such calls, held the phone at arm's length— allowing a colleague, Assistant Attorney General Robert Mardian, to listen in. "You understand," Mardian heard Edgar say, "that if I am called upon to testify before the Congress, I will have to tell *all* that I know about this matter."

The threat was lost on Kleindienst, who knew nothing of the buggings Nixon had ordered. Mardian, who did, thought Edgar had "threatened the President of the United States." He reported the conversation to the White House—and, two years later, to Watergate investigators.

Edgar went further, according to a note by William Sullivan found among Mardian's private papers. On April 10, still furious that Kleindienst had welcomed an inquiry, the Director called the President himself at Camp David. Should he be called before Congress to discuss bugging, Edgar said, he "would have to lay bare the FBI's sensitive operations, and this would be very undesirable and damaging."

There was no inquiry into Boggs' allegations. In May, celebrating his forty-seventh year in office, Edgar said he had no thought of retiring. "I intend to remain as Director of the FBI as long as I can be of service to my country." On June 12 he appeared at the wedding of Nixon's daughter Tricia, smiling and waving for photographers as though all were well between him and the President.

All was not well, and events the next day made things immeasurably worse. That morning, a Sunday, *New York Times* readers across the country were regaled with seven pages of revelatory material on the escalation of the Vietnam War. These were the Pentagon Papers, secret documents supplied to the *Times*—as the FBI quickly established—by former government analyst Daniel Ellsberg. The *Times* continued to pump out the information, in spite of frantic government litigation. It was the most blatant leak of all, and it led Nixon an irreversible step closer to the follies of Watergate. For Edgar, it brought fateful clashes with both Nixon and William Sullivan.

These shifts were set in motion by a comedy of errors involving Louis Marx, the elderly millionaire who happened to be both Ellsberg's father-in-law and a long-standing friend of Edgar's. Nixon, convinced Ellsberg was part of a Communist conspiracy, wanted every scrap of information on the man. He was enraged to hear that, because Marx was a friend, Edgar had ordered agents not to question him.

Edgar had issued such an order, and for the very reason reported to Nixon, that he was "sorry for Louis." Ironically, however, the order was not carried out. Charles Brennan, the head of Domestic Intelligence at the FBI, is said to have misread Edgar's scribbled "No H" as "OK H." By the time he realized his mistake, Marx had been interviewed. Edgar flew into a tantrum and ordered Brennan demoted and transferred to Ohio. This in turn upset William Sullivan, Brennan's superior and longtime friend, triggering extraordinary events.

Sullivan had reached boiling point. Given free rein to run the COINTELPRO program, he had put up with Edgar's ways like everyone else. Now he was frustrated, by Edgar's stonewalling over domestic intelligence, and by the ending of COINTELPRO. He was angry, too, about Edgar's latest empire building abroad. This included a new office in Bern, Switzerland, which seemed to exist mainly to provide hospitality to Edgar's cronies during their travels, and a totally useless one in La Paz, Bolivia. Edgar seemed to think that, since Cuban Communist Che Guevara had been killed in Bolivia, it must be a useful place for the FBI to be.

Unlike submissive colleagues, Sullivan had argued openly with Edgar on such matters. He had had the temerity to say publicly that race riots and student unrest should not be blamed on the Communist Party. Edgar had been furious. Now there was Edgar's hysterical treatment of Charles Brennan, an outstanding agent, over the Louis Marx misunderstanding.

Losing patience, Sullivan began covert contacts with Nixon officials who shared his feelings, and especially with Assistant Attorney General Mardian. Mardian, who knew the Director had called him "a goddamned Lebanese Jew," thought Edgar "garrulous, full of wind. Mean, like a mean old dog."

To hammer home the criticism, Sullivan supplied Mardian with sheaves of Edgar's internal correspondence. Mardian sent some of it to John Mitchell and filed the rest nervously in a folder marked "Jones." The belief that sooner or later Edgar would find out about everything had spread beyond the FBI.

At the height of the Pentagon Papers furor, Sullivan shared with Mardian his conviction that Edgar was "not of sound mind." "He told me," Mardian recalled, "that he had in his possession documents that were 'out of channel,' wiretap information. He said Hoover had used such information against previous Presidents and was liable to use these documents to blackmail Nixon. As long as he had those files, Nixon could not relieve him."

Sullivan was referring to the Bureau copies of Nixon's taps on government officials and newsmen, now held under tight security in his office. Mardian passed on the blackmail warning, and the President—then in California—took it in deadly earnest. Mardian was ordered to fly to the Western White House at once, by Air Force jet, for consultations.

John Ehrlichman's handwritten notes of the meeting reflect the mood of urgency. "OK . . . Obtain and destroy all logs. . . . Tell Hoover to destroy . . . Haig request the FBI (Sullivan) to destroy all special coverage."

In Washington, Sullivan handed over two battered satchels containing the wiretap summaries. Mardian placed them in a locked vault, then waited for further instructions from the White House.

At the FBI, Edgar and Sullivan were at loggerheads. On August 28, after discussions with twenty-two colleagues, Sullivan sent Edgar a long letter laying out their differences. "I would like to convince you," he wrote, "that those of us who disagree with you are trying to help you and not hurt you. . . . This letter will probably anger you. In view of your absolute power you can fire me . . . or in some other way work out your displeasure with me. So be it. . . ."

Edgar began the ensuing meeting with Sullivan with a harangue. He said he had given the matter "a good deal of prayer." Then he began to sputter and stammer. When Sullivan advised him to retire, he said he would not. On the contrary, it was Sullivan who had to go. He was told to take leave due to him and apply for retirement.

Not knowing that the Nixon wiretap transcripts had been passed to Mardian, Edgar ordered other aides to look for them in Sullivan's office while he was at home in New Hampshire. The aides searched every file cabinet and drawer and found nothing. When Sullivan returned, he refused to say what had become of the transcripts. "If you want to know more," he said curtly, "you'll have to talk to the Attorney General."

On October 1, pointedly leaving behind only his autographed photograph of the Director, Sullivan left the FBI for good. Mark Felt, who replaced him as Edgar's key assistant, briefed Edgar on the fruitless hunt for the wiretap records. Uncharacteristically, Edgar was lost for words. Then he shook his head. "The greatest mistake I ever made," he murmured, "was to promote Sullivan." He stood there, lost in thought, as Felt slipped quietly from the room.

Months later, when Edgar was dead and when the full significance of the wiretaps emerged—along with so many other Nixonian secrets—Felt wondered about the Director's silence. "It is very strange," he mused, "that Hoover did not explain the entire situation to me. . . . He knew the whole story."

CHAPTER 34

"Anyone who opposes us, we'll destroy. As a matter of fact, anyone who doesn't support us we'll destroy."

Egil Krogh, aide to President Nixon, 1971

ON OCTOBER 3, 1971, A SUNDAY, ASSISTANT ATTORNEY GENERAL Mardian asked John Ehrlichman to come and see him at home. The man who had custody of the wiretap transcripts was panicking.

"Mardian was very afraid," Ehrlichman recalled, "not only of the integrity of the files but also of his own personal safety. He felt he was being surveilled by Hoover, that it was only a matter of time before Hoover caused agents of the FBI to break into his office vault and recover the records. . . ."

At a meeting in the Oval Office that week, Ehrlichman and Attorney General Mitchell asked the President for guidance on what to do with the transcripts. What they said emerged only in 1991, on newly released tape recordings:

Mitchell: Hoover is tearing the place up over there trying to get at them. The question is, should we get them out of Mardian's office before Hoover blows the safe . . . and bring them over here?

Ehrlichman: My impression from talking with Mardian is that Hoover feels very insecure without having his own copy of those things. Because, of course, that gives him leverage with Mitchell and with you.

Nixon: Yeah.

Ehrlichman: Because they're illegal. Now he doesn't have any copies and he has agents all over this town interrogating people, trying to find out where they are. He's got Mardian's building under surveillance.

Nixon: Now, why the hell didn't he have a copy, too?

Ehrlichman: If he does, he'll beat you over the head with it.

Nixon: Oh . . . you've gotta get them out of there.

Mitchell: Hoover won't come and talk to me about it. He's just got his Gestapo all over the place.

Nixon: Yeah . . . just say [to Mardian] that we want to see them. Put them in a special safe.

As Nixon ordered, so it was done. The telltale wiretap evidence was moved from Mardian's office to a secure White House strongbox. Sullivan, moreover, told the President's men that, before leaving, he had ordered the Washington field office to destroy its file on the compromising wiretap operation.

Nixon's aides had been discussing how to remove Edgar from office for nearly a year. Once it had seemed politically risky to dump him, because he seemed too popular in the country. Now there were polls that showed the enthusiasm had waned, and a constant tattoo of criticism in the press.

Edgar made a speech about "journalistic prostitutes" and issued orders that no one in the Bureau was to speak, ever, with *The Washington Post, The New York Times,* the *Los Angeles Times,* CBS or NBC. Such tantrums, though, served only to convince White House advisers that the Director had become an embarrassing liability.

As early as January, the President himself had said Edgar was "a question." Deputy Attorney General Kleindienst now made a habit of holding the phone away from his ear when Edgar called, grinning hugely and making circular motions in the air. "That man has been out of his mind for three years," he told Sullivan after one such call. "How much longer do we have to put up with him?"

For all his public support of Edgar, Attorney General Mitchell assured colleagues privately that "we'll get rid of him soon." According to Henry Kissinger, Nixon himself was "determined to get rid of Hoover at the earliest opportunity."

One morning shortly before Sullivan's showdown with Edgar, Mardian had called several senior FBI officials, including Sullivan, into his office at the Justice Department. The atmosphere was conspiratorial. At a quarter to ten Mardian pointed to the clock. "At ten A.M.," he said, "our problem with Hoover will be solved. It will all be over. The President has asked Hoover to see him at the White House at ten, and he's going to ask Hoover to resign."

The call never came. Anticipation turned to doubt, doubt to frustration, and the men drifted disconsolately away. They soon learned that, back in his office after seeing Nixon, Edgar was triumphantly dictating memos. Far from firing him, the President had cleared Edgar to open a string of new FBI offices around the world, an expansion opposed by the Attorney General, the Secretary of State and several of the Director's own aides.

In the privacy of his office, Mardian called the White House to find out what had happened. "Nothing happened," Ehrlichman told him irritably. "Nothing. Nixon couldn't pull the string. . . . He got cold feet."

"I'm willing to fight him, but I don't," the President said lamely at the Oval Office meeting on October 8, 1971. "We've got to avoid the situation where he could leave with a blast. . . . I sorta, I went all around with him. . . . There are some problems. If I fire Hoover, if you think we've got an uprising and a riot now . . . If he does go, he's got to go of his own volition. . . ."

Two weeks later, Ehrlichman handed the President a special report on Edgar and the FBI. Further delay, it warned, could be disastrous:

> The concern with image, the cultism, has finally taken its toll. Virtually any genuine innovation or imaginative approach is stifled. . . . Morale of FBI agents in the field has deteriorated badly. . . . All clandestine activities have been terminated. Liaison with the intelligence

community has been disrupted and key men forced out. . . . Hoover has reportedly threatened the President. . . . Years of intense adulation have inured Hoover to self-doubt. He remains realistic, however, and on June 30 his most trusted confidant, Clyde Tolson, stated to a reliable source, "Hoover knows that, no matter who wins in '72, he's through."

Sullivan has been "keeping book" on Hoover for some time. He is a skilled writer. His book could be devastating should he choose to expose such matters as the supervisor who handled Hoover's stock portfolio and tax matters; the painting of Hoover's house by the FBI Exhibits Section; the ghostwriting of Hoover's books by FBI employees; the rewriting of FBI history and the "donation" by "admiring" facility owners of accommodations and services which are often in fact underwritten by employee contributions. . . . The situation was probably best stated by Alfred Tennyson in *The Idylls of the King:*

> The old order changeth, yielding place to new;
> And God fulfils himself in many ways,
> Lest one good custom should corrupt the world.

The report recommended that Edgar retire before the end of 1971, and Nixon agreed wholeheartedly. "Hoover," he told colleagues, "has to realize that he can't stay forever . . . he's too old." "I guess, I guess . . . I think I could get him to resign, if I put it to him directly that without it he's going to be hurt politically. . . . But I want this closely held—it's just got to be."

This time the operation was carefully planned, starting with a phone call from John Mitchell to Edgar's former aide Cartha DeLoach. "I walked into the Attorney General's office," DeLoach recalled, "and he told me to close the door. Then right out of a clear blue sky he told me, 'We've got to get rid of Hoover, but we don't want him kicking over the traces. Can you suggest a way we might be able to do it without him saying or doing anything?' I said, 'Well, if you're going to do it, you've got to allow him to save face. Let him keep his bulletproof car and his chauffeur. That's a mark of prestige, and he likes that. Let him keep Helen Gandy as his secretary, because she does ordering of groceries for him and paying of bills, all the things he's never had to do himself. Make him Director Emeritus, or Ambassador of Internal Security. And have the President call him once in a while, to ask for counsel and advice. . . .'"

At the White House, a nervous Nixon worked out a slick compromise. Instead of firing Edgar abruptly he would tell him he could stay until the 1972 election. That way, the FBI would not become a political football during the campaign. To defuse the critics, however, the retirement plan would be announced at once. And, to preserve Edgar's dignity, he would be allowed to do it himself.

With Ehrlichman taking notes, Nixon rehearsed the little speech he intended to make, still preserved in the archives. "Edgar," it ran. "As you can imagine I've been giving your situation a great deal of thought. I am absolutely delighted that you have weathered the attacks upon you and the Bureau so well. . . . Obviously, If I am reelected, your replacement would be someone who would carry on your tradition. . . . I sincerely think this is in our mutual best interests. . . ."

And so on, in that vein. Nixon may have tried this ploy in late December, when Edgar arrived for a talk at the President's home in Key Biscayne. Yet Edgar stayed on for dinner on the terrace afterward, stone crabs and Grand Marnier soufflé, washed down with red wine.

If Nixon flinched from confrontation that night, he may have considered trying again at New Year's, when he asked Edgar to fly back to Washington with him on Air Force One. "The President," Edgar told a colleague before the flight, "wants to talk to me about something."

Yet again, however, Nixon apparently failed to read his script. The White House let it be known that the flight was a sign of presidential favor to celebrate Edgar's seventy-seventh birthday, and Nixon presented him with a cake.

Far from talk of dismissal, the press now reported that

Nixon "wants Hoover to remain in office." In the last major interview of his life, granted before the Florida trip, Edgar declared himself determined to carry on. "Many of our great artists and composers," he said, "did their best work in their eighties. They were judged on performance, not age. . . . Look at Bernard Baruch; he was brilliant in his nineties—and Herbert Hoover and Douglas MacArthur in their eighties. That is my policy. . . ." Attorney General Mitchell, who had privately been recommending Edgar's retirement for months, agreed. Talk about replacing Edgar, he said, was "spurious speculation."

The President of the United States had now gone into at least two meetings assuring his aides he was about to give Edgar his marching orders. Edgar had emerged unscathed, and Nixon's advisers did not know why.

The first time, in the fall, John Ehrlichman had waited for a few hours, then asked Haldeman what had happened. The President, Haldeman said, was refusing to discuss the matter. Twenty-four hours later Ehrlichman asked again. "Don't ask," the Chief of Staff replied. "He doesn't want to talk about it." Later, Haldeman told Ehrlichman to forget the breakfast had ever taken place.

Many months later, after Edgar's death, Nixon would confide a little in Ehrlichman. "The meeting was a total strikeout," he said. "He told me I'd have to force him out." "It was my conclusion," the President was to write in his memoirs, "that Hoover's resignation before the election would raise more problems than it would solve."

Yet Nixon denies to this day that Edgar had a hold on him. "Hoover," he said in 1988, "never gave any indication to me of blackmail." Specifically, Nixon denied that Edgar threatened to disclose his wiretapping of newsmen. He was less coy at the time with his colleague Henry Kissinger. "Nixon thought," Kissinger recalled, "Hoover was quite capable of using the knowledge he acquired as part of his investigations to blackmail the President."

Contrary to what Nixon imagined at first, the threat had not evaporated when Sullivan handed over the FBI copies of the wiretap transcripts to Assistant Attorney General

Mardian. When Mardian checked the list, he discovered some of the transcripts were missing. They had been retained, all along, by Edgar.

As of New Year's Day 1972, then, the President still had cause to fear Edgar over the taps. Not least as he prepared for his groundbreaking visit to China—there was the continuing embarrassment of his woman friend from Hong Kong. And there was now something else—something that had to be hidden at all costs.

"We may have on our hands here," Nixon had told Ehrlichman, "a man who will pull down the temple with him, including me. . . ."

Six months earlier, Nixon had lost his temper—and fashioned a new trap for himself. In spite of intense legal efforts, he had failed to prevent *The New York Times* from continuing to publish the Pentagon Papers. He was afraid future installments might reflect badly on him, that the man who had leaked the Papers—Daniel Ellsberg—was part of some sinister radical conspiracy. The President was angry at stories that Edgar was, as Nixon put it in his memoirs, "dragging his feet" on the Ellsberg investigation. "If the FBI was not going to pursue the case," he decided, "then we would have to do it ourselves."

Nixon had railed about this in late June 1971, seated in the Oval Office at the mahogany desk that had once been Woodrow Wilson's. With him was his aide Charles Colson. "I don't give a damn how it is done," Colson recalls the President saying, "do whatever has to be done to stop these leaks and prevent further unauthorized disclosures; I don't want to be told why it can't be done. . . . I want to know who is behind this. . . . I want results. I want it done, whatever the cost."

They did do it, and the cost, when it all came out two years later, would be monstrous. Nixon's frustration over Edgar's failings, or what the President saw as failings, was the first step on the road that led to the loss of his presidency.

Two young men, Egil Krogh and David Young, were installed in a warren of underground offices in the Executive Office Building next to the White House. They had a conference room, a special alarm system, a three-way combination safe and "sterile" phones. And since their job was to plug leaks, Young indulged a whimsical impulse. He fixed a sign on the door that read "Mr. Young—Plumber." As Plumbers they will always be remembered.

The cast of characters is now well known. The chain of command went from Nixon to Ehrlichman to Krogh and Young, with Colson and the President's Counsel, John Dean, putting in their nickel's worth. In the field, assigned to do the White House's dirty work, were Howard Hunt and Gordon Liddy. Hunt was a fifty-two-year-old career CIA officer who had, technically, retired from the Agency and gone free-lance. Liddy had served as an Assistant District Attorney in New York, then as a special assistant in the Nixon Treasury Department, since leaving the FBI in 1962.

Liddy was obsessed, by his own account, with guns, violence and the elemental power of the human will. He liked to discuss the more exotic ways of killing, and reportedly claimed he had killed a man while serving in the FBI. A former FBI official described Liddy as both "wild man" and "superklutz," qualities that made him well suited for work in the Nixon White House in 1971. Krogh took him on board, at $26,000 a year, to coordinate field operations for the President's Plumbers. Liddy had entered a world of conspiracies.

His predecessor, John Caulfield, had worked on such projects as setting up an apartment rigged with bugging devices, for the seduction of a woman who might provide seamy information on Senator Edward Kennedy. Charles Colson had recently urged Caulfield to set fire to the Brookings Institution, as a cover for the theft of documents related to the Ellsberg case.

While that scheme was abandoned, an equally crazy one was not. On the night of September 4, 1971, under the command of Liddy and Hunt, three Cuban exiles broke into the Los Angeles office of Daniel Ellsberg's psychiatrist. His files, the Plumbers hoped, would produce evidence of conspiracy in the Pentagon Papers case along with sex material with which to smear Ellsberg. According to Ehrlichman, the President knew of the planned break-in in advance, as he had known of the plot to firebomb the Brookings Institution.

The operation against Ellsberg failed. The Cuban hired hands ransacked the psychiatrist's records only to emerge empty-handed. Their fruitless crime would one day become a major part of the Watergate scandal and lead to jail sentences for almost everyone involved. In the fall of 1971, however, it remained a dark secret. Any outsider who learned it would gain extraordinary power over the President. And Edgar had the secret.

He knew because, in his anger about Edgar's "foot-dragging" over Ellsberg, Nixon had told him. "It was obvious," Ehrlichman told the Senate Watergate Committee, "that the President had, at Mr. Krogh's request, shaken up the Director . . . told the Director that he was having to resort to sending two people out there from the White House. . . ."

Quite apart from what Nixon volunteered, Edgar may have known presidential secrets thanks to electronic surveillance. In August 1970, according to reporter Tad Szulc, a specialist on intelligence matters, the Secret Service had discovered a minute bugging device concealed in the wall of the Oval Office. It had been planted there during routine repainting by an interior decorator employed by the General Services Administration. "My sources believed it was Hoover's operation," Szulc said recently. "And if you are getting that kind of seed information you have a total mastery of what's going on in the mind of the President."

Edgar may not have needed a bug to learn about some of the President's most secret conversations, including those about himself. He reportedly had access to the tapes Nixon himself made for posterity, the recordings we now know as the Watergate Tapes. For although the taping system had been installed by the Secret Service, it was reportedly insecure from the moment of its inception in early 1971.

In 1977, shortly before his death, William Sullivan talked with the film producer Larry Cohen, then embarking on a movie about Edgar's life. "He told me," said Cohen, "that Hoover was aware Nixon was taping his own conversations. He knew about it because several of the Secret Service agents involved were former FBI agents. He said FBI officials knew where the tapes were kept—room 175½ of the Executive Office Building, a place other people had access to. Hoover aides had been able to go in there on more than one occasion and borrow tapes, and even played them at parties—particularly tapes where Nixon made embarrassing faux pas. They would play them and people would laugh, and then they'd put the tapes back again. It was a slipshod affair; it wasn't like they were locked up in a safe or anything. How Nixon could've allowed this to happen is beyond our ken. I guess he thought he was immune."

In fact, Nixon became more vulnerable with every passing month. If, as Ehrlichman testified, he confided in Edgar about the burglary of Ellsberg's psychiatrist, he presumably did so on the assumption Edgar would never tell. Yet in October 1971 the President did something guaranteed to infuriate Edgar, should he find out.

It was then that, as reported earlier, Nixon approved the internal White House report on Edgar's incompetence, urging that Edgar be eased out as soon as possible. Its author was Gordon Liddy, who was still in regular contact with former FBI colleagues. Within weeks, moreover, Liddy became general counsel for CREEP (the Committee to Re-elect the President) and there worked alongside another former FBI—and CIA—agent, James McCord. McCord, unlike most of Nixon's henchmen, thought Edgar "the finest law enforcement officer the world has ever seen."

Then there was Fred LaRue, a White House political operative also about to join CREEP. He was the son of Ike LaRue, an oilman friend of Clint Murchison's who had been friendly with Edgar at the Del Charro. John Caulfield, up to his neck in White House dirty tricks, was close to Joseph Woods, former FBI agent and brother of the President's secretary, Rose Mary. Woods was intensely loyal to Edgar.

With potential sources like that, and with his other intelligence pipelines out of the White House, it is likely that Edgar knew a great deal about the plotting against him. By New Year's 1972, in spite of the public show of trust, the trip with the President on Air Force One, the birthday cake and the smiles, Edgar's relations with Nixon were threadbare.

During a delay before the flight that day, Edgar spent forty-five minutes in the back of a limousine talking gloomily with his Special Agent in Charge in Miami, Kenneth Whittaker. "He was upset," Whittaker recalled. "He told me about his problems with Sullivan, and he talked about Nixon. He wasn't high on Nixon. 'Let me tell you, Whittaker,' he said, 'Pat Nixon would make a better president than him.' It was the last time I saw Mr. Hoover alive."

Back in Washington, Edgar took a remarkable step. He asked Andrew Tully, a journalist he trusted, to join him for lunch in his private dining room. "I have some things to say," he told Tully, "but I don't want you to publish it until after I'm dead." Tully agreed, asked one question, then sat back and listened. The question was: "Is the President pressuring you to retire?"

"Not anymore he's not," Edgar replied. "I put the kibosh on those jaspers who want to get rid of me. . . . The President asked me what thoughts I had about retirement and I said none, then I told him why. I told him he needed me around to protect him from those people around him. Some of those guys don't know a goddamned thing about due process of law. They think they can get away with murder. I told the President I hoped I'd live long enough to keep those people from getting him into bad trouble."

Edgar was scathing about Nixon's advisers. "John Mitchell," he said, "he's never even been in a courtroom. He's not equipped to be Attorney General. Ehrlichman, Haldeman and [Ron] Ziegler [Nixon's press spokesman] . . . they don't know anything except how to sell advertising. That counsel, Dean—he doesn't know law. I ignore the son of a bitch."

Edgar spoke of men in "the President's kindergarten" who kept "coming up with half-baked schemes." He told how he had squashed the 1970 White House plan for a coordinated campaign against internal unrest. Then, with chilling prescience, he effectively predicted the Watergate disaster. "The President," he said, "is a good man. He's a patriot. But he listens to some wrong people. By God, he's got some former CIA men working for him that I'd kick out of my office. Someday that bunch will serve him up a fine mess."

Whether or not Edgar still had any protective feelings toward Nixon, they were not reciprocated. "The hatr d of Hoover by Nixon and his staff," said James McCord, "appeared to be becoming intense. . . . My own experience at CREEP verified this. . . . It was an open secret there that Nixon was out to get Hoover . . . by any means he possibly could."

Within days of giving his secret interview to Tully, Edgar provoked the administration even further. A year earlier, against Edgar's wishes, Attorney General Mitchell had approved secret FBI surveillance of a foreign embassy that the CIA regarded as essential. On February 3, 1972, a report reveals:

> Hoover had advised that he was to testify in Congress and would advise the Congress that the installation in the [Chilean mission] was initiated at CIA request.

Edgar was threatening to expose domestic snooping, snooping the administration wanted continued. It fit the scenario painted by McCord, then regularly in touch with his contacts at the CIA and the FBI. "Nixon," he said, "planned to fire Hoover. Hoover learned of it and resolved that he would have to go to Congress with the facts of Nixon's wiretapping of the news media, the National Security Council staff and of Ellsberg. This Nixon feared."

The coverage Edgar objected to was discontinued. Edgar made no reference to it in his routine appearance before Congress' Appropriations Committee, on March 2, 1972. Already, though, he was about to cross Nixon again. In late February, the columnist Jack Anderson had shaken the government with a story claiming the Republicans had accepted a huge cash donation from International Telephone and Telegraph as a payoff for government intervention in an antitrust suit against the company. The story was based on a memo apparently written by Dita Beard, an ITT lobbyist, and authenticated by Anderson before publication. Now, knowing Edgar detested Anderson, Nixon's counsel John Dean went to see the Director. His mission— to have the Bureau prove the Beard memorandum was a forgery.

"Hoover," Dean recalled, "was poised at the end of a long, polished conference table, waiting for me as if I were there to photograph him." Dean noticed Edgar was wearing perfume, then launched into his request. Edgar, all sweetness and light, agreed that Anderson, the journalist who had organized the raid on his garbage, was "the lowest form of human being to walk the earth . . . a muckraker who lies, steals . . . he'll go lower than dog shit for a story." Certainly, he said, he would be happy to have the Bureau Laboratory examine the Beard memorandum.

A confident Dean concluded that the memo, so compromising to the government, would soon be exposed as a fake. He was wrong. Far from demolishing the document, the Bureau report concluded it was probably genuine. When Dean called Edgar's office to bring pressure, Edgar exploded. "Call Dean right back," an aide remembers him saying. "Tell him I said for him to go jump in the lake! . . . This request is completely improper."

Improper it was, but the President himself tried to intervene—by penning a personal note to Edgar. Still the Director refused to budge. Nixon, Colson told colleagues, was angrier than he had ever seen him. There was renewed talk of firing the Director, or at least of shifting him to a grand-sounding new post that carried no power.

At the height of the row, the President was embarrassed by a damning exposé in *Life* magazine. It spelled out, in detail, how the White House had intervened to help the banker Arnholt Smith, one of Nixon's best friends, and a bookmaker called John Alessio, another Nixon backer, to shake off corruption and tax charges. Edgar, *Life* reported, had used his personal influence to help defeat the White House moves and to see that Alessio faced trial. It was this, McCord believed from his White House contacts, that had really set Nixon at Edgar's throat. And now it was all coming out.

CHAPTER 35

"Nixon was determined to get rid of Hoover at the earliest opportunity after the 1972 election, and he wanted to supply no hostages that might impede the process."

Henry Kissinger,
former National Security Adviser

IN LATE MARCH 1972, GORDON LIDDY SAT CLOSETED WITH THE President's adviser Charles Colson. When they finished talking, Colson picked up the phone. "Gordon Liddy," he told CREEP organizer Jeb Magruder, "can't get a decision out of you people on an intelligence program. I don't want to get into a debate of the merits. . . . Let's get on with it."

The program at issue was the project code-named "Gemstone" and it was about to be approved. This was Liddy's brainchild, his response to a high-level White House request. Two months earlier, in the office of the Attorney General of the United States, he had explained his concept to John Mitchell, John Dean and Magruder.

Gemstone, Liddy suggested, should include electronic surveillance of the Democratic National Convention, including a chase plane to intercept radio-telephone communications; break-ins to obtain and photograph documents; kidnapping teams to capture radical leaders and smuggle them, drugged, to a safe house in Mexico; mugging squads to beat up demonstrators; prostitutes to lure Democratic politicians to a specially rigged yacht, there to be filmed as they had sex; and sabotage of the air-conditioning in the Convention hall. It was all to cost around $1 million.

Liddy's superiors did not fire him out of hand for

proposing such a scheme. They merely sent him back to the drawing board, with orders to "tone the plan down a little." The next version of Gemstone, which concentrated on surveillance, wiretapping and surreptitious photography, was better received. Several targets were discussed, one of them the office of the Democratic National Committee. Though there would be no go-ahead until April, the die had been cast for the break-ins at the Watergate.

In the weeks that followed, Liddy and Howard Hunt ran around the country pursuing harebrained schemes. They flew to Los Angeles with orders to snatch damaging documents that would "blow [Democratic hopeful Senator] Muskie out of the water." The plan aborted. Sporting a red wig, Hunt rushed to Colorado to persuade ITT lobbyist Dita Beard to deny authorship of the memo that, according to columnist Jack Anderson, proved Republican corruption. Then, around March 24, Hunt and Liddy had lunch at the Hay Adams Hotel, just across the street from the White House, with a former CIA doctor. Their mission this time was an operation to "stop" Anderson—perhaps by killing him.

The columnist had aroused the fury of the Nixon administration time after time, publishing more than seventy articles based on intelligence sources. He was already, illegally, under CIA surveillance. Hunt, himself a former CIA officer reported to have been involved in plots to assassinate foreign leaders, told Liddy that Anderson had finally gone too far. As a result of one of his columns, he asserted, a key U.S. intelligence source abroad had been fatally exposed.

Hunt later told associates that the order to kill Anderson came from a "senior White House official." Liddy claimed the idea as his own. The man said to have admitted to one past killing had—by his own account—recently acquired a CIA 9mm parabellum pistol, "for use in the event Bud Krogh or other of my White House superiors tasked me with an assassination."

In the paneled luxury of the Hay Adams dining room, Hunt, Liddy and the "retired" CIA physician discussed the possibilities. Should Anderson be killed in a staged car accident? Should he become the victim of a fatal mugging? Or should they try "Aspirin Roulette" and plant poison pills in his medicine cabinet?

The CIA had been hatching such plans for years. Its Technical Services Division had produced botulism-injected cigarettes to kill President Nasser of Egypt, a poisoned handkerchief to do away with General Kassem of Iraq, a chemical to be smeared on the toothbrush of Congolese Prime Minister Lumumba, gelatine capsules and a booby-trapped ballpoint pen to murder Cuba's Fidel Castro. While none of these plots came to fruition, governmental murder by poison was an accepted concept in the secret world.[1]

"I was willing to obey an order to kill Jack Anderson," Liddy wrote later, ". . . this killing would not be retributive but preventive." Whichever method was to be used, he and Hunt decided the plot should include exiled Cubans—as had the break-in at Ellsberg's psychiatrist's office and as would the Watergate operation. Liddy was to be disappointed. After arranging to obtain a poison that would leave no traces, Hunt was told the plan to kill the columnist had been called off. The pair resumed work on the nefarious schemes that would lead to Watergate.

Some believe Watergate was only the tip of the iceberg. During the Nixon administration, unidentified intruders invaded the homes and offices of numerous people whom the administration considered to be its "enemies." There were at least a hundred such break-ins, all apparently politically motivated, all unsolved. Radicals and foreign diplomats deemed to be subversive were regular targets. But so were respected reporters. There was a break-in at the home of CBS White House correspondent Dan Rather in April 1972, and later at the office of his colleague Marvin Kalb. Tad Szulc, a thorn in the Nixonian flank, was raided, too. So were prominent politicians—Democratic Party Treasurer Robert Strauss in 1972, Senator Lowell Weicker the following year. And there may have been an even more famous victim—J. Edgar Hoover.

Some of the victims of the mysterious break-ins possessed documents thought to be compromising to the Nixon regime. Edgar, more than any other potential target, had knowledge of a whole range of sins, and an unknown quantity of documentary proof.

A year after Watergate, Mark Frazier, a young reporter working in Washington, was to pick up an intriguing lead. Three sources, he learned, had given affidavits to the Senate Watergate Committee referring to two break-in operations at Edgar's home in Rock Creek Park. They were, allegedly, "directed by Gordon Liddy."

In the welter of news arising from Watergate, Frazier was unable to get the story published in a Washington paper. Instead, it ran in a university publication, *The Harvard Crimson*. The article drew on interviews with a source on the Watergate Committee, with a "past associate of Howard Hunt" and with Felipe DeDiego, a Cuban who worked with Hunt and Liddy on both the raid against Ellsberg's psychiatrist and the first of the two Watergate raids.

Edgar had been the target of two operations, according to these sources. A first break-in attempt, in "late winter of 1972," was designed to "retrieve documents that were thought to be used as potential blackmail against the White House." It failed, but was followed by a second, successful break-in. "This time," Frazier reported, "whether through misunderstanding or design, a poison of the thiophosphate genre was placed on Hoover's personal toilet articles."

Thiophosphate is a compound used in insecticides, highly toxic to human beings if taken orally, inhaled or absorbed through the pores of the skin. Ingestion can result in a fatal heart seizure and can be detected only if an autopsy is performed within hours of death.

Former staff members of both the Watergate Committee and the Special Prosecution Force remember being told of operations against Edgar's house. The files of the Prosecution Force reflect an inquiry to the FBI about "possible burglaries" at his home. Former Force attorney Nathaniel Akerman remembers the matter as "something that certainly didn't fall into the nut category."[2]

481

Gordon Liddy today denies knowledge of any break-in at Edgar's house. Hunt, contacted in Mexico, said curtly it was "a matter of total disinterest to me." Nixon's former Chief of Staff, Haldeman, however, accepted that something of the kind may have happened. "I have to concede the possibility," he said. "I think Nixon was capable at the time of saying to Colson, 'I want this done. I don't want any arguments about it. I don't want you to talk to Haldeman because he'll just say, Don't do it. Just go ahead and get it done. . . .'"

Watergate burglar Felipe DeDiego, who today claims ignorance of the Hoover break-ins, was interviewed by Frazier twice in 1973. At first he said he knew about the operation and hoped soon to be able "to talk about everything." Then, questioned again, he withdrew his comments. At home in Florida, however, he told Dade County State's Attorney Richard Gerstein that he had information on "other burglaries of a political nature."[3]

Another of the Watergate burglars, Frank Sturgis, said in 1988 that DeDiego told him about the Hoover break-ins immediately after Edgar's death. "Felipe told me about it," he said. "I suspected the CIA was behind it. I told him, 'I guess our friends probably wanted to go over there and see what kind of documents Hoover had stashed away.' Felipe laughed and said, 'That's dangerous. It's dangerous. . . .' And we didn't talk about it anymore."

Sturgis admitted that the burglars were active in Washington earlier than emerged from the official Watergate investigation. Asked if he himself was involved in the Hoover break-ins, he hedged. "I'm not saying yes to my involvement. Let me say 'no' to that. It opens up a can of worms."

One day in early April 1972, Edgar had his usual lunch at his usual spot—grapefruit and cottage cheese salad in a dim corner of Washington's Mayflower Hotel. With him were Clyde and Thomas Webb, the trusted attorney and FBI veteran whom Edgar had long ago recommended to serve Clint Murchison. They listened, taken aback, as Edgar talked about his struggles with President Nixon.

Edgar was tired now. Weeks earlier, when he had told reporter Andrew Tully about Nixon's "kindergarten," he had paused and closed his eyes. "I'm getting old," he sighed. "I know that. Hell, even I can't live forever."

Sometime earlier, Washington plastic surgeon Gordon Bell had surgically removed a small skin cancer from Edgar's face. "He was a big baby," Dr. Bell's widow recalled, "a classic hypochondriac. He had a great fear of surgery, and Clyde Tolson stood beside him and did everything a female would do to console him. Hoover made Clyde look at what we were injecting, and said, 'I don't want you injecting any truth serum.' Afterwards, he brought us copies of his books with flowery inscriptions. 'You know,' my husband said then, 'the man's losing his mind.'"

On another occasion, Clyde phoned the doctor in the early hours of the morning. "He said Mr. Hoover had suffered a bad fall," said Mrs. Bell. "We opened up our office and they came in. Hoover had gashed his forehead and an eyebrow—to the bone. I would say they'd been drinking. My husband, who had a dry wit, turned to Clyde and said, 'Next time you hit your boss, you should try to miss the eyebrow.' Clyde got so upset that he left the room. People don't fall at home and gash themselves every day, and my husband gave Hoover a lecture and told him it was time to start making allowances for his age."

For months past, Edgar had spent much of his time in the office staring out the window, as the girders of the new FBI building rose, very slowly, across the street. He kept a photo album of it on his desk, which aides updated constantly. "At the rate it is going up," he would say, "none of us will be around by the time it is finished."

Many of "us" were already gone. Of his oilmen friends, Billy Byars had died in 1965, Clint Murchison in 1969, and Sid Richardson was long gone. The previous fall, looking unsteady himself, Edgar had buried the old classmate he had been close to in the early days at the Bureau, Frank Baughman. Baughman was one of the few who still called Edgar by the old nickname, Speed. Two months earlier,

Walter Winchell had died of cancer in Los Angeles. Edgar had not bothered to go to the funeral.

Others were failing fast. Lewis Rosenstiel had suffered a stroke. Clyde had been in the hospital again with heart problems. Edgar himself was talking about God more than usual. "For me," he told a writer for an Evangelist magazine, "Jesus is a living reality. . . . I know that I can count on our Redeemer." Edgar had recently made his last will, leaving almost his entire fortune to Clyde.

In late April, when Cartha DeLoach saw him at a Hearst Newspapers lunch in New York, Edgar seemed feisty enough. Roy Cohn, his protégé from the McCarthy days, was there, too. He thought the Director looked well, younger than his seventy-seven years. "I had a checkup and everything is fine," Edgar said. "If I retired, I'd fall apart and rot away. That's what happens when you quit. I'm staying."

There was another reason to hang on. "You've been through the same type of persecution," he told Cohn. "My time had to come. But I've got the bums on the run. And I'm staying right where I am."

Back in Washington, Edgar dined at the Cosmos Club and attended the Saturday racing at Pimlico as usual. On Sunday, April 30, he drank martinis with neighbors across the street, pottered about in the garden and watched "The FBI" on television.

Edgar's last day alive, by a great irony, was May Day, the workers' holiday celebrated by the Left, the Left he had struggled all his life to suppress. Edgar arrived at work alone, without the ailing Clyde.

It was not a pleasant day at the office. That morning, in his *Washington Post* column, Jack Anderson offered revelations about FBI dossiers on the private lives of political figures, black leaders, newsmen and show business people. Hours later, in a carefully timed appearance on Capitol Hill, he promised to prove it.

"The executive branch," the columnist testified to a congressional committee, "conducts secret investigations of prominent Americans. . . . FBI chief J. Edgar Hoover has demonstrated an intense interest in who is sleeping with whom in Washington. . . . I should make clear that I am not offering hearsay testimony. I have seen FBI sex reports; I have examined FBI files. . . . I am willing to make some of these documents available to the Committee."

These were astonishing claims in 1972, and the FBI corridors were abuzz with talk about Anderson that day. This, however, was only one in a salvo of new attacks. Earlier, Edgar had obtained advance copies of two books about himself. *Citizen Hoover,* by Jay Robert Nash, was a savage attack on Edgar's entire career. Americans, Nash wrote, no longer knew what to make of Edgar. He was both "benefactor and bully, protector and oppressor, truth-giver and liar. . . . The truth is the FBI of our collective memory never really existed outside of the very fertile and imaginative mind of its eternal Director. . . . To him, all high adventure was possible in the cause of Right, all moral victories over obvious evil inevitable, so long as faith in the all-encompassing power of his good office was absolute."

The second book, which the FBI had obtained by covert means in proof form, was more damaging. In a daring exposé called simply *John Edgar Hoover,* award-winning reporter Hank Messick hinted at the dark truths behind Edgar's compliant attitude toward organized crime. He highlighted, too, the relationship with Lewis Rosenstiel that placed Edgar close to top mobsters.

"Besides," reads a de Tocqueville quotation on the flyleaf of the Messick book,

> what is to be feared is not so much the immorality of the great as the fact that immorality may lead to greatness.

The Nash book would be found on Edgar's night table after his death, and Messick's book may have been in the house as well. Secret FBI intervention no longer cowed publishers. These books were going to be published whether Edgar liked it or not.

Edgar stayed at work until nearly six that last day, late by his standards, then went to Clyde's apartment for dinner. He probably arrived home about 10:15 P.M., to be greeted by the two yapping cairn terriers. Edgar liked to have a nightcap, a glass of his favorite bourbon, Jack Daniel's Black Label, poured from a musical decanter. When raised from its rest, the decanter tinkled "For he's a jolly good fellow." Edgar was fond of it.

If there was such a quiet moment that night, it was reportedly shattered by an unwelcome telephone call. Later, Helen Gandy would claim that, somewhere between ten and midnight, President Nixon called Edgar at home. His purpose, Gandy said, was to tell Edgar once and for all that he must quit. Afterward, Edgar phoned Clyde to talk about the call. Clyde subsequently told Gandy, and that is how the story survives.

If Gandy's account is accurate, Edgar must have gone to bed feeling shattered. He would have walked into the hall, past the bust of himself waiting to greet visitors, past the pictures and inscriptions that spoke of fifty-nine years in government service; one showed him with a smiling Richard Nixon. Then he would have climbed the stairs, passing an oil painting of himself on the landing, to the master bedroom with its maplewood four-poster.

May 2, a Tuesday, began as a typical Washington spring day—too hot for comfort even in the early morning. Edgar's black housekeeper, Annie Fields, always came up from her basement apartment to fix breakfast, and Edgar always came down to eat at 7:30 A.M. But today he did not.

The chauffeur reportedly arrived at 7:45, to be followed by his predecessor in the job, James Crawford. Crawford, one of the blacks Edgar had once elevated to agent rank to avoid accusations of discrimination, still worked on, in retirement, with Edgar, as handyman and gardener. He was there that morning by appointment with Edgar, to discuss where to plant some new rosebushes.

The Director, however, did not appear. As the servants waited, the dogs scurried about, eager for the morning ritual of scraps from the master's table. Then it was 8:30, and the old retainers began to worry. There had been no sound from upstairs, not this morning.

Annie Fields, it is said, went upstairs to investigate.[4] She knocked timorously at the bedroom door, then—answered only by silence—tried the door. It was unlocked, which was highly unusual.

The housekeeper saw Edgar's body the moment she stepped into the room. It was dressed in pajama trousers, naked from the waist up, and lying beside the bed. She went no farther and ran downstairs to find Crawford, the longest-serving member of the household staff. Crouched on the bedroom floor, holding the rigid, cold hand in his, Crawford knew at once that his boss was dead.

Crawford rushed to telephone first the doctor and then Clyde, the one other person he knew should be alerted at once. Clyde nearly missed the call. He was already out of the apartment, on his slow way to the limousine he assumed was about to arrive, when he realized he had forgotten something. So he came limping back, one leg dragging because of the strokes he had suffered, to hear the phone that was ringing and ringing.

Edgar's doctor, Robert Choisser, was at the house within an hour of the discovery of the body. "Mr. Hoover had been dead for some hours," he recalled. "I was rather surprised by his sudden death, because he was in good health. I do not recall prescribing him medication for blood pressure or heart disease. There was nothing to lead anyone to expect him to die at that time, except for his age."

The body was in rigor mortis, suggesting Edgar had been dead for many hours—since about 2:00 or 3:00 A.M., Choisser thought. Later that morning, because deaths at home must be reported to the coroner's office, he contacted Dr. Richard Welton, a former classmate working as a Medical Examiner. Routinely in such cases the coroner takes the doctor's word for it and simply registers the death. Welton and Coroner James Luke, however, decided the death of a man as prominent as Edgar required their presence at the scene.

The two medical examiners arrived at the house soon

after 11:00 A.M., and, except that Dr. Welton believes the body had been moved from the floor to the bed, found the scene as described by Dr. Choisser. "It was totally normal," Welton recalled. "There was nothing to suggest trauma. Hoover was in an age group where it could be expected. . . . It is common for such a person to be found dead after apparently trying to get to the bathroom during the night."[5]

On the way to the car, Welton wondered aloud whether there should be an autopsy. "What if," he asked Luke, "someone should pop up six months from now and say someone had been feeding Hoover arsenic? We'll think we should have done an autopsy." It was only a passing thought. Back at the office, however, Dr. Luke consulted by telephone with the Medical Examiner for New York City, Dr. Milton Helpern, perhaps the world's most renowned forensic detective.

Neither pathologist had any reason to suppose anyone had been feeding Edgar arsenic, or any other poison. No one then knew that the Watergate burglars even existed, let alone that two of them had consulted a CIA expert about ways of killing columnist Jack Anderson, including the option of planting poison in his medicine cabinet. They knew nothing of alleged break-ins at Edgar's home, nothing of the suggestion that a poison might have been "placed on Hoover's personal toilet articles"—a poison capable of inducing cardiac arrest, detectable only if an autopsy was speedily performed.

Nor, on the other hand, did the doctors have any notion of the stress Edgar had been under, of the latest threats to his reputation—Jack Anderson's congressional testimony promising to produce proof of Edgar's snooping on public figures and Hank Messick's forthcoming book hinting at his links with organized crime. They knew nothing of the call Nixon had reportedly made to Edgar late the previous night, telling him it was time to step down.

Three days after Edgar's death, having decided an autopsy was unnecessary, Coroner Luke signed the death certificate:

John Edgar Hoover, male, white.
Occupation: Director, FBI.
Immediate cause: Hypertensive cardiovascular disease.

On May 5, three days after Edgar died, the men who were to break into Democratic Party headquarters moved into Room 419 at the Howard Johnson Motor Lodge, directly opposite the Watergate building they were to make so famous. Their first break-in attempt, three weeks later, failed. It was followed by one successful entry, then a second—in June—when they were caught. The Watergate saga followed, leading to the resignation of President Nixon and jail terms for most of the burglars and for John Mitchell, H. R. Haldeman, John Ehrlichman, John Dean, Charles Colson, Egil Krogh and others.

Krogh, Nixon intimate and chief Plumber, wound up serving time in Allenwood minimum security prison in Pennsylvania. Also in Allenwood in early 1974 was former Congressman Neil Gallagher, once a victim of Edgar's rage for his failure to cooperate in smearing Robert Kennedy, now serving time for the income-tax conviction that followed.[6] According to Gallagher, Krogh had something strange to say about Edgar's death.

"I was the prison librarian," Gallagher recalled in 1991, "and Krogh would come in with his two Bibles. He was very religious, a Christian Scientist. He'd sit writing letters at the big table in the library, and sometimes we'd talk. One night, when I was about to close the place and there were only the two of us there, we talked about Hoover.

"I said I thought the circumstances of Hoover's death were a bit strange. Because of my war with Hoover, I'd followed everything about him closely. I said to Krogh, 'Hoover knew everything that was going on in Washington. He must surely have known about the Plumbers and everything. Do you think Hoover was blackmailing the President?' And then I said, and it surprises me now, 'Did you guys knock Hoover off? You had the troops to do it, and the reason. . . .'

"It took several seconds for it to sink in. Then Krogh literally jumped out of his chair. And in a highly charged voice he sort of screamed, 'We didn't knock off Hoover. He knocked himself off.' And I said, 'My God, that explains a lot about the bastard's death coming the way it did.' And with that Krogh jumped up, gathered his papers and his Bibles and rushed out of the library. We never had another conversation the rest of the time we were in Allenwood."

Interviewed in 1991, Krogh recalled knowing Gallagher in the prison. Told what Gallagher had said of their discussion about Edgar's death, he replied, "I might have had a conversation like that, but it was a long time ago. A lot of water has passed under the bridge since then. I don't remember it." Gallagher, for his part, has signed an affidavit swearing to the truth of his account.

There is no way, now, to know why Nixon's adviser should have said Edgar committed suicide—nor why the subject upset him so much. If evidence along those lines was known to the White House, it has vanished along with so many other mysteries of the Watergate period. Nor is it possible, today, to make a judgment on the allegation that Watergate investigators were unable to track further—that there were break-ins at Edgar's home before he died. The most troubling claim, that the second break-in involved planting a poison chemical designed to cause death by simulated heart attack, cannot be further assessed outside the judicial system.

After he heard the news of Edgar's death, Clyde Tolson made two telephone calls. The first was to Helen Gandy, the secretary who had served the Director since 1919. The second was to the office of the Attorney General, and from there the word passed to H. R. Haldeman at the White House. He in turn informed the President—at 9:15 A.M., according to his handwritten notes.

As Haldeman recalls it, the news "wasn't a great surprise" to Nixon. He said nothing that reflected his reported exchange with Edgar on the phone the previous night. He wrote in his diary, or so we are told in his memoirs:

> Hoover . . . died at the right time; fortunately, he died in office. It would have killed him had he been forced out of office or had he resigned even voluntarily. I remember the last conversation I had with him about two weeks ago when I called him and mentioned the fine job the Bureau had done on the hijacking cases. . . .

Ehrlichman and Haldeman do not recall any reaction by the President to Edgar's death, aside from his concern for the files. John Mitchell, who had left the post of Attorney General in order to run Nixon's reelection campaign, had the same worry. His orders that morning, Haldeman noted at the time, were to hunt down "the skeletons." It was decided not to announce Edgar's death publicly until eleven o'clock.

Gordon Liddy, Nixon's dirty-tricks specialist, thought it was vital to find the skeletons. As an FBI veteran, he had once worked with some of Edgar's most sensitive political files. "I called the White House at once," Liddy recalled. "I said, 'You've got to get those files. They are a source of enormous power. You don't have much time. There's going to be a race on. Get those files.' "

Liddy thinks he spoke to Ehrlichman, who could speak directly to the President, and to Howard Hunt to get him to talk with Charles Colson. Ehrlichman confirms he did discuss the danger with Nixon, and someone that morning took drastic action.

When the undertakers reached Edgar's house around 12:30 P.M., they walked into a scene out of Orwell's darkest imaginings. "They were virtually tearing the place apart," undertaker William Reburn remembered. "There were men in suits, fifteen or eighteen of them, swarming all over the place, ransacking it, going through everything he had. I assumed they were government agents. They were going through Hoover's books, desk, drawers, like they were looking for something. . . .

"They were methodical. One agent was assigned to a bookcase, going through all the books kind of page by page. They were taking all the books off the shelves and looking under and behind the shelves. There had been this rumor that Hoover had secret files, and that was the thought that entered my mind, that they were hunting for his files."

Whoever the searchers were, someone may have got there before them. Early that morning two of Edgar's neighbors had seen something mysterious. "It was early in the morning," Anthony Calomaris recalled in 1992. "I was seventeen then, and I was getting ready for school. And my mother called me into her room, onto the balcony we had then. There were two men carrying something out of Mr. Hoover's kitchen door, and Annie the housekeeper was at the door. What they were carrying was long and obviously heavy, wrapped in something like a quilt. They heaved it into a station wagon parked in the alley and drove away."

Because of the shape of the bundle, Calomaris and his mother assumed at the time that it contained a body—that Edgar had died in the night and that these were undertakers, working early to avoid the press. The documented record, however, is that Edgar's body was not removed until much later, around lunchtime. At the hour the neighbors saw the men with a bundle, the body had not, according to all available testimony, even been discovered.

Yet Calomaris and his mother are adamant that they saw something being removed before Anthony left for school. The men were surely not interlopers—had they been, the housekeeper would not have been calmly seeing them to the door. Given the known desire of others to get at Edgar's secrets, were allies removing something before the death became generally known, to thwart later searchers?

Whatever was or was not found at Edgar's home, Nixon's men were worried about the contents of his office. That same morning, after a conversation with the White House, Acting Attorney General Kleindienst ordered that it be sealed—to secure Edgar's files. That afternoon, the man

Nixon had picked as Acting FBI Director, L. Patrick Gray, arrived to ask John Mohr where the "secret files" were. Mohr told him there were none.

Gray was back, asking the same question, before nine o'clock the next morning. "Judging from his conversation and his comments," Mohr recalled, "I thought he was looking for secret files that would embarrass the Nixon administration. . . . I told him in no uncertain terms that there were no secret files." There was a stand-up row, with Gray yelling that he was "a hardheaded Irishman and nobody pushes me around." Mohr said he was a hard-headed Dutchman—no one pushed him around, either. The shouting could be heard several offices away.

Gray, who later narrowly escaped prosecution for destroying documents after Watergate, may in the end have had some success. Joe Diamond, a young file clerk who joined the FBI a week after Edgar's death, recalls a curious episode.

"It was my second day on the job, and the Supervisor asked me and three other men to go upstairs to do a job. We went up, and there were four gentlemen in suits there. And they had us take these crates stuffed with papers down to the basement to the shredder. We picked up the crates and it was like we were carrying gold or something the way they acted. It took about two hours to get the stuff shredded, and then they took the sacks and left. . . . I recognized two of the men in suits. One of them was L. Patrick Gray and the other was [Deputy Associate Director] Mark Felt."

Almost certainly, a mass of documents were gone even before Gray took over. "I learned later," recalled Kleindienst, "that certain files were removed even before I called to order that Hoover's office be locked." "It was reported to me by my FBI sources," said Liddy, "that by the time Gray went in to get the files, Miss Gandy had already got rid of them."

Kleindienst's instructions to seal Edgar's office had no effect anyway, because John Mohr placed a literal interpretation on the order. He locked up only Edgar's personal office, which contained no files at all. The other nine rooms in the office suite, which were bulging with documents, remained unsecured. They housed some of the most secret documents of all, including the Official and Confidential files stored in locked file cabinets under the eagle eye of Helen Gandy.

Three years later a congressional committee would make what it could of the stories told by Gandy, Mohr, Felt and others. It would conclude only one thing for certain: that a mass of documents were trucked to Edgar's home in the weeks that followed his death. According to Gandy, these were merely Edgar's personal files, containing private correspondence, investment records and the like. In line with Edgar's known wishes, she said, she sorted through them, then sent them to be destroyed in the office shredder.

The staff of Congress' Government Information Subcommittee, which heard Gandy's testimony, were convinced she was lying. Surviving records indicated that the truckload taken to Edgar's home had included official records. Gandy, who said the consignment consisted of just four file cabinets and thirty-five cardboard boxes, was contradicted by Raymond Smith, the truck driver who made the delivery. He said he transported at least twenty, possibly twenty-five, cabinets from headquarters to the basement of Edgar's house. A file drawer came open during the transfer, and he saw that it was crammed with folders, each about an inch thick. Edgar's housekeeper Annie Fields told neighbors the files were kept under tight security from the moment they arrived.

Finally, it is clear that in Edgar's office the label "Personal" had a significance quite different from the ordinary sense of the word. Early in his tenure, Edgar had established a procedure designated "Personal and Confidential," under which senior officials could communicate with him in total secrecy, outside the central records system.

In the opinion of the scholar who has done most to expose FBI secret dossiers, Professor Athan Theoharis of Marquette University, the Personal and Confidential files probably contained material even more explosive than the Official and Confidential dossiers that have since so shocked the public.

It is not certain that all the files removed to Edgar's home were eventually destroyed. *Newsweek* reported in 1975 that dossiers "very, very damaging to the Nixon White House" remained in Clyde Tolson's custody. When he in turn died, *Newsweek* said, FBI agents descended on the house to cart the documents away. Clyde's former secretary, Dorothy Skillman, told a story similar to Helen Gandy's. She destroyed Clyde's correspondence, she said, and it was "mostly birthday cards." Anthony Marro, the *Newsweek* reporter, stands by his story.

"I find your testimony very difficult to believe," Congressman Andrew Maguire told Helen Gandy when she testified in December 1975 about the fate of the files. "That," she answered haughtily, "is your privilege."

"You're beating a dead horse," Mark Felt told congressional investigators. "So what, you won't find out what was destroyed. Only Miss Gandy knows that. And what if you do? . . . There's no serious problem if we lose some papers. I didn't see anything wrong, and I still don't."

EPILOGUE

> "You know, he was the last reigning monarch in the Western World."
>
> *Tom Huston, former Nixon aide, 1975*

AT MIDDAY WASHINGTON TIME ON THE DAY EDGAR DIED, THE Stars and Stripes slid down to half-staff on American government buildings, military installations and Navy ships around the world. President Nixon, relieved of his Hoover problem at last, was diverting the nation with a show of public grief.

The President now claimed the man he had been trying to dump had been "one of my closest personal friends and advisers." Edgar, he said, had been "the symbol and embodiment of the values he cherished most: courage, patriotism, dedication to his country and a granite-like honesty and integrity."

Vice President Spiro Agnew, who would soon face trial for bribery and tax evasion, said Edgar had endeared himself to Americans for "his total dedication to principle and his complete incorruptibility." John Mitchell, who had urged Edgar's dismissal, called the death "a great tragedy." Acting Attorney General Kleindienst, who used to hold the phone away from his ear when Edgar called, now thought him "a giant among patriots" who never allowed the taint of political influence. Ronald Reagan, then Governor of California, declared that "No twentieth-century man has meant more to this country than Hoover."

In Congress, politicians rushed to praise Edgar. John Rooney, who had been party to many of Edgar's abuses, spoke of Edgar's "deep respect for his fellowman." Congressman Hale Boggs, who had called for Edgar's retirement the previous year, now claimed he had never criticized him personally at all. Even Senator Edward Kennedy spoke of Edgar's "honesty, integrity and his desire to do what he thought best for the country." In all, 149 representatives and senators eventually paid tribute.

The few that raised their voices in dissent included Martin Luther King's widow, Coretta. She spoke of Edgar's "deplorable and dangerous" legacy and of a file system "replete with lies and sordid material on some of the highest people in government, including presidents." Dr. Benjamin Spock was glad Edgar was dead. "It's a great relief, especially if his replacement is a man who better understands democratic institutions and the American process."

At FBI headquarters, a telex went out to the furthest corners of Edgar's empire, asking Bureau employees to offer up prayers. It was signed by Clyde, but probably penned by John Mohr. In Miami, Agent in Charge Whittaker said Edgar's passing was "like losing a father." From retirement, Cartha DeLoach told the press Edgar had been "a great American, a compassionate man with unswerving loyalty and dedication."

In private, DeLoach had reservations. "I respected him," he recalled, "but I never loved him as a true friend." "For me," said Mark Felt, "it was no personal loss. I never did feel emotional about it. My main thought that day was about the problems created by his death."

There was little solemnity at FBI field offices around the country. In California, Agent Cril Payne arrived at a colleague's retirement party expecting gloom. "I couldn't believe my eyes," he recalled. "The place was packed! The older agents had showed up in record number. Had a stranger wandered into the room he might have thought it was the office Christmas party! Instead of the somber gathering I had envisioned, the luncheon became a time for joyous celebration. If the truth were known, I think the great majority of agents felt an overwhelming sense of relief. . . ."

"It was fitting," quipped another agent, "that the Director

passed away in his sleep. That's the way the Bureau was run lately."

For years now a joke had been going the rounds in the Bureau—about the day Clyde told Edgar how much burial lots for the two of them would cost. "I'm not going to pay that for a burial lot," cried Edgar. "I'll tell you what you do. Go ahead and buy your own lot and rent a vault for me for three days. I'll only be there three days."

When Edgar died, FBI Mafia specialist Neil Welch remembered that story. "The last resurrection had been sometime previously," he said dryly in 1988. "I wanted to see if history repeated itself. So a group of us in Detroit got together and flew to Washington, not out of a sense of great grief or anything, just out of curiosity to see the changeover. I wanted to see what machinations were going on in that temple of his over there. . . ."

In New York, at the Aqueduct Racetrack, three mobsters in the Gambino family spotted the news in the paper. "You know what I feel about this," shrugged the senior man in the group. "Absolutely nothing. This guy meant nothing to us, one way or the other."

At the tracks Edgar had frequented, people felt differently. His regular table at Pimlico was dressed out in black cloth. At Bowie, his table was adorned with his name card. Edgar's lunch table at the Mayflower, where he had eaten the previous day, was draped with red, white and blue sashes.

"The shock of Brother Hoover's loss," a speaker told fellow Masons in Washington, "was felt far beyond the boundaries of our great nation. . . . When Brother Hoover died, a giant fell and the gods wept."

The undertakers who handled Edgar's body, from Gawler's on Wisconsin Avenue, were used to the deaths of the famous. The company had looked after the remains of many of Edgar's friends and enemies: Joseph McCarthy and Dwight Eisenhower, John Kennedy and Estes Kefauver—a long list of prominent Americans. Even so, the half hour spent at Edgar's house left them shaken.

"The place was like a museum," recalled undertaker William Reburn, "like a shrine the man had made to himself. He must've had some ego. The picture of him at the top of the stairs was almost like the one of Napoleon with the hand inside the jacket." A colleague, John van Hoesen, remembered the statuary: "Busts, like Roman busts of Caesar, but of J. Edgar Hoover."

Edgar's corpse was obese, a heavy burden to maneuver downstairs, onto a mortuary cot and out a side entrance into an old sedan—a subterfuge designed to conceal the operation from the press. At Gawler's the body was embalmed, dressed in a suit and tie chosen by Clyde and laid out in a $3,000 casket.

"He looked very good," said Edgar's niece Margaret Fennell, "but smaller than I remembered. I guess death does that to you." For the first time in years Edgar was without the various devices—the built-up shoes, the raised desk— that he had used to make himself appear taller than he really was. "My former colleagues," said DeLoach, "couldn't stand to see that great dissipation of power in a man that should be revered. Miss Gandy talked to Mr. Tolson and John Mohr, and they decided to have the casket closed."

Mohr and Gandy gave up plans for a quiet Masonic ceremony, which Edgar had said he wanted, when President Nixon decided to treat him like a national hero. The next morning, in heavy rain, a hearse brought the remains to lie in the Rotunda of the Capitol. The entire Supreme Court, the Cabinet and members of the Congress were on hand to receive the casket. It was laid, wrapped in the flag, on Lincoln's catafalque—an honor that had previously been extended to only twenty-one people. Edgar was the first civil servant to be so honored, and 25,000 people flocked to the Capitol to pay homage.[1]

It was Nixon, the following day, who delivered the eulogy at the funeral service in the National Presbyterian Church. "America," he intoned, "has revered this man, not only as the Director of an institution, but as an institution in his own right. For nearly half a century, nearly one fourth of the whole history of this Republic, J. Edgar Hoover has exerted a great influence for good in our national life. While eight Presidents came and went, while other leaders of morals and manners and opinion rose and fell, the Director stayed at his post. . . . Each of us stand forever in his debt. . . . His death only heightens the respect and admiration felt for him across this land and in every land where men cherish freedom."

The Watergate tapes show that ten months later, at the height of the crisis that was to bring him down, Nixon discussed Edgar with John Dean. The transcript runs as follows:

Dean: Now, the other thing is . . . everything is cast that we're the political people and they're not—that Hoover was above reproach . . .

Nixon: Bullshit! Bullshit!

Dean: Total bullshit. The, uh, person who could, would destroy Hoover's image is going to be this man Bill Sullivan. . . . Also, it's going to tarnish quite severely some of the FBI and a former president.

Nixon: Fine . . .

Policemen from across the country lined the route to Congressional Cemetery, where Edgar's parents lay buried. Clyde had insisted that his friend's wish was to be buried there rather than at Arlington, as Nixon suggested. The cortege was now reduced to ten limousines, carrying Clyde, Congressman John Rooney, a few colleagues and the handful of relatives, nephews and nieces and their children.

The cemetery, one of Washington's oldest, was somewhat neglected in those days—an unlikely final destination for a man of Edgar's stature. The limousines inched their way between the narrow gateposts, and the mourners gathered for the final ceremony. Clyde was pushed to the site in a wheelchair. "I was shocked," said Edgar's nephew Fred Robinette. "It looked like he didn't know where he was. He had this vacant stare."

In the absence of a widow, it was Clyde who received the flag from the coffin. Then it was over. Minutes after the mourners had left, neighborhood children ran to pilfer the flowers from the grave.

Clyde now became a virtual recluse. He refused to accept a condolence call from Acting FBI Director Gray, and he never set foot in the office again. His resignation letter, pleading ill health, was composed by another Bureau official, its signature forged by a secretary. Clyde moved into Edgar's house and remained there for the rest of his life.

He received the bulk of Edgar's fortune, officially valued at half a million dollars—$1.5 million at today's rates—although Justice Department investigators would later suspect that his true wealth was hidden by secret investment accounts. Clyde soon began selling off the myriad collectibles his friend had gathered over the years. They went under the hammer at Sloan's Auction Gallery, with the vendor's name concealed by the code name "JET"—for "J. Edgar" and "Tolson."

In his will, Edgar had entrusted the welfare of his two cairn terriers to Clyde. Clyde, however, soon had the dogs put down. He sank into a listless existence, whiling away his days munching candy—a longtime addiction—and watching television.

In the time that remained to him, Clyde would be stirred to action only once, in 1973, when William Sullivan spoke out about the transfer of wiretap records to the Nixon White House. The administration, Sullivan said, had feared Edgar would resort to blackmail to hold on to his job—not least because he "had been of unsound mind for the past few years."

This moved Clyde to write a letter of protest to *The Washington Post,* dismissing Sullivan as "a disgruntled former employee." A month or so later, however, when Watergate investigators interviewed Clyde, they doubted his own "mental competency."

Clyde had become a pathetically lonely figure, visited mainly by thoughtful neighbors. One, Betty Nelson, came in to give him chocolate bars and a kiss on Valentine's Day 1975. He was taken to the hospital in early April and died there of heart failure a few days later.

A new FBI Director, Clarence Kelley, would say Clyde's death left "a great void in the law enforcement field." The truth was that he was virtually forgotten. In his final three years, reportedly, his only excursions had been to visit Edgar's grave at Congressional Cemetery. Now Clyde lay buried there, too, about ten yards from the man he loved. According to cemetery officials, each man had asked to be buried near the other.

President Nixon had responded cynically on the morning of Edgar's death as he wondered how to replace him. His first choice had been Clyde, not in spite of but because of the fact that he was a virtual invalid. "Tolson's incapacity," the President told H. R. Haldeman—a thought duly minuted for the record—"may be an advantage." Nixon wanted the control of the FBI Edgar had denied him, and a sick man seemed just the candidate.

"We have not used the power in the first four years," the President would remark to his aide John Dean. "We have never used it. We haven't used the Bureau, and we haven't used the Justice Department, but things are going to change. . . ."

It was when Clyde declined the Director's job that Nixon decided on L. Patrick Gray as a stopgap, an uncontroversial Acting Director for election year. Gray was a former Navy man whose career watchword, unkind critics say, had been "Aye, aye, sir." For a long time now, the "sir" in question had been Nixon himself—and the President liked that.

Edgar had run his fiefdom as though he would live forever, and it remained in disarray for years, not least because of the chaos that followed Watergate. Gradually, however, first under Gray, then under FBI veteran and former police chief Clarence Kelley and—above all—during the nine-year directorship of William Webster, the Bureau entered the modern world. Women were admitted as agents, and staff across the country were released from the sillier of Edgar's rules and regulations. Men no longer lived in constant fear of irrational punishment. The aging leaders Edgar had gathered around him were gradually forced out or left of their own accord. And, it is believed, the worst abuses of FBI power—against the Congress and ordinary citizens—have since been exposed and eradicated.

"J. Edgar Hoover's greatness," his old adjutant Louis Nichols wrote confidently in late 1972, "will grow with the passage of time." To fulfill that hope, loyalists busied themselves trying to perpetuate Edgar's memory. They pressed Congress for a bill to create commemorative medals, commissioned portraits and sculptures. Edgar's FBI badge—No. 1—was presented to the Smithsonian Institution. His gun, a .32 Colt Pocket Positive, was solemnly preserved. FBI stalwarts, members of the old guard, made an annual pilgrimage to the cemetery. Their numbers soon dwindled, however, and Edgar's grave has often lain untended, overrun by vines and weeds.[2]

Even twenty years after his death, however, the name J. Edgar Hoover still stirs controversy. Americans either yearn for the certainties he seemed to embody, or wonder how it was that his abuses were tolerated for so long. To understand the phenomenon better, we may ask what drove Edgar, what led him to the narrow world of the mind he came to inhabit—the world in which, with some success, he sought to confine his countrymen as well.

The vast library Edgar left behind, now preserved at the FBI National Academy, offers few answers—just the predictable mountain of books on Communism, a stack of books on religion and health and some whodunits. There is no evidence that Edgar was steeped in any particular philosophy, nor that his life was the execution of any conscious plan.

Leading psychologists and psychiatrists, however, asked to study the information gathered for this book, all recognize a distinct pattern in Edgar's makeup, one that began forming in childhood and led to serious mental disorder in the grown man.[3] Separated by twelve years from his youngest sibling, conceived when his parents were mourning the death of his infant sister Sadie, Edgar had been rather more than the apple of his mother's eye.

Annie Hoover saw herself as "a lady," with pretensions to a certain social status. If she ever nursed hopes that her husband would improve himself, rise above his origins, they were gone by the time Edgar was born. They vanished altogether when Dickerson was overwhelmed by serious mental illness. Instead, Annie had great expectations of Edgar, too great perhaps for his emotional well-being.

Edgar missed a vital stage of normal childhood development: the end of total dependence on the mother, a growing bond to a supportive father and the discovery of himself as an independent personality. Rather than working out a set of moral values for himself, he had little more to work with than the unreasoned rules of behavior imposed in childhood. Pushed by his forceful mother, he came to believe that only greater achieving could make him "good." His was a childhood that left him prone to lifelong insecurity and lack of self-esteem.

Studies now suggest that, being especially vulnerable, people with such a background tend to block their feelings, cut themselves off from meaningful relationships. They come to think of life in terms of the Good, represented by themselves, and the Bad, represented by everyone and everything that seems to run counter to their way of thinking. Such people often gravitate to groups or organizations, groups that reflect their own limited view of the world. They surround themselves with acolytes who will reinforce the notion that they are always right about everything. Such factors are typical of the state psychologists call *paranoia*.

Edgar fit the profile. Annie's expectations account for his compulsion to perform not just well but perfectly. Edgar's early obsession with record-keeping, his excessive misery when the school Cadet Corps troop failed to carry off a prize, his insistence on tidiness and his neurotic concern about germs are characteristic of his personality type.

Early on, at an age when a healthy youngster will have an open, inquiring mind, Edgar had rigid, backward-looking attitudes. Even then there was the rapid-fire speech for which the grown man would become famous, talking rather than listening, defense by way of constant attack, the snuffing out of potential argument by never letting the other side have its say. At the FBI, Edgar achieved the paranoid's ideal. He not only joined a highly disciplined group, he joined one he could mold and totally control for the rest of his life.

"There is no doubt," concluded psychiatrist Dr. Harold Lief, Professor Emeritus of Psychiatry at the University of Pennsylvania, "that Hoover had a personality disorder, a narcissistic disorder with mixed obsessive features. I picked up some paranoid elements, undue suspiciousness and some sadism. A combination of narcissism and paranoia produces what is known as an Authoritarian Personality. Hoover would have made a perfect high-level Nazi."

While Dr. Lief reached this conclusion spontaneously, on the basis of the information in this book, he was later struck by parallels in the personality of Nazi Germany's secret police chief Heinrich Himmler. Like Edgar, Lief noted, Himmler had a weak father and was heavily dependent on his mother. He too kept precise records and diaries from an abnormally early age. He was at the top of his class at school, but too frail for sports. He involved himself in his college fraternity and had fixed right-wing ideas from an early age. Though a zealous officer cadet, he tried to avoid military service. He was a chatterbox who dominated all conversations, excessively strict with subordinates and outwardly submissive to superiors. He denounced others at every opportunity. He cut himself off emotionally, distanced himself from women and took an unhealthy interest in the "immoral" behavior of others.

The psychologist Erich Fromm concluded that Himmler was a classic, sadistic Authoritarian. "There are thousands of Himmlers living among us," he wrote. "One must not underestimate the number of people whom they damage and make thoroughly unhappy. The potential Himmler looks like anyone else, except to those who have learned to read character and who do not have to wait until circumstances permit the 'monster' to show his colors."

It is the social system in which a person lives, however, that determines the outcome of his Authoritarianism. Happily, Edgar and his crippled psyche existed in a society very different from that of Nazi Germany. While he persecuted innumerable people, there were limits to how far he could go. Medically, nevertheless, he was constantly at risk. "Had Hoover been unsuccessful or had the world he created for himself collapsed," said Dr. Lief, "it would have been shattering for him. He would certainly have required treatment. As it was, he was able to use his personality successfully. He attained huge power and managed to stay in the system for many, many years. He was, you might say, a successful narcissist and sociopath."

A sociopath is a person who, because of mental illness, lacks a sense of social or moral responsibility. Edgar ran his course as head of the FBI, for half a century, by presenting himself as the precise opposite.

Edgar's sexuality comes as no surprise to the psychologists. "His basic problem," said Dr. Lief, "seems to me to have been that he was both attracted and repelled by women. Because he separated lust and love it's likely that he idealized mother figures and lusted after the degraded woman, which would explain his reported liking of pornography. If I hadn't known anything about his alleged homosexual tendencies, my guess would have been that his primary adaptation was to transvestism, which indeed turns out to have been part of the picture."

For Edgar, transvestism may have offered a form of release. Like his homosexuality, however, it surely brought terrible inner torment. Studies of transvestism are filled with stories of emotional turmoil. Many transvestites attempt suicide, and almost all live in terror of being exposed.

It is surely no coincidence that the earliest report of Edgar's cross-dressing refers to the postwar years, when worries about sex drove him to consult a psychiatrist.

Edgar's puritanism seems to have been the hypocrisy of a public man overcompensating for private weaknesses. In 1957, the year before the cross-dressing episodes involving sex with young males at New York's Plaza Hotel, Edgar had launched a call for the suppression of pornography. "If we act now," he declared, "we can look forward to a new generation of young people with clean minds and healthy bodies living in a better, cleaner America."

According to Dr. John Money, Professor of Medical Psychology at Johns Hopkins University, Edgar's sexual conflicts fit a familiar pattern, one seen quite often in policemen. "You find this sort of thing in officers who work for the Vice Squad. They may hang out in men's toilets in order to arrest other men, but they make sure they get themselves serviced first. They may look like knights in shining armor, but they're undercover agents psychologically as much as by profession.

"Hoover's whole life," observed Dr. Money, "was one of haunting and hounding people over their sexuality, brutalizing them one way or another because of it. He took on the role of being the paragon, keeping the country morally clean, yet hid his own sexual side. His terrible thing was that he needed constantly to destroy other people in order to maintain himself. Many people like that break down and end up needing medical help. Hoover managed to live with his conflict—by making others pay the price."

Noting that some personality types are now universally known by the names of famous case histories—sadism for the Marquis de Sade, masochism for Leopold von Sacher-Masoch and so on—Dr. Money proposes that Edgar's name be used in similar fashion. "Hoover," he believes, "is a model to describe those who exhibit a paraphiliac, or perverted, type of sexuality by sacrificing other people to exorcise their own demands. He had what I call 'malignant bisexuality,' and I suggest quite seriously that his condition should henceforth be called the 'J. Edgar Hoover Syndrome.' "

On September 30, 1975, a Marine band struck up a specially composed "J. Edgar Hoover March" in the courtyard of the vast concrete complex that Edgar had hoped to see finished, and which is now the FBI headquarters. Hours earlier, workmen had raised a glittering name high on the facade that faces Pennsylvania Avenue. This was to be the J. Edgar Hoover Building, as decided by Richard Nixon immediately after Edgar's death.

The headquarters was inaugurated by Nixon's successor, President Ford. He chose his words carefully, offering most of his praise not to the memory of Edgar, but to the "special agents, legendary symbols of American justice for decades." He spoke of Edgar little and with reserve, calling him only "a pioneering public servant."

By late 1975, caution had become essential. The evils of the Hoover years were beginning to leak out. Appalled senators and congressmen were perusing the documents and listening to the testimony that confirmed Edgar's abuse of power and of civil liberties.

The golden name on FBI headquarters has become more tarnished, literally and figuratively, with every passing year. "Why does society continue to honor someone like Hoover?" asked Professor Lief in 1992. "Of course, he thrived in an era when anti-Communism was the unifying theme in the West. Society seems always to need its devils, and Communism was the Devil in this century—though in different circumstances it could have been the Jew or some other 'demon.' Hoover seized above all on anti-Communism, so I guess he was honored because he was perceived to be fighting the Devil.

"American society has a strangely polarized attitude toward its heroes. On the one hand people love to discover the idol has clay feet, to find the flaw in the famous man. On the other hand, thousands and thousands of people seem to have a need to identify with a hero, to increase their own sense of strength by believing in someone who presents himself as wiser or more powerful than themselves. And they are reluctant to take the hero off his pedestal, even when they discover that he was not what he seemed. This is a curious contradiction in our society, and sometimes a dangerous one."

"You affect the future," *Washington Post* columnist Richard Cohen observed in 1990, "by what you do with the past, how you interpret it. All over the world, when regimes change, so do names. Danzig becomes Gdansk. The Moldau becomes Vltava. Images of Lenin come down all over Eastern Europe, and in the Soviet Union Stalingrad becomes Volgograd. These are all political statements. They say, 'There's a new way of doing things.' But an FBI agent walking into that building looks up and sees J. Edgar Hoover's name. What's the lesson to him—that efficiency and bureaucratic success condone abuse of office?"

That Edgar created an efficient law enforcement Bureau should not have been enough to secure him a position as an American hero for half a century. Someone else, more balanced and with more respect for the rights of citizens, could have set up the FBI. To take Edgar at face value was as perilous as tolerating a dictator simply because he "makes the trains run on time."

When Edgar was alive, a perceptive writer noted that he had entered "the realm of the untouchables, a remote roseate country of mind, mood and attitude, beyond the harsh ridges of reality." Today, now that it is clear what the harsh realities were, it is not enough to complain that Edgar fooled America. The survival of a J. Edgar Hoover for so many years, and in such an atmosphere of phony adulation, could have occurred only in a society led by men who condoned his secret abuses and public hypocrisies, while maintaining otherwise. Edgar had many accomplices, including Presidents—Democrats and Republicans alike—who went along with his excesses because it suited their political purposes.

If there is a moral here, it is perhaps the one drawn by future Vice President Walter Mondale while taking part in the Senate probe of the CIA and FBI in 1975. "The lesson we learn from this history," he said, "is that we cannot keep our liberty secure by relying alone on the good faith of men with great power."

AFTERWORD

(For the Paperback Edition)

ON MARCH 28, 1993, PRESIDENT CLINTON ROSE TO ADDRESS THE annual Gridiron Club dinner in Washington, D.C., traditionally an evening for topical satire. In the audience was FBI Director William Sessions, then fighting a losing battle against accusations of abuse of office, and the President gave him no encouragement. "I might have to pick an FBI director," he said, grinning, "and it's going to be hard to fill J. Edgar Hoover's . . . pumps."

Everyone understood the allusion. For the past month, since the hardback publication of this book, America had been tittering at the allegation that Hoover liked dressing up in women's clothes. On television, Jay Leno and David Letterman made cracks. The "Saturday Night Live" team ran a news item reporting that an application by Hoover to join the Army had been posthumously rejected. *The New York Times Magazine* devoted a page of commentary to the sex angle, and John Updike penned a spoof for *The New Yorker*. In a reference to the transvestite in the movie *The Crying Game,* the *Times* ran a cartoon featuring the "Jaye Edgar Hoover Building." On the same theme, *The Nation* advertised an imaginary movie called *The Lying Game*. And so on—for months.

Although this book is about issues far wider and more serious than Hoover's sexual preferences, it was the sex that preoccupied the media. Some, meanwhile, sought to assail my reporting on the subject, and my sources. Here, therefore, I offer relevant new information that has reached me since the hardback edition was published last year.

I was contacted by Marie Gladhill, an octogenarian whose father, Wilhelm Buch, was a Danish newspaperman based in Washington, D.C. "Many Danes used to call on my father when they came to Washington," Mrs. Gladhill told me. "I was present, in the early thirties, when he received a visit from a young Danish sailor about nineteen years old, who had recently been arrested for some homosexual offense. My father asked him how he had got out of jail. The young fellow laughed and said, 'Mr. Hoover got me out.' And he told how Hoover had taken him home with him. As if to explain, he said: 'Mr. Hoover is homosexual . . .' "

In a speech to a writers' conference in the eighties, novelist William Styron said Hoover had once been spotted with Clyde Tolson on the patio of a beach house in Malibu, California. "There was the head of the FBI," said Styron, "painting the toenails of his longtime male friend." In 1993, Styron told me that he received this information from a source he considered reliable. He believes the story to be "absolutely true."

Following publication of *Official and Confidential,* the *New York Post* reported that Hoover and Tolson were drawn into a 1966 probe of a nationwide extortion racket. A member of the U.S. Congress, two deans of Eastern universities, and William Church, the admiral in charge of the New York naval yards, were among the many victims of a blackmail ring that systematically entrapped homosexuals. Although not publicly named at the time, Clyde Tolson was one of the ring's victims, according to the *Post* story. A photograph of Hoover with one of the extortionists, apparently taken at a social occasion, reportedly surfaced during the police inquiry—then vanished. While independent research has failed to confirm the details, interviews conducted in 1993 with former detectives—and with two of the blackmailers themselves—established that Hoover's name did come up during the investigation. *Post* reporter Murray Weiss said: "I stand a hundred percent by everything I wrote."

There has been a fresh development on the subject of the claim that a sexy photograph of Hoover and Tolson was in the possession of James Angleton, the CIA counterintelligence chief, in the sixties. Former intelligence officer John Weitz, like Angleton a veteran of the wartime intelligence organization OSS, has revealed that it was Angleton who, years earlier, showed him a similar picture of the two men. Authentic or not, there can now be little doubt that such photographs did exist, and that Angleton believed they could be used to intimidate Hoover (see Chapter 22).

The furor over this book was triggered, above all, by the allegation that Hoover on occasion dressed up in female clothing—a claim offered in lurid detail by Susan Rosenstiel, a former wife of liquor millionaire Lewis Rosenstiel.

Hoover defenders maintain that Mrs. Rosenstiel is not a credible source because, in 1971, she pleaded guilty to an attempted perjury charge. I told readers about that in the hardback edition of this book and, unlike those who now attack Mrs. Rosenstiel, also explained the circumstances. The charge was brought in connection with a two-year-old civil suit—a move considered unprecedented and bizarre by lawyers—the very week that the New York State Legislative Committee on Crime had planned to produce Mrs. Rosenstiel as a witness to her husband's Mafia links. Outraged Committee officials believed the charge was instigated by Lewis Rosenstiel, using his wealth and influence to obstruct the committee's inquiry by discrediting his former wife. Court records show the tycoon had used similar tactics in the recent past, to pervert the course of justice.

Those trying to discredit Mrs. Rosenstiel today claim that she was "reputedly an alcoholic with mental problems, known as 'Snow White' in [unnamed] circles." During six years' work on *Official and Confidential,* including extended interviews with the woman, I found no evidence to support such accusations. Nor were any such weaknesses even rumored until after publication of my book. On the contrary, the former Chief Counsel of the Crime Committee, New York Judge Edward McLaughlin, and committee investigator William Gallinaro, found Mrs. Rosenstiel an exceptionally good witness. "I thought her absolutely truthful," Judge McLaughlin told me. "The woman's power of recall was phenomenal. Everything she said was checked and double-checked, and everything that was checkable turned out to be true." Although this assessment of Mrs. Rosenstiel is in this book, it has not been quoted in a single newspaper.

I have now received FBI files on Lewis Rosenstiel—files withheld during the years I worked on the book, in spite of an early application under the Freedom of Information Act. They contain nothing to discredit Mrs. Rosenstiel. They do show that, as early as 1939, Hoover was interested in and concerned about the FBI's handling of Mr. Rosenstiel. They contain what appears to be the record of a first meeting between the two men in 1956, although other evidence suggests they met earlier. That year, when Rosenstiel asked to see Hoover, the Director saw him within hours. Mrs. Rosenstiel has alleged that Hoover brought pressure on politicians to help further her husband's business interests —and the file shows that the millionaire did lobby the Director's office about his business problems. In 1957, the unctuous Rosenstiel was assuring Hoover that "your wish is my command." Later, when Rosenstiel was sick, Hoover sent him flowers.

Susan Rosenstiel mentioned to me that she had once possessed a photograph of Hoover in the company of her husband's mobster friends. That she did have such evidence was confirmed following publication of this book by Mary Nichols of the *Philadelphia Inquirer*, who met Mrs. Rosenstiel years ago. "She did have suitcases of photographs that she had hauled away from her marriage to Lewis Rosenstiel," Nichols recalled. "The ones I saw showed Hoover, lawyer Roy Cohn and Rosenstiel at all sorts of social events with mobsters."

Susan Rosenstiel's credibility aside, I ran her story not least because it was buttressed by similar accounts from two other witnesses. In 1993, moreover, I learned that allegations about cross-dressing by Hoover were current in the East Coast homosexual community as early as 1963.

Historically, Hoover's sexuality matters because of the allegations that Mafia bosses used their knowledge of his private life to blackmail him, thus incapacitating the FBI in the fight against organized crime. That the FBI was delinquent in that fight for most of Hoover's career is now beyond argument. In 1993, congressional crime consultant Ralph Salerno drew a startling historical conclusion.

Hoover's attitude, said Salerno, "allowed organized crime to grow very strong in economic and political terms, so that it became a much bigger threat to the well-being of this country than it would have been if it had been addressed much sooner. I think if they could have been attacked before they grew, before they got the wealth, before they got the knowledge, organized crime could have been nipped in the bud, and never would have grown as strong as it got to be in later decades."

The case can be made that, had Hoover not been so delinquent, the Godfather-style Mafia in the United States, the Mafia of insidious nationwide power, might never have existed.

Neil Welch, a former FBI Agent in Charge and a legendary fighter against organized crime after Hoover's death, has called the information in this book "a powerful indictment of both the presidents and the Congress that allowed one man to have such enormous power over the nation's law enforcement machinery—with no real accountability. FBI agents in the field could have been vastly more effective in their war against crime if the issues now raised had been responsibly addressed in the public dialogue while Hoover lived."

A former FBI supervisor, Laurence Keenan, offers troubling new information on another controversial episode: Hoover's handling of the assassination of President Kennedy. Sent to Mexico City to investigate the alleged assassin's visit there before the tragedy, Keenan returned deeply frustrated. "I remember arriving there two or three days after the assassination," he recalled, "with the authority to coordinate all the investigations by the FBI and the CIA. But my attempt to talk to the witnesses was aborted. I had the authority from Director Hoover to conduct the investigation. But on having telephone contact with Washington, I realized that these orders were somewhat paper orders— not to be taken literally. My efforts were frustrated from day one. It was agreed that I should return to headquarters and submit my report. I went in and talked to the Director, and there really wasn't too much excitement. Oswald was seen as the lone assassin, and the investigation was to be wrapped up. We could say the investigation was effectively over within days. 'Conspiracy' was a word that was *verboten*. It was not to be heard on anybody's lips. The idea that Oswald had a confederate or was part of a group or a conspiracy was definitely enough to place a man's career in jeopardy. The realization soon came to me that my efforts in Mexico City had been window dressing. I knew the FBI had the capacity and the facilities to conduct a world-class investigation. When the FBI was told to do something and had the backing of the front office—meaning Mr. Hoover—there were no limits to what we could do. However, looking back, I feel a certain amount of shame. This one investigation disgraced a great organization."

There should be no doubt, finally, about Hoover's blackmailing of politicians. In 1993, in his memoirs, former British Home Secretary Roy—now Lord—Jenkins told of an extraordinary encounter he'd had with the Director in 1966. "I suppose," Jenkins recalled, "he did not think it much mattered what he said to 'Brits,' and he talked with the wildest indiscretion. He denounced the Kennedys [Jack just three years dead, Bobby just two years away from being his nominal boss as Attorney General]. He said he had somewhat, but not all that much, more respect for Lyndon Johnson. He implied that he had such detailed and damning material on every U.S. politician of note, particularly those of liberal persuasion, that his position was impregnable. No one could afford to fire or discipline him. The country was in a pretty terrible state, both morally and politically, but was just about held together by FBI agents, who patrolled it like a chosen race of prefects."

Members of the public who have contacted me since the original hardback publication have expressed outrage. "The information in your book," one woman wrote, "made me want to retch. I don't think I will ever believe anything about our form of government again—nor will I ever have confidence in anyone in office, ever. They named a building for him, and it is still there!"

They did, and it is. But democracy is not dead. As this edition went to press, outraged by fresh information about Hoover's abuse of Congress, seven U.S. senators, led by Howard Metzenbaum, introduced a bill that would—if passed—remove the Director's name from the headquarters of the FBI.

As a signal of real change, FBI Director Louis Freeh marked his arrival in office in 1993 by announcing a string of appointments. The new lineup of Assistant Directors included a woman, a black man and a Hispanic. In Congressional Cemetery, J. Edgar Hoover must be spinning in his grave. May he and his abuses soon spin out of current concern and into the dark place in American history to which he belongs.

A.S.
Co. Waterford, Ireland
1994

AUTHOR'S NOTES

See List of Abbreviations on pages 573–575.

Prologue

1. White House tape transcripts, Oct. 8, 25, 1971.

Chapter 1

1. As an alert reader of the hardback edition of this book pointed out, January 1, 1895, was in fact a Tuesday. The mistake is in Hoover's original note, in HC.

2. Sullivan served with the FBI for thirty years, from 1941 to 1971, by which time he had risen to the number three post in the Bureau—Assistant to the Director. Because he left the FBI after a quarrel with Hoover, described in detail in a later chapter, it has been suggested that his criticisms may have been more sour grapes than hard fact. Yet conversations with the co-author of Sullivan's book, former NBC journalist Bill Brown, and analysis of his tape-recorded conversations with congressional investigator Robert Fink, indicated that Sullivan was essentially truthful. His comments may sometimes have been self-serving, but the accusations leveled at Hoover are consistent with other information. His comments remain a unique high-level resource for any study of Hoover. Sullivan was shot dead in 1977 in an apparent hunting accident, shortly before a scheduled appearance before the House committee investigating the assassination of President Kennedy. (*The Bureau,* by William Sullivan, NY, Norton, 1979, transcript of int. by DES investigator Robert Fink, May 2, 1976, notes of Arthur Schlesinger int., July 26, 1976, ints. Ann Barniker, Charles Bates, Bill Brown, Fred Clancy, Mark Felt, Robert Fink, Richard Helms, Harold Leinbaugh, John McGrail, Robert Mardian, 1988, 1990, David Garrow notes of int. with Charles Brennan.)

Chapter 3

1. Rauh is best remembered as a cofounder of Americans for Democratic Action.

2. Hoover never registered to vote, according to the Washington, D.C., Board of Elections. D.C. residents could not vote at all until 1956, but from 1964 on could vote in presidential elections and for a nonvoting House delegate.

Chapter 4

1. Herbert Hoover was not related to J. Edgar Hoover.

2. While these innovations are generally credited to Hoover, his predecessor Bruce Bielaski insisted they were part of a program he drafted years earlier. (1958 int. of Bielaski, reported to author by Wm. Dufty, 1992.)

3. The best summation of Hoover's complex file systems is in *From the Secret Files of J. Edgar Hoover*, edited by Athan Theoharis, Chicago, Ivan Dee, 1991.

Chapter 5

1. Amos aside, it seems three other blacks may have worked as genuine agents. Even that is not certain; they served in New York and Chicago and may also have been used as chauffeurs when Hoover was in town.

2. This alleged surveillance of Farley is distinct from a later operation Roosevelt ordered for political reasons in 1940. In 1933, relations between Roosevelt and Farley were still cordial.

Chapter 6

1. A reader points out that, in Ireland, plainclothesmen of the old G Division of the Dublin police were long known as "G-Men." Given that so many FBI agents were of Irish extraction, it seems possible that the appellation was originated not by criminals but within the FBI itself. (Corr. Peter McDermott, 1993.)

2. Dr. Rubye Johnson, Associate Professor of Social Work at Tulane University, suggests that Hoover derived his notions about women and crime from the idea of women as intrinsically evil that circulated around 1900. The notion

has long since been refuted, not least by FBI statistics. The "red hair" thesis is ridiculous. (Int. Dr. Rubye Johnson, 1992.)

3. It seems three agents fired: Charles Winstead, Clarence Hurt and perhaps Purvis. Winstead is generally credited with firing the shots that killed Dillinger. (FBI HQ 67-3900, et al.)

Chapter 7

1. The woman with the toy gun has been wrongly identified in picture captions as Cobina Wright. Interviews with Wright and Stuart establish that this was an error. Stuart has original copies of the photographs, supplied to her by the Stork Club photographer. The pictures were taken at New Year's 1936, not 1935, as cited elsewhere.

Chapter 8

1. Recent examples of similar behavior by homosexual officials include President Reagan's adviser Terry Dolan and Rep. Robert Bauman. (*WP,* May 11, 1987, *Advocate,* Apr. 15, 1982, *NYT,* Oct. 4, 1980, *Playboy,* Aug. 1990.)

Chapter 9

1. The only serious attempt at independent reporting on Hoover between 1937 and the sixties was a *New York Post* series in the fall of 1959. Writer William Dufty and David Gelman, now a senior editor at *Newsweek,* remember the palpable fear they encountered and the countermeasures taken by Hoover. The series was denounced in Congress, and by the National Association of Manufacturers, before it had even been written. Hoover falsely told Joseph Eckhouse, a top Gimbels executive (and thus a vital *Post* advertiser) that *Post* editor James Wechsler's wife had been fired from a previous post for being a Communist. Hoover also ordered the bugging of Wechsler's Washington hotel room, and a *Post* reporter's room was searched. (*NYP,* Oct. 5–20, 1959, Dorothy Schiff to author, Mar. 30, 1988, ints. Wm. Dufty, David Gelman, Ed Kosner, Joseph Barry, Carl Pelleck, Nancy Wechsler, Cartha DeLoach, 1988, Sullivan

to Belmont, Dec. 1, 1958, FBI 94-8-173, H to Hoffman, Jan. 27, 1960, FBI 94-8-180, Wechsler/H corr., Wechsler Papers, State Historical Society of Wisconsin, *Time,* Oct. 19, 1959, *NAM News,* Feb. 20, 1959, *The FBI Nobody Knows,* by Fred Cook, NY, Macmillan, 1964, p. 416, Robert Spivack file, FBI 10018954, *NYT,* Jul. 22, 1975, int. John Crewdson, 1988, Nichols to H, Oct. 17, 1957, Private Collection.)

Chapter 10

1. Harry Vaughan, President Truman's aide, years later said flatly that Corcoran had been tapped during the Roosevelt era—as he was to be during the Truman presidency. No records survive of such a tap during the Roosevelt period, but that does not necessarily mean it did not happen. Not all such records survived. (*D,* p. 109, and see *B,* pp. 163ff.)

Chapter 11

1. Britain did not fully share the secret with the U.S. until 1943.

2. Some scholars have questioned whether Stephenson really had access to Roosevelt. The President's appointment records do not reflect such visits, but the Roosevelt Library Archivist notes that he often had "off the record" meetings, which went unrecorded. Stephenson's secretary, Grace Garner, has said he "certainly" saw the President, and repeatedly. She personally handled much of the relevant cable traffic. (Raymond Teichman, FDR Library Supervisory Archivist, in letter to author, June 16, 1992, int. Garner, 1992.)

3. A copy of the official British history of the Stephenson operation surfaced in 1989 in Canada.

4. von Auenrode was using the name "von Karsthoff" at the time. (Popov Papers.)

5. "Good riddance" was a characteristic Hoover phrase, one he used in writing when an agent he disliked quit the Bureau. (Davidson to Callahan re. Nelson Gibbons, Sept. 24, 1962, FBI 67-528050.)

6. Sir William Stephenson confirmed before his death that he did discuss Popov with Hoover. (Response to author's question, 1988.)

7. Popov's private papers show Masterman addressed him as "My dear Popov," while Popov addressed him as "JC."

8. Popov's ghostwriter, and his son Marco, say he was initially reluctant to include the anecdote at all, because it was such a bitter memory.

9. The widows of two other British officers who worked with Popov, Ewen Montagu and Bill Luke, said in 1990 their husbands had no doubt Popov saw Hoover. Popov also discussed the episode with a friend, the Yugoslav author Branko Bokun, in 1946. "He told me then, and many times afterwards," Bokun recalled, "there are some things in life that shock so much they never leave you. It marked him for the rest of his life." (Ints. Iris Montagu, Anne Luke and Branko Bokun, 1990.) The official files neither support nor impugn Popov's account. The British do not release intelligence records. One of the official histories of wartime intelligence, co-authored by former MI-5 Deputy Director Charles Simkins, says there is nothing in MI-5 or MI-6 files about Popov's talks with Jebsen, nor about his confrontation with Hoover. It may be significant that, as official accounts admit, there were frequent turf battles between the foreign and domestic arms of British Intelligence. John Pepper, who worked for William Stephenson and who arrived in New York with Popov, said in 1990, "We didn't tell MI-5 anything about the case." MI-5, which had handled Popov's early European operations, lost effective control and contact once his American mission began. Popov's U.S. sojourn may have been covered by the files of British Security Coordination—William Stephenson's organization—but their contents remain an unknown quantity. (*British Intelligence in the Second World War,* vol. 5, by Michael Howard, London, HMSO, 1990, and *British Intelligence in the Second World War,* vol. 4, by F. H. Hinsley and C. A. G. Simkins, London, HMSO, 1990, [turf battles] ibid., p. 181, ints. Pepper, 1988, 1990.)

10. According to Japanese sources, the Taranto precedent was a key factor in planning Pearl Harbor. By August 1941, when Popov arrived in the U.S. with his warning, Japanese

pilots were training hard—in the words of a surviving pilot—"for torpedo bombing runs on an enclosed harbor." (*And I Was There,* by Edwin Layton, with Roger Pineau and John Costello, NY, Morrow, 1985, p. 72, int. Hirata Matsumura, *International Herald Tribune,* Dec. 7, 1991.)

Chapter 12

1. There were football (as opposed to baseball) teams thus named in 1941.

2. These arrests were quite separate from the later internment of some 111,000 Japanese Americans and resident aliens, which Hoover rightly opposed as "based primarily on public hysteria and political pressure." As late as 1989, a special law was passed to ensure that surviving internees were paid compensation. (*NYT,* Jun. 30, 1985, *WP,* Oct. 27, and *NYT,* Nov. 9, 1989.)

3. Popov and Hoover were to clash again. In 1946, in a signed article in *Reader's Digest,* Hoover told a distorted version of the original Popov contact, implying his loyalties were to Nazi Germany and taking credit for the discovery of the microdot system. Confronted by a furious Popov, Hoover agreed changes would be made in future editions of the article. The FBI file records Popov's visit to HQ that year, but suggests he met only with aides. He insisted he met with Hoover himself. (*Reader's Digest,* Apr. 1946, *Spy Counterspy,* by Dusko Popov, St. Albans (UK), Panther, 1976, pp. 176ff, Popov to H, Sept. 6, H to Popov, Sept. 11, Ladd to H, Sept. 11, 1946, unsigned memo, Aug. 16, SAC to Director, Aug. 31, Kelley to Dunn, Oct. 1, 1973, FBI 65-36994, Popov to Iverson, Oct. 10, 1973, Popov Papers.)

4. The intimate nature of Hoover's relations with the officials Ketchum named makes it plausible that he dined with them regularly, as described. In light of everything else now known about Hoover's Machiavellian activity over Pearl Harbor, Ketchum's account cannot be dismissed. (Ints. Betty Rowell, Mrs. Edward Tindall, Harold Jinks, Betty Keenan, Mrs. Ernest Stevenson and Robert Donihi, 1990, Joseph Keenan to H, Sept. 30, 1947, Keenan Papers, Harvard Law School Library, but see *P,* p. 544*n59*.)

5. For his World War II service, William Stephenson became the first non-American to receive the Medal for Merit. He also received a British knighthood, as did William Donovan and, later, Hoover. Had he been British, Hoover would have been entitled to style himself *Sir* J. Edgar Hoover. Less than impressed, probably because of his poor wartime relations with the British, Hoover soon had the British honor deleted from the official list of his awards. (*Intrepid's Last Case,* by William Stevenson, NY, Ballantine, 1984, p. 172, *A Man Called Intrepid,* by William Stevenson, London, Macmillan, 1976, p. 461, *Washington Times Herald,* Mar. 8, 1946, *London Daily Telegraph* and *Times,* Oct. 18, *Business Week,* Nov. 11, entry HSF 5, *Time,* Dec. 22, 1947.)

Chapter 13

1. For coverage of Hoover's role in the Welles affair, see Chapter 8.

Chapter 14

1. Suspicion had first been aroused by a news story on February 9, 1945, suggesting that Roosevelt's plans for intelligence, made with Donovan at his elbow, would lead to a "police state." The story was based on a top-secret Donovan memo that had gone only to a handful of officials, including Hoover. The *Chicago Tribune* correspondent who obtained it, Walter Trohan, has repeatedly denied Hoover was his source and said Roosevelt aide Steve Early gave him the lead. Yet Early was away from Washington for three weeks before the story broke and would hardly have leaked information certain to embarrass his boss. Trohan was at this time becoming close to Hoover—they would eventually become so pally that they addressed each other in jest as "Comrade." General Donovan, meanwhile, is said to have marked the various copies of the memo in question with tiny textual differences—and it was those inserted in Hoover's copy that reportedly turned up in the Trohan story. (*Donovan and the CIA,* by Thomas Troy, Frederick, MD, University Publications of America, 1981, pp. 253ff,

Chicago Tribune, Feb. 9, 1945, ints. Trohan, 1988, Walter Pforzeheimer, Larry Houston, Thomas Powers, 1991, [Early] *FDR,* by Ted Morgan, NY, Simon & Schuster, 1985, p. 744, [H/Trohan] int. Trohan, 1988, Trohan Papers, HHL, [Donovan belief] Thomas Troy, op. cit., pp. 258ff, ["marked"] *NYP,* Oct. 11, 1959, int. Wm. Dufty, 1988.)

2. See Chapter 8.

Chapter 15

1. It is clear today that there was indeed a Communist espionage operation in the early forties and that documents were leaked by sources in Washington. Some of the Bentley/Chambers testimony fits the skein of evidence in the Rosenberg and Fuchs spy cases. There is still no certainty, however, that either White or Hiss was wittingly involved.

2. For coverage of COINTELPRO, see Chapter 32.

3. As of the 1948 elections, Mundt became a Senator.

4. "I never played poker in my life," Hoover claimed in a 1946 note. McGaughey's account, and other anecdotes, shows that he lied. His congressional poker circle in the forties included Representatives Michael Kerwin, Thomas Martin and Ben Jensen, and Senator Stiles Bridges. (H notation, Jan. 16, 1946, OC 51, Cooper article, NY *Journal,* Dec. 3, 1937, *Infamy, Pearl Harbor and Its Aftermath,* by John Toland, NY, Berkley Books, 1983, p. 342.)

5. The four convicted were Julius and Ethel Rosenberg, Morton Sobell and David Greenglass, all in connection with the Rosenberg spy case. For all the controversy, little doubt now remains that the Rosenbergs did betray nuclear secrets. Nikita Khrushchev's memoirs, published in 1990, acknowledged the Rosenbergs' "significant help" in accelerating Soviet development of the atomic bomb. Hoover had been the first to suggest the prosecution of Ethel, in spite of a lack of hard evidence against her, in the hope that it would "serve as a lever" to force Julius to crack. He never did, but Hoover waited hopefully at an open telephone line until the very moment of the couple's execution in 1953. At home in Virginia that night, according to his son, FBI propaganda boss Louis Nichols and the friendly journalist Rex Collier

"went around the house turning off the lights, so they would have more electricity at Sing Sing to electrocute the Rosenbergs. It was symbolic." (Ints. Ann Ginger, Director, Meiklejohn Institute, and Gene Dennis, archivist, ILWU, San Francisco, 1992, *Rosenberg File*, by Ronald Radosch and Joyce Milton, NY, Holt, Rinehart and Winston, 1983, *Ethel Rosenberg: Beyond the Myths*, by Irene Philipson, NY, Franklin Watts, 1988, [Khrushchev] *Khrushchev Remembers*, ed. Jerrold Schecter and Vyacheslav Luchkov, Boston, Little, Brown, 1990, pp. 193ff, Anthony Villano, op. cit., pp. 25ff, int. J. Edgar Nichols, 1988.)

6. In 1953, when the Republicans had returned to the White House, Edgar made a sensational congressional appearance in support of Attorney General Brownell's claim that Truman had ignored FBI warnings about Harry Dexter White. Hoover claimed he appeared only because Brownell ordered him to, but Brownell said in 1988 that Hoover "volunteered." (Int. Brownell, 1988, OC 67, *NYT*, Nov. 7, 14–19, 22–27, 1953, *Life*, Nov. 23, 1953, *P*, p. 318, *Drew Pearson Diaries*, 1949–59, ed. Tyler Abell, NY, Holt, Rinehart & Winston, 1974, p. 284.)

Chapter 17

1. There is no report that Hoover ever expressed any sympathy for the likes of Rockwell.

2. In 1956, again before an election, Hoover would feed information on Stevenson to Richard Nixon. He would later tell a Kennedy aide that Stevenson was a "notorious homosexual." (*Nation*, May 7, 1990, citing FBI records.)

3. A source interviewed for this book contradicts a note in FBI files suggesting that Hoover ceased providing McCarthy with information in the summer of 1953. The interviewee, an electronics specialist who bugged McCarthy and his aides on behalf of the military during the Army-McCarthy hearings, said the secret help continued to the end. "I was listening in," he recalled, "two, sometimes three times a day, to calls between Hoover and Roy Cohn. Cohn and McCarthy were still getting everything they had from Hoover." (Int. with source, anonymous by request—he still

works for the government, and Athan Theoharis, *Secret Files,* p. 264.)

Chapter 18

1. Former agent Woods has been named as having been used by Hoover, in retirement, to offer material on Martin Luther King's sex life to the press. He denied it in a 1990 interview and said he could not remember ever having filed a report on a senator's sex activity.

2. Supreme Court Justice Abe Fortas resigned in 1969 after disclosures that he was taking money from a convicted criminal whose appeal was pending. In 1965, responding to pressure from President Johnson, Hoover had smoothed the way for Fortas' Senate confirmation. In 1966, he and the FBI improperly exchanged information on a case then pending before the Court. (*Cloak and Gavel,* by Alexander Charns, Chicago, University of Illinois Press, 1992, pp. 53–57, et al.)

3. There is indeed a mass of FBI material on Smathers, including allegations about his sex life. (Smathers FBI docs., FOIPA Release 293, 982/190-47115, Jul. 19, 1991.)

Chapter 19

1. During the furor, the file shows, Hoover engaged in a complex debate with Deputy Attorney General Kleindienst over precisely how to answer a press inquiry into whether or not the FBI had ever "instituted" electronic surveillance of a member of Congress. Hoover tried to avoid answering at all, then settled for saying the FBI had "never installed" a bugging device against a politician. According to a surveillance expert who then worked for the government, the FBI was at the time using a new, secret system, one that did not require a bug as such but functioned thanks to something normally present in all homes and offices. The system is still secret. (H to T, Apr. 13, 1971, TSF 8.)

2. Dowdy was being investigated for bribery and was eventually jailed.

3. Illicit FBI tapping was reportedly not restricted to members of Congress. Robert Amory, a CIA Deputy Direc-

tor in the fifties, said he saw evidence that the Bureau tapped his office phone. Secretary of State Dean Rusk suspected the FBI of bugging him. And, according to former Agent Norman Ollestad, Hoover sometimes bugged his own colleagues. (*WP*, Feb. 7, 1971, *As I Saw It,* by Dean Rusk, NY, Norton, 1990, pp. 197, 559, *Waging Peace and War,* by Thomas Schoenbaum, NY, Simon & Schuster, 1988, p. 280, *Inside the FBI,* by Norman Ollestad, NY, Lyle Stuart, 1967, pp. 68, 105.)

4. Gallagher has insisted that the bonds in the IRS case had belonged to the Democratic Party and brought him no profit. He believes the charges were a natural sequel to the *Life* magazine episode.

5. Zicarelli was overheard in 1964 and 1965—but not in 1960—talking with a crony about asking for Gallagher's help with a deportation case. The mobsters also mentioned other public officials in hopeful terms—three judges, a U.S. Senator and a Republican Congresswoman. (Newark *Star-Ledger, NYT,* Jun. 11, 1969.)

6. As the Watergate tapes show, Smith's close relations with the FBI were later discussed with President Nixon in the Oval Office. (Transcript, Feb. 16, 1973, p. 7, WHT.)

Chapter 21

1. Lombardozzi died in 1992. His comments were obtained through an intermediary, with the help of London attorney William Pepper, in 1990.

2. In 1948, when Hoover received a Justice Department request for information on the racketeer Longy Zwillman, he said FBI records reflected "no investigation" on the man. This circumlocution concealed the fact that Bureau files contained 600 pages on the mobster. (*Gangster,* by Mark Stuart, London, Star, 1987, p. 141.)

3. A review of Anslinger's FBI file suggests that—contrary to the mythology—he and Hoover were friendly toward each other. (FBI 72-56284.)

4. McClanahan went to jail for thirteen months, following a trial featuring mob witnesses from Chicago to Las Vegas.

5. In 1949, when members of the Licavoli mob family

asked Davidson how they could thank him for having helped a relative, he suggested they donate $5,000 to a J. Edgar Hoover foundation then being set up to combat juvenile delinquency—no connection with the foundation of that name that exists today. The Licavolis made the donation. (H to T, et al., Jun. 29, 1949, FBI 94-8-350-371, *Life*, May 2, 1969, int. Davidson, 1990.)

6. At Maryland tracks Edgar dealt with a Damon Runyonesque tipster called "Washington Jake." In California he dealt with Harry Hall, a bookmaker with a prison record. Hall recalls giving Hoover a tip while accompanied by Joe Matranga, son-in-law of a mobster high in the Detroit Mafia. (Int. Jimmy Raftery, 1988, ints. Harry Hall, 1988, 1990, corr. John Hunt, 1993.)

Chapter 22

1. Chuck and Sam Giancana's 1992 book *Double Cross* attracted criticism for some of its claims about the assassination of President Kennedy. Portions of the book do appear to have been embroidered, but interviews with co-author Sam Giancana (Chuck's son and his namesake, the mobster's godson) indicate that its principal assertions are based on Chuck's account of what the mobster told him. (Ints. Sam Giancana, 1991, 1992.)

2. Guilemo Santucci, a confidant of Costello and Lansky, said much the same. He would talk, recalled his driver John Dellafera, "of the good old days, when Hoover and the other big shots would look the other way. He told me they would do Hoover favors and he would do them favors in return. Hoover agreed to this as if they had something on him." (Int. and written statement of Dellafera, 1991.)

3. In the late forties, the FBI did carry out surveillance against Costello, planting bugs at New York's Copacabana Club, where the mobster held court each day. This was highly productive until, out of the blue, the agents were suddenly called off. "We were never told why," recalled former agent Jack Danahee. (Int. 1988.)

4. See end of Chapter 7.

5. See Chapter 7.

6. Police sources told Hamill they, too, had heard of the compromising photographs.

7. Lansky did come under heavy FBI surveillance in 1961, but this was part of the push against organized crime under Attorney General Robert Kennedy. (*Little Man,* by Robert Lacey, Boston, Little, Brown, 1991, pp. 288ff, corr. Lacey, 1992.)

8. The U.S. Intelligence/Mafia connection in World War II was a high-risk relationship, the precursor of the arrangement in the sixties, when the CIA and the mob collaborated to plot the murder of Fidel Castro.

9. The CIA's James Angleton, said to have been in possession of a Hoover sex picture, served in the OSS in Rome at the end of the war—at the time Lansky's associate Lucky Luciano arrived there, following his release from a U.S. jail in recognition of his services to U.S. Intelligence. (*Cold Warrior,* by Tom Mangold, NY, Simon & Schuster, 1991, pp. 22ff.)

10. The spying on the brothel, near the Brooklyn Naval Yard, occurred because of suspicion that U.S. Senator David Walsh, Chairman of the Naval Affairs Committee, was a patron. Walsh was exonerated, following a controversial probe in which the FBI played a key role. Afterward, Walsh sent Hoover an effusive letter of thanks. (OC 123, 153, *Trading With the Enemy,* by Charles Higham, NY, Delacorte, 1983, p. 88, *NYP,* May 1–22, 1942, *NYT,* Oct. 6, 1942, *Meyer Lansky: Mogul of the Mob,* by Dennis Eisenberg, Uri Dan, and Eli Landau, NY, Paddington Press, 1979, p. 199.)

Chapter 23

1. Judge McLaughlin and former committee investigator William Gallinaro were outraged when a charge of perjury was brought against Mrs. Rosenstiel in an unrelated New York case in January 1971. They believed then, and still do, that this was the work of Rosenstiel himself, using money and influence to obstruct the committee inquiry by discred-

iting his former wife. The millionaire's attorney in the divorce case, Benjamin Javits, was disbarred for conniving at his client's attempt to subvert the judicial system. (*NYT*, Feb. 9, 1971, *Village Voice*, Feb. 18, 1971, ints. Wm. Gallinaro, Edward McLaughlin, 1988, [Javits] *NYT*, Jan. 6, 1971.)

2. In 1959, Hoover rebuffed Dr. Robert Hutchins, President of the Fund for the Republic, who offered $4 million to help the struggle against organized crime and asked the FBI for advice. Hoover sent William Sullivan to tell Hutchins flatly that none of the mob bosses mentioned by Hutchins—all prominent mafiosi—were known to the FBI. Hoover's advice was that the fund would do better making a study of why blacks committed such a high percentage of violent crime. (Ints. W. H. Ferry, 1988, 1991, *Nation*, Apr. 26, 1971, corr. Jan. 27–Mar. 30, 1953, FBI 100-368336, FBI cross-refs. on W. H. Ferry.)

Chapter 24

1. Johnson's biographer Robert Caro concluded in 1990 that it was "blindingly clear" there was ballot-rigging, as did the early exhaustive study by Mary Kahl. (*The Years of Lyndon Johnson: Means of Ascent,* by Robert Caro, NY, Alfred Knopf, 1990, pp. xxxi, 384, *Ballot Box 13*, by Mary Kahl, Jefferson, NC, McFarland, 1983, pp. 231, 241, int. Madeleine Brown, 1989, *People*, Aug. 3, 1987.)

2. The accepted wisdom on why Kennedy picked Johnson has been the reconstruction of events by historian and former Kennedy aide Arthur Schlesinger. Drawing on talks with Robert Kennedy, he established that John at first invited Johnson onto the ticket merely as a ploy to unite the party—not dreaming he would accept. He was chagrined when Johnson did accept, a move Schlesinger surmised was because Johnson felt it was his last chance to become a national figure. Had he been free to do so, Robert recalled, "Jack . . . wanted to get rid of" Johnson. Yet when he tried to palm Johnson off with the chairmanship of the party, the Texan turned him down flat. "I want the vice presidency

and intend to get it," he was quoted as saying. (See sources for "Convention" for this chapter.)

3. Lincoln's diary, covering most of her Kennedy service, remains locked in a deposit box.

4. On August 18, 1960, Hoover sent an FBI report about Kennedy to his Republican opponent, Richard Nixon. Though heavily censored as released, it apparently concerned Kennedy's womanizing. (SAC Washington to H, Aug. 18, 1960, FBI 94-37374, int. Hervé Alphand, 1988, *A Hero for Our Time,* by Ralph Martin, NY, Macmillan, 1983, p. 342, *L'Étonnement d'Être,* by Hervé Alphand, Paris, Fayard, 1977, p. 382.)

Chapter 25

1. See Chapter 5.

Chapter 26

1. Giancana's half brother, Chuck, has offered an equally startling and wholly unsubstantiated explanation. By his account, some of the packages contained copies of FBI reports on organized crime—reports that allowed Giancana to think he was getting vital insights into FBI operations against the mob. Soon, however, the mobster realized that there were great gaps in the intelligence he was sent—that the President was withholding key information. From then on, supposedly, his rage against Kennedy knew no bounds. (*Double Cross,* by Sam and Chuck Giancana, NY, Warner, 1992, p. 296, and int. Sam Giancana, 1992.)

2. A communication in Hoover's Official and Confidential file, dated March 30, 1962, advised him that the dismantling of the alleged marriage involved a Reno divorce, followed by another in New Jersey when the first was invalidated. A papal annulment was granted in 1953, the writer claimed, following pressure from Cardinal Cushing. (OC 13.2.)

3. See *Goddess: The Secret Lives of Marilyn Monroe,* by Anthony Summers, NY, New American Library, 1986, for a full account of the surveillance and of the actress' death.

4. The phone logs, however, record several calls after August 1962, some with the word "No" by them, and others without it.

5. The only such photograph ever published was taken by a photographer affiliated with the White House, and it was withheld until 1987, when it appeared in the June issue of *Life*.

Chapter 27

1. Hoover responded by planting press leaks to discredit Yarmolinsky. (See Yarmolinsky entry in sourcing for this chapter.)

2. Yevgeny Ivanov, the Soviet Naval Attaché at the center of the Profumo scandal, was in reality a GRU (military intelligence) agent. He said in 1992 that Moscow advised him it indeed had an interest in Novotny. Ivanov himself talked with her in London. (*The Naked Spy*, by Yevgeny Ivanov, London, John Blake, 1992, pp. 144ff.)

3. The FBI used Mollenhoff in the early sixties as a go-between to pass Bureau information to members of Congress. In 1970, when Mollenhoff was an aide to President Nixon, he would write to Hoover to warn that the *Los Angeles Times* was planning a series critical of the FBI. (Theodore Sorensen, Oral History, JFKL, Transcript, Feb. 27, 1973, p. 5, WHT, corr. Edwin Guthman, Jun. 1991, Mollenhoff to H, Feb. 23, 1970, White House Staff files, NP.)

Chapter 28

1. Some theorize that Johnson wanted a "lone nut" version because he feared rumors of Soviet involvement could lead to nuclear war. This may have been a factor.

2. For the second official's recollection, received after the hardback edition went to press, see the Afterword.

3. Hoover tried to discredit citizens who publicly challenged the "lone gunman" thesis. He authorized the mailing of a phony anonymous letter attacking the attorney Mark Lane and ordered circulation of a photograph that allegedly

showed Lane engaged in sexual activity. The photograph and memo went to at least one member of the Warren Commission: Congressman Hale Boggs. (Baumgartner to Sullivan, Feb. 24, 1964, IC 6, p. 762, H to SAC NY, Oct. 16, 1964, FBI 100-11844, DeLoach to T, Sept. 26, 1966, Mark Allen FOIA release Civil Action 81-1206, [photo] blind memo, Feb. 29, 1968, Fred Graham Papers, LC, ints. Graham, 1990, and Thomas Boggs, 1988, *Mother Jones,* Aug. 1979.)

4. Also excised from the original address book page is a (scored-through) name that appears to be "Gandy." It may be pure coincidence that this was the name of Hoover's secretary (Helen Gandy). But the record suggests Oswald was so angry with what he saw as FBI harassment before the assassination that he intended to complain to "the proper authorities." It is possible that, like countless callers over the years, Oswald had tried calling Hoover, was brushed off by Gandy and scrawled her name in his address book. While under arrest he made "derogatory remarks" about Hoover personally. (WC docs. 205, 16.64, WR IV, 466ff.)

5. Two reporters, Alonzo Hudkins of *The Houston Post* and Hugh Aynesworth of *The Dallas Morning News,* have since said that the "informant number" published by Hudkins—S-172—was fabricated, by Aynesworth, according to his own account in 1976. Their different accounts have failed to satisfy students of the case. Other concerns aside, the number S-172 is very close to the code by which the FBI did refer to security informants at that time. In 1975, Dallas FBI Agent Joe Pearce told Bureau Inspectors that Oswald had been Hosty's "informant or source." (*Esquire,* Feb. 1976, *New Times,* Jul. 11, 1975, HSCA Report, pp. 185ff, McNiff to Adams, Dec. 31, 1975, FBI 62-116395.)

6. The Commission did not even interview Deputy Sheriff Sweatt. It seems that the FBI, for its part, failed to tell the Commission about a similar allegation, by former Army Intelligence Colonel Philip Corso. (DeLoach to Mohr, two memos, Feb. 7, and another, Feb. 10, 1964, FBI 1977

release, no serial, Rosen to Belmont, Feb. 7, 1964, FBI 105-82555, ints. Mary and Julian Sourwine, 1991, int. Corso, 1992.)

7. Congress' Assassinations Committee reported that Aleman's FBI "contact" at that time, "denied ever being told such information by Aleman." It is not clear whether this refers to Scranton, who refused comment as late as 1992. (HSCA Report, p. 175, and int. 1992.)

8. Congress' Assassinations Committee quoted Becker as saying he did not report the Marcello threat to the FBI in 1962. In 1992 he insisted that he did report it, and noted that the committee's questioning of him was merely superficial. Its investigators spoke with him on the phone, but never in person. And he never testified. (HSCA IX, 83, int. Becker, 1992.)

9. Professor Robert Blakey, former Chief Counsel of Congress' Assassinations Committee, recalled in 1992 that the mob's violent talk on the wiretaps was circulated within the Justice Department. Independent research, however, shows no sign that it went to the Secret Service. Failure to circulate reports is sometimes justified on the grounds that it might risk exposure of an agency's sources and methods. There can be no recourse to that excuse in the case of threats against the President's life. (Ints. Robert Blakey, Mark Allen, 1992.)

10. One of Murchison's friends, D. H. "Dryhole" Byrd, owned the Texas School Book Depository. He and Paul Raigorodsky, who testified to the Warren Commission about Oswald's activity in Dallas, had—like Hoover—been guests at Murchison's California hotel. (*Dallas Conspiracy,* by Peter Dale Scott, unpub. ms., p. vi, 21, *Clint,* by Ernestine van Buren, Austin, TX, Eakin Press, 1986, p. 96, *Wall Street Journal,* Apr. 20, 1970, [Raigorodsky] ints. Allan Witwer, 1990, *Crossfire,* by Jim Marrs, NY, Carroll & Graf, 1989, p. 282.)

11. Discussed in the chapter that follows.

12. See Chapter 7. Gordon Novel, quoted in Chapter 22 as saying he was shown compromising photographs of Hoover by a senior CIA official, also claimed to have had a

conversation on the subject years later, with Marcello. According to Novel, Marcello said he too had been shown such a picture—in the course of contacts with those involved in the joint CIA-Mafia plots to kill Fidel Castro in the early sixties. Marcello said other top Mafia bosses had long since had access to the smear material, and had used it to keep Hoover's FBI at bay. (Int. Gordon Novel, 1992.)

Chapter 29

1. There were subplots to the Jenkins affair. President Johnson was principally concerned that it would lead to the discovery of his affair with the wife of one of his aides, who regularly joined him at social occasions with a homosexual companion as "beard." In 1964, several Washington officials received copies of what purported to be a compromising letter from Edgar to Jenkins. Edgar responded by having Senator Bourke Hickenlooper denounce the letter as part of a "Communist smear campaign." Agents who investigated the letter dubbed their probe REPULSE—for "Russian Efforts to Publish Unsavory Love Secrets of Edgar." (Evans to Belmont, Oct. 17, DeLoach to Mohr, Oct. 30, 1964, FBI 94-4-3830, int. Robert Baker, 1990, [Hickenlooper] H/Hickenlooper corr., Jan. 1966, Hickenlooper Papers, HHL, *CR*, Jan. 17, 1966, p. 367, *NYT*, Jan. 15, 1966, [dubbed] Trenton, NJ, *Times*, Mar. 13, 1980.)

Chapter 30

1. While he reacted viscerally against those who promoted racial equality, Hoover did not seek to promote the interests of white supremacists. On the contrary, the Bureau clamped down effectively on the Ku Klux Klan early in his career and—most notably—in the mid-sixties. (*P*, pp. 140ff, 373ff, 407ff, Athan Theoharis, *Secret Files*, p. 129, int. Neil Welch, 1988.)

2. See Chapter 27. In fact, Robert Kennedy granted wiretap permission only subject to review within thirty days. There was no review until 1965, because the assassination of President Kennedy, on November 22, 1963, put Robert virtually out of action for months. Hoover quietly

ignored the condition Kennedy had set, and the King wiretapping went on and on. (Athan Theoharis, *Secret Files,* p. 99.)

3. FBI records show that Dr. King once discussed Rustin's homosexuality with a colleague, in a warning way. The original FBI surveillance material remains sealed at the National Archives until 2027, and only then will historians learn what it reveals about King's sex life. (*Parting the Waters,* by Taylor Branch, NY, Simon & Schuster, 1988, p. 861.)

4. Joseph Woods, the former agent named by Royko, said in 1968 that the reporter might be "mixed up." As a serving agent, Woods had been one of those who supplied Hoover with sex information on politicians. (Int. Woods, 1988, and see Chapter 18.)

5. Although Sullivan's attempt to minimize his role was self-serving, former Assistant Directors Courtney Evans and Charles Bates totally rejected the notion that he might have sent the tape without Hoover's approval. Sullivan's longtime secretary, Ann Barniker, said the entire anti-King operation was "Mr. Hoover's thing." (Ints. Evans, Bates, Lish Whitsun, Nate Ferris, Ray Wannall, John McGrail, Larry Cohen, Bill Brown, Nicholas Horrock, 1988, Ann Barniker, 1990, *S,* p. 142, SRIA, p. 160, *GF,* p. 161, and David Garrow notes of Charles Brennan int.)

6. While Ray's claims have received little credence, students of the case cite leads indicating that Ray had contacts with an FBI informant before the assassination and that the FBI received advance intelligence that King would be killed in Memphis, yet failed to alert him. (Ints. Harold Weisberg, James Lesar, 1988, Philip Melanson, 1991.)

Chapter 31

1. The Democratic Convention in Chicago turned out to be a week of mayhem in which hundreds of anti-Vietnam demonstrators were injured in battles with the police. Edgar praised the police and said the media had distorted the facts. Later, a presidential commission concluded the police

behavior had been gratuitous and malicious, "a police riot." A Senate probe showed Edgar had urged agents to look not for the facts but for information that would weigh in favor of the police. (IC 6, p. 254, *NYT,* Sept. 19, Dec. 2, 1968.)

2. Rose Mary Woods' brother Joseph was a retired FBI agent. He was one of those who fed Hoover derogatory information on politicians and later—according to one reporter—tried to spread smear material on Martin Luther King. (See index references.)

3. There was a Hearthside restaurant, and there was such a reservoir. In 1988, Billy Byars, Jr., remembered the two adolescents named by Krebs and agreed that one of them had visited the Del Charro. While he said he knew nothing of the alleged sex activity, three of Krebs' associates recalled hearing elements of the story at the time.

Chapter 32

1. Hoover had declared himself "extremely pleased" with the sending of a phony letter smearing a New York Communist Party worker, William Albertson, as an FBI informant. His widow was paid $170,000, as late as 1989, as compensation for the fact that the operation wrecked Albertson's career. Hoover personally supervised the thirty-year persecution of Frank Wilkinson, a Los Angeles housing official who had first come to the FBI's attention for leading protests against plans for segregated housing in 1942. For no offense other than a stubborn commitment to civil rights and the abolition of the House Un-American Activities Committee, Wilkinson was surveilled, his phone tapped and his office burgled. Propaganda against him was mailed from nonexistent organizations, and his meetings were disrupted—on one occasion by American Nazis acting at the instigation of FBI agents. The FBI once learned precise details of a plot to kill Wilkinson and failed to warn him. Hoover's notes and initials are all over the Wilkinson file, which runs to 132,000 pages. (*NYT,* Oct. 26, 1989, *People,* Nov. 20, 1989, [Wilkinson] files of *LAT,* esp. Oct. 18, 1987, int. Frank Wilkinson, 1989, parts of FBI 100-112434, *It Did*

Happen Here, by Bud and Ruth Schulz, Berkeley, University of California Press, 1989, p. 263, and Athan Theoharis, *Secret Files,* p. 129.)

2. There is evidence that the FBI triggered events that led to other Panther deaths. In New Haven, Connecticut, Alex Rackley was executed by his own comrades following the leak of false information that he was a government informant. (*In These Times,* May 9, 1990.)

Chapter 33

1. See Chapter 8.
2. See Chapter 20.
3. See Chapter 19.
4. Mitchell said nothing about a resignation offer in eighty hours of conversation with Len Colodny, co-author of *Silent Coup,* before his death in 1988. (Int. Len Colodny, 1991.)

Chapter 35

1. The Soviet KGB, for its part, chalked up numerous confirmed kills with the use of poisoning techniques. (*KGB,* by John Barron, NY, Bantam, 1974, pp. 423ff.)

2. The FBI claimed in 1991 it had nothing on this subject in its files. Then, confronted with a memo from Prosecution Force files, it produced a document reflecting Akerman's inquiry and establishing that his source was independent of the *Crimson* article. Its author, former Agent Forrest Putman, said he could not remember writing the report. (John Wright [FBI] to James Lesar, Feb. 17, 1989, Kevin O'Brien [FBI] to Lesar, Nov. 20, 1991, Forrest Putman to CENSORED, Nov. 26, 1973, FBI 62-115870, int. Putman, 1991.)

3. According to the *Crimson* article, DeDiego suggested that two Cubans, Humberto Lopez and Jaime Ferrer, might supply information on the break-ins. Lopez, who was a Hunt-Liddy operative, said in 1988 that he knew nothing about them. Jaime Ferrer was not traced. In the early sixties, during the CIA's secret war against Castro, DeDiego was a member of Operation 40, a group whose members were

trained to capture Castro government documents and—in some cases—to commit assassinations. (Int. Humberto Lopez, 1988, and see DeDiego sourcing for this chapter.)

4. Clyde Tolson's brother, Hillory, is said to have claimed privately that Hoover in fact died at Clyde's apartment and that his body was returned to his home by agents in an FBI vehicle—to avoid the obvious embarrassment. While the story is not implausible, it is so indirectly sourced that it can here be treated only as rumor. (Ints. Robert Simmons, 1988, 1991.)

5. Dr. Luke told the press Hoover had been "suffering from a heart ailment for some time." It is odd that Dr. Choisser, Hoover's longtime GP, denies that there was any such history. (Death Cert. No. 72-03405, HSF 8, *NYT, WP,* May 3, 1972, but see, too, unattributed ref. to a much earlier heart ailment in *J. Edgar Hoover: The Man and the Secrets,* by Curt Gentry, NY, Norton, 1991, p. 461.)

6. See Chapter 19.

Epilogue

1. Realizing that Edgar's lying-in-state would coincide with antiwar rallies near the Capitol, Nixon's adviser Charles Colson issued orders to disrupt the demonstrations. Gordon Liddy and Howard Hunt brought in a team of Cubans, including some who were to take part in the Watergate break-ins, and they provoked fights in the crowd. Afterward, those involved claimed their purpose had been to protect Edgar's catafalque, which in fact was already perfectly well secured by the police and the military. (*Nightmare,* by Anthony Lukas, London, Penguin, 1988, p. 194, *Undercover,* by Howard Hunt, NY, Putnam, 1974, p. 211, *Will,* by Gordon Liddy, NY, St. Martin's Press, 1980, p. 220, *Secret Agent,* by Jim Hougan, NY, Morrow, 1978, pp. 133ff, *WP,* May 26, 1974, *Miami Herald,* Apr. 22, 1973, *NYT,* Mar. 9, 1973, ints. Gordon Liddy, Rolando Martinez, Felipe DeDiego, Frank Sturgis, Humberto Lopez, William Kunstler, 1988.)

2. The grave was well tended in 1992, following a change

in management of the cemetery. The Society of Former Agents now contributes to the upkeep, and Washington Masons also help. (Int. John Hanley, 1992.)

3. The content of this book was discussed with two eminent professors of psychiatry and psychology, a child psychologist and an Army psychologist who has worked with dysfunctional families. They are Dr. Harold Lief, Professor Emeritus at the University of Pennsylvania and past President of the American Academy of Psychoanalysts, Dr. John Money, Professor of Medical Psychology at Johns Hopkins University School of Medicine, Dr. Norris Haynes, Research Director at Yale University's Child Study Center, and Gaye Humphreys, a family therapist now working with the Army in Ireland.

SOURCE NOTES

Everything reported in this book was documented by the author, and all sources—of both human and print origin—appeared in the 1993 hardback edition. While the main text remains unabridged in this edition, the Source Notes are summarized—in the interest of brevity and to ensure that the book is affordable to a wider public. Readers who wish to obtain the full Source Notes should write to the author, who will be glad to provide them. Please address requests to: Anthony Summers, c/o Pocket Books, 1230 Avenue of the Americas, New York, NY 10020.

J. Edgar Hoover left no diaries or intimate letters—with the single exception of his bizarre correspondence with Melvin Purvis, quoted in this book. His personal files, which probably contained private letters as well as highly sensitive office documents, were mostly destroyed on his orders following his death. A mass of personal material—photographs, childhood journals, even Hoover's christening robe and baby bootees—has survived as a permanent exhibit at the Masons' Supreme Council headquarters in Washington, D.C. For real information, however, the researcher must forage among the millions of documents that passed across the Director's desk during his tenure. The notes he scrawled on them in his rounded script, known as Blue Gems because they are written in blue ink, reveal a good deal about the man.

Hoover's obsession with all that concerned himself, coupled with the inexorable efficiency of his bureaucratic machine, created another historical treasure. Every single clipping that mentioned his name—from national newspapers to the most obscure local journal—was clipped, perused personally by Hoover, then filed away. Crammed into thirty-three cardboard boxes, they have found their way to the National Archives.

These paper sources, along with tens of thousands of FBI documents obtained under the Freedom of Information Act—and more than 800 interviews conducted for this book—are the pieces of the jigsaw that lead to this portrait of Hoover.

To interpret abbreviations used below, see pages 573–575

Prologue

Interviews included undertakers William Reburn and John van Hoesen, Watergate figures Frank Sturgis and Felipe DeDiego, Nixon aides H. R. Haldeman and John Ehrlichman, Justice Department officials Robert Mardian, Mitchell Rogovin, and Harold Tyler, psychiatrists Dr. Harold Lief and Dr. John Money. Events at the Nixon White House were documented by WHT, 587-003, 601-033, Haldeman's note, 9:15 A.M., May 2, 1972, WHSF, NP. Nixon's reaction to H's death draws on *J. Edgar Hoover: The Man and the Secrets,* by Curt Gentry, NY, Norton, 1991, p. 28, and a 1992 interview of Gentry (supplied to the author by Ingrid Young) regarding passage in unpublished Watergate tape transcript.

Chapter 1

Interviews included Hoover relatives Dorothy Davy, Fred Robinette, Virginia Hoover, Anna Hoover Kienast, and Marjorie Stromme, childhood acquaintances Monica Dwyer and Francis Gray, and aide and intimate friend Guy Hottel. Medical information was supplied by Dr. Lawrence McDonald. Documents on Hoover's childhood include his parents' letters, school reports, and his own notes at HC, his 1949–50 correspondence with Harold Burton, Burton Papers, LC, publications of Central High School Alumni Association, and his father's death certificate, D.C. no. 2645955.

SOURCE NOTES

Chapter 2

Interviews included former FBI Assistant Director Cartha DeLoach and—on church attendance—former agent Leo McClairen. Schoolmates' recollections came from Dave Stephens' letter to H., May 25, 1955, in HSF, and C.W. Collier's letter in *Time*, Jun. 1, 1936. Hoover's degree was described in an interview with the George Washington University Registrar. Details of H.'s early career drew on William Dufty's research for the *NYP*, 1958 (which included an interview with Bruce Bielaski), the John Lord O'Brian Papers at the University of Buffalo Law School, H.'s World War I memos in DJ files, RG60, NA, the Felix Frankfurter Papers, LC, and Hoover and Clyde Tolson's staff files. Hoover's wartime status drew on the exemption list in *CR*, vol. 56, p. 8138, and an interview with Barbie Richardson of the Selective Service Commission. H.'s relations with Alice were based on an interview with a serving FBI archival source who requested anonymity, and Cartha DeLoach.

Chapter 3

Interviews included H.'s godson, J. Edgar Ruch, Guy Hottel, Justice Frankfurter's former law clerk Joseph Rauh, and James Thompson of Aspin Hill pet cemetery. *Without Understanding: The FBI and Political Surveillance, 1908–1941,* a doctoral dissertation by David Williams (See Bibliography), was especially useful, as were the papers of Sen. Thomas Walsh, LC, the several 1920 congressional probes of illegal practices at the Justice Department under Attorney General Palmer, Hse. of Reps. 66th Cong., 2nd and 3rd Sessions, the *Drew Pearson Diaries, 1949–59,* ed. Tyler Abell, NY, Holt, Rinehart & Winston, 1974, the Felix Frankfurter Papers, LC, and the papers of Denis Dickason in the collection of Harriet Pickering. A list of H.'s library books was supplied by the FBI Library at Quantico. His Masonic record is in HSF. Frank Baughman's inscribed photo is in HC, and his FBI file is no. 67-691-2.

Chapter 4

Interviews included a second godson of H., J. Edgar Nichols, author Ralph de Toledano, Roger Baldwin of the ACLU, former FBI Assistant Directors Charles Bates and Cartha DeLoach, former agents Edward Armbruster Jr., Robert Domalewsky, Aubrey Lewis, Neil Welch, Leo McClairen, Ed Duff, Erwin Piper, Kenneth Whittaker, Wm. South, and Mervin O'Melia. Lavonne Cowley, widow of agent Sam Cowley, and reporter Fletcher Knebel on letters written to an agent's wife. The papers of President Herbert Hoover, at HHL, were especially useful, as were the Harlan Stone Papers, gen. corr. 1889–1946, at LC, the Melvin Purvis personnel file, FBI 67-7489, the Denis Dickason letters in Harriet Pickering's collection, and the chapter on H. in *Public Entrepreneurship: Toward a Theory of Bureaucratic Political Power,* by Eugene Lewis (see Bibliography), and the lecture outline for agent recruits, by Bernard Suttler, at RG65NA.

Chapter 5

Interviews included neighbor Anthony Calomaris, TV journalist Eames Yates, former agents Duane Eskridge, Erwin Piper, Joseph Schott, and Kenneth Whittaker and author Ralph de Toledano on H.'s habits, FBI historian Susan Falb on FBI women, Guy Hottel's relative Chandler Brossard, Florida restaurateur Jo-Ann Weiss, and former Asst. AG Robert Mardian on H. and Jews, former *Washington Post* editor Ben Bradlee on H.'s xenophobia, former Asst. AG Harold Tyler and John Howe on his limousines, Kennedy era officials Wm. Hundley, Edwin Guthman, John Seigenthaler, and former Attorney General Ramsey Clark on H. and Robert Kennedy, Aubrey Lewis, James Barrow, Donald Stewart, Gerard Tracey, and Cartha DeLoach on black agents, hotelier Mara Forbes on red ties, Michael Fooner, Arthur Murtagh and—in 1972—journalist Guy Richards on FBI bugging of James Farley. Victor Navasky's book *Kennedy Justice,* NY, Atheneum, 1971, provided H.'s "baloney" comment on the Mafia, and Jack Levine's report to Asst. AG Miller, Jan. 23, 1962, illuminated H.'s handling of agents. Also used were the files of the National Association for the Advancement of Colored People, at LC, the Joseph Bayliss letter to Cong. Carl Mapes, Mar. 26, 1929, HH, HHL, and the Cummings Papers at the University of Virginia. Herbert Hoover's talk with incoming President Roosevelt came from Scheidt's note to H., Jun. 2, 1950, and Nichols' note to Tolson, Feb. 24, 1956, in Crime Records Research, RG65NA. The Ku Klux Klan allegation is at Drew Pearson's *Diaries,* op. cit., p. 285, and Garvan's recommendation to FDR appears in a letter from Garvan to FDR, Jun. 16, 1933, Personal Files, FDRL.

Chapter 6

For my reporting of H.'s relationship with Melvin Purvis I am grateful to Purvis' son Alston, who gave me access to the remarkable Purvis/H. letters in the Purvis Collection at the University of Boston. Interviews included Alston Purvis and Doris Lockerman, H.'s niece Marjorie Stromme on threats made by "Machine Gun" Kelly, former agent William Turner on Kathryn Kelly, and Anita Colby on H.'s claim that Tolson shot Dillinger. "FBI Summaries of Interesting Cases," preserved in the private collection of a former Assistant Director's family, were useful on the Thirties' Bandits, as was *Scanlon's* May 1970 on Kathryn Kelly. H.'s comments on women and crime were drawn from an undated *NYT* clip of 1932, *Hearst's Progress* of Jun. 1939, and *Secret Intelligence Agent,* by Montgomery Hyde, London, Constable, 1982, p. 242. The suggestion that agents mutinied at Little Bohemia is in a memo to DeLoach, May 11, 1966, FBI 948-350. The suggestion that the real Dillinger survived is elaborated in *Dillinger Dossier,* by Jay Robert Nash, Highland Park, IL, December Press, 1983.

Chapter 7

Interviews included Katherine Miller, Betty Kelly, JoAnn Weiss, former Assistant Directors Cartha DeLoach, Mark Felt, and Charles Bates, former agents Ken Clawson, Neil Welch, John O'Beirne, John Doyle, Harry Whidbee, Pete Pitchess, Joseph Schott, and Leo McClairen, and hotelier Arthur Forbes, on Clyde Tolson. Harvey's employees Pooch Miller, Charles Harvinson, George Dunson, and Aaron Shainus and H.'s reporter friend Walter Trohan described H.'s use of the restaurant. Jokes about H. and Tolson were gleaned from H.'s nephew Fred Robinette, Julia Cameron, and Jan Wenner. The Corcoran episode was described by Joseph Shimon, and additional information supplied by Thomas Corcoran, Betty Corcoran, James G.C. Corcoran II, and James Dowd. H.'s relationship with Winchell was described by Herman Klurfeld and Curly Harris, and his patronage of the Stork Club by Guy Hottel, Chandler Brossard, Anita Colby, and Luisa Stuart. The H./Tolson "tiff" was reported by William Turner. Documentary sources used included: the H./Tolson correspondence in TSF & HSF; *WH*, Aug. 28, 1933, and FBI file 62-68973 on Ray Tucker; an H. note and Nichols to H., Jan. 21, 1938, FBI 62-320-1, and *Inquisition In Eden*, by Alvah Bessie, NY, Macmillan, 1965, p. 194, on H.'s use of perfume. The Joe Pasternak interview was kindly supplied by Charles Higham, and Ethel Merman's comment appeared in the *San Francisco Chronicle*, May 23, 1978.

Chapter 8

Interviews included Curtis Lynum, quoting Raymond Suran on Tolson being jilted, Edna Daulyton, former agents Joe Wickman and Jim Barrow, and acquaintance Alvin Malnik on H.'s guilt about his mother, nephew Fred Robinette, Ginger Rogers, Effie Cain, Leo McClairen, Walter Trohan, Richard Auerbach, and Guy Hottel on Lela Rogers. Joan, Richard, and Manee Thompson, and Katherine Porter were interviewed about Frances Marion. Charles Harvinson, John Howard, Joseph Schott, Joseph Griffin, and Arthur and Mara Forbes discussed Dorothy Lamour. Walter Trohan and Beatrice Berle recalled the Sumner Welles episode, and David Wise reported a conversation with Assistant AG James Rowe. Former agent Joe Wickman spoke of H.'s standing order about allegations of homosexuality. Frank Kameny, Harry Hay, and Dan

Simenovsky discussed the Mattachine Society, and Dr. Marshall Ruffin's treatment of H. was described by his wife, Monteen—with additional information supplied by Dr. Hill Carter, Jack Anderson, and Dr. Robert Sjogren. William Stutz recalled delivering flowers for H. The depositions of Hillory Tolson and Dorothy Skillman, TWF, were useful on Tolson's family life. Dorothy Lamour wrote to the author, who made use of Lamour's book, *My Side of the Road*, Englewood Cliffs, NJ, Prentice-Hall, 1980. Harold Ickes' unpub. diaries, LC, were a valuable source on the Welles affair, and the information on John Monroe was gleaned from FBI documents kindly supplied by Dan Simenovsky.

Chapter 9

Interviews included: former agent C. W. Toulme on the arrest of Alvin Karpis, J. Edgar Nichols on his father, former agent Joseph Purvis on H. and newspapers, Jeremiah O'Leary on his relations with the FBI, and Karl Hess, Fletcher Knebel, and Nancy Weehsier on interference with the press. Roland Evans, Mrs. Stewart Alsop, and Mrs. E. Chubb discussed Joseph Alsop, and the Jack Nelson episode was described by Nelson himself, and David Kraslow. Former Assistant Directors Charles Bates and Cartha DeLoach spoke of the FBI relationship with Jimmy Stewart. The report that Karpis was tracked by a Treasury agent is in *Surreptitious Entry*, by Willis George, NY, Appleton-Century, 1946, p. 45. Information on Louis Nichols came from a private family collection. The Raymond Henle letter, dated Feb. 19, 1958, is in the Henle Papers at the State Historical Society of Wisconsin. References to Jeremiah O'Leary come from H. to OC file, Feb. 25, 1966, OC92, Jones to Bishop, Jun. 11, 1968, FBI 1/11-38861-45, Shanklin to HQ, Nov. 22, 1963, FBI 89-4324, Jones to Bishop, Apr. 7, 1970, FBI 1/11-399961-45, and *WP*, Jan. 28, 1978. Vice President Henry Wallace referred to surveillance of Drew Pearson in *The Price of Vision: The Diary of Henry A. Wallace*, ed. John Morton, Boston, Houghton

Mifflin, 1973, p. 406. H.'s claim that Alsop was a homosexual is in a Feb. 15, 1962, memo in the Lewis Strauss Papers, HHL. The Jack Alexander description of H.'s office is in FBI file 62-11607.

Chapter 10

Edward Turrou, son of former star agent Leon Turrou, provided information on the 1938 Nazi trial, and Thomas DeWald kindly shared his research on Ford executive Harry Bennett. Former Assistant AG Norman Littell expanded on his diary entries, and reporter William Dufty supplied his unpublished manuscript with its interview of Federal Communications Chairman James Fly. Former FBI surveillance specialist Wesley Swearingen granted extensive interviews. Secretary of State Cordell Hull's "cocksucker" exclamation comes from Ralph de Toledano's book *J. Edgar Hoover: The Man in his Time* (see Bibliography), p. 152. The Supervisory Archivist at the Roosevelt Library advised the author in an Apr. 4, 1990, letter that there is no trace of an FDR memorandum about investigating Soviet and Fascist espionage, as claimed by H. with The Francis Biddle Papers, FDRL, were used in connection. AG Frank Murphy. The writings of James Lawrence Fly are in the Fly Collection at the Butler Library, Columbia University. The reference to 1944 taps of Republicans came from the *NY Star*, Sept. 28, 1948, and the author's conversations with the late Guy Richards. The most scholarly work on FBI surveillance has been done by Prof. Athan Theoharis, of Marquette University, and I used his article in *Political Science Quarterly*, vol. 107, No. 1, Spring 1992.

Chapter 11

The description of H.'s house drew on interviews with Hilton Simmons, Robert Fink, Anthony Calomaris, and Anthony Cave Brown, reporting his interview with Sir William Stephenson. Stephenson's "grip" is noted in William Stephenson's April 25, 1993, letter to the author. William Corson recalled an interview of H. on having received a written presidential instruction to cooperate with

Stephenson, but FDRL Archivist Raymond Teichman reported no trace of such a document in a Jun. 16, 1992, letter to the author. The official British history of Stephenson's operation, *An Account of Secret Activities in the Western Hemisphere,* is unpublished, and was shown to the author by William Stevenson. The Van Deman Papers are in the Military Reference Branch, NA. The Popov episode was discussed by Jill and Marco Popov, Celia Jackson, Rodney Dennys, Col. T. A. Robertson, author William Stevenson, Chloe MacMillan, and former FBI official Arthur Thurston. For a full reading of the sources used for this controversial episode, it is especially essential to see the hardback edition. Notable, however, are the Popov Papers preserved by his family, FBI file 65-36994, "The British Assault on J. Edgar Hoover: The Tricycle Case," by Thomas Troy, *Intelligence and Counterintelligence,* III, No. 3, 1989, *British Intelligence in the Second World War,* vol. 4, by F. H. Hinsley and C.A.G. Simkins, London, HMSO, 1990, and *American Historical Review,* article by John Bratzel and Leslie Rout, Dec. 1982.

Chapter 12

Interviews on Pearl Harbor included Duane Eskridge, George Allen, Tom Flynn, and Saburu Chiwa. Col. Carlton Ketchum's son, David, discussed his father's claims and provided correspondence. A. M. Ross-Smith and Deborah Payne provided information on H.'s allegations against British intelligence, and J. Edgar Nichols reported H.'s Hitler assassination scheme. Former agents John Holtzman, Duane Traynor, and Norval Wills, and attorney Lloyd Cutler, discussed the Nazi saboteurs. Key among Pearl Harbor sources were *And I Was There,* by Edwin Layton, Roger Pineau, and John Costello, NY, William Morrow, 1985, and *Pearl Harbor: Final Judgment,* by Henry Clausen and Bruce Lee, NY, Crown, 1992, Dec. 7–12 correspondence at FDRL, John A. Burns Oral History Project, Univ. of Hawaii, and H. phone and office logs showing that H. was on vacation when asked to testify. *Eight Spies Against America,* by George Dasch, NY, Robert

McBride, 1959, and the *Atlanta Constitution*, Jul. 4–6, 1980, contain essential information on the Nazi saboteurs.

Chapter 13

Cartha DeLoach supplied the story about H. mimicking Eleanor Roosevelt, G. Gordon Liddy recalled H. describing her as dangerous, and Edna Daulyton the encounter in the hotel. Trude Lash spoke about her husband Joseph and Mrs. Roosevelt, and Bernard Fensterwald reported the comments of Col. Roger Pierce on the alleged sex recording. Dr. Beatrice Berle described the collapse of H.'s relations with Pres. Roosevelt. The H. "hoot owl" comment is from a notation, Dec. 1958, cited in *WP*, Jun. 6, 1982. *FDR* by Ted Morgan, NY, Simon & Schuster, 1985, and *Eleanor Roosevelt* by Blanche Wiesen Cook, NY, Viking, 1992, were vital resources. The H./Eleanor Roosevelt correspondence is in FBI file 62-62-735. FDRL Archivist Raymond Teichman confirmed the absence of records of H./FDR contacts late in the presidency.

Chapter 14

The Steelman anecdote was told by former agent Curtis Lynum. General William Quinn described H.'s check on the remnants of the OSS, and former CIA Director Richard Helms discussed H.'s antipathy to CIA. I drew on *Off the Record: The Private Papers of Harry S Truman,* ed. Robert Ferrell, NY, Harper & Row, 1980, and *Dear Bess: Letters from Harry to Bess Truman,* ed. Robert Ferrell, London, Norton, 1983, and *Truman,* by David McCullough, NY, Simon & Schuster, 1992. The James Angleton comments are from IC 2, p. 67.

Chapter 15

Dr. Edward Elson was interviewed. Alger Hiss' attorney Cal Barksdale spoke about the Hiss case on behalf of his client, and Stephen Salant and William Reuben were also interviewed. Robert Morgenthau discussed his father's view of Harry White, and Robert McGaughey described Mundt's access to Hiss files. David Garrow supplied notes of his interview with Charles Brennan, and Truman's "Gestapo" comment came from a George Elsey note, May 2, 1947, from the George Elsey Papers, HSTL. *Dangerous Dossiers,* by Herbert Mitgang, and *Alien Ink,* by Natalie Robins (see Bibliography), were main sources on FBI meddling with writers and artists. Charlie Chaplin's FBI file is number 96100-127090. "Ghost of a Typewriter," by Fred Cook, *Nation,* May 12, 1962, and "Forgery by Typewriter," by Gil Green, *Nation,* Nov. 10, 1984, were useful. Prof. Herbert Parmet kindly supplied his 1988 interview of Richard Nixon. Dmitri Volkogonov's quote came from *NYT,* Oct. 29, 1992. Information on Thomas Dewey came from the Dewey folder, Nichols OC, FBI 62-116758.

Chapter 16

Professor Howard Higman, of the Univ. of Colorado, kindly obtained his FBI file on my behalf. Prof. John Murphy analyzed it, and Marilyn Van Derbur was interviewed. John Lowenthal, Al Bernstein, Telford Taylor, and Joseph Rauh discussed H.'s attack on Max Lowenthal. The "bad news" report to Truman is covered by an unsigned memo, Aug. 20, Rosen to Ladd, Aug. 28, and Powers to H., Aug. 28, 1953, HSF5. Merle Miller's assistant Carol Hanley corresponded with the author. Sen. Hickenlooper's involvement in the Lowenthal affair is at *CR,* Nov. 27, 1950, Hickenlooper Papers, HHL, and see *CR,* Jan. 17, 1966. Truman's part in the matter is reflected in H. to Admiral Souers, Jul. 20, HT to Lowenthal, Jul. 25, Aug. 2, Lowenthal to HT, Jul. 31, 1950, Pres. Sec.'s files, HSTL.

Chapter 17

Guy Hottel, Donald Surine, Walter Trohan, and Thomas Reeves discussed H.'s relationship with Sen. McCarthy. Barbara Coffman Burns reported H.'s hosting of a Nixon fundraiser. Virginia Murchison Linthicum, Madeleine Brown, and Jim Johnson spoke about Sid Richardson and Clint Murchison. Former AG William Rogers was interviewed on H.'s relations with Eisenhower. H.'s vacationing at Del Charro was discussed by Allan Witwer, former agents Harry Whidbee, Erwin Piper, and Frenchie LaJeunesse, hoteliers Arthur and Mara Forbes, Donald King, former

SAC Richard Auerbach, Billy Byars, Jr., Effie Cain, and others. John Connally described H.'s connections with oilmen, and Peter Sprague, Leland Redline, Henry Darlington, Robert Morgenthau, William Hundley, John Dowd, and William Pennington discussed his oil investments. Cornelius Gallagher was interviewed about H. and Roy Cohn, as was David Schine. H.'s broadcast on behalf of McCarthy is documented in Nichols to T., Apr. 5, 1949, and transcribed in FBI 94-37708. Wm. Sullivan's comments are in part from notes of an Arthur Schlesinger interview, Jul. 26, 1976. David Kraslow allowed quotation from contemporaneous notes of his Oct. 13, 1971, meeting with H. George Allen's "juice" quote is from *Washington Exposé*, by Jack Anderson, Washington, DC, Public Affairs Press, 1967, pp. 209ff. I used notes of interviews with Allan Witwer by Drew Pearson, in the Pearson Papers, Texas Oilmen file, G300, LBJL, and by Wm. Lambert, in his collection. The Director's Daily Log proved the length of his vacations. Official findings on diversion of Recreation Fund money are from AG Griffin Bell's US Recording Report, Jan. 10, 1978. I cited the Valuation of Securities, Estate of Clyde Tolson, Apr. 14, 1975, in TSF9. Myer Schine's admission of a deal with the mob is from the Schine transcript, Sen. Special Cttee. to Investigate Org. Crime in Interstate Commerce, 1950, Pt. 2.

Chapter 18

John Williams, citing Allard Lowenstein, reported the meeting of worried US senators. Henry Eakins quoted Sen. Mundt on H. as "most dangerous." Former agent Harold Leinbaugh, Peter Eikenberry, Leon Friedman, and Ralph Salerno discussed Rep. John Rooney. Robert Winter-Berger was interviewed about John McCormack, and Jack Anderson about Thomas Dodd. Curtis Lynum described the Zero file system. Judge George McKinnon, Edna Daulyton, Julius Knutson, Quentin Burke, and Joseph Shimon provided information on Rep. Knutson. Former agents Amos Teasley, Joseph Woods, John Tierney, Paul Ertzinger, Conrad Trahern, Alfred Nicholas, Joseph Purvis, and Harold

Charron talked about the Official and Confidential files. I interviewed Gordon Liddy and former CIA Director Richard Helms about H.'s pressure on politicians. David Gelman recalled the *NYP* contact with Rep. Celler. I interviewed Arthur Murtagh, Walter Trohan, and former Sen. George Smathers. Sullivan's comments drew on an unpublished interview by DES investigator Robert Fink, May 2, 1976. *The Washington Pay-off,* by Robert Winter-Berger, Secaucus, NJ, Lyle Stuart, 1972, was a main source on congressional corruption. I used the McCormack Papers, Boston University, and the Keenan Papers, Harvard Law School Library, to document those politicians' relations with H., and *Above the Law,* by James Boyd, NY, New American Library, 1968, and FBI file 58-6157, OC92 on Thomas Dodd. For the passage about Emmanuel Celler, I used the Celler Papers, LC, and a letter from Dorothy Schiff of Mar. 30, 1988. Arthur Murtagh's congressional testimony of Nov. 1975 is at IC3, pp. 1047, 1068.

Chapter 19

I drew on interviews with former AG Laurence Silberman, Sen. Ralph Yarborough, Abigail McCarthy, and —on Rep. Boggs—with Thomas Boggs, Thomas P. O'Neill, Gary Hymel, Henry Reuss, Charles Percy, and Birch Bayh. I discussed Sen. Long with his former aide Robert Bevin, with Bernard Fensterwald, and former FBI Assistant Director Cartha DeLoach. The Gallagher affair was reported on the basis of multiple interviews with Cornelius Gallagher and his family, with Charles Joelson, William Lambert, Russell Sackett, Elizabeth May, Joseph Zicarelli Jr., Larry Weisman, former AG Ramsey Clark, former Justice Dept. official Mitchell Rogovin, and FBI agents John Lelwica, John Connors, Lincoln Stokes, and Victor Carelli. Former Justice Dept. official William Hundley, journalist Mike Royko, and former agent William Turner discussed *Life* magazine reporter Sandy Smith. On the FBI and the Supreme Court, I used the "Now It Can Be Told" syndicated TV program, Sept. 16, 1991, and *Cloak and Gavel,* by Alexander Charns, Chicago, Univ. of Illinois Press, 1992.

SOURCE NOTES

An unpublished manuscript by Robert Bevin was useful on
surveillance of Congress, as was the unpublished manuscript *The Intruders,* by Edward Long, and draft chapters for
a book from Bernard Fensterwald's personal papers. Bernard Fensterwald signed an affidavit on Oct. 22, 1990, about
the alleged DeLoach visit to Sen. Long. The discussion of
Sandy Smith drew on *Playboy,* 1981, Wm. Helmer to
Turner, Sept. 1980, with enclosures, SAC Chicago to H.,
Mar. 16, DeLoach to Mohr, Mar. 16, 1965, FBI file 07-
455829, and a *Life* memo by Smith, Aug. 21, 1968.

Chapter 20
Cartha DeLoach described H. weeping. Mrs. L. B. Brown
described her husband's ordeal, and former agents Wm.
Turner, Nate Ferris, Gordon Liddy, Joseph Schott, Francis
Flanagan, Jack Shaw, Bernard Conners, and Nelson Gib-
bons discussed agent conditions. Dr. Robert Choisser and
Marilyn Bell spoke about H.'s health. John Dowd, Joseph
Griffin, Homer Boynton, Mrs. Leo Gauthier, John Dunphy,
Martin Kaiser, and Assistant AG Harold Tyler discussed the
1977 FBI corruption probe. Documents used included
Nelson Gibbons' FBI file, held by his attorney, AG Griffin
Bell's statement on release of the *US Recording Report,* Jan.
10, 1978, and the Nov. 11, 1976, report to Michael
Shaheen, Council on Professional Responsibility, by John
Dowd, Special Attorney, Crim. Div., DJ, obtained under
Freedom of Information Act.

Chapter 21
The Lombardozzi quote was obtained for the author by
attorney Wm. Pepper. Guy Hottel discussed H. and
horseracing, and former agents Pete Pitchess, Wm. Roemer,
and Neil Welch described early FBI attitudes to organized
crime. Former Assistant Cttee. Counsel Joseph Nellis, Wm.
Turner, and Jack Anderson were interviewed about Sen.
Kefauver. Former AGs Herbert Brownell, Wm. Rogers, and
Ramsey Clark, NY DA Robert Morgenthau, former LA
Police Chief Tom Reddin, crime consultant Ralph Salerno
former Justice Dept. officials Robert Pelaquin, Wm

Hundley, and Edwin Guthman, Prof. Fred Inbau, former FBI Assistant Directors Courtney Evans, Mark Felt, and Cartha DeLoach, and fourteen former FBI agents, were consulted about H.'s inaction against organized crime. Herman Klurfeld, and Mrs. Meyer Lansky, reported by Michael Fooner, discussed Winchell's links to the mob. Restaurateurs Jesse, Grace, and Jo-Ann Weiss discussed H. and Joe's Stone Crabs. Allan Witwer talked about Ed Levinson, Wm. Gallinaro about Art Samish and John Daly, Robert Baskett, Wm. Wilson, and Wm. Gallinaro about Dub McClanahan. Irving Davidson and Bobby Baker were interviewed, and former agent Wm. Roemer reported Murray Humphries' comments about H. and Murchison. Among 22 interviewees on H. and horse-racing, Virginia Linthicum, Effie Cain, Bud Brubaker, Guy Hottel, Curly Harris, Cliff Wickman, and Chick Lang were especially helpful. H.'s request to Phil Kovolick was reported in interviews and corr. with Hank Messick. Reporter Fletcher Knebel and former Justice Dept. aide Ed Guthman added to reports that H. placed larger bets than he publicly admitted. For the massive body of specialist literature on organized crime used, readers are referred to the hardback edition. This chapter drew on an uned. ms. in the papers of Leon Turrou, held by his son, the Harold Robinson Papers, HSTL, H.'s testimony to the US Sen. Cttee. to Investigate Crime in Interstate Commerce, Mar. 26, 1951, pp. 524ff., and—on Kefauver—the Apr. 21, 1952, report by Auerbach to H., and Sullivan to Belmont, Dec. 28, 1961, in FBI file 62-77208. Del Webb's registration at the Del Charro was seen in Allan Witwer's collection, and *Dallas Conspiracy,* an unpub. ms. by Prof. Peter Dale Scott, VI, 16, provided information on John Drew. Reporting on Del Mar used the Hearings, Cal. Sen. Factfinding Cttee. on Govt. Admin., Examination of 22nd Agricultural Assn., 1960, and orig. *Life* research files on Boys Inc.

Chapter 22

The late Norma Abrams was interviewed in 1988, as was Eduardo Disano. Herman Klurfeld, Joseph DiMona, and

Lyle Stuart discussed the Lepke case, and Wm. Hundley
described his encounter with Costello. Sam Giancana
(nephew) recounted his father's version of the Chicago
mobster's attitude to H., and Wm. Pepper (*supra.*) arranged
the contact with Lombardozzi. Seymour Pollack was interviewed twice. The late Jimmy Fratianno was interviewed in
1990, and Nicholas Lore, Jim Henderson, and George Carr
discussed the encounter with H. that Fratianno described.
Irving Resnick and his daughter Dana were interviewed,
and Resnick's story was discussed with Pete Hamill, Jim
Doyle, and Wm. Roemer. At Gatti's Restaurant, owner
Mike Gatti and Edidio Crolla recalled H. and Lansky. Wm.
Gallinaro told of the Royal Canadian Mounted Police
taping a Lansky conversation. John Weitz and Gordon
Novel were interviewed about alleged H./Tolson sex photographs, and see *Esquire,* May 1993, p. 57, and author's reply
in August edition. An earlier report of the Hundley-Costello
meeting was found in 1978 memos of Mike Ewing in HSCA
files. Possible deportation of Costello is discussed in memos
re Drew Pearson, Mar.–Sept. 1952, and Jun. 1, 1954, in FBI
file 94-8-350. Documentation on Pollack was found at
Hearings, House Select Cttee. on Crime, Dec. 7, 1971, p. 3.

Chapter 23

The head of the Justice Dept.'s Special Group, Milton
Wessel, and Laurence Walsh discussed H.'s response to
Apalachin. Susan Rosenstiel was interviewed in France, and
signed an affidavit swearing to the truth of her account. NY
Crime Cttee. Chief Counsel Edward McLaughlin, investiga-
tor Wm. Gallinaro, Hank Messick, Jackie Somerville, Sid-
ney Stricker, Stanley Penn, Jim Savage, Dr. Elaine Needel,
Dr. Henry Foster, Robert Morgenthau, and former Asst.
Director Cartha DeLoach were interviewed about
Rosenstiel. Kenneth Wells discussed the Freedoms Founda-
tion. The author used FBI files on the Special Group
obtained by Milton Wessel, and used Hearings, Subcttee. 5,
House Judiciary Cttee., Serial 16, p. 102, and Hearings,
Approp. Cttee. Subcttee., Mar. 6, 1961, p. 432. The testimo-
nies of James Kelly, Yolanda Lora, John Harrington, Jere-

miah McKenna, and Louis Nichols on Rosenstiel are in the
files of the NY State Joint Legislative Cttee. on Crime, Its
Causes, Control, Effects on Society, 1971. The author
obtained a Dept. of Justice memo from Wm. Gallinaro to
Henry Peterson, Jul. 27, 1970. Nichols' retirement corr. is
in a private collection. H.'s office logs, May 6, Jul. 15, 1958,
established his contacts with Rosenstiel. The 1958 FBI
report on the mob is Belmont to Boardman, Jul. 14, 1958,
FBI file 94-8-350-943. After hardback publication, the
author received material on Lewis Rosenstiel from FBI file
94-41753, and on Susan Rosenstiel from FBI file 163-
1486-2 (FOIPA release 298-462). The account of H.'s reaction is in *Kennedy Justice,* by Victor Navasky, *supra.,* p. 44.
H.'s denial of a mob coalition is in *Law Enforcement
Bulletin,* Jan. 1962.

Chapter 24

Former agent Kenneth Whittaker and Jesse Weiss discussed H.'s relations with Joseph Kennedy. Lady Bird
Johnson, Lynda Robb, Curtis Lynum, Robert Parker, Joseph Schott, Bobby Baker, and Cartha DeLoach were interviewed in connection with H. and Lyndon Johnson. Joseph
Shimon recalled Joseph Kennedy's mob friendships, as did
Edna Daulyton. Judith Campbell Exner was interviewed on
several occasions. Evelyn Lincoln and Pierre Salinger discussed the 1960 Convention, and Ben Bradlee, Igor Cassini,
Gore Vidal, and Jack Anderson described John Kennedy's
attitude to H.. Philip Hochstein reported H.'s assertion that
JFK had not legitimately won the election. The documentation of this and other Kennedy chapters is so vast that
scholars are strongly advised to use only the hardback
edition. The references that follow are highly selective.
Joseph Kennedy's 1955 letter to H. is in *The FBI Pyramid,*
by Mark Felt (see Bibliography), p. 195, and his role as FBI
"Contact" is in OC14. British reports on JFK drew on
Honeytrap, by the author and Stephen Dorril, London,
Weidenfeld & Nicolson, 1987. FBI reports on Inga Arvad
are in OC7, i, ii, iii, and JFK's early courting of H. is in FBI

file 94-37373. His father's similar corr. is in file 94-37308. The FBI's "highlights" of JFK's behavior are in Jones to DeLoach, Jul. 13, 1960, OC96. JFK and Lansky are covered in the transcript of "60 Minutes," CBS-TV, Jun. 25, 1989, and Battaglia is in Rosen to Boardman, Mar. 4, 1958, FBI file 94-37374. The approach to Marcello is in *Pay-off*, by Michael Dorman, NY, David McKay, 1972, p. 109. JFK's activity at the Convention is covered in the author's book *Goddess: The Secret Lives of Marilyn Monroe*, NY, New American Library, 1986, and *Kennedy and Johnson* (NY, Holt, Rinehart, and Winston, 1968) and *My Thirteen Years with John F. Kennedy* (NY, David McKay, 1965) by Evelyn Lincoln, and ints. Lincoln. H.'s post-election letter to JFK is at Nov. 9, 1960, in FBI file 94-37374.

Chapter 25

Mitchell Rogovin told the anecdote about the bust of Stanley Finch. Danny Selznick supplied his interview of Cartha DeLoach on Robert Kennedy's consultative visit to H., and the interaction of H. and RFK was based on interviews with former Asst. Director Courtney Evans, former agents Curtis Lynum, Joseph Schott, Jack Danahee, Gordon Liddy, and with Arthur and Mara Forbes, Wm. Hundley, Joe Dolan, and Angie Novello. Jesse and Grace Weiss, and Billy Byars, Jr., discussed H.'s relations with the Weiss and Byars families, and Edward Munden and Robert Garvey spoke of the Alicia Purdom case. John Seigenthaler and Wm. Hundley talked about H. and black agents, while Kenneth Whittaker reported Joseph Kennedy's comments after golf, and H.'s outburst about RFK. Robert Morgenthau and Joe Dolan recalled the Des Moines fiasco. Documents on the Purdom episode are in OC13, i, ii. H.'s Jan. 10, 1961, memo to RFK about Communism is in IC6, p. 821. H.'s letters to JFK are in JFKL, and the warning to H. of possible dismissal is in Millen to Conrad, Dec. 5, 1961, HSF6.

Chapter 26

The Mar. 22, 1962, H. meeting with JFK was discussed by Evelyn Lincoln and Judith Exner. The "first marriage" story was recalled by Ben Bradlee, Tom Wicker, Courtney Evans, Igor Cassini, Walter Trohan, J. B. Stoner, and Bobby Baker. Cartha DeLoach, former agent Homer Young, and Dick Schumacher talked about JFK and Angie Dickinson. Gordon Liddy, Eunice Murray, Cartha DeLoach, John Sherlock, Harry Hall, Liz Renay, Billy Byars, Jr., Arthur and Mara Forbes, and Anthony Calomaris spoke of the relationship between the Kennedys and Marilyn Monroe. The duration of the Mar. 1962 H.-JFK meeting is established in JFKL records, and O'Donnell's account is from Dec. 7, 1976, interview supplied to the author by Prof. Herbert Parmet. Evidence that H. knew of the JFK-Campbell affair is in Evans to Belmont, Mar. 20, 1962, OC96. Angie Dickinson is discussed in *A Woman Named Jackie*, by David Heymann, London, Heineman, 1989, and in *Those Wild Wild Kennedy Boys*, by Stephen Dunleavy and Peter Brennan, NY, Pinnacle, 1976, p. 49. My book *Goddess, supra.*, was the main source for the Monroe material, but Peter Lawford's description of the affair came from David Heymann's book *Jackie, supra*. Winchell's article about Monroe and JFK is in Jones to DeLoach, Jul. 9, 1963, FBI file 105-40018.

Chapter 27

The 1963 decision to dump H. drew on interviews with Edwin Guthman, former AG Nicholas Katzenbach, Abba Schwartz, Robert Morgenthau, and Wm. Hundley. The notion of Yarmolinsky as a replacement was discussed with Joe Dolan and Yarmolinsky. Abba Schwartz described JFK's reference to keeping a file on H.. Ben Bradlee and Bobby Baker discussed the Rometsch episode, and members of Bill Thompson's family spoke of his relationship with JFK. The coverage of the Profumo case drew on *Honeytrap*, by the author and Stephen Dorril, *supra.*, FBI file 65-68218, and State Dept. and CIA documents released to the author. JFK's conversation with Martin Luther King is from an interview of Andrew Young in *Christianity In Crisis*, Feb. 16, 1976, and *My Soul Is Rested*, by Howell Raines, NY, Putnam, 1977, p. 430. Sources on Rometsch included FBI files 105-122316, WFO 105-54487, OC22, *Des Moines Register,* Oct. 26, 1963, and letters in the possession of Bobby Baker.

Chapter 28

The assassination of President Kennedy is a vast subject served by myriad books. This author's expertise derives from his work on the book *Conspiracy,* NY, Paragon, 1989, and TV documentaries. For this chapter, Robert Morgenthau, Burke Marshall, William Manchester, Edwin Guthman, Mark Felt, and Joseph Schott discussed the way H. and RFK heard the news. Bill Koras and Joe Kelly recalled H.'s visit to the races the day after. Other new interviews included those with former FBI Asst. Director Courtney Evans, Rep. Hale Boggs' son Thomas, Ruth Paine, James Hosty—the agent who handled Oswald before the assassination—and Oswald's widow Marina. Col. Philip Corso discussed early information about an Oswald "double," and the late Aaron Kohn described Guy Banister. Former agents Paul Scranton and George Davis were asked about FBI contacts with Aleman, and Ed Becker and former agents Julian Blodgett and George Bland discussed the FBI and the Marcello threat. Col. Corso also recalled H. saying the case remained a "mess." Joe Dolan told of RFK saying the FBI now no longer worked for "us." H.'s "shock" is in the Nov. 22 note in F6135-6, WHCF, Box 188, LBJL. Johnson's concern about his own safety is in H. to Tolson, Nov. 29, OC92. Schlei's memory is in his Oral History, JFKL. Johnson's note of H. telling him "Evidence not strong" is in LBJ notes, Nov. 23, Appointment file (Diary Backup), Box 1, LBJL. H.'s "big mouth" comment about Earl Warren is a notation on a UPI report, Apr. 24, 1964, in FBI file 62-109060. A study of Hosty's name in Oswald's address book is in HSCA, *Report,* p. 232, and *The Oswald Papers,* an unpub. ms. by Paul Hoch. Parts of Banister's FBI file were kindly supplied by Dale Myers, and John Davis shared an interview of Aaron Kohn. Johnson's theories on the case are drawn from DeLoach to T., Apr. 4, 1967, FBI file 44-24696, a Walter Cronkite int. of LBJ, Oct. 3, 1969

LBJL, *Atlantic Monthly*, Jul. 1973, and *Wall Street Journal*, Jan. 30, 1992. The Malnik/Weiss conversation is in FBI log MM877-C, kindly supplied by Hank Messick. Of course, I have referred throughout to the Reports and accompanying volumes of the Warren Commission and the House Committee on Assassinations.

Chapter 29

William Manchester described his 1964 meeting with H., and George Ball and Nicholas Katzenbach described their impressions of H.. H.'s relations with Lyndon Johnson were described by Mrs. Johnson, Hugh Sidey, George Reedy, Madeleine Brown, Richard Goodwin, and Cartha DeLoach. Allan Witwer was discussed by Wm. Lambert, Robert Pelaquin, Wallace Turner, David Nevin, Joseph Dolan, and Richard Billings, and himself granted an interview. Robert Sherrill spoke of White House pressure on *Life*. Former Asst. Director Charles Bates and George Ball recalled H.'s intervention when British Prime Minister Wilson visited. Former Deputy AG Laurence Silberman described his examination of the Official and Confidential files, and former agents Harold Leinbaugh and Kenneth Whittaker, and former AG Ramsey Clark, Bill Brown, and Dr. Joseph Rankin discussed the Walter Jenkins affair. Laurence Silberman and former Asst. AG Robert Mardian discussed the Goldwater incident, as did John Daley, Edwin Guthman, and Jeffrey Shulman. LBJ FBI files include 58-7086, 94-4-3830, 47-50152, and 47-44945. FBI reports on Peter Lisagor were released to the author in 1989 and 1991. Congressional investigation of FBI abuses at the Atlantic City Convention are in IC6. The FBI report alleging that a Goldwater aide used prostitutes is Jones to DeLoach, Oct. 23, 1964, Mardian Papers, HIW.

Chapter 30

The late Ralph Abernathy was interviewed in 1989. Wm. Dufty and Gore Vidal spoke of rumors that H. had black blood, and Robert Parker recalled H.'s early comments on King. The FBI attitude to civil rights was discussed by John

Williams, former agents Roy Moore, Neil Welch, former Asst. Directors Cartha DeLoach and Charles Bates, and Tip O'Neill, Cornelius Gallagher, Don Edwards, and Joe Waggoner described H.'s leaks about King to the Congress. Efforts to smear him in the press were covered in interviews with Ben Bradlee, former AG Nicholas Katzenbach, John Herbers, David Kraslow, Mike Royko, Eugene Patterson, Newbold Noyes, and former agent Joseph Woods. The FBI's response to King's assassination was discussed with former AG Ramsey Clark, Mitchell Rogovin, and former agents Arthur Murtagh and Donald Wilson. Philip Melanson, the late Gregory Stone, and former agent Frenchie LaJeunesse were interviewed on the murder of RFK, while Connie Ring and Donald King spoke of H.'s attitude to Edward Kennedy. The best source books on King are those by David Garrow (*Bearing the Cross*, NY, Morrow, 1986, and *The FBI and Martin Luther King Jr.*, NY, Norton, 1981), and by Taylor Branch (*Parting the Waters*, NY, Simon & Schuster, 1988). H.'s birth certificate, filed only on September 21, 1938, is DC no. 419530-D. Daniel Selznick kindly provided his interview of Cartha DeLoach talking about King and prostitutes. Arthur Murtagh testified to a colleague's joyous reaction to the Mississippi killings in Nov. 1978, HSCA, VI, p. 117. Pres. Johnson's comment on "the sovereignties" is in the Burke Marshall Oral History, Oct. 28, 1968, p. 30, LBJL. H.'s "mores" and "alley cat" notations are at Oct. 7, 1964, FBI file 94-8-350-1323, and Oct. 14, 1964, FBI file 100-106670480/4. The undated draft of the anonymous letter to King is in OC24. Useful sources on King's death are the HSCA Final Report, and *The Murkin Conspiracy*, by Philip Melanson, NY, Praeger, 1989. Tolson's "Goddamn the Kennedys" is in *The Bureau*, by Wm. Sullivan (see Bibliography), p. 48. The RFK autopsy pictures are in OC97. The FBI reaction to Chappaquiddick is at Boston to H., Jul. 19, 1969, FBI 94-55752-108.

Chapter 31

Dr. Edmund Keeney and Dr. Robert Choisser were interviewed on H.'s health, Mark Felt and Jack Danahee on

Tolson's. J. Edgar Nichols told of his father's role as Nixon advisor, and H. R. Haldeman, John Ehrlichman, Pete Pitchess, John Connally, and Kenneth Whittaker described H.'s relations with Pres. Nixon. Former Hong Kong Legat Dan Grove was a key source on Marianna Liu. Ehrlichman, Haldeman, Joe Trento, and Jack Anderson recalled H.'s attempt to smear Nixon aides as homosexuals, and Charles Krebs, Billy Byars Jr., the late Skitch Hendrix, Roy Parkin, David Rowell, and detective Don Smith provided information on H.'s alleged behavior with young boys. Documents on alleged bugging of Nixon are in John Dean's testimony, WAC, III, 981, staff memo, Jun. 12, 1973, NP; WHT, Sept. 15, 1972, Feb. 16, Feb. 23, Feb. 27, and the transcript of a Nixon/Dean conversation, Mar. 13, 1973, Submission of Recorded Presidential Conversations to House Committee on Judiciary; and cf. (Agnew) IC6, pp. 164, 193ff, 483. Nixon and Liu are the subject of Director to SAC San Francisco, Aug. 18, 1976, FBI file 105-40947-8. The INLET coverage is at IC6, pp. 19, 52, 642ff. The homosexual smear of Nixon aides is in DeLoach to T., Jun. 11, 1969, OC119; H. to RN, Sept. 3, 1969, W. Hse. Staff Files, JDE, NP.

Chapter 32

Kenneth Clawson discussed the FBI and Vietnam protests. Former Asst. Director Charles Bates, SAC Richard Held Jr., Bill Thomas, Larry Heim, and George Moore filled in the details of the smearing of Jean Seberg. Wesley Swearingen and Lynn Atkinson talked of the FBI and the Black Panthers, and Ray Cline, Noel Gayler, and former CIA Director Richard Helms discussed H.'s attitude to the CIA. H.'s comments on Kent State are in H. to Tolson, May 11, 1970, FBI file 44-45339. Good sources on COINTELPRO are *COINTELPRO,* by Nelson Blackstock, and *The COINTELPRO Papers,* by Ward Churchill and Jim Vander Wall (see Bibliography). Robert Hardy's testimony is in Hearings, House Select Committee on Intelligence, 94th Cong., 1st Sess., Pt. 3, pp. 1050ff, 1133. The FBI and the Black Panthers are extensively covered in IC3 and 6. The smear of Jean Seberg is in FBI files 157-13876, 157-

3912, 157-13870, and in *Played Out: The Jean Seberg Story*, by David Richards, NY, Berkley, 1983. The Dick Gregory episode is at *WP*, Mar. 10, 1978; H. to SAC Chicago, May 15, 1968, p. 104 of Ward Churchill's book, *supra.;* and H. to SAC Chicago, Apr. 23, 1968, Black Nationalist files, RR; IC3, p. 189. Prof. Herbert Parmet kindly supplied his Nov. 1988 interview of Richard Nixon. Tom Huston's testimony is in IC2, pp. 3ff. Dean's remark that H. had "lost his guts" is Dean to N., Apr. 30, 1974, submission of Recorded Presidential Conversations to House Committee on Judiciary.

Chapter 33

The raid on H.'s garbage was recalled by Charles Elliott and Jack Anderson. Kenneth Clawson described H.'s "jellyfish" comment on former AG Ramsey Clark, and Edmund Muskie and Henry Reuss discussed FBI surveillance. Former Asst. AG Robert Mardian recalled H.'s threat to "tell *all.*" Daniel and Patricia Ellsberg, and John Ehrlichman, were interviewed on the Ellsberg affair. Daniel Selznick's interview of Cartha DeLoach provided information on the aging H.'s schedule. Patrick Buchanan's advice to N. of Feb. 12, 1971, is in *From: The President, Richard Nixon's Secret Files*, ed. Bruce Oudes, NY, Harper & Row, 1989, p. 217. H.'s view of Women's Liberation as "subversive" is at H. to SAC SF, May 7, 1970, FBI file on WL Movement, RR. The assertion that H. proposed the Kissinger taps is in *RN*, I, by Richard Nixon, NY, Grosset & Dunlap, 1978, p. 479, in *Years of Upheaval*, by Henry Kissinger, Boston, Little, Brown, 1982, pp. 120, 1115, and in *White House Years*, by Henry Kissinger, Boston, Little, Brown, 1979, p. 252. Sullivan's assertion that H. was "not of sound mind" was in *LAT*, May 15, 1973. While the description of Sullivan's fall was from many sources, an especially useful source for this final phase was the Mardian Papers, HIW.

Chapter 34

Robert Mardian and John Ehrlichman discussed their Oct. 3, 1971, meeting, and Mardian was most helpful for the chapter as a whole. H. R. Haldeman and former SAC Kenneth Whittaker recalled H. and RN at Key Biscayne. David Young and Gordon Liddy described events prior to Watergate, Larry Cohen passed on Sullivan's comments on H.'s knowledge of Nixonian taping, and Andrew Tully recalled his revealing interview with H.. N.'s White House discussion about the transcripts is in WHT, Oct. 8, 1971. The report on H. is Ehrlichman to N., Oct. 23, 1971, WHSF, NP. Nixon's denial of any H. blackmail is in his book, *RN*, II, by Richard Nixon, NY, Grosset & Dunlap, 1978, p. 75, and in a Nixon interview kindly supplied by Prof. Herbert Parmet. Seymour Hersh's book, *The Price of Power*, NY, Summit, 1983, refers to missing transcripts at p. 398, and see Glanzer to Silbert, May 7, 1973, and the statement of Robert Mardian, taken by FBI Inspector Meincke, May 11, 1973, Mardian Papers, HIW. Nixon's fear that H. would "pull down the temple" is at WHT, Oct. 25, 1971, p. 3. Liddy's reported claim that he had killed a man is in *An American Life*, by Jeb Magruder, NY, Atheneum, 1974, p. 175.

Chapter 35

Former reporter Mark Frazier was interviewed about his *Harvard Crimson* report, and forensic toxicologist Dr. Michael Slade described thiophosphate. Scott Armstrong, Emily Sheketoff, and Nathaniel Akerman confirmed that Watergate investigators were told of operations against H.'s house, and Gordon Liddy, Howard Hunt, H. R. Haldeman, and Felipe DeDiego were interviewed on the subject. Frank Sturgis' comments were kindly obtained by Dan Christensen. Dr. Bell's widow Marilyn recalled H.'s plastic surgery, and Cartha DeLoach spoke of H.'s last days. Jack Anderson described his congressional testimony about FBI snooping, and Jay Robert Nash and Hank Messick said their books were found in H.'s house after his death. James Crawford, Dr. Robert Choisser, Dr. James Luke, and Dr. Richard Welton discussed H.'s death, and Neil Gallagher and Egil Krogh were asked about Krogh's alleged later comment. H. R. Haldeman, John Ehrlichman, Richard

Kleindienst, and Gordon Liddy were interviewed about Administration reactions to the death, and undertaker Wm. Reburn and neighbors Helen and Anthony Calomaris described events at H.'s house. Former FBI clerk Joe Diamond told of the destruction of documents, and congressional investigators Mark Gittenstein and Robert Fink described the inquiry into the fate of H.'s files. Former *Newsweek* reporter Anthony Marro was interviewed about the FBI's reported removal of documents after Tolson's death. Hunt's reported involvement in assassination plots is in Jim Hougan's book *Secret Agenda,* NY, Morrow, 1978, p. 5, and in *Life,* Mar. 1990. The numerous burglaries suspected to be linked to the Watergate crew are listed in "The Unsolved Break-Ins," by Robert Fink, in *Rolling Stone,* Oct. 10, 1974. A document on "possible burglaries" at H.'s home is Director, FBI, to Special Prosecution force, DJ, Nov. 28, 1973, NA. Roy Cohn recalled his last meeting with H. in *Esquire,* Nov. 1972. Jack Anderson's testimony on FBI snooping is in Hearings, Subcttee. of Cttee. on Govt. Operations, 92 Cong., 2nd Sess., May 1, 1972, pp. 2437ff. N.'s reported call to H. on the last night is in notes of a conversation with Helen Gandy by Ladislas Farago, Farago Collection, Mugar Library, Univ. of Boston. H.'s death certificate, no. 72-03405, is at HSF8. Nixon's response to the news was described by John Ehrlichman to the author, but see also *J. Edgar Hoover: The Man and the Secrets,* by Curt Gentry (see Bibliography), p. 28. Haldeman's note on "skeletons," dated 9:15 A.M., May 2, 1972, is in WHSF, NP. Richard Kleindienst's testimony on action after H.'s death was Dec. 1, 1975, in DES, p. 2, and DES—with the draft staff report obtained by the author—is the principal source. Mark Felt's "dead horse" remark is cited in the DES staff report.

Epilogue

Former Asst. Directors Cartha DeLoach and Mark Felt, Neil Welch, race official Bill Koras, Dr. Edward Elson, nephew Fred Robinette, goddaughter Marianita Mattusch, neighbor Anthony Calomaris, cemetery staff Ethel Robertson, Lee Jenney, and Audrey Jones discussed H.'s burial and events following his death. Godson J. Edgar Nichols described visits to the grave, and niece Dorothy Davy recalled Annie Hoover's social aspirations. Psychiatrist Dr. Harold Lief and psychologists Dr. John Money and Capt. Gaye Humphreys offered opinions on H.'s personality. Documents used included *J. Edgar Hoover Memorial Tributes in the Congress,* Washington, DC, US Govt. Printing Office, 1974, and the Masons' *Tribute of Admiration and Affection,* Oct. 1, 1972, Scottish Rite Temple. The Dean/Nixon exchange is in *Blind Ambition,* by John Dean, NY, Simon & Schuster, 1976, p. 265, citing Watergate tapes, Mar. 13, 1973, but (for variant) cf. submission of Recorded Presidential Conversations to House Judiciary Committee, Mar. 13, 1973, p. 122. Doubt about Tolson's "mental competency" is in a report by investigator Philip Haire, Jul. 9, 1973, WAC, NA. Medical texts used were "Some Aspects of the Development of Authority," *Journal of Analytic Psychology,* Jul. 1977, and (on Himmler) *The Anatomy of Human Destructiveness,* by Erich Fromm, London, Pelican, 1987, pp. 398ff. H.'s comments on pornography were in *This Week,* Aug. 25, 1957 (reprinted for circulation by FBI), H. testimony Hse. Appropriations Subcommittee, Jan. 30, 1957, p. 203, *American Legion* magazine, May 1961, and *Inside the FBI,* by Norman Ollestad (see Bibliography), p. 62. The closing quote by Walter Mondale is from IC6, p. 64.

Afterword

The Clinton speech is drawn from *NYT,* Mar. 29, 1993, and an interview with the secretary of the Gridiron Club, and Styron's speech from *The Complete Guide to Writing Fiction,* by Barnaby Conrad, Cincinnati, Ohio, Writers Digest Books, 1990, p. 26, and interviews with William Styron, 1993. The reference to the extortion racket draws on the *New York Post,* Feb. 11, 1993, and interviews with Murray Weiss, John Pyne, Sherman Kaminsky, George Hammock, and James McDonnell. John Weitz revealed Angleton's identity to writer Peter Maas, in *Esquire,* May 1993. Fresh Rosenstiel sources include FBI files 139-2163

and 94-41753, and Mary Perot Nichols in *Philadelphia
Inquirer*, Mar. 28, 1993. Elizabeth Brown was informative
on stories about Hoover in the homosexual community.
Ralph Salerno and Laurence Keenan were interviewed for
the "Frontline" program. Lord Jenkins' anecdote is in *A
Life at the Center*, Random House, NY, 1993, p. 189.

LIST OF
ABBREVIATIONS
USED IN NOTES

B	*The Boss,* by Athan Theoharis and John Stuart Cox, Philadelphia, Temple, 1988
BI	Bureau of Investigation document
CP	Cummings Papers
CR	*Congressional Record*
D	*The Director,* by Ovid Demaris, New York, Harper's Magazine Press, 1975
DES	Inquiry into the Destruction of Former FBI Director J. Edgar Hoover's Files and FBI Recordkeeping, Hearings, House Government Information and Individual Rights Subcommittee, 1975
DJ	Department of Justice
EL	Dwight D. Eisenhower Library
EPUA	Morris Ernst Papers, University of Texas at Austin
ER	Eleanor Roosevelt
F	*From the Secret Files of J. Edgar Hoover,* edited by Athan Theoharis, Chicago, Ivan Dee, 1991
FBI	FBI document number
FDRL	Franklin D. Roosevelt Library
G	Cornelius Gallagher
GC	*Bearing the Cross,* by David Garrow, New York, William Morrow, 1986
GF	*The FBI and Martin Luther King, Jr.,* by David Garrow, New York, Norton, 1981
H	J. Edgar Hoover
HC	Hoover Collection, (J. Edgar Hoover Foun-

ABBREVIATIONS

	dation), Temple of the Supreme Council, Thirty-third Degree, Scottish Rite of Freemasonry, Washington, D.C.
HH	Herbert Hoover Papers
HHL	Herbert Hoover Library
HIW	Hoover Institution on War, Revolution and Peace
HSCA	Hearings and Appendices of the House Committee on Assassinations, 1979
HSF	Hoover Staff File
HSTL	Harry S Truman Library
HT	Harry Truman
IC	Hearings before the Select Committee to Study Governmental Operations with Respect to Intelligence Activities of United States Senate, 94th Congress, 1st Session, 1976
INTPERF	*Summary Report, The Investigation of the Assassination of President John F. Kennedy: Performance of the Intelligence Agencies, Final Report of the Select Committee to Study Governmental Operations with Respect to Intelligence Activities, U.S. Senate, Book V, 1976*
JFK	John F. Kennedy
JFKL	John F. Kennedy Library
LAT	*Los Angeles Times*
LBJ	Lyndon Baines Johnson
LBJL	Lyndon Baines Johnson Library
LC	Library of Congress
MLK	Martin Luther King, Jr.
NA	National Archives
N	Richard Nixon
NP	Nixon Papers
NYP	*New York Post*
NYT	*The New York Times*
OC	Official and Confidential Files (OC1, for example, refers to OC vol. 1)

ABBREVIATIONS

POF	President's Official Files, Franklin Delano Roosevelt Library
PC	Private Collection (Lou Nichols' papers)
RFK	Robert F. Kennedy
RG65NA	Record Group 65, Civil Reference Division of the National Archives (mostly scrapbooks containing Hoover news clippings)
RR	FBI Reading Room
SRIA	Supplementary Detailed Staff Reports on Intelligence Activities and the Rights of Americans, Book III, Final Report of Select Committee to Study Governmental Activities, U.S. Senate, 1976
T	Clyde Tolson
TSF	Tolson Staff File
TWF	Tolson Will File, Superior Court of the District of Columbia, Plaintiff Hillory A. Tolson vs. John P. Mohr, Administration No: 868–75
WAC	Hearings, Senate Committee on Presidential Campaign Activities, 93rd Congress, 1st Session, 1973–74 (Watergate and Related Activities)
WES	*Washington Evening Star*
WH	*Washington Herald*
WHSF	White House Special Files, Nixon Papers
WHT	White House Tape transcripts, Watergate Special Prosecution Force File segment, Record Group 460, National Archives
WMP	Wayne Morse Papers, University of Oregon
WP	*The Washington Post*
WR	Report volume of the President's Commission on the Assassination of President Kennedy, 1964 (WC + number denotes a Warren Commission Volume of Hearings or Exhibits)
WS	*Washington Star*
WT	*The Washington Times*

ACKNOWLEDGMENTS

Aside from those credited at the front of the book, a vast number of people helped bring this project to fruition. Thanks cannot go to the FBI as an agency, which resents probing and obstructs the proper functioning of the Freedom of Information Act. Nevertheless, FBI historian Susan Falb, Leslie Clemens and Sally Sparks at the Research Unit of the Office of Public Affairs, the Reading Room staff and Larry Heim, editor of *The Grapevine,* the journal of the Society of Former Agents, were helpful. Dozens of agents and retired agents were interviewed, and the names of those who agreed to be quoted are cited in the Source Notes section. Former Assistant Directors Charles Bates, Cartha DeLoach, Courtney Evans and Mark Felt were all generous with their time. So too was the late Guy Hottel, sometime confidant of both Hoover and Clyde Tolson, who agreed to be interviewed for the first time at the age of eighty-six. Clark Schoaff, guardian of the Hoover memorabilia at the Temple of the Supreme Council, Thirty-third Degree, Scottish Rite of Freemasonry, gave us repeated access to the collection. The sons of two of the men closest to Hoover, John Edgar Nichols and John Edgar Ruch, allowed access to their fathers' papers and photographs.

My researchers perused the papers of all the presidents Hoover served, and special thanks are due to Raymond Teichman, Supervisory Archivist of the Franklin Delano Roosevelt Library, and William Johnson, Chief Archivist at the John F. Kennedy Library. Also to John Taylor, Archivist of the Military History Division at the National Archives, and Jean Smith at the Library of Congress.

Some of the new evidence on the Pearl Harbor saga was found in the pigeon loft at the former residence of the Bishop of Grasse, now the home of Marco Popov, son of World War II agent Dusko Popov. Alston Purvis, son of

ACKNOWLEDGMENTS

Melvin, gave me access to his father's voluminous correspondence with Hoover—the only known extensive example of the Director's private letter-writing. The author James Rusbridger readily dug into his Pearl Harbor files. Gaye Humphreys, in Ireland, led me by the hand into the world of psychiatry, where I had never ventured before. The attorney and author Bill Pepper provided key contacts in the world of organized crime.

The Assassination Archive and Research Center in Washington, which houses a massive collection of FBI material on President Kennedy's murder, was again a vital resource —one so valuable that it deserves more solid support than a handful of private individuals can provide. With them, I mourn the death in 1991 of its founder, Bernard Fensterwald, whose experience as a congressional Chief Counsel helped me understand the way Hoover manipulated the Congress. I thank Mark Allen, Mary Ferrell and Paul Hoch, Professor Philip Melanson and Harold Weisberg —those most responsible of assassination scholars. Gary Miller, Dale Myers, Larry Happanen, Gus Russo, Dennis Lee Effle, Ed Tatro and Scott Van Wynsberghe kindly supplied contacts and information.

Two distinguished authors who have previously written about Hoover, David Garrow and Richard Gid Powers, ransacked their files and their memories. John Flanagin and Sondra Feldstein, who both hold advanced degrees in American history, performed the often thankless task of plowing through the papers of former presidents and countless government officials. Margot Edman and Julie Ziegler in New York, Robert Fink and Margaret St. John in Washington, Peter Frumkin in Boston and Mike Spears in Dallas all gave sterling service as researchers. In California, former IRS agent John Daley provided valuable contacts. K. B. Basseches in Washington and Terry Murphy in Ireland photographed ancient photographs with scrupulous care. At Putnam in New York, Dolores McMullan handled the logistics of transatlantic editing with courtesy and enthusiasm. In Virginia, Audrey Atkins, Kathy Titus, Barbara Warren and Shirley Yoder faithfully logged hundreds of hours of tape-recorded interviews. Debbie Roberts helped bring order to our chaotic Virginia office, as did John Lombard in Ireland. Denise Fitzgerald came to the rescue with secretarial help on the final lap. Pip Printing in Manassas and Mail Boxes Etc. in Georgetown copied many thousands of documents—and that is no idle credit in a book of this genre. James Ronayne drove thousands of uncomplaining miles on my behalf.

I am indebted once again to my attorney James Lesar, a master of the Freedom of Information Act, and my financial adviser, Peter Metcalf. Nine talented journalists, Fred Cook in New Jersey, Hank Messick and Dan Christensen in Florida, Anthony Cook in Beverly Hills, William Dufty in Michigan, Jeff Goldberg and Jim Hougan in Washington, and Stephen Dorril and Tom Mangold in the UK, were foremost among the many colleagues who shared expertise without asking for reward. I salute the producers of "Frontline," at WGBH in Boston, and director Bill Cran, of Invision in London, who defended their Hoover program and my role in it with integrity, and who have permitted me to quote from "Frontline" interviews in this paperback edition. And long-suffering friends Bob Dorff, Fanny Dubes, Tamara Glenny and Henry Ehrlich, Monica Gruler, Sheelagh Power and Rupert Murray, and Paddy and Joyce O'Keeffe of Knocklofty House in County Tipperary, supplied all manner of help—above all laughter.

PHOTO CREDITS

PHOTO CREDITS

34. Aubrey Lewis
35. *San Diego Union Tribune*
36. Hong Kong Hilton
37. AP/Wide World Photos
38. National Archives
39. *The Washington Post*
40. National Archives
41. AP/Wide World Photos

SELECTED BIBLIOGRAPHY

In the hardback edition, there was an extensive Bibliography, covering some 260 titles. To keep this paperback edition compact, only those books on or by J. Edgar Hoover and on the FBI are listed.

On J. Edgar Hoover

Comfort, Mildred. *J. Edgar Hoover, Modern Knight Errant.* Minneapolis: T. S. Denison, 1959.

Demaris, Ovid. *The Director.* New York: Harper's Magazine Press, 1975.

Fowler, Blonde. *FBI Woman.* Privately published, 1976.

Gentry, Curt. *J. Edgar Hoover: The Man and the Secrets.* New York: Norton, 1991.

Gibson, Dirk. *Neither God Nor Devil: A Rhetorical Perspective on the Political Myths of J. Edgar Hoover.* Ann Arbor, MI: University Microfilms International, 1983.

Lewis, Eugene. *Public Entrepreneurship: Toward a Theory of Bureaucratic Political Power.* Bloomington: Indiana University Press, 1984.

Memorial Tributes to J. Edgar Hoover in the Congress of the United States and Various Articles and Editorials Relating to His Life and Work. Washington, D.C.: U.S. Government Printing Office, 1974.

Messick, Hank. *John Edgar Hoover.* New York: David McKay, 1972.

Nash, Jay Robert. *Citizen Hoover.* Chicago: Nelson Hall, 1972.

Powers, Richard Gid. *Secrecy and Power.* New York: Free Press, 1987.

Theoharis, Athan. *From the Secret Files of J. Edgar Hoover.* Chicago: Ivan Dee, 1991.

SELECTED BIBLIOGRAPHY

Theoharis, Athan, and John Stuart Cox. *The Boss*. Philadelphia: Temple, 1988.

Toledano, Ralph de. *J. Edgar Hoover: The Man in His Time*. New York: Manor, 1974.

By J. Edgar Hoover

Hoover, J. Edgar. *J. Edgar Hoover on Communism*. New York: Random House, 1969.

———. *J. Edgar Hoover Speaks*. Edited by James D. Bales. Washington, D.C.: Capitol Hill Press, 1971.

———. *Masters of Deceit*. New York: Henry Holt, 1958.

———. *Persons in Hiding*. Boston: Little, Brown, 1938.

———. *A Study of Communism*. New York: Holt, Rinehart and Winston, 1962.

On the FBI

Blackstock, Nelson. *COINTELPRO*. New York: Pathfinder, 1988.

Charns, Alexander. *Cloak and Gavel*. Chicago: University of Illinois Press, 1992.

Churchill, Ward, and Jim Vander Wall. *The COINTELPRO Papers*. Boston: South End Press, 1990.

Clark, Ramsey. *Crime in America*. New York: Simon & Schuster, 1970.

Cochran, Louis. *FBI Man*. New York: Duell, Sloan & Pearce, 1966.

Collins, Frederick. *The FBI in Peace and War*. New York: Putnam, 1943.

Conners, Bernard. *Don't Embarrass the Bureau*. Indianapolis: Bobbs-Merrill, 1972.

Cook, Fred. *The FBI Nobody Knows*. New York: Macmillan, 1964.

Donner, Frank. *The Age of Surveillance*. New York: Vintage, 1981.

Felt, Mark. *The FBI Pyramid*. New York: Putnam, 1979.

Keller, William. *The Liberals and J. Edgar Hoover*. Princeton, NJ: Princeton University Press, 1989.

SELECTED BIBLIOGRAPHY

Kelley, Clarence, and James Davis. *Kelley: The Story of an FBI Director.* Kansas City, MO: Andrews, McMeel & Parker, 1987.

Lamphere, Robert, and Tom Shactman. *The FBI-KGB War.* New York: Random House, 1986.

Look magazine editors. *The Story of the FBI.* New York: Dutton, 1947.

Lovegrove, Richard, and Tom Orwig. *The FBI.* New York: Brompton, 1989.

Lowenthal, Max. *The Federal Bureau of Investigation.* New York: Harcourt Brace Jovanovich, originally published by William Sloane, 1950.

Lynum, Curtis. *The FBI and I.* Bryn Mawr, PA: Dorrance, 1987.

Millspaugh, Arthur. *Crime Control by the National Government.* Washington, D.C.: Brookings Institution, 1937.

Mitgang, Herbert. *Dangerous Dossiers.* New York: Donald Fine, 1988.

Munves, James. *The FBI and the CIA.* New York: Harcourt Brace Jovanovich, 1975.

Nelson, Jack, and Ronald Ostrow. *The FBI and the Berrigans.* New York: Coward, McCann, 1972.

Ollestad, Norman. *Inside the FBI.* New York: Lyle Stuart, 1967.

O'Reilly, Kenneth. *Racial Matters.* New York: Macmillan Free Press, 1989.

Payne, Cril. *Deep Cover.* New York: Newsweek Books, 1979.

Purvis, Melvin. *American Agent.* Garden City, NY: Doubleday, Doran, 1936.

Robins, Natalie. *Alien Ink.* New York: Morrow, 1992.

Rosenfeld, Susan. *The History of the J. Edgar Hoover Building.* Washington, D.C.: FBI Office of Congressional and Public Affairs, 1987.

Schott, Joseph. *No Left Turns.* New York: Praeger, 1975.

Sullivan, William. *The Bureau: My Thirty Years in Hoover's FBI.* New York: Norton, 1979.

Theoharis, Athan. *Spying on Americans.* Philadelphia: Temple, 1978.

SELECTED BIBLIOGRAPHY

Tully, Andrew. *Inside the FBI*. New York: Dell, 1987.

Turner, William. *Hoover's FBI: The Men and the Myth*. Los Angeles: Sherbourne Press, 1970.

Turrou, Leon. *Where My Shadow Falls*. Garden City, NY: Doubleday, 1949.

Ungar, Sanford. *FBI*. Boston: Atlantic Monthly Press, 1975.

Villano, Anthony, and Gerald Astor. *Brick Agent*. New York: New York Times Books, 1977.

Watters, Pat, and Stephen Gillers, eds. *Investigating the FBI*. Garden City, NY: Doubleday, 1973.

Welch, Neil, and David Marston. *Inside Hoover's FBI*. New York: Doubleday, 1984.

Whitehead, Don. *The FBI Story*. New York: Random House, 1956.

Williams, David. *Without Understanding: The FBI and Political Surveillance 1908–1941*. Ann Arbor, MI: University Microfilms International, 1981.

Wright, Richard. *Whose FBI?* LaSalle, IL: Open Court, 1974.

INDEX

Key to page references: 444c.15n.6, for example, indicates note 6 to chapter 15, on page 444.

587

INDEX

INDEX

INDEX

INDEX

INDEX